Penguin Books

Helter Skelter

Vincent Bugliosi was Deputy District Attorney
for Los Angeles and Professor of Criminal Law
at the Beverly School of Law and is now in
private practice.

Curt Gentry is a well-known non-fiction writer
and has recently written *Frameup*, a re-creation
of the famous Mooney-Billings murder case.

Helter Skelter

An Investigation Into Motive

Vincent Bugliosi

Prosecutor in the Tate-LaBianca Trials

with

Curt Gentry

Penguin Books

Penguin Books Ltd, Harmondsworth,
Middlesex, England
Penguin Books, 625 Madison Avenue,
New York, New York 10022, U.S.A.
Penguin Books Australia Ltd, Ringwood,
Victoria, Australia
Penguin Books Canada Ltd, 2801 John Street,
Markham, Ontario, Canada L3R 1B4
Penguin Books (N.Z.) Ltd, 182-190 Wairau Road,
Auckland 10, New Zealand

First published in Great Britain by The Bodley Head 1975
This abridged edition first published in Penguin Books 1977
Reprinted 1980 (twice)

The excerpts from the Beatles' songs, *Blackbird, Cry Baby Cry,
Helter Skelter, I Will, Honey Pie, Revolution* and *Sexy Sadie*,
by Lennon/McCartney, are used by permission of
Northern Songs Limited, 12 Bruton Street, London W1X 7AH

Made and printed in Australia at
The Dominion Press, Blackburn, Victoria
Set in Intertype Plantin

CIP

Bugliosi, Vincent.
  Helter skelter.

  Index
  First published, New York: Norton, 1974.
  ISBN 0 14 004296 2

  1. Murder — California — Hollywood — Case studies.
  I. Gentry, Curt, 1931-, joint author. II. Title.

364.1'523'0922

To Gail and Blanche

'We are what you have made us. We were brought up on your TV. We were brought up watching "Gunsmoke", "Have Gun Will Travel", "FBI", "Combat". "Combat" was my favourite show. I never missed "Combat".'

Brenda

'I became Charlie. Everything I once was, was Charlie. There was nothing left of me any more. And all of the people in the Family, there's nothing left of them any more, they're all Charlie too.'

Paul Watkins

'Whatever is necessary, you do it. When somebody needs to be killed, there's no wrong. You do it, and then you move on. And you pick up a child and you move him to the desert. You pick up as many children as you can and you kill whoever gets in your way. That is us.'

Sandy

'If you find an apple that has a little spot on it, you cut out that spot.'

Squeaky

'You just better hope I never get out.'

Bobby Beausoleil

Contents

Publisher's Note

Mention of Manson's interpretation of the Beatles' lyrics is critical to the understanding of the workings of Manson's weird mind and to an appreciation of the prosecution case on motivation. It must be emphasized that the hidden meanings found by Manson in these songs were hidden to everyone except Manson. No rational, normal person could possibly find in the words of the lyrics any justification for any of the features of Manson's creed or any of his actions. That they were an influence on Manson is indisputable, but so too is the fact that this was no responsibility of the Beatles.

Note to Readers

The acronym 'aka', which is used throughout the book, stands for 'also known as'.

Part One

The Murders

'How does it feel
To be
One of the
Beautiful People ?'

The Beatles,
'Baby You're a Rich Man',
Magical Mystery Tour album

Saturday, August 9, 1969

It was so quiet, one of the killers would later say, you could almost hear the sound of ice rattling in cocktail shakers in the homes way down the canyon.

The canyons above Hollywood and Beverly Hills play tricks with sounds. A noise clearly audible a mile away may be indistinguishable at a few hundred feet.

It was hot that night, but not as hot as the night before, when the temperature hadn't dropped below 92 degrees. The three-day heat wave had begun to break a couple of hours before, about 10 P.M. on Friday – to the psychological as well as the physical relief of those Angelenos who recalled that on such a night, just four years ago, Watts had exploded in violence. Though the coastal fog was now rolling in from the Pacific Ocean, Los Angeles itself remained hot and muggy, sweltering in its own emissions, but here, high above most of the city, and usually even above the smog, it was at least 10 degrees cooler. Still, it remained warm enough so that many residents of the area slept with their windows open, in hopes of catching a vagrant breeze.

All things considered, it's surprising that more people didn't hear something.

But then it was late, just after midnight, and 10050 Cielo Drive was secluded.

Being secluded, it was also vulnerable.

Cielo Drive is a narrow street that abruptly winds upward from Benedict Canyon Road. One of its cul-de-sacs, easily missed though directly opposite Bella Drive, comes to a dead end at the high gate of 10050. Looking through the gate, you could see neither the main residence nor the guest house some distance beyond it, but you could see, toward the end of the paved parking area, a corner of the garage and, a little farther on, a split-rail fence which, though it was only August, was strung with Christmas-tree lights.

The lights, which could be seen most of the way from the Sunset Strip, had been put up by actress Candice Bergen when she was living with the previous tenant of 10050 Cielo Drive, TV and record producer Terry Melcher. When Melcher, the son of Doris Day, moved to his mother's beach house in Malibu, the new tenants left the lights up. They were on this night, as they were every night, adding a year-round holiday touch to Benedict Canyon.

From the front door of the main house to the gate was over a hundred feet. From the gate to the nearest neighbor on Cielo, 10070, was almost a hundred yards.

At 10070 Cielo, Mr and Mrs Seymour Kott had already gone to bed, their dinner guests having left about midnight, when Mrs Kott heard, in close sequence, what sounded like three or four gunshots. They seemed to have come from the direction of the gate of 10050. She did not check the time but later guessed it to be between 12:30 and 1 A.M. Hearing nothing further, Mrs Kott went to sleep.

About three-quarters of a mile directly south and downhill from 10050 Cielo Drive, Tim Ireland was one of five counselors supervising an overnight camp-out for some thirty-five children at the Westlake School for Girls. The other counselors had gone to sleep, but Ireland had volunteered to stay up through the night. At approximately 12:40 A.M. he heard from what seemed a long distance away, to the north or northeast, a solitary male voice. The man was screaming, '*Oh, God, no, please don't! Oh, God, no, don't, don't, don't . . .*'

The scream lasted ten to fifteen seconds, then stopped, the abrupt silence almost as chilling as the cry itself. Ireland quickly checked the camp, but all the children were asleep. He awoke his supervisor, Rich Sparks, who had bedded down inside the school, and, telling him what he had heard, got his permission to drive around the area to see if anyone needed help. He observed nothing unusual, though he did hear a number of dogs barking.

There were other sounds in the hours before dawn that Saturday.

Emmett Steele, 9951 Beverly Grove Drive, was awakened by the barking of his two hunting dogs. The pair usually ignored ordinary sounds but went wild when they heard gunshots. Steele went out to look around but, finding nothing out of place, returned to bed. He estimated the time as between 2 and 3 A.M.

Robert Bullington, an employee of the Bel Air Patrol, a private security force used by many of the homeowners in the affluent area, was parked in front of 2175 Summit Ridge Drive, with his window down, when he heard what sounded like three shots, spaced a few seconds apart. Bullington called in; Eric Karlson, who was working the desk at patrol headquarters, logged the call at 4:11 A.M. Karlson in turn called the West Los Angeles Division of the Los Angeles Police Department (LAPD), and passed on the report. The officer who took the call remarked, 'I hope we don't have a murder; we just had a woman-screaming call in that area.'

Los Angeles *Times* delivery boy Steve Shannon heard nothing unusual when he pedaled his bike up Cielo Drive between 4:30 and 4:45 A.M. But as he put the paper in the mailbox of 10050, he did notice what looked like a telephone wire hanging over the gate. He also observed, through the gate and some distance away, that the yellow bug light on the side of the garage was still on.

Seymour Kott also noticed the light and the fallen wire when he went out to get his paper about 7:30 A.M.

About 8 A.M., Winifred Chapman got off the bus at the intersection of Santa Monica and Canyon Drive. A light-skinned black in her mid-50s, Mrs Chapman was the housekeeper at 10050 Cielo, and she was upset because, thanks to L.A.'s terrible bus service, she was going to be late to work. Luck seemed with her, however; just as she was about to look for a taxi, she saw a man she had once worked with, and he gave her a ride almost to the gate.

She noticed the wire immediately, and it worried her.

13

In front and to the left of the gate, not hidden but not conspicuous either, was a metal pole on the top of which was the gate-control mechanism. When the button was pushed, the gate swung open. There was a similar mechanism inside the grounds, both being positioned so a driver could reach the button without having to get out of the car.

Because of the wire, Mrs Chapman thought the electricity might be off, but when she pushed the button, the gate swung open. Taking the *Times* out of the mailbox, she walked hurriedly on to the property, noticing an unfamiliar automobile in the driveway, a white Rambler, parked at an odd angle. But she passed it, and several other cars nearer the garage, without much thought. Overnight guests weren't that uncommon. Someone had left the outside light on all night, and she went to the switch at the corner of the garage and turned it off.

At the end of the paved parking area was a flagstone walkway that made a half circle to the front door of the main house. She turned right before coming to the walk, however, going to the service porch entrance at the back of the residence. The key was secreted on a rafter above the door. Taking it down, she unlocked the door and went inside, walking directly to the kitchen, where she picked up the extension phone. It was dead.

Thinking that she should alert someone that the line was down, she proceeded through the dining room toward the living room. Then she stopped suddenly, her progress impeded by two large blue steamer trunks, which hadn't been there when she had left the previous afternoon – and by what she saw.

There appeared to be blood on the trunks, on the floor next to them, and on two towels in the entryway. She couldn't see the entire living room – a long couch cut off the area in front of the fireplace – but everywhere she could see she saw the red splashes. The front door was ajar. Looking out, she saw several pools of blood on the flagstone porch. And, farther on, on the lawn, she saw a body.

Screaming, she turned and ran back through the house, leaving the same way she had come in but, on running down the driveway, changing her course so as to reach the gate-control button. In so doing, she passed on the opposite side of the white Rambler, seeing for the first time that there was a body inside the car too.

Once outside the gate, she ran down the hill to the first house, 10070, ringing the bell and pounding on the door. When the Kotts didn't answer, she ran to the next house, 10090, banging on that door and screaming, '*Murder, death, bodies, blood!*'

Fifteen-year-old Jim Asin was outside, warming up the family car. It was Saturday and, a member of Law Enforcement Unit 800 of the Boy Scouts of America, he was waiting for his father, Ray Asin, to drive him to the West Los Angeles Division of LAPD, where he was scheduled to work on the desk. By the time he got to the porch, his parents had opened the door. While they were trying to calm the hysterical Mrs Chapman, Jim dialed the police emergency number. Trained by the Scouts to be exact, he noted the time: 8:33.

Officer Jerry Joe DeRosa, driving patrol car 8L5, arrived first, light flashing and siren blaring. DeRosa began interviewing Mrs Chapman, but had a difficult time of it. Not only was she still hysterical, she was vague as to what she had seen – 'blood, bodies everyplace' – and it was hard to get the names and relationships straight. Polanski. Altobelli, Frykowski.

Ray Asin, who knew the residents of 10050 Cielo, stepped in. The house was owned by Rudi Altobelli. He was in Europe, but had hired a caretaker, a young man named William Garretson, to look after the place. Garretson lived in the guest house to the back of the property. Altobelli had rented the main residence to Roman Polanski, the movie director, and his wife. The Polanskis had gone to Europe, however, in March, and while they were away, two of their friends, Abigail Folger and Voytek Frykowski, had moved in. Mrs Polanski had returned less than a month ago, and Frykowski and Folger were staying on with her until her husband returned. Mrs Polanski was a movie actress. Her name was Sharon Tate.

Questioned by DeRosa, Mrs Chapman was unable to say which, if any, of these people were the two bodies she had seen.

To the names she added still another, that of Jay Sebring, a noted men's hair stylist and a friend of Mrs Polanski's. She mentioned him because she remembered seeing his black Porsche with the other automobiles parked next to the garage.

Getting a rifle from his squad car, DeRosa had Mrs Chapman show him how to open the gate. Walking cautiously up the driveway to the Rambler, he looked in the open window. There *was* a body inside, in the driver's seat but slumped toward the passenger side. Male, Caucasian, reddish hair, plaid shirt, blue denim pants, both shirt and pants drenched with blood. He appeared to be young, probably in his teens.

About this time Unit 8L62, driven by Officer William T. Whisenhunt, pulled up outside the gate. DeRosa walked back and told him he had a possible homicide. The two officers, both armed, proceeded up the driveway. As Whisenhunt passed the Rambler, he looked in, noting that the window on the driver's side was down and both lights and ignition were off. The pair then checked out the other automobiles and, finding them empty, searched both the garage and the room above it. Still no one.

A third officer, Robert Burbridge, caught up with them. As the three men reached the end of the parking area, they saw not one but two inert forms on the lawn. From a distance they looked like mannequins that had been dipped in red paint, then tossed haphazardly on the grass.

They seemed grotesquely out of place on the well-cared-for lawn, with its landscaped shrubbery, flowers, and trees. To the right was the residence itself, long, rambling, looking more comfortable than ostentatious, the carriage light outside the main door shining brightly. Farther on, past the south end of the house, they could see a corner of the swimming pool, shimmering blue green in the morning light. To the left was a split-rail fence, intertwined with Christmas-tree lights, still on. And beyond the fence was a sweeping, panoramic view that stretched all the way from downtown Los Angeles to the beach. Out there life was still going on. Here it had stopped.

The first body was eighteen to twenty feet past the front door of the residence. The closer they came, the worse it looked. Male,

Caucasian, probably in his 30s, about five feet ten, wearing short boots, multicolored bell bottoms, purple shirt, casual vest. He was lying on his side, his head resting on his right arm, his left hand clutching the grass. His head and face were horribly battered, his torso and limbs punctured by literally dozens of wounds. It seemed inconceivable that so much savagery could be inflicted on one human being.

The second body was about twenty-five feet beyond the first. Female, Caucasian, long dark hair, probably in her late 20s. She was lying supine, her arms thrown out. Barefoot, she was wearing a full-length nightgown, which, before the many stab wounds, had probably been white.

The stillness now got to the officers. Everything was quiet, too quiet. The serenity itself became menacing. Those windows along the front of the house: behind any a killer could be waiting, watching.

Leaving DeRosa on the lawn, Whisenhunt and Burbridge went back toward the north end of the residence, looking for another way to get in. They'd be open targets if they entered the front door. They noticed that a screen had been removed from one of the front windows and was leaning up against the side of the building. Whisenhunt also observed a horizontal slit along the bottom of the screen. Suspecting this might have been where the killer or killers entered, they looked for another means of entry. They found a window open on the side. Looking in, they saw what appeared to be a newly painted room, devoid of furniture. They climbed in.

DeRosa waited until he saw them inside the house, then approached the front door. There was a patch of blood on the walk, between the hedges; several more on the right-hand corner of the porch; with still others just outside and to the left of the door and on the doorjamb itself. He didn't see, or later didn't recall, any footprints, though there were a number. The door being open, inward, DeRosa was on the porch before he noticed that something had been scrawled on its lower half. Printed in what appeared to be blood were three letters: PIG.

Whisenhunt and Burbridge had finished checking out the

kitchen and dining room when DeRosa entered the hallway. Turning left into the living room, he found his way partly blocked by the two blue steamer trunks. DeRosa also observed, next to the trunks and on the floor, a pair of horn-rimmed glasses. Burbridge, who followed him into the room, noticed something else: on the carpet, to the left of the entrance, were two small pieces of wood. They looked like pieces of a broken gun grip. (A third piece was found later.)

They had arrived expecting two bodies, but had found three. They were now looking not for more death, but some explanation. A suspect. Clues.

The room was light and airy. Desk, chair, piano. Then something odd. In the center of the room, facing the fireplace, was a long couch. Draped over the back was a huge American flag.

Not until they were almost to the couch did they see what was on the other side.

She was young, blond, very pregnant. She lay on her left side, directly in front of the couch, her legs tucked up toward her stomach in a fetal position. She wore a flowered bra and matching bikini panties, but the pattern was almost indistinguishable because of the blood, which looked as if it had been smeared over her entire body. A white nylon rope was looped around her neck twice, one end extending over a rafter in the ceiling, the other leading across the floor to still another body, that of a man, which was about four feet away.

The rope was also looped twice around the man's neck, the loose end going under his body, then extending several feet beyond. A bloody towel covered his face, hiding his features. He was short, about five feet six, and was lying on his right side, his hands bunched up near his head as if still warding off blows. His clothing – blue shirt, white pants with black vertical stripes, wide modish belt, black boots – was blood-drenched.

None of the officers, thought about checking either body for pulse. As with the body in the car and the pair on the lawn, it was so obviously unnecessary.

Shaken, the officers fanned out to search the rest of the house. There was a loft above the living room. DeRosa climbed up the wooden ladder and nervously peeked over the top, but saw no one. A hallway connected the living room with the south end of the residence. There was blood in the hall in two places. To the left, just past one of the spots, was a bedroom, the door of which was open. The blankets and pillows were rumpled and clothing strewn about, as if someone – possibly the nightgown-clad woman on the lawn – had already undressed and gone to bed before the killer or killers appeared. Sitting atop the headboard of the bed, his legs hanging down, was a toy rabbit, ears cocked as if quizzically surveying the scene. There was no blood in this room, nor any evidence of a struggle.

Across the hall was the master bedroom. Its door was also open, as were the louvered doors at the far end of the room.

This bed was larger and neater, the white spread turned back to reveal a gaily flowered top sheet and a white bottom sheet with a gold geometric pattern. In the center of the bed, rather than across the top, were two pillows, dividing the side that had been slept on from the side that hadn't. Across the room, facing the bed, was a TV set, on each side of which was a handsome armoire. On top of one was a white bassinet.

Cautiously, adjoining doors were opened: dressing room, closet, bath, closet. Again no signs of a struggle.

However, there was blood on the inside left side of the louvered French door, suggesting that someone, again possibly the woman on the lawn, had run out this way, attempting to escape.

Stepping outside, the officers were momentarily blinded by the glare from the pool. Asin had mentioned a guest house behind the main residence. They spotted it now, or rather the corner of it, some sixty feet to the southeast, through the shrubbery.

Approaching it quietly, they heard the first sounds they had heard since coming onto the premises: the barking of a dog, and a male voice saying, 'Shhh, be quiet.'

Whisenhunt went to the right, around the back of the house. DeRosa turned left, proceeding around the front, Burbridge following as backup. Stepping onto the screened-in porch, DeRosa could see, in the living room, on a couch facing the front door, a youth of about 18. He was wearing pants but no shirt, and though he did not appear to be armed, this did not mean, DeRosa would later explain, that he didn't have a weapon nearby.

Yelling '*Freeze!*' DeRosa kicked in the front door.

Startled, the boy looked up to see one, then, moments later, three guns pointing directly at him. Christopher, Altobelli's large Weimaraner, charged Whisenhunt, chomping the end of his shotgun. Whisenhunt slammed the porch door on his head, then held him trapped there until the youth called him off.

As to what then happened, there are contrary versions.

The youth, who identified himself as William Garretson, the caretaker, would later state that the officers knocked him down, handcuffed him, yanked him to his feet, dragged him outside onto the lawn, then knocked him down again.

DeRosa would later be asked, re Garretson:

Q. 'Did he fall or stumble to the floor at any time?'
A. 'He may have; I don't recall whether he did or not.'
Q. 'Did you direct him to lay on the ground outside?'
A. 'I directed him, yes, to lay on the ground, yes.'
Q. 'Did you help him to the ground?'
A. 'No, he went down on his own.'

Garretson kept asking, 'What's the matter? What's the matter?' One of the officers replied, 'We'll show you!' and, pulling him to his feet, DeRosa and Burbridge escorted him back along the path toward the main house.

Whisenhunt remained behind, looking for weapons and blood-stained clothing. Though he found neither, he did notice many small details of the scene. One at the time seemed so insignificant that he forgot it until later questioning brought it back to mind. There was a stereo next to the couch. It had been off when they entered the room. Looking at the controls, Whisenhunt noticed that the volume setting was between 4 and 5.

Garretson, meantime, had been led past the two bodies on the lawn. It was indicative of the condition of the first, the young woman, that he mistakenly identified her as Mrs Chapman, the

Negro maid. As for the man, he identified him as 'the young Polanski'. If, as Chapman and Asin had said, Polanski was in Europe, this made no sense. What the officers couldn't know was that Garretson believed Voytek Frykowski to be Roman Polanski's younger brother. Garretson failed completely when it came to identifying the young man in the Rambler.*

At some point, no one recalls exactly when, Garretson was informed of his rights and told that he was under arrest for murder. Asked about his activities the previous night, he said that although he had remained up all night, writing letters and listening to records, he had neither heard nor seen anything. His highly unlikely alibi, his 'vague, unrealistic' replies, and his confused identification of the bodies led the arresting officers to conclude that the suspect was lying.

Five murders – four of them probably occurring less than a hundred feet away – and he had heard nothing?

Escorting Garretson down the driveway, DeRosa located the gate-control mechanism on the pole inside the gate. He noticed that there was blood on the button.

The logical inference was that someone, quite possibly the killer, had pressed the button to get out, in so doing very likely leaving a fingerprint.

Officer DeRosa, who was charged with securing and protecting the scene until investigating officers arrived, now pressed the button himself, successfully opening the gate but also creating a superimposure that obliterated any print that may have been there.

At 9:40, DeRosa called in, reporting five deaths and a suspect in custody. While Burbridge remained behind at the residence, awaiting the arrival of the investigating officers, DeRosa and Whisenhunt drove Garretson to the West Los Angeles police

---

*Why he failed to identify the youth, whom he did know, is unknown. A good guess would be that Garretson was in shock. Also, adding to his confusion, it was about this time that, in looking toward the gate, he saw Winifred Chapman, whom he presumed dead, alive and talking to a police officer.

station for questioning. Another officer took Mrs Chapman there also, but she was so hysterical she had to be driven to the UCLA Medical Center and given sedation.

In response to DeRosa's call, four West Los Angeles detectives were dispatched to the scene. Lieutenant R. C. Madlock, Lieutenant J. J. Gregoire, Sergeant F. Gravante, and Sergeant T. L. Rogers would all arrive within the next hour. By the time the last pulled up, the first reporters were already outside the gate.

Monitoring the police radio bands, they had picked up the report of five deaths. It was hot and dry in Los Angeles, and fire was a constant concern, especially in the hills, where within minutes lives and property could vanish in an inferno. Someone apparently presumed the five people had been killed in a fire. Jay Sebring's name must have been mentioned in one of the police calls, because a reporter phoned his residence and asked his butler, Amos Russell, if he knew anything about 'the deaths by fire'. Russell called John Madden, president of Sebring International, and told him about the call. Madden was concerned: neither he nor Sebring's secretary had heard from the hair stylist since late the previous afternoon. Madden placed a call to Sharon Tate's mother in San Francisco. Sharon's father, a colonel in Army Intelligence, was stationed at nearby Fort Baker and Mrs Tate was visiting him. No, she hadn't heard from Sharon. Or Jay, who was due in San Francisco sometime that same day.

Prior to her marriage to Roman Polanski, Sharon Tate had lived with Jay Sebring. Though thrown over for the Polish film director, Sebring had remained friends with Sharon's parents, as well as Sharon and Roman, and whenever he was in San Francisco he usually called Colonel Tate.

When Madden hung up, Mrs Tate called Sharon's number. The phone rang and rang, but there was no answer.

It was quiet inside the house. Though anyone who called got a ringing signal, the phones were still out. Officer Joe Granado, a forensic chemist with SID, the Scientific Investigation Division of LAPD, was already at work, having arrived about 10 A.M. It was Granado's job to take samples from wherever there appeared to be blood. Usually, on a murder case, Granado would be done in hour or two. Not today. Not at 10050 Cielo Drive.

Sometime between 10 and 11 A.M., Raymond Kilgrow, a telephone company representative, climbed the pole outside the gate to 10050 Cielo Drive and found that four phone wires had been cut. The cuts were close to the attachment on the pole, indicating that the person responsible had probably climbed the pole too. Kilgrow repaired two of the wires, leaving the others for the detectives to examine.

Later, in the police lab, Granado would give his blood samples the Ouchterlony test, to determine if the blood was animal or human. If human, other tests would be applied to determine the blood type – A, B, AB, or O – and the subtype. There are some thirty blood subtypes; however, if the blood is already dry when the sample is taken, it is only possible to determine whether it is one of three – M, N, or MN. It had been a warm night, and it was already turning into another hot day. By the time Granado got to work, most of the blood, except for the pools near the bodies inside, had already dried.

Within the next several days Granado would obtain from the Coroner's Office a blood sample from each of the victims, and would attempt to match these with the samples he'd already collected. In an ordinary murder case the presence of two blood types at the crime scene might indicate that the killer, as well as the victim, had been wounded, information which could be an important clue to the killer's identity.

But this was no ordinary murder. Instead of one body, there were five.

There was so much blood, in fact, that Granado overlooked some spots. In all he took forty-five blood samples. However, for some reason never explained, he didn't run subtypes on twenty-one of them. If this is not done a week or two after collection, the components of the blood break down.

Later, when an attempt was made to re-create the murders, these omissions would cause many problems.

Just before noon William Tennant, Polanski's business manager, arrived, still dressed in tennis clothes, and was escorted through the gate by the police. It was like being led through a nightmare, as he was taken first to one body, then another. He didn't recognize the young man in the automobile. But he identified the man on the lawn as Voytek Frykowski, the woman as Abigail Folger, and the two bodies in the living room as Sharon Tate Polanski and, tentatively, Jay Sebring. When the police lifted the bloody towel, the man's face was so badly contused Tennant couldn't be sure. Then he went outside and was sick.

Like the shock waves from an earthquake, news of the murders spread.

'FIVE SLAIN IN BEL AIR,' read the headline on the first AP wire story. Though sent out before the identity of the victims had become known, it correctly reported the location of the bodies; that the telephone lines had been cut; and the arrest of an unnamed suspect. There were errors: one, to be much repeated, that 'one victim had a hood over his head . . .'

LAPD notified the Tates, John Madden, who in turn notified Sebring's parents, and Peter Folger, Abigail's father. On reaching home, William Tennant made what was, for him, the most difficult call. He was not only Polanski's business manager but a close friend. Tennant checked his watch, automatically adding nine hours to get London time. Though it would be late in the evening, he guessed that Polanski might still be working, trying to tie up his various film projects before returning home the following Tuesday, and he tried the number of his town house. He guessed right. Polanski and several associates were going over a scene in the script of *The Day of the Dolphin* when the telephone rang.

Polanski would remember the conversation as follows:

'Roman, there's been a disaster in a house.'

'Which house?'

'Your house.' Then, in a rush, 'Sharon is dead, and Voytek and Gibby and Jay.'

'*No, no, no, no!*' Surely there was a mistake. Both men now crying, Tennant reiterated that it was true; he had gone to the house himself.

'How?' Polanski asked. He was thinking, he later said, not of fire but a landslide, a not uncommon thing in the Los Angeles hills, especially after heavy rains; sometimes whole houses were buried, which meant that perhaps they could still be alive. Only then did Tennant tell him that they had been murdered.

Voytek Frykowski, LAPD learned, had a son in Poland but no relatives in the United States. The youth in the Rambler remained unidentified, but was no longer nameless; he had been designated John Doe 85.

The specialists had begun arriving about noon.

Officers Jerrome A. Boen and D. L. Girt, Latent Prints Section, Scientific Investigation Division, LAPD, dusted the main residence and the guest house for prints.

After dusting a print with powder ('developing the print'), a clear adhesive tape was placed over it; the tape, with the print showing, would then be 'lifted' and placed on a card with a contrasting background. Location, date, time, officer's initials were noted on the back. It took six hours to cover both residences. Later that afternoon the pair were joined by officer D. E. Dorman and Wendell Clements, the latter a civilian fingerprint expert, who concentrated on the four vehicles.

Contrary to popular opinion, a readable print is more rare than common. Many surfaces, such as clothing and fabrics, do not lend themselves to impressions. Even when the surface is such that it will take a print, one usually touches it with only a portion of the finger, leaving a fragmentary ridge, which is useless for comparison. If the finger is moved, the result is an unreadable smudge. And, as officer DeRosa demonstrated with the gate button, one print placed atop another creates a superimpose, also useless for identification purposes. Thus, at any crime scene, the number of clear, readable prints, with enough points for comparison, is usually surprisingly small.

Not counting those prints later eliminated as belonging to LAPD personnel at the scene, a total of fifty lifts were taken from the residence, guest house, and vehicles at 10050 Cielo Drive. Of these, seven were eliminated as belonging to William Garretson (all were from the guest house; none of Garretson's prints were found in the main house or on the vehicles); an additional fifteen were eliminated as belonging to the victims; and three were not clear enough for comparison. This left a total of twenty-five unmatched latent prints, any of which might – or might not – belong to the killer or killers.

It was 1:30 P.M. before the first homicide detectives arrived. On verifying that the deaths were not accidental or self-inflicted, Lieutenant Madlock had requested that the investigation be reassigned to the Robbery–Homicide Division. Lieutenant Robert J. Helder, supervisor of investigations, was placed in charge. He in turn assigned Sergeants Michael J. McGann and Jess Buckles to the case. (McGann's regular partner, Sergeant Robert Calkins, was on vacation and would replace Buckles when he returned.) Three additional officers, Sergeants E. Henderson, Dudley Varney, and Danny Galindo, were to assist them.

On being notified of the homicides, Los Angeles County Coroner Thomas Noguchi asked the police not to touch the bodies until a representative of his office had examined them. Deputy Coroner John Finken arrived about 1:45, later to be joined by Noguchi himself. Finken made the official determination of death; took liver and environmental temperatures (by 2 P.M. it was 94 degrees on the lawn, 83 degrees inside the house); and severed the rope connecting Tate and Sebring, portions of which were given to the detectives so that they could try to determine where it had been manufactured and sold. It was white, three-strand nylon, its total length 43 feet 8 inches. Granado took blood samples from the rope, but didn't take subtypes. After plastic bags had been placed over the hands of the victims, to preserve any hair or skin that might have become lodged under the nails during a struggle, Finken assisted in covering and placing the bodies on stretcher carts, to be wheeled to ambulances and taken to the Coroner's Office, Hall of Justice, downtown Los Angeles.

Besieged by reporters at the gate, Dr Noguchi announced he would have no comment until making public the autopsy results at noon the following day.

Both Noguchi and Finken, however, privately had already given the detectives their initial findings.

There was no evidence of sexual molestation or mutilation.

Three of the victims – the John Doe, Sebring, and Frykowski – had been shot. Aside from a defensive slash wound on his left hand, which also severed the band of his wristwatch, John Doe had not been stabbed. But the other four had – many, many times. In addition, Sebring had been hit in the face at least once, and Frykowski had been struck over the head repeatedly with a blunt object.

Though exact findings would have to await the autopsies, the coroners concluded from the size of the bullet holes that the gun used had probably been .22 caliber. The police had already suspected this. In searching the Rambler, Sergeant Varney had found four bullet fragments between the upholstery and the exterior metal of the door on the passenger side. Also found, on the cushion of the rear seat, was part of a slug. Though all were too small for comparison purposes, they appeared to be .22 caliber.

As for the stab wounds, someone suggested that the wound pattern was not dissimilar to that made by a bayonet. In their official report the detectives carried this a step further, concluding, 'the knife that inflicted the stab wounds was probably a bayonet'. This not only eliminated a number of other possibilities, it also presumed that only one knife had been used.

The depth of the wounds (many in excess of 5 inches), their width (between 1 and 1½ inches), and their thickness (⅛ to ¼ inch) ruled out either a kitchen or a regular pocketknife.

Coincidentally, the only two knives found in the house *were* a kitchen knife and a pocketknife. Tests soon eliminated the kitchen knife. The pocketknife was found in the living room, less than three feet from Sharon Tate's body. It was wedged behind

27

the cushion in one of the chairs, with the blade sticking up. A Buck brand clasp-type pocketknife, its blade was ¾ inch in diameter, $3^{13}\!/_{16}$ inches in length, making it too small to have caused most of the wounds. Noticing a spot on the side of the blade, Granado tested it for blood: negative. Girt dusted it for prints: an unreadable smudge.

Mrs Chapman could not recall ever having seen this particular knife. This, plus the odd place where it was found, indicated that it might have been left by the killer(s).

In literature a murder scene is often likened to a picture puzzle. If one is patient and keeps trying, eventually all the pieces will fit into place.

Veteran policemen know otherwise. A much better analogy would be two picture puzzles, or three, or more, no one of which is in itself complete. Even after a solution emerges – if one does – there will be leftover pieces, evidence that just doesn't fit. And some pieces will always be missing.

There was the American flag, its presence adding still another bizarre touch to a scene already horribly macabre. The possibilities it suggested ranged from one end of the political spectrum to the other – until Winifred Chapman told the police that it had been in the residence several weeks.

Few pieces of evidence were so easily eliminated. There were the bloody letters on the front door. In recent years the word 'pig' had taken on a new meaning, one all too familiar to the police. But what did it mean printed here?

There was the rope. Mrs Chapman flatly stated that she had never seen such a rope anywhere on the premises. Had the killer(s) brought it? If so, why?

What significance was there in the fact that the two victims bound together by the rope, Sharon Tate and Jay Sebring, were former lovers? Or was 'former' the right word? What was Sebring doing there, with Polanski away? It was a question that many of the newspapers would also ask.

The horn-rimmed glasses – negative for both prints and blood – did they belong to a victim, a killer, or someone totally unconnected with the crime? Or – with each question the possibilities proliferated – had they been left behind as a false clue?

The two trunks in the entryway. The maid said they hadn't been there when she left at 4:30 the previous afternoon. Who delivered them, and when, and had this person seen anything?

Why would the killer(s) go to the trouble of slitting and removing a screen when other windows, those in the newly painted room that was to be the nursery for the Polanskis' unborn child, were open and screenless?

John Doe 85, the youth in the Rambler. Chapman, Garretson, and Tennant had failed to identify him. Who was he and what was he doing at 10050 Cielo Drive? Had he witnessed the other murders, or had he been killed before they took place? If before, wouldn't the others have heard the shots? On the seat next to him was a Sony AM–FM Digimatic clock radio. The time at which it had stopped was 12:15 A.M. Coincidence or significant?

As for the time of the murders, the reports of gunshots and other sounds ranged from shortly after midnight to 4:10 A.M.

Not all of the evidence was as inconclusive. Some of the pieces fitted. No shell casings were found anywhere on the property, indicating that the gun was probably a revolver, which does not not eject its spent shells, as contrasted to an automatic, which does.

Placed together, the three pieces of black wood formed the right-hand side of a gun grip. The police therefore knew the gun they were looking for was probably a .22 caliber revolver that was minus a right grip. From the pieces it might be possible to determine both make and model. Though there was human blood on all three pieces, only one had enough for analysis. It tested O-MN. Of the five victims, only Sebring had O-MN, indicating that the butt of the revolver could have been the blunt object used to strike him in the face.

The bloody letters on the front door tested O-M. Again, only one of the victims had this type and subtype. The word PIG had been printed in Sharon Tate's blood.

There were four vehicles in the driveway, but one which should have been there wasn't – Sharon Tate's red Ferrari. It was possible that the killer(s) had used the sports car to escape, and a 'want' was broadcast for it.

Long after the bodies had been removed, the detectives remained on the scene, looking for meaningful patterns.

They found several which appeared significant.

There were no indications of ransacking or robbery. McGann found Sebring's wallet in his jacket, which was hanging over the back of a chair in the living room. It contained $80. John Doe had $9 in his wallet, Frykowski $2.44 in his wallet and pants pocket, Folger $9.64 in her purse. On the nightstand next to Sharon Tate's bed, in plain view, were a ten, a five, and three ones. Obviously expensive items – a videotape machine, TV sets, stereo, Sebring's wristwatch, his Porsche – had not been taken. While this didn't completely eliminate the possibility that the murders had occurred during a residential burglary – the victims surprising the burglar(s) while at work – it certainly put it way down the list.

Other discoveries provided a much more likely direction.

A gram of cocaine was found in Sebring's Porsche, plus 6.3 grams of marijuana and a two-inch 'roach', slang for a partially smoked marijuana cigarette.

There were 6.9 grams of marijuana in a plastic bag in a cabinet in the living room of the main residence. In the nightstand in the bedroom used by Frykowski and Folger were 30 grams of hashish, plus ten capsules which, later analyzed, proved to be a relatively new drug known as MDA. There was also marijuana residue in the ashtray on the stand next to Sharon Tate's bed, a marijuana cigarette on the desk near the front door, and two more in the guest house.

Had a drug party been in progress, one of the participants 'freaking out' and slaying everyone there? The police put this at the top of their list of possible reasons for the murders, though well aware this theory had several weaknesses, chief among them the presumption that there was a single killer, wielding a gun in one hand, a bayonet in the other, at the same time carrying 43 feet of rope, all of which, conveniently, he just happened to bring along. Also, there were the wires. If they had been cut *before* the murders, this indicated premeditation, not a spontaneous flare-up. If cut *after*, why?

Or could the murders have been the result of a drug 'burn', the killer(s) arriving to make a delivery or buy, an argument over money or bad drugs erupting into violence? This was the second, and in many ways the most likely, of the five theories the detectives would list in their first investigative report.

The third theory was a variation of the second, the killer(s) deciding to keep both the money and the drugs.

The fourth was the residential burglary theory.

The fifth, that these were 'deaths by hire', the killer(s) being sent to the house to eliminate one or more of the victims, then, in order to escape identification, finding it necessary to kill all. But would a hired killer choose as one of his weapons something as large, conspicuous, and unwieldy as a bayonet? And would he keep stabbing and stabbing and stabbing in a mad frenzy, as so obviously had been done in this case?

The drug theories seemed to make the most sense. In the investigation that followed, as the police interviewed acquaintances of the victims, and the victims' habits and life styles emerged into clearer focus, the possibility that drugs were in some way linked to the motive became in some minds such a certainty that when given a clue which could have solved the case, they refused even to consider it.

The police were not the only ones to think of drugs.

On hearing of the deaths, actor Steve McQueen, long-time friend of Jay Sebring, suggested that the hair stylist's home should be rid of narcotics to protect his family and business. Though McQueen did not himself participate in the 'housecleaning', by the time LAPD got around to searching Sebring's residence, anything embarrassing had been removed.

Others developed instant paranoia. No one was sure who the police would question, or when. An unidentified film figure told a *Life* reporter: 'Toilets are flushing all over Beverly Hills; the entire Los Angeles sewer system is stoned.'

FILM STAR, 4 OTHERS
DEAD IN BLOOD ORGY
Sharon Tate Victim
In 'Ritual' Murders

The headlines dominated the front pages of the afternoon papers, became the big news on radio and TV. The bizarre nature of the crime, the number of victims, and their prominence – a beautiful movie star, the heiress to a coffee fortune, her jet-set playboy paramour, an internationally known hair stylist – would combine to make this probably the most publicized murder case in history, excepting only the assassination of President John F. Kennedy. Even the staid New York *Times*, which rarely reports crime on its front page, did so the next day, and many days thereafter.

The accounts that day and the next were notable for the unusual amount of detail they contained. So much information had been given out, in fact, that the detectives would have difficulty in finding 'polygraph keys' for questioning suspects.

In any homicide, it is standard practice to withhold certain information which presumably only the police and the killer(s) know. If a suspect confesses, or agrees to a polygraph examination, these keys can then be used to determine if he is telling the truth.

Owing to the many leaks, the detectives assigned to the 'Tate case', as the press was already calling the murders, could only come up with five: (1) That the knife used was probably a bayonet. (2) That the gun was probably a .22 caliber revolver. (3) The exact dimensions of the rope, as well as the way it was looped and tied. And (4) and (5), that a pair of horn-rimmed glasses and a Buck knife had been found.

The amount of information unofficially released so bothered LAPD brass that a tight lid was clamped on further disclosures. This didn't please the reporters; also, lacking hard news, many turned to conjecture and speculation. In the days that followed a monumental amount of false information was published. It was widely reported, for example, that Sharon Tate's unborn child had been ripped from her womb; that one or both of her breasts had been slashed off; that several of the victims had been sexually mutilated. The towel over Sebring's face became a white hood (KKK ?) or a black hood (satanists?), depending on which paper or magazine you read.

When it came to the man charged with the murders, however, there was a paucity of information. It was presumed, initially, that the police were maintaining silence to protect Garretson's rights. It was also presumed that LAPD had to have a strong case against him or they wouldn't have arrested him.

During the first few days a total of forty-three officers would visit the crime scene, looking for weapons and other evidence. In searching the loft above the living room, Sergeant Mike McGann found a film can containing a roll of video-tape. Sergeant Ed Henderson took it to the Police Academy, which had screening facilities. The film showed Sharon and Roman Polanski making love. With a certain delicacy, the tape was not booked into evidence but was returned to the loft where it had been found.

In addition to searching the premises, detectives interviewed neighbors, asking if they had seen any strange people in the area.

Ray Asin recalled that two or three months before there had been a large party at 10050 Cielo Drive, the guests arriving in 'hippie garb'. He got the impression, however, that they weren't actually hippies, as most arrived in Rolls-Royces and Cadillacs.

Emmett Steele, who had been awakened by the barking of his hunting dogs the previous night, remembered that in recent weeks someone had been racing a dune buggy up and down the hills late at night, but he never got a close look at the driver and passengers.

Most of those interviewed, however, claimed they had neither seen nor heard anything out of the ordinary.

The detectives were left with far more questions than answers. However, they were hopeful one person could put the puzzle together for them: William Garretson.

The detectives downtown were less optimistic. Following his arrest, the 19-year-old had been taken to West Los Angeles jail and interrogated. The officers found his answers 'stuporous and non-responsive', and were of the opinion that he was under the residual effect of some drug. It was also possible, as Garretson himself claimed, that he had slept little the previous night, just a few hours in the morning, and that he was exhausted, and very scared.

Shortly after this, Garretson retained the services of attorney Barry Tarlow. A second interview, with Tarlow present, took place at Parker Center, headquarters of the Los Angeles Police Department. As far as the police were concerned, it too was unproductive. Garretson claimed that although he lived on the property, he had little contact with the people in the main house. He said that he'd only had one visitor the previous night, a boy named Steve Parent, who showed up about 11:45 and left about a half hour later. Questioned about Parent, Garretson said he didn't know him well. He'd hitched a ride up the canyon with him one night a couple of weeks ago and, on getting out of the car at the gate, had told Steve if he was ever in the neighborhood to drop in. Garretson, who lived by himself in the back house, except for the dogs, said he'd extended similar invitations to others. When Steve showed up, he was surprised: no one else ever had. But Steve didn't stay long, leaving after learning that Garretson wasn't interested in buying a clock radio Steve had for sale.

The police did not at this time connect Garretson's visitor with the youth in the Rambler, possibly because Garretson had earlier failed to identify him.

After conferring with Tarlow, Garretson agreed to take a polygraph examination, and one was scheduled for the following afternoon.

All day Wilfred and Juanita Parent had waited, and worried. Their 18-year-old son Steven hadn't come home the previous night. 'He didn't call, didn't leave word. He'd never done anything like that before,' Juanita Parent said.

About 8 P.M., aware that his wife was too distraught to cook dinner, Wilfred Parent took her and their three other children to a restaurant. Maybe when we get back, he told his wife, Steve will be there.

LAPD discovered the identity of John Doe 85 through a print and license check. Shortly after the Parents returned home, an El Monte policeman appeared at the door and handed Wilfred Parent a card with a number on it and told him to call it. He left without saying anything else.

Parent dialled the number.

'County Coroner's Office,' a man answered.

Confused, Parent identified himself and explained about the policeman and the card.

The call was transferred to a deputy coroner, who told him, 'Your son has apparently been involved in a shooting.'

'Is he dead?' Parent asked, stunned. His wife, hearing the question, became hysterical.

'We have a body down here,' the deputy coroner replied, 'and we believe it's your son.' He then went on to describe physical characteristics. They matched.

Parent hung up the phone and began sobbing. Later, understandably bitter, he'd remark, 'All I can say is that it was a hell of a way to tell somebody that their boy was dead.'

About nine that same Saturday night, August 9, 1969, Leno and Rosemary LaBianca and Susan Struthers, Rosemary's 21-year-old daughter by a previous marriage, left Lake Isabella for the long drive back to Los Angeles. The lake, a popular resort area, was some 150 miles from L.A.

Susan's brother, Frank Struthers, Jr, 15, had been vacationing at the lake with a friend, Jim Saffie, whose family had a cabin there. Rosemary and Leno had driven up the previous Tuesday, to leave their speedboat for the boys to use, then returned Saturday morning to pick up Frank and the boat. However, the boys were having such a good time the LaBiancas agreed to let Frank stay over another day, and they were returning now, without

35

him, driving their 1968 green Thunderbird, towing the speed-boat on a trailer behind.

Because of the boat, they couldn't drive at the speed Leno preferred, and fell behind most of the Saturday night freeway traffic that was speeding toward Los Angeles and environs. Like many others that night, they had the radio on and heard the news of the Tate murders. According to Susan, it seemed particularly to disturb Rosemary, who, a few weeks earlier, had told a close friend, 'Someone is coming in our house while we're away. Things have been gone through and the dogs are outside the house when they should be inside.'

Sunday, August 10, 1969

About 1 A.M. the LaBiancas dropped Susan off at her apartment on Greenwood Place, in the Los Feliz district of Los Angeles. Leno and Rosemary lived in the same neighborhood, at 3301 Waverly Drive, not far from Griffith Park.

The LaBiancas did not immediately return home but first drove to the corner of Hillhurst and Franklin.

John Fokianos, who had a newsstand on that corner, recognized the green Thunderbird-plus-boat as it pulled into the Standard station across the street, and while it was making a U-turn that would bring it alongside his stand, he reached for a copy of the Los Angeles *Herald Examiner*, Sunday edition, and a racing form. Leno was a regular customer.

To Fokianos, the LaBiancas seemed tired from their long trip. Business was slow, and they chatted for a few minutes, 'about Tate, the event of the day. That was the big news.' Fokianos would recall that Mrs LaBianca seemed very shaken by the deaths. He had some extra news fillers for the Sunday Los Angeles *Times*, which featured the murders, and he gave them one without charge.

He watched as they drove away. He did not notice the exact time, except that it was sometime between 1 and 2 A.M., probably closer to the latter, as not long after they left the bars closed and there was a flurry of business.

As far as is known, John Fokianos was the last person – excluding their killer(s) – to see Rosemary and Leno LaBianca alive.

At noon on Sunday the hall outside the autopsy room on the first floor of the Hall of Justice was packed with reporters and TV cameramen, all awaiting the coroner's announcement.

They would have a long wait. Although the autopsies had begun at 9:50 A.M., and a number of deputy coroners had been pressed into service, it would be 3 P.M. before the last autopsy was completed.

Dr R. C. Henry conducted the Folger and Sebring autopsies, Dr Gaston Herrera those of Frykowski and Parent. Dr Noguchi supervised and directed all four; in addition, he personally conducted the other autopsy, which began at 11:20 A.M.

Sharon Marie Polanski, 10050 Cielo Drive, female Caucasian, 26 years, 5–3, 135 pounds, blond hair, hazel eyes. Victim's occupation, actress . . .

Much of Sharon Tate's story sounded like a studio press release. It seemed she had always wanted to be an actress. At age 6 months she had been Miss Tiny Tot of Dallas, at 16 years Miss Richland, Washington, then Miss Autorama. When her father, a career army officer, was assigned to San Pedro, she would hitchhike into nearby Los Angeles, haunting the studios.

In addition to her ambition, she had at least one other thing in her favor: she was a very beautiful girl. She acquired an agent who succeeded in getting her a few commercials, then, in 1963, an audition for the TV series 'Petticoat Junction'. Producer Martin Ransohoff saw the pretty 22-year-old on the set and according to studio flackery, told her, 'Sweetie, I'm going to make you a star.'

The star was a long time ascending. Singing, dancing, and acting lessons were interspersed with bit parts, usually wearing a black wig, in 'The Beverly Hillbillies', 'Petticoat Junction', and two Ransohoff films, *The Americanization of Emily* and *The Sandpiper*. While the latter film, starring Elizabeth Taylor and Richard Burton, was being filmed in Big Sur, Sharon fell in love with the magnificently scenic coastline. Whenever she wanted to escape the Hollywood hassle, she fled there. Scrubbed of makeup, she would check into rustic Deetjen's Big Sur Inn, often alone, sometimes with girl friends, and walk the trails, sun at the beach, and blend in with the regulars at Nepenthe.

According to close friends, though Sharon Tate looked the part of the starlet, she didn't live up to at least one portion of that image. She was not promiscuous. Her relationships were few, and rarely casual, at least on her part. She seemed attracted to dominant men. In 1963 Jay Sebring spotted Sharon at a studio preview, prevailed upon a friend for an introduction, and, after a brief but much publicized courtship, they became lovers, a relationship which lasted until she met Roman Polanski.

It was 1965 before Ransohoff decided his protégée was ready for her first featured role, in *Eye of the Devil*, which starred Deborah Kerr and David Niven. Listed seventh in the credits, Sharon Tate played a country girl with bewitching powers. She had less than a dozen lines; her primary role was to look beautiful, which she did. This was to be true of almost all her movies.

Though set in France, the film was made in London, and it was here, in the summer of 1966, that she met Roman Polanski.

Polanski was at this time 33, and already acclaimed as one of Europe's leading directors. He had been born in Paris, his father a Russian Jew, his mother Polish of Russian stock. When Roman was 3, the family moved to Cracow. They were still there in 1940 when the Germans arrived and sealed off the ghetto. With his father's help, Roman managed to escape and lived with family friends until the war ended. Both his parents, however, were sent to concentration camps, his mother dying in Auschwitz.

Following the war, he spent five years at the Polish National Film Academy at Lodz. As his senior thesis, he wrote and directed *Two Men and a Wardrobe*, a much acclaimed surrealistic short. He made several other short films, among them *Mammals*, in which a Polish friend, Voytek Frykowski, played a thief. After an extended trip to Paris, Polanski returned to Poland to make *Knife in the Water*, his first feature-length effort. It won the Critics Award at the Venice Film Festival, was nominated for an Academy Award, and established Polanski, then only 27, as one of Europe's most promising filmmakers.

In 1965, Polanski made his first film in English, *Repulsion*, starring Catherine Deneuve. *Cul de Sac* followed, which won the

Best Film Award in the Berlin Film Festival, the Critics Award in Venice, a Diploma of Merit in Edinburgh, and the Giove Capitaliano Award in Rome. In the news stories following the Tate murders, reporters were quick to note that in *Repulsion* Miss Deneuve went mad and murdered two men, while in *Cul de Sac* the inhabitants of an isolated castle each meet a bizarre fate until only one man is left alive. They also noted Polanski's 'penchant for violence', without adding that most often in Polanski's films the violence was less explicit than implied.

When Ransohoff introduced Roman and Sharon at a large party, neither was at first particularly impressed. The introduction was not accidental. On learning that Polanski was considering doing a film spoof of horror movies, Ransohoff had offered to produce it. He wanted Sharon for the female lead. Polanski gave her a screen test and decided she would be acceptable for the part. The film was *The Fearless Vampire Killers*.

Before the filming was over, and after what was for Polanski a very long courtship, Sharon and Roman became off-screen lovers too. When Sebring flew to London, Sharon told him the news. If he took it hard, he was careful not to show it, very quickly settling into the role of family friend. Those who claimed that Sebring was still in love with Sharon were guessing – though Sebring knew hundreds of people, he apparently had few really close friends, and kept his inner feelings very much to himself – but it was a safe guess that although the nature of that love had changed, some deep attachment remained.

Paramount asked Polanski to do the film version of Ira Levin's novel *Rosemary's Baby*. The film, in which Mia Farrow played a young girl who had a child by Satan, was completed late in 1967. On January 20, 1968, to the surprise of many friends to whom Polanski had vowed never again to marry, he and Sharon were wed in a mod ceremony in London.

Rosemary's Baby premiered that June. That same month the Polanskis rented actress Patty Duke's home at 1600 Summit Ridge Drive in Los Angeles. It was while they were living there that Mrs Chapman began working for them. In early 1969 they heard that 10050 Cielo Drive might be vacant. Though they never met in person, Sharon talked to Terry Melcher on the phone several times, making arrangements to take over his unexpired lease. The Polanskis signed a rental agreement on February 12, 1969, at $1,200 a month, and moved in three days later.

Though *Rosemary's Baby* was a smash success, Sharon's own career had never quite taken off. Her biggest role came in the 1967 film *Valley of the Dolls*, in which she played the actress Jennifer who, on learning that she had breast cancer, takes an overdose of sleeping pills. Not long before her death, Jennifer remarks, 'I have no talent. All I have is a body.'

There were reviewers who felt that adequately summed up Sharon Tate's performance. To be fairer, to date she hadn't been given a single role which gave her a chance to bring out whatever acting ability she may have had.

She was not a star, not yet. Her career seemed to hesitate on the edge of a breakthrough, but it could easily have remained stationary, or gone the other way.

But for the first time in her life, Sharon's ambition had slipped to second place. Her marriage and her pregnancy had become her whole life. According to those closest to her, she seemed oblivious to all else.

Hollywood is a bitchy town. In interviewing acquaintances of the victims, LAPD would encounter an incredible amount of venom. Interestingly enough, in the dozens of interview sheets, no one who actually knew Sharon Tate said anything bad about her. Very sweet, somewhat naïve – these were the words most often used.

That Sunday a Los Angeles *Times* reporter who had known Sharon described her as 'an astonishingly beautiful woman with a statuesque figure and a face of great delicacy'.

But then he didn't see her as Coroner Noguchi did.

Cause of death: Multiple stab wounds of the chest and back, penetrating the heart, lungs, and liver, causing massive hemorrhage. Victim was stabbed sixteen times, five or which wounds were in and of themselves fatal.

Jay Sebring, 9860 Easton Drive, Benedict Canyon, Los Angeles,

*male Caucasian, 35 years, 5–6, 120 pounds, black hair, brown
eyes. Victim was a hair stylist and had a corporation known as
Sebring International . . .*

Born Thomas John Kummer, in Detroit, Michigan, he had
changed his name to Jay Sebring shortly after arriving in Hollywood, following a four-year stint as a Navy barber, borrowing
the last name from the famous Florida sports-car race because he
liked the image it projected.

In his personal life, as in his work, appearances were all-important. He drove an expensive sports car, frequented the 'in'
clubs, even had his Levi jackets custom-made. He employed a
full-time butler, gave lavish parties, and lived in a 'jinxed' mansion, 9860 Easton Drive, Benedict Canyon. Once the love nest of
actress Jean Harlow and producer Paul Bern, it was here, in
Harlow's bedroom, that Bern had committed suicide, two
months after their marriage. According to acquaintances, Sebring
had bought the house because of its 'far out' reputation.

It was widely reported that a motion-picture studio had flown
Sebring to London just to cut George Peppard's hair, at a cost of
$25,000. While the report was probably as factual as another also
current, that he had a black belt in karate (he had taken a few
lessons from Bruce Lee), there was no question that he was the
leading men's hair stylist in the United States. In addition to
Peppard, his customers included Frank Sinatra, Paul Newman,
Steve McQueen, Peter Lawford, and other motion-picture stars,
many of whom had promised to invest in his new corporation,
Sebring International.

On April 9, 1968, Sebring had signed an application for a
$500,000 executive protection policy with the Occidental Life
Insurance Company of California. A background investigation,
conducted by the Retail Credit Company, estimated his net
worth at $100,000, of which $80,000 was the appraised worth of
his residence. Sebring, Inc., the original business, had assets of
$150,000, with liabilities of $115,000.

The investigators also looked into Sebring's personal life. He
had married once, in October 1960, he and his wife, Cami, a

model, separating in August 1963, their divorce becoming final in March 1965, the couple having had no children. The report also stated that Sebring had never 'used drugs as a habit'. LAPD knew otherwise.

They also knew something else the credit company investigators had never discovered. There was a darker side to Jay Sebring's nature that surfaced during numerous interviews conducted by the police. As noted in the official report: 'He was considered a ladies' man and took numerous women to his residence in the Hollywood hills. He would tie the women up with a small sash cord and, if they agreed, would whip them, after which they would have sexual relations.'

Rumors of this had long circulated around Hollywood. Now picked up by the press, they became the basis for numerous theories, chief among them that some sort of sadomasochistic orgy had been in progress on the night of August 9, 1969, at 10050 Cielo Drive.

LAPD never seriously considered Sebring's odd sexual habits a possible cause of the murders. None of the girls interviewed – and the number was large, Sebring frequently dating five or six different girls a week – claimed that Sebring had actually hurt them, though he often asked them to pretend pain. Nor, as far as could be determined, was Sebring involved in group sex: he was too afraid his private quirks would subject him to ridicule.

Cause of death: Exsanguination – victim literally bled to death. Victim had been stabbed seven times and shot once, at least three of the stab wounds, as well as the gunshot wound, being in and of itself fatal.

Abigail Anne Folger, female Caucasian, 25 years, 5–5, 120 pounds, brown hair, hazel eyes, residence since the first of April, 10050 Cielo Drive. Prior to that she lived at 2774 Woodstock Road. Occupation, heiress to the Folger coffee fortune...

Abigail 'Gibby' Folger's coming-out party had been held at the St Francis Hotel in San Francisco on December 21, 1961. The Italianate ball was one of the highlights of the social season.

After that she had attended Radcliffe, graduating with honors;

worked for a time as publicity director for the University of California Art Museum in Berkeley; quit that to work in a New York bookstore; then became involved in social work in the ghettos. It was while in New York, in early 1968, that Polish novelist Jerzy Kosinski introduced her to Voytek Frykowski. They left New York together that August, driving to Los Angeles. Through Frykowski, she met the Polanskis, Sebring, and others in their circle. She was one of the investors in Sebring International.

Shortly after arriving in Southern California, she registered as a volunteer social worker for the Los Angeles County Welfare Department, and would get up at dawn each day for assignments that took her into Watts, Pacoima, and other ghetto areas. She continued this work until the day before she and Frykowski moved into 10050 Cielo Drive.

Something changed after that. Probably it was a combination of things. She became depressed over how little such work actually accomplished, how big the problems stayed. 'A lot of social workers go home at night, take a bath, and wash off their day,' she told an old San Francisco friend. 'I can't. The suffering gets under your skin.' She was also disturbed about the way her affair with Frykowski was going, and with their use of drugs, which had passed the point of experimentation.

The police were unable to determine exactly when Folger and Frykowski began to use drugs heavily, on a regular basis. It was learned that on their cross-country trip they had stopped in Irving, Texas, staying several days with a big dope dealer well known to local and Dallas police. Dealers were among their regular guests both before and after they moved to Cielo Drive. William Tennant told police that whenever he visited the latter residence, Abigail 'always seemed to be in a stupor from narcotics'. When her mother last talked to her, about ten that Friday night, she said Gibby had sounded lucid but 'a little high'.

The coroners discovered 2.4 mg. of methylenedioxyamphetamine – MDA – in Abigail Folger's system. That this was a larger amount than was found in Voytek Frykowski's body – 0.6 mg. –

did not necessarily indicate that she had taken a larger quantity of the drug, but could mean she had taken it at a later time.

Effects of the drug vary, depending on the individual and the dosage, but one thing was clear. That night she was fully aware of what was happening.

Victim had been stabbed twenty-eight times.

Wojiciech 'Voytek' Frykowski, male Caucasian, 32 years, 5–10, 165 pounds, blond hair, blue eyes. Frykowski had been living with Abigail Folger in a common-law relationship . . .

'Voytek,' Roman Polanski would later tell reporters, 'was a man of little talent but immense charm.' The two had been friends in Poland, Frykowski's father reputedly having helped finance one of Polanski's early films. Even in Poland, Frykowski had been known as a playboy. According to fellow émigrés, he had once taken on, and rendered inoperative, two members of the secret police, which may have had something to do with his exit from Poland in 1967. He had married twice, and had one son, who had remained behind when he moved to Paris. Both there and, later, in New York, Polanski had given him money and encouragement, hopeful – but knowing Voytek well, not too optimistic – that one of his grand plans would come through. None ever quite did. He told people that he was a writer, but no one could recall having read anything he had written.

Friends of Abigail Folger told the police that Frykowski had introduced her to drugs so as to keep her under his control. Friends of Frykowski said the opposite – that Folger had provided the drugs so as not to lose him.

According to the police report: 'He had no means of support and lived off Folger's fortune . . . He used cocaine, mescaline, LSD, marijuana, hashish in large amounts . . . He was an extrovert and gave invitations to almost everyone he met to come visit him at his residence. Narcotic parties were the order of the day.'

He had fought hard for his life. Victim was shot twice, struck over the head thirteen times with a blunt object, and stabbed fifty-one times.

Steven Earl Parent, male Caucasian, 18 years, 6–0, 175 pounds, red hair, brown eyes . . .

He had graduated from Arroyo High School in June; dated several girls but no one in particular; had a full-time job as a delivery boy for a plumbing company, plus a part-time job, evenings, as salesman for a stereo shop, holding down the two jobs so he could save money to attend junior college that September.

Victim had one defensive slash wound, and had been shot four times.

During the fluoroscopy examination that preceded the Sebring autopsy, Dr Noguchi discovered a bullet lodged between Sebring's back and his shirt. Three more bullets were found during the autopsies: one in Frykowski's body, two in Parent's. These – plus the slug fragments found in Parent's automobile – were turned over to Sergeant William Lee, Firearms and Explosives Unit, S I D, for study. Lee concluded that all the bullets had probably been fired from the same gun, and that they were .22 caliber.

While the autopsies were in progress, Sergeants Paul Whiteley and Charles Guenther, two homicide detectives from the Los Angeles Sheriff's Office, approached Sergeant Jess Buckles, one of the Los Angeles Police Department detectives assigned to the Tate homicides, and told him something very curious.

On July 31 they had gone to 964 Old Topanga Road in Malibu, to investigate a report of a possible homicide. They had found the body of Gary Hinman, a 34-year-old music teacher. He had been stabbed to death.

The curious thing: as in the Tate homicides, a message had been left at the scene. On the wall in the living room, not far from Hinman's body, were the words POLITICAL PIGGY, printed in the victim's own blood.

Whiteley also told Buckles that they had arrested a suspect in connection with the murder, one Robert 'Bobby' Beausoleil, a young hippie musician. He had been driving a car that belonged to Hinman, there was blood on his shirt and trousers, and a knife had been found hidden in the tire well of the vehicle. The arrest had occurred on August 6; therefore he had been in custody at the time of the Tate homicides. However, it was possible that he hadn't been the only one involved in the Hinman murder. Beausoleil had been living at Spahn's Ranch, an old movie ranch near the Los Angeles suburb of Chatsworth, with a bunch of other hippies. It was an odd group, their leader, a guy named Charlie, apparently having convinced them that he was Jesus Christ.

Buckles, Whiteley would later recall, lost interest when he mentioned hippies. 'Naw,' he replied, 'we know what's behind these murders. They're part of a big dope transaction.'

Whiteley again emphasized the odd similarities. Like mode of death. In both cases a message had been left. Both printed. Both in a victim's blood. And in both the letters PIG appeared. Any one of these things would be highly unusual. But *all* – the odds against its being a coincidence must be astronomical.

Sergeant Buckles, LAPD, told Sergeants Whiteley and Guenther, LASO, 'If you don't hear from us in a week or so, that means we're on to something else.'

A little more then twenty-four hours after the discovery of the Tate victims, the Los Angeles Police Department was given a lead by the Los Angeles Sheriff's Office, which, if followed, could possibly have broken the case.

Buckles never did call, nor did he think the information important enough to walk across the autopsy room and mention the conversation to his superior, Lieutenant Robert Helder, who was in charge of the Tate investigation.

At Lieutenant Helder's suggestion, Dr Noguchi withheld specifics when he met with the press. He did not mention the number of wounds, nor did he say anything about two of the victims having ingested drugs. He did, again, deny the already much repeated reports that there had been sexual molestation and/or mutilation.

Asked about Sharon's child, he said that Mrs Polanski was in the eighth month of her pregnancy; that the child was a perfectly formed boy; and that had he been removed by post-mortem cesarean within the first twenty minutes after the mother's death, his life probably could have been saved. 'But by the time the bodies were discovered, it was too late.'

Lieutenant Helder also talked to the press that day. Yes, Garretson was still in custody. No, he could not comment on the evidence against him, except to say that the police were now investigating his acquaintances.

Pressed further, Helder admitted, 'There's no solid information that will limit us to a single suspect. It could've been one man. It could've been two. It could've been three.

'But,' he added, 'I don't feel that we have a maniac running around.'

Lieutenant A. H. Burdick began the polygraph examination of William Garretson at 4:25 that afternoon, at Parker Center.

Burdick did not immediately hook up Garretson. In accordance with routine, the initial portion of the examination was conversational, the examiner attempting to put the suspect at ease while eliciting as much background information as possible.

Though obviously frightened, Garretson loosened up a little as he talked. He told Burdick that he was nineteen, from Ohio, and had been hired by Rudi Altobelli in March, just before Altobelli left for Europe. His job was simple: to look after the guest house and Altobelli's three dogs. In return, he had been given a place to stay, thirty-five dollars a week, and the promise of an airline ticket back to Ohio when Altobelli returned.

He had little to do with the people who lived in the main house, Garretson claimed. Several of his replies seemed to bear this out. He still referred to Frykowski, for example, as 'the younger Polanski', while he appeared unfamiliar with Sebring, either by name or description, though he had seen the black Porsche in the driveway on several occasions.

About 8:30 or 9 P.M. Friday, Garretson said, he went down to the Sunset Strip, to buy a pack of cigarettes and a TV dinner. He guessed the time of his return at about ten, but couldn't be sure, not having a watch. As he passed the main house, he noticed the lights were on, but he didn't see anyone. Nor did he observe anything out of the ordinary.

Then 'about a quarter of twelve or something like that, Steve [Parent] came up and, you know, he brought his radio with him. He had a radio, clock radio; and I didn't expect him or anything, and he asked me how I'd been and everything...' Parent plugged in the radio, to demonstrate how it worked, but Garretson wasn't interested.

Then 'I gave him a beer ... and he drank it and then he called somebody – somebody on Santa Monica and Doheny – and he said that he would be going there, and so then he left, and, you know, that's when – that's the last time I saw him.'

When found in Parent's car, the clock radio had stopped at 12:15 A.M., the approximate time of the murder. Although it could have been a remarkable coincidence, the logical presumption was that Parent had set it while demonstrating it to Garretson, then unplugged it just before he left. This would coincide with Garretson's estimate of the time.

According to Garretson, after Parent left, he wrote some letters and played the stereo, not going to sleep until just before dawn. Though he claimed to have heard nothing unusual during the night, he admitted that he had been 'scared'.

Why? Burdick asked. Well, Garretson replied, not long after Steve left, he noticed that the handle of the door was turned down, as if someone had tried to open it. And when he tried to use the phone, to learn the time, he found it was dead.

Like the other officers, Burdick found it difficult to believe that Garretson, though admittedly awake all night, heard nothing, while neighbors even farther away heard shots or screams. Garretson insisted, however, that he had neither heard nor seen anything. He was less sure on another point – whether he had gone out into the back yard when he let Altobelli's dogs out. To Burdick he appeared evasive about this. From the yard, however, he couldn't see the main house, though he might have heard something.

As far as LAPD was concerned, the moment of truth was now arriving. Burdick began setting up the polygraph, at the same time reading Garretson the list of questions he intended to ask.

This, too, was standard operating procedure, and more than a little psychological. Knowing a certain question was going to be asked, but not when, built tension, accentuating the response. He then began the test.

Q. 'Is your true last name Garretson?'

A. 'Yes.'

No significant response.

Q. 'Concerning Steve, did you cause his death?'

A. 'No.'

Facing forward, Garretson couldn't see Burdick's face. Burdick kept his voice matter of fact as he moved on to the next question, in no way indicating that the steel pens had jerked across the graph.

Q. 'You understood the question?'

A. 'Yes.'

Q. 'Do you feel responsible for Steve's death?'

A. 'That he even knew me, yes.'

Q. 'Huh?'

A. 'That he even knew me. I mean he wouldn't have come up that night, and nothing would have happened in other words to him.'

Burdick relieved the pressure cup on Garretson's arm, told him to relax, talked to him informally for a while. Then again the pressure, and the questions, only slightly changed this time.

Q. 'Is your true last name Garretson?'

A. 'Yes.'

Q. 'Did you shoot Steve?'

A. 'No.'

No significant response.

More test questions, followed by 'Do you know who caused Mrs Polanski's death?'

A. 'No.'

Q. 'Did you cause Mrs Polanski's death?'

A. 'No.'

Still no significant response.

Burdick now accepted Garretson's explanation, that he felt responsibility for Parent's death, but had no part in causing it or the other murders. The examination went on for another half hour or so, during which Burdick closed off several avenues of investigation. Garretson was not gay; he had never had sex with any of the victims; he had never sold drugs.

There was no indication that Garretson was lying, but he remained nervous throughout. Burdick asked him why. Garretson explained that when he was being taken to his cell, a policeman had pointed at him, saying, 'There's the guy that killed all those people.'

Although legally inadmissible as evidence, the police believed in the polygraph.* Though uninformed of it at the time, Garretson had passed. 'At the conclusion of the examination,' Captain Don Martin, commander, SID, wrote in his official report, 'it was the examiner's opinion that Mr Garretson was truthful and not criminally involved in the Polanski homicides.'

For all intents and purposes, with the polygraph William Eston Garretson ceased to be a 'good suspect'. Yet a bothersome question remained: Every single human being at 10050 Cielo Drive had been slaughtered save one; why?

Because there was no immediate answer, and certainly in part because, having been the only warm body on the premises, he had seemed such a likely suspect, Garretson was held for another day.

That Sunday, LAPD not only lost their best suspect to date, another promising lead fizzled out. Sharon Tate's red Ferrari, which the police had thought might have been used as a getaway

* In 1972 a Los Angeles Superior Court judge broke with precedent and permitted the results of a polygraph test to be received into evidence in a marijuana case.

car, was located in a Beverly Hills garage where Sharon had taken it the previous week for repairs.

That evening Roman Polanski returned from London. Reporters who saw him at the airport described him as 'terribly crushed' and 'beaten by the tragedy'. Though he refused to talk with the press, a spokesman for him denied there was any truth to the rumors of a marital rift. Polanski had remained in London, he said, because he hadn't finished his work there. Sharon had returned home early, by boat, because of airline restrictions against travel during the last two months of pregnancy.

Frank Struthers also returned to Los Angeles that Sunday night. About 8:30 P.M. the Saffies dropped him off at the end of the long driveway leading to the LaBianca residence. Lugging his suitcase and camping equipment up the driveway, the fifteen-year-old noticed that the speedboat was still on the trailer behind Leno's Thunderbird. That seemed odd; his stepfather didn't like to leave the boat out overnight. Stowing his equipment in the garage, he went to the back door of the residence.

Only then did he notice that all the window shades had been pulled down. He couldn't recall ever seeing them that way before, and it frightened him just a little bit. The light was on in the kitchen, and he knocked on the door. There was no response He called out. Again no answer.

Really upset now, he walked to the closest pay phone, which was at a hamburger stand at Hyperion and Rowena. He dialed the number of the house, then, getting no response, tried to reach his sister at the restaurant where she worked. Susan wasn't working that night, but the manager offered to try her apartment. Frank gave him the number of the pay phone.

Shortly after nine she called. She hadn't seen or heard from their mother and stepfather since they had dropped her off at her apartment the previous night. Telling Frank to remain where he was, she called her boy friend, Joe Dorgan, and told him Frank thought something was wrong at the house. About 9:30, Joe and Susan picked up Frank at the hamburger stand, the three driving directly to 3301 Waverly Drive.

Rosemary often left a set of house keys in her own car. They found them and opened the back door. Dorgan suggested that Susan remain in the kitchen while he and Frank checked out the rest of the house. They proceeded through the dining room. When they got to the living room, they saw Leno.

He was sprawled on his back between the couch and a chair. There was a throw pillow over his head, some kind of cord around his neck, and the tops of his pajamas were torn open so his stomach was bare. Something was protruding from his stomach.

He was so still they knew he was dead.

Afraid Susan would follow and see what they had, they returned to the kitchen. Joe picked up the kitchen phone to call the police, then, worried that he might be disturbing evidence, put it back down, telling Susan, 'Everything's O.K.; let's get out of here.' But Susan knew everything wasn't O.K. On the refrigerator door someone had written something in what looked like red paint.

Hurrying back down the driveway, they stopped at a duplex across the street, and Dorgan rang the bell of 3308 Waverly Drive. The peephole opened. Dorgan said there had been a stabbing and he wanted to call the police. The person inside refused to open the door, saying, 'We'll call the police for you.'

LAPD's switchboard logged the call at 10:26 P.M., the caller complaining about some juveniles making a disturbance.

Unsure whether the person had really made the call, Dorgan had already pushed the bell of the other apartment, 3306. Dr and Mrs Merry J. Brigham let the three young people in. However, they were so upset Mrs Brigham had to complete the call. At 10:35, Unit 6A39, a black-and-white manned by officers W. C. Rodriquez and J. C. Toney, was dispatched to the address, arriving very quickly, five to seven minutes later.

While Susan and Frank remained with the doctor and his wife, Dorgan accompanied the two Hollywood Division officers to the LaBianca residence. Toney covered the back door while Rodriquez went around the house. The front door was closed but not locked. After one look inside, he ran back to the car and called for a backup unit, a supervisor, and an ambulance.

Within a few minutes, Ambulance Unit G-1 arrived, and Leno LaBianca was pronounced DOA – dead on arrival. In addition to the pillow Frank and Joe had seen, there was a bloody pillowcase over his head. The cord around his neck was attached to a massive lamp, the cord knotted so tightly it appeared he had been throttled with it. His hands were tied behind his back with a leather thong. The object protruding from his stomach was an ivory-handled, bi-tined carving fork. In addition to a number of stab wounds in the abdomen, someone had carved the letters WAR in the naked flesh.

The backup unit, 6L40, manned by Sergeant Edward L. Cline, arrived just after the ambulance. A veteran of sixteen years, Cline took charge, obtaining a pink DOA slip from the two attendants before they left.

The pair were already on their way down the driveway when Rodriquez called them back. Cline had found another body, in the master bedroom.

Rosemary LaBianca was lying face down on the bedroom floor, parallel to the bed and dresser, in a large pool of blood. She was wearing a short pink nightgown and, over it, an expensive dress, blue with white horizontal stripes which Susan would later identify as one of her mother's favorites. Both nightgown and dress were bunched up over her head, so her back, buttocks, and legs were bare. Cline didn't even try to count the stab wounds, there were so many. Her hands were not tied but, like Leno, she had a pillowcase over her head and a lamp cord was wrapped around her neck. The cord was attached to one of a pair of bedroom lamps, both of which had overturned. The tautness of the cord, plus a second pool of blood about two feet from the body, indicated that perhaps she had tried to crawl, pulling the lamps over while doing so.

A second pink DOA slip was filled out, for Mrs Rosemary LaBianca. Joe Dorgan had to tell Susan and Frank.

There was writing, in what appeared to be blood, in three places in the residence. High up on the north wall in the living room, above several paintings, were printed the words DEATH TO

PIGS. On the south wall, to the left of the front door, even higher up, was the single word RISE. There were two words on the refrigerator door in the kitchen, the first of which was misspelled. They read HEALTER SKELTER.

Monday, August 11, 1969

At 12:15 A.M. the case was assigned to Robbery-Homicide. Sergeant Danny Galindo, who had spent the previous night on guard duty at the Tate residence, was the first detective to arrive, at about 1 A.M. He was joined shortly after by Inspector K. J. McCauley and several other detectives, while an additional unit, ordered by Cline, sealed off the grounds.

Galindo made a detailed search of the one-story residence. Except for the overturned lamps, there were no signs of a struggle. Nor was there any evidence that robbery had been the motive. The items logged into the County Public Administrator's Report included jewelry, watches, camera equipment, guns and numerous other easily fenced items.

Several days later Frank Struthers returned to the residence with the police. The only missing items, as far as he could determine, were Rosemary's wallet and her wristwatch.

Galindo was unable to find any indications of forced entry. However, testing the back door, he found it could be jimmied very easily. He was able to open it with only a strip of celluloid.

The detectives made a number of other discoveries. The ivory-handled carving fork found protruding from Leno's stomach belonged to a set found in a kitchen drawer. There were some watermelon rinds in the sink. There were also blood splatters, both there and in the rear bathroom. And a piece of blood-soaked paper was found on the floor in the dining room, its frayed end suggesting that possibly it had been the instrument used to print the words.

In many ways the activities at 3301 Waverly Drive the rest of that night were a replay of those that had occurred at 10050 Cielo

Drive less than forty-eight hours earlier, except that in this case Sergeant Joe Granado didn't take *any* subtypes.

The blood sample from the kitchen sink wasn't sufficient to determine if it was animal or human, but all the other samples tested positive on the Ouchterlony test, indicating they were human blood. The blood in the rear bathroom, as well as all the blood in the vicinity of Rosemary LaBianca's body, was type A – Rosemary LaBianca's type. All the other samples, including that taken from the rumpled paper and the various writings, were type B – Leno LaBianca's type.

The fingerprint men from SID, Sergeants Harold Dolan and J. Claborn, lifted a total of twenty-five latents, all but six of which would later be identified as belonging to Leno, Rosemary, or Frank. It was apparent to Dolan, from examining those areas where fingerprints should have been but weren't, that an effort had been made to eradicate prints. For example, there was not even a smudge on the ivory handle of the carving fork, on the chrome handle of the refrigerator door, or on the enamel finish of the door itself – all surfaces that readily lent themselves to receiving latent fingerprints. The refrigerator door on close examination showed wipe marks.

After the police photographer had finished, a deputy coroner supervised the removal of the bodies. The pillowcases were left in place over the heads of the victims; the lamp cords were cut near the bases, so the knots remained intact for study. A representative of the Animal Regulation Department removed the three dogs, which, when the first officers arrived, had been found inside the house.

Left behind were the puzzle pieces. But this time at least a partial pattern was discernible, in the similarities:

Los Angeles, California; consecutive nights, multiple murders; victims affluent Caucasians; multiple stab wounds; incredible savagery; absence of a conventional motive; no evidence of ransacking or robbery; ropes around the necks of two Tate victims, cords around the necks of both LaBiancas. And the bloody printing.

Yet within twenty-four hours the police would decide there was no connection between the two sets of murders.

SECOND RITUAL
KILLINGS HERE
Los Feliz Couple Slain;
Link to 5-Way Murder Seen

The headlines screamed from the front pages that Monday morning; TV programs were interrupted for updates; to the millions of Angelenos who commuted to work via the freeways their car radios seemed to broadcast little else.*

It was then the fear began.

When the news of the Tate homicides broke, even those acquainted with the victims were less fearful than shocked, for simultaneously came the announcement that a suspect had been arrested and charged with the murders. Garretson, however, had been in custody when these new murders took place. And with his release that Monday – still looking as puzzled and frightened as when the police 'captured' him – the panic began. And spread.

Sometimes fear can be measured. Among the barometers: In two days one Beverly Hills sporting goods store sold 200 firearms; prior to the murders, they averaged three or four a day. Some of the private security forces doubled, then tripled, their personnel. Guard dogs, once priced at $200, now sold for $1,500; those who supplied them soon ran out. Locksmiths quoted two-week delays on orders. Accidental shootings, suspicious persons reports – all suddenly increased.

The news that there had been twenty-eight murders in Los Angeles that weekend (the average being one a day) did nothing to decrease the apprehension.

It was reported that Frank Sinatra was in hiding; that Mia Farrow wouldn't attend her friend Sharon's funeral because, a

---

* Some of the details were garbled. It was reported, for example, that the pillowcases were white hoods; that the phrase DEATH TO PIGS had been printed in blood on the refrigerator door, when it actually appeared on the wall in the living room. But enough information had leaked out for the detectives again to have trouble finding polygraph keys.

relative explained, 'Mia is afraid she will be next'; that Tony Bennett had moved from his bungalow on the grounds of the Beverly Hills Hotel to an inside suite 'for greater security'; that Steve McQueen now kept a weapon under the front seat of his sports car; that Jerry Lewis had installed an alarm system in his home complete with closed circuit TV.

A cloud of fright hung over southern California more dense than its smog. It would not dissipate for months. As late as the folowing March, William Kloman would write in *Esquire*: 'In the great houses of Bel Air, terror sends people flying to their telephones when a branch falls from a tree outside.'

POLITICAL PIGGY – Hinman.
PIG – Tate.
DEATH TO PIGS – LaBianca.

In each case, written in the blood of one of the victims.

Sergeant Buckles still didn't think it important enough to check further.

Deputy Medical Examiner David Katsuyama conducted the LaBianca autopsies. Before starting, he removed the pillowcases from the heads of the victims. Only then was it discovered that in addition to the carving fork embedded in his abdomen, a knife had been stuck in Leno LaBianca's throat.

Since none of the personnel at the scene had observed the knife, this became one of the LaBianca polygraph keys. There were two others. For some reason, though the phrase DEATH TO PIGS had leaked to the press, neither RISE nor HEALTER SKELTER had.

Leno A. LaBianca, 3301 Waverly Drive, male Caucasian, 44 years, 6–0, 220 pounds, brown eyes, brown hair ...

Born in Los Angeles, son of the founder of the State Wholesale Grocery Company, Leno had gone into the family business after attending the University of Southern California, eventually becoming president of Gateway Markets, a Southern California chain.

As far as the police were able to determine, Leno had no enemies. Yet they soon discovered that he too had a secret side. Friends and relatives described him as quiet and conservative; they were amazed to learn, after his death, that he owned nine thoroughbred horses, the most prominent being Kildare Lady, and that he was a chronic gambler, frequenting the tracks nearly every racing day, often betting $500 at a time. Nor did they know that he was, at the time of his death, some $230,000 in debt.

In the weeks ahead the LaBianca detectives would do a re-remarkable job of tracking their way through the tangled maze of Leno LaBianca's complex financial affairs. The possibility that Leno might have been the victim of loan sharks, however, fell apart when it was learned that Rosemary LaBianca was quite wealthy herself, having more than sufficient assets to pay off Leno's debts.

One of Leno's former partners, also Italian, who knew of his gambling habits, told the police he thought the murders might have been committed by the Mafia. He admitted he had no evidence to support this; however, the detectives did learn that for a short time Leno had been on the board of directors of a Hollywood bank which LAPD and LASO intelligence units believed was backed by 'hoodlum money'. They had been unable to prove this, though several other broad members were indicated and convicted of a kiting scheme. The possibility of a Mafia link became one of a number of leads that would have to be checked out.

Cause of death: Multiple stab wounds. Victim had twelve stab wounds, plus fourteen puncture wounds made by a double-tined fork, for a total of twenty-six separate wounds, any one of six of which could in and of itself have been fatal.

Rosemary LaBianca, 3301 Waverly Drive, female Caucasian, 38 years, 5–5, 125 pounds, brown hair, brown eyes . . .

It was probable that even Rosemary did not know a great deal about her early years. It was believed that she had been born in Mexico, of American parents, then orphaned or abandoned in Arizona. She remained in an orphanage there until the age of twelve, when she was adopted by a family named Harmon, who took her to California. She had met her first husband while working as a carhop at the Brown Derby Drive-In in Los Feliz in the late 1940s, while still in her teens. They were divorced in 1958, and it was shortly after this, while working as a waitress at the Los Feliz Inn, that she met and married Leno LaBianca.

According to Ruth Sivick, her partner in Boutique Carriage, the dress shop she owned, Rosemary had a good head for business; not only was the shop successful, Rosemary also invested in stocks and commodities, and did well. How well was not known until her estate was probated, and it was learned she had left $2,600,000. Abigail Folger, the heiress in the Cielo slayings, had left less than one-fifth that.

Mrs Sivick had last seen Rosemary on Friday, when they went buying for the store. Rosemary had called on Saturday morning, telling her they planned to drive to Lake Isabella, and wondering if she could drop by that afternoon and feed the dogs. The LaBiancas had three dogs. All had barked loudly when she approached the house at about 6 P.M. After feeding them – taking the dog food out of the refrigerator – Mrs Sivick checked the doors – all were locked – and left.

Mrs Sivick's testimony established that whoever wiped the refrigerator handle of prints had done so sometime after she had been there.

Rosemary LaBianca – carhop to millionairess to murder victim.

Cause of death: Multiple stab wounds. Victim had been stabbed a total of forty-one times, any one of six of which could in and of itself have been fatal.

All but one of Leno LaBianca's wounds were to the front of his body; thirty-six of the forty-six inflicted on Rosemary LaBianca were to her back and buttocks. Leno had no defensive wounds, indicating that his hands had probably been bound before he was stabbed. Rosemary had a defensive slash wound on her left jaw. This wound, plus the knife in Leno's throat, indicated that the placing of the pillowcases over the heads of the victims was a belated act, possibly even occurring after they had died.

The pillowcases were identified as the LaBiancas' own, having been removed from the two pillows on their bed.

The knife found in Leno's throat was also theirs; though it was from a different set than the fork, it matched others found in a kitchen drawer. The dimensions of its blade were: length, $4\frac{7}{8}$ inches; thickness, just under $\frac{1}{16}$ inch; width at widest point, $\frac{13}{16}$ inch; width at narrowest point, $\frac{3}{8}$ inch.

The LaBianca detectives later noted in their report: 'The knife recovered from his throat appeared to be the weapon used in both homicides.'

It was a presumption, and nothing more, since for some reason Dr Katsuyama, unlike his superior Dr Noguchi, who handled the Tate autopsies, did not measure the dimensions of the wounds. Nor did the detectives assigned to the LaBianca case ask for these statistics.

The ramifications of this one presumption were immense. A single weapon indicated that there was probably a single killer. That the weapon used belonged in the residence meant that the killer had probably arrived unarmed, his decision to kill the pair occurring sometime after he entered the premises. This in turn suggested: (1) that the killer had arrived to commit a burglary or some other crime, then had been surprised when the LaBiancas returned home; or (2) that the victims knew the killer, trusting him enough to let him in at two in the morning or thereafter.

One little presumption, but it would cause many, many problems later.

As would the estimated time of death.

Asked by the detectives to determine the time, Katsuyama came up with 3 P.M. Sunday. When other evidence appeared to contradict this, the detectives went back to Katsuyama and asked him to recalculate. He now decided Leno LaBianca had died sometime between 12:30 A.M. and 8:30 P.M. on Sunday, and that Rosemary had died an hour earlier. However, Katsuyama cautioned, the time could be affected by room temperature and other variables.

All this was so indecisive that the detectives simply ignored it. They knew, from Frank Struthers, that Leno was a creature of habit. Every night he bought the paper, then read it before going to bed, always starting with the sports section. That section had been open on the coffee table, with Leno's reading glasses beside it. From this and other evidence (Leno was wearing pajamas, the bed hadn't yet been slept in, and so forth) they concluded that the murders had probably taken place within an hour or so after the La Biancas had left Fokianos' newsstand, or sometime between 2 and 3 A.M. on Sunday.

As early as Monday, police were minimizing the similarities between the two crimes. Inspector K.J. McCauley told reporters: 'I don't see any connection between this murder and the others. They're too widely removed. I just don't see any connection.' Sergeant Bryce Houchin observed: 'There is a similarity, but whether it's the same suspect or a copycat we just don't know.'

There were several reasons for discounting the similarities. One was the absence of any apparent link between the victims; another the distance between the crimes. Still another, and more important in formulating a motive, drugs were found at 10050 Cielo Drive, while there were none at 3301 Waverly Drive.

There was one more reason, perhaps the most influential. Even before Garretson was released, the Tate detectives had not one but several very promising new suspects.

August 12–15, 1969

From William Tennant, Roman Polanski's business manager, LAPD learned that in mid-March the Polanskis had given a catered party at Cielo with over a hundred guests. As at any large Hollywood gathering, there were crashers, among them +Herb Wilson, +Larry Madigan, and +Jeffrey Pickett, nicknamed 'Pic'.* The trio, all in their late twenties, were reputedly dope dealers. During the party Wilson apparently stepped on Tennant's foot. An argument ensued, Madigan and Pickett taking Wilson's side. Irritated, Roman Polanski had the three men evicted.

It was a minor incident, in and of itself hardly cause for five savage murders, but Tennant had heard something else: 'Pic' had once threatened to kill Frykowski. This information had come to him through a friend of Voytek's, Witold Kaczanowski, an artist professionally known as Witold K.

Not unmindful of the similarity between 'Pic' and the bloody-lettered PIG on the front door of the Tate residence, detectives interviewed Witold K. From him they learned that after the Polanskis had left for Europe, Wilson, Pickett, Madigan, and a fourth man, +Gerold Jones, were frequent visitors to the Cielo residence, Wilson and Madigan, according to Witold, supplying Voytek and Gibby with most of their drugs, including the MDA they had taken before they died. As for Jeffrey Pickett, when Gibby and Voytek took over Cielo, he moved into their

---

*Everything in this book is based on fact. In a few instances the names of persons only tangentially involved have been changed for legal reasons, the cross symbol (+) indicating the substitution of a pseudonym for the true name. The persons were and are real, however, and the incidents depicted are entirely factual.

Woodstock residence. Witold was staying there also. Once, during an argument, Pickett tried to strangle the artist. When Voytek learned of this, he told Pickett to get out. Enraged, Pic swore, 'I'll kill them all and Voytek will be the first.'

Numerous others also felt one or more of the men might be involved, and passed on their suspicions to the police. John and Michelle Phillips, formerly of the Mamas and Papas group and friends of four of the five Tate victims, said Wilson once drew a gun on Voytek. Various Strip habitués claimed Wilson often bragged that he was a hired killer; that Jones was an expert with knives, always carrying one for throwing; and that Madigan was Sebring's 'candy man', or cocaine source.

More than ever convinced that the Tate homicides were the result of a drug burn or freakout, LAPD began looking for Wilson, Madigan, Pickett, and Jones.

On August 12 the police told reporters that they had officially ruled out any connection between the Tate and LaBianca homicides. According to the Los Angeles *Times*, 'Several officers indicated they were inclined to believe the second slayings were the work of a copycat.'

From the start, the two investigations had proceeded separately, with different detectives assigned to each. They would continue this way, each team pursuing its own leads.

They had one thing in common, though that similarity widened the distance between them. Both were operating on a basic assumption: in nearly 90 percent of all homicides the victim knows his killer. In both investigations the chief focus was now on aquaintances of the victims.

In checking out the Mafia rumor, the La Bianca detectives interviewed each of Leno's known business associates. All doubted the murders were Mafia originated. One man, active in the Sons of Italy, told the detectives that if the Mafia had been responsible, he 'probably would have heard about it'. It was a thorough investigation, the detectives even checking to see if the San Diego company where Leno had purchased his speedboat during their 1968 vacation was Mafia financed; it wasn't, though numerous other businesses in the Mission Bay area were allegedly backed by 'Jewish Mafia money'.

They even questioned Leno's mother, who told them, 'He was a good boy. He never did belong to the association.'

> *Beloved Wife of Roman*
> *Sharon Tate Polanski*
> *1943   1969*
> *Paul Richard Polanski*
> *Their Baby*

Wednesday was a day of funerals. More than 150 persons attended Sharon Tate's last rites at Holy Cross Cemetery. Among those present were Kirk Douglas, Warren Beatty, Steve McQueen, James Coburn, Lee Marvin, Yul Brynner, Peter Sellers, John and Michelle Phillips. Roman Polanski, wearing dark glasses and accompanied by his doctor, broke down several times during the ceremony, as did Sharon's parents and her two young sisters, Patricia and Deborah.

Many of the same people, including Polanski, later attended the services for Jay Sebring, at Wee Kirk o' the Heather, Forest Lawn. Additional celebrities included Paul Newman, Henry and Peter Fonda, Alex Cord, and George Hamilton, all former Sebring clients.

There were fewer people, and fewer flashbulbs, as, across the city, six of his high-school classmates carried Steven Parent's body from the small El Monte church where his services had taken place.

Abigail Folger was buried near where she had grown up in Northern California on the San Francisco Peninsula, following a requiem mass in Our Lady of the Wayside Church, which had been built by her grandparents.

Voytek Frykowski's body remained in Los Angeles until relatives in Poland could arrange for it to be returned there for burial.

While the Tate victims were being interred, the police were attempting to re-create their lives, in particular their last day.

Friday, August 8.

About 8 A.M. Mrs Chapman arrived at Cielo. She did what dishes there were, then commenced her regular household chores.

About 8:30 Frank Guerrero arrived, to paint the room at the north end of the residence. This was to be the nursery. Before starting, Guerrero removed the screens from the windows.

At 11 A.M. Roman Polanski called from London. Mrs Chapman overheard Sharon's side of the conversation. Sharon was worried that Roman wouldn't be home in time for his birthday, August 18. He apparently assured her that he would be back on August 12 as planned, as Sharon later told Mrs Chapman this. Sharon informed Roman that she had enrolled him in a course for expectant fathers.

Most of the day Sharon wore only bikini panties and a bra. This, according to Mrs Chapman, was her usual at-home attire in hot weather.

Shortly before noon Mrs Chapman, noticing that there were paw prints and dog splatters on the front door, washed down the whole exterior with vinegar and water. A small detail, which later would become extremely important.

Steven Parent had lunch at his home in El Monte. Before returning to work at the plumbing supply company, he asked his mother if she would lay out clean clothes so he could make a quick change before going to his second job, at the stereo shop, later that afternoon.

About 12:30 two of Sharon's friends, Joanna Pettet (Mrs Alex Cord) and Barbara Lewis, arrived at Cielo for lunch. Mrs Chapman served them. It was all small talk, the women would later recall, mostly about the expected baby. Sharon showed the two women the nursery, and introduced them to Guerrero.

About 1 P.M. Sandy Tennant called Sharon. Sharon told her she wasn't planning a party that evening, but did invite her to drop by, an invitation Sandy declined.

Having finished the first coat of paint, Guerrero left about 1:30. He didn't replace the screens, since he intended to return Monday to give the room a final coat. The police later concluded the killer(s) either didn't notice they were off or feared entering a freshly painted room.

About 2 P.M. David Martinez, one of Altobelli's two gardeners, arrived at 10050 Cielo and began work. Voytek and Abigail arrived not long after this, joining Sharon and her guests for a late lunch.

About 3 P.M. the second gardener, Tom Vargas, arrived. As he came in the gate, Abigail was driving out in her Camaro. Five minutes later Voytek also left, driving the Firebird.

Joanna Pettet and Barbara Lewis departed about 3:30.

At about that same time Sebring's butler, Amos Russell, served Jay and his current female companion coffee in bed. About 3:45 Jay called Sharon, apparently telling her he would be over earlier than expected. He later called his secretary, to pick up his messages, and John Madden, to discuss his visit to the San Francisco salon the next day. He didn't mention to either his plans for that evening, but he did tell Madden he had spent the day hard at work on a crest for the new franchise shops.

Just after Sebring called Sharon, Mrs Chapman told her she had finished her work and was leaving for the day. Since it was so hot in the city, Sharon asked her if she would like to stay over. Mrs Chapman declined. It was undoubtedly the most important decision she ever made.

David Martinez was just leaving, and he gave Mrs Chapman a ride to the bus stop. Vargas remained behind, completing his work. While gardening near the house, he noticed Sharon asleep on the bed in her room. When a deliveryman from the Air Dispatch Company arrived with the two blue steamer trunks, Vargas, not wishing to disturb Mrs Polanski, signed for them. The time, 4:30 P.M., was noted on the receipt. The trunks contained Sharon's clothing, which Roman had shipped from London.

Abigail kept her 4:30 appointment with Dr Flicker.

Before Vargas left, about 4:45, he went back to the guest house and asked Garretson if he would do some watering over the weekend, as the weather was extremely hot and dry.

Across the city, in El Monte, Steven Parent hurried home,

changed clothes, waved to his mother, and was off to his second job.

Between 5:30 and 6 P.M. Mrs Terry Kay was backing out of her driveway at 9845 Easton Drive when she observed Jay Sebring driving down the road in his Porsche, seemingly in a hurry. Perhaps because her car was blocking his progress, he did not wave in his usual genial manner.

Sometime between 6 and 6:30 P.M. Sharon's thirteen-year-old sister Debbie called her, asking if she could drop by that evening with some friends. Sharon, who tired easily because of her advanced pregnancy, suggested they make it another time.

Between 7:30 and 8 P.M. Dennis Hurst arrived at the Cielo address to deliver a bicycle Abigail had purchased in his father's shop earlier that day. Sebring (whom Hurst later identified from photographs) answered the door. Hurst saw no one else and observed nothing suspicious.

Between 9:45 and 10 P.M. John Del Gaudio, manager of the El Coyote Restaurant on Beverly Boulevard, noted Jay Sebring's name on the waiting list for dinner: party of four. Del Gaudio didn't actually see Sebring or the others, and it is probable that he was off at the time, as waitress Kathy Palmer, who served the four, recalled they waited in the bar fifteen to twenty minutes before a table was available, then, after finishing dinner, left about 9:45 or 10. Shown photographs, she was unable to positively identify Sebring, Tate, Frykowski, or Folger.

If Abigail was along, they must have left the restaurant before ten, as it was about this time that Mrs Folger called the Cielo number and talked to her, confirming that she planned to take the 10 A.M. United flight to San Francisco the next morning. Mrs Folger told the police that 'Abigail did not express any alarm or anxiety as to her personal safety or the situation at the Polanski house'.

About 11 P.M. Steve Parent stopped at Dales Market in El Monte and asked his friend John LeFebure if he wanted to go for a ride. Parent had been dating John's younger sister Jean. John suggested they make it another night.

About forty-five minutes later Steve Parent arrived at the Cielo address, hoping to sell William Garretson a clock radio. Parent left the guest house about 12:15 A.M. He got as far as his Rambler.

There was another barometer to the fear: the difficulty the police had in locating people. To have suddenly moved a few days after a crime would, in ordinary circumstances, be considered suspicious. But not in this case. From a not untypical report: 'Asked why she had moved right after the murders, she replied that she wasn't sure why, that like everyone else in Hollywood she was just afraid . . .'

August 16–30, 1969

Though the police told the press there had been 'no new developments', there were some that went unreported. After testing them for blood, Sergeant Joe Granado gave the three pieces of gun grip to Sergeant William Lee of the Firearms and Explosives Unit of SID. Lee didn't even have to consult his manuals; one look and he knew the grip was from a Hi Standard gun. He called Ed Lomax, product manager for the firm that owns Hi Standard, and arranged to meet him at the Police Academy. Lomax also made a quick ID. 'Only one gun has a grip like that,' he told Lee, 'the Hi Standard .22 caliber Longhorn revolver.' Popularly known as the 'Buntline Special' – patterned after a pair of revolvers Western author Ned Buntline had made for Marshal Wyatt Earp – the gun had the following specifications: capacity 9 shots, barrel 9½ inches, over-all length 15 inches, walnut grips, blue finish, weight 35 ounces, suggested retail price $69.95. It was, Lomax said, 'rather a unique revolver'; introduced in April 1967, only 2,700 had been manufactured with this type grip.

Lee obtained from Lomax a list of stores where the gun had been sold, plus a photograph of the model, and LAPD began preparing a flyer which they planned to send to every police department in the United States and Canada.

The evening of Saturday, August 16, Roman Polanski was interviewed for several hours by LAPD. The following day he returned to 10050 Cielo Drive for the first time since the murders. He was accompanied by a writer and a photographer for *Life* and Peter Hurkos, the well-known psychic, who had been hired by friends of Jay Sebring to make a 'reading' at the scene.

As Polanski identified himself and drove through the gate, the premises still being secured by LAPD, he commented bitterly to Thomas Thompson, the *Life* writer and a long-time acquaintance, 'This must be the world-famous orgy house.' Thompson asked him how long Gibby and Voytek had been staying there. 'Too long, I guess,' he answered.

The blue bedsheet that had earlier covered Abigail Folger was still on the lawn. The bloody lettering on the door had faded, but the three letters were still decipherable. The havoc inside seemed to take him aback for a minute, as did the dark stains in the entryway, and, once inside the living room, the even larger ones in front of the couch. He walked from room to room, here and there touching things as if he could conjure up the past. The pillows were still bunched up in the center of the bed, as they had been that morning. They were always that way when he was gone, he told Thompson, adding simply, 'She hugged them instead of me.' He lingered a long time at the armoire where, in anticipation, Sharon had kept the baby things.

Hurkos later told the press: 'Three men killed Sharon Tate and the other four – and I know who they are. I have identified the killers to the police and told them that these men must be stopped soon. Otherwise they will kill again.' The killers, he added, were friends of Sharon Tate, turned into 'frenzied homicidal maniacs' by massive doses of LSD. The killings, he was quoted as saying, erupted during a black magic ritual known as 'goona goona', its suddenness catching the victims unawares.

If Hurkos did identify the three men to LAPD, no one bothered to make a report on it. All publicity to the contrary notwithstanding, those in law enforcement have a standard procedure for handling such 'information': listen politely, then forget it. Being inadmissible as evidence, it is valueless.

There was an interesting juxtaposition of stories on the B, or lead local news, page of the Los Angeles *Times* that Sunday.

The big story, Tate, commandeered the top spot, with its headline, 'ANATOMY OF A MASS/MURDER IN HOLLYWOOD.'

Below it was a smaller story, its one-column head reading, 'LABIANCA COUPLE,/VICTIMS OF SLAYER,/GIVEN FINAL RITES.'

To the left of the Tate story, and just above an artist's drawing of the Tate premises, was a much briefer, seemingly unrelated item, chosen, one suspected, because it was small enough to fit the space. Its headline read, 'POLICE RAID RANCH./ARREST 26 SUSPECTS/IN AUTO THEFT RING.'

It began: 'Twenty-six persons living in an abandoned Western movie set on an isolated Chatsworth ranch were arrested in a daybreak raid by sheriff's deputies Saturday as suspects in a major auto theft ring.'

According to deputies, the group had been stealing Volkswagens, then converting them into dune buggies. The story, which did not contain the names of any of those arrested but did mention that a sizable arsenal of weapons had been seized, concluded: 'The ranch is owned by George Spahn, a blind, 80-year-old semi-invalid. It is located in the Simi Hills at 12000 Santa Susana Pass Road. Deputies said Spahn, who lives alone in a house on the ranch, apparently knew there were people living on the set but was unaware of their activity. They said he couldn't get around and he was afraid of them.'

It was a minor story, and didn't even rate a follow-up when, a few days later, all the suspects were released, it being discovered they had been arrested on a misdated warrant.

Following a report that Wilson, Madigan, Pickett, and Jones were in Canada, LAPD sent the Royal Canadian Mounted Police a 'want' on the four men; RCMP broadcast it; alert reporters picked it up; and within hours the news media in the United States were heralding 'a break in the Tate case'.

Although LAPD denied that the four men were suspects, saying they were only wanted for questioning, the impression remained that arrests were imminent. There were phone calls, among them one from Madigan, another from Jones.

Jones was in Jamaica, and said he would fly back voluntarily if the police wished to talk to him. They admitted they did.

Madigan showed up at Parker Center with his attorney. He cooperated fully, agreeing to answer any questions except those which might tend to involve him in the use or sale of narcotics. He admitted having visited Frykowski at the Cielo residence twice during the week before the murders, so it was possible his prints were there. On the night of the murders, Madigan said, he had attended a party given by an airline stewardess who lived in the apartment below his. He had left about 2 or 3 A.M. This was later verified by LAPD, which also checked his prints against the unmatched latents found at the Cielo address, without success.

Madigan was given a polygraph, and passed, as did Jones, when he arrived from Jamaica. Jones said that he and Wilson had been in Jamaica from July 12 to August 17, at which time he had flown to Los Angeles and Wilson had flown to Toronto. Asked why they had gone to Jamaica, he said they were 'making a movie about marijuana'. Jones' alibi would have to be checked out, but after his polygraph, and a negative print check, he ceased to be a good suspect.

The publicity had been bad. There was no disputing that. As Steven Roberts, Los Angeles bureau chief for the New York *Times*, later put it, 'All the stories had a common thread – that somehow the victims had brought the murders on themselves . . . The attitude was summed up in the epigram: "Live freaky, die freaky." '

Given Roman Polanski's affinity for the macabre; rumors of Sebring's sexual peculiarities; the presence of both Miss Tate and her former lover at the death scene while her husband was away; the 'anything goes' image of the Hollywood jet set; drugs; and the sudden clamp on police leaks, almost any kind of plot could be fashioned, and was. Sharon Tate was called everything from 'the queen of the Hollywood orgy scene' to 'a dabbler in satanic arts'. Polanski himself was not spared. In the same newspaper a reader could find one columnist saying the director was so grief-stricken he could not speak, while a second had him night-clubbing with a bevy of airline stewardesses. If he wasn't personally responsible for the murders, more than one paper implied, he must know who committed them.

From a national news weekly:

> Sharon's body was found nude, not clad in bikini pants and a bra as had first been reported ... Sebring was wearing only the torn remnants of a pair of boxer shorts ... Frykowski's trousers were down to his ankles. Both Sebring and Tate had X's carved on their bodies ... One of Miss Tate's breasts had been cut off, apparently as the result of indiscriminate slashing ... Sebring had been sexually mutilated ...

The rest was equally accurate: 'No fingerprints were found anywhere ... no drug traces were found in any of the five bodies ...' And so on.

Though it read like something from the old *Confidential*, the article had appeared in *Time*, its writer apparently having some tall explaining to do when his editors became aware of his imaginative embellishments.

Angered by 'a multitude of slanders', Roman Polanski called a press conference on August 19, where he castigated newsmen who 'for a selfish reason' wrote 'horrible things about my wife'. There had been no marital rift, he reiterated; no dope; no orgies. His wife had been 'beautiful' and 'a good person', and 'the last few years I spent with her were the only time of true happiness in my life ...'

Madigan and Jones had been eliminated as suspects. Herb Wilson and Jeffrey Pickett remained.

Because of his familiarity with the case, it was decided to send Lieutenant Deemer east to interview the two.

Jeffrey 'Pic' Pickett had been contacted through a relative, and a meeting was set up in a Washington, D.C., hotel room. The son of a prominent State Department official, Pickett appeared to Deemer to be 'under the influence of some narcotic, probably an excitant drug'. He also had a bandaged hand. When Deemer expressed curiosity about it, Pickett vaguely replied that he had cut it on a kitchen knife. Though he agreed to a polygraph, Deemer found that Pickett couldn't remain still or follow instructions, so he interviewed him informally. He claimed that on the day of the murders he had been working in an auto company in Sheffield, Massachusetts. Asked if he owned any weapons, he admitted he had a Buck knife, purchased, he said, in Marlboro, Massachusetts, on a friend's credit card.

Later Pickett gave Deemer the knife. It was similar to the one found at Cielo. He also turned over a roll of videotape which he claimed showed Abigail Folger and Voytek Frykowski using drugs at a party at the Tate residence. Pickett didn't say how he came into possession of the film or what use he had intended to make of it.

Accompanied by Sergeant McGann, Deemer went to Massachusetts. A check of the time cards at the auto company in Sheffield revealed that Pickett's last workday was August 1, eight days before the homicides. Moreover, though two stores in Marlboro sold Buck knives, neither had ever stocked this particular model.

Pickett's status as a suspect rose appreciably, until the detectives interviewed the friend he had mentioned. Going through his credit card receipts, he produced the one for the Buck knife. It had been purchased in Sudbury, Massachusetts, on August 21, long after the murders. The friend and his wife also recalled something Pickett had apparently forgotten. He had gone to the beach with them the weekend of August 8–10. Pickett was subsequently polygraphed, twice. Both times it was decided he was telling the truth and was not involved. Eliminate Pickett.

Flying to Toronto, Deemer interviewed Herb Wilson. Although initially reluctant to submit to a polygraph, Wilson consented when Deemer agreed not to ask any questions that might make him liable to Canadian prosecution on narcotics charges. He passed. Eliminate Wilson.

The fingerprints of both Pickett and Wilson were checked against the unmatched Tate latents, with no match.

The videotape Pickett gave Deemer was viewed in the SID lab. Apparently filmed during the period the Polanskis were away, it showed Abigail Folger, Voytek Frykowski, Witold K, and an unidentified young lady having dinner in front of the fire-place of the Tate residence. The video machine was simply turned on and left to run, those present after a time seeming to forget it.

Abigail wore her hair tied back in a rather severe chignon effect. She looked both older and more tired than in her other photos; Voytek looked dissipated. Though what appeared to be marijuana was smoked, Voytek seemed more drunk than high. At first Abigail treated him with the exasperated affection one would accord a spoiled child.

But then the mood gradually changed. In an obvious attempt to exclude Abigail, Voytek began speaking Polish. Abigail, in turn, was playing the grand dame, responding to his crude jests with witty repartee. Voytek began calling her 'Lady Folger', then, as he became drunker, 'Lady F'. Abigail talked about him in the third person, as if he wasn't present, commenting upon, with some disgust, his habit of coming down off his drug trips by getting drunk.

To those viewing the tape it must have seemed nothing more than an overly long, exceedingly boring chronicle of a domestic argument. Except for two incidents, which, considering what would happen to two of those present, in this very house, gave it an eeriness as chilling as anything in *Rosemary's Baby*.

As she was serving the dinner, Abigail recalled a time when Voytek, stoned on drugs, looked into the fireplace and saw a strange shape. He had rushed for a camera, hoping to capture the image, a blazing pig's head.

The second incident was, in its own way, even more disturbing. The microphone had been left on the table, next to the roast. As the meat was being carved, it picked up, amazingly loud, over and over and over again, the sound of the knife grating on the bone.

At the end of August there was a summing up, for both the Tate and the LaBianca detectives.

The 'First Homicide Investigation Progress Report – Tate' ran to thirty-three pages. Nowhere in it was there any mention of the LaBianca murders.

The 'First Homicide Investigation Progress Report – La-Bianca' was seventeen pages long. Despite the many similarities between the two crimes, it contained not one reference to the Tate homicides.

They remained two totally separate investigations.

Although Lieutenant Bob Helder had over a dozen detectives working full time on the Tate case, Sergeants Michael McGann, Robert Calkins, and Jess Buckles were the principal investigators. All were long-time veterans on the force, having worked their way up to the status of detective the hard way, from the ranks. They were experienced, and inclined to be set in their ways.

The LaBianca team, under Lieutenant Paul LePage, consisted, at various times, of from six to ten detectives, with Sergeants Frank Patchett, Manuel Gutierrez, Michael Nielsen, Philip Sartuchi, and Gary Broda the principal investigators. The LaBianca detectives were generally younger, better educated, and far less experienced. Graduates of the Police Academy for the most part, they were more inclined to the use of modern investigative techniques. For example, they obtained the fingerprints of almost everyone they interviewed; gave more polygraph examinations; made more *modus operandi* (MO) and fingerprint runs through the California State Bureau of Criminal Investigation and Identification (CII); and dug deeper into the backgrounds of the victims, even checking the outgoing calls Leno LaBianca had made from a motel while on vacation seven years ago.

They were also more inclined to consider 'far out' theories. For example, while the Tate report didn't attempt to explain that bloody word on the front door, the LaBianca report speculated as to the meaning of the writings found inside the residence on Waverly Drive. It even suggested a connection so remote it couldn't even be called a wild guess. The report noted: 'Investigation revealed that the singing group the Beatles' most recent album, No. SWBO 101, has songs titled "Helter Skelter" and "Piggies" and "Blackbird". The words in the song "Blackbird" frequently say "Arise, arise", which might be the meaning of "Rise" near the front door.'

The idea was just sort of tossed in, by whom no one would later remember, and just as promptly forgotten.

The two sets of detectives had one thing in common, however. Though to date the LaBianca team had interviewed some 150 persons, the Tate investigators more than twice that, neither was much closer to 'solving' the case than when the bodies were first discovered.

The Tate report listed five suspects – Garretson, Wilson, Madigan, Pickett, and Jones – all of whom had by this time been eliminated.

The LaBianca report listed fifteen – but included Frank and Susan Struthers, Joe Dorgan, and numerous others who were never serious suspects. Of the fifteen, only Gardner remained a good possible, and, though lacking a palm print for positive elimination (one had been found on a bank deposit slip on Leno's desk), his fingerprints had already been checked against those found in the residence with no match.

The progress reports were strictly intradepartmental; the press would never see them.

But already a few reporters were beginning to suspect that the real reason for the official silence was that there was nothing to report.

September 1969

About noon on Monday, September 1, 1969, 10-year-old Steven Weiss was fixing the sprinkler on the hill behind his home when he found a gun.

Steven and his parents lived at 3627 Longview Valley Road in Sherman Oaks. Running parallel to Longview, atop the hill, was Beverly Glen.

The gun was lying next to the sprinkler, under a bush, about seventy-five feet – or halfway – up the steep hill. Steven had watched 'Dragnet' on TV; he knew how guns should be handled. Picking it up very carefully by the tip of the barrel, so as not to eradicate prints, Stevens took the gun back to his house and showed it to his father, Bernard Weiss. The senior Weiss took one look and called LAPD.

Officer Michael Watson, on patrol in the area, responded to the radio call. More than a year later Steven would be asked to describe the incident from the witness stand:

Q. 'Did you show him [Watson] the gun?'
A. 'Yes.'
Q. 'Did he touch the gun?'
A. 'Yes.'
Q. 'How did he touch it?'
A. 'With both hands, all over the gun.'
So much for 'Dragnet'.

Officer Watson took the cartridges out of the cylinder; there were nine – seven empty shell casings and two live rounds. The gun itself was a .22 caliber Hi Standard Longhorn revolver. It had dirt on it, and rust. The trigger guard was broken, the barrel loose and slightly bent, as if it had been used to hammer something. The gun was also missing the right-hand grip.

Officer Watson took the revolver and shells back to Valley Services Division of LAPD, located in Van Nuys, and after booking them as 'Found Evidence' turned them over to the Property Section, where they were tagged, placed in manila envelopes, and filed away.

Between September 3 and 5, LAPD sent out the first batch of confidential 'flyers' on the wanted Tate gun. In addition to a photograph of a Hi Standard .22 caliber Longhorn revolver, and a list of Hi Standard outlets supplied by Lomax, Deputy Chief Robert Houghton sent a covering letter which asked police to interview anyone who had purchased such a gun, and to 'visually check the weapon to see if the original grips are intact'. To avoid leaks to the media, he suggested the following cover story: such a gun had been recovered with other stolen property and the police wished to determine its ownership.

LAPD sent out approximately three hundred of the flyers, to various law-enforcement agencies in California, other parts of the United States, and Canada.

Someone neglected to mail one to the Valley Services Division of the Los Angeles Police Department in Van Nuys.

On September 10 – one month after the Tate murders – a large advertisement appeared in newspapers in the Los Angeles area:

REWARD
$25,000

Roman Polanski and friends of the Polanski family offer to pay a $25,000 reward to the person or persons who furnish information leading to the arrest and conviction of the murderer or murderers of Sharon Tate, her unborn child, and the other four victims.

Information should be sent to
Post Office Box 60048,
Terminal Annex,
Los Angeles, California 90069.

Persons wishing to remain anonymous should provide sufficient means for later identification, one method of which is to tear this newspaper page in half, transmit one half with the information submitted and save the remaining half for matching-up later. In the event more than one person is entitled to the reward, the reward will be divided equally between them.

Although unannounced in the press, others had already begun their own unofficial inquiries. Sharon's father, Colonel Paul Tate, had retired from the Army in August. Growing a beard and letting his hair grow long, the former intelligence officer began frequenting the Sunset Strip, hippie pads, and places where drugs were sold, looking for some lead to the killer(s) of his daughter and the others.

The police were fearful Colonel Tate's private investigation might become a private war, since there were reports he did not go on his forays unarmed.

Nor were the police happy about the reward. Besides the implication that LAPD wasn't capable of solving the case on its own, such an announcement usually yields only crackpot calls, and of these they already had a surplus.

Most had come in following the release of Garretson, the callers blaming the murders on everyone from the Black Power movement to the Polish Secret Police, their sources imagination, hearsay, even Sharon herself – returned during a seance. One wife called the police to accuse her husband: 'He was evasive as to his whereabouts that night.'

For such a well-publicized crime there were surprisingly few 'confessions'. It was as if the murders were so horrible that even the chronic confessors didn't want to become involved. A recently convicted felon, anxious to 'make a deal', did claim another man had bragged of involvement in the killings, but, after investigation, the story proved bogus.

Though almost forgotten for a time, by mid-September the pair of prescription glasses found near the trunks in the living room of the Tate residence had, simply by the process of attrition, become one of the most important remaining clues.

Early that month the detectives showed the glasses to various optical company representatives. What they learned was in part discouraging. The frames were a popular model, the 'Manhattan' style, readily available, while the prescription lenses were also a stock item, meaning they didn't have to be ground to order. But, on the plus side, they also learned several things about the person who had worn them.

Their owner was probably a man. He had a small, almost volley-ball-shaped head. His eyes were far apart. His left ear was approximately ¼ to ½ inch higher than his right ear. And he was extremely myopic – if he didn't have an extra pair, he would probably have to replace the glasses soon.

It was at least something to go on. Another flyer, with the exact specifications of the prescription, was sent to all members of the American Optometric Association, the California Optometric Association, the Los Angeles County Optometric Association, and the Ophthalmologists of Southern California, in hopes that it would yield more than had the flyer on the gun.

Of the 131 Hi Standard Longhorn revolvers sold in California, law-enforcement agencies had been able to locate and eliminate 105, a surprisingly large percentage, since many of the owners had moved to other jurisdictions. The search continued, but to date it hadn't yielded a single good suspect. A second gun letter was sent to thirteen different gunshops in the United States which, in recent months, had ordered replacement grips for the Longhorn model. Though the replies to this one wouldn't come back until much later, it too drew a blank.

Nor were the LaBianca detectives having any better luck. To date they had given eleven polygraphs; all had been negative. As a result of an MO run through the CII computer, the finger-prints of 140 suspects were checked; a palm print found on a bank deposit slip was checked against 2,150 suspects; and a fingerprint found on the liquor cabinet was checked against a total of 41,034 suspects. All uniformly negative.

At the end of September neither the Tate nor the LaBianca detectives bothered to write up a progress report.

October 1969

On October 17, Lieutenant Helder and Deputy Chief Houghton told reporters that they had evidence which, if it could be traced, might lead to 'the killers' – plural – of Sharon Tate and the four others. They refused to be more specific.

The press conference had been called in attempt to relieve some of the pressure on LAPD. No solid information was released, but a number of current rumors were denied.

Less than a week later, on October 23, LAPD very hastily called another press conference, to announce that they had a clue to the identity of 'the killer' – singular – of the five Tate victims: a pair of prescription eyeglasses that had been found at the scene.

The announcement was made only because several papers had that same day already printed the 'wanted' flyer on the glasses.

Approximately 18,000 eye doctors had received the flyer from their various member associations; in addition, it had been printed verbatim in the *Optometric Weekly* and the *Eye, Ear, Nose, and Throat Monthly*, which had a combined national circulation of over 29,000. What was surprising was not that the story had leaked, but that it had taken so long for it to do so.

Starved for solid news, the press heralded 'a major breakthrough in the case', overlooking the obvious fact that the police had had the glasses in their possession since the day the Tate victims were discovered.

Lieutenant Helder refused comment when a reporter, obviously with excellent connections inside the department, asked if it was true that to date the glasses flyer had yielded only seven suspects, all of whom had already been eliminated.

It was indicative of the desperation of the Tate detectives that the second, and last, Tate progress report, prepared the day before the press conference, stated: 'At this time Garretson has not been positively eliminated.'

The Tate report, covering the period September 1–October 22, 1969, ran to twenty-six pages, most of which were devoted to closing out the cases against Wilson, Pickett, et al.

The LaBianca report, closed out on October 15, was a little shorter, twenty-two pages, but far more interesting.

In one section of the report the detectives mentioned their use of the CII computer: 'A MO run on all crimes where the victims were tied is presently being run. Future runs will be made concentrating on the peculiarities of the robberies, used gloves, wore glasses or disabled the phone.'

Robberies. Plural. *Wore glasses, disabled the phone.* The phone at the LaBianca residence was not disabled, nor was there evidence that a LaBianca assailant wore glasses. These references were to *Tate*.

The conclusion is inescapable: The LaBianca detectives had decided – on their own, and without consulting the Tate detectives – to see if they could solve the Tate, as well as the LaBianca, case.

The second LaBianca report was interesting for still another reason.

It listed eleven suspects, the last of whom was one MANSON, CHARLES.

Part Two

The Killers

'You couldn't meet a nicer group of people.'
            Leslie Van Houten, describing
            the Manson Family
            to Sergeant Michael McGann

'At twelve o'clock a meeting round the table
For a seance in the dark
With voices out of nowhere
Put on especially by the children for a lark.'
            The Beatles
            'Cry Baby Cry',
            'White Album'

'You have to have a real love in your heart to
do this for people.'
            Susan Atkins, telling
            Virginia Graham why she
            stabbed Sharon Tate

October 15–31, 1969

The physical distance between Parker Center, headquarters of the Los Angeles Police Department, and the Hall of Justice, which houses the Los Angeles County Sheriff's Office, is four blocks. That distance can be traversed in the time it takes to dial a telephone.

But it isn't always that easy. Though LAPD and LASO cooperate on investigations that involve both jurisdictions, there exists between them a certain amount of jealousy.

One of the LaBianca detectives would later admit that he and his fellow officers *should* have checked with LASO homicide detectives in mid-August to see if they had any similar murders. But it wasn't until October 15, after most of their other leads had evaporated, that they did so.

When they did, they learned of the Hinman murder. And, unlike Sergeant Buckles of the Tate team, they found the similarities striking enough to merit further investigation.

There had been some recent developments in the Hinman case, Sergeants Whiteley and Guenther told them. Less than a week before, Inyo County officers had raided isolated Barker Ranch, located in an extremely rugged, almost inaccessible area south of Death Valley National Monument. The raid, based on charges ranging from grand theft to arson, had netted twenty-four members of a hippie cult known as the 'Manson Family'. Many of these same people – including their leader, Charles Manson, a 34-year-old ex-con with a long and checkered criminal history – had also been arrested in an earlier raid conducted by LASO, which had occurred on August 16, at Spahn's Movie Ranch in Chatsworth.

During the Barker raid, which took place over a three-day

period, two young girls had appeared out of the bushes near a road some miles from the ranch, asking the officers for protection. They claimed they had been attempting to flee the 'Family' and were afraid for their lives. One was named Stephanie Schram, the other Kitty Lutesinger.

Whiteley and Guenther had been looking for Kitty Lutesinger ever since learning that she was a girl friend of Bobby Beausoleil, the suspect in the Hinman murder. Informed of her arrest, they drove 225 miles to Independence, the Inyo County seat, to question her.

Kitty, a freckled, frightened 17-year-old, was five months pregnant with Beausoleil's child. Though she had lived with the Family, she apparently was not trusted by them. When Beausoleil disappeared from Spahn Ranch in early August, no one would tell her where he had gone. Only after several weeks did she learn that he had been arrested, and, much later, that he had been charged with the murder of Gary Hinman.

Questioned about the murder, Kitty said she had heard that Manson had sent Beausoleil and a girl named Susan Atkins to Hinman's home to get money from him. A fight had ensued, and Hinman had been killed. Kitty couldn't recall who told her this, just that it was the talk at the ranch. She did recall, however, another conversation in which Susan Atkins told her and several other girls that she had been in a fight with a man who had pulled her hair, and that she had stabbed him three or four times in the legs.

Susan Atkins had been arrested in the Barker raid and booked under the name 'Sadie Mae Glutz'. She was still in custody. On October 13, the day after they talked to Kitty, Sergeants Whiteley and Guenther questioned her.

She told them that she and Bobby Beausoleil were sent to Gary Hinman's house to get some money he had supposedly inherited. When he wouldn't give it to them, Beausoleil pulled out a knife and slashed Hinman's face. For two days and two nights the pair had taken turns sleeping, so Hinman wouldn't escape. Then, on their last evening at the residence, while she was in the kitchen, she had heard Gary say, 'Don't, Bobby!' Hinman then staggered into the kitchen bleeding from a chest wound.

Even after this, Hinman didn't die. After wiping the house of prints (not effectively, since both a palm print and a fingerprint belonging to Beausoleil were found), they were going out the front door when they heard Hinman moaning. Beausoleil went back in, and she heard Gary cry out, 'Oh, no, Bobby, please don't!' She also heard 'a sound like gurgling as when people are dying'.

Beausoleil then hot-wired Hinman's 1965 Volkswagen bus and they drove back to Spahn Ranch.

Whiteley and Guenther asked Susan if she would repeat her statement on tape. She declined. She was transported to the San Dimas sheriff's station, where she was booked for suspicion of murder.

Susan Atkins' statement did not implicate Manson in the Hinman murder. Nor, contrary to what Kitty had said, did Susan admit to having stabbed anyone. Whiteley and Guenther strongly suspected she was telling only what she thought they already knew.

Nor were the two LaBianca detectives very impressed. Hinman had been close to the Manson Family; several of its members – including Beausoleil, Atkins, even Manson himself – had lived with him at various times in the past. In short, there was a link. But there was no evidence that Manson or any of his followers knew the LaBiancas or the people at 10050 Cielo Drive.

Still, it was a lead, and they proceeded to check it out. Kitty had been released into the custody of her parents, who had a local address, and they interviewed her there. From LASO, Inyo County officials, Manson's parole officer, and others, they began assembling names, descriptions, and fingerprints of persons known to belong to or associate with the Family. Kitty had mentioned that while the Family was still living at Spahn, Manson had tried to enlist a motorcycle gang, the Straight Satans, as his personal bodyguard. One biker named Danny had stuck around for several months.

On learning that the motorcycle gang hung out in Venice, California, the LaBianca detectives asked Venice PD if they could locate a Straight Satan named Danny.

Something in Kitty Lutesinger's statement puzzled Whiteley and Guenther. According to Kitty, Susan Atkins had admitted stabbing a man three or four times in the legs.

Gary Hinman hadn't been stabbed in the legs.

But Voytek Frykowski had.

Although rebuffed once before, on October 20 the sheriff's deputies again contacted the Tate detectives at LAPD, telling them what they had learned.

It is possible to measure the Tate detectives' interest with some exactness. Not until October 31, eleven days later, did they interview Kitty Lutesinger.

November 1–12, 1969

November was a month for confessions. Which, initially, no one believed.

After being booked for the Hinman murder, Susan Denise Atkins, aka* Sadie Mae Glutz, was moved to Sybil Brand Institute, the women's house of detention in Los Angeles. On November 1, after completing orientation, she was assigned to Dormitory 8000, and given a bunk opposite one Ronnie Howard. Miss Howard, a buxom former call girl who over her 30-some years had been known by more than a dozen and a half aliases, was at present awaiting trial on a charge of forging a prescription.

On the same day Susan moved into Dormitory 8000, one Virginia Graham did also. Miss Graham, herself an ex-call girl with a sizable number of aka's, had been picked up for violating her parole. Although they hadn't seen each other for five years, Ronnie and Virginia had not only been friends and business associates in the past, going out on 'calls' together, but Ronnie had married Virginia's ex-husband.

As their work assignments, Susan Atkins and Virginia Graham were given jobs as 'runners', carrying messages for the prison authorities. In the slow periods when there wasn't much work, they would sit on stools in 'control', the message center, and talk.

At night, after lights-out, Ronnie Howard and Susan talked also.

Susan loved to talk. And Ronnie and Virginia proved rapt listeners.

* Police shorthand for 'also known as'; 't/n' means 'true name'.

On November 2, 1969, one Steve Zabriske appeared at the Portland, Oregon, Police Department and told Detective Sergeant Ritchard that a 'Charlie' and a 'Clem' had committed both the Tate and LaBianca murders.

He had heard this, the 19-year-old Zabriske said, from Ed Bailey and Vern Plumlee, two hippie types from California whom he had met in Portland. Zabriske also told Ritchard that Charlie and Clem were at present in custody in Los Angeles on another charge, grand theft auto.

Bailey had told him something else, Zabriske said: that he had personally seen Charlie shoot a man in the head with a ·45 caliber automatic. This had occurred in Death Valley.

Sergeant Ritchard asked Zabriske if he could prove any of this. Zabriske admitted he couldn't. However, his brother-in-law, Michael Lloyd Carter, had also been present during the conversations, and would back him up if Sergeant Ritchard wanted to talk to him.

Sergeant Ritchard didn't. Since Zabriske 'did not have last names, nor did he have anything concrete to establish that he was telling the truth', Sergeant Ritchard, according to the official report, 'did not place any credence on this interview and did not notify the Los Angeles Police Department . . .'

The girls in Dormitory 8000 called Sadie Mae Glutz – as Susan Atkins insisted on being known – 'Crazy Sadie'. It wasn't just that ridiculous name. She was much too happy, considering where she was. She would laugh and sing at inappropriate times. Without warning, she would stop whatever she happened to be doing and start go-go dancing. She did her exercise sans underpants. She bragged that she had done everything sexual that could be done, and on more than one occasion propositioned other inmates.

Virginia Graham thought she was sort of a 'little girl lost', putting on a big act so no one would know how frightened she really was.

One day while they were sitting in the message center, Virginia asked her, 'What are you in for?'

'First degree murder,' Susan matter-of-factly replied.

The next day Susan told Virginia that the man she was accused of killing was named Gary Hinman. She said that she, Bobby, and another girl were involved. The other girl hadn't been charged with the murder, she said, though she had been in Sybil Brand not too long ago on another charge; right now she was out on bail and had gone to Wisconsin to get her baby.*

Virginia asked her, 'Well, did you do it?'

Susan looked at her and smiled and said, 'Sure.' Just like that.

Only the police had it wrong, she said. They had her holding the man while the boy stabbed him, which was silly, because she couldn't hold a big man like that. It was the other way round; the boy held him and she had stabbed him, four or five times.

Susan's conversations were not limited to murder. Subjects ranged from psychic phenomena to her experiences as a topless dancer in San Francisco. It was while there, she told Virginia, that she met 'a man, this Charlie'. He was the strongest man alive. He had been in prison but had never been broken. Susan said she followed his orders without question – they all did, all the kids who lived with him. He was their father, their leader, their love.

It was Charlie, she said, who had given her the name Sadie Mae Glutz.

Virginia remarked that she didn't consider that much of a favor.

Charlie was going to lead them to the desert, Susan said. There was a hole in Death Valley, only Charlie knew where it was, but deep down inside, in the center of the earth, there was a whole civilization. And Charlie was going to take the 'family', the chosen few, and they were going to go to this bottomless pit and live there.

Charlie, Susan confided to Virginia, was Jesus Christ.

* She was referring to Mary Brunner, first member of the Family, who had had a child by Manson. At this time the police were unaware of her involvement in the Hinman homicide.

Susan, Virginia decided, was nuts.

On the night of Wednesday, November 5, a young man who might have been able to provide a solution to the Tate-LaBianca homicides ceased to exist.

At 7:35 P.M. officers from Venice PD, responding to a telephone call, arrived at 28 Clubhouse Avenue, a house near the beach rented by a Mark Ross. They found a youth – approximate age 22, nickname 'Zero', true name unknown – lying on a mattress on the floor in the bedroom. Deceased was still warm to the touch. There was blood on the pillow and what appeared to be an entrance wound in the right temple. Next to the body was a leather gun case and an eight-shot .22 caliber Iver & Johnson revolver. According to the other persons present – a man and three girls – Zero had killed himself while playing Russian roulette. The stories of the witness – who identified themselves as Bruce Davis, Linda Baldwin, Sue Bartell, and Catherine Gillies, and who said they had been staying at the house while Ross was away – tallied perfectly. Linda Baldwin stated that she had been lying on the right side of the mattress, Zero on the left side, when Zero noticed the leather case in a stand next to the bed and remarked, 'Oh, here's a gun.' He removed the gun from the case, Miss Baldwin said, commenting, 'There's only one bullet in it.' Holding the gun in his right hand, he had then spun the cylinder, placed the muzzle against his right temple, and pulled the trigger.

The others, in various parts of the house, had heard what sounded like a firecracker popping, they said. When they entered the bedroom, Miss Baldwin told them, 'Zero shot himself, just like in the movies.' Bruce Davies admitted he picked up the gun. They had then called the police.

The officers were unaware that all those present were members of the Manson Family, who had been living at the Venice residence since their release following the Barker Ranch raid. Since when questioned separately all told essentially the same story, the police accepted the Russian roulette explanation and listed the cause of death as suicide.

They had several very good reasons to suspect that explanation, although apparently no one did.

When officer Jerrome Boen later dusted the gun for latents, he found no prints. Nor were there prints on the leather gun case.

And when they examined the revolver, they found that Zero had really been bucking the odds. The gun contained seven live rounds and one spent shell. It had been fully loaded, with no empty chambers.

A number of Family members, including Manson himself, were still in jail in Independence. On November 6, LaBianca detectives Patchett and Sartuchi, accompanied by Lieutenant Burdick of SID, went there to interview them.

Patchett asked Manson if he knew anything about either the Tate or LaBianca homicides. Manson replied, 'No,' and that was that.

Patchett was so unimpressed with Manson that he didn't even bother to write up a report on the interview. Of the nine Family members the detectives talked to, only one rated a memorandum. About 1:30 that afternoon Lieutenant Burdick interviewed a girl who had been booked under the name Leslie Sankston.

I inquired of Miss Sankston if she was aware that Sadie [Susan Atkins] was reportedly involved in the Gary Hinman homicide. She replied that she was. I inquired if she was aware of the Tate and LaBianca homicides. She indicated that she was aware of the Tate homicide but seemed unfamiliar with the LaBianca homicide. I asked her if she had any knowledge of persons in her group who might possibly be involved in either the Tate or LaBianca homicides. She indicated that there were some 'things' that caused her to believe someone from her group might be involved in the Tate homicide. I asked her to elaborate on the 'things' [but] she declined to indicate what she meant and stated that she wanted to think about it overnight, and that she was perplexed and didn't know what to do. She did indicate she might tell me the following day.

However, when Burdick again questioned her the next morning, 'she stated she had decided she did not want to say anymore about the subject and the conversation was terminated'.

Though the interviews yielded nothing, the LaBianca detectives did pick up one possible lead. Before leaving Independence, Patchett asked to see Manson's personal effects. Going through the clothing Manson had been wearing when arrested, Patchett noticed that he used leather thongs both as laces in his moccasins and in the stitching of his trousers. Patchett took a sample thong from each back to Los Angeles for comparison with the thong used to tie Leno LaBianca's hands.

A leather thong is a leather thong, SID in effect told him; though the thongs were similar, there was no way to tell whether they had come from the same piece of leather.

LAPD and LASO have no monopoly on jealousy. To a certain extent it exists between almost all law-enforcement agencies, and even within some.

The Homicide Division of the Los Angeles Police Department is a single room, 318, on the third floor of Parker Center. Although it is a large room, rectangular in shape, there are no partitions, only two long tables, all the detectives working at either one or the other. The distance between the Tate and LaBianca detectives was only a few feet.

But there are psychological as well as physical distances. As a result, none of the LaBianca detectives walked those few feet to tell the Tate detectives that they were following a lead which might connect the two homicides. No one informed Lieutenant Helder, who was in charge of the Tate investigation, that they had gone to Independence and interviewed one Charles Manson, who was believed involved in a strikingly similar murder, or that while there one of his followers, a girl who went by the name of Leslie Sankston, had admitted that someone in their group might be involved in the *Tate* homicides.

The LaBianca detectives continued to go it on their own.

On Thursday, November 6, at about 4:45 P.M., Susan Atkins had walked over to Virginia Graham's bed and sat down. They had finished work for the day, and Susan/Sadie was in a talkative mood. She began rapping about the LSD trips she had taken, karma, good and bad vibrations, and the Hinman murder.

Virginia cautioned her that she shouldn't be talking so much; she knew a man who had been convicted just on what he told a cellmate.

Susan replied, 'Oh, I know. I haven't talked about it to anyone else. You know, I can look at you and there's something about you, I know I can tell things to you.' Also, she wasn't worried about the police. They weren't all that good. 'You know, there's a case right now, they are so far off the track they don't even know what's happening.'

Virginia asked, 'What are you talking about?'

'That one on Benedict Canyon.'

'Benedict Canyon? You don't mean Sharon Tate?'

'Yeah.' With this Susan seemed to get very excited. The words came out in a rush. 'You know who did it, don't you?'

'No.'

'Well, you're looking at her.'

Virginia gasped, 'You've got to be kidding!'

Susan just smiled and said, 'Huh-uh.'*

Later Virginia Graham would be unable to remember exactly how long they had talked – she would estimate it as being between thirty-five minutes and an hour, maybe longer. She would also admit confusion as to whether some details were discussed that afternoon or in subsequent conversations, and the order in which some topics came up.

But the content she remembered. That, she would later say, she would never forget as long as she lived.

She asked the big question first: Why, Sadie, why? Because, Susan replied, we 'wanted to do a crime that would shock the world, that the world would have to stand up and take notice'. But why the Tate house? Susan's answer was chilling in its simplicity: 'It is isolated.' The place had been picked at random.

---

*The Atkins–Graham–Howard conversations have been taken from LAPD's taped interviews with Virginia Graham and Ronnie Howard; my interviews with both; their trial testimony; and my interview with Susan Atkins. There are, of course, minor variations in wording. Major discrepancies will be noted.

They had known the owner, Terry Melcher, Doris Day's son, from about a year back, but they didn't know who would be there, and it didn't matter; one person or ten, they had gone there prepared to do everybody in.

'In other words,' Virginia asked, 'you didn't know Jay Sebring or any of the other people?'

'No,' Susan replied.

'Do you mind me asking questions? I mean, I'm curious.' Susan didn't mind. She told Virginia that she had kind brown eyes, and if you look through a person's eyes you can see the soul.

Virginia told Susan she wanted to know exactly how it had come down. 'I'm dying of curiosity,' she added.

Susan obliged. Before leaving the ranch, Charlie had given them instructions. They had worn dark clothing. They also brought along a change of clothes in the car. They drove up to the gate, then drove back down to the bottom of the hill, parked the car, and walked back up.

Virginia interrupted, 'Then it wasn't just you?'

'Oh, no,' Susan told her. 'There were four of us.' In addition to herself, there were two other girls and a man.

When they reached the gate, Susan continued, 'he' cut the telephone wires. Virginia again interrupted to ask whether he wasn't worried he'd cut the electrical wires, extinguishing the lights and alerting the people that something was wrong. Susan replied, 'Oh, no, he knew just what to do.' Virginia got the impression, less from her words than from the way she said them, that the man had been there before.

Susan didn't mention how they got past the gate. She said they had killed the boy first. When Virginia asked why, Susan replied that he had seen them. 'And he had to shoot him. He was shot four times.'

At this point Virginia became somewhat confused. Later she would state, 'I think she told me – I'm not positive – I think she said that this Charles shot him.' Earlier Virginia had got the impression that, although Charlie had instructed them what to do, he hadn't come along. But now it appeared he had.

What Virginia didn't know was that there were two men

named Charles in the Family: Charles Manson and Charles 'Tex' Watson. The complications this simple misunderstanding would later cause would be immense.

On entering the house – Susan didn't say how they got in – they saw a man on the couch in the living room, and a girl, whom Susan identified as 'Ann Folger', sitting in a chair reading a book. She didn't look up.

Virginia asked her how she knew their names. 'We didn't,' Susan replied, 'not until the next day.'

At some point the group apparently split up, Susan going on to the bedroom, while the others stayed in the living room.

'Sharon was sitting up in bed. Jay was sitting on the edge of the bed talking to Sharon.'

'Oh, really?' Virginia asked. 'What did she have on?'

'She had on a bikini bra and panties.'

'You're kidding. And she was pregnant?'

'Yeah. And they looked up, and were they surprised!'

'Wow! Wasn't there some kind of a big hassle?'

'No, they were too surprised and they knew we meant business.'

Susan skipped on. It was as if she was 'tripping out', jumping abruptly from one subject to another. Suddenly they were in the living room and Sharon and Jay were strung up with nooses around their necks so if they tried to move they would choke. Virginia asked why they'd put a hood over Sebring's head. 'We didn't put any hood over his head,' Susan corrected her. 'That's what the papers said, Sadie.' 'Well, there wasn't any hood,' Susan reiterated, getting quite insistent about it.

Then the other man [Frykowski] broke and ran for the door. 'He was full of blood,' Susan said, and she stabbed him three or four times. 'He was bleeding and he ran to the front part,' out the door and onto the lawn, 'and would you believe that he was there hollering "Help, help, somebody please help me," and nobody came?'

Bluntly, without elaboration, 'Then we finished him off.'

Virginia wasn't asking any questions now. What had begun as

a little girl's fairy tale had become a horror-filled nightmare.

There was no mention of what had happened to Abigail Folger or Jay Sebring, only that 'Sharon was the last to die'. On saying this, Susan laughed.

Susan said that she had held Sharon's arms behind her, and that Sharon looked at her and was crying and begging, 'Please don't kill me. Please don't kill me. I don't want to die. I want to live. I want to have my baby. I want to have my baby.'

Susan said she looked Sharon straight in the eye and said, 'Look, bitch, I don't care about you. I don't care if you're going to have a baby. You had better be ready. You're going to die, and I don't feel anything about it.'

Then Susan said, 'In a few minutes I killed her and she was dead.'

After killing Sharon, Susan noticed there was blood on her hand. She tasted it. 'Wow, what a trip!' she told Virginia. 'I thought "To taste death, and yet give life." ' Had she ever tasted blood? she asked Virginia. 'It's warm and sticky and nice.'

Virginia managed to ask a question. Hadn't it bothered her to kill Sharon Tate, with her pregnant?

Susan looked at Virginia quizzically and said, 'Well, I thought you understood. I loved her, and in order for me to kill her I was killing part of myself when I killed her.'

She had wanted to cut out the baby, Susan said, but there hadn't been time. They wanted to take out the eyes of the people, and squash them against the walls, and cut off their fingers. 'We were going to mutilate them, but we didn't have a chance to.'

Virginia asked her how she felt after the murders. Susan replied, 'I felt so elated; tired, but at peace with myself. I knew this was just the beginning of helter skelter. Now the world would listen.'

Virginia didn't understand what she meant by 'helter skelter', and Susan tried to explain it to her. However, she talked so quickly and with such obvious excitement that Virginia had trouble following. As Virginia understood it, there was this group, these chosen people, that Charlie had brought together, and they were elected, this new society, to go out, all over the country and all over the world, to pick out people at random and execute them, to release them from this earth. 'You have to have a real love in your heart to do this for people,' Susan explained.

Four or five times while Susan was talking, Virginia had to caution her to keep her voice down. Susan smiled and said she wasn't worried about that. She was very good at playing crazy.

After they'd left the Tate residence, Susan continued, she discovered that she had lost her knife. She thought maybe the dog had got it. 'You know how dogs are sometimes.' They had thought about going back to look for it but had decided against it. She had also left her hand print on a desk. 'It dawned on me afterwards,' Susan said, 'but my spirit was so strong that obviously it didn't even show up, or they would have had me by now.'

As Virginia understood it, after leaving the Tate residence, they had apparently changed clothes in the car. Then they had driven some distance, stopping at a place where there was a fountain or water outside, to wash their hands. Susan said a man came outside and wanted to know what they were doing. He started to holler at them. 'And,' Susan asked, 'guess who he was?'

'I don't know,' Virginia replied.

'It was the sheriff of Beverly Hills!'

Virginia said she didn't think Beverly Hills had a sheriff.

'Well,' Susan said petulantly, 'the sheriff or mayor or something.'

The man had started to reach into the car to grab the keys, and 'Charlie turned on the key. Boy, we made it. We laughed all the way,' Susan said, adding, 'if he had only known!'

For a moment Susan remained silent. Then, with her little girl's smile, she asked, 'You know the other two the next night?'

Virginia flashed on the grocery store owner and his wife, the LaBiancas. 'Yeah,' she said, 'was that you?'

Susan winked and said, 'What do you think?'

But Virginia had heard enough for one day. She excused herself to go take a shower.

Virginia would later recall thinking, She's got to be kidding! She's making all this up. This is just too wild, too fantastic!

But then she remembered what Susan was in for – first degree murder.

Virginia decided not to say anything to anyone. It was just too incredible. She also decided, if possible, to avoid Susan.

The following day, however, Virginia walked over to Ronnie Howard's bed to tell her something. Susan, who was lying on her own bed, interrupted: 'Virginia, Virginia, remember that beautiful cat I was telling you about? I want you to dig on his name. Now listen, his name is Manson – *Man's Son!*' She repeated it several times to make sure Virgina understood. She said it in a tone of childlike wonder.

She just couldn't keep it to herself any longer. It was just too much. The first time she and Ronnie Howard were alone together, Virginia Graham told her what Susan Atkins had said. 'Hey, what do you do?' she asked Ronnie. 'If this is true – My God, this is terrible. I wish she hadn't told me.'

Ronnie thought Sadie was 'making it all up. She could have gotten it out of the papers.'

The only way to know for sure, they decided, would be for Virginia to question her further, to see if she could learn something that only one of the killers would know.

Virginia had an idea how she could do this without arousing Susan's suspicions. Though she hadn't mentioned it to Susan Atkins, Virginia Graham had more than a passing interest in the Tate homicides. She had known Jay Sebring. A girl friend, who was working as a manicurist for Sebring, had introduced them at the Luau some years ago, shortly after Sebring opened his shop on Fairfax. But there was another coincidence even odder. Virginia had been to 10050 Cielo Drive. Back in 1962 she and her then husband and another girl had been looking for a quiet place, away from things, and had learned 10050 Cielo Drive was up for lease. There had been no one there to show them around, so they had just looked in the windows of the main house. She could remember little about it, only that it looked like a red barn, but the next day at lunch she told Susan about having been there and asked if the interior was still decorated in gold and white. It was just a guess. Susan replied, 'Huh-uh,' but didn't elaborate. Virginia then told her about knowing Sebring, but Susan didn't appear very interested. This time Susan wasn't as talkative, but Virginia persisted, picking up miscellaneous bits and pieces of information.

They'd met Terry Melcher through Dennis Wilson, one of the Beach Boys rock group. They – Charlie, Susan, and the others – had lived with Dennis for a time. Virginia got the idea they were hostile toward Melcher, that he was too interested in money. Virginia also learned that the Tate murders had taken place between midnight and one in the morning; that 'Charlie is love, pure love'; and that when you stab someone 'it feels good when the knife goes in'.

She also learned that besides the Hinman, Tate, and LaBianca murders, 'there's more – and more before . . . There's also three people out in the desert . . .'

That afternoon Susan walked over and sat down on Virginia's bed. Virginia had been leafing through a movie magazine. Susan saw it and began talking. The story she related, Virginia would say much later, was even more bizarre than what Susan had already told her. It was so incredible that Virginia didn't even mention it to Ronnie Howard. No one would believe it, she decided. For Susan Atkins, in one spurt of non-stop talking, gave her a 'death list' of persons who would be murdered next. All were celebrities. She then, according to Virginia, described in gruesome detail exactly how Elizabeth Taylor, Richard Burton, Tom Jones, Steve McQueen, and Frank Sinatra would die.

On Monday, November 10, Susan Atkins had a visitor at Sybil Brand, Sue Bartell, who told her about the death of Zero. After Sue left, Susan told Ronnie Howard. Whether she embellished it or not is unknown. According to Susan, one of the girls had been holding Zero's hand when he died. When the gun went off, 'he climaxed all over himself'.

Susan didn't seem disturbed to hear of Zero's death. On the contrary, it excited her. 'Imagine how beautiful to be there when it happened!' she told Ronnie.

On Wednesday, November 12, Susan Atkins was taken to court for a preliminary hearing on the Hinman murder. While there, she heard Sergeant Whiteley testify that it was Kitty Lutesinger – not Bobby Beausoleil – who had implicated her. On being returned to jail, Susan told Virginia that the prosecution had a surprise witness; but she wasn't worried about her testimony: 'Her life's not worth anything.'

That same day Virginia Graham received some bad news. She was being transferred to Corona Women's Prison, to serve out the rest of her sentence. She was to leave that afternoon. While she was packing, Ronnie came up to her and asked, 'What do you think?'

'I don't know,' Virginia replied. 'Ronnie, if you want to take it from here – '

'I've been talking to that girl every night,' Ronnie said. 'Boy, she's really weird. She could have, you know.'

Virginia had forgotten to ask Susan about the word 'pig', which the papers had said was printed in blood on the door of the Tate residence. She suggested that Ronnie question her about this, and anything else she could think of that might indicate whether she was telling the truth.

In the meantime, they decided not to mention it to anyone else.

That same day the LaBianca detectives received a call from Venice PD. Were they still interested in talking to one of the Straight Satans? If so, they were questioning one, a guy named Al Springer, on another charge.

The LaBianca detectives had Springer brought over to Parker Center, where they intereviewed him on tape. What he told them was so unexpected they had trouble believing it. For Springer said that on August 11 or 12 – two or three days after the Tate homicides – Charlie Manson had bragged to him about killing people, adding, 'We knocked off five of them just the other night.'

November 12–16, 1969

LaBianca detectives Nielsen, Gutierrez, and Patchett interviewed Springer on tape, in one of the interrogation cubicles of LAPD Homicide. Springer was 26, five feet nine, weighed 130 pounds, and, except for his dusty, ragged 'colors', as bikers' jackets are known, was surprisingly neat for a member of an 'outlaw' motorcycle band.

Springer, it turned out, prided himself on his cleanliness. Which was one of the reasons he personally hadn't wanted to have anything to do with Manson and his girls, he said. But Danny DeCarlo, the club treasurer of the Straight Satans, had got mixed up with them and had missed meetings, so around August 11 or 12, he, Springer, had gone to Spahn Ranch to persuade Danny to come back. '. . . and there was flies all over the place and they were just like animals up there, I couldn't believe it, you know. You see, I'm really clean, really. Some of the guys get pretty nasty, but I myself, I like to keep things clean.

'Well, in comes this Charlie . . . He wanted Danny up there because Danny had his colors on his back, and all these drunkards, they come up there and start harassing the girls and messing with the guys and Danny walks out with his Straight Satan colors on, and nobody messes with Charlie, see.

'So I tried to get Danny to come back, and Charlie is standing there, and Charlie says, he says, "Now wait a minute, maybe I can give you a better thing than you've got already." I said, "What's that?" He says, "Move up here, you can have all the girls you want, all the girls," he says, "are all yours, at your disposal, anything." And he's a brainwashing type guy. So I said, "Well, how do you survive, how do you support these twenty, thirty fucking broads, man?" And he says, "I got them all

hoofing for me." He said, "I go out at night and I do my thing."
"Well," I said, "what's your thing, man; run your trip down."
He figured me being a motorcycle rider and all, I'd accept any-
thing including murder.

'So he starts getting in my ear and says how he goes up and he
lives with the rich people, and he calls the police "pigs" and what
not, he knocks on the door, they'll open the door, and he'll just
drive in with his cutlass and start cutting them up, see.'

Q. 'This is what he told you?'

A. 'This is what he told me verbally, right to my face.'

Q. 'You're kidding, is that what you really heard?'

A. 'Yeah. I said, "When's the last time you did it?" He says,
"Well, we knocked off five of them," he says, "just the other
night." '

Q. 'So he told you that – Charlie stated that he knocked over
five people?'

A. 'Right. Charlie and Tex.'

Springer couldn't recall the exact word Manson used: it wasn't
'people'; it might have been 'pigs' or 'rich pigs'.

The LaBianca detectives were so startled they had Springer
run through it a second time, and a third.

A. 'I think you've got your man right here, I really do.'

Q. 'I'm pretty sure we have, but in this day and age of feeding
people their rights, if we're going to make a decent case on him,
we can't do it with his statement.'

Exactly when had Manson told him this? Well, it was the first
time he went to Spahn, and that was either August 11 or 12 – he
couldn't remember which. But he sure remembered the scene.
'I've never seen anything like it in my life. I've never been to a
nudist colony or I've never seen real idiots on the loose ...'
Everywhere he looked there were naked girls. Maybe a dozen and
a half were of age, 18 or over, but about an equal number weren't.
The young ones were hiding in the bushes. Charlie had told him
he could have his pick. He'd also offered to buy him a dune
buggy and a new motorcycle if he would stay.

It was a true turnabout. Charlie Manson, aka Jesus Christ,
trying to tempt a Straight Satan.

That Springer resisted the temptation may have been due in part to his knowledge that other members of his gang had been there on previous occasions: 'Everybody got sick of catching the clap . . . the ranch was just out of hand . . .'

During Springer's first visit, Manson had demonstrated his prowess with knives, in particular a long sword. Springer had seen Charlie throw it maybe fifty feet, sticking it, say, eight times out of ten. This was the sword, Springer said, that Charlie used when he 'put the chop' to people.

'Did you ever get a corpse with his ear cut off?' Springer abruptly asked. Apparently one of the detectives nodded, as Springer said, 'Yeah, there's your man.' Charlie had told him about cutting some guy's ear off. If Danny would come in, he could tell them about it. The only problem was, 'Danny's scared of these creeps, they've tried to kill him already.'

Springer had also mentioned a Tex and a Clem. The detectives asked him to describe them.

Clem was a certified idiot, Springer said: he was an escapee from Camarillo, a state mental hospital. Whatever Charlie said, Clem would parrot it. As far as he could tell, 'Charlie and Tex are the ones that had the brains out there.' Unlike Clem, Tex didn't say much; he 'kept his mouth shut, real tight. He was real clean-cut. His hair was a little long, but he was – just like a college student.' Tex seemed to spend most of his time working on dune buggies.

Charlie had a thing about dune buggies. He wanted to fix them with a switch on the dash that would turn the tail-lights off. Then, when the CHP (California Highway Patrol) pulled them over to cite them, there would be two guys armed with shotguns in the back, and as the CHPs came up alongside, 'Pow, blow them up.'

Q. 'Why did he say he wanted to do that?'

A. 'Ah, he wants to build up a thing where he can be leader of the world. He's crazy.'

Q. 'Does he have a name for his group?'

A. 'The Family.'

Back to that sword, could Springer describe it? Yeah, it was a cutlass, a real pirate's sword. Up until a few months ago, Springer said, it had belonged to the ex-president of the Straight Satans, but then it had disappeared, and he guessed one of the members had given it to Charlie.

He had heard, from Danny, that the sword had been used when they had killed a guy 'called Henland, I believe it was'. This was the guy who had his ear cut off.

What did he know about the 'Henland' killing? they asked. According to Danny, a guy named 'Bausley' and one or two other guys had killed him, Springer said. Danny had told him that 'almost beyond a reasonable doubt he could prove that Bousley or Bausley or whatever killed this guy and evidently Charlie was in on it or something. Well, anyway, somebody cut his ear.' Clem had also told him, Springer, 'how they had cut some fucking idiot's ear off and wrote on the wall and put the Panther's hand or paw up there to blame the Panthers. Everything they did, they blamed on the niggers, see. They hate niggers because they had killed a nigger prior to that.'

Five. Plus 'Henland' (Hinman). Plus 'a nigger'. Total thus far: seven. The detectives were keeping track.

Had he seen any other weapons while at Spahn? Yeah, Charlie had shown him a whole gunrack full, the first time he went up there. There were shotguns, deer rifles, .45 caliber hand guns, 'and I heard talk of and was told by Danny that they had a .22 Buntline long barrel, a nine-round. This came from Danny, and he knows guns. And this is what was supposed to have killed that, ah, Black Panther.'

Charlie had told him about it. As Al remembered it, Tex had burned this black guy in a deal for a whole bunch of grass. When Charlie refused to give back the guy's money, the black had threatened to get all his Panther brothers up to Spahn Ranch and wipe out the place. 'So Charlie pulls out a gun, somebody else was going to do it, but Charlie pulls out a gun and he points it at the guy, and he goes click, click, click, click and the gun didn't go off, four or five times, and the guy stood up and he said, "Ha, you coming here with an empty gun on me," and Charlie says click, bam, in the heart area somewhere, and he told me this personally right to my face and that was what the Buntline was used on, the long-barrel job.'

After the murder, which had occurred somewhere in Hollywood, the Panther's buddies 'took the carcass off supposedly to some park, Griffith Park or one of them . . . This is all hearsay, but it is hearsay right from Charlie.'

A. 'Now, did anybody have their refrigerator wrote on?'

There was a sudden silence, then one of the LaBianca detectives asked, 'Why does this come up?'

A. ' 'Cause he told me something about writing something on the refrigerator.'

Q. 'Who said he wrote it on the refrigerator?'

A. 'Charlie did. Charlie said they wrote something on the fucking refrigerator in blood.'

Q. 'What did he say he wrote?'

A. 'Something about pigs or niggers or something like that.'

If Springer was telling the truth, and *if* Manson wasn't just bragging to impress him, then it meant that Manson was probably also involved in the LaBianca murders. Bringing the total thus far to nine.

But the LaBianca detectives had good reason to doubt this statement, for, contrary to the press reports, DEATH TO PIGS hadn't been printed in blood on the refrigerator door; the phrase had actually been printed on the living-room wall, as had the word RISE. What had been printed on the refrigerator door was HEALTER SKELTER.

While Springer was being questioned, one of the LaBianca detectives left the room. When he returned a few minutes later, another man was with him.

Q. 'Here's another partner, Mike McGann, Al. Let me shove this table down here. He just came in, so you might want to bring him up on what we've talked about.'

McGann was one of the Tate detectives. The LaBianca detectives had finally decided to walk those few feet, and share what they had learned. But this time the temptation to say 'Hey, look what *we* found' must have been irresistible.

They had Springer run through it again. McGann listened, unimpressed. Springer then began talking about still another murder, that of a cowboy named 'Shorty', whom he had met when he first visited the ranch. How and what had he heard about Shorty's death? one of the detectives asked. 'I heard about that from Danny.' Danny heard, from the girls, that Shorty 'got to know too much and hear too much and got worried too much' and 'so they just cut his arms and his legs and his head off . . .' Danny had felt very badly about this, because he had liked Shorty.

Ten. *If.*

Q. (*to McGann*) 'Anything you want to get in on this?'

Q. 'Yeah, I want to ask about why they killed this colored – the Panther supposedly. When did this take place, do you know?'

Springer wasn't sure, but he thought it was about a week before he went up to the ranch. Danny could probably tell them about that.

Q. 'Did you connect up the five people that Charlie said that he killed in early August with any particular crime?'

A. 'Right, the Tate crime.'

Q. 'You put that together?'

A. 'Right.'

They began zeroing in. Anybody else present when Charlie supposedly confessed those five murders to you? No. Was Tate ever specifically mentioned? No. Did you see anyone at the ranch who wore glasses? No. Ever see Manson with a gun? No, only a knife: 'he's a knife freak'. Were the cutlass and the other knives you saw sharpened on both sides? He thought so but wasn't sure; Danny had mentioned Charlie sending them out someplace to be sharpened. Ever see any rope up there? Yeah, they used all kinds of rope. Do you know there's a $25,000 reward on the Tate murders? Yeah, and 'I sure could use it'.

Springer had been to Spahn Ranch three times, his second visit occurring the day after his first. He'd lost his hat riding out and had gone back to look for it, but then his bike had broken down and he'd had to stay overnight to repair it. Again Charlie, Tex, and Clem had worked on him to join them. His third and last visit had taken place on the night of Friday, August 15. The detectives were able to establish the date because it was the night before the sheriff's raid on Spahn Ranch. Also, the Straight Satans held their club meetings on Friday, and they had discussed getting Danny away from Charlie. 'A lot of the guys in the club were going to go up there and beat his ass, teach him a lesson not to brainwash our members . . .' Eight or nine of them did go to Spahn that night, 'but it didn't happen that way'.

Charlie had conned some of them. The girls had lured others into the bushes. And when they started breaking up things, Charlie told them that he had guns trained on them from the rooftops. Springer had one of his brothers check the gunrack that Charlie had shown him on his first visit. A couple of rifles were missing. After a time they'd left, in a cloud of exhaust fumes and threats, leaving one of their more sober members, Robert Reinhard, to bring Danny back the following day. But the next morning 'the police were all over the place', arresting not only Charlie and the others but also DeCarlo and Reinhard.

All had been released a few days later and, according to Danny, Shorty had been killed not long after this.

Fearing he would be next, Danny had taken his truck and split to Venice. Late one night Clem and Bruce Davis, another of Charlie's boys, had snuck up on the truck. They had succeeded in prying open the door when Danny heard them and grabbed his .45. Danny felt sure, Springer said, that they had come 'to off him'. And he was scared now, not only for himself but because his little boy was living with him. Springer thought Danny was frightened enough to talk to them. Talking to the Venice detectives would be no problem, since 'he's known them most of his life', but getting him to come down to Parker Center was something else. Springer, however, promised he'd try to get Danny to come in voluntarily, if possible the next day.

Springer didn't have a phone. The detectives asked if there

was somewhere they could call 'without putting any heat on you? Is there some gal you see quite a bit of?'

A. 'Just my wife and kids.'

The clean, neat, monogamous Springer didn't conform to their stereotype of a biker. As one of the detectives remarked, 'You're going to give the motorcycle gang a whole new image in the world.'

Although Al Springer appeared to be telling the truth, the detectives were not greatly impressed with his story. He was an outsider, not a member of the Family, yet the very first time he goes to Spahn Ranch, Manson confesses to him that he's committed at least nine murders. It just didn't make sense. It appeared far more likely that Springer was just regurgitating what Danny DeCarlo, who had been close to Manson, had told him. It was also possible that Manson, to impress the cyclists, had bragged about committing murders in which he wasn't even involved.

Although the interview had been taped, the LaBianca detectives had only one portion transcribed, and that not the section on their case, but the part, less than a page in length, with Manson's alleged confession, 'We knocked off five of them just the other night.' The LaBianca detectives then filed the tape and that single page in their 'tubs', as police case files are known. With other developments in the case, they apparently forgot them.

Yet the Springer interview of November 12, 1969, was in a sense an important turning point. Three months after the Tate–LaBianca homicides, LAPD was finally seriously considering the possibility that the two crimes were not, as had long been believed, unrelated. And the focus of at least the LaBianca investigation was now on a single group of suspects, Charlie Manson and his Family.

There is some confusion as to exactly when Susan Atkins first discussed the Tate–LaBianca murders with Ronnie Howard. Whatever the date, there was a similarity in the way it came about, Susan first admitting her participation in the murder of

Hinman, then, in her little-girl manner, attempting to surprise Ronnie with other, more startling revelations.

According to Ronnie, one evening Susan came over, sat down on her bed, and started rapping about her experiences. Susan said that she had 'dropped acid' (taken L S D) many times, in fact she had done everything there was to do; there was nothing left; she'd reached a stage where nothing shocked her any more.

Ronnie replied that there wasn't much that would shock her, either. Since age 17, when she'd been sent to a federal penitentiary for two years for extortion, Ronnie had seen quite a lot.

'I bet I could tell you something that would really blow your mind,' Susan said.

'I don't think so,' Ronnie responded.

'You remember the Tate deal?'

'Yes.'

'I was there. We did it.'

'Really, anyone can say that.'

'No, I'll tell you.' And tell her Susan Atkins did.

Susan would flash from one thought to another with such rapidity that Ronnie was often left confused. Too, Ronnie's recollection of details – especially names, dates, places – was not as good as Virginia's. But she also recalled details Susan either hadn't told Virginia or Virginia had forgotten. Charlie had a a gun; the girls all had knives. Charlie had cut the telephone wires, shot the boy in the car, then awakened the man on the couch (Frykowski), who looked up to see a gun pointing in his face.

Sharon Tate's plea and Susan's brutal response were nearly identical in both Ronnie's and Virginia's accounts. However, the description of how Sharon died differed somewhat. As Ronnie understood it, two other people held Sharon while, to quote Susan, 'I proceeded to stab her.'

'It felt so good the first time I stabbed her, and when she screamed at me it did something to me, sent a rush through me, and I stabbed her again.'

Ronnie asked where. Susan replied in the chest, not the stomach.

'How many times?'

'I don't remember. I just kept stabbing her until she stopped screaming.'

Ronnie knew a little bit about the subject, having once stabbed her ex-husband. 'Did it feel sort of like a pillow?'

'Yeah,' Susan replied, pleased that Ronnie understood. 'It was just like going into nothing, going into air.' But the killing itself was something else. 'It's like a sexual release,' Susan told her. Especially when you see the blood spurting out. It's better than a climax.'

Remembering Virginia's question, Ronnie asked Susan about the word 'pig'. Susan said that she printed the word on the door, after first dipping a towel in Sharon Tate's blood.

At one point in the conversation Susan asked, 'Don't you remember that guy that was found with the fork in his stomach? We wrote "arise" and "death to pigs" and "helter skelter" in blood.'

'Was that you and your same friends?' Ronnie asked.

'No, just three this time.'

'All girls?'

'No, two girls and Charlie. Linda wasn't in on this one.'

Susan rapped on about a variety of subjects: Manson (he was both Jesus Christ and the Devil); helter skelter (Ronnie admittedly didn't understand it but thought it meant 'you have to be killed to live'); sex ('the whole world is like one big intercourse – everything is in and out – smoking, eating, stabbing'); how she would play crazy to fool the psychiatrists ('All you have to do is act normal,' Ronnie advised her); children (Charlie had helped deliver her baby, whom she had named Zezozose Zadfrack Glutz; within a couple of months after his birth she had begun fellating him); bikers (with the motorcycle gangs on their side, they 'would really throw some fear into the world'); and murder. Susan loved to talk about murder. 'More you do it, the better you like it.' Just the mention of it seemed to excite her. Laughingly, she told Ronnie about some man whose head 'we cut off', either out in the desert or in one of the canyons.

She also told Ronnie, 'There are eleven murders that they will never solve.' And there were going to be more, many more. Although Charlie was in jail 'in Indio', most of the Family was still free.

As Susan talked, Ronnie Howard realized that there were still some things that could shock her. One was that this little girl, who was 21 but often seemed much younger, probably *had* committed all these murders. Another was Susan's assertion that this was only the beginning, that more murders would follow.

Ronnie Howard would later state: 'I'd never informed on anyone in the past, but this one thing I could not go along with. I kept thinking that if I didn't say anything these people would probably be set free. They were going to pick other houses, just at random. I just couldn't see all those innocent people being killed.'

It would seem that if one were in jail, talking to a policeman would be relatively easy. Ronnie Howard discovered otherwise.

The dates, again, are vague, but according to Ronnie, she told +Sergeant Broom,* one of the female deputies at Sybil Brand, that she knew who had committed the Tate and LaBianca murders; that the person who told her had been involved and was now in custody; but that the other killers were on the loose and unless they were apprehended soon there would be more murders. Ronnie wanted permission to call LAPD.

Sergeant Broom said she would pass the request to her superior, +Lieutenant Johns.

After waiting three days and hearing nothing, Ronnie asked Sergeant Broom about the request. Lieutenant Johns didn't think there was anything to the story, the sergeant told her. By this time the lieutenant had probably forgotten all about it, Sergeant Broom said, adding, 'Why don't you do the same thing, Ronnie?'

By now, according to Ronnie, she was literally begging. People were going to die unless she warned the police in time. Could you call *for* me? Ronnie asked. *Please!*

* Since neither the deputy nor her lieutenant was available for interviews, therefore making it impossible to present their version of these incidents, pseudonyms have been used for both.

It was against the rules for a guard to make a call for an inmate, Sergeant Broom informed her.

On Thursday, November 13, biker Danny DeCarlo came down to Parker Center, where he was interviewed by the LaBianca detectives. It was not a long interview, and it was not taped. Although DeCarlo had a great deal of information about the activities of Manson and his group, having lived with them for more than five months, at no time had Charlie admitted to him that he was involved in either the Tate or the LaBianca murders.

This made the officers even more skeptical about Springer's tale, and it was probably at this point that they decided to write him off as a reliable source. When Springer came back the following week, he was given some photos to identify but was asked few questions.

Arrangements were made to interview DeCarlo on tape, and at length, on Monday, November 17. He was to come in about 8:30 in the morning.

Ronnie Howard kept after Sergeant Broom, who finally mentioned the subject to Lieutenant Johns a second time. The lieutenant suggested that she ask Ronnie for some details.

Sergeant Broom did, and Ronnie – still without identifying the people involved – told her a little of what she had learned. The killers knew Terry Melcher. They had shot the boy, Steven Parent, first, four times, because he saw them. Sharon Tate had been the last to die. The word 'pig' had been written in her blood. They were going to cut out Sharon's baby, but didn't. Again she stressed that more killings were planned.

Sergeant Broom apparently misunderstood Ronnie, for she told Lieutenant Johns that they *had* cut out the baby. And Lieutenant Johns knew this wasn't true.

Your informant is lying, Sergeant Broom informed Ronnie, and told her why.

Ronnie, now almost hysterical, told Sergeant Broom that she had misunderstood what she'd said. Could she talk to Lieutenant Johns herself?

But Sergeant Broom decided that she had already bothered the lieutenant enough. As far as she was concerned, she informed Ronnie, the matter was closed.

There was an irony here, although Ronnie Howard was unaware of it, and wouldn't have appreciated it had she known: Sergeant Broom dated one of the Tate detectives. But apparently they had other, more important things to talk about.

Virginia Graham was having her own troubles with bureaucracy. Although, unlike Ronnie Howard, she was not yet completely convinced that Susan Atkins was telling the truth, the possibility that there might be more murders worried her too. On November 14, two days after her transfer to Corona, she decided she had to tell someone what she had heard. There was one person at the prison she knew and trusted, Dr Vera Dreiser, a staff psychologist.

Virginia made out a request form, writing on it, 'Dr Dreiser, it is very important that I speak with you.'

The form was returned with a notation stating that Miss Graham should fill out another blue slip, to see Dr Owens, administrator of the unit to which she was assigned. But Virginia didn't want to speak to Dr Owens. Again she requested a personal interview with Dr Dreiser.

The request was granted. But not until December. And by then the whole world knew what Virginia Graham had wanted to tell Dr Dreiser.

November 17, 1969

Danny DeCarlo was due at LAPD Homicide at 8:30 that Monday morning. He didn't show. It was possible DeCarlo had skipped. He had been very frightened when the detectives talked to him the previous Thursday.

There was another possibility, one that they didn't want to think about.

That same day Ronnie Howard had a court appearance in Santa Monica, on the forgery charge. When inmates of Sybil Brand are due in court, they are first transported to the men's jail on Bochet Street, where a bus picks them up and delivers them to the assigned departments. Before the arrival of the bus, there are usually a few minutes during which each girl is permitted to make one call from a pay phone.

Ronnie saw her chance and got in line. However, time began running out and there were still two girls ahead of her. She paid each fifty cents to let her call first.

Ronnie called the Beverly Hills Police Department and asked to speak to a homicide detective. When one came on the line, she gave him her name and booking number, and told him she knew who had committed the Tate and LaBianca murders. The officer said those cases were being handled by the Hollywood Division of LAPD, and suggested she call there.

Ronnie then called Hollywood PD, giving a second homicide officer the same information. He wanted to send someone over immediately, but she told him she would be in court the rest of the day.

She hung up, however, before the officer could ask which court she would be in.

All day in court Ronnie Howard had the feeling that she was being watched. She was sure that two men, sitting in the back of the courtroom, were homicide detectives, and expected at any minute they would arrange to speak to her. But they never did. When court adjourned, she was taken by bus back to Sybil Brand, Dormitory 8000, and Susan Atkins.

Shortly before 5 P.M., Danny DeCarlo arrived at LAPD Homicide. He had been on his way downtown earlier when he noticed he was low on gas and had pulled into a service station. On leaving, he had made an illegal turn, had been spotted by a black-and-white, and, after the officers checked and found he had some outstanding traffic tickets, had been hauled in. It had taken all day to secure his release.

Unlike Al Springer, Danny DeCarlo looked, talked, and acted like a biker. He was short, five feet four, weighed 130 pounds, had a handlebar mustache, tattoos on both arms, and burn scars on one arm and both legs from motorcycle pile-ups. Wary, frequently glancing back over his shoulder as if expecting to find someone there, he spoke in a colorful jargon that the interviewing officers – Nielsen, Gutierrez, and McGann – unconsciously adopted. Now 25, he had been born in Toronto, then given U.S. citizenship after serving four years in the Coast Guard, his job: weapons expert. Currently he was in business with his father, selling firearms. When it came to the guns at Spahn Ranch, the detectives couldn't have found a better source. When he wasn't getting drunk and chasing girls – which he admitted occupied most of his time – he looked after the weapons. He not only cleaned and repaired them, he slept in the gunroom.

He also knew a great deal about Spahn's Movie Ranch, which was located in Chatsworth, not more than twenty miles from downtown Beverly Hills, yet, seemingly, a world away. Once William S. Hart, Tom Mix, Johnny Mack Brown, and Wallace Beery had made movies here; it was said that Howard Hughes had come to Spahn, to oversee personally the filming of portions of *The Outlaw*; and the rolling hills behind the main buildings provided settings for *Duel in the Sun*. Now, except for an occasional Marlboro commercial or a 'Bonanza' episode, the main business was renting horses to weekend riders. The movie sets – Longhorn Saloon, Rock City Cafe, Undertaking Parlor, Jail – which fronted on Santa Susana Pass Road, were old now, run down, as was George Spahn, the 81-year-old, near blind owner of the ranch. For years Ruby Pearl, a onetime circus bareback rider turned horse wrangler, had run the riding stable part of the business for George: getting hay, hiring and firing cowboys, making sure they looked after the horses and stable and kept their hands off the too young girls who came for riding lessons. Almost sightless, George depended on Ruby, but at the end of the day she went home to a husband and another life. When the Manson Family arrived, in August 1968, George was living alone in a filthy trailer, feeling old, lonely, and neglected.

Manson, who originally asked Spahn's permission to stay for a few days, but neglected to mention that there were twenty-five to thirty people with him, assigned Squeaky to look after George.

Squeaky – t/n Lynette Fromme – had been with Manson more than a year at that time, having been one of the first girls to join him. She was thin, red-headed, covered with freckles. Though 19, she looked much younger. DeCarlo told the detectives, 'She had George in the palm of her hand. She cleaned for him, cooked for him, balanced his checkbook, made love with him.'

Q. (*unbelievingly*) 'She did?! That old son of a gun!'

A. 'Yeah . . . Charlie's trip was to get George so he had so much faith in Squeaky that come time for George to go off into the happy hunting ground he'd turn the ranch over to Squeaky. That was their thing. Charlie'd always tell her what to tell George . . . and she'd report back to Charlie anything anyone else told him.'

Squeaky maintained that she was George's eyes. According to DeCarlo, they saw only what Charlie Manson wanted them to see.

Possibly because he suspected, possibly because his own children on their occasional visits strongly resisted the idea, George never did get around to willing the property to Squeaky. Which, the detective surmised, was probably why he was still alive out at Spahn Ranch.

George Spahn had frustrated one of Charlie's plans. Danny DeCarlo had played along with, then failed to come through on, another – Manson's scheme to get the motorcycle gangs to join him in 'terrorizing society', as DeCarlo put it. Danny had met Manson in March 1969, just after separating from his wife. He had gone to Spahn to repair some bikes, and had stayed; 'I had a ball,' he later admitted. Manson's girls had been taught that having babies and caring for men were their sole purpose in life. DeCarlo liked being cared for, and the girls, at least at first, appeared very affectionate toward 'Donkey Dan', a nickname they had bestowed upon him because of certain physical endowments.

There were problems. Charlie was against drinking; Danny liked nothing better than to swill beer and lie in the sun – later he testified that while at Spahn he was smashed 'probably 90 percent of the time'. And, with the exception of a couple of 'special sweeties', DeCarlo eventually tired of most of the girls: 'They would always try preaching to me. It was always the same shit Charlie preached to them.'

With the August 15 visit of the Straight Satans, Manson must have realized that he would never succeed in getting the bikers to join him. After that, Danny was ignored, left out of Family conferences, while the girls denied him their favors. Though he went to Barker Ranch with the group, he stayed only three days. He split, DeCarlo said, because he had begun to believe all the 'murder talk' he had heard, and because he had strong suspicions that unless he left he might be next. 'After that,' he said, 'I started watching my back.'

When the LaBianca detectives had talked to DeCarlo the previous Thursday, he'd promised to try to locate Manson's sword. He turned it over to Sergeant Gutierrez, who booked it as the personal property of 'Manson, Charles M.,' probable crime '187 PC' – murder.

The sword had accumulated a history. A few weeks after Danny moved to Spahn, the president of the Straight Satans,

George Knoll, aka '86 George', had visited him. Manson had admired George's sword and had conned him out of it by promising to pay a twenty-dollar traffic ticket George owed. According to Danny, the sword became one of Charlie's favorite weapons; he had a metal scabbard built for it, next to the steering wheel of his personal dune buggy. When the Straight Satans came to get Danny the night of August 15, they spotted the sword and reclaimed it. On learning that it was 'dirty', i.e., had been used in a crime, they had broken it in half. It was in two pieces when DeCarlo handed it over to Gutierrez.

Over-all length, 20 inches; blade length, 15 inches. The width of its razor-sharp blade, the tip of which had been honed on both sides, was 1 inch.

This was the sword, according to DeCarlo, that Manson had used to slice Gary Hinman's ear.

From DeCarlo the detectives now learned that, in addition to Bobby Beausoleil and Susan Atkins, three others had been involved in the murder of Hinman: Manson, Mary Brunner, and Bruce Davis. DeCarlo's primary source was Beausoleil, who, on returning to Spahn after the murder, had bragged to DeCarlo about what he had done. Or, as Danny put it, 'He came back with a big head the next day, you know, just like he got him a cherry.'

The story, as DeCarlo claimed Beausoleil had related it to him, went as follows. Mary Brunner, Susan Atkins, and Bobby Beausoleil had dropped in on Hinman, 'bullshitting about old times and everything like that'. Bobby then asked Gary for all his money, saying they needed it. When Gary said he didn't have any money, Bobby pulled out a gun – a 9 mm. Polish Rodom automatic – and started pistol-whipping him. In the scuffle the gun went off, the bullet hitting no one but ricocheting through the kitchen.

Beausoleil then called Manson at Spahn Ranch and told him, 'You'd better get up here, Charlie. Gary ain't cooperating.' A short time later Manson and Bruce Davis arrived at the Hinman residence. Puzzled and hurt, Gary pleaded with Charlie, asking him to take the others and leave; he didn't want any trouble; he couldn't understand why they were doing this to him; they had always been friends. According to DeCarlo, 'Charlie didn't say anything. He just hit him with the sword. Whack. Cut part of his ear off or all of it. [Hinman's left ear had been split in half.]

'So Gary went down, and was really going through some changes about losing his ear . . .' Manson gave him a choice: sign over everything he had, or die. Manson and Davis then left.

Though Beausoleil did obtain the 'pink slips' (California automobile ownership papers) on two of Hinman's vehicles, Gary continued to insist he had no money. When more pistol-whipping failed to convince him, Bobby again called Manson at Spahn, telling him, 'We ain't going to get nothing out of him. He ain't going to give up nothing. And we can't just leave. He's got his ear hacked off and he'll go to the police.' Manson replied, 'Well, you know what to do.'

'Bobby said he went up to Gary again. Took the knife and stuck him with it. He said he had to do it three or four times . . . [Hinman] was really bleeding, and he was gasping for air, and Bobby said he knelt down next to him and said, "Gary, you know what? You got no reason to be on earth any more. You're a pig and society don't need you, so this is the best way for you to go, and you should thank me for putting you out of your misery." Then [Hinman] made noises in his throat, his last gasping breath, and wow, away he went.'

Q. 'So Bobby told him he was a "pig"?'

A. 'Right. You see, the fight against society was the number one element in this – '

Q. (*skeptically*) 'Yeah. We'll get into his philosophy and all that bullshit later . . .'

They never did.

DeCarlo went on. Before leaving the house, they wrote on the wall ' "white piggy" or "whitey" or "kill the piggies", something along that line'. Beausoleil also dipped his hand in Hinman's blood and, using his palm, made a paw print on the wall; the plan was 'to push the blame onto the Black Panthers', who used the paw print as their symbol. Then they hot-wired Hinman's Volkswagen microbus and his Fiat station wagon and drove both back to Spahn Ranch, where Beausoleil bragged about his exploits to DeCarlo.

Later, apparently fearful that the palm print might be identifiable, Beausoleil returned to the Hinman residence and attempted, unsuccessfully, to wipe it off the wall. This was several days after Hinman's death, and Beausoleil later told DeCarlo that he 'could hear the maggots eating away on Gary'.*

As killers, they had been decidedly amateurish. Not only was the palm print identifiable, so was a latent fingerprint Beausoleil had left in the kitchen. They kept Hinman's Volkswagen and his Fiat at the ranch for several days, where a number of people saw them. Hinman had played bagpipes, a decidedly uncommon musical instrument. Beausoleil and the girls took his set back to Spahn Ranch, where for a time they remained on a shelf in the kitchen; DeCarlo for one had tried to play them. And Beausoleil did not discard the knife but continued to carry it with him; it was in the tire well when he was arrested on August 6, driving Hinman's Fiat.

DeCarlo drew a picture of the knife Beausoleil claimed he had used to stab Hinman. It was a pencil-thin, miniature bowie, with an eagle on the handle and a Mexican inscription. It tallied perfectly with the knife recovered from the Fiat. DeCarlo also sketched the 9 mm. Radom, which as yet hadn't been recovered.

The detectives asked him what other hand guns he had seen at Spahn.

A. 'Well, there was a .22 Buntline. When they did that Black Panther, I didn't want to touch it. I didn't want to clean it. I didn't want to be nowhere around it.'

DeCarlo claimed he didn't know whose gun it was, but he said, 'Charlie always used to carry it in a holster on the front of him. It was more or less always with him.'

---

* Beausoleil, Brunner, and Atkins went to Hinman's residence on Friday, July 25, 1969. Manson slashed Hinman's ear sometime late that night. Hinman was not killed, however, until Sunday, July 27, and it was not until the following Thursday, July 31, that his body was discovered by LASO, following a report from a friend who had been trying to reach Hinman for several days.

Sometime 'around July, maybe June', the gun 'just popped up'. When was the last time he saw it? 'I know I didn't see it for at least a week before the raid.'

The Spahn Ranch raid had taken place on August 16. A week earlier would be August 9, the date of the Tate homicides.

Q. 'Did you ever ask Charlie, "Where's your gun?"'

A. 'He said, "I just gave it away." He liked it, so I figured it was maybe just stashed.'

The detectives had DeCarlo draw the Buntline. It was nearly identical with the photo of the Hi Standard Longhorn model sent out in the LAPD flyer. Later DeCarlo was shown the flyer and asked, 'Does this look like the gun you mentioned?'

A. 'It sure does.'

Q. 'What's the difference between that gun and the gun that you saw?'

A. 'No difference at all. Only the rear sight blade was different. It didn't have any.'

The detectives had DeCarlo run down what he knew about the murder of the Black Panther. Springer had first mentioned the killing to them when they interviewed him. In the interim they had done some checking and had come up with a slight problem: no such murder had ever been reported.

According to DeCarlo, after Tex burned the guy for $2,500 on a grass deal, the Panther had called Charlie at Spahn Ranch, threatening that if he didn't make good he and his brothers were going to wipe out the whole ranch. That same night Charlie and a guy named T.J. went to the Panther's place, in North Hollywood. Charlie had a plan.

He put the .22 Buntline in his belt in back. On a signal T.J. was to yank out the gun, step out from behind Charlie, and plug the Panther. Nail him right there. Only T.J. had chickened out, and Manson had to do the shooting himself. Friends of the black, who were present when the shooting occurred, had later dumped the body in Griffith Park, Danny said.

Danny had seen the $2,500 and had been present the next morning when Manson criticized T.J. for backing down. DeCarlo described T.J. as 'a really nice guy; his front was trying to be one of Charlie's boys, but he didn't have it inside'. T.J. had gone along with Manson on everything up to this, but he told him, 'I don't want to have nothing to do with snuffing people.' A day or two later he 'fled in the wind'.

Q. 'Who else got murdered up there? What about Shorty? Do you know anything about that?'

There was a long pause, then: 'That was my ace in the hole.'

Q. 'How so?'

A. 'I was going to save that for the last.'

Q. 'Well, might as well clear the thing up now. Has Charlie got something he can smear on you that – '

A. 'No, no way at all. Nothing.'

One thing did worry DeCarlo, however. In 1966 he had been convicted of a felony, smuggling marijuana across the Mexican border, a federal charge; he was currently appealing the sentence. He was also under indictment on two other charges: along with Al Springer and several other Straight Satans, he had been charged with selling a stolen motorcycle engine, which was a local charge, and giving false information while purchasing a firearm (using an alias and not disclosing that he had a prior felony conviction), which was federal. Manson was still on parole from a federal pen. 'So what if they send me to the same place? I don't want to feel a shank in my back and find that little son of a bitch behind me.'

Q. 'Let me explain something to you, Danny, so you know where you stand. We're dealing with a guy here who we are pretty sure is responsible for about thirteen murders. Some of which you don't know about.'

The figure thirteen was just a guess, but DeCarlo surprised them by saying, 'I know about – I'm pretty sure he did Tate.'

Q. 'O.K., we've talked about the Panther, we've talked about Gary Hinman, we're going to talk about Shorty, and you think he did Tate, that's eight. Now, we've got five more. All right? Now, our opinion of Charlie is that he's got a little mental problem.

'But we're in no way going to jeopardize you or anyone else if, for no other reason, we don't want another murder. We're in business to stop murders. And in this business there's no sense in solving thirteen murders if somebody else is going to get killed. That just makes fourteen.'

A. 'I'm a nasty motorcycle rider.'

Q. 'I don't care what you are personally.'

A. 'The police's general opinion of me is nothing.'

Q. 'That's not my opinion.'

A. 'I'm not an outstanding citizen – '

Q. 'As I told you the other day, Danny, you level with us, all the way, right down the line, no bullshitting – I'm not going to bullshit you, you're not going to bullshit me – we level with each other and I'll go out for you a hundred percent. And I mean it. So that you don't have to go to the joint.'

Q. (*another detective*) 'We've dealt with motorcycle riders before, and with all kinds of people. We've gone out on a limb to help them because they've helped us. We'll do our very best to make sure that nobody gets killed, whether he's a motorcycle rider or the best citizen in the world . . .

'Now tell us what you know about Shorty.'

Early that same evening, two LAPD homicide officers, Sergeants Mossman and Brown, appeared at Sybil Brand and asked to see one Ronnie Howard.

The interview was brief. They heard enough, however, to realize they were on to something big. Enough, too, to decide it wasn't the best idea to leave Ronnie Howard in the same dormitory with Susan Atkins. Before leaving Sybil Brand, they arranged to have Ronnie moved to an isolation unit. Then they drove back to Parker Center, anxious to tell the other detectives that they had 'cracked the case'.

Nielsen, Gutierrez, and McGann were still questioning DeCarlo about the murder of Shorty. They already knew something about it, even before talking to Springer and DeCarlo, since Sergeants Whiteley and Guenther had begun their own investigation into the 'possible homicide' after talking to Kitty Lutesinger.

They knew 'Shorty' was Donald Jerome Shea, a 36-year-old male Caucasian who had worked at Spahn Ranch on and off for some fifteen years as a horse wrangler. Like most of the other cowboys who drifted in and out of Spahn's Movie Ranch, Shorty was just awaiting the day when some producer discovered he had all the potentials of a new John Wayne or Clint Eastwood. Whenever the prospect of any acting job materialized, Shorty would quit work and go in search of that ever elusive stardom. Which explained why, when in late August he disappeared from Spahn, no one thought too much about it. At first.

Kitty had also told LASO that Manson, Clem, Bruce, and possibly Tex had been involved in the killing, and that some of the girls in the Family had helped obliterate all traces of the crime. One thing they didn't know, and now asked Danny, was, 'Why did they do it?'

A. 'Because Shorty was going to old man Spahn and snitching. And Charlie didn't like snitches.'

Q. 'Just about the petty bullshit at the ranch?'

A. 'That's right. Shorty was telling old man Spahn that he should put him in charge and he would clean everybody up.' He would, in short order, run off Manson and his Family. Shorty, however, made a fatal mistake: he forgot that little Squeaky was not only George's eyes, she was also Charlie's ears.

There were other reasons, which Danny enumerated. Shorty had married a black topless dancer; Charlie 'had a thing' about interracial marriages, and blacks. ('Charlie had two enemies,' DeCarlo said, 'the police and the niggers, in that order.') Charlie also suspected that Shorty had helped set up the August 16 raid on Spahn – Shorty had been 'offed' about ten days later.* And there was the possibility, though this was strictly conjecture on DeCarlo's part, that Shorty had overheard something about some of the other murders.

Bruce Davis had told him about Shorty's murder, DeCarlo said. Several of the girls had also mentioned it, as had both Clem

---

* The exact date of Shea's death still remains unknown. It is believed to have occurred on either the night of Monday, August 25, or Tuesday, August 26, 1969.

and Manson. Danny was unclear as to some of the details – how they had managed to catch Shorty off guard, and where – but as for the mode of death, he was more than graphic. 'Like they were going to do Caesar,' they went to the gunroom and picked up a sword and four German bayonets, the latter purchased from an Army surplus store for a buck each and honed to razor sharpness, then, getting Shorty off by himself, they 'stuck him like carving up a Christmas turkey . . . Bruce said they cut him up in nine pieces. They cut his head off. Then they cut his arms off too, so there was no way they could possibly identify him. They were laughing about that.'

After killing him, they covered the body with leaves; some of the girls had helped dispose of Shorty's bloody clothing, his automobile, and other possessions; then 'Clem came back the next day or that night and buried him good'.

Q. (*unidentified voice*) 'Can we break this up for about fifteen minutes, maybe send Danny up to get some coffee? There's been an accident and they want to talk to you guys.'

A. 'Sure.'

Q. 'I'm going to send Danny up to the eighth floor. I want him back down here in fifteen minutes.'

A. 'I'll wait right here.' Danny was not anxious to be seen wandering the halls of LAPD.

Q. 'It won't take more than fifteen minutes. We'll close the door so nobody will know you're in here.'

There had been no accident. Mossman and Brown had returned from Sybil Brand. As they related what they had heard, the fifteen minutes stretched to nearly forty-five. Although the Atkins-Howard conversations left many unanswered questions, the detectives were now convinced that the Tate and LaBianca cases had been 'solved'. Susan Atkins had told Ronnie Howard details – the unpublished words written at the LaBianca residence, the lost knife at Tate – which only one of the killers could know. Lieutenants Helder (Tate) and LePage (LaBianca) were notified.

When the detectives returned to the interrogation room, they were in a lighthearted mood.

Q. 'Now, when we left Shorty, he was in nine pieces and his head and arms were off . . .'

DeCarlo was not told what they had learned. But he must have sensed a change in the questioning. The matter of Shorty was quickly wrapped up. Tate was now the topic. Exactly why did Danny think Manson was involved?

Well, there were two incidents. Or maybe it was the same incident, Danny was not sure. Anyway, 'they went out on one caper and they came back with seventy-five bucks. Tex was in on that. And he fucked up his foot, fucking somebody out of it. I don't know whether he put his lights out or not, but he got seventy-five bucks.'

There were no calendars at Spahn Ranch, DeCarlo had told them earlier; no one paid much attention to what day it was. The one date everyone at the ranch remembered, however, was August 16, the day of the raid. It was before this.

Q. 'How much before?'

A. 'Oh, two weeks.'

If DeCarlo's estimate was correct, this would also be before Tate. What was the other incident?

A. 'They went out one night, everybody went but Bruce.'

Q. 'Who went?'

A. 'Charlie, Tex, and Clem. Them three. O.K., the next morning –'

One of the detectives interrupted. Had he actually seen them leave? No, only the next morning – Another interruption: Did any of the girls go that night?

A. 'No, I think – No, I am almost positive it was just them three that went.'

Q. 'Well, do you remember, were the rest of the girls there that night?'

A. 'See, the girls were scattered all over the place, and there is no possible way that I could have kept track of who was there and who wasn't there . . .'

So it was possible the girls could have gone without DeCarlo's knowing about it. Now, what about the date?

This one Danny remembered, more or less, because he was rebuilding the engine on his bike and had to go into town to get a bearing. It was 'around the ninth, tenth, or eleventh' of August. 'And they split that night and they came back the next morning.'

Clem was standing in front of the kitchen, DeCarlo said. Danny walked up to him and asked, 'What'd you do last night?' Clem, according to Danny, smiled 'that real stupid smile of his'. Danny glanced back over his shoulder and saw that Charlie was standing behind him. He got the impression that Clem had been about to answer but that Charlie had signaled him to be quiet. Clem said something like 'Don't worry about it, we did all right.' At this point Charlie walked off. Before starting after him, Clem put his hand on Danny's arm and said, 'We got five piggies.' There was a great big grin on his face.

Clem told DeCarlo, 'We got five piggies.' Manson told Springer, 'We knocked off five of them just the other night.' Atkins confessed to Howard that she stabbed Sharon Tate and Voytek Frykowski. Beausoleil confessed to DeCarlo that he had stabbed Hinman. Atkins told Howard that *she* had done the stabbing. Suddenly the detectives had a surfeit of confessors. So many that they were thoroughly confused as to who was involved in which homicides.

Skipping Hinman, which, after all, was the sheriff's case, and concentrating on Tate, they had two versions:

(1) DeCarlo felt that Charlie, Clem, and Tex – without the help of any of the girls – had killed Sharon Tate and the others.

(2) Ronnie Howard understood Susan Atkins to say that she, two other girls (the names 'Linda' and 'Katie' had been mentioned, but whether they were involved in this particular homicide was unclear), plus 'Charles', plus possibly one other man, had gone to 10050 Cielo Drive.

As for the LaBianca murders, all they knew was that there were 'two girls and Charlie', that 'Linda wasn't in on this one', and that Susan Atkins was somehow involved in that collective 'we'.

The detectives decided to try another approach – through the other girls at the ranch. But first they wanted to wrap up a few loose ends. What clothing had the three men been wearing? Dark clothing, DeCarlo replied. Charlie had on a black sweater, Levi's, moccasins; Tex was dressed similarly, he thought, though he may have been wearing boots, he wasn't sure; Clem wore Levi's and moccasins, too, plus an olive-drab field jacket. Had he noticed any blood on their clothes when he saw them the next morning? No, but then he hadn't been looking for any. Did he have any idea which vehicle they took? Sure, Johnny Swartz's '59 Ford; it was the only car working at that time. Any idea where it was now? It had been hauled off during the August 16 raid and, so far as Danny knew, was probably still in the impound garage in Canoga Park. Swartz was one of the ranch hands at Spahn, not a Family member, but he let them borrow his car. Any idea what Tex's true name was? 'Charles' was his first name, Danny said; he'd seen the last name once, on a pink slip, but couldn't recall it. Was it 'Charles Montgomery'? the detectives asked, using a name Kitty Lutesinger had supplied. No, that didn't sound familiar. What about Clem – does the name 'Tufts' ring any bell? No, he'd never heard Clem called that, but, 'That boy that was found shot up in Topanga Canyon, the 16-year-old kid. Wasn't his name Tufts?' One of the detectives replied, 'I don't know. That's the sheriff's case. We got so many murders now.'

O.K., now about the girls. 'How well did you know the broads out there?'

A. 'Pretty well, man.' [Laughter]

The detectives began going through the names the girls had used when arrested in the Spahn and Barker raids. And they immediately encountered problems. Not only had they used aliases when booked, they also used them at the ranch. And not a single alias but several, seemingly changing names like clothes, whenever the mood hit them. As a further complication, they even traded aliases.

As if these weren't problems enough, Danny provided another. He was extremely reluctant to admit that any of the girls might be capable of murder.

The guys were something else. Bobby, Tex, Bruce, Clem, any

would kill, DeCarlo felt, if Charlie told him to. (All, it later turned out, had.)

Ella Jo Bailey was eliminated; she'd left Spahn Ranch before the murders, Mary Brunner and Sandra Good were out also; they'd been in jail both nights.

What about Ruth Ann Smack, aka Ruth Ann Huebelhurst? (These were booking names. Her true name was Ruth Ann Moorehouse, and she was known in the Family as 'Ouisch'. Danny knew this, but for personal reasons didn't bother to enlighten the detectives.)

Q. 'What do you know about her?'

A. 'She used to be one of my favorite sweeties.'

Q. 'Do you think she would have the guts to get into a cold-blooded murder?'

Danny hesitated a long time before answering. 'You know, that little girl there is so sweet. What really made me sick to my stomach is when she came up one night, when I was up there in the desert, and she said, "I can hardly wait to get my first pig."

'Little 17-year-old! I looked on her like she was my daughter, just the sweetest little thing you would ever want to meet in your life. She was so beautiful and so sweet. And Charlie fucked her thinking around so much it turned your guts.'

The date when she told DeCarlo this was determined to be about September 1. If she hadn't killed by then, she couldn't have been in on LaBianca or Tate. Eliminate Ruth Ann.

Ever know a Katie? Yeah, but he didn't know what her real name was. 'I never knew anyone by their real name,' DeCarlo said. Katie was an older broad, not a runaway. She was from down around Venice. His description of her was vague, except that she had so much hair on her body that none of the guys wanted to make it with her.

What about a Linda? She was a short broad, Danny said. But she didn't stay long, maybe only a month or so, and he didn't know much about her. She'd left by the time they raided Spahn Ranch.

When Sadie went out on 'creepy-crawly' missions, did she carry any weapons? one of the detectives asked.

A. 'She carried a little knife . . . They had a bunch of little hunting knives, Buck hunting knives.'

Q. 'Buck knives?'

A. 'Buck knives, right . . .'

They now began firing specific questions at DeCarlo. Ever see any credit cards with an Italian name on them? Anybody ever talk about somebody who owned a boat? Ever hear anyone use the name 'LaBianca'? Danny gave 'No' answers to all.

What about glasses, anybody at Spahn wear them? 'None of 'em wore glasses because Charlie wouldn't let 'em wear glasses.' Mary Brunner had had several pairs; Charlie had broken them.

DeCarlo was shown some two-strand nylon rope. Ever see any rope like this up at Spahn? No, but he had seen some three-strand. Charlie had bought about 200 feet of it at the Jack Frost surplus store in Santa Monica, in June or July.

Was he sure about that? Sure he was sure; he'd been along when Charlie bought it. Later he'd coiled it so it wouldn't develop snags. It was the same as they used in the Coast Guard, on PT boats; he'd handled it hundreds of times.

Although DeCarlo was unaware of it, the Tate-Sebring rope was also three-strand.

Probably by prearrangement, the detectives began to lean on DeCarlo.

Q. 'Did you ever caper with any of the guys?'

A. 'Fuck no. No way at all. Ask any of the girls.'

Q. 'Did you have anything to do with Shorty's death?'

DeCarlo denied it, vehemently. Shorty had been his friend; besides, 'I've got no balls for putting anybody's lights out.' But there was just enough hesitation in his reply to indicate he was hiding something. Pressed, DeCarlo told them about Shorty's guns. Shorty had a matched pair of Colt .45s. He was always hocking, then reclaiming the pistols. In late August or early September – after Shorty had disappeared but supposedly before DeCarlo knew what had happened to him – Bruce Davis had given him Shorty's pawn tickets on the guns, in repayment for some money he owed DeCarlo. Danny had reclaimed the pistols.

Later, learning that Shorty had been killed, he'd sold the guns to a Culver City shop for seventy-five dollars.

Q. 'That puts you in a pretty shitty spot, you're aware of that?'

Danny was. And he got in even deeper when one of the detectives asked him if he knew anything about lime. When arrested, Mary Brunner was carrying a shopping list made up by Manson. 'Lime' was one of the items listed. Any idea why Charlie would want some lime?

Danny recalled that Charlie had once asked him what to use 'to decompose a body'. He had told him lime worked best, because he had once used it to get rid of a cat that had died under a house.

Q. 'Why did you tell him that?'

A. 'No particular reason, he was just asking me.'

Q. 'What did he ask you?'

A. 'Oh, the best way to ah, ah, you know, to get rid of a body real quick.'

Q. 'Did you ever think to say, "Now what in the fuck makes you ask a question like that, Charlie?" '

A. 'No, because he was nuts.'

Q. 'When did that conversation take place?'

A. 'Right around, ah, right around the time Shorty disappeared.'

It looked bad, and the detectives left it at that. Although privately they were inclined to accept DeCarlo's tale, it gave them some additional leverage to try and get what they wanted.

They wanted two things.

Q. 'Anybody left up at Spahn Ranch that knows you?'

A. 'Not that I know of. I don't know who's up there. And I don't want to go up there to find out. I don't want nothing to do with the place.'

Q. 'I want to look around there. But I need a guide.'

Danny didn't volunteer.

They made the other request straight out.

Q. 'Would you be willing to testify?'

A. '*No, sir!*'

There were two charges pending against him, they reminded

him. On the stolen motorcycle engine, 'Maybe we can get it busted down to a lesser charge. Maybe we can go so far as to get it knocked off. As far as the federal thing is concerned, I don't know how much weight we can push on that. But here again we can try.'

A. 'If you try for me, that's fine. That's all I can ask of you.'

If it came down to being a witness or going to jail –

DeCarlo hesitated. 'Then when *he* gets out of jail – '

Q. 'He isn't going to get out of jail on no first degree murder beef when you've got over five victims involved. If Manson was the guy that was in on the Tate murder. We don't know that for a fact yet. We've got a great deal of information that way.'

A. 'There's also a reward involved in that.'

Q. 'Yes, there is. Quite a bit of a reward. Twenty-five grand. Not to say that one guy is going to get it, but even split that's a hell of a piece of cash.'

A. 'I could send my boy through military school with that.'

Q. 'Now, what do you think, would you be willing to testify against this group of people?'

A. 'He's going to be sitting there looking at me, Manson is, isn't he?'

Q. 'If you go to trial and testify, he is. Now, how scared of Manson are you?'

A. 'I'm scared shitless. I'm petrified of him. He wouldn't hesitate for a second. If it takes him ten years, he'd find that little boy of mine and carve him to pieces.'

Q. 'You give that motherfucker more credit than he deserves. If you think Manson is some kind of a god that is going to break out of jail and come back and murder everybody that testified against him – '

But it was obvious DeCarlo didn't put that past Manson.

Even if he remained in jail, there were the others.

A. 'What about Clem? Have you got him locked up?'

Q. 'Yeah. Clem is sitting in the cooler up in Independence, with Charlie.'

A. 'What about Tex and Bruce?'

Q. 'They're both out. Bruce Davis, the last I heard, sometime earlier this month, was in Venice.'

A. 'Bruce is down in Venice, huh? I'll have to watch myself ... One of my club brothers said he spotted a couple of the girls down in Venice, too.'

The detectives didn't tell DeCarlo that when Davis was last seen, on November 5, it was in connection with another death, the 'suicide' of Zero. By this time LAPD had learned that Zero – aka Christopher Jesus, t/n John Philip Haught – had been arrested in the Barker raid. Earlier, in going through some photographs, DeCarlo had identified 'Scotty' and 'Zero' as two young boys from Ohio, who had been with the Family for a short time but 'didn't fit in'. One of the detectives had remarked, 'Zero's no longer with us.'

A. 'What do you mean he's "no longer with us"?'

Q. 'He's among the dead.'

A. *'Oh, shit, is he?'*

Q. 'Yeah, he got a little too high one day and he was playing Russian roulette. He parked a bullet in his head.'

While the detective had apparently bought the story of Zero's death, as related by Bruce Davis and the others, Danny didn't, not for a minute.

No, Danny didn't want to testify.

The detectives left it at that. There was still time for him to change his mind. And, after all, they now had Ronnie Howard. They let Danny go, after making arrangements for him to call in the next day.

The DeCarlo interview had lasted over seven hours. It was now past midnight on Tuesday, November 18, 1969. I was already asleep, unaware that in a few hours I would be handed the job of prosecuting the Tate-LaBianca killers.

Part Three

The Investigation –
Phase Two

'No sense makes sense.'
    Charles Manson

November 18, 1969

By now the reader knows a great deal more about the Tate-LaBianca murders than I did on the day I was assigned that case. In fact, since large portions of the foregoing story have not been made public before this, the reader is an insider in a sense highly unusual in a murder case. And, in a way, I'm a newcomer, an intruder. The sudden switch from an unseen background narrator to a very personal account is bound to be a surprise. The best way to soften it, I suspect, would be to introduce myself; then, when we've got that out of the way, we'll resume the narrative together. This digression, though unfortunately necessary, will be as brief as possible.

A conventional biographical sketch would probably read more or less as follows: Vincent T. Bugliosi, age thirty-five, Deputy District Attorney, Los Angeles, California. Born Hibbing, Minnesota. Graduate Hollywood High School. Attended the University of Miami on a tennis scholarship, B.A. and B.B.A. degrees. Deciding on the practice of law, attended UCLA, LL.B degree president graduating class 1964. Joined the Los Angeles County District Attorney's Office same year. Has tried a number of highly publicized murder cases – Floyd-Milton, Perveler-Cromwell, etc – obtaining convictions in all. Has tried 104 felony jury trials, losing only one. In addition to his duties as deputy DA, Bugliosi is a professor of criminal law at Beverly School of Law, Los Angeles. Served as technical consultant and edited the scripts of two pilot films for Jack Webb's TV series 'The D.A.' Series star Robert Conrad patterned his part after the young prosecutor. Married. Two children.

That's probably about how it would read, yet it tells nothing about how I feel toward my profession, which is even more important.

'*The primary duty of a lawyer engaged in public prosecution is not to convict, but to see that justice is done . . .*'

Those words are from the old Canon of Ethics of the American Bar Association. I'd thought of them often during the five years I'd been a deputy DA. In a very real sense they had become my personal credo. If, in a given case, a conviction is justice, so be it. But if it is not, I want no part of it.

The Tate-LaBianca case was the farthest thing from my mind on the afternoon of November 18, 1969. I'd just completed a long trial and was on my way back to my office in the Hall of Justice when Aaron Stovitz, head of the Trials Division of the District Attorney's Office, grabbed me by the arm and, without a word of explanation, hurried me down the hall into the office of J. Miller Leavy, director of Central Operations.

Leavy was talking to two LAPD lieutenants I'd worked with on previous cases, Bob Helder and Paul LePage. Listening for a minute, I heard the word 'Tate'. Turning to Aaron, I asked, 'Are *we* going to handle it?'

He nodded affirmatively.

My only comment was a low whistle.

Helder and LePage gave us a sketchy résumé of what Ronnie Howard had said. As a follow-up to Mossman and Brown's visit the previous night, two other officers had gone to Sybil Brand that morning and talked to Ronnie for a couple of hours. They had obtained considerably more detail, but there were still huge gaps in the story.

To say that the Tate and LaBianca cases had been 'solved' at this point would be a gross overstatement. Obviously, in any murder case finding the killer is extremely important. But it's only a first step. Neither the finding, the arresting, nor the indicting of a defendant has evidentiary value and none are proof of guilt. Once the killer is identified, there remains the difficult (and sometimes insurmountable) problem of connecting him with the crime by strong, admissible evidence, then proving his guilt beyond a reasonable doubt, be it before a judge or a jury.

And as yet we hadn't even made the first step, much less the second. In talking to Ronnie Howard, Susan Atkins had implicated herself and 'Charles', presumably meaning Charles Manson. But Susan had also said that others were involved, and we lacked their actual identities. This was on Tate. On LaBianca there was virtually no information.

One of the first things I wanted to do, after reviewing the Howard and DeCarlo statements, was to go to Spahn Ranch. Arrangements were made for me to go out the next morning with several of the detectives.

When I returned home late that afternoon and told my wife, Gail, that Aaron and I had been assigned the Tate case, she shared my excitement. But with reservations. She had been hoping that we could take a vacation. It had been months since I'd taken a full day off. Although every day I made sure I spent some time with our two children, when I was on a big case I totally immersed myself in it. I promised Gail I'd try to take a few days off, but I honestly had to admit that it might be a while before I could do so.

At that time we were, fortunately, unaware that I would be living with the Tate-LaBianca cases for almost two years, averaging close to hundred-hour work-weeks. And that the few moments Gail, the kids, and I had together would be devoid of privacy, our home transformed into a fortress, a bodyguard not only living with us but accompanying me everywhere I went, following a threat by Charles Manson that he would 'kill Bugliosi'.

November 19–21, 1969

We'd picked a hell of a day for a search. The wind was incredible. By the time we reached Chatsworth, it was almost buffeting us off the road.

It wasn't a long drive, well under an hour. From the Hall of Justice in downtown Los Angeles it's about thirty miles to Chatsworth. Going north on Topanga Canyon Boulevard past Devonshire for about two miles, we made a sharp left onto Santa Susana Pass Road. Once heavily traveled but in recent years bypassed for a faster freeway, the two-lane road winds upward a mile or two. Then suddenly around a bend and to the left, there it was, Spahn's Movie Ranch.

Its ramshackle Main Street was less than twenty yards from the highway, in plain view. Wrecked automobile and truck bodies littered the area. There wasn't a sign of life.

There was an unreality to the place, accentuated by the roaring wind and the appearance of total desertion, but even more so by the knowledge, if the Atkins-Howard story was true, of what had begun and ended here. A run-down movie set, off in the middle of nowhere, from which dark-clad assassins would venture out at night, to terrorize and kill, then return before dawn to vanish into the surroundings. It might have been the plot of a horror film, except that Sharon Tate and at least eight other real human beings were now dead.

We pulled off onto the dirt road, stopping in front of the Long Branch Saloon. In addition to myself, there were Lieutenant Helder and Sergeant Calkins of the Tate team; Sergeant Lee of SID; Sergeants Guenther, Whiteley, and William Gleason from LASO; and our guide, Danny DeCarlo. Danny had finally agreed to accompany us, but only on one condition: that we handcuff him. That way, if any members of the Family were still around, they wouldn't think he was voluntarily 'flapping to the fuzz'.

Though the sheriff's deputies had been to the ranch before, we needed DeCarlo for a specific purpose: to point out the areas where Manson and the Family target-practiced. The object of our search: any .22 caliber bullets and/or shell casings.

But first I wanted to obtain George Spahn's permission to search the ranch. Guenther pointed out his shack, which was to the right and apart from the Western set. We knocked and a voice, that of a young girl, said, 'Come right in.'

It was as if every fly in the area had taken shelter there during the storm. Eighty-one-year-old George Spahn was sitting in a decaying armchair, wearing a Stetson and dark glasses. In his lap was a Chihuahua, at his feet a cocker spaniel. A hippie girl of about 18 was fixing his lunch, while a transistor radio, tuned to a cowboy station, blared 'Young Love' by Sonny James.

Once we had identified ourselves, Spahn seemed to relax. Asked for permission to search, he magnanimously replied, 'It's my ranch and you're welcome to search it any time you want to, day or night, and as often as you like.' I explained his legal rights. Under the law, no search warrant was required, only his permission. If he did give permission, however, it might be necessary at some later date for him to testify to this in court. Spahn still agreed.

Once we went back outside, people began appearing from almost every building. There must have been ten to fifteen, most of them young, most in hippie-type clothes, although a few appeared to be ranch hands. How many, if any, were actual members of the Family we didn't know. While looking around, I heard some odd sounds coming from a doghouse. Leaning down and looking in, I saw two dogs and, crouched in the corner, a toothless, white-haired old woman of about 80. I later checked with one of the ranch hands to see if she needed help, but he said she was happy where she was.

It was a very strange place.

About a hundred yards behind the main cluster of buildings

there was a drop down to a creek, then, beyond it, the hills rose up and became a part of the Santa Susana mountain range. Rocky, brush covered, the area looked far more rugged than it actually was. I wondered how many times as a boy I'd seen this scene in B-grade cowboy films. According to Lutesinger and DeCarlo, it was here, in the canyons and gullies behind the ranch, and across the road, in Devil's Canyon, that the Family hid out from the police. Here, too, somewhere in this area, if the various accounts were correct, were the remains of Donald 'Shorty' Shea.

While we were searching the creek bed for shell casings, I kept thinking about George Spahn, alone and almost defenseless in his blindness. I asked, 'Anybody bring a tape recorder?' Calkins had; it was in the back of his car. 'Let's go back and get Spahn's consent on tape,' I said. 'Between now and the time we go to trial, I don't want some s.o.b. putting a knife to Spahn's throat, forcing him to say he didn't give us permission.' We went back and taped Spahn's consent. It was for his protection as well as our own; knowing the tape existed could be discouragement.

Altogether, that day we found approximately sixty-eight .22 caliber bullets (approximate because some were fragments rather than whole slugs) and twenty-two shell casings of the same caliber.

While looking around the corral area, I spotted some white nylon rope, but it was two-strand, not three.

Guenther and Whiteley had made their own find, in Danny DeCarlo. That afternoon they interviewed him on the Hinman murder and Beausoleil's confession. The only problem was that the Beausoleil trial had been going on for a week now, and both the prosecution and defense had rested.

Against the objections of Beausoleil's attorney, a continuance was obtained until the following Monday, at which time the prosecution hoped to reopen its case to introduce the confession.

It was agreed that if DeCarlo testified in the Beausoleil trial, LASO would drop the motorcycle engine theft charge against him.

On my return to the Hall of Justice there was a meeting in the office of the then Assistant District Attorney, Joseph Busch. The police wanted to wrap up the case, Lieutenant LePage informed us. The public pressure on LAPD to solve these murders was unbelievable. LAPD wanted to offer Susan Atkins immunity, in exchange for telling what she knew about the murders.

I was in total disagreement. 'If what she told Ronnie Howard is true, Atkins personally stabbed to death Sharon Tate, Gary Hinman, and who knows how many others! *We don't give that gal anything!*'

Chief Davis wanted to rush the case to the grand jury, LePage said. But before that he wanted to break the news that we had caught the killers in a big press conference.

'We don't even *have* a case to take to the grand jury,' I told LePage. 'We're not even sure who the killers are, or if they're free or in custody. All we have is a good lead, but we're getting there. Let's see if, on our own, we can get enough evidence to nail all of them. If we can't, then, as a last resort – a very, very last resort – we can turn to Atkins.'

I could sympathize with LAPD; the media were blasting the department almost daily. On the other hand, it would be nothing compared to the public response if we let Susan Atkins walk off scot-free. I couldn't forget Susan describing how it felt to taste Sharon Tate's blood: 'Wow, what a trip!'

LePage was firm; LAPD wanted to make a deal. I conferred with Busch and Stovitz; they were far less adamant than I. Against my very strong objections, Busch told LePage that the DA's Office would be willing to settle for a second degree murder plea for Atkins.

Susan Atkins would be offered a deal. The precise terms, or whether she would even accept them, remained unknown.

At eight that night two cars sped out of Los Angeles, their destination the last home of the Manson Family: Death Valley.

Sergeants Nielsen, Sartuchi, and Granado were in one car, Sergeants McGann, Gene Kamadoi, and I were in the other. We broke a few speed limits along the way, arriving in Independence, California, at 1:30 A.M.

Independence, seat of Inyo County, is not a large town. The county itself, though second largest in the state, has less than 16,000 residents, just over one per square mile. If a person were looking for a place to hide, he could find few better.

Before leaving Los Angeles, I had telephoned Frank Fowles, Inyo County DA, and we had arranged to meet at a nearby café at 6 A.M. Fowles, his deputy Buck Gibbens, and their investigator Jack Gardiner were already there. The three men were, I would soon learn, very conscientious; the help they would give us in the months ahead would be considerable.

Fowles told me that although they had seized some of Manson's belongings during the October raid on Barker Ranch, a number of things remained there, including an old school bus, which was littered with clothing and other items. I suggested that before leaving Independence we obtain a search warrant for the ranch that specifically mentioned the bus.

This caught Fowles by surprise. I explained that if we did find evidence, and wished to use it in a trial, we didn't want it suppressed just because someone suddenly appeared with a pink slip saying, 'I'm the real owner of the bus. I only loaned it to Charlie, and you didn't get my permission.'

Fowles understood that. It was only, he explained cryptically, that they didn't do things quite that way in Inyo County. We returned to his office and, after waiting for the typist to come to work, I dictated the warrant, which was later signed by Judge John P. McMurray.

The trip to Barker Ranch would take three hours, leaving us little more than an hour to search before the sun set. En route Fowles told me some of the things he had learned about the Manson Family. The first few members – in effect, a scouting party – had appeared in the area in the fall of 1968. Since you have to be somewhat different to want to live on the edge of Death Valley, residents of the area had developed a tolerance for people who elsewhere would have been considered odd types.

The hippies were no stranger than others who passed through – prospectors, desert rats, chasers after legendary lost mines. There were only a few minor brushes with the authorities – the girls were advised to desist from panhandling in Shoshone, and one made the mistake of giving a marijuana cigarette to a 15-year-old girl, who just happened to be the sheriff's niece – until September 9, 1969, when National Park Rangers discovered that someone had attempted to burn a Michigan loader, a piece of earth-moving equipment that was parked in the race-track area of Death Valley National Monument. It appeared a senseless act of vandalism. Automobile tracks leading away from the area were determined to belong to a Toyota. Several persons recalled seeing the hippies driving a red Toyota and a dune buggy. On September 21, Park Ranger Dick Powell spotted a 1969 red Toyota in the Hail and Hall area. The four females and one male who were riding in it were questioned but not detained. Powell later ran a license check, learning that the plates on the Toyota belonged to another vehicle. On September 24, Powell returned to look for the group, but they had gone. On September 29, Powell, accompanied by California Highway Patrolman James Pursell, decided to check out Barker Ranch. They found two young girls there, but no vehicles. As they had found standard in their contacts with this group, the girls gave vague, uncommunicative answers to their questions. As the officers were leaving the area, they encountered a truck driven by Paul Crockett, forty-six, a local miner. With him was Brooks Poston, 18, who had previously been a member of the hippie band but was now working for Crockett. On hearing that there were two girls at the ranch, Crockett and Poston appeared apprehensive and, when questioned, finally admitted that they feared for their lives.

Powell and Pursell decided to accompany them back to Barker. The two girls had vanished, but the officers presumed they were still nearby, probably watching them. They began questioning Crockett and Poston.

The officers had come looking for arson suspects, and a possible stolen vehicle. They found something totally unexpected. From Pursell's report:

The interview resulted in some of the most unbelievable and fantastic information we had ever heard: tales of drug use, sex orgies, the actual attempt to re-create the days of Rommel and the Desert Corps by tearing over the countryside by night in numerous dune buggies, the stringing of field phones around the area for rapid communication, the opinion of the leader that he is Jesus Christ and seemed to be trying to form a cult of some sort . . .

The surprises weren't over. Before leaving Barker, Powell and Pursell decided to check out some draws back of the ranch. To quote Powell: 'In doing so we stumbled into a group of seven females, all nude or partially so, hiding behind various clumps of sagebrush.' They saw one male, but he ran away when they approached. They questioned the girls but received no useful information. In searching the area, the officers found the red Toyota and a dune buggy, carefully camouflaged with tarps.

The officers had a problem. Because of the Panamint mountain range, they couldn't use their police radio. They decided to leave and return later with more men. Before departing, they removed several parts from the engine of the Toyota, rendering it inoperative; the dune buggy had no engine, so they weren't concerned with it.

They would later learn that 'as soon as we left, the suspects pulled a complete Volkswagen engine from under a pile of brush, put it in the disabled dune buggy, and drove off within two hours'.

A check on the two vehicles revealed 'wants' on both. The Toyota had been rented from a Hertz agency in Encino, a town near Los Angeles, on a credit card stolen in a residential burglary. The dune buggy had been stolen off a used-car lot only three days before Powell and Pursell saw it.

On the night of October 9, officers from the California Highway Patrol, the Inyo County Sheriff's Office, and National Park rangers assembled near Barker for a massive raid on the ranch, to commence the following morning.

At about 4 A.M., as several of the officers were proceeding down one of the draws some distance from the ranch, they spotted two males asleep on the ground. Between them was a sawed-off shotgun. The two, Clem Tufts [t/n Steve Grogan] and

Randy Morglea [t/n Hugh Rocky Todd], were placed under arrest. Though the officers were unaware of it, the pair had been stalking human game: Stephanie Schram and Kitty Lutesinger, two 17-year-old girls who had fled the ranch the previous day.

Another male, Robert Ivan Lane [aka Soupspoon], was apprehended on a hill overlooking the ranch. Lane had been acting as lookout but had fallen asleep. There was still another lookout post, this one a very well disguised dugout, its tin roof hidden by brush and dirt, on a hill south of the ranch. The officers had almost passed it when they saw a female emerge from the brush, squat, and urinate, then disappear back into the bushes. While two officers covered the entrance with their rifles, one climbed above the dugout and dropped a large rock on the tin roof. The occupants rushed out. Apprehended were: Louella Maxwell Alexandria [t/n Leslie Van Houten, aka Leslie Sankston]; Marnie Kay Reeves [t/n Patricia Krenwinkel]; and Manon Minette [t/n Catherine Share, aka Gypsy].

Those inside the ranch house were caught unawares, and offered no resistance. They were: Donna Kay Powell [t/n Susan Denise Atkins, aka Sadie Mae Glutz]; Elizabeth Elaine Williamson [t/n Lynette Fromme, aka Squeaky]; and Linda Baldwin [t/n Madaline Cottage, aka Little Patty].

Other members of the raiding party surrounded nearby Myers Ranch, where the group had also been staying, arresting: Sandra Collins Pugh [this was her married name; her maiden name was Sandra Good, aka Sandy]; Rachel Susan Morse [t/n Ruth Ann Moorehouse, aka Ouisch]; Mary Ann Schwarm [t/n Diane Von Ahn]; and Cydette Perell [t/n Nancy Pitman, aka Brenda McCann].

A total of ten females and three males were arrested during this first sweep of the Barker Ranch area. They ranged in age from 16 to 26, with the average 19 or 20. Two babies were also found: Zezozose Zadfrack Glutz, age 1 year, whose mother was Susan Atkins; and Sunstone Hawk, age 1 month, whose mother was Sandra Good. Both were badly sunburned. Mrs Powell, wife of ranger Dick Powell, who had been brought along as matron, took care of them.

A search of the area revealed a number of hidden vehicles, mostly dune buggies, mostly stolen; a mailbag with a .22 Ruger single-shot pistol inside, also stolen; a number of knives; and caches of food, gasoline, and other supplies. Also found were more sleeping bags than people, indicating that there might be others still in the area.

The officers decided to take the prisoners into Independence and book them, then make a surprise raid at a later date, in case others returned.

The strategy paid off. The second raid occurred on October 12, two days after the first. CHP officer Pursell and two Park rangers arrived in the area before their support and were hiding in the brush, waiting for the others, when they saw four males walk from one of the washes to the ranch house and enter. Pursell spotted sheriff's deputy Don Ward of the backup unit approaching in the distance. It was already after 6 P.M., the dusk rapidly becoming dark. Not wanting to risk a gunfight at night, Pursell decided to act. While Powell covered the front of the building, Pursell drew his gun and, to quote from his report, 'I quickly moved to the back door, flung it open, and making as much use of the wall on the left of the doorway as possible, I ordered all occupants to remain still and place their hands on their heads.'

The group, most of whom had been sitting around the kitchen table, were ordered outside, lined up, and searched. There were three females: Dianne Bluestein [t/n Dianne Lake, aka Snake]; Beth Tracy [t/n Collie Sinclair]; and Sherry Andrews [t/n Claudia Leigh Smith]. Plus four males: Bruce McGregor Davis [aka Bruce McMillan]; Christopher Jesus [t/n John Philip Haught, aka Zero, who in less than a month would be shot to death while allegedly playing Russian roulette]; Kenneth Richard Brown [aka Scott Bell Davis, Zero's partner from Ohio]; and one Lawrence Bailey [aka Larry Jones].

There was no sign of the group's leader, Charles Manson. Pursell decided to recheck the house. It was completely dark now. However, a homemade candle was burning in a glass mug on the table, and, taking that, he began searching the rooms. On entering the bathroom, 'I was forced to move the candle around quite a bit, as it made a very poor light. I lowered the candle toward the hand basin, and small cupboard below, and saw long hair hanging out of the top of the cupboard, with was partially open.' It seemed impossible that a person could get into such a small space, but, without Pursell's having to say anything,

a figure began to emerge from the tiny cupboard. After I recovered from the initial shock, I advised the subject to continue out and not make any false moves. As he emerged, he made a comment, more or less in a humorous vein, about being glad to get out of that cramped space.

The subject was dressed entirely in buckskins, much differently than all the others we had found ... I asked the subject who he was. He immediately replied, 'Charlie Manson'. He was taken to the back door and turned over to the officers outside.

On re-entering the house, Pursell found still another male, who was just emerging from the bedroom. He was David Lee Hamic [aka Bill Vance, an ex-con with more aliases than Manson].

None of the suspects were armed, although several sheath knives were found on the kitchen table.

The prisoners were handcuffed and, hands on heads, walked single file toward Sourdough Springs, where the officers had left two pickups. En route they encountered two more females driving a car loaded with groceries. Also placed under arrest were: Patti Sue Jardin [t/n Catherine Gillies], and Sue Bartell [aka Country Sue]. All the suspects were loaded in the back of one pickup, the second following immediately behind to provide illumination.

On the way to Independence, Manson told Pursell and Ward that the blacks were going to take over the country and that he and his group only wanted to find a quiet, peaceful place away from the conflict. But the establishment, as represented by the police, wouldn't let them alone. He also told them that they, being both cops and white, were in deep trouble and should escape to the desert or somewhere while they still had the chance.

Also during the ride, again according to Pursell, 'two things happened which indicated to me the leadership exerted over the group by subject Manson. At least twice Charlie made statements that would cause the others to say "amen" two or three times in unison. Also, a few times when the others would become involved in whispered, giggly conversations, Charlie would simply look at them and immediately they would fall silent.

'The amazing part of the stare,' Pursell noted, 'was how obvious the results were without a word being spoken.'

On arriving in Independence, the suspects were charged with grand theft auto, arson, and various other offenses. The leader of the Family was fingerprinted, photographed, and booked as 'MANSON, CHARLES M., aka JESUS CHRIST, GOD.'

According to Frank Fowles, although all but three of the eleven vehicles recovered were stolen, there was insufficient evidence to link most of the group with the thefts, and after a few days more than half of those arrested were released. Though most had left the area, two of the girls, Squeaky and Sandy, had rented a motel room and were staying in Independence, so they could run errands for Manson and the others still in custody.

I asked Fowles if he knew why the group had come to the area in the first place. He told me that one of the girls, Cathy Gillies, was the granddaughter of the woman who owned Myers Ranch. The Family had apparently camped there first, then moved to nearby Barker. After the raid a sheriff's deputy interviewed Mrs Arlene Barker, who was living at Indian Ranch in the Panamint Valley. She told him that about a year ago Manson had visited her, asking permission to camp at Barker Ranch. Like George Spahn, Mrs Barker presumed there were only a few people and that they intended to stay only a few days. On this visit Manson gave her a gold record which had been presented to the Beach Boys, commemorating one million dollars in sales of their LP 'The Beach Boys Today'. Manson told her that he was the composer or arranger for the group. Manson had contacted her again, two or three weeks before the October raid, wanting to buy Barker Ranch. She told him she wanted cash; Manson said he'd see her again when he had it.

Apparently Manson felt that if he actually owned the property he would have fewer problems with local law-enforcement agencies.

I was unaware until much later that Manson supposedly had an alternate plan to get control of Myers Ranch, which called for murdering Cathy's grandmother, and that the plan had been frustrated by something very simple and commonplace: while en route to her home, the three killers he'd chosen had a flat tire.

I asked Fowles about the evidence recovered in the raids and subsequent searches. Were any of the knives Buck brand? Yes, several. Any rope? No. What about wire cutters? Yes, there was a big red pair; they'd found them in the back of what they later learned was Manson's personal, or command, dune buggy. Aside from the Ruger .22 and Clem's shotgun, any other firearms? Not one, Fowles said. In none of the searches did the officers turn up the machine guns, shotguns, rifles, pistols, and large stores of ammunition Crockett, Poston, and others said the Family had.

Throughout the trials that followed, we would remain very aware that those members of the Family still at large probably had access to a sizable cache of arms and ammunition.

Barker Ranch was located in Golar Wash, one of seven dry washes in the Panamint range, approximately twenty-two miles southeast of Ballarat. He had been all over the country, Fowles told me; those dry washes comprised the roughest terrain he had ever seen; we'd have to walk much of it, he said, otherwise our heads would bounce through the roof of the four-wheel-drive jeep Fowles had chosen for the trip.

The washes were extremely narrow and rock-strewn. Going up them, we'd frequently gain one foot, then with an angry screech of rubber, slide back two. You could smell the tires burning. Finally, Fowles and I got out of the vehicle and walked in front of it, removing boulders as McGann drove forward, foot after foot. It took us two hours to travel five miles.

No one would have chosen to live at either Barker or Myers Ranch, which were about a quarter of a mile apart, except for one thing: there was water. There was even a swimming pool at

Barker, though, like the stone ranch house and outlying shacks, it was in disrepair. The house was small – living room, bedroom, kitchen, bathroom. The cabinet under the sink where Manson hid measured 3 by 1½ by 1½ feet. I could see why Pursell was so surprised.

When I saw the large school bus, I couldn't believe Manson had brought it up one of the washes. He hadn't, Fowles told me; he'd driven it in over the road on the Las Vegas side. Even that had been an ordeal, and the condition of the bus showed it. It was a battered green and white. On the side was an American flag decal with the slogan AMERICA – LOVE IT OR LEAVE IT. While Sartuchi and the others searched the house, I went to work on the abandoned bus.

The placement of the warrant took some thought. It had to be left in sight. However, if it was, anyone could come along and remove it. I didn't want a defense attorney contending we hadn't fulfilled the requirements of the search. I put it on one of the racks just under the roof of the bus. You *could* see it, if you looked up.

At least a foot of clothing was piled on the floor. I later learned that wherever the Family stayed, they kept a community clothing pile. When an item was needed, they'd root through the pile until they found it. I got down on my hands and knees and began rooting too. I was looking for two things in particular: clothing with bloodstains, and boots. A bloody boot-heel print had been found on the front porch of the Tate residence. There was a small mark, a little indentation, in the heel that I was hoping we could match up. Although I found several boots, none had such a mark. And when Joe Granado applied the benzidine test to the clothing, the results were uniformly negative. I had all the clothing taken back to LA anyway, hoping SID might come up with something in the lab.

There were eight to ten magazines in the bus, half of which were *National Geographics*. Looking through them, I noticed something curious: all dated from 1939 to 1945 and all had articles on Hitler. One also had photographs of Rommel and his Desert Corps.

But that was all we found. Our search appeared to have yielded little, if anything, of evidentiary value. However, I was anxious to go through the items picked up in the raids.

On the way back to Independence we stopped in Lone Pine. While I was nursing a beer with the officers, Sartuchi remarked that he and Patchett had interviewed Manson in Independence some weeks earlier, questioning him about the Tate as well as the LaBianca murders. The following day when I called Lieutenant Helder, I mentioned this, thinking he probably had a report on the interview. Helder was amazed; he had no idea anyone from LAPD had ever talked to Manson. This was my first indication that the Tate and LaBianca detectives hadn't exactly been working hand in glove.

Helder did have some news. It wasn't good. Sergeant Lee had run a ballistics comparison on the .22 caliber bullets we'd found at Spahn: all were negative to those recovered at 10050 Cleo Drive.

I wasn't about to give up that easily. I still wanted a much more thorough search of Spahn Ranch.

We stayed in Independence again that night. Up early the next morning, I walked to the courthouse. A couple of blocks from it I saw two young girls, one carrying a baby. It was a wild guess but I asked, 'Are you Sandy and Squeaky?' They admitted they were. I identified myself and said that I would like to talk to them in the District Attorney's office at 1 P.M. They said they would come if I would buy them some candy. I said I would.

In the DA's office, Fowles opened his files and gave me everything he had on the Manson Family. Sartuchi set to work photocopying.

In going through the documents, I spotted a reference to Crockett and Poston: 'Inyo County Deputy Sheriff Don Ward talked to the two miners in Shoshone and has their entire conversation recorded.' I wanted to interview the pair, but it would save time if I heard the tape first, so I asked McGann to contact Ward and get it for me.

There was also an October 2, 1969, California Highway Patrol report in which it was stated: 'Deputy Dennis Cox has F.I.R. card on suspect Charles Montgomery, 23 years of age (dob 12–2–45).' Field Interrogation Reports are three-by-five cards that are made whenever a person is stopped and questioned. I wanted to see that card. We still knew very little about Tex, who hadn't been arrested in either the Spahn or Barker raids.

After going through the large stack of documents, I started on the evidence seized in the October 10–12 raid. I had Granado test the knives for blood: negative. The wire cutters were large and heavy. It would have been difficult to shinny up a telephone pole with them; still, maybe they were the only pair available. I gave them to the officers so SID could make comparison cuts on the Tate telephone wires. Boots, but no discernible heel mark; I put them aside for SID. I checked the labels on all the clothing, noting that a number of the women's garments, though now filthy, came from expensive shops. I had them taken to L.A. for analysis. I also wanted Winifred Chapman and Susan Struthers to look at them, to see if any of the items might have been the property of Sharon Tate, Abigail Folger, or Rosemary LaBianca.

Squeaky and Sandy kept the appointment. I'd done a little checking before talking to them. Though the information was sketchy, I knew that both had been born in Southern California, and had come from fairly well-to-do families. Squeaky's parents lived in Santa Monica; her father was an aeronautical engineer. Sandy's parents had divorced and remarried; her father was a San Diego stockbroker. According to DeCarlo, when Sandy joined the Family, sometime early in 1968, she had some $6,000 in stocks, which she sold, giving the money to Manson. She and her baby were now on welfare. Both girls had started college, then dropped out, Squeaky attending El Camino Junior College in Torrance, Sandy the University of Oregon and San Francisco State. Squeaky had been one of the earliest members of the Family, I later learned, casting her lot with Manson just months after he got out of prison in 1967.

They were the first Family members I had talked to, other than DeCarlo, who was a fringe member at best, and I was immediately struck by their expressions. They seemed to radiate inner contentment. I'd seen others like this – true believers, religious fanatics – yet I was both shocked and impressed. Nothing seemed to faze them. They smiled almost continuously, no matter what was said. For them all the questions had been answered. There was no need to search any more, because they had found the truth. And their truth was 'Charlie is love'.

Tell me about this love, I asked them. Do you mean this in the male-female sense? Yes, that too, they answered, but that was only a part. More all-encompassing? Yes, but 'Love is love; you can't define it.'

Did Charlie teach you this? I asked, genuinely curious. Charlie did not need to teach them, they said. Charlie only turned them around so they could look at themselves and see the love within. Did they believe that Charlie was Jesus Christ? They only smiled enigmatically.

Is your love for Charlie, say, different from your love for George Spahn? I asked Squeaky. No, love is love, Squeaky said; it's all the same. But she'd hesitated just a moment before answering, giving the impression that though these were the words she was supposed to say, there was heresy in them, in denying that Charlie was special. Perhaps to overcome this, she told me about her relationship with George Spahn. She was in love with George, Squeaky said; if he asked her to marry him, she would. George was, she went on, a beautiful person inside. He was also, she added, in an obvious attempt to shock me, very good in bed. She was quite graphic.

'Frankly, I'm not interested in your sex life, Squeaky,' I told her. 'But I am very, very interested in what you know about the Tate, LaBianca, Hinman, and other murders.'

Neither expression changed in the slightest. The smiles remained. They knew nothing about any crimes. All they knew about was love.

I talked to them for a long time, asking specific questions now, but still getting pat answers. On asking where they were on a certain date, for example, they'd reply, 'There is no such thing as time.' The answers were both non-responsive and a guard. I wanted to get past that guard, to learn what they really felt. I couldn't.

I sensed something else. Each was, in her own way, a pretty girl. But there was a sameness about them that was much stronger than their individuality. I'd notice it again later that afternoon, in talking to other female members of the Family. Same expressions, same patterned responses, same tone of voice, same lack of distinct personality. The realization came with a shock: they reminded me less of human beings than Barbie dolls.

Looking at Sandy's almost beatific smile, I remembered something that Frank Fowles had told me, and a chill ran up and down my spine.

While she was still in jail in Independence, Sandy had been overheard talking to one of the other girls in the Family. Sandy had told her, 'I've finally reached the point where I can kill my parents.'

Leslie, Ouisch, Snake, Brenda, Gyspy – Frank Fowles arranged to have them brought over from the jail, where they were still being held on charges stemming from the Barker raid. Like Squeaky and Sandy, they accepted my 'bribe', candy and gum, and told me nothing of importance. Their answers were as if rehearsed; often they gave identical responses.

If we were to get any of them to talk, I knew, we would have to separate them. There was a cohesion, a kind of cement, that held them together. A part of it was undoubtedly their strange – and to me still puzzling – relationship with Charles Manson. Part of their shared experiences, the world known as the Family. But I couldn't help wondering if another of the ingredients wasn't fear: fear of what the others would say if they talked, fear of what the others would do.

The only way we could find out would be to keep them apart, and owing to the smallness of the jail, it couldn't be done in Independence.

Besides Manson, there was only one male Family member still

in custody: Clem Tufts, t/n Steve Grogan. Jack Gardiner, Fowles' investigator, gave me the 18-year-old Grogan's rap sheet:

3-23-66, Possession dangerous drugs, 6 mos. probation; 4-27-66, Shoplifting, Cont'd on probation; 6-23-66, Disturbing the peace, Cont'd on probation; 9-27-66, Probation dismissed; 6-5-67, Possession marijuana, Counseled & released; 8-12-67, Shoplifting, Bail forfeiture; 1-22-68, Loitering, Closed after investigation; 4-5-69, Grand theft money & Prowling, Released insuff. evidence; 5-20-69, Grand theft auto, Released insuff. evidence; 6-11-69, Child molesting & Indecent exposure . . .

Grogan had been observed exposing himself to several children, ages 4 to 5 years. 'The kids wanted me to,' he explained to arresting officers, who had caught him in the act. 'I violated the law, the thing fell out of my pants and the parents got excited,' he later told a court-appointed psychiatrist. After interviewing Grogan, the psychiatrist ruled *against* committing him to Camarillo State Hospital, because 'the minor is much too aggressive to remain in a setting which does not provide containment facilities'.

The court decided otherwise, sending him to Camarillo for a ninety-day observation period. He remained a grand total of two days, then walked away, aided, I would later learn, by one of the girls from the Family.

His escape had occurred on July 19, 1969. He was back at Spahn in time for the Hinman, Tate, and LaBianca murders. He was arrested in the August 16 Spahn raid, but was released two days later, in time to behead Shorty Shea.

Currently, as a result of the Barker raid, he was charged with grand theft auto and possession of an illegal weapon, i.e., the sawed-off shotgun. I asked Fowles the present status of the case.

He said that, at the instigation of Grogan's attorney, he had been examined by two psychiatrists, who had decided that he was 'presently insane'.

I told Fowles I hoped he would request a jury trial and fight the insanity plea. If I brought Clem to trial in Los Angeles, charged with participating in the Tate murders, I didn't want the defense introducing evidence that a court in Inyo County had already found him insane. Frank agreed to go along with this.

At the moment our case against Grogan was so thin as to be nonexistent. There was no proof that Donald 'Shorty' Shea was even dead; to date, no body had been found. As for the Tate murders, all we had was DeCarlo's statement that Clem had told him, 'We got five piggies.'

There was no way we could use that statement in court if there was a joint trial. In 1965 the California Supreme Court ruled, in the case of *People* vs. *Aranda*, that the prosecution cannot introduce into evidence a statement made by one defendant which implicates a co-defendant.

Since *Aranda* would have a bearing on all the trials involving the Manson Family members, a simplified explanation is in order. For example, if there were a joint trial, with more than one defendant, we couldn't use Susan Atkins' statement to Ronnie Howard, 'We did it,' the plural being inadmissible because it implicated co-defendants. We could, however, use her statement, 'I stabbed Sharon Tate.' It is possible to 'sanitize' some statements so they don't violate *Aranda*. Susan Atkins' admission to Whiteley and Guenther, 'I went to Gary's house with Bobby Beausoleil' could be edited to 'I went to Gary's house,' although a good defense attorney can fight, and – depending on the prosecutor and judge – sometimes win the exclusion of even that. But when it came to the pronoun 'we', there was no way we could get around it.

Therefore, Manson's statement to Springer, 'We knocked off five of them just the other night,' was useless. As was Clem's remark to DeCarlo, 'We got five piggies.'

Manson and Grogan could have made such confessions on nationwide TV and, if there was a joint trial, we could never use their remarks against them.

So we had virtually nothing on Clem.

In going through Grogan's file, I noticed that one of his brothers had made application for the California Highway Patrol; I made note of this, thinking maybe his brother could influence Clem to cooperate with us. DeCarlo had described

Grogan in two words: 'He's nuts.' In his police photograph – big, wide grin, chipped front tooth, moronic stare – he did look idiotic. I asked Fowles for copies of the recent psychiatric reports.

Asked, 'Why do you hate your father?' Grogan replied, 'I'm my father and I don't hate myself.' He denied the use of drugs. 'I have my own bennies, adrenalin. It's called fear.' He claimed that 'love is everything', but, according to one psychiatrist, 'he also revealed that he could not accept the philosophy of interracial brotherhood. Quotes supposedly from the Bible with sexual correlation were given in defense of his attitude.'

Other quotes from Clem: 'I'm dying a little every day. My ego is dying and knows he's dying and struggles hard. When you're free of ego you're free of everything . . . Whatever you say is right for yourself . . . Whoever you think I am, that's who I am.'

The philosophy of Clem? Or Charles Manson? I'd heard the same thoughts, in several instances even identical words, from the girls.

If the psychiatrists had examined one of Manson's followers and, on the basis of such responses, found him insane, what of his leader?

I saw Charles Manson for the first time that day. He was walking from the jail to the courtroom for arraignment on the Michigan loader arson charge, and was accompanied by five sheriff's deputies.

I hadn't realized how small he was. He was just five feet two. He was thin, of slight build, a shade hunchbacked, wore his brown hair very long, almost to his shoulders, and had a good start on a beard, grown – I'd noticed in comparing the LASO and Inyo mug shots – after his arrest in the Spahn Ranch raid. He wore fringed buckskins, which were not inexpensive. Though handcuffed, his walk was casual, not stiff, as though he was completely at ease.

I could not believe that this little guy had done all the things it was said he had. He looked anything but a heavyweight. Yet I knew that to underrate him would be the biggest mistake I could make. For if the Atkins and DeCarlo stories were true, he was not only capable of committing murder himself, he also possessed the incredible power to command others to kill for him.

November 22–23, 1969

That weekend I went through LAPD's files on the Tate-LaBianca murders; the Inyo County files; LASO's reports on the Spahn Ranch raid and other contacts with the Family; and numerous rap sheets. LAPD had conducted over 450 interviews on Tate alone; although they had netted less than had a ten-cent phone call from an ex-hooker, I had to familiarize myself with what had and hadn't been done. I was especially interested in seeing if I could find any link between the Tate-LaBianca victims and the Manson clan. Also, I was looking for some clue as to the motive behind the slayings.

Occasionally writers refer to 'motiveless crimes'. I've never encountered such an animal, and I'm convinced that none such exists. It may be unconventional; it may be apparent only to the killer or killers; it may even be largely unconscious – but every crime is committed for a reason. The problem, especially in this case, was finding it.

After listening to the seven-hour taped interview with Daniel DeCarlo, I began studying the criminal record of one Manson, Charles M.

I wanted to get to know the man I would be up against.

Charles Manson was born 'no name Maddox' on November 12, 1934, in Cincinnati, Ohio, the illegitimate son of a 16-year-old girl named Kathleen Maddox.*

Though Manson himself would later state that his mother was

* As with almost everything else written about Manson's early years, even his date of birth is usually given erroneously, although for an understandable reason. Unable to remember her child's birthday, the mother changed it to November 11, which was Armistice Day and an easier date to remember.

a teen-age prostitute, other relatives say she was simply 'loose'. One remarked, 'She ran around a lot, drank, got in trouble.' Whatever the case, she lived with a succession of men. One, a much older man named William Manson, whom she married, was around just long enough to provide a surname for the youth.

The identity of Charles Manson's father was something of a mystery. In 1936 Kathleen filed a bastardy suit in Boyd County, Kentucky, against one 'Colonel Scott', a resident of Ashland, Kentucky. On April 19, 1937, the court awarded her a judgment of $25, plus $5 a month for the support of 'Charles Milles Manson'. Though it was an 'agreed judgment', Colonel Scott apparently didn't honor it, for as late as 1940 Kathleen was attempting to file an attachment on his wages. Most accounts state that Colonel Scott died in 1954; though this has never been officially verified, Manson himself apparently believed it. He also stated on numerous occasions that he never met his father.

According to her own relatives, Kathleen would leave the child with obliging neighbors for an hour, then disappear for days or weeks. Usually his grandmother or maternal aunt would have to claim him. Most of his early years were spent with one or the other, in West Virginia, Kentucky, or Ohio.

In 1939 Kathleen and her brother Luther robbed a Charleston, West Virginia, service station, knocking out the attendant with Coke bottles. They were sentenced to five years in the state penitentiary for armed robbery. While his mother was in prison, Manson lived with his aunt and uncle in McMechen, West Virginia. Manson would later tell his counselor at the National Training School for Boys that his uncle and aunt had 'some marital difficulty until they became interested in religion and became very extreme'.

A very strict aunt, who thought all pleasures sinful but who gave him love. A promiscuous mother, who let him do anything he wanted, just so long as he didn't bother her. The youth was caught in a tug-of-war between the two.

Paroled in 1942, Kathleen reclaimed Charles, then 8. The next several years were a blur of run-down hotel rooms and newly introduced 'uncles', most of whom, like his mother, drank heavily.

In 1947 she tried to have him put in a foster home, but, none being available, the court sent him to the Gibault Schol for Boys, a caretaking institution in Terre Haute. Indiana. He was 12 years old.

According to school records, he made a 'poor institutional adjustment' and 'his attitude toward schooling was at best only fair'. Though 'during the short lapses when Charles was pleasant and feeling happy he presented a likable boy', he had 'a tendency toward moodiness and a persecution complex . . .' He remained in Gibault ten months, then ran away, returning to his mother.

She didn't want him, and he ran away again. Burglarizing a grocery store, he stole enough money to rent a room. He then broke into several other stores, stealing, among other things, a bicycle. Caught during a burglary, he was placed in the juvenile center in Indianapolis. He escaped the next day. When he was apprehended, the court – erroneously informed that he was Catholic – made arrangements through a local priest to have him accepted at Father Flanagan's Boys Town.

He didn't make its distinguished alumni list. Four days after his arrival, he and another boy, Blackie Nielson, stole a car and fled to the home of Blackie's uncle in Peoria, Illinois. En route they committed two armed robberies – one a grocery store, the other a gambling casino. Among criminals, as in the law itself, a distinction is made between non-violent and violent crimes. Manson had 'graduated', committing his first armed robbery at age 13.

The uncle was glad to see them. Both boys were small enough to slip through skylights. A week after their arrival in Peoria, the pair broke into a grocery store and stole $1,500. For their efforts, the uncle gave them $150. Two weeks later they tried a repeat, but this time they were caught. Both talked, implicating the uncle. Still only 13, Charles Manson was sent to the Indiana School for Boys at Plainfield.

He remained there three years, running away a total of eighteen times. According to his teachers, 'He professed no trust in anyone' and 'did good work only for those from whom he figured he could obtain something'.

In February 1951, Charles Manson and two other 16-year-olds escaped and headed for California. For transportation they stole cars. For support they burglarized gas stations – Manson would later estimate they hit fifteen or twenty – before, just outside Beaver, Utah, a roadblock set up for a robbery suspect netted them instead.

In taking a stolen vehicle across a state line, the youths had broken a federal law, the Dyer Act. This was the beginning of a pattern for Charles Manson of committing federal crimes, which carry far stiffer sentences than local or state offenses.

On March 9, 1951, Manson was ordered confined to the National Training School for Boys, in Washington, D.C., until reaching his majority.

Detailed records were kept on Charles Manson during the time he was there.* On arrival, he was given a battery of aptitude and intelligence tests. Manson's IQ was 109. Though he had completed four years of school, he remained illiterate. Intelligence, mechanical aptitude, manual dexterity: all average. Subject liked best: music. Observed his first case worker, with considerable understatement, 'Charles is a 16-year-old boy who has had unfavorable family life, if it can be called family at all.' He was, the case worker concluded, aggressively antisocial.

One month after his arrival: 'This boy tries to give the impression that he is trying hard to adjust although he actually is not putting forth any effort in this respect . . . I feel in time he will try to be a wheel in the cottage.'

After three months: 'Manson has become somewhat of an "institution politician". He does just enough work to get by on . . . Restless and moody most of the time, the boy would rather spend his class time entertaining his friends.' The report concluded: 'It appears that this boy is a very emotionally upset youth who is definitely in need of some psychiatric orientation.'

Manson was anxious to be transferred to Natural Bridge Honor Camp, a minimum security institution. Because of his run-away record, school officials felt the opposite – i.e., transfer

* I would not obtain the results of these until much later; however, portions are quoted here.

to a reformatory-type institution – was in order, but they decided to withhold decision until after the boy had been examined by a psychiatrist.

On June 29, 1951, Charles Manson was examined by a Dr Block. The psychiatrist noted 'the marked degree of rejection, instability, and psychic trauma' in Manson's background. His sense of inferiority in relation to his mother was so pronounced, Block said, that he constantly felt it necessary 'to suppress any thoughts about her'. Because of his diminutive stature, his illegitimacy, and the lack of parental love, 'he is constantly striving for status with the other boys'. To attain this, Manson had 'developed certain facile techniques for dealing with people. These for the most part consist of a good sense of humor' and an 'ability to ingratiate himself ... This could add up to a fairly "slick" institutionalized youth, but one is left with the feeling that behind all this lies an extremely sensitive boy who has not yet given up in terms of securing some kind of love and affection from the world.'

Though the doctor observed that Manson was 'quite unable to accept any kind of authoritative direction', he found that he 'accepted with alacrity the offer of psychiatric interviews'.

If he found this suspicious, the doctor did not indicate it in his report. For the next three months he gave Manson individual psychotherapy. It may be presumed that Charles Manson also worked on the doctor, for in his October 1 report Dr Block was convinced that what Manson most required were experiences which would build up his self-confidence. In short, he needed to be trusted. The doctor recommended the transfer.

It would appear that Charles Manson had conned his first psychiatrist. Though the school authorities considered him at best a 'calculated risk', they accepted the doctor's recommendation, and on October 24, 1951, he was transferred to Natural Bridge Camp.

That November he turned 17. Shortly after his birthday he was visited by his aunt, who told the authorities that she would supply a home and employment for him if he was released. He was due for a parole hearing in February 1952, and, with her offer, his chances looked good. Instead, less than a month before the hearing, he took a razor blade and held it against another boy's throat while he sodomized him.

As a result of the offense, he lost ninety-seven days good time and, on January 18, 1952, he was transferred to the Federal Reformatory at Petersburg, Virginia. He was considered 'dangerous', one official observing, 'He shouldn't be trusted across the street.' By August he had committed eight serious disciplinary offenses, three involving homosexual acts. His progress report, if it could be called that, stated, 'Manson definitely has homosexual and assaultive tendencies.' He was classified 'safe only under supervision'. For the protection of himself as well as others, the authorities decided to transfer him to a more secure institution, the Federal Reformatory at Chillicothe, Ohio. He was sent there on September 22, 1952.

From the Chillicothe files: 'Associates with trouble makers ... seems to be the unpredictable type of inmate who will require supervision both at work and in quarters ... In spite of his age, he is criminally sophisticated ... regarded as grossly unsuited for retention in an open reformatory type institution such as Chillicothe ...' This from a report written less than a month after his transfer there.

Then, suddenly, Manson changed. For the rest of the year there were no serious disciplinary offenses. Except for minor infractions of the rules, and a consistently 'poor attitude toward authority', his good conduct continued into 1953. A progress report that October noted 'Manson has shown a marked improvement in his general attitude and cooperation with officers and is also showing an active interest in the educational program ... He is especially proud of the fact that he raised his [educational level from lower fourth to upper seventh grade] and that he can now read most material and use simple arithmetic.'

Because of his educational advancement and his good work habits in the transportation unit, where he repaired and maintained vehicles belonging to the institution, on January 1, 1954, he was given a Meritorious Service Award. Far more important to Charles Manson, on May 8, 1954, he was granted parole. He was 19.

One of the conditions of his parole was that he live with his aunt and uncle in McMechen. He did, for a time, then, when his mother moved to nearby Wheeling, he joined her. They seemed drawn together, yet unable to stand each other for any length of time.

Since 14, Charles Manson's only sexual contacts had been homosexual. Shortly after his release he met a seventeen-year-old McMechen girl, Rosalie Jean Willis, a waitress in the local hospital. They were married in January 1955. For support Manson worked as a busboy, service-station helper, parking lot attendant. He also boosted cars. He would later admit to stealing six. He appeared to have learned nothing; he took at least two across state lines. One, stolen in Wheeling, West Virginia, he abandoned in Fort Lauderdale, Florida. The second, a 1951 Mercury, he drove from Bridgeport, Ohio, to Los Angeles in July 1955, accompanied by his now pregnant wife. Manson had finally made it to the Golden State. He was arrested less than three months later, and admitted both Dyer Act violations. Taken to federal court, he pleaded guilty to the theft of the Mercury, and asked for psychiatric help, stating, 'I was released from Chillicothe in 1954 and, having been confined for nine years, I was badly in need of psychiatric treatment. I was mentally confused and stole a car as a means of mental release from the confused state of mind that I was in.'

The judge requested a psychiatric report. Manson was examined on October 26, 1955, by Dr Edwin McNiel. He gave the psychiatrist a much abbreviated version of his past, stating that he was first sent to an institution 'for being mean to my mother'. Of his wife, Manson said, 'She is the best wife a guy could want. I didn't realize how good she was until I got in here. I beat her at times. She writes to me all the time. She is going to have a baby.'

He also told McNiel that 'he spent so much time in institutions that he never really learned much of what "real life on the outside was all about". He said that now he has a wife and is about to become a father it has become important to him to try to be on the outside and be with his wife. He said she is the only one he has ever cared about in his life.'

Dr McNiel observed: 'It is evident that he has an unstable personality and that his environmental influences throughout most of his life have not been good . . . In my opinion this boy is a poor risk for probation; on the other hand, he has spent nine years in institutions with apparently little benefit except to take him out of circulation. With the incentive of a wife and probable fatherhood, it is possible that he might be able to straighten himself out. I would, therefore, respectfully recommend to the court that probation be considered in this case under careful supervision.' Accepting the suggestion, on November 7, 1955, the court gave Manson five years' probation.

There remained the Florida charge. Though his chances of getting probation on it were excellent, before the hearing he skipped. A warrant was issued for his arrest. He was picked up in Indianapolis on March 14, 1956, and returned to Los Angeles. His probation was revoked, and he was sentenced to three years' imprisonment at Terminal Island, San Pedro, California. By the time Charles Manson, Jr, was born, his father was back in jail.

'This inmate will no doubt be in serious difficulty soon,' wrote the orientation officer. 'He is young, small, baby-faced, and unable to control himself . . .'

Given another battery of tests, Manson received average marks in all the categories except 'word meaning', where he had a high score. His IQ was now 121. With some perception, when it came to his work assignment Manson requested 'a small detail where he is not with too many men. He states he has a tendency to cut up and misbehave if he is around a gang . . .'

Rosalie moved in with his mother, now living in Los Angeles, and during his first year at Terminal Island she visited him every week, his mother somewhat less frequently. 'Manson's work habits and attitudes range from good to poor,' noted his March 1957 progress report. 'However, as the time of his parole hearing approaches, his work performance report has jumped from good to excellent, showing that he is capable of a good adjustment if he wants to.'

His parole hearing was set for April 22. In March his wife's visits ceased. Manson's mother told him Rosalie was living with another man. In early April he was transferred to the Coast Guard unit, under minimal custody. On April 10 he was found in the Coast Guard parking lot, dressed in civilian clothes, wiring the ignition of a car. Subsequently indicted for attempted escape, he pleaded guilty, and an extra five years probation was tacked onto the end of his current sentence. On April 22 the parole request was denied.

Rosalie filed for divorce not long after this, the divorce becoming final in 1958. She retained custody of Charles, Jr, remarried, and had no further contact with Manson or his mother.

April 1958, annual review: His work performance was 'sporadic', his behavior continued to be 'erratic and moody'. Almost without exception, he would let down anyone who went to bat for him. Manson was called 'an almost classic text book case of the correctional institutional inmate ... His is a very difficult case and it is impossible to predict his future adjustment with any degree of accuracy.'

He was released September 30, 1958, on five years' parole.

By November, Manson had found a new occupation: pimping. His teacher was +Frank Peters, a Malibu bartender and known procurer, with whom he was living.

Unknown to Manson, he was under surveillance by the FBI, and had been since his release from prison. The federal agents, who were looking for a fugitive who had once lived with Peters, told Manson's parole officer that his 'first string' consisted of a 16-year-old girl named Judy, whom he had personally 'turned out'; as additional support, he was getting money from 'Fat Flo', an unattractive Pasadena girl who had wealthy parents.

His parole officer called him in for a talk. Manson denied he was pimping; said he was no longer living with Peters; promised never to see Judy again; but stated that he wished to continue his relationship with Flo, 'for money and sex'. After all, he said, he had 'been in a long time'. After the interview the parole officer wrote 'This certainly is a very shaky probationer and it seems just a matter of time before he gets in further trouble.'

On May 1, 1959, Manson was arrested attempting to cash a forged U.S. Treasury check for $37.50 in Ralph's, a Los Angeles supermarket. According to the arresting officers, Manson told them he had stolen the check from a mailbox. Two more federal offenses.

L A P D turned Manson over to Secret Service agents for questioning. What then happened was somewhat embarrassing. 'Unfortunately for them,' read a report of the incident, 'the check itself has disappeared; they feel certain subject took it off the table and swallowed it when they momentarily turned their backs.' The charges remained, however.

In mid-June an attractive 19-year-old girl named Leona called on Manson's parole officer and told him she was pregnant by Charlie. The parole officer was skeptical and wanted to see a medical report. He also began checking her background.

With the aid of an attorney, Manson obtained a deal: if he would plead guilty to forging the check, the mail theft charge would be dropped. The judge ordered a psychiatric examination, and Dr McNiel examined Manson a second time.

When Manson appeared in court on September 28, 1959, Dr McNiel, the U.S. Attorney's Office, and the probation department *all* recommended against probation. Leona also appeared and made a tearful plea in Manson's behalf. They were deeply in love, she told the judge, and would marry if Charlie were freed. Though it was proved that Leona had lied about being pregnant, and that she had an arrest record as a prostitute under the name Candy Stevens, the judge, evidently moved by Leona's plea and Manson's promise to make good, gave the defendant a ten-year sentence, then suspended it and placed him on probation.

Manson returned to pimping and breaking federal laws.

By December he had been arrested by L A P D twice: for grand theft auto and the use of stolen credit cards. Both charges were dismissed for lack of evidence. That month he also took Leona-aka-Candy and a girl named Elizabeth from Needles, California, to Lordsburg, New Mexico, for purposes of prostitution, violating the Mann Act, still another federal beef.

Held briefly, questioned, then released, he was given the impression that he had 'beat the rap'. He must have suspected that the investigation was continuing, however. Possibly to prevent Leona from testifying against him, he did marry her, though he didn't inform his probation officer of this. He remained free throughout January 1960, while the FBI prepared its case.

Late in February, Manson's probation officer was visited by an irate parent, +Ralph Samuels, from Detroit. Samuels' daughter +Jo Anne, 19, had come to California in response to an ad for an airline stewardess school, only to learn, after paying her tuition, that the school was a fraud. She had $700 in savings, however, and together with another disillusioned student, +Beth Beldon, had rented an apartment in Hollywood. About November 1959, Jo Anne had the misfortune to meet Charles Manson, who introduced himself, complete with printed card, as 'President, 3-Star-Enterprises, Nit: Club, Radio and TV Productions'. Manson conned her into investing her savings in his nonexistent company; drugged and raped her roommate; and got Jo Anne pregnant. It was an ectopic pregnancy, the fetus growing in one of the Fallopian tubes, and she nearly died.

The probation officer could offer little more than a sympathetic ear, however, for Charles Manson had disappeared. A bench warrant was issued, and on April 28 a federal grand jury indicted him on the Mann Act violation. He was arrested June 1 in Laredo, Texas, after police picked up one of his girls on a prostitution charge, and brought back to Los Angeles, where, on June 23, 1960, the court ruled he had violated his probation and ordered him returned to prison to serve out his ten-year sentence. The judge observed: 'If there ever was a man who demonstrated himself completely unfit for probation, he is it.' This was the same judge who had granted him probation the previous September.

The Mann Act charge was later dropped. For a full year Manson remained in the Los Angeles County Jail, while appealing the revocation. The appeal was denied, and in July 1961 he was sent to the United States Penitentiary at McNeil Island, Washington. He was 26.

According to staff evaluation, Manson had become something of an actor: 'He hides his loneliness, resentment, and hostility behind a façade of superficial ingratiation ... An energetic, young-appearing person whose verbalization flows quite easily, he gestures profusely and can dramatize situations to hold the listener's attention.'

Manson gave as his claimed religion 'Scientologist', stating that he 'has never settled upon a religious formula for his beliefs and is presently seeking an answer to his question in the new mental health cult known as Scientology'.

Scientology, an outgrowth of science-fiction writer L. Ron Hubbard's Dianetics, was just coming into vogue at this time. Manson's teacher, i.e., 'auditor', was another convict, Lanier Rayner. Manson would later claim that while in prison he achieved Scientology's highest level, 'beta clear'.*

Although Manson remained interested in Scientology much longer than he did in any other subject except music, it appears that he stuck with it only as long as his enthusiasm lasted, then dropped it, extracting and retaining a number of terms and phrases ('auditioning', 'cease to exist', 'coming to Now') and some concepts (karma, reincarnation, etc.) which, perhaps fittingly, Scientology had borrowed in the first place.

The annual report that September took a close, hard look at the 28-year-old convict:

Charles Manson has a tremendous drive to call attention to himself. Generally he is unable to succeed in positive acts, therefore he often resorts to negative behavior to satisfy this drive. In his effort to 'find' himself, Manson peruses different religious philosophies, e.g., Scientology and Buddhism; however, he never remains long enough with any given teachings to reap meaningful benefits. Even these attempts and his cries for help represent a desire for attention, with only

---

* In one of his pamphlets, Hubbard defined a 'clear' as 'one who has straightened up this lifetime'. It is rather hard to see how this might apply to Charles Manson.

superficial meaning. Manson has had more than the usual amount of staff attention, yet there is little indication of change in his demeanor. In view of his deep-seated personality problems ... continuation of institutional treatment is recommended.

On October 1, 1963, prison officials were informed, 'according to court papers received in this institution, that Manson was married to a Leona Manson in 1959 in the State of California, and that the marriage was terminated by divorce on April 10, 1963, in Denver, Colorado, on grounds of mental cruelty and conviction of a felony. One child, Charles Luther Manson, is alleged to have been of this union.'

This is the only reference, in any of Manson's records, to his second marriage and second child.

Manson's annual review of September 1964 revealed a clear conduct record, but little else encouraging. 'His past pattern of employment instability continues ... seems to have an intense need to call attention to himself ... remains emotionally insecure and tends to involve himself in various fanatical interests.'

Those 'fanatical interests' weren't identified in the prison reports, but at least several are known. In addition to Scientology and his guitar, there was now a third. In January 1964 'I Want To Hold Your Hand' became the No. 1 song on U.S. record charts. With the New York arrival of the 'four Liverpool lads' the following month, the United States experienced the phenomenon known as Beatlemania. According to former inmates at McNeil, Manson's interest in the Beatles was almost an obsession. It didn't necessarily follow that he was a fan. There was more than a little jealousy in his reaction. He told numerous people that, given the chance, he could be much bigger than the Beatles.

May 1966:

Manson continues to maintain a clear conduct record ... Recently he has been spending most of his free time writing songs, accumulating about 80 or 90 of them during the past year, which he ultimately hopes to sell following release ... He also plays the guitar and drums, and is hopeful that he can secure employment as a guitar player or as a drummer or singer ...

He shall need a great deal of help in the transition from institution to the free world.

In June 1966, Charles Manson was returned to Terminal Island for release purposes.

August 1966: 'Manson is about to complete his ten-year term. He has a pattern of criminal behavior and confinement that dates to his teen years. This pattern is one of instability whether in free society or a structured institutional community. Little can be expected in the way of change in his attitude, behavior, or mode of conduct ...' This last report noted that Manson had no further interest in academic or vocational training; that he was no longer an advocate of Scientology; that 'he has come to worship his guitar and music'; and, finally, 'He has no plans for release as he says he has nowhere to go.'

The morning Charles Manson was to be freed, he begged the authorities to let him remain in prison. Prison had become his home, he told them. He didn't think he could adjust to the world outside.

His request was denied. He was released at 8:15 A.M. on March 21, 1967, and given transportation to Los Angeles. That same day he requested and received permission to go to San Francisco. It was there, in the Haight-Ashbury section, that spring, that the Family was born.

Charles Manson was 32 years old. Over seventeen of those years – more than half his life – had been spent in institutions.

I was surprised, in studying Manson's record, to find no sustained history of violence – armed robbery age 13, homosexual rape age 17, wife beating age 20, that was it. I was more than surprised, I was amazed at the number of federal offenses. Probably ninety-nine out of one hundred criminals never see the inside of a federal court. Yet here was Manson, described as 'criminally sophisticated', violating the Dyer Act, the Mann Act, stealing from the mails, forging a government check, and so on. Had Manson been convicted of comparable offenses in state courts, he probably would have served *less than five years* instead of over seventeen.

Why? I could only guess. Perhaps, as he said before his reluctant release from Terminal Island, prison was the only home he had. It was also possible that, consciously or unconsciously, he sought out those offenses that carried the most severe punishments. A third speculation – and I wasn't overlooking the possibility that it could be a combination of all three – was a need, amounting almost to a compulsion, to challenge the strongest authority.

I was a long way from understanding Charles Manson. Though I could see patterns in his conduct, which might be clues to his future actions, a great deal was missing.

Burglar, car thief, forger, pimp – was this the portrait of a mass murderer?

I had far more questions than answers. And, as yet, not even a clue as to the motive.

Although Lieutenants Helder and LePage remained in charge of the Tate and LaBianca cases, the assignments were more jurisdictional than operational, since each was in charge of numerous other homicide investigations. Nineteen detectives had originally been assigned to the two cases. That number had now been cut to six. Moreover, for some odd reason, though there were only two victims in the LaBianca slayings, four detectives remained assigned to that case: Sergeants Philip Sartuchi, Mike Nielsen, Manuel 'Chick' Gutierrez, and Frank Patchett. But on Tate, where there were five victims, there were only two detectives: Sergeants Robert Calkins and Mike McGann.

I called Calkins and McGann in for a conference and gave them a list of things I needed done. A few samples:

Interview Terry Melcher.

Check the fingerprints of every known Family member against the twenty-five unmatched latents found at 10050 Cielo Drive.

Put out a 'want' on Charles 'Tex' Montgomery, using the description on Inyo Deputy Sheriff Cox's August 21, 1969, F.I.R. card (M/C/6 feet/145 pounds/slim build/ruddy complexion/born December 2, 1945). If the case breaks before we arrest him, I told them, we may never find him.

Show photos of every Family member to Chapman; Garretson; the Tate gardeners; and the families, friends, and business associates of the victims. If there's a link, I want to know about it.

Check everyone in the Family to see who wears glasses, and determine if the pair found at the Tate murder scene belongs to a Family member.

After Calkins and McGann left, I got in touch with the

LaBianca detectives and gave them similar instructions regarding the photos and the Waverly Drive latents.

Five of the Manson girls were still in jail in Independence. LAPD decided to bring them to Los Angeles for individual interrogation. They would be confined at Sybil Brand but a 'keep away' would be placed on each. This meant they could have no contact with each other or with anyone else LAPD designated – for example, Susan Atkins.

It was a good move on LAPD's part. There was a chance that, questioned separately, one or more might decide to talk.

On Tuesday, the twenty-fifth, Frank Fowles, the Inyo County DA, called, and we traded some information.

Fowles told me that Sandra Good had been overheard talking again. She had told another Family member that Charlie was going to 'go alibi'. If he was brought to trial for the Tate-LaBianca murders, they would produce evidence showing he wasn't even in Los Angeles at the time the murders occurred.

I told Fowles of a rumor I'd heard. According to McGann, a police informant in Las Vegas had told him that Charles 'Tex' Montgomery and Bruce Davis had been seen there the previous day, driving a green panel Volkswagen. They had allegedly told someone that they were attempting to raise enough money to bail out Manson; failing in that, they intended to kill someone.

Fowles had heard similar rumblings among the Manson girls. He took them seriously enough to send his own family out of Inyo County over the Thanksgiving weekend. He remained behind, however, ready to forestall any bail attempt.

After hanging up, I called Patchett and Gutierrez of the LaBianca team and told them I wanted a detailed report on Manson's activities the week of the murders. Their report eventually gave me evidence which, together with other information we obtained, would blow any alibi defense to smithereens.

Wednesday, November 26. 'Hung jury on Beausoleil,' one of

the deputy D As yelled in the door of my office. 'Eight to four for conviction.'

The case had been so weak our office hadn't sought the death penalty. Also, the jury hadn't believed Danny DeCarlo. Brought in at the last minute, without adequate preparation, he had not been a convincing witness.

Later that day LASO asked my office if I would take over the prosecution of Beausoleil in his new trial, and I was assigned this case in addition to the two cases I was already handling.

That same morning Virginia Graham decided she had to tell someone what she knew. Having failed to get an appointment with Dr Dreiser, Virginia instead went to her counselor. The authorities at Corona called LAPD. At 3:15 that afternoon Sergent Nielsen arrived at the prison and began taping her story.

Unlike Ronnie, who was unsure whether four or five people were involved in the Tate homicides, Virginia recalled Sadie's saying there were three girls and one man. Like Ronnie, however, she presumed the man, 'Charles', was Manson.

The individual questioning of the five girls took place that afternoon and evening at Sybil Brand.

Sergeant Manuel 'Chick' Gutierrez interviewed Dianne Bluestein, aka Snake, t/n Dianne Lake, given age 21, true age 16. Listening later to the tapes, I was appalled to hear him threaten her with the gas chamber. In an interview lasting nearly two hours he gained little more from her than an admission that she liked candy bars.

Having got nothing intelligible from Dianne, he next interviewed Rachel Morse, aka Ouisch, t/n Ruth Ann Moorehouse, age 18. Ruth Ann was the girl Danny DeCarlo identified as his 'favorite sweetie', the same girl who at Barker Ranch had told him she couldn't wait to get her first pig.

Unlike Dianne, Ruth Anne answered Gutierrez' questions, though most of her replies were lies. She claimed she'd never heard of Shorty, Gary Hinman, or anyone named Katie. The

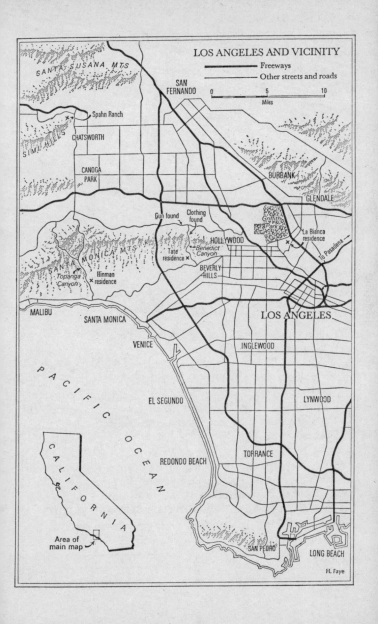

LOS ANGELES AND VICINITY

Freeways
Other streets and roads

0   5   10
Miles

SANTA SUSANA MTS
SAN FERNANDO
Spahn Ranch
SIMI HILLS
CHATSWORTH
CANOGA PARK
BURBANK
GLENDALE
Gun found
Clothing found
Griffith Park
La Bianca residence
To Pasadena
SANTA MONICA MTS
HOLLYWOOD
Tate residence
Benedict Canyon
SANTA MONICA MTS
Topanga Canyon
Hinman residence
BEVERLY HILLS
MALIBU
SANTA MONICA
LOS ANGELES
VENICE
INGLEWOOD
PACIFIC OCEAN
EL SEGUNDO
LYNWOOD
CALIFORNIA
REDONDO BEACH
TORRANCE
Area of main map
SAN PEDRO
LONG BEACH
H. Faye

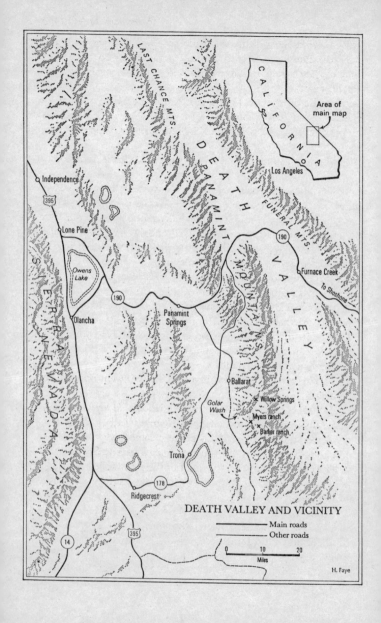

DEATH VALLEY AND VICINITY

——— Main roads
- - - - - Other roads

0   10   20
Miles

H. Faye

reason she knew so little, she explained, was that she had been with the Family only a short time, a month or so before the Spahn Ranch raid (all five girls said this, obviously by pre-arrangement).

Manon Minette, aka Gypsy, t/n Catherine Share, who at 27 was the oldest female member of the Family, gave the detectives nothing of value. Nor did Brenda McCann, t/n Nancy Pitman, age 18.

It was otherwise, however, with 20-year-old Leslie Sankston.

Leslie, whose true name, Van Houten, was not known to us at this time, was interviewed by Mike McGann. McGann tried using her parents, conscience, the hideousness of the murders, the implication that others had talked and involved her – none worked. What did work was Leslie's little-girl cuteness, her I-know-something-you-don't game playing.

Q. 'What did you hear about the Tate murders up there?'

A. 'I'm deaf. I didn't hear nothing.' [Laughs]

Q. 'Five people were killed up there, on the hill. And I know three for sure that went up there. I think I know the fourth. And I don't know the fifth. But I suspect you do. Why are you holding back? You know what happened.'

A. 'I have a pretty good idea.'

Q. 'I want to know who was involved. How it went down. The little details.'

A. 'I told Mr Patchett [in Independence] I'll tell him if I changed my mind. I haven't changed my mind yet.'

Q. 'You're going to have to talk about it someday.'

A. 'Not today . . . How did you ever trace it back to Spahn?'

Q. 'Who did you see leave the night of the eighth of August?'

A. [Laughs] 'Oh, I went to bed early that night. Really, I don't want to talk about it.'

Q. 'Who went?'

A. 'That's what I don't want to talk about.'

All these were little admissions, if not of participation, at least of knowledge.

Though she didn't want to talk about the murders, she didn't mind talking about the Family. 'You wouldn't meet a nicer group of people,' she told McGann. 'Of all the guys at the ranch, I liked Clem the best; he's fun to be with.' Clem, with the idiotic grin, who liked to expose himself to little children. Sadie was 'really kind of a nice person. But she tends to be on the rough side ...' As Sharon Tate, Gary Hinman, and others had discovered. Bruce Davis was all talk, Leslie continued, always going on about how he was going to dynamite someone, but she was sure it was 'only talk'. She commented on some of the others, but not Charlie. In common with the four other girls who had been brought down from Independence, she avoided the subject of Manson.

Q. 'The Family is no more, Leslie.' Charlie was in jail; Clem was in jail; Zero had killed himself playing Russian roulette –
A. *'Zero!'*

Obviously shocked, she dropped her little-girl role and pressed McGann for details. He told her that Bruce Davis had been present.

A. 'Was Bruce playing it too?'
Q. 'No.'
A. (*sarcastically*) 'Zero was playing Russian roulette all by himself!'
Q. 'Kind of odd, isn't it?'
A. 'Yeah, it's odd!'

Sensing an advantage, McGann moved in. He told her that he knew five people had gone to the Tate residence, three girls and two men, and that one of the men was Charles Manson.

A. 'I don't think Charlie was in on any of them.'

Leslie said she had heard only four people went to Tate. 'I would say that three of them were girls. I would say that there were probably more girls involved than men.' Then, later, 'I heard one girl who didn't murder someone while they was, they were up there.'

Q. 'Who is that?'
A. 'A girl by the name of Linda.'

Susan Atkins had told Ronnie Howard, in regard to the killings the second night, 'Linda wasn't in on this one,' presumably meaning she had been along the first night, but until now we had been unsure of this.

Questioned, Leslie said she didn't know Linda's last name; that she was at Spahn only a short time and hadn't been arrested with them; and that she was a small girl, maybe five feet two, thin, with light-brown hair.

McGann asked her *who* had told her that Linda had been along on Tate. Leslie replied, petulantly, 'I don't remember. I don't remember who told me little details!' Why was she so upset? McGann asked. 'Because so many of my friends are getting knocked off, for reasons I don't even know about.'

McGann showed her the mug shots taken after the Barker raid. Though she had been present, she claimed she couldn't recognize most of the people. When handed one of a girl booked as 'Marnie Reeves', Leslie said, 'That's Katie.'

Q. 'Katie is Marnie Reeves?'

Leslie equivocated. She wasn't sure. She really didn't know any of these people all that well. Though she had lived with the Family at both Spahn and Barker, she associated mostly with the motorcycle riders. She thought they were neat.

McGann brought the questioning back to the murders. Leslie began playing games again, and in the process making admissions. She implied that she knew of eleven murders – Hinman 1, Tate 5, LaBianca 2, Shea 1, for a total of 9 – but she declined to identify the other two. It was as if she were keeping score in a baseball game.

After a break in the questioning, McGann decided to shock Leslie some more.

Q. 'Sadie has already told fifteen people in the jailhouse that she was there, that she took part in it.'

A. 'That's incredible.' Then, after a thoughtful pause, 'Didn't she mention anyone else?'

Q. 'No. Except for Charlie. And Katie.'

A. 'She mentioned Charlie and Katie?'

Q. 'That's right.'

A. 'That's pretty nauseating.'

Q. 'She said Katie was there, and I know it was Marnie Reeves, and you know it was Marnie Reeves.'

At this point, McGann told me, Leslie nodded her head affirmatively.

Q. 'Sadie also said, "I went out the next night and killed two more people, out in the hills." '

A. *'Sadie said that!'*

Leslie was astonished. With good reason. Though we were as yet unaware of it, Leslie knew Susan Atkins had never entered the LaBianca residence. She knew that because she was one of the persons who had.

After this, Leslie refused to answer any further questions. McGann asked her why.

A. 'Because if Zero was suddenly found playing Russian roulette I could be found playing Russian roulette.'

Q. 'We'll give you twenty-four-hour protection from now on.'

A. *(laughing sarcastically)* 'Oh, that would really be nice! I'd rather stay in jail.'

From Leslie we learned that three girls had gone to the Tate residence: Sadie, Katie, and Linda. We also learned that Linda was 'one girl who didn't murder someone', the clear implication being that the two other girls had. Beyond Leslie's limited description of Linda, however, we knew nothing about her.

We also knew that Katie was 'Marnie Reeves'. According to her Inyo arrest sheet, she was five feet six, weighed 120 pounds, had brown hair and blue eyes. Her photograph revealed a not very attractive girl, with very long hair and a somewhat mannish face. She looked older than 22, the age she gave. In comparing the Barker and Spahn photos, it was discovered that she had been arrested in the earlier raid also, at that time giving the name 'Mary Ann Scott'. It was possible that 'Katie', 'Marnie Reeves', and 'Mary Ann Scott' were all three aliases. She had been released a few days after her arrest at Barker, and her current whereabouts were unknown.

In return, Leslie had learned a few things from McGann: that

Tex, Katie, and Linda were still free; and, more important, that Susan Atkins, aka Sadie Mae Glutz, was the snitch.

Even with a 'keep away' on the girls, it wouldn't be long before this information got back to Manson.

November 27–30, 1969

On Saturday, Sergeant Patchett interviewed Gregg Jakobson. A talent scout, who was married to the daughter of old-time comedian Lou Costello, Jakobson had first met Charles Manson about May 1968, at the Sunset Boulevard home of Dennis Wilson, one of the Beach Boys rock group.

It was Jakobson who had introduced Manson to Terry Melcher, Doris Day's son, while Melcher was still living at 10050 Cielo Drive. In addition to producing his mother's TV show, Melcher was involved in a number of other enterprises, including a record company, and Jakobson had attempted to persuade him to record Manson. After listening to him play and sing, Melcher said no.

Though Melcher had been unimpressed by Manson, Jakobson had been fascinated with the 'whole Charlie Manson package', songs, philosophy, life style. Over a period of about a year and a half, he'd had many talks with Manson. Charlie loved to rap about his views on life, Gregg said, but Patchett wasn't particularly interested in this, and moved on to other subjects.

Did he know a Charles 'Tex' Montgomery? Patchett asked. Yes, very well, Jakobson replied; only his real name wasn't Montgomery – it was Watson.

Sunday, November 30. At LAPD from 8:30 A.M. to midnight.
Charles Denton Watson had been arrested in Van Nuys, California, on April 23, 1969, for being on drugs. Though he had been released the next day, he had been fingerprinted at the time of his arrest.

10:30 A.M. Latent Prints Section called Lieutenant Helder. The print of Watson's right ring finger matched a latent found on the front door of the Tate residence.

Helder and I jumped up and down like little kids. This was the first physical evidence connecting the suspects to the crime scene.

Helder sent out fifteen detectives to see if they could locate Watson at any of his old addresses, but they had no luck. They did learn, however, that Watson was from a small town in Texas, McKinney.

Checking an atlas, we found that McKinney was in Collin County. Patchett called the sheriff of Collin, informing him that a former local resident, Charles Denton Watson, was wanted for 187 PC murder, in California.

The sheriff's name was Tom Montgomery. A coincidence, Watson's using as alias the last name of the local sheriff? It was more than that: Sheriff Montgomery was Watson's second cousin.

'Charles is living here now,' Sheriff Montgomery said. 'He has an apartment in Denton. I'll bring him in.'

The sheriff, we later learned, called Watson's uncle, Maurice Montgomery, saying, 'Can you bring Charles over to the jail? We've got some trouble.'

Maurice picked up his nephew and drove him to McKinney in his pickup truck. 'He didn't say much on the way,' the uncle later said. 'I didn't know what it was all about, but I guess he knew all the time.'

Watson supposedly refused comment and was lodged in the local jail.

Manson, Atkins, and Watson were now in custody, but two other suspects were still at large. From one of the ranch hands at Spahn, LAPD heard that Linda's last name was Kasabian, and that she was supposedly in a convent in New Mexico. Marnie Reeves was rumored to be on a farm outside Mobile, Alabama.

That same day Patchett interviewed Terry Melcher regarding his contacts with Manson. He confirmed what Jakobson had already said: he had gone to Spahn Ranch twice, to hear Manson and the girls perform, and was 'not enthused'; he had also seen Manson twice before this, while visiting Dennis Wilson. Melcher, however, added one important detail Jakobson hadn't mentioned.

On one of the latter occasions, late at night, Wilson had given him a ride back to his house on Cielo Drive. Manson had come along, sitting in the back seat of the car, singing and playing his guitar. They'd driven up to the gate and let him out, Melcher said, Wilson and Manson then driving off.

We now knew that Charles Manson had been to 10050 Cielo Drive on at least one occasion prior to the murders, although there was no evidence that he had ever been inside the gate.

At 5:30 that Sunday afternoon, while still at LAPD, I talked to Richard Caballero. A former deputy DA now in private practice, Caballero was representing Susan Atkins on the Hinman charge. Earlier Caballero had contacted Aaron Stovitz, wanting to know what the DA's Office had on his client. Aaron laid it out for him: while at Sybil Brand, Susan Atkins had confessed to two other inmates that she was involved not only in the Hinman but also the Tate and LaBianca murders. Aaron gave Caballero copies of the taped statements Ronnie Howard and Virginia Graham had given LAPD.

Under the law of discovery, the prosecution must make available to a defense attorney any and all evidence against his client. This is a one-way street. While the defense therefore knows in advance exactly what evidence the prosecution has, the defense isn't required to tell the prosecution anything. Although discovery usually occurs after a formal request to the Court, Aaron wanted to impress Caballero with the strength of our case, hoping his client would decide to cooperate.

Caballero came to Parker Center to see me and the detectives, wanting to know what kind of deal we could offer. In accordance with the earlier discussion between our office and LAPD, we said that if Susan would cooperate with us, we would probably let her plead guilty to second degree murder – i.e., we would not seek the death sentence, but we would ask for life imprisonment.

Caballero went to Sybil Brand and talked to his client. He would later testify: 'I told her what the problems were, what the evidence was against her as it was related to me. That included the Hinman case (to which she had already confessed to LASO) and the Tate-LaBianca case. As a result of all this, I indicated to her that there is no question in my mind but they were going to seek the death penalty and that they would probably get it. I told her. "They have enough evidence to convict you. You will be convicted." '

About 9:30, Caballero returned to LAPD. Susan was undecided. She might be willing to testify before the grand jury, but he was sure she would never testify against the others at the trial. She was still under Manson's domination. Any minute she could bolt back to him. He said he'd let me know what she finally decided.

It was left hanging there. Though we had the Howard-Graham statements implicating Atkins, and physical evidence linking Watson to the Tate murder scene, our whole case against Manson and the others rested on the decision of Sadie Mae Glutz.

December 1, 1969

7 A.M. Aaron reached me at home. Sheriff Montgomery had just called. If he didn't have a warrant in two hours, he was going to release Watson.

I rushed down to the office and made out a complaint. McGann and I took it to Judge Antonio Chavez, who signed the warrant, LAPD teletyping it to Sheriff Montgomery with just minutes to spare.

I also made out two other complaints: one against Linda Kasabian, the other against Patricia Krenwinkel. The latter, LAPD had learned from LASO, was the real name of Marnie Reeves, aka Katie. Following the Spahn raid, her father, Joseph Krenwinkel, an Inglewood, California, insurance agent, had arranged for her release. On learning this, Sergeant Nielsen had called Krenwinkel, asking where he could reach his daughter. He had told him she was staying with relatives in Mobile, Alabama, and had given him the address. LAPD had then contacted Mobile Police Chief James Robinson, and he had men out looking for her now. Judge Chavez signed these warrants also.

Buck Compton, the Chief Deputy District Attorney, called to inform me that Chief Davis had scheduled a press conference for two that afternoon. Aaron and I were to be in his office at 1:30. 'Buck, this is way too premature!' I told him. 'We don't even have enough on Manson for an indictment, much less a conviction. As for Krenwinkel and Kasabian, if the story breaks before they're picked up, we may never catch them. Can't we persuade Davis to hold off?' Buck promised to try.

At least part of my worry was unnecessary. Patricia Krenwinkel was arrested in Mobile a few minutes before we arrived in Compton's office. Mobile police had gone to the home of her aunt. Mrs Garnett Reeves, but Patricia wasn't there. However, Sergeant William McKellar and his partner were driving down the road that runs in front of the residence when they saw a sports car with a boy and girl inside. As the two cars passed, McKellar 'noticed the female passenger pulled her hat down lower over her face'. Convinced this was 'an effort to avoid identification', the officers pulled a quick U and sirened the car to a halt. Though the girl fitted the teletype description, she said her name was Montgomery. On being taken to the aunt's home, however, she admitted her true identity. The young man, a local acquaintance was questioned and released. Patricia Krenwinkel was read her rights and placed under arrest at 3:20 P.M. Mobile time.

1:30 P.M. Buck, Aaron, and I met with Chief Davis. I told Davis that I'd scraped together barely enough evidence against Krenwinkel and Kasabian to get warrants, but it was all inadmissible hearsay: Leslie Sankston's statement to McGann; Susan Atkins' statements to Virginia Graham and Ronnie Howard. We can't get a grand jury indictment on this, I told him, adding, 'If Susan Atkins doesn't cooperate, we've had it.'

There were over two hundred reporters and cameramen waiting in the police auditorium, Davis said, representing not only all the networks and wire services but newspapers from all over the world. There was no way he could call it off now.

Shortly before the press conference Lieutenant Helder called both Roman Polanski and Colonel Paul Tate, telling them the news. For Colonel Tate, the news meant the end of his months-long private investigation; despite his diligence, he had not come up with anything that was of use to us. But at least now the wondering and suspicion were over.

2 P.M. Facing fifteen microphones and dozens of bright lights, Chief Edward M. Davis announced that after 8,750 hours of police work LAPD had 'solved' the Tate case. Warrants had been issued for the arrests of three persons: Charles D. Watson,

24, who was now in custody in McKinney, Texas; Patricia Krenwinkel, 21, who was in custody in Mobile, Alabama; and Linda Kasabian, age and present whereabouts unknown. It was anticipated that an additional four or five persons would be named in indictments which would be sought from the Los Angeles County grand jury. (Neither Charles Manson nor Susan Atkins was mentioned by name in the press conference.)

These persons, Davis continued, were also involved in the murder deaths of Rosemary and Leno LaBianca.

This came as a big surprise to most of the newsmen, since LAPD had maintained almost from the start that there was no connection between the two homicides. Though a few reporters had suspected the crimes were linked, they had been unable to sell their theories to LAPD

Caballero called Aaron. He wanted to interview Susan Atkins on tape, but he didn't want to do it at Sybil Brand, where there was a chance one of the other Manson girls would hear of it. Also, he felt Susan would be inclined to talk more freely in other surroundings. He suggested having her brought to his own office.

Though unusual, the request wasn't unprecedented. Aaron made up a removal order, which was signed by Judge William Keene, and that evening Susan Atkins, escorted by two sheriff's deputies, was taken to Caballero's office, where Caballero and his associate, Paul Caruso, interviewed her on tape.

The tape was for two purposes, Caballero told Aaron. He wanted it for the psychiatrists in case he decided on an insanity plea. And if we went ahead on the deal, he would let us listen to it before we took the case to the grand jury.

December 2, 1969

LAPD called a few minutes after I arrived at the office. All five suspects were now in custody, Linda Kasabian just having voluntarily surrendered to Concord, New Hampshire, police. According to her mother, Linda had admitted to being present at the Tate residence but claimed she had not participated in the murders. It looked as if she wasn't going to fight extradition.

A somewhat different decision had been reached in Texas.

McKinney was less than thirty miles north of Dallas, and only a few miles from Farmersville, where Charles Watson had grown up and gone to school. Audie Murphy had been a Farmersville boy. Now they had another local celebrity.

Stories in the Texas papers described Watson as having been an A student in high school, a football, basketball, and track star, who still held the state record for the low hurdles. Most local residents expressed shocked disbelief. 'Charles was the boy next door,' one said. 'It was drugs that did it,' an uncle told reporters. The principal of Farmsville High was quoted as saying, 'It almost makes you afraid to send your kids off to college any more.'

On the instruction of Watson's attorney, Bill Boyd, the Los Angeles detectives Sartuchi and Nielsen were not allowed to speak to his client. Sheriff Montgomery wouldn't even permit them to fingerprint him. Sartuchi and Nielsen did see Watson, however. According to their report, he was well dressed, clean-shaven, with short, not long, hair. He appeared in good health and looked like 'a clean-cut college boy'.

While in McKinney, the detectives established that Watson had gone to California in 1967 and that he hadn't moved back until November 1969 – long after the murders.

Sartuchi and Nielsen returned to Los Angeles convinced we'd have little cooperation from the local authorities. It wasn't only a matter of relatives; somehow the whole affair had become involved in state politics!

'Little cooperation' would be a gross exaggeration.

Reporters were busy tracing the wanderings of the nomadic Family and interviewing those members not in custody. I asked Gail to save the papers, knowing the interviews might be useful at a later date. Though still uncharged with the murders, Charles Manson had now taken center stage. Sandy: 'The first time I heard him sing it was like an angel . . .' Squeaky: 'He gave off a lot of magic. But he was sort of a changeling. He seemed to change every time I saw him. He seemed ageless . . .'

There were also interviews with acquaintances and relatives of the suspects. Joseph Krenwinkel recalled how in September 1967 his daughter Patricia left her Manhattan Beach apartment, her job, and her car, not even picking up a paycheck due her, to join Manson. 'I am convinced he was some kind of hypnotist.'

Krenwinkel was not the only one to make that suggestion. Attorney Caballero talked to reporters outside the Santa Monica courtroom where his client had just entered a not guilty plea to the Hinman murder. Susan Atkins was under the 'hypnotic spell' of Manson, Caballero said, and had 'nothing to do with the murders' despite her presence at the Hinman and Tate residences.

Caballero also told the press his client was going to go before the grand jury and tell the complete story. This was the first confirmation we had that Susan Atkins had agreed to cooperate.

That same day LAPD interviewed Barbara Hoyt, whose parents had persuaded her to contact the police. Barbara had lived with the Family off and on since April 1969, and had been with them at the Spahn, Myers, and Barker ranches.

The pretty 17-year-old's story came out in bits and pieces, over several interviews. Among her disclosures:

One evening while at Spahn, about a week after the August 16 raid, she had heard screams that seemed to come from down the creek. They lasted a long time, five to ten minutes, and she was sure they were Shorty's. After that night she never saw Shorty again.

The next day she heard Manson tell Danny DeCarlo that Shorty had committed suicide, 'with a little help from us'. Manson had also asked DeCarlo if lime would dispose of a body.

While at Myers Ranch, in early September 1969, Barbara had overheard Manson tell someone – she wasn't sure who – that it had been real hard killing Shorty, once he had been 'brought to Now'. They'd hit him over the head with a pipe, Manson said, then everyone stabbed him, and finally Clem had chopped his head off. After that they'd cut him up in nine pieces.

While still at Myers, Barbara had also overhead Sadie tell Ouisch about the murders of Abigail Folger and Sharon Tate. Sometime later Ouisch told Barbara that she knew of ten other people the group had murdered.

Not long after this, Barbara and another girl – Sherry Ann Cooper, aka Simi Valley Sherri – fled the Family's Death Valley hideout. Manson caught up with them in Ballarat, but, because other people were present, had let them go, even giving them twenty dollars for their bus fare to Los Angeles.

Although very frightened, Barbara agreed to cooperate with us.

That cooperation would nearly cost her life.

About this same time another of Manson's girls agreed to help the police. She was the last person from whom I expected cooperation – Mary Brunner, the first member of the Manson Family.

Following his release from prison in March 1967, Charles Manson had gone to San Francisco. A prison acquaintance found him a room across the bay in Berkeley. In no hurry to find a job, subsisting mostly by panhandling, Manson would wander Telegraph Avenue or sit on the steps of the Sather Gate entrance to the University of California, playing his guitar. Then one day along came this librarian. As Charlie related the story to Danny DeCarlo, 'She was out walking her dog. High-button blouse.

Nose stuck up in the air, walking her little poodle. And Charlie's fresh out of the joint and along he comes talking his bullshit.'

Mary Brunner, then 23, had a B.A. degree in history from the University of Wisconsin and was working as an assistant librarian at the University of California. She was singularly unattractive, and Manson apparently was one of the first persons who thought her worth cultivating. It was possible he recalled the days when he lived off Fat Flo.

'So one thing led to another,' DeCarlo resumed. 'He moved in with her. Then he comes across this other girl. "No, there will be no other girls moving in with me!" Mary says. She flatly refused to consider the idea. After the girl had moved in, two more came along. And Mary says, "I'll accept one other girl but never three!" Four, five, all the way up to eighteen. This was in Frisco. Mary was the first.'

The Family had been born.

By this time Manson had discovered the Haight. According to a tale Manson himself often told his followers, one day a young boy handed him a flower. 'It blew my mind,' he'd recall. Questioning the youth, he learned that in San Francisco there was free food, music, dope, and love, just for the taking. The boy took him to Haight-Ashbury, Manson later told Steve Alexander, a writer for the underground paper *Tuesday's Child*: 'And we slept in the park and we lived on the streets and my hair got a little longer and I started playing music and people liked my music and people smiled at me and put their arms around me and hugged me – I didn't know how to act. It just took me away. It grabbed me up, man, that there were people that are real.'

They were also young, naïve, eager to believe, and, perhaps even more important, belong. There were followers aplenty for any self-styled guru. It didn't take Manson long to sense this. In the underground milieu into which he'd stumbled, even the fact that he was an ex-convict conferred a certain status. Rapping a line of metaphysical con that borrowed as much from pimping as joint jargon and Scientology, Manson began attracting followers, almost all girls at first, then a few young boys.

'There are a lot of Charlies running around, believe me,' observed Roger Smith, Manson's parole officer during his San Francisco period.

But with one big difference: somewhere along the line – I wasn't yet sure *how* or *where* or *when* – Manson developed a control over his followers so all-encompassing that he could ask them to violate the ultimate taboo – say 'Kill' and they would do it.

Many automatically assumed the answer was drugs. But Dr David Smith, who got to know the group through his work in the Haight-Ashbury Free Medical Clinic, felt 'sex, not drugs, was the common denominator' in the Manson family. 'A new girl in Charlie's Family would bring with her a certain middle-class morality. The first thing Charlie did was to see that all this was worn down. That way he was able to eliminate the controls that normally govern our lives.'

Sex, drugs – they were certainly part of the answer, and I'd soon learn a great deal more about how Manson used both – but they were only part. There was something more, a lot more.

Manson himself de-emphasized the importance of drugs, at least as far as he was concerned. During this period he took his first L S D trip. He later said that it 'enlightened my awareness' but added 'being in jail for so long had already left my awareness pretty well open'.

Manson claimed he foresaw the decline of the Haight even before it came into full flower. Saw police harassment, bad trips, heavy vibes, people ripping off one another and OD'ing in the streets. During the famous Summer of Love, with free rock concerts and Owsley's acid and a hundred more young people arriving every day, he got an old school bus, loaded up his followers, and split, 'looking for a place to get away from the Man'.

Mary Brunner eventually left her job and joined Manson's wandering caravan. She had a child by him, Michael Manson, the whole Family participating in the delivery, Manson himself biting through the umbilical cord.

Interviewed in Eau Claire, Wisconsin, where she had gone following her release from jail, Mary Brunner agreed to cooperate with the police in return for immunity in the Hinman murder. She supplied numerous details regarding that crime. She also said that in the latter part of September 1969, Tex Watson had told her about the murder of Shorty. They had buried his body near the railroad tracks at Spahn, Tex said, and Gypsy abandoned his car in Canoga Park near a residence the Family had previously occupied on Gresham Street. On the basis of this information, L A S O began a search for both the body and the vehicle.

Obviously, Mary Brunner would be an important witness in both the Hinman and Shea cases. Though she had been in jail when the Tate and LaBianca murders occurred, for a time I even considered using her as a witness in that case, since she could testify to the beginnings of the Family. But I remained very leery of her. According to others I interviewed, her devotion to Manson was fanatical. I just couldn't visualize her testifying against the father of her child.

The Tate case had been big news abroad since the murders occurred, eclipsing even the incident at Chappaquiddick. The arrests commanded just as much attention.

Because of the time difference, it was nearly midnight of December 1 before reports of the 'hippie kill cult' reached London. As in the United States, the sensational dispatches dominated the headlines of the papers the next day, led off radio and T V broadcasts.

At eleven that morning a maid in the Tagarth Hotel, on Tagarth Road in London, tried to open the door of a room occupied by an American youth named Joel Pugh. It was locked from the inside. Shortly after 6 P.M. the hotel manager unlocked the door with a passkey. 'It only opened about one foot,' he stated. 'There seemed to be a weight behind it.' Kneeling down and reaching in, 'I felt what seemed like an arm.' He hastily called the police. A constable from Hammersmith station arrived minutes later and pushed the door open. Behind it was the body of Joel Pugh. He was lying on his back, unclothed except for a sheet over the lower half of his body. His throat had been slit, twice. There was a bruise on his forehead, slash marks on both wrists, and two bloody razor blades, one less than two feet from the body. There were no notes, although there were some 'writings' in reverse on the mirror, along with some 'comic-book type drawings'.

According to the manager, Pugh had checked into the room on October 27 with a young lady who had left after three weeks. A 'hippie in appearance', Pugh was quiet, went out rarely, seemed to have no friends.

There being 'no wound not incapable of being self-inflicted', the coroner's inquest concluded that Pugh 'took his own life while the balance of his mind was disturbed'.

Although the circumstances of the death, including the wounds themselves, were equally if not more consistent with murder, it was considered a routine suicide. No one thought the drawings or writings important enough to take down (the manager later recalled only the words 'Jack and Jill'). No attempt was made to determine the time of death. Nor, though Pugh's room was on the ground floor and could be entered and left through the window, did anyone feel it necessary to check for latent prints.

At the time no one connected the death with the big American news that day. If it hadn't been for a brief reference in a letter over a month later, we probably would have remained unaware that Joel Dean Pugh, age 29, former Manson Family member and husband of Family member Sandra Good, had joined the lengthening list of mysterious deaths connected with the case.

When she and Squeaky moved out of their motel room in Independence, Sandy left some papers behind. Among them was a letter from an unidentified former Family member which contained the line: 'I would not want what happened to Joel to happen to me.'

December 3, 1969

About eight that night Richard Caballero brought the Susan Atkins tape to LAPD. He requested that no copy be made; however, I was allowed to take notes. In addition to myself, both Lieutenants Helder and LePage and four or five detectives were present while the tape was being played. We said little as, with all the casualness of a child reciting what she did that day in school, Susan Atkins matter-of-factly described the slaughter of seven people.

The voice was that of a young girl. But except for occasional giggles – 'And Sharon went through quite a few changes [laughs], quite a few changes' – it was flat, emotionless, dead. It was as if all the human feelings had been erased. *What kind of creature is this?* I wondered.

I'd soon know. Caballero had agreed that before we took the case to the grand jury, I could personally interview Susan Atkins.

The tape lasted about two hours. Although the monumental job of proving their guilt remained, when the tape had ended – Caballero saying to Susan, 'O.K., now we're going to get you something to eat, including some ice cream' – we at least knew, for the first time, exactly who had been involved in the Tate and LaBianca murders.

Though Manson had sent the killers to 10050 Cielo Drive, he had not gone along himself. Those who did go were Charles 'Tex' Watson, Susan Atkins, Patricia Krenwinkel, and Linda Kasabian. One man, three girls, who would mercilessly shoot and stab five people to death.

Manson, however, did enter the Waverly Drive residence the next night, to tie up Rosemary and Leno LaBianca. He then sent in Watson, Krenwinkel, and Leslie Van Houten, aka Sankston, with instructions to 'kill them'.

Susan Atkins herself hadn't been inside the LaBianca residence. She had remained in the car with Clem and Linda. But she had heard – from Manson, Krenwinkel, and Van Houten – what had occurred inside.

Though the tape cleared up some mysteries, many remained. And there were discrepancies. For example, although Susan admitted stabbing the big man (Frykowski) five or six times, 'in self-defense', she said nothing about stabbing Sharon Tate. In contrast to what she had told Virginia Graham and Ronnie Howard, Susan now claimed that she had held Sharon while Tex stabbed her.

Returning to my office, I did what I do after every interview – converted my notes into a tentative interrogation. I had a lot of questions I wanted to ask Sadie Mae Glutz.

Linda Kasabian waived extradition proceedings and was flown back to Los Angeles that same day. She was booked into Sybil Brand at 11:15 P.M. Aaron was there, as was Linda's attorney, Gary Fleischman. Though Fleischman permitted her to ID some photographs of various Family members which Aaron had, he would not let Aaron question her. Aaron did ask her how she felt, and she replied, 'Tired, but relieved.' Aaron got the impression that Linda herself was anxious to tell what she knew but that Fleischman was holding out for a deal.

December 4, 1969

Confidential Memorandum

To: Evelle J. Younger
           District Attorney

From: Aaron H. Stovitz
           Head, Trials Division

Subject: Susan Atkins

A meeting was held today in Mr Younger's office, commencing at 10:20 A.M. and concluding at 11 A.M. Present at the meeting were Mr Younger, Paul Caruso, Richard Caballero, Aaron Stovitz and Vincent Bugliosi.

Discussion was had as to whether or not immunity should be given to Susan Atkins in exchange for her testimony at the Grand Jury hearing and subsequent trial. It was decided that she would *not* be given immunity.

Mr Caballero made it known that at this moment his client may not testify at the trial due to her fear of the physical presence of Charles Manson and the other participants in the Sharon Tate murders.

Discussion was held concerning the value of Susan Atkins' testimony. Agreement was reached upon the following points:

1. That Susan Atkins' information has been vital to law enforcement.

2. In view of her past cooperation and in the event that she testifies truthfully at the Grand Jury, the prosecution will not seek the death penalty against her in any of the three cases that are now known to the police; namely, the Hinman murder, the Sharon Tate murders, and the LaBianca murders.

4. The extent to which the District Attorney's Office will assist Defense Counsel in an attempt to seek less than a first degree murder, life sentence, will depend upon the extent to which Susan Atkins continues to cooperate.

4. That in the event that Susan Atkins does not testify at the trial or

that the prosecution does not use her as a witness at the trial, the prosecution will not use her testimony, given at the Grand Jury, against her.

Caballero had made an excellent deal, as far as his client was concerned. If she testified truthfully before the grand jury, we could not seek the death penalty against her in the Hinman, Tate, and LaBianca cases; nor could we use her grand jury testimony against her or any of her co-defendants when they were brought to trial. As Caballero later put it, 'She gave up nothing and got everything in return.'

For our part, I felt we got very much the short end. Susan Atkins would tell her story at the grand jury. We'd get an indictment. And that would be all we would have, a scrap of paper. For Caballero was convinced she would never testify at the trial. He was worried that even now she might suddenly change her mind.

We had no choice but to rush the case to the grand jury, which was meeting the following day.

Our case was getting a little stronger. The previous day Sergeant Sam McLarty of the Mobile Police Department had taken Patricia Krenwinkel's prints. On receiving the exemplar from Mobile, Sergeant Frank Marz of LAPD 'made' one print. The print of the little finger on Krenwinkel's left hand matched a latent print officer Boen had lifted from the frame on the left French door *inside* Sharon Tate's bedroom. This was the blood-spattered door that led outside to the pool.

We know had a second piece of physical evidence linking still another of the suspects to the crime scene.

But we didn't have either suspect. Like Watson, Krenwinkel intended to fight extradition. She would be held fourteen days without bond. If extradition papers were not there before the fifteenth day, she would be released.

Caballero drove me to his office in Beverly Hills. By the time we arrived, about 5:30 P.M., Susan Atkins was already there, having been taken out of Sybil Brand on the basis of another court order, requested by Aaron. Caballero had suggested that Susan would be much more apt to speak freely with me in the relaxed atmosphere of his office than at Sybil Brand, and Miller Leavy, Aaron, and I had agreed.

Although she had opened up to both Virginia Graham and Ronnie Howard, my interview with Susan Atkins on the Tate-LaBianca murders was the first she had had with any law-enforcement officer. It would also be the last.

Twenty-one years old, five feet five, 120 pounds, long brown hair, brown eyes, a not unattractive face, but with a distant, far-off look, similar to the expressions of Sandy and Squeaky but even more pronounced.

Although this was the first time I had seen Susan Atkins, I already knew quite a bit about her. Born in San Gabriel, California, she had grown up in San Jose. Her mother had died of cancer while Susan was still in her teens, and, after numerous quarrels with her father, she'd dropped out of high school and drifted to San Francisco. Hustler, topless dancer, kept woman, gun moll – she'd been all these things even before meeting Charles Manson. I had a certain amount of pity for her. I tried my best to understand her. But I couldn't summon up very much compassion, not after having seen the photographs of what had been done to the Tate victims.

After Caballero introduced us, I informed her of her constitutional rights and obtained permission to interview her.

'Were you, Tex, or any of the others under the influence of LSD or any other drug on the night of the Tate murders?'

'No.'

'What about the next night, the night the LaBiancas were killed?'

'No. Neither night.'

There was something mysterious about her. She would talk rapidly for a few minutes, then pause, head slightly cocked to the side, as if sensing voices no one else could.

'You know,' she confided, 'Charlie is looking at us right now and he can hear everything we are saying.'

'Charlie is up in Independence, Sadie.'

She smiled, secure in the knowledge that she was right and I, an outsider, an unbeliever, was wrong.

Looking at her, I thought to myself, This is the star witness for the prosecution? I'm going to build my case upon the testimony of this very, very strange girl?

She was crazy. I had no doubt about it. Probably not legally insane, but crazy nonetheless.

As on the tape, she admitted stabbing Frykowski but denied stabbing Sharon Tate. I'd conducted hundreds of interviews; you get a sort of visceral reaction when someone is lying. I felt that she *had* stabbed Sharon but didn't want to admit it to me.

I had to interview over a dozen witnesses that same night: Winifred Chapman, the first police officers to arrive at Cielo and Waverly, Granado and the fingerprint men, Lomax from Hi Standard, Coroner Noguchi and Deputy Medical Examiner Katsuyama, DeCarlo, Melcher, Jakobson. Danny DeCarlo hadn't been believable in the Beausoleil trial: I had to make sure the grand jury believed him. It was necessary not only to extract from very disparate witnesses, many of them experts in their individual fields, exactly what was relevant, but to bring these pieces together into a solid, convincing case.

Seven murder victims, multiple defendants: a case like this was not only probably unprecedented, it required weeks of preparation. Because of Chief Davis' rush to break the news, we'd had only days. Next morning we had to take the Tate and LaBianca cases before the Los Angeles County grand jury.

December 5, 1969

In Los Angeles the grand jury consists of twenty-three persons, picked by lot from a list of names submitted by each Superior Court judge. Of that number twenty-one were present, two-thirds of whom would have to concur to return an indictment. The proceedings themselves are usually brief. The prosecution presents just enough of its case to get an indictment and no more. Though in this instance the testimony would extend over two days, the 'star witness for the prosecution' would tell her story in less than one.

THE SERGEANT AT ARMS. 'Susan Atkins.'

The jurors, seven men and fourteen women, looked at her with obvious curiosity.

Aaron informed Susan of her rights, among which was her right not to incriminate herself. She waived them. I then took over the questioning, establishing that she knew Charles Manson and taking her back to the day they first met. It was over two years ago. She was living in a house on Lyon Street in the Haight-Ashbury district of San Francisco, with a number of other young people, most of whom were into drugs.

A. '. . . and I was sitting in the living room and a man walked in and he had a guitar with him and all of a sudden he was surrounded by a group of girls.' The man sat down and began to play, 'and the song that caught my attention most was "The Shadow of Your Smile", and he sounded like an angel'.

Q. 'You are referring to Charles Manson?'

A. 'Yes. And when he was through singing, I wanted to get some attention from him, and I asked him if I could play his guitar . . . and he handed me the guitar and I thought, "I can't play this," and then he looked at me and said, "You can play that if you want to."

'Now he had never heard me say "I can't play this," I only thought it. So when he told me I could play it, it blew my mind, because he was inside my head, and I knew at that time that he was something that I had been looking for ... and I went down and kissed his feet.'

A day or two later Manson returned to the house and asked her to go for a walk. 'And we walked a couple of blocks to another house and he told me he wanted to make love with me.

'Well, I acknowledged the fact that I wanted to make love with him, and he told me to take off my clothes, so I uninhibitedly took off my clothes, and there happened to be a full-length mirror in the room, and he told me to go over and look at myself in the mirror.

'I didn't want to do it, so he took me by the hand and stood me in front of the mirror, and I turned away and he said, "Go ahead and look at yourself. There is nothing wrong with you. You are perfect. You always have been perfect." '

Q. 'What happened next?'

A. 'He asked me if I had ever made love with my father. I looked at him and kind of giggled and I said, "No." And he said, "Have you ever thought about making love with your father?" I said, "Yes." And he told me, "All right, when you are making love ... picture in your mind that I am your father." And I did, I did so, and it was a very beautiful experience.'

Susan said that before she met Manson she felt she was 'lacking something'. But then 'I gave myself to him, and in return for that he gave me back to myself. He gave me the faith in myself to be able to know that I am a woman.'

A week or so later, she, Manson, Mary Brunner, Ella Jo Bailey, Lynette Fromme, and Patricia Krenwinkel, together with three or four boys whose names she couldn't remember, left San Francisco in an old school bus from which they had removed most of the seats, furnishing it with brightly colored rugs and pillows. For the next year and a half they roamed – north to Mendocino, Oregon, Washington; south to Big Sur, Los Angeles, Mexico,

Nevada, Arizona, New Mexico; and, eventually, back to L.A., living first in various residences in Topanga Canyon, Malibu, Venice, and then, finally, Spahn Ranch. En route others joined them, a few staying permanently, most only temporarily. According to Susan, they went through changes, and learned to love. The girls made love with each of the boys, and with each other. But Charlie was complete love. Although he did not have sex with her often – only six times in the more than two years they were together – 'he would give himself completely'.

Q. 'Were you very much in love with him, Susan?'

A. 'I was in love with the reflection and the reflection I speak of is Charlie Manson's.'

Q. 'Was there any limit to what you would do for him?'

A. 'No.'

I was laying the foundation for the very heart of my case against Manson, that Susan and the others would do anything for him, up to and including murder at his command.

Q. 'What was it about Charlie that caused you girls to be in love with him and to do what he wanted you to do?'

A. 'Charlie is the only man I have ever met . . . on the face of this earth . . . that is a complete man. He will not take back-talk from a woman. He will not let a woman talk him into doing anything. He is a man.'

Charlie had given her the name Sadie Mae Glutz because 'in order for me to be completely free in my mind I had to be able to completely forget the past. The easiest way to do this, to change identity, is by doing so with a name.'

According to Susan, Charlie himself went under a variety of names, calling himself the Devil, Satan, Soul.

Q. 'Did Mr Manson ever call himself Jesus?'

A. 'He personally never called himself Jesus.'

Q. 'Did you ever call him Jesus?' From my questioning the night before, I anticipated that Susan would be evasive about this, and she was.

A. 'He represented a Jesus Christ-like person to me.'

Q. 'Do you think Charlie is an evil person?'

A. 'In your standards of evil, looking at him through your eyes,

I would say yes. Looking at him through my eyes, he is as good as he is evil, he is as evil as he is good. You could not judge the man.'

Although Susan didn't state that she believed Manson was Christ, the implication was there. Though I was at this time far from understanding it myself, it was important that I give the jury some explanation, however partial, for Manson's control over his followers. Incredible as all this was to the predominantly upper-middle-class, upper-middle-aged grand jurors, it was nothing compared to what they would hear when she described those two nights of murder.

I worked up to them gradually, having her describe Spahn Ranch and the life there, and asking her how they survived. People gave them things, Susan said. Also, they panhandled. And 'the supermarkets all over Los Angeles throw away perfectly good food every day, fresh vegetables and sometimes cartons of eggs, packages of cheese that are stamped to a certain date, but the food is still good, and us girls used to go out and do "garbage runs" '.

They also stole – credit cards, other things.

Q. 'Did Charlie ask you to steal?'

A. 'No, I took it upon myself. I was – we'd get programmed to do things.'

Q. 'Programmed by Charlie?'

A. 'By Charlie, but it's hard for me to explain it so that you can see the way – the way I see. The words that would come from Charlie's mouth would not come from inside him, [they] would come from what I call the Infinite.'

And sometimes, at night, they 'creepy-crawled'. They would pick a house at random, anywhere in Los Angeles, slip in while the occupants were asleep, creep and crawl around the rooms silently, maybe move things so when the people awakened they wouldn't be in the same place they had been when they went to bed. Everyone carried a knife. Susan said she did it 'because everybody else in the Family was doing it' and she wanted that experience.

These creepy-crawling expeditions were, I felt sure the jury would surmise, dress rehearsals for murder.

Q. 'Did you call your group by any name, Susan?'

A. 'Among ourselves we called ourselves the Family.' It was, Susan said, 'a family like no other family'.

I thought I heard a juror mutter, 'Thank God!'

Q. 'Susan, were you living at Spahn Ranch on the date of August the eighth, 1969?'

A. 'Yes.'

Q. 'Susan, on that date did Charlie Manson instruct you and some other members of the Family to do anything?'

A. 'I never recall getting any actual instructions from Charlie other than getting a change of clothing and a knife and was told to do exactly what Tex told me to do.'

Q. 'Did Charlie indicate to you the type of clothing you should take?'

A. 'He told me . . . wear dark clothes.'

Susan ID'd photos of Watson, Krenwinkel, and Kasabian, as well as a photo of the old Ford in which the four of them left the ranch. Charlie waved to them as they drove off. Susan didn't notice the time, but it was night. There was a pair of wire cutters in the back seat, also a rope. She, Katie, and Linda each had a knife; Tex had a gun and, she believed, a knife too. Not until they were en route did Tex tell them, to quote Susan, that they 'were going to a house up on the hill that used to belong to Terry Melcher, and the only reason why we were going to that house was because Tex knew the outline of the house'.

Q. 'Did Tex tell you why you four were going to Terry Melcher's former residence?'

Matter-of-factly, with no emotion whatsoever, Susan replied, 'To get all of their money and to kill whoever was there.'

Q. 'It didn't make any difference who was there, you were told to kill them: is that correct?'

A. 'Yes.'

They got lost on the way. However, Tex finally recognized the turnoff and they drove to the top of the hill. Tex got out, climbed the telephone pole, and, using the wire cutters, severed the wires. When Tex returned to the car, they drove back down the hill, parked at the bottom, then, bringing along their extra clothing, walked back up. They didn't enter the grounds through the gate 'because we thought there might be an alarm system or electricity'. To the right of the gate was a steep, brushy incline. The fence wasn't as high here. Susan threw over her clothing bundle, then went over herself, her knife in her teeth. The others followed.

They were stowing their clothing in the bushes when Susan saw the headlights of a car. It was coming up the driveway in the direction of the gate. 'Tex told us girls to lie down and be still and not make a sound. He went out of sight . . . I heard him say "Halt".' Susan also heard another voice, male, say 'Please don't hurt me, I won't say anything.' 'And I heard a gunshot and I heard another gunshot and another one and another one.' Four shots, then Tex returned and told them to come on. When they got to the car, Tex reached inside and turned off the lights; then they pushed the car away from the gate, back up the driveway.

I showed Susan a photo of the Rambler. 'It looked similar to it, yes.' I then showed her the police photograph of Steven Parent inside the vehicle.

A. 'That is the thing I saw in the car.'

There were audible gasps from the jurors.

Q. 'When you say "thing", you are referring to a human being?'

A. 'Yes, human being.'

The jurors had looked at the heart of Susan Atkins and seen ice.

They went on down the driveway, past the garage, to the house. Using a scale diagram I'd had prepared, Susan indicated their approach to the dining-room window. 'Tex opened the window, crawled inside, and the next thing I knew he was at the front door.'

Q. 'Did all of you girls enter at that time?'

A. 'Only two of us entered, one stayed outside.'

Q. 'Who stayed outside?'

A. 'Linda Kasabian.'

Susan and Katie joined Tex. There was a man lying on the

couch (Susan ID'd a photo of Voytek Frykowski). 'The man stretched his arms and woke up. I guess he thought some of his friends were coming from somewhere. He said, "What time is it?" ... Tex jumped in front of him and held a gun in his face and said, "Be quiet. Don't move or you're dead." Frykowski said something like "Who are you and what are you doing here?" '

Q. 'What did Tex say to that, if anything?'

A. 'He said, "I am the Devil and I'm here to do the Devil's business ..." '

Tex then told Susan to check for other people. In the first bedroom she saw a woman reading a book. (Susan ID'd a photo of Abigail Folger.) 'She looked at me and smiled and I looked at her and smiled.' She went on. A man and a woman were in the next bedroom. The man, who was sitting on the edge of the bed, had his back to Susan. The woman, who was pregnant, was lying on the bed. (Susan ID'd photos of Jay Sebring and Sharon Tate.) The pair were talking and neither saw her. Returning to the living room, she reported to Tex that there were three more people.

Tex gave her the rope and told her to tie up the man on the couch. After she'd done this, Tex ordered her to get the others. Susan walked into Abigail Folger's bedroom, 'put a knife in front of her, and said, "Get up and go into the living room. Don't ask any questions. Just do what I say." ' Katie, also armed with a knife, took charge of Folger while Susan got the other two.

None offered any resistance. All had the same expression on their faces, 'Shock.'

On entering the living room, Sebring asked Tex, 'What are you doing here?' Tex told him to shut up, then ordered the three to lie on their stomachs on the floor in front of the fireplace. 'Can't you see she's pregnant?' Sebring said. 'Let her sit down.'

When Sebring 'didn't follow Tex's orders ... Tex shot him'.

Q. 'Did you see Tex shoot Jay Sebring?'

A. 'Yes.'

Q. 'With the gun that he had taken from Spahn Ranch?'

A. 'Yes.'

Q. 'What happened next?'

A. 'Jay Sebring fell over in front of the fireplace and Sharon and Abigail screamed.'

Tex ordered them to be quiet. When he asked if they had any money, Abigail said she had some in her purse in the bedroom. Susan went with her to get it. Abigail handed her seventy-two dollars and asked if she wanted her credit cards. Susan said she didn't. On their return to the living room, Tex told Susan to get a towel and retie Frykowski's hands; she did, she said, but couldn't get the knot very tight. Tex then took the rope and tied it first around Sebring's neck, then the necks of Abigail and Sharon. He threw the end of the rope over the beam in the ceiling and pulled on it, 'which made Sharon and Abigail stand up so they wouldn't be choked to death . . .' Then, 'I forget who said it, but one of the victims said, "What are you going to do with us?" and Tex said, "You are all going to die." And at that time they began to plead for their lives.'

Q. 'What is the next thing that happened?'

A. 'Then Tex ordered me to go over and kill Frykowski.'

As she raised her knife, Frykowski, who had managed to free his hands, jumped up and 'knocked me down, and I grabbed him as best I could, and then it was a fight for my life as well as him fighting for his life.

'Somehow he got ahold of my hair and pulled it very hard and I was screaming for Tex to help me, or somebody to help me, and Frykowski, he was also screaming.

'Somehow he got behind me, and I had the knife in my right hand and I was – I was – I don't know where I was at but I was just swinging with the knife, and I remember hitting something four, five times repeatedly behind me. I didn't see what it was I was stabbing.'

Q. 'But did it appear to be a human being?'

A. 'I never stabbed a human being before, but I just know it was going into something.'

Q. 'Could it have been Frykowski?'

A. 'It could have been Frykowski, it could have been a chair, I don't know what it was.'

Susan had changed her story. In my interview with her, and

on the tape, she had admitted to stabbing Frykowski 'three or four times in the leg'. Also, if the story she told Virginia Graham was true, she knew exactly how it felt to stab someone, i.e., Gary Hinman.

Frykowski ran for the front door, 'yelling for his life, for somebody to come help him'. Tex got to him and hit him over the head several times with 'I believe a gun butt'. Tex later told her that he had broken the gun hitting Frykowski and that it wouldn't work any more.* Apparently Tex had a knife ready, as he began stabbing Frykowski 'as best he could because Frykowski was still fighting'. Meanwhile, 'Abigail Folger had gotten loose from the rope and was in a fight with Katie, Patricia Krenwinkel . . .'

THE FOREMAN. 'We have a grand juror who would like to be excused for just a couple of minutes.'

A recess was taken. There was more than one pale face in the jury box.

We resumed where Susan had left off. Someone was moaning, she said. Tex ran over to Sebring, 'and bent down and viciously stabbed him in the back many times . . .

'Sharon Tate, I remember seeing her struggling with the rope.' Tex ordered Susan to take care of her. Susan locked her arm around Sharon's neck, forcing her back onto the couch. She was begging for her life. 'I looked at her and said, "Woman, I have no mercy for you." And I knew that I was talking to myself, not to her . . .'

Q. 'Did Sharon say anything about the baby at that point?'

A. 'She said, "Please let me go. All I want to do is have my baby."'

'There was a lot of confusion going on . . . Tex went over to help Katie . . . I saw Tex stab Abigail Folger and just before he stabbed – maybe an instant before he stabbed her – she looked at him and let her arms go and looked at all of us and said, "I give up. Take me."'

I asked Susan how many times Tex had stabbed Abigail. 'Only

---

* Although Frykowski had been shot twice, Susan couldn't recall the shooting, leaving in doubt exactly when this occurred.

once,' Susan replied. 'She grabbed her middle section of her body and fell to the floor.'

Tex then ran outside. Susan released her grip on Sharon but continued to guard her. When Tex returned, he told Susan, 'Kill her.' But according to the story Susan was now telling, 'I couldn't.' Instead, 'in order to make a diversion so that Tex couldn't see that I couldn't kill her, I grabbed her hand and held her arms, and then I saw Tex stab her in the heart area around the chest'. Sharon then fell from the couch to the floor. (Susan only mentioned Tex stabbing Sharon Tate once. According to the autopsy report, she had been stabbed sixteen times. According to Ronnie Howard, Susan told her, 'I just kept stabbing her until she stopped screaming.')

The next thing she remembered, Susan now testified, was that she, Tex, and Katie were outside, and 'I saw Abigail Folger on the front lawn, bent over falling onto the grass . . . I didn't see her go outside . . . and I saw Tex go over and stab her three or four – I don't know how many times . . .' (Abigail Folger had twenty-eight stab wounds.) 'While he was doing that, Katie and I were looking for Linda, because she wasn't around . . . and then Tex walked over to Frykowski and kicked him in the head.' Frykowski was on the front lawn, away from the door. When Tex kicked him, 'the body didn't move very much. I believe it was dead at that time.' (Which was not surprising, since Voytek Frykowski had been shot twice, struck over the head thirteen times with a blunt object, and stabbed fifty-one times.)

Then 'Tex told me to go back into the house and write something on the door in one of the victims' blood . . . He said, "Write something that will shock the world" . . . I had previously been involved in something similar to this [Hinman], where I saw "political piggy" written on the wall, so that stuck very heavily in my mind . . .' Re-entering the house, she picked up the same towel she had used to tie Frykowski's hands, and walked over to Sharon Tate. Then she heard sounds.

Q. 'What kind of sounds were they?'

A. 'Gurgling sounds like blood flowing into the body out of the heart.'

Q. 'What did you do then?'

A. 'I picked up the towel and turned my head and touched her chest, and at the same time I saw she was pregnant and I knew that there was a living being inside of that body and I wanted to but I didn't have the courage to go ahead and take it ... And I got the towel with Sharon Tate's blood, walked over to the door, and with the towel I wrote PIG on the door.'

Susan then threw the towel back into the living room; she didn't look to see where it landed. (It fell on Sebring's face, hence the 'hood' referred to in the press.)

Sadie, Tex, and Katie then picked up the bundles of spare clothing they'd hidden in the bushes. They left by the gate, Tex pushing the button, and hurried down the hill. 'When we got to the car, Linda Kasabian started the car, and Tex ran up to her and said, "What do you think you're doing? Get over on the passenger side. Don't do anything until I tell you to do it." Then we drove off.'

They changed clothing in the car, all except Linda, who, not having been in the house, had no blood on her. As they were driving away, Susan realized she had lost her knife, but Tex was against going back.

They drove somewhere along 'Benedict Canyon, Mulholland Drive, I don't know [which street] ... until we came to what looked like an embankment going down like a cliff with a mountain on one side and a cliff on the other.' They pulled off and stopped, and 'Linda threw all the bloody clothes over the side of the hill ...' The weapons, the knives and gun, were tossed out at 'three or four different places, I don't remember how many'.

Susan then described, as she had to Virginia Graham and Ronnie Howard, how after they'd pulled off onto a side street and used a garden hose to wash off the blood, a man and a woman rushed out of the house and threatened to report them to the police. 'And Tex looked at him and said, "Gee, I'm sorry. I didn't think you were home. We were just walking around and wanted a drink of water. We didn't mean to wake you up or disturb you." And the man looked down the street and said, "Is that your car?" And Tex said, "No, I told you we were just walking." The man said, "I know that is your car. You better get in and get going".'

They got in the car, and the man, apparently having decided to detain them, reached in to get the keys. Tex quickly started the car, however, and drove off fast.

After stopping at a service station on Sunset Boulevard, where they took turns going to the bathroom to check for 'any other blood spots', they drove back to Spahn Ranch, arriving there, Susan guessed, about 2 A.M.

When they pulled up in front of the boardwalk of the old movie set, Charles Manson was waiting for them. He walked over to the car, leaned inside, and asked, 'What are you doing home so early?'

According to Susan, Tex told Manson 'basically just what we had done. That it all happened perfectly. There was a lot of – it happened very fast – a lot of panic, and he described it, "Boy, it sure was helter skelter".'

While at the service station, Susan had noticed blood on the door handles and steering wheel. She now went into the ranch kitchen and got a rag and a sponge and wiped it off.

Q. 'How was Charles Manson acting when you arrived back at Spahn Ranch?'

A. 'Charles Manson changes from second to second. He can be anybody he wants to be. He can put on any face he wants to put on at any given moment.'

Patricia 'was very silent'. Tex was 'nervous like he had just been through a traumatic experience'.

Q. 'How did you feel about what you had just done?'

A. 'I almost passed out. I felt as though I had killed myself. I felt dead. I feel dead now.'

After she'd finished cleaning the car, Susan and the others had gone to bed. She thought she had made love to someone, maybe Clem, but then again maybe she had imagined it.

The noon recess was called.

Throughout her testimony Susan had referred to the victims by name. After the recess I established that she hadn't known their names that night, nor had she ever seen any of them before. '. . . when I first saw them, my reaction was, "Wow, they sure are beautiful people." '

Susan first learned their identities the day after the murders, while watching the news on TV in the trailer next to George Spahn's house. Tex, Katie, and Clem were also there, and maybe Linda, though Susan wasn't sure.

Q. 'As you were watching the television news coverage, did anyone say anything?'

Someone – Susan thought the words came from her own mouth, but she wasn't positive – said either, 'The Soul sure did pick a lulu,' or 'The Soul sure did a good job.' She did remember saying that what had happened had 'served its purpose'. Which was? I asked.

A. 'To instill fear into the establishment.'

I asked Susan if any other members of the Family knew they had committed the Tate murders.

A. 'The Family was so much together that nothing ever had to be said. We all just knew what each other would do or had done.'

We came now to the second night, the evening of August 9 and the early-morning hours of August 10.

That evening Manson again told Susan to get an extra set of clothing. 'I looked at him and I knew what he wanted me to do, and I gave a sort of sigh and went and did what he asked me to do.'

Q. 'Did he say what you were going to go out and do that night?' I asked.

A. 'He said we were going to go out and do the same thing we did the last night . . . only two different houses . . .'

It was the same car and the same cast – Susan, Katie, Linda, and Tex – with three additions: Charlie, Clem, and Leslie. Susan didn't notice any knives, only a gun, which Charlie had.

They stopped in front of a house, 'somewhere in Pasadena, I believe', Charlie got out, and the others drove around the block, then came back and picked him up. 'He said he saw pictures of children through the window and he didn't want to do that house.' In the future, however, Manson explained, they might have to kill the children also.

They stopped in front of another house, but saw some people nearby so remained in the car and after a few minutes drove off. At some point Susan fell asleep, she said. When she awakened, they were in a familiar neighborhood, near a house where, about a year before, she, Charlie, and about fifteen others had gone to an LSD party. The house had been occupied by a 'Harold'. She couldn't recall his last name.

Charlie got out, only he didn't walk up the driveway of this particular house but the one next door. Susan went back to sleep. She woke up when Charlie returned. 'He said, "Tex, Katie, Leslie, go into the house. I have the people tied up. They are very calm."

'He said something to the effect that last night Tex let the people know they were going to be killed, which caused panic, and Charlie said that he reassured the people with smiles in a very quiet manner that they were not to be harmed ... And so Tex, Leslie, and Katie got out of the car.'

Susan ID'd photographs of Tex, Leslie, and Katie. Also of the LaBianca residence, the long driveway, and the house next door.

I asked Susan what else Charlie told the trio. She replied that she 'thought', but it may be 'my imagination that tells me this', that 'Charlie instructed them to go in and kill them'. She did recall him saying that they were 'to paint a picture more gruesome than anybody had ever seen'. He'd also told them that after they were done they were to hitchhike back to the ranch.

When Charlie returned to the car, he had a woman's wallet with him. Then they drove around 'in a predominantly colored area'.

Q. 'What happened next?'

Susan said they stopped at a gas station. Then 'Charlie gave Linda Kasabian the woman's wallet and told her to put it in the bathroom in the gas station and leave it there, hoping that somebody would find it and use the credit cards and thus be identified with the murder ...'

I wondered about that wallet. To date, none of Rosemary LaBianca's credit cards had been used.

After leaving the station, Susan said, she went back to sleep. 'It was like I was drugged' though 'I was not on drugs at the time'. When she woke up, they were back at the ranch.

(At this time we were unaware that Susan Atkins had made some significant omissions in her grand jury testimony – including three other attempts at murder that night. Had we known of them, we probably would have asked for an indictment of Clem. As it was, however, all we had against him was Susan's statement that he had been in the car. And we still had a slim hope that his brother, whom we'd contacted at the Highway Patrol Academy, might persuade him to cooperate with us.)

Susan had not entered the LaBianca residence. However, the next morning Katie told her what had happened inside.

A. 'She told me that when they got in the house they took the woman in the bedroom and put her on the bed and left Tex in the living room with the man . . . And then Katie said the woman heard her husband being killed and started to scream, "What are you doing to my husband?" And Katie said that she then proceeded to stab the woman . . .'

Q. 'Did she say what Leslie was doing while – '

A. 'Leslie was helping Katie hold the woman down because the woman was fighting all the way up until she died . . .' Later Katie told Susan that the last words the woman spoke – 'What are you doing to my husband?' – would be the thought she would carry with her into infinity.

Afterwards, Katie told Susan, they wrote ' "Death to all pigs" on the refrigerator door or on the front door, and I think she said they wrote "helter skelter" and "arise".'

Then Katie walked into the living room from the kitchen with a fork in her hand, and 'she looked at the man's stomach and she had the fork in her hand and she put the fork in the man's stomach and watched it wobble back and forth. She said she was fascinated by it.'

Susan also said that it was 'Katie, I believe,' who carved the word 'war' on the man's stomach.

The three then took a shower and, since they were hungry, they went to the kitchen and fixed themselves something to eat.

According to Susan, Katie also told her that they presumed the couple had children and that they would probably find the bodies when they came over for Sunday dinner later that day.

After leaving the residence, 'they dumped the old clothing in a garbage can a few blocks, maybe a mile, away from the house'. Then they hitchhiked back to Spahn Ranch, arriving about dawn.

I had only a few more questions for Susan Atkins.

Q. 'Susan, did Charlie oftentimes use the word "pig" or "pigs"?'

A. 'Yes.'

Q. 'How about "Helter skelter"?'

A. 'Yes.'

Q. 'Did he use the words "pigs" and "helter skelter" very, very frequently?'

A. 'Well, Charlie talks a lot . . . In some of the songs he wrote, "helter skelter" was in them and he'd talk about helter skelter. We all talked about helter skelter.'

Q. 'You say "we"; are you speaking of the Family?'

A. 'Yes.'

Q. 'What did the word "pig" or "pigs" mean to you and your Family?'

A. ' "Pig" was a word used to describe the establishment. But you must understand that all words had no meanings to us and that "helter skelter" was explained to me.'

Q. 'By whom?'

A. 'Charlie. I don't even like to say Charlie – I'd like to say the words came from his mouth – that helter skelter was to be the last war on the face of the earth. It would be all the wars that have ever been fought built one on top of the other, something that no man could conceive of in his imagination. You can't conceive of what it would be like to see every man judge himself and then take it out on every other man all over the face of the earth.'

After a few more questions, I brought Susan Atkins' testimony to an end. As she nonchalantly stepped down from the witness stand, the jurors stared at her in disbelief. Not once had she shown a trace of remorse, sorrow, or guilt.

There were only four more witnesses that day. After Susan Atkins was taken from the room, Wilfred Parent was brought in to identify his son in a high-school prom picture. After identifying photos of the other Tate victims, Winifred Chapman testified that she had washed the front door of the Tate residence shortly before noon on Friday, August 8. This was important, since it meant that in order to leave a print Charles 'Tex' Watson had to have been on the premises sometime after Mrs Chapman left at four that afternoon.

Aaron questioned Terry Melcher. He described meeting Manson; told of how Manson had been along when Dennis Wilson drove him home to 10050 Cielo Drive one night; and described, very briefly, his two visits to Spahn Ranch, the first to audition Manson, the second to introduce him to Michael Deasy, who had a mobile recording unit and who he felt might be more interested in recording Manson than he was.

According to various Family members, Melcher had made numerous promises to Manson, and hadn't come through on them. Melcher denied this: the first time he went to Spahn, he had given Manson fifty dollars, all the money he had in his pocket, because 'I felt sorry for these people'; but it was for food, not an advance on a recording contract; and he'd made no promises. As for Manson's talent, he 'wasn't impressed enough to allot the time necessary' to prepare and record him.

I wanted to interview Melcher in depth – I had a feeling that he was withholding something – but, like most of the other grand jury witnesses, he was here for a very limited purpose, and any real digging would have to wait.

Los Angeles Coroner Thomas Noguchi testified to the autopsy findings on the five Tate victims. When he had concluded, the session was adjourned until Monday.

That the proceedings were secret encouraged speculation, which, in some cases, appeared not as conjecture but fact. The headline on the Los Angeles *Herald Examiner* that afternoon read:

TATE KILLERS WILD ON LSD,
GRAND JURORS TOLD

It wasn't true; Susan Atkins had stated the very opposite, that the killers were not on drugs either night. But the myth was born, and it persisted, perhaps because it was the easiest explanation for what had happened.

Though, as I'd soon learn, drugs were one of several methods Manson used to obtain control over his followers, they had no part in these crimes, for a very simple reason: on these two nights of savage slaughter, Charles Manson wanted his assassins in complete control of their faculties.

The reality, and its implications, were far more frightening than the myth.

December 6–8, 1969

'I just had a talk with Gary Fleischman, Vince,' Aaron said. 'He wants a deal for his client Linda Kasabian. Complete immunity in exchange for her testimony at the trial. I told him maybe we could go along with her pleading to voluntary manslaughter, but we couldn't give her – '

'Christ, Aaron,' I interrupted. 'It's bad enough that we had to give Susan Atkins something! Look at it this way – Krenwinkel's in Alabama, Watson's in Texas; for all we know, we may not be able to extradite them before the others go on trial; and Van Houten wasn't along on the night of the Tate murders. If we give deals to Atkins and Kasabian, who are we going to prosecute for the five Tate killings? Just Charlie? The people of this city won't tolerate that.'

According to Fleischman, Linda was anxious to testify. He had urged her to fight extradition; she'd gone against his advice and come back to California because she wanted to tell the whole story.

'O.K., what can she testify to? According to Susan, Linda never entered either the Tate or LaBianca residences. As far as we know, she wasn't an eyewitness to any of the murders, with the possible exception of Steven Parent. More important, as long as we have Susan, Linda's testimony would be valueless to us, since Susan and Linda are both accomplices. As you well know, the law is clear on this: the testimony of one accomplice can't be used to corroborate the testimony of another accomplice. What we really need, more than anything else, is corroboration.'

This was one of our biggest problems. In a sense it didn't matter who ended up as our star witness; without corroboration our case would be lost as a matter of law. We not only had to find corroboration against *each* of the defendants, that corroborating evidence had to be completely independent of the accomplice's testimony.

Aaron had seen Linda briefly, when she was booked into Sybil Brand. I'd never seen her. For all I knew, she was probably just as freaky as Sadie Mae Glutz.

'Now if Susan bolts back to Charlie,' I told Aaron, 'and we're left without a major witness for the trial – as well we might be – then we can talk about a deal for Linda. In fact, if that happens, Linda may be our only hope.'

When the grand jury reconvened on Monday, we moved quickly through the remaining testimony. Sergeant Michael McGann described what he had found at 10050 Cielo Drive on the morning of August 9, 1969. Sergeant Frank Escalante testified to having rolled Charles Watson's prints on April 23, 1969, when he was arrested on a drug charge; Jerrome Boen of SID described how he lifted the latent from the front door of the Tate residence; and Harold Dolan, also of SID, testified to having compared it to the Watson exemplar, finding eighteen points of identity, eight more than LAPD requires for a positive identification. Sergeant William Lee testified regarding the pieces of gun grip and the .22 caliber bullets. Edward Lomax of Hi Standard matched the grips with his firm's .22 caliber Longhorn revolver, and gave statistics indicating that the gun itself, because of its low production figures, was 'rather unique'. Gregg Jakobson told of touting Manson to Melcher. Granado testified regarding the rope, the blood on the gun grips, and his discovery of the Buck knife.

It was for the most part highly technical testimony, and the appearance of Daniel DeCarlo provided a respite, as well as more than a little local color.

Aaron asked Danny: 'Did you have any particular reason for staying at the ranch?'

A. 'Lots of pretty girls up there.'

How did he get along with particular girls – for example, Katie?

A. 'We talked, that is about it, but I never did nothing. You know, I never snatched her up or anything.'

Q. 'And is your motorcycle club the kind that goes into a town and scares everybody?'

A. 'No, that only happens in the movies.'

DeCarlo's appearance, however, was intended for more than comic relief. He testified that Manson, Watson, and others, including himself, target-practiced with a .22 caliber Buntline revolver at Spahn. He said that he had last seen the gun 'maybe a week, week and a half' before the sixteenth of August, and never after that. DeCarlo also recalled how he and Charlie had bought the three-strand nylon rope (which, being an ex-Coast Guardsman, he called 'line') at the Jack Frost store in Santa Monica in June 1969, and, shown the rope found at Cielo, said it was 'identical'.

After Susan Atkins, the outlaw motorcyclist looked almost like a model citizen.

Of the five girls brought down from Independence, Catherine Share, aka Gypsy, refused to testify, and we had not called Leslie Van Houten, since we were now aware that she was one of the LaBianca killers. The three remaining – Dianne Lake, aka Snake; Nancy Pitman, aka Brenda; and Ruth Ann Moorehouse, aka Ouisch – all denied any knowledge of the murders.

I'd anticipated this. However, I had another reason for calling them. If they appeared as defense witnesses when we went to trial, any discrepancy between what they told the grand jury and the trial jury would give me a prior inconsistent statement with which to impeach their testimony.

At 4.17 P.M. the Los Angeles County grand jury began their deliberations. Exactly twenty minutes later they returned the following indictments: Leslie Van Houten, two counts of murder and one count of conspiracy to commit murder; Charles Manson, Charles Watson, Patricia Krenwinkel, Susan Atkins, and Linda Kasabian, seven counts of murder and one count of conspiracy to commit murder.

We'd got the indictments. And that was about all we had.

December 9–12, 1969

Neither Aaron nor I logged the calls we received, but it would be a safe guess that we were getting upward of a hundred a day, to most of which our only response was 'no comment'. The press was frantic. Although the indictments had been made public, the grand jury transcript itself had been 'sealed'; it would remain secret until a week to ten days after the last defendant was arraigned. It was rumored that one magazine offered $10,000 just to look at a copy.

Each day brought new developments. Thus far, although sheriff's deputies had dug up a sizable portion of Spahn Ranch, no trace of the remains of Donald 'Shorty' Shea had been found. However, acting on the information supplied by Mary Brunner, LASO searched the neighborhood adjacent to 20910 Gresham Street, Canoga Park, and found, just around the corner from the former Family residence, Shea's 1962 Mercury. It was dirt-covered and rain-streaked, apparently having been abandoned some months before. Inside the vehicle was a footlocker containing Shea's personal effects; dusting it, LASO found a set of palm prints, which were later matched to Family member Bruce Davis. Shea's cowboy boots were also in the car. They were caked with dried blood.

Independence, California, 4 P.M., December 9, Charles Milles Manson, aka Jesus Christ, age 35, address transient, occupation musician, was charged with the Tate-LaBianca murders. Sartuchi and Gutierrez were bringing him to Los Angeles.

We scheduled Manson's arraignment on a different date than that of the other defendants, fearing that if Atkins and Manson met in the courtroom he'd persuade her to repudiate her testimony. For Susan, I realized, the Family was her only family. I understood now why Caballero felt it was only a matter of time before she returned to the fold.

On December 10, Susan Atkins, Linda Kasabian, and Leslie Van Houten were brought before Judge William Keene. All three requested and were granted continuances before entering pleas.

This was the first time I had seen Kasabian. She was short, about five feet one, with long, dark-blond hair and green eyes, and was quite obviously pregnant. She looked older than twenty. In contrast to Susan and Leslie, who smiled and giggled through most of the proceedings, Linda seemed on the edge of tears.

Following the grand jury hearing, Judge Keene had called Aaron and me into chambers. At that time he'd told us that since the DA's Office was not discussing the case with the press, he saw no need to issue a 'publicity order' (or, as it is most often called, a 'gag order') covering the case. However, owing to the incredible amount of pre-trial publicity Judge Keene, without consulting our office, now went ahead and issued a detailed publicity order. In essence, it forbade anyone connected with the case – prosecutors, defense attorneys, police officers, witnesses, and so forth – to discuss the evidence with any representative of the media.

Though unknown to me at the time, the order was already too late to prevent an inside account of the murders from making headlines around the world. The previous evening, attorney Richard Caballero, acting on the basis of an agreement with Susan Atkins, had arranged the sale of the publication rights to her story.

Call from LAPD. Charles Koenig, an attendant at the Standard service station at 12881 Ensenada Boulevard in Sylmar, was cleaning the women's rest room when he noticed the toilet was running. Lifting the lid off the tank, he found, on top of the mechanism, damp but above the waterline, a woman's wallet. He'd checked the driver's license and credit cards, saw the name 'Rosemary LaBianca', and immediately called LAPD.

SID was checking the wallet for prints but, because of both the material and the dampness, they doubted they'd find any.

Just the discovery of the wallet was enough for me, for it provided another piece of independent evidence supporting Susan Atkins' story. Apparently the wallet had been there, undiscovered, since Linda Kasabian placed it there the night of the LaBianca murders, exactly four months ago.

At 11 A.M. on December 11 buckskin-clad Charles Manson was brought before Judge William Keene. The courtroom was so packed with reporters and spectators you couldn't have squeezed another person in with a shoehorn. Since Manson lacked funds to hire an attorney, Keene appointed Paul Fitzgerald of the Public Defender's Office to represent him. I'd come up against Paul before on several jury trials and knew he had a good reputation in his office. Manson was arraigned, and a postponement granted until December 22 for the entering of his plea.

In Independence, Sandra Good had told me that once, in the desert, Charlie had picked up a dead bird, breathed on it, and the bird had flown away. Sure, Sandy, sure, I replied. Since then I'd heard a great deal about Manson's alleged 'powers'; Susan Atkins, for example, felt he could see and hear everything she did or said.

Midway through the arraignment I looked at my watch. It had stopped. Odd. It was the first time I could remember that happening. Then I noticed that Manson was staring at me, a slight grin on his face.

It was, I told myself, simply a coincidence.

Following the arraignment, Paul Fitzgerald told Ron Einstoss, veteran crime reporter for the Los Angeles *Times*: 'There's no case against Manson and these defendants. All the prosecution has are two fingerprints and Vince Bugliosi.'

Fitzgerald was not the only one who felt we had no case. The consensus in the DA's Office and the Los Angeles legal community – which I picked up from many sources, usually with some such remark as 'Too bad you had to get involved in such a bummer' – was that the case against Manson and most of the other defendants would be thrown out on an 1118 motion.

Under section 1118.1 of the California Penal Code, if at the end of the People's case the court feels the prosecution has failed to put on enough evidence to sustain a conviction on appeal, the judge is empowered to acquit the defendants. They aren't even required to put on a defense to the charges.

Such talk, in addition to the national exposure that would be accorded any defense attorney connected with the case, was, I suspected, the reason Manson was having so many visitors at the Los Angeles County Jail. As one deputy sheriff put it, 'It's like a bar association convention over here.' (Between December 11, 1969, and January 21, 1970, Manson had 237 separate visits, 139 of which were by one or more attorneys.) Among the first lawyers to call on him were Ira Reiner, Daye Shinn, and Ronald Hughes, none of whom I knew at that time, though I'd know all three much better before the trial ended.

December 14, 1969

SUSAN ATKINS' STORY OF 2 NIGHTS OF MURDER

The story in Sunday's Los Angeles *Times* covered nearly three pages. Though obviously edited and rewritten, with some additional material on her childhood, it was essentially the same story Susan Atkins had related on the tape made in Caballero's office.

Not until the trial itself would the story-behind-the-story come out. The following is reconstructed from the courtroom testimony. I can make no claim as to its accuracy, only that this is what the various participants testified under oath.

Before the imposition of the gag order, Lawrence Schiller, a self-described Hollywood 'journalist and communicator', approached Richard Caballero and his law associate, Paul Caruso, asking if they would be interested in selling Susan Atkins' first-person account of the murders. After consulting with Susan, an agreement was reached and a 'ghost' – Los Angeles *Times* reporter Jerry Cohen, on leave of absence from the paper – was hired to write the account.* Using as his main source the December 1 tape, Cohen completed the story in just two days, while locked in a room in Schiller's home. To make sure he maintained 'exclusivity', Schiller saw that Cohen had neither carbon paper

---

* Schiller, though listed as co-author, not only didn't write the story, he never even met Susan Atkins.

According to evidence introduced during the trial, the terms of the agreement were: 25 percent to Schiller; of the remaining 75 percent, 60 percent to Susan Atkins, 40 percent to her attorneys.

nor access to a phone, and he destroyed all but the finished draft.

According to their subsequent courtroom testimony, Caballero and Caruso understood that initially the story was to appear in Europe only, with a publication date of Sunday, December 14.

According to Schiller, on December 12 he made three Xerox copies of the manuscript: one was given to Caballero; one to a German editor who had bought the rights for his magazine and who translated it as he flew back to Germany; and the third flown by special courier to the London *News of the World,* which had paid $40,000 for exclusive English rights. Schiller put the original in his own safe.

The following day, Saturday, December 13, Schiller learned (1) that the Los Angeles *Times* also had a Xerox copy of the manuscript, and (2) that the *Times* intended to run it in full the following day. Screaming copyright infringement, Schiller tried, unsuccessfully, to stop publication.

Exactly how the Los Angeles *Times* obtained the story remains unknown. During the trial Caballero more than hinted that he suspected Schiller, while Schiller attempted to put the blame on Caballero.

Whatever the ethics of the whole matter, the Atkins story created immense problems which would plague both the defense and the prosecution throughout the trial. The story was not only reprinted in newspapers all over the world; even before the trial started it appeared as a paperback book, titled *The Killing of Sharon Tate.** It was felt by some that the Atkins revelations would make it impossible for the defendants to obtain a fair trial. Although neither Aaron nor I nor, eventually, the trial judge, shared this view, we were all too aware, from the moment the story broke, that finding twelve jurors who hadn't read or heard of the account, and then keeping any mention of it out of the courtroom itself, would be a difficult task.

Few of the Angelenos who read Susan Atkins' story in the *Times* that Sunday were aware that she was at the same time

* Published by New American Library, which is owned by the Times Mirror Company, which also owns the Los Angeles *Times.*

riding around Los Angeles and its environs in a nondescript, though heavily guarded, automobile. We were hoping she would point out the places where the clothing and weapons had been discarded following the Tate murders.

On returning to Sybil Brand that night, Susan wrote a letter to a former cellmate, Kitt Fletcher, in which she told of her excursion: 'My attorney is great. He has had me out to his office twice and today he got me out for 7 hours. We went riding in a car up to the Tate mansion and through the canyons. The LAPD wanted me to see if I could recall where certain things happened. It was such a beautiful day my memory vanished.'

As in most jails, the mail at Sybil Brand was censored, both letters received and letters sent being read by the authorities. Those which contained what appeared to be incriminating statements were photocopied and given to our office. Under existing case law, this could be done without violating a prisoner's constitutional rights.

Susan/Sadie was in a letter-writing mood. Several of her letters contained damaging admissions which, unlike her grand jury testimony, could be used against her in the trial, if we chose to do so. A 'kite'* Susan sent Ronnie Howard read as follows:

I can see your side of this clearly. Nor am I mad at you. I am hurt in a way only I understand. I blame no one but myself for even saying anything to anybody about it ... Yes, I wanted the world to know M. It sure looks like they do now. There was a so called motive behind all this. It was to instill fear into the pigs and to bring on judgment day which is here now for all.

In the word kill, the only thing that dies is the ego. All ego must die anyway, it is written. Yes, it could have been your house, it could have been my fathers house also. In killing someone phisally (*sic*) you are only releasing the soul. Life has no boundris (*sic*) and death is only an illusion. If you can believe in the second coming of Crist (*sic*), M is he who has come to save ... Maybe this will help you to understand ... I did not admit to being in the 2nd house because I was not in the 2nd house.

I went before the grand jury because my attorney said your testimony was enough to convict me and all the others. He also said it was

* In jail parlance a kite is any illegal communication.

my only chance to save myself. Then I was out to save myself. I have gone through some changes since then . . . I know now it has all been perfect. Those people died not out of hate or anything ugly. I am not going to defend our beliefs. I am just telling you the way it is . . . As I write to you I feel more at ease inside. When I first heard you were the informer I wanted to slit your throat. Then I snapped that I was the real informer and it was my throat I wanted to cut. Well that's all over with now as I let the past die away from my mind. You know it will all turn out ok in the end anyway, M or no M, Sadie or no Sadie, love will still run forever. I am giving up me to become that love a little more every day . . .

Quoting a lyric from one of Manson's songs, Susan ended the letter: 'Cease to exist, just come and say you love me. As I say I love you or I should say I love Me (my love) in you.

'I hope now you understand a little more. If not, ask.'

Ronnie, who was now living in deathly fear of Susan, turned the letter over to her attorney, Wesley Russell, who passed it on to our office. It would prove far more damaging to Susan Atkins than the confession which appeared in the Los Angeles *Times*.

December 15–25, 1969

When on a case, I made it a habit periodically to scour LAPD's 'tubs', or files, often finding something useful to my case whose evidentiary value wasn't apparent to the police.

In going through the LaBianca tubs, I made two discoveries. The first was the Al Springer interview. Only one page had been transcribed, the one on which Springer related how Manson told him, 'We knocked off five of them just the other night.' I took the tape and had it transcribed, adding 'Interview Al Springer' to my own already lengthy list of Things to Do. Though, because of *Aranda*, Manson's confession couldn't be used against him at the trial, it was quite possible he had made other admissions that could.

The second find was a photocopy of a letter mailed to Manson while he was in jail in Independence. The content was innocuous; however, it was signed 'Harold'. Susan Atkins had told the grand jury that a guy named 'Harold' had been living at the house next door to the LaBianca residence when she, Charlie, and a number of others had gone there for an LSD party a year or so earlier. I had a feeling this might be the same person, and made another note for the LaBianca detectives: 'Find Harold.' This shouldn't be too difficult, as he had given an address in Sherman Oaks and two telephone numbers.

In her printed 'confession' Susan Atkins had described how, after changing clothes in the car, the Tate killers drove 'along a steep embankment', with a mountain on one side, a ravine on the other. 'We stopped and Linda got out of the car and threw all the clothes, all drippy with blood . . . over the side.'

With the *Times* story on the seat beside them, a TV camera

crew from Channel 7, KACB-TV, attempted to re-create the scene. Driving from the gate at 10050 Cielo Drive, they proceeded down Benedict Canyon, all but the driver changing clothes on the way. It took them six minutes and twenty seconds – during which they later admitted they felt more than a little foolish – to complete their change of apparel. At the first spot where they could pull off the road – a wide shoulder opposite 2901 Benedict Canyon Road – they stopped and got out.

Mountain on one side, ravine on the other. Newscaster Al Wiman looked down the steep embankment and, pointing to some dark objects about fifty feet down, said, laughing, 'Looks like clothing down there.' King Baggot, the cameraman, and Eddie Baker, the sound man, looked too and had to agree.

It was just too easy – if the clothing was in plain view from the road, surely LAPD would have found it by now. Still, they decided to check it out. They were about to descend the slope when the car radio buzzed: they were needed on another story.

While on the other assignment they couldn't get those dark objects out of mind. About 3 P.M. they returned to the spot. Baker went down first, followed by Baggot. They found three sets of clothing: one pair of black trousers, two pairs of blue denim pants, two black T-shirts, one dark velour turtleneck, and one white T-shirt which was spotted with some substance that looked like dried blood. Some of the clothing was partly covered by dirt slides; all of it, however, was in an area about twelve feet square, as if thrown there in one bundle.

They yelled the news up to Wiman, who called LAPD. By the time McGann and three other detectives arrived, shortly before five, it was beginning to get dark, so the TV crew set up artificial lighting. While the detectives placed the clothing in plastic bags, Baggot filmed the incident.

On learning of the find, I asked the Tate detectives to conduct a thorough search of the area, to see if they could locate any of the weapons. I had to make the request not once but many, many times. In the interim, a week after the initial discovery, Baggot and Baker returned to the scene and conducted their own search, finding a knife. It was an old, badly rusted kitchen knife, which, because of its dimensions and dull edge, was eliminated as one of the murder weapons, but it was in plain view less than a hundred feet from where the clothing had been found.

That a TV crew had found the clothing was an embarrassment to LAPD. Faces at Parker Center, however, would be far redder before the end of the following day.

On Tuesday, December 16, Susan Atkins appeared before Judge Keene and pleaded not guilty to all eight counts of the indictment. Keene set a trial date of February 9, 1970. Since this was the same date set for the retrial of Bobby Beausoleil, I was taken off the Beausoleil-Hinman case, and it was assigned to Deputy DA Burton Katz. I wasn't unhappy about this; I had more than enough to do on Tate-LaBianca.

That Tuesday was, for Bernard Weiss, a most trying day.

Weiss hadn't read Susan Atkins' story when it appeared in the Los Angeles *Times* but a colleague at work had, and he mentioned to Weiss that a .22 caliber revolver had definitely been used in the Tate murders. Odd coincidence, wasn't it, his boy finding a similar type gun?

Weiss thought it might be something more than that. After all, his son had found the revolver on September 1, a little over two weeks after the Tate murders; they lived not far from the Tate residence; and the road right above the hill where Steven had found the gun was Beverly Glen. That morning Weiss called the Valley Services Division of LAPD in Van Nuys and told them he thought they might have the missing Tate gun. Van Nuys referred him to LAPD Homicide at Parker Center.

Weiss called there about noon, and repeated his story. He observed that the gun his son had found had a broken trigger guard and part of the wooden grip was missing. 'Well, it sounds enough like the gun,' the detective told him. 'We'll check it out.'

Weiss anticipated that the detective would call him back; he didn't. That evening on arriving home, Weiss read the Atkins story. It convinced him. About 6 P.M. he again called LAPD Homicide. The officer he'd talked to at noon was out, so he had to repeat the story a third time. This officer told him, 'We don't keep guns that long. We throw them in the ocean after a while.' Weiss said, 'I can't believe you'd throw away what could be the single most important piece of evidence in the Tate case.' 'Listen, mister,' the officer replied, 'we can't check out every citizen report on every gun we find. Thousands of guns are found every year.' The discussion became an argument, and they hung up on each other.

Weiss then called one of his neighbors, Clete Roberts, a newscaster for Channel 2, and told Roberts the story. Roberts in turn called someone at LAPD.

Although it remains unclear which of the five calls triggered a response, at least one did. At 10 P.M. – three and a half months after Weiss gave the gun to officer Watson – Sergeants Calkins and McGann drove over to Van Nuys and picked up the .22 caliber Hi Standard Longhorn revolver.

POLICE FIND GUN BELIEVED USED
IN SLAYING OF 3 TATE VICTIMS

News of the find 'leaked' to the Los Angeles *Times* four days later. It was a somewhat selective leak. There were no details as to when or where the gun was found, or by whom, the implication being that it had been discovered by LAPD sometime after the clothing, and in the same general area.

The cylinder contained two live rounds and seven empty shell casings. This tallied perfectly with the original autopsy reports, which stated that Sebring and Frykowski had each been shot once, and Parent five times. There was only one problem: I'd already discovered the autopsy reports were in error.

After Susan Atkins testified that Tex Watson shot Parent four (not five) times, I'd asked Coroner Noguchi to re-examine the Parent autopsy photos. When he did, he found that two of the wounds had been made by the same bullet. This reduced the number of times Parent was shot to four; it also left one bullet unaccounted for.

This time I had Noguchi re-examine *all* the autopsy photos. In doing so, he found that Frykowski had been shot not once but twice, the coroners performing the autopsy having overlooked a gunshot wound in the left leg. So the count was again consistent, even if the reports were not.

Bill Lee of SID compared the three pieces of gun grip with the butt of the revolver: a perfect fit. Joe Granado tested some brown spots on the barrel: blood, human, same type and subtype as Jay Sebring's. After test-firing the gun, Lee placed the test bullets and the Tate bullets under a comparison microscope. Three of the four bullets recovered after the Tate murders were either too fragmented or battered for the stria to be matched up. With the fourth, the Sebring bullet, he made a positive ID. There was no doubt whatsoever, he told me, that it had been fired from the .22 Longhorn.

One very important step remained: linking the gun to Charles Manson. I asked the Tate detectives to show it to DeCarlo, to determine if it was the same gun with which Manson and the other men used to target-practice at Spahn. I also requested as complete a history of the gun as they could manage, from the day it was manufactured by Hi Standard to the day it was found by Steven Weiss.

It was decided that there was insufficient evidence to convict either Gypsy or Brenda, and the two hard-core Manson Family members were released from custody. Although Brenda returned to her parents for a short time, both soon rejoined Squeaky, Sandy, and the other Family members at Spahn, lonely George having weakened and let them move back to the ranch.

Manson's frequent court appearances gave me opportunities to study him. Though he'd had little formal schooling, he was fairly articulate, and definitely bright. He picked up little nuances, seemed to consider all the hidden sides of a question before answering. His moods were mercurial, his facial expressions chameleonlike. Underneath, however, there was a strange intensity. You felt it even when he was joking, which, despite the seriousness of the charges, was often. He frequently played to the always packed courtroom, not only to the Family faithful but to the press and spectators as well. Spotting a pretty girl, he'd often smile or wink. Usually they appeared more flattered than offended.

Though their responses surprised me, they shouldn't have. I'd already heard that Manson was receiving a large volume of mail, including many 'love letters', the majority of which were from young girls who wanted to join the Family.

On December 17, Manson appeared before Judge Keene and asked to have the Public Defender dismissed. He wanted to represent himself, he said.

Judge Keene told Manson that he was not convinced that he was competent to represent himself, or, in legal jargon, to proceed 'in pro per' (in propria persona).

MANSON. 'Your Honor, there is no way I can give up my voice in this matter. If I can't speak, then our whole thing is done. If I can't speak in my own defense and converse freely in this courtroom, then it ties my hands behind my back, and if I have no voice, then there is no sense in having a defense.'

Keene agreed to reconsider Manson's motion on the twenty-second.

Manson's insistence that only he could speak for himself, as well as his obvious enjoyment at being in the spotlight, led to one conclusion: when the time came, he probably wouldn't be able to resist taking the stand.

I began keeping a notebook of questions I intended to ask him on cross-examination. Before long there was a second notebook, and a third.

On the nineteenth Leslie Van Houten also asked to have her present attorney, Donald Barnett, dismissed. Keene granted the motion and appointed Marvin Part to be Miss Van Houten's attorney of record.

Only later would we learn what was happening behind the scenes. Manson had set up his own communications network. Whenever he heard that an attorney for one of the girls had initiated a move on behalf of his client which could conceivably run counter to Manson's own defense, within days that attorney would be removed from the case. Barnett had wanted a psychiatrist to examine Leslie. Learning of this, Manson vetoed the idea, and when the psychiatrist appeared at Sybil Brand, Leslie refused to see him. Her request for Barnett's dismissal came immediately after.

Manson's goal: to run the entire defense himself. In court as well as out, Charlie intended to retain complete control of the Family.

Manson wanted to represent himself, he told the court, because 'lawyers play with people, and I am a person and I don't want to be played with in this matter'. 'I am in a difficult position,' he continued. 'The news media has already executed and buried me . . . If anyone is hypnotized, the people are hypnotized by the lies being told to them . . . There is no attorney in the world who can represent me as a person. I have to do it myself.'

Judge Keene had a suggestion. He would arrange for an experienced attorney to confer with him. Unlike other attorneys to whom Manson had talked, this attorney would have no interest in representing him. His function would be solely to discuss with him the legal issues, and the possible dangers, of defending himself. Manson accepted the offer and, after court, Keene arranged for Joseph Ball, a former president of the State Bar Association and former senior counsel to the Warren Commission, to meet with Manson.

Manson talked to Ball and found him 'a very nice gentleman', he told Judge Keene on the twenty-fourth. 'Mr Ball probably understands maybe everything there is to know about law, but he doesn't understand the generation gap; he doesn't understand free love society; he doesn't understand people who are trying to get out from underneath all of this . . .'

Ball, in turn, found Manson 'an able, intelligent young man, quiet-spoken and mild-mannered . . .' Although he had attempted to persuade him, without success, that he could benefit

247

from the services of a skilled lawyer, Ball was obviously impressed with Manson. 'We went over different problems of law, and I found he had a ready understanding ... Remarkable understanding. As a matter of fact, he has a very fine brain. I complimented him on the fact. I think I told you that he had a high IQ. Must have, to be able to converse as he did.' Manson 'is not resentful against society', Ball said. 'And he feels that if he goes to trial and he is able to permit jurors and the Court to hear him and see him, they will realize he is not the kind of man who would perpetrate horrible crimes.'

After Ball had finished, Judge Keene questioned Manson for more than an hour about his knowledge of courtroom procedure, and the possible penalties for the crimes with which he was charged, throughout almost begging him to reconsider his decision to defend himself.

MANSON. 'For all my life, as long as I can remember, I've taken your advice. Your faces have changed, but it's the same court, the same structure ... All my life I've been put in little slots, Your Honor. And I went along with it ... I have no alternative but to fight you back any way I know because you and the District Attorney and all the attorneys I have ever met are all on the same side. The police are on the same side and the newspapers are on the same side and it's all pointed against me, personally... No. I haven't changed my mind.'

THE COURT. 'Mr Manson, I am imploring you not to take this step; I am imploring you to either name your own attorney, or, if you are unable to do so, to permit the Court to name one for you.'

Manson's mind was made up, however, and Judge Keene finally concluded: 'It is, in this Court's opinion, a sad and tragic mistake that you are making by taking this course of action, but I can't talk you out of it ... Mr Manson, you are your own lawyer.'

It was Christmas Eve. I worked until 2 A.M., then took the next day off.

December 26–31, 1969

A call from LAPD. A cook at the Brentwood Country Club says that the chief steward there, Rudolf Weber, was the man in front of whose house the Tate killers stopped to hose off about 1 A.M. on August 9.

Bringing along a police photographer to take photos of the area, Calkins and I went to see Weber at his home at 9870 Portola Drive, a side street just off Benedict Canyon Drive, less than two miles from the Tate residence. As I listened to Weber's story, I knew he was going to be a good witness. He had an excellent memory, told exactly what he remembered, didn't try to fill in what he did not. He was unable to make a positive identification from the large batch of photos I showed him, but his general description fitted: all four were young (Watson, Atkins, Krenwinkel, and Kasabian were all in their early twenties), the man was tall (Watson was six feet one), and one of the girls was short (Kasabian was five feet one). His description of the car – which had never appeared in the press – was accurate down to the faded paint around the license plates. How was it he could recall such a detail about the car but not their faces? Very simple: when he followed the four down to the car, he turned the flashlight on the license plate; when he saw them on the street, near the hose, they were in the dark.

Weber had a surprise – a big one. Following the incident, thinking perhaps the four people had committed a burglary in the area, he had written down the license number of the vehicle. He had since thrown the piece of paper away – my heart sank – but he still remembered the number. It was GYY 435.

How in the world could he remember that? I asked him. In his job as steward he had to remember numbers, he replied.

Anticipating that this point might be brought up by the defense, I asked Weber if he had read the Atkins story. He said he hadn't.

On returning to my office, I checked the impound report on John Swartz's car: 1959 Ford 4 Dr, Lic. # GYY 435.'

When I interviewed Swartz, the former Spahn ranch hand told me that Manson and his girls often borrowed the car; in fact, he had taken the back seat out so they could fit the big boxes in when they went on their 'garbage runs'. With the exception of one particular night, they always asked his permission before taking the car.

What night was that? Well, he wasn't exactly sure of the date, but it was a week, two weeks before the raid. What happened that particular night? Well, he'd already gone to bed in his trailer when he heard his car start up. He got up and looked out the window just in time to see the tail-lights pulling away. Any idea what time that was? Well, he usually went to bed around ten or thereabouts, so it was after that. When he woke up the next morning, Swartz said, the car was back. He'd asked Charlie why they'd taken the car without asking, and Charlie had told him that he hadn't wanted to wake him up.

Any other nights during this same period when Manson borrowed the car? I inquired. Yeah, one other night Charlie, the girls, and some other guys – he was unable to remember which girls and guys – said they were going downtown to play some music.

Swartz was unable to date this particular night except that it was around the same time they took the car without permission. Before or after? He couldn't remember. Consecutive nights? Couldn't remember that either.

I asked Swartz if he had ever belonged to the Family. '*Never*,' he very emphatically replied. One time, after the raid, and after Shorty had dropped from sight, he and Manson had an argument, Swartz said. Charlie had told him, 'I could kill you any time. I could come into your sleeping quarters any time.' After that Swartz quit his job at Spahn, where he had been working off and on since 1963, and got a job at another ranch.

What did he know about Shorty's disappearance? Well, a week or two after the raid Shorty just wasn't around any more. He'd asked Charlie if he knew where he was, and Charlie had told him, 'He's gone to San Francisco about a job. I told him about a job there.' He didn't exactly feel confident with that explanation, he said, not after having noticed that Bill Vance and Danny DeCarlo each had one of Shorty's .45 caliber pistols.

Shorty would never willingly part with those matched pistols, Swartz said, no matter how hard up he was.

Under the Constitution of the United States, extradition is mandatory, not discretionary. When a state has a valid and duly executed indictment – as we did in the case of Charles 'Tex' Watson – there is no legitimate reason why the accused shouldn't be extradited forthwith.

Certain powers in Collin County, Texas, felt otherwise. Bill Boyd, Watson's attorney, told the press he'd fight to keep his client in Texas if it meant going all the way to the United States Supreme Court.

Bill Boyd's father, Roland Boyd, was a powerful southern politician of the Sam Rayburn school. He was also the campaign manager of a candidate who was running for attorney general of Texas. It was his candidate, Judge David Brown, who heard the Watson extradition request, and granted delay after delay after delay to young Boyd's client.

Bill Boyd was himself an aspiring politician. Tom Ryan, the local DA, told a Los Angeles *Times* reporter: 'I've heard it said that Bill wants to be President of the United States. And after that he wants to be God.'

Meanwhile, Tex apparently wasn't suffering unduly. We heard, from various sources, that his one-man cell was comfortably furnished, that he had his own record player and records. His vegetarian meals were cooked by his mother. He also wore his own clothing, which she laundered. And he was not completely lacking company, his cell adjoining that occupied by the female prisoners.

Though the extradition of Watson was proving difficult, there were indications that Katie Krenwinkel might decide to return voluntarily, on Manson's orders. Squeaky, acting as Charlie's liaison, had sent Krenwinkel a barrage of letters and telegrams, photocopies of which we received from the Mobile, Alabama, authorities: 'Together we stand . . . If you go extra is good . . .'

I also presumed that the togetherness referred to in each of the messages meant that Manson intended to conduct a joint, or umbrella, defense.

Since the Family had contacted Krenwinkel but, as far as we could determine, not Watson, I carried my conjecture a step further, guessing that when the case went to trial Manson and the girls would try to put the hat on Watson.

Presuming they would try to prove that Tex, not Charlie, was the mastermind behind the Tate-LaBianca murders, I began collecting every bit of evidence I could find on the Manson-Watson relationship, and the role each played in the Family.

When interrogated in Los Angeles by Gutierrez, 16-year-old Dianne Lake had been threatened with the gas chamber. And had said nothing. Inyo County Deputy DA Buck Gibbens and investigator Jack Gardiner tried kindness, something Dianne had known little of during her life.

Dianne's parents had 'turned hippy' while she was still a child. By age 13 she was a member of the Hog Farm commune, and had been introduced to group sex and LSD. When she joined Manson, just before her 14th birthday, it was with her parents' approval.

Apparently not finding Dianne submissive enough, Manson had, on various occasions: punched her in the mouth; kicked her across a room; hit her over the head with a chair leg; and whipped her with an electrical cord. Despite such treatment, she stayed. Which implies something tragic about the alternatives available to her.

After her return to Independence, Gibbens and Gardiner had a number of lengthy conversations with Dianne. They convinced her that other people did care about her. Gardiner's wife and children visited her regularly. Hesitantly at first, Dianne began telling the officers what she knew. And, contrary to what she had told the grand jury, she knew a great deal. Tex, for example, had admitted to her that he'd stabbed Sharon Tate. He did it, he told her, because Charlie had ordered the killings.

On December 30, Sartuchi and Nielsen interviewed Dianne in Independence. She told them that one morning, maybe a week or two weeks before the August 16 raid, Leslie had come into the back house at Spahn with a purse, a rope, and a bag of coins. She hid them under a blanket. When, a short time later, a man arrived and knocked on the door, Leslie hid herself. She told Dianne the man had given her a ride from Griffith Park and she didn't want him to see her.

The two LaBianca detectives exchanged looks. Griffith Park was not far from Waverly Drive.

After the man left, Leslie came out from under the blanket and Dianne helped her count the money. There was about eight dollars in change, in a plastic sack.

Because of Leno LaBianca's coin collection, the detectives were very interested in that bag of change.

Q. 'O.K., you say you helped Leslie count the money or coins. Did you see any coins in there from another country?'

A. 'Canada.'

Leslie then built a fire and burned the purse (Dianne recalled it as being brown leather), some credit cards (one was an oil company card), and the rope (it was about 4 feet long and 1 to 1½ inches in diameter). Then she took off her own clothing and burned it too. Had Dianne noticed any blood spots on the clothing? No.

Later, in late August or early September, while they were at Willow Springs, about ten miles from Barker Ranch, Leslie told Dianne that she had stabbed someone who was already dead. Was it a woman or a man? Leslie hadn't said.

Leslie also told Dianne that the murder had occurred someplace near Griffith Park, near Los Feliz; that someone had written something in blood on the refrigerator door, and that she, Leslie, then wiped everything so there would be no prints, even wiping things they hadn't touched. When they left, they took some food with them. What kind of food? A carton of chocolate milk.

Had Leslie said anything about the Tate murders? Leslie had told her she wasn't in on that.

Sartuchi attempted to get more details. The only other thing Dianne could recall was that there had been a big boat outside the house. But she couldn't remember whether Leslie had told her about the boat or whether she had read it in the paper. She did, however, remember Leslie describing it.

Prior to this, the only evidence we had linking Leslie Van Houten with the LaBianca murders was the testimony of Susan Atkins. Since Susan was an accomplice, this would not stand up in court without independent corroboration.

Dianne Lake supplied it.

There was a question, however, as to whether Dianne would be able to testify at the trial. She was obviously emotionally disturbed. She had occasional LSD flashbacks. She feared Manson, and she loved him. At times she thought he was inside her head. Shortly after the first of the year the Inyo County court arranged for her to be sent to Patton State Hospital, in part for treatment for her emotional problems, in part because the court didn't know what else to do with her.

Additions to my list of Things to Do: Check to see if any LaBianca credit cards are still missing. When doctors permit, interview Dianne; find out if anyone else present during backhouse incident or Willow Springs conversation. Check with Katsuyama to see if any of the LaBianca stab wounds were postmortem, i.e., inflicted after death. Ask Susan Struthers if her mother had a brown leather purse and if it is missing. Ask Susan and/or Frank Struthers if either Rosemary or Leno liked chocolate milk.

Tiny details, but they could be important.

Charles Manson was not without a sense of humor. While in the County Jail he had somehow managed to obtain an application for a Union Oil Company credit card. He filled it in, giving his correct name and jail address. He listed 'Spahn's Movie Ranch' as his previous residence, and gave George Spahn as a reference. As for his occupation, he put 'Evangelist'; type of business, 'Religious'; length of employment, '20 years'. He also wrote, in the blank for wife's first name, 'None', and gave as his number of dependents '16'.

The card was smuggled out of jail and mailed from Pasadena. Someone at Union Oil – obviously not a computer – recognized the name, and Charles Manson didn't get the two credit cards he'd requested.

Another characteristic I'd noticed while observing Manson in court was his cockiness. One possible reason for this was his new notoriety. At the beginning of December 1969 few had ever heard of Charles Manson. By the end of that month the killer had already upstaged his famous victims. An enthusiastic Family member was heard to brag, 'Charlie made the cover of *Life*!'

But it was something more. You got the feeling that, despite his verbal utterances, Manson was convinced that he was going to beat the rap.

He wasn't the only one to feel this. Leslie Van Houten wrote her parents that even if convicted she'd be out in seven years (in California a person given life imprisonment is eligible for parole in seven years), while Bobby Beausoleil wrote several of his girl friends that he expected to be acquitted in his new trial, after which he was going to start his own Family.

The problem, at year's end, was that there was a very good chance that at least Manson would be right.

'What if Manson demands an immediate trial?'

Aaron and I discussed this at length. A defendant has a constitutional right to a speedy trial and a statutory right to go to trial within sixty days after the return of the indictment. If Manson insisted on this, we were in deep trouble.

We needed more time, for two reasons. We still desperately

lacked evidence to corroborate the testimony of Susan Atkins, presuming – and it was a very big presumption – that she agreed to testify. And two of the defendants, Watson and Krenwinkel, were still out of state. They just happened to be the only two defendants against whom there was scientific evidence of guilt, i.e., the fingerprints at the Tate residence. If there was to be a joint trial, which we wanted, we needed at least one of the two sitting behind that defense table.

I suggested we bluff. Every time we were in court, we should indicate that we wanted to go to trial as quickly as possible. Our hope was that Manson would think this was bad, and start stalling himself.

It was a gamble. There was a very real possibility that Charlie might call our bluff, saying, with his strange little grin, 'O.K., let's go to trial right now.'

Part Four

The Search For
The Motive

The Bible, the Beatles,
and Helter Skelter

'If I'm looking for a motive, I'd look for something which
doesn't fit your habitual standard, with which you use to
work as police – something much more far out.'
> Roman Polanski to
> Lieutenant Earl Deemer

January 1970

Confidential Memo. From: Deputy DA Vincent Bugliosi. To: District Attorney Evelle Younger. Subject: Status of Tate & LaBianca cases.

The memo ran to thirteen pages, but the heart of it consisted of a single paragraph:

'Without Susan Atkins' testimony on the Tate case, the evidence against two out of the five defendants [Manson and Kasabian] is rather anemic. Without her testimony on the LaBianca case, the evidence against five out of the six defendants [everyone except Van Houten] is non-existent.'

That was it. Without Sadie, we still didn't have a case.

On January 2, I called a meeting of the Tate and LaBianca detectives, giving them a list of forty-two things that had to be done.

Many were repeat requests: Go to the areas where the clothing and the gun were found and search for knives. Has Granado been able to 'make' the boots we picked up in November with the bloody boot-heel print on the Tate walkway? SID must have something by now on the wire cutters, also the clothing the TV crew found. Where is the tape Inyo County Deputy Sheriff Ward made with the two miners, Crockett and Poston? Where are the reports on the Tate, LaBianca, and Spahn Ranch toll calls? Telephone company destroys its records after six months; hurry on this.

Many of the requests were elementary follow-up steps that I felt the detectives should have already done on their own, without our prompting: Get Atkins printing exemplar and compare it with PIG on the front door at Tate. Get same on defendants Van

Houten, Krenwinkel, and Watson and compare with printing at the LaBianca residence. Submit a complete report on the stolen credit cards involved in this case (we were hoping to find a sales slip on the rope or the Buck knives). DeCarlo said he was along when Manson purchased the three-strand nylon rope at the Jack Frost store in Santa Monica in June 1969: ask Frost employees if they sold such a rope; also show them the 'Family album' to see if they can recall Manson and/or DeCarlo. Also show photos of Manson, Atkins, Kasabian, and the others to employees of the Standard station in Sylmar where Rosemary LaBianca's wallet was found.

If it was any consolation to the police – and I'm sure it wasn't – my own list was much longer than theirs. It ranged from such simple items as a reminder to get the Beatles' album that contained the song 'Helter Skelter' to more than fifty names of potential witnesses I needed to interview. It also included such detailed specifics as: Obtain exact measurements of all LaBianca wounds – original officers failed to ask Deputy Medical Examiner Katsuyama for this – in order to determine dimensions of knives used.

The measurements of the LaBianca wounds were extremely important. If the wound patterns were consistent with those made by the LaBianca kitchen knives, then the logical inference was that the defendants had entered the residence unarmed, then killed the LaBiancas with their own knives. If Manson had intended to kill these people, the defense would surely ask, would he have sent in unarmed people to do the job?

Of even greater importance was another item which appeared on all the assignment lists: Get incidents – and witnesses who can testify to same – where Manson ordered or instructed *anyone* to do *anything*.

Put yourself in the jury box. Would you believe the prosecutor if he told you that a little runt out at Spahn Ranch sent some half dozen people, the majority of them young girls, out to murder for him, their victims not persons they knew and had a grudge against but complete strangers, including a pregnant woman, and that without argument they did it?

To convince a jury of this, I would have first to convince them of Manson's domination over the Family, and particularly over his co-defendants. A domination so total, so complete, that they would do anything he told them to do. Including murder.

As the defense attorneys requested discovery, I'd take them to my office and let them go through our files on the case. Since Manson was now acting as his own attorney, the files were also made available to him, the only difference being that they carted over to the County Jail and he examined them there. there. Eventually, by a court order, secretaries in our office photostated everything in our files, with a copy for each defense counsel.

Only two things were held back. I argued to the court, 'We would vehemently resist furnishing Mr Manson with addresses, and particularly telephone numbers, of prospective witnesses, Your Honor.' I also strongly opposed providing the defense with copies of the death photos. We had heard that a German magazine had a standing offer of $100,000 for them. I did not want the families of the victims to open a magazine and see the terrible butchery inflicted on their loved ones.

With only these two exceptions – the court ruling in our favor on both – the prosecution, by law, gave the defense anything they wanted and, discovery being a one-way street, they in turn gave us *nothing*. We couldn't even get a list of the witnesses they intended to call. I was still reading newspaper and magazine articles to pick up leads.

Even this wasn't as simple as it sounds. Many former associates of the Family were in fear of their lives. Several, including Dennis Wilson of the Beach Boys, had received death threats. Since few sources wished to be quoted by name, pseudonyms were often used in the articles. In several instances, I tracked down someone only to find a person I'd already interviewed.

On August 9, 1968 – exactly a year before the Tate murders – Gregg Jakobson had arranged a recording session for Manson at a studio in Van Nuys. I went there to listen to the tapes, which were now in the possession of Herb Weiser, a Hollywood attorney representing the studio.

My own admittedly unprofessional appraisal was that Manson was no worse than many performers in current vogue.* However, Charlie's musical ability was not my major concern. Both Atkins and DeCarlo had said that the words 'helter skelter' appeared in at least one of Manson's own songs. I'd asked both, 'Are you sure he wasn't just playing the Beatles' song "Helter Skelter"? No, each had replied; this was Charlie's own composition. If anywhere in his lyrics I could find 'helter skelter', 'pig', 'death to pigs', or 'rise', it would be strong circumstantial evidence.

No luck.

It looked, for a time, as if we'd have better luck with the Watson extradition. On January 5, following a hearing in Austin, Texas Secretary of State Martin Dies, Jr, ordered Watson returned to California. Boyd returned to McKinney and filed a writ of habeas corpus, asking that Dies' order be vacated. The writ was filed with Judge Brown. On January 16, Brown granted a thirty-day continuance on Boyd's request. Tex remained in Texas.

In Los Angeles, Linda Kasabian was arraigned on the sixth and pleaded 'not guilty'. That same day attorney Marvin Part requested that a court-appointed psychiatrist examine his client, Leslie Van Houten. Judge Keene appointed Dr Blake Skrdla, who was to make a confidential report to Part. Earlier Part had requested and received permission to interview Leslie on tape. Though the prosecution would neither hear the tape nor see the report, it was a fairly safe assumption that Part, like his predecessor Barnettt, was considering an insanity plea.

---

*A folk-song expert later listened to the tapes and found the songs 'extremely derivative'. From his notes: 'Somewhere along the line Manson has picked up a pretty good guitar beat. Nothing original about the music. But the lyrics are something else. They contain an amazing amount of hostility ('You'll get yours yet," etc.). This is rare in folk songs, except in the old murder ballads, but even there it is always past tense. In Manson's lyrics these are things that are *going to happen*. Very spooky. Overall judgment: a moderately talented amateur.'

We didn't have to wait very long for Manson's reaction.

On the nineteenth Leslie requested that Part be relieved as her attorney and Ira Reiner appointed instead.

Owing to the possibly sensitive nature of her testimony, Judge George M. Dell decided to hear the matter in chambers, outside the presence of the public and press.

Part opposed the substitution, arguing that Leslie Van Houten was mentally incapable of making a rational decision. 'This girl will do anything that Charles Manson or any member of this so-called Manson Family says ... This girl has no will of her own left ... Because of this hold that Charles Manson and the Family has over her, she doesn't care whether she is tried together and gets the gas chamber, she just wants to be with the Family.'

The appointment of Reiner, Part claimed, would constitute a conflict of interest, one that would definitely hurt Miss Van Houten.

Part told the court how the switch had come about. A week or so ago Squeaky had visited Leslie. Although Part was present, Squeaky had told her, '*We* think you ought to have another lawyer,' and had shown her Reiner's card. Leslie had replied, 'I'll do anything that Charlie wants me to do.' A few days later Leslie (1) refused to be examined by the psychiatrist, and (2) informed Part that he was no longer her attorney and that Reiner was.

Part wanted Judge Dell to listen to the tape he had made with Leslie. He was sure that, having heard it, the Court would realize that Leslie Van Houten was incapable of acting in her own best interests.

It was now obvious that Part felt a joint trial and an 'umbrella' defense would hurt his client. The other defendants were charged with seven murders, Leslie with only two. And the evidence against her was slight. 'To the best of my knowledge,' Part said, referring to the Dianne Lake statement which he had received through discovery, 'all she did was perhaps stab somebody who was already dead.'

Judge Dell then questioned Ira Reiner, who admitted that he had talked to Manson 'roughly a dozen times'. He also admitted that Manson was one of several people who had suggested he represent Leslie. He had never actually represented Manson, however, and he had only gone to see Miss Van Houten after receiving a written request from her.

Judge Dell questioned Leslie outside the presence of the two attorneys. She remained firm in her resolve: she wanted Reiner.

Part, literally, begged Judge Dell to listen to the tape he had made with Leslie. Part said, 'That girl is insane in a way that is almost science fiction.'

Judge Dell said he would rather not hear the tape. He was concerned with one issue only: whether Miss Van Houten's mental state was such that she could intelligently make a substitution of counsel. To determine this, he appointed three psychiatrists to listen to the tape and examine Leslie, their confidential report, on that single issue, to be made directly to him.

Manson himself appeared before Judge Dell on the seventeenth.

MANSON. 'I have a motion here – it's a strange motion – probably never been a motion like this ever before – '

THE COURT. 'Try me.'

After examining it, the judge had to agree: 'It certainly is an interesting document.'

'Charles Manson, also known as Jesus Christ, Prisoner', assisted by six other pro pers, who called themselves 'The Family of Infinite Soul, Inc.', had filed a habeas corpus motion on behalf of Manson-Christ, charging that the sheriff was depriving him of his spiritual, mental, and physical liberty, in an unconstitutional manner not in harmony with man's or God's law, and asking that he be released forthwith.

Judge Dell denied the motion.

MANSON. 'Your Honor, behind the big words and all the confusion and the robes you hide the truth.'

THE COURT. 'Not intentionally.'

MANSON. 'Like sometimes I wonder if you know what is going on.'

THE COURT. 'Sometimes I do too, Mr Manson. I admit there

is some self-doubt ... Yet we in the black robes do our thing, too.'

Manson requested a number of items – a tape recorder, unlimited telephone privileges, and so on – which he claimed both the Sheriff's Office and the DA's Office were denying him. Dell corrected him.

THE COURT. 'The prosecutor is willing to go further than the sheriff has, as a matter of fact.'

MANSON. 'Well, I was going to ask him if he would call the whole thing off. It would save a lot of trouble.'

THE COURT. 'Disappoint all these people? Never, Mr Manson.'

When Manson again appeared before Judge Dell, on the twenty-eighth, he was still complaining about the limitations of his pro per privileges. For example, he wanted to interview Robert Beausoleil, Linda Kasabian, and Sadie Mae Glutz, but their attorneys had denied permission. Judge Dell informed him they had that right.

MANSON. 'I got a message from Sadie. She told me that the District Attorney had made her say what she had said.'

Manson was playing to the press, certain that they would pick up the charge, and they did. It was the next best thing to calling Susan on the phone and telling her how to recant.

Aaron played out our bluff, stating that the People were prepared to go to trial.

Manson, to our relief, wanted more time.

Judge Dell assigned the case to Judge William Keene, and granted a continuance to February 9, at which time the trial date would be set.

Our relief was real. Not only was our case still weak, Aaron and I couldn't even agree on the motive.

The prosecution does not have the legal burden of proving motive. But motive is extremely important evidence. A jury wants to know why. Just as showing that a defendant has a motive for committing a crime is circumstantial evidence of guilt, so is the absence of motive circumstantial evidence of innocence.

In this case, even more than in most others, proving motive was important, since these murders appeared completely senseless. It was doubly important in Manson's case, since he was not present when the murders took place. If we could prove to the jury that Manson, and Manson alone, had a motive for these murders, then this would be very powerful circumstantial evidence that he also ordered them.

It wasn't that we lacked a motive. Though Aaron and LAPD disagreed with me, I felt we had one. It was just that it was almost unbelievably bizarre.

When I interviewed Susan Atkins on December 4, she told me, 'The whole thing was done to instill fear in the establishment and cause paranoia. Also to show the black man how to take over the white man.' This, she said, would be the start of 'Helter Skelter', which, when I questioned her before the grand jury the next day, she defined as 'the last war on the face of the earth. It would be all the wars that have ever been fought built one on top of the other . . .'

'There was a so called motive behind all this,' Susan wrote Ronnie Howard. 'It was to instill fear into the pigs and to bring on judgment day which is here now for all.'

Judgment Day, Armageddon, Helter Skelter – to Manson they were one and the same, a racial holocaust which would see the black man emerge triumphant. 'The karma is turning, it's blackie's turn to be on top.' Danny DeCarlo said Manson preached this incessantly. Even a near stranger such as biker Al Springer, who visited Spahn Ranch only a few times, told me he thought 'helter skelter' must be Charlie's 'pet words', he used them so often.

That Manson foresaw a war between the blacks and the whites was not fantastic. Many people believe that such a war may someday occur. What *was* fantastic was that he was convinced he could personally start that war himself – that by making it look as if blacks had murdered the seven Caucasian victims he could turn the white community against the black community.

The jury would never buy Helter Skelter, Aaron said, suggesting that we offer something they would understand. I told him it wouldn't take me two seconds to dump the whole Helter Skelter theory if he could find another motive in the evidence.

Aaron, however, was right. The jury would never accept Helter Skelter, as is. We were missing far too many bits and pieces, and one all-important link.

Presuming that Manson actually believed that he could start a race war with these acts, what would he, Charlie Manson, personally gain by it?

To this I had no answer. And without it the motive made no sense.

'Always think of the Now ... No time to look back ... No time to say how.' This rhyme was repeated in almost every letter Sandy, Squeaky, Gypsy, or Brenda sent to the defendants. Its meaning was obvious: Don't tell them anything.

Through a barrage of letters, telegrams, and attempted visits, the Manson girls tried to get Beausoleil, Atkins, and Kasabian to dump their present attorneys, repudiate any incriminating statements they may have made, and engage in a united defense.

Though Beausoleil agreed that 'the whole thing balances on whether the Family stays together in their heads & doesn't break up & start testifying against itself', he decided, 'I'm going to keep my present lawyer.'

Bobby Beausoleil had always been somewhat independent. Less handsome than 'pretty' (the girls had nicknamed him 'Cupid'), Beausoleil had had bit parts in several movies, written music, formed a rock group, and had his own harem, all before meeting Manson. Leslie, Gypsy, and Kitty had all lived with Bobby before joining Charlie.

Beausoleil requested that Squeaky and the others not visit him so often. They were taking up all his visiting time, when the person he really wanted to see was Kitty, who was expecting his child in less than a month.

Beausoleil wasn't the only one being pressured. Without Susan Atkins, the prosecution had no case against Manson, and Manson knew it. Family members called Richard Caballero at all hours of the day and night. When cajoling didn't work, they tried threats. Less because of their pressure than that of his own client, Caballero finally gave in and let some of the Manson girls – though not Manson himself – visit Susan.

It was, at best, a holding action. At any moment Susan could insist on seeing Charlie, and Caballero would be unable to prevent it. After Susan's story had appeared in the Los Angeles *Times*, little signs had appeared on the walls at Sybil Brand reading, 'SADIE GLUTZ IS A SNITCH.' This greatly upset Susan. And each time something like this happened, the scales seemed to tip a little more in Manson's favor.

Manson was also aware that if Susan Atkins refused to testify at the trial, our only hope lay with Linda Kasabian. After a time Linda's attorney, Gary Fleischman, refused to see Gypsy, so persistent had her visits become. If Linda didn't testify, Gypsy told him on numerous occasions, everyone would get off. Fleischman did take her along one time when he went to see his client. Gypsy told Linda – in the presence of several persons – that she should lie and say that on the night of the Tate-LaBianca murders she had never left Spahn Ranch but remained with her at the waterfall. Gypsy promised to back up her story.

Given a choice between Susan and Linda as the star witness for the prosecution, I much preferred Linda: she hadn't killed anyone. But in the rush to get the case to the grand jury, we'd made the deal with Susan and, like it or not, we were stuck with it. Unless Susan bolted.

Yet this posed its own problems. If Susan didn't testify, we'd need Linda, but without Susan's testimony we had no evidence against Linda, so what could we offer her? Fleischman wanted immunity for his client, yet from Linda's standpoint it would be better to be tried and acquitted than get immunity, testify against Manson and the others, and risk retribution by the Family.

We were very worried at this point. Exactly how worried is evidenced by a telephone call I made. After Manson had been indicted for the Tate-LaBianca murders, the Inyo county authorities had dropped the arson charges against him, though they had a strong case. I called Frank Fowles and asked him to refile the charges, which he did, on February 6. We were that afraid that Manson would be set free.

February 1970

That an accused mass murderer could emerge a countercultural
hero seemed inconceivable. But to some Charles Manson had
become a cause.

Just before she went underground, Bernadine Dohrn told
Students for a Democratic Society convention: 'Offing those rich
pigs with their own forks and knives, and then eating a meal in
the same room, far out! The Weathermen dig Charles Manson.'

The underground paper *Tuesday's Child*, which called itself
the Voice of the Yippies, blasted its competitor the Los Angeles
Free Press for giving too much publicity to Manson – then
spread his picture across the entire front page with a banner
naming him MAN OF THE YEAR.

The cover of the next issue had Manson on a cross.

Manson posters and sweat shirts appeared in psychedelic
shops, along with FREE MANSON buttons.

Gypsy and other spokesmen for the Family took to the late-
night radio talk shows to play Charlie songs and denounce the
prosecution for 'framing an innocent man'.

Stretching his pro per privileges to their utmost limits,
Manson himself granted a number of interviews to the underground press. He was also interviewed, by phone from the County
Jail, by several radio stations. And his visitor's list now included,
among the 'material witnesses', some familiar names.

'I fell in love with Charlie Manson the first time I saw his
cherub face and sparkling eyes on TV,' exclaimed Jerry Rubin.
On a speaking tour during a recess in the Chicago Seven trial,
Rubin visited Manson in jail, giving rise to the possibility that
Manson might be considering the use of disruptive tactics during
his own trial. According to Rubin, Charlie rapped for three

hours, telling him, among other things, 'Rubin, I am not of your world. I've spent all my life in prison. When I was a child I was an orphan and too ugly to be adopted. Now I am too beautiful to be set free.'

'His words and courage inspired us,' Rubin later wrote. 'Manson's soul is easy to touch because it lays quite bare on the surface.'*

Yet Charles Manson – revolutionary martyr was a difficult image to maintain. Rubin admitted being angered by Manson's 'incredible male chauvinism'. A reporter for the *Free Press* was startled to find Manson both anti-Jewish and anti-black. And when one interviewer tried to suggest that Manson was as much a political prisoner as Huey Newton, Charlie, obviously perplexed, asked, 'Who's he?'

As yet the pro-Mansonites appeared to be a small, though vocal minority. If the press and TV reports were correct, a majority of the young people whom the media had lumped together under the label 'hippies' disavowed Manson. Many stated that the things he espoused – such as violence – were directly contrary to their beliefs. And more than a few were bitter about the guilt by association. It was almost impossible to hitchhike any more, one youth told a New York *Times* reporter. 'If you're young, have a beard, or even long hair, motorists look at you as if you're a "kill crazy cultist", and jam the gas.'

The irony was that Manson never considered himself a hippie, equating their pacifism with weakness. If the Family members had to have a label, he told his followers, he much preferred calling them 'slippies', a term which, in the context of their creepy-crawly missions, was not inappropriate.

What was most frightening was that the Family itself was growing. The group at Spahn had increased significantly. Each time Manson made a courtroom appearance, I spotted new faces among the known Family members.

It could be presumed that many of the new 'converts' were sensation seekers, drawn like moths to the glare of publicity.

* *We Are Everywhere*, by Jerry Rubin (New York: Harper & Row, 1971).

What we didn't know, however, was how far they would go to gain attention or acceptance.

Leslie Van Houten was legally sane, Judge Dell ruled on February 6, basing his decision on the confidential reports of the three psychiatrists, and granting her motion for a substitution of attorneys.

In court the same day, Manson unexpectedly called our bluff: 'Let's have an early trial setting. Let's go tomorrow or Monday. That's a good day for a trial.' Keene set a trial date of March 30, the date already assigned Susan Atkins. That gave us a little more time, but not nearly enough.

At the start of February there were still huge holes in our case, big areas where we had almost no information whatsoever. For example, I still had very little insight into what made Charles Manson tick.

By the end of the month I had that, and a great deal more. For by then I understood, for the first time, Manson's motive – the reason why he'd ordered these murders.

I rarely interview a witness just once. Often the fourth or fifth interview will bring out something previously forgotten or deemed insignificant, which, in proper context, may prove vital to my case.

When I had questioned Gregg Jakobson before the grand jury, my primary concern had been to establish the link between Manson and Melcher.

Reinterviewing the talent scout, I was surprised to discover that since meeting Manson at Dennis Wilson's home in the early summer of 1968, Jakobson had had over a hundred long talks with Charlie, mostly about Manson's philosophy. An intelligent young man, who flirted off and on with the hippie life style, Gregg had never joined the Family, though he'd often visited Manson at Spahn Ranch. Besides seeing in Manson certain commercial possibilities, Jakobson had found him 'intellectually stimulating'. He was so impressed that he often touted him to others, such as Rudi Altobelli, the owner of 10050 Cielo Drive, who had been both Terry Melcher's and Sharon Tate's landlord.

I was surprised at the wide variety of people Manson knew. Charlie was a chameleon, Gregg said; he often professed that 'he had a thousand faces and that he used them all – he told me that he had a mask for everyone'.

Including the jury? I wondered, realizing that if Manson put on the mask of the peace-loving hippie at the trial, I'd be able to use Gregg's remark to unmask him.

I asked Gregg why Manson felt it necessary to don masks.

A. 'So he could deal with everyone on their own level, from the ranch hand at Spahn, to the girls on the Sunset Strip, to me.'

I was curious as to whether Manson had a 'real' face. Gregg thought he had. Underneath it all he had very firm beliefs. 'It was rare to find a man who believed in his convictions as strongly as Charlie did – who couldn't be swayed.'

Did Charlie ever quote anyone? I asked Gregg.

Yes, he replied, 'the Beatles and the Bible'. Manson would quote, verbatim, whole lyrics from the Beatles' songs, finding in them a multitude of hidden meanings. As for the Bible, he most often quoted Revelation 9. But in both cases he usually used the quotations as support for his own views.

Though I was very interested in this odd coupling, and would later question Gregg in depth about it, I wanted to know more about Manson's personal beliefs and attitudes.

Q. 'What did Manson say, if anything, about right and wrong?'

A. 'He believed you could do no wrong, no bad. Everything was good. Whatever you do is what you are supposed to do; you are following your own karma.'

The philosophical mosaic began taking shape. The man I was seeking to convict had no moral boundaries. It was not that he was immoral, but totally amoral. And such a person is always dangerous.

Q. 'Did he say it was wrong to kill a human being?'

A. 'He said it was not.'

Q. 'What was Manson's philosophy re death?'

A. 'There was no death, to Charlie's way of thinking. Death was only a change. The soul or spirit can't die . . . That's what we used to argue all the time, the objective and the subjective and the marriage of the two. He believed it was all in the head, all subjective. He said that death was a fear that was born in man's head and can be taken out of man's head, and then it would no longer exist . . .

'Death to Charlie,' Gregg added, 'was no more important than eating an ice cream cone.'

Yet once, in the desert, Jakobson had run over a tarantula, and Manson had angrily berated him for it. He had denounced others for killing rattlesnakes, picking flowers, even stepping on a blade of grass. To Manson it was not wrong to kill a human being, but it was wrong to kill an animal or plant. Yet he also said that nothing was wrong, everything that happened was right.

That Manson's philosophy was riddled with such contradictions apparently bothered his followers little if at all. Manson said that each person should be independent, but the whole Family was dependent on him. He said that he couldn't tell anyone else what to do, that they should 'do what your love tells you', but he also told them, 'I am your love', and his wants became theirs.

I asked Gregg about Manson's attitude toward women. I was especially interested in this because of the female defendants.

Women had only two purposes in life, Charlie would say: to serve men and to give birth to children. But he didn't permit the girls in the Family to raise their own children. If they did, Charlie claimed, they would give them their own hangups. Charlie believed that if he could eliminate the bonds created by parents, schools, churches, society, he could develop 'a strong white race'. Like Nietzsche, whom Manson claimed to have read, Charlie 'believed in a master race'.

'According to Charlie,' Gregg continued, 'women were only as good as their men. They were only a reflection of their men, all the way back to daddy. A woman was an accumulation of all the men she had been close to.'

Then why were there so many women in the Family? I asked; there were at least five girls to every man.

It was only through the women, Gregg said, that Charlie could attract the men. Men represented power, strength. But he needed the women to lure the men into the Family.

As with others I interviewed, I asked Gregg for examples of Manson's domination. Gregg gave me one of the best I'd yet found: he said he had had dinner with the Family on three occasions; each time Manson sat alone on the top of a large rock, the other members of the Family sitting on the ground in a circle around him.

Q. 'Did Tex Watson ever get up on the rock?'

A. 'No, of course not.'

Q. 'Did anyone else in the Family get up there?'

A. 'Only Charlie.'

I needed many, many more examples like this, so that when I offered all of them at the trial, the jury would be led to the irresistible conclusion that Manson had such a hold over his followers, and specifically his co-defendants, that never in a million years would they have committed these murders without his guidance, directions, and orders.

I asked Gregg Charlie's ambitions. 'Charlie wanted to be a successful recording artist,' Gregg said. 'Not so much as a means to making money as to get his word out to the public. He needed people to live with him, to make love, to liberate the white race.'

What was Manson's attitude toward blacks?

Gregg replied that Charlie 'believed there were different levels when it came to race, and the white man occupied a higher level than the black'. This was why Charlie was so strongly opposed to black-white sex; 'you would be interfering with the path of evolution, you would be mixing up nervous systems, less evolved with more evolved.'

According to Jakobson, 'Charlie believed that the black man's sole purpose on earth was to serve the white man. He was to serve the white man's needs.' But blackie had been on the bottom too long, Charlie said. It was now his turn to take over the reins of power. This was what Helter Skelter, the black-white revolution, was all about.

Gregg and I would talk about this on more than a half dozen

separate occasions. What before had been only fragments, bits and pieces, now began slipping into place.

The picture that eventually emerged, however, was so incredibly bizarre as to be almost beyond belief.

There is a special feeling you develop over years of interviewing people. When someone is lying or not telling everything he knows, you can often sense it.

On reinterviewing Terry Melcher, I became convinced that he was withholding something. There wasn't time for pussyfooting. I told Terry I wanted to talk to him again, only this time he should have his attorney, Chet Lappen, present. When we met in Lappen's office on the seventeenth, I put it to him bluntly: 'You're not leveling with me, Terry. You're keeping something back. Whatever it is, eventually it will come out. It would be far better if you told me about it now rather than have the defense surprise us with it on cross-examination.'

Terry wavered for a few minutes, then decided to tell me.

The day after news of Manson's involvement in the Tate murders broke, Terry had received a telephone call from London. The caller was Rudi Altobelli, the owner of 10050 Cielo Drive. Rudi had told him, in confidence, that one day in March 1969, while he was taking a shower in the guest house, Manson had knocked on the door. Manson claimed to be looking for Terry, who had moved out some months before, but Altobelli, who was a successful business manager for a number of theatrical stars, suspected that Manson had actually come looking for him, as Manson had worked the conversation around to his own music and songs. In a rather subtle fashion, Altobelli had made it clear that he wasn't interested, and Manson had left.

The guest house! 'Terry,' I said, 'why didn't you tell me this before?'

'I wasn't sure it was relevant.'

'Christ, Terry, this places Manson inside the gate of the Tate residence. As you well know, to reach the guest house he'd have to first pass the main house. This means Manson was familiar with the layout of the house and grounds. I don't know what could be any *more* relevant. Where's Altobelli now?'

'Cape Town, South Africa,' Melcher reluctantly replied. Checking his address book, he gave me the number of the hotel where he was staying.

I called Cape Town. Mr Altobelli had just checked out of the hotel, leaving no forwarding address. However, Terry told me that Rudi was planning to return to Los Angeles for a few days sometime soon.

'The minute he hits L.A. I want to know it,' I told him. As a safeguard I put out a few feelers of my own, asking others who knew Altobelli to contact me if they saw or heard from him.

The same day I talked to Melcher, half our extradition problems were solved: Patricia 'Katie' Krenwinkel waived further proceedings and asked to be returned to California immediately. When she made her first courtroom appearance on the twenty-fourth, she requested Paul Fitzgerald of the Public Defender's Office as her attorney. Fitzgerald told the judge that, barring a possible conflict of interest, his office would be willing to represent her.

Terry Melcher didn't call. But another of my contacts did, reporting that Rudi Altobelli had returned to Los Angeles the previous day. I called Altobelli's attorney, Barry Hirsch, and arranged a meeting. Before leaving the office, I prepared a subpoena and stuck it in my pocket.

Rather than ask Altobelli whether the guest house incident really occurred, and risk a possible denial, I simply laid it out: 'Rudi, the reason I'm here is because I want to ask you about the time Manson came to the guest house. Terry told me about it.' *Fait accompli.*

Yes, Manson had been there, Rudi said. But did this mean he would have to testify?

Rudi Altobelli was a bright, urbane, and, as I'd later discover, at times quite witty man. The roster of entertainment figures he'd represented included such stars as Katherine Hepburn, Henry

Fonda (who for a time had rented the guest house at 10050 Cielo Drive), Samantha Eggar, Buffy Sainte-Marie, Christopher Jones, and Sally Kellerman, to name only a few. However, in common with almost all the other witnesses in this case, he was scared.

On his return from Europe following the murders, he'd found that 10050 Cielo Drive had been sealed by the police. Needing a place to stay, and unsure whether he might have been one of the intended victims – and still might be – he picked the safest place he could think of. He moved in with Terry Melcher and Candice Bergen, who were occupying a beach house in Malibu owned by Terry's mother, Doris Day. Though Terry and Rudi had spent many hours discussing the murders, and possible suspects, Manson's name was never mentioned, Rudi said. When the news broke that Manson had been accused of the murders, a possible motive being his grudge against Melcher, Altobelli decided that he had probably chosen the least safe place in Southern California. He still shivered when recalling it.

He had another reason for fear. In a sense, he too had rejected Manson.

'Tell me about it, Rudi,' I suggested. 'Then we'll discuss whether you have to testify or not. But first, how do you know it was Manson?'

Because he'd met Manson once before, Altobelli said, during the summer of 1968, at Dennis Wilson's house. Manson was living there at the time, and Rudi had dropped in while Dennis was playing a tape of Manson's music. He'd listened politely, commented that it was 'nice', the minimal courtesy possible, then left.

At various times Dennis and Gregg had tried to interest him in Manson and his philosophy. Having worked hard for what money he had, Altobelli said, he was not sympathetic to Manson's sponging, and had told them exactly that.

The incident had occurred about eight or nine on the evening of Sunday, March 23, 1969 – Rudi remembered the date because he and Sharon had flown to Rome together the next day, Rudi on business, Sharon to rejoin her husband and to make a movie there. Rudi was alone in the guest house, taking a shower, when Christopher started barking. Grabbing a robe, he went to the door and saw Manson on the porch. While it was possible that Manson had knocked and the shower had muffled the sound, Rudi was irritated that he had opened the outside door and walked onto the porch uninvited.

Manson started to introduce himself but Rudi, somewhat brusquely, without opening the screen door that separated the porch from the living room, said, 'I know who you are, Charlie, who do you want?'

Manson said he was looking for Terry Melcher. Altobelli said Terry had moved to Malibu. When Manson asked for his address, Altobelli said he didn't know it. Which was not true.

Prolonging the conversation, Manson asked him what business he was in. Though Altobelli felt sure Manson already knew the answer, he replied, 'The entertainment business.' He added, 'I'd like to talk to you longer, Charlie, but I'm leaving the country tomorrow and have to pack.'

Manson said he would like to talk to him when he returned. Rudi told him that he wouldn't be back for over a year. Another untruth, but he had no desire to talk further with Manson.

Before Manson left, Rudi asked him why he had come back to the guest house. Manson replied that the people at the main house had sent him back. Altobelli said that he didn't like to have his tenants disturbed, and he would appreciate it if he wouldn't do so in the future. With that Manson left.

Though one question was uppermost in my mind, before asking it I had Altobelli describe Manson, the lighting on the porch, exactly where each was standing. Since he had met Manson on a prior occasion, there was no question that this was a positive identification, but I wanted to be absolutely sure.

Then I asked it, and held my breath until he answered. 'Rudi, who was up front that night?'

'Sharon, Gibby, Voytek, and Jay.'

Four of the five Tate victims! This meant that Manson could have seen any or all of them. Prior to my talking to Rudi, we had assumed that Manson had never seen the people he had ordered killed.

'Rudi, all those people are dead. Was there anyone else up front who could testify to this?'

Rudi thought a moment. He had been up at the main house earlier in the evening, actually returning to the guest house only a few minutes before Manson arrived. 'I'm not sure,' he said, 'but I'm almost positive Hatami was there.'

Shahrokh Hatami, a native of Iran, was Sharon's personal photographer, and a good friend of both Polanskis. Hatami had been at the house that afternoon, Rudi knew, photographing Sharon while she was packing for her trip.

Rudi then told me something he said he had never told anyone else. I knew there was no way I could use it in the trial; it was hearsay, and though there are many exceptions to the hearsay rule, this couldn't come in under any of them.

On the flight to Rome, Sharon had asked him: 'Did that creepy-looking guy come back there yesterday?'

So Sharon had seen Manson, the creepy-looking little guy who four and a half months later would mastermind her murder!

Something must have happened to have caused such a strong reaction. A confrontation of some sort. Could it be that Voytek, who had an unpredictable temper, and got into an argument with Manson? Or that Manson had said something offensive to Sharon, and Jay had come to her defense?

I called LAPD and told them to find Shahrokh Hatami.

Lieutenant Helder contacted a friend of Colonel Tate's, who in turn located Hatami. I interviewed him in my office. Very emotionally, the Iranian photographer told me how much he had loved Sharon. 'Not romantic, but' – he apologized for his broken English – 'one human being loving qualities other human being has.'

Yes, he'd once sent someone to the back house. One time. He didn't know the date, but it was the day before Sharon left for Europe. It was in the afternoon. He'd looked out the window and noticed a man walking into the yard, hesitant, as if he didn't know where he was going, yet cocky, as if he thought he owned the place. His manner irritated Hatami, and he went out on the porch and asked him what he wanted.

I asked Hatami to describe the man. He said he was short, like Roman Polanski (Polanski was five feet five, Manson five feet two), late twenties, thin, with long hair. What colour hair? Dark brown. He didn't have a beard but looked as if he needed a shave. How could he tell that? He'd walked off the porch onto the stone walk to confront him; they were at most three or four feet apart.

With the exception of the age – Manson was thirty-four, but could easily have been mistaken for younger – the description fitted.

The man said he was looking for someone, mentioning a name Hatami did not recognize.

Could it have been Melcher? I asked. Possible, Hatami said, but he really couldn't remember. It had meant nothing to him at the time.

'This is the Polanski residence,' Hatami told him. 'This is not the place. Maybe the people you want is back there,' pointing. 'Take the back alley.'

By 'back alley' Hatami meant the dirt pathway in front of the residence which led to the guest house. But, as I'd later argue to the jury, to an American 'back alley' meant a place where there were garbage cans, refuse. Manson must have felt he was being treated like an alley cat.

I asked Hatami, 'What tone of voice did you use?' He illustrated, speaking loudly and angrily. Roman was away, Hatami said, and he felt protective of Sharon. 'I wasn't happy that he was coming on the property, and looking at people he doesn't know.'

How did the man react? He appeared upset, Hatami said; he turned and walked away without saying 'excuse me' or anything.

Just before this, however, Sharon came to the door and said, 'Who is it, Hatami?' Hatami told her that a man was looking for someone.

Showing Hatami a diagram of the house and grounds, I had

him point to the spots where each was standing. Sharon was on the porch, the man on the walk not more than six to eight feet away, with no obstruction between them. There could be no question that Charles Manson saw Sharon Tate, and she him. Sharon had undoubtedly looked right into the eyes of the man who would order her death. We now had, for the first time, evidence that prior to the murders, Manson had seen one of his victims.

Hatami had remained on the walk, Sharon on the porch, while the man went down the path toward the guest house. According to Hatami, he came back up the path in 'a minute or two, no more', and left the premises without saying anything.

It was not as abrasive an incident as I'd anticipated, but, together with Melcher's rejection and Altobelli's subtle putdown, Hatami's 'take the back alley' was more than sufficient cause for Manson to have strong feelings against 10050 Cielo Drive. Too, not only were these people obviously establishment, they were establishment in the very fields – entertainment, recording, motion pictures – in which Manson had tried to make it and failed.

There was one discrepancy: the time. Hatami was positive the incident had occurred during the afternoon. Altobelli, however, was equally insistent that it was between eight and nine in the evening when Manson appeared on the guest house porch. While it was possible one or the other was confused, the most logical explanation was that Manson had gone to the guest house that afternoon, found no one there (Altobelli was out most of the afternoon, making arrangements for his trip), then returned that evening. This was supported by Hatami's statement that Manson had come back up the path after 'a minute or two, no more', which hardly left time for his conversation with Altobelli.

Finally, nearly three months after first requesting it, I obtained the tape Inyo County Deputy Sheriff Don Ward had made with the two miners, Paul Crockett and Brooks Poston.

Crockett, a weather-worn miner in his mid-40s, had been prospecting in the Death Valley area in the spring of 1969 when he came across Manson's advance party at Barker Ranch. At this time it consisted of only two persons, a young runaway named Juanita Wildebush and Brooks Poston, a slender, rather docile 18-year-old who had been with the Family since June 1968. Nights, Crockett would visit the pair, and the talk would invariably turn to one subject, Charlie. 'And I couldn't believe what they were saying,' Crockett observed. 'I mean, it was so utterly ridiculous.' It became obvious to Crockett that these people believed this Charlie to be the second coming of Christ. It was just as obvious that they feared him. And so Crockett, who was no stranger to mysticism, did something perhaps a little odd but at least psychologically effective. He told them that, just like Charlie, he too had powers. And 'I planted them with the idea that I had the power to keep Charlie from coming back up there'.

Other Family members – including Paul Watkins, Tex Watson, Brenda McCann, and Bruce Davis – would occasionally show up at Barker with messages and supplies, and it didn't take long for the word to get back to Manson.

Initially he scoffed at the idea. But each time he tried to go to Barker something happened: the truck broke down, Spahn Ranch was raided, and so on. Meanwhile Juanita eloped with Bob Berry, Crockett's parner, and Crockett succeeded in 'unconverting' several of Manson's most important male followers: Poston; Paul Watkins, who often acted as Manson's second in command; and, somewhat later, Juan Flynn, a tall, strapping Panamanian cowboy who had worked at Spahn.

When Crockett first met young Poston, he was 'a zombie'. The phrase was Poston's own. He said that he had wanted to leave the Family many times, but 'Manson had a vise grip on my mind and I couldn't break the grip. I didn't know how to leave . . .'

Crockett discovered that Manson had 'programmed all his people to the extent that they're just like him. He has put all kinds of things in their heads. I didn't believe it could be done, but he has done it and I seen it working.' Crockett began 'deprogramming' Poston. He put him to work in his various mining ventures, built up his body, got him to thinking of other things than Manson.

When Manson finally reached Barker, in September 1969, Crockett, meeting him for the first time, found him 'a very clever man – he borders on genius'. Then Manson told him 'some of the weirdest stories. I thought it was all make-believe, to start with.' Before long, Crockett was not only convinced that Manson was insane, he was sure 'he would think no more of killing one of us than he would of stepping on a flower; in fact, he'd rather do that than step on a flower'.

Deciding that his own life expectancy was directly proportionate to his usefulness to Manson, Crockett made himself very useful, volunteering his truck to haul in supplies, and so forth. He and the former Mansonites now living with him in a small cabin near Barker also began taking precautions.

Among the weird tales Manson had told Crockett: That the black man 'was getting ready to blow the whole thing open ... Charlie has set up the whole thing, it's kind of like a storybook ... He says Helter Skelter is coming down.'

'Helter Skelter is what he calls the Negro revolt,' Poston explained. 'He says the Negroes are going to revolt and kill all the white men except the ones that are hiding in the desert ...' Long before this Manson had told Poston, 'When Helter Skelter comes down, the cities are going to be mass hysteria and the cops – the piggies, he calls them – won't know what to do, and the beast will fall and the black man will take over ... that the battle of Armageddon will be at hand.'

God's chosen people were the Family, Charlie said. He would lead them to the desert, where they would multiply until they numbered 144,000. He got this, Poston said, 'from reading things into the Bible, from Revelation'.*

Also in Revelation, as well as in Hopi Indian legends, there was mention of a 'bottomless pit', Poston said. The entrance to this pit, according to Charlie, was 'a cave that he says is underneath Death Valley that leads down to a sea of gold that the Indians knew about'. Charlie claimed that

---

* Manson apparently got the 144,000 figure from Revelation 7, which mentions the twelve tribes of Israel, each numbering 12,000.

every tuned-in tribe of people that's ever lived have escaped the destruction of their race by going underground, literally, and they're all living in a golden city where there's a river that runs through it of milk and honey, and a tree that bears twelve kinds of fruit, a different fruit each month, or something like that, and you don't need to bring candles nor any flashlights down there. He says it will be all lit up because . . . the walls will glow and it won't be cold and it won't be too hot. There will be warm springs and fresh water, and people are already down there waiting for him.

Both Atkins and Jakobson had already told me about Charlie's 'bottomless pit'. The Family loved to hear Charlie sermonize about this hidden 'land of milk and honey'. They not only believed, they were so convinced that such a place existed that they spent days searching for the hole in the ground which would lead them to the underground paradise.

There was also a kind of desperation in the search, because it was here, underground in the bottomless pit, that they intended to hide and wait out Helter Skelter.

It was obvious to both Crockett and Poston that Manson believed Helter Skelter was imminent. And there were the preparations. Manson had arrived at Barker Ranch in September 1969 with about eight others, all heavily armed. More Family members arrived the following week, driving stolen dune buggies and other vehicles. They began setting up lookout posts and fortifications, hiding caches of guns, gasoline, and supplies.

(It did not occur to Crockett and Poston – since neither was aware of the Family's involvement in the Tate–LaBianca murders – that Manson might be fearful of something other than blacks.)

Manson hadn't given up on Poston, but Crockett's 'deprogramming' had been very effective. Manson was even more upset about Paul Watkins' leaving him, since Watkins, a good-looking youth with a way with women, had been Manson's chief procurer of young girls.

Crockett, Poston, and Watkins had begun sleeping with their shotguns within reach. On at least three occasions Charlie, Clem, and/or the girls tried to creepy-crawl the cabin. Each time the trio had been lucky and had heard something, aborting the plan. Then one night Juan Flynn arrived 'to shoot some bull', and admitted Manson had suggested he kill Crockett. Crockett persuaded Juan – who was far too independent to ever join the Family – that he should leave the area.

Crockett, accustomed to living as free and unencumbered as a mountain goat, was a mite stubborn. He felt he had as much right to be in Death Valley as Manson did. But he was also a realist. With Flynn gone and Watkins in town getting supplies, he and Poston were vastly outnumbered. Figuring 'my usefulness to Charlie had already vanished and that he would, if he considered it necessary, liquidate me immediately, if not sooner', Crockett had Poston fill the canteens and pack some grub. Under cover of night they fled the area on foot, walking over twenty rugged miles to Warmsprings, then catching a ride to Independence, where they told Deputy Sheriff Ward about Charles Manson and his family.

After hearing the tape, I arranged through Frank Fowles for Crockett and Poston to come to Los Angeles.

Though it was Crockett who had broken Manson's hold over Poston, the latter was by far the most articulate. Incidents, dates, places – snap, snap, snap. Crockett, by contrast, was evasive. 'I can feel their vibrations. I can't talk freely to you because they might know what I am saying.'

Crockett had helped Poston, Watkins, and Flynn break away from Manson. To do this he must have gained some insight into how Manson had gained control over them in the first place. Others had also said that Manson 'programmed' his followers. Did he understand how he accomplished this?

Crockett said he did, but when he tried to articulate it, he became bogged down in a morass of words and definitions, finally saying, 'I can't explain it. It's all part of the occult.'

I decided I wouldn't be able to use Crockett as a witness.

It was otherwise with Brooks Poston. The tall, gangly youth, with the air of the hayseed about him, was a fund of information about Manson and the Family.

A highly impressionable 17-year-old, Brooks Poston had met Manson at Dennis Wilson's house, and from that moment until he finally broke with Manson more than a year later to follow Crockett, 'I believed Charlie was JC.'

Q. 'Did Manson ever tell you that he was J C, or Jesus Christ?'

It wasn't so much stated as implied, Brooks said. Charlie claimed that he had lived before, nearly two thousand years ago, and that he had once died on the cross. (Manson had also told Gregg Jakobson that he had already died once, and that 'death is beautiful'.)

Charlie had a favorite story which he was fond of telling the Family, complete with dramatic gestures and moans of pain. Brooks had heard it often. According to Charlie, while he was living in Haight-Ashbury, he had taken a 'magic mushroom' (psilocybin) trip. He was lying on a bed, but it became a cross, and he could feel the nails in his feet and hands and the sword in his side, and when he looked down at the foot of the cross he saw Mary Magdalene (Mary Brunner), and she was crying, and he said, 'I'm all right, Mary.' He had been fighting it, but now he gave up, surrendered himself to death, and when he did, he could suddenly see through the eyes of everyone at the same time, and at that moment he became the whole world.

With such clues, his followers had little trouble guessing his true identity.

I was curious about something. Up until his arrest in Mendocino County on July 28, 1967,* Charlie had always used his real name, Charles Milles Manson. On that occasion, however, and thereafter, he called himself Charles *Willis* Manson. Had Manson ever said anything about his name? I asked. Crockett and Poston both told me that they had heard Manson say, very

* Manson was charged with interfering with the questioning of a suspected runaway juvenile, Ruth Ann Moorehouse. He was given thirty days, suspended, and placed on three years probation. Asked his occupation when booked, he said he was a minister.

slowly, that his name was 'Charles' Will Is Man's Son', meaning that his will was that of the Son of Man.

Although Susan Atkins had emphasized Charlie's surname in talking to Virginia Graham, I hadn't really thought, until now, how powerful that name was. Man Son. It was tailor-made for the Infinite Being role he was now seeking to portray.

But Charlie carried all this yet a step further, Poston said. Manson claimed that the members of the Family were the original Christians, reincarnated, and that the Romans had returned as the establishment.

It was now time, Manson told his closest followers, for the Romans to have their turn on the cross.

Exactly how did Manson 'program' someone? I asked Brooks.

He had various techniques, Poston said. With a girl, it would usually start with sex. Charlie might convince a plain girl that she was beautiful. Or, if she had a father fixation, have her imagine that he was her father. (He'd used both techniques with Susan Atkins.) Or, if he felt she was looking for a leader, he might imply that he was Christ. Manson had a talent for sensing, and capitalizing on, a person's hangups and/or desires. When a man first joined the group, Charlie would usually take him on an LSD trip, ostensibly 'to open his mind'. Then, while he was in a highly suggestible state, he would talk about love, how you had to surrender yourself to it, how only by ceasing to exist as an individual ego could you become one with all things.

As with Jakobson, I queried Poston as to the sources of Manson's philosophy. Scientology, the Bible, and the Beatles. These three were the only ones he knew.

A peculiar triumvirate. Yet by now I was beginning to suspect the existence of at least a fourth influence. The old magazines I'd found at Barker, Gregg's mention that Charlie claimed to have read Nietzsche and that he believed in a master race, plus the emergence of a startling number of disturbing parallels between Manson and the leader of the Third Reich, led me to ask Poston: 'Did Manson ever say anything about Hitler?'

Poston's reply was short and incredibly chilling.

A. 'He said that Hitler was a tuned-in guy who had leveled the karma of the Jews.'

I spent most of the two days interviewing Crockett and Poston, obtaining much new information, some of it very incriminating. For example, Manson had once suggested Poston take a knife, go into Shoshone, and kill the sheriff. In the first real test of his newly found independence, Poston had refused to even consider the idea.

Before Crockett and Poston returned to Shoshone, I told them I wanted to talk to Juan Flynn and Paul Watkins. They weren't sure if Juan would talk to me – that big Panamanian cowboy was an independent cuss – but they thought Paul might. Since he was no longer procuring girls for Charlie, he had some free time on his hands.

Watkins agreed to the interview, and I arranged for Watkins, Poston, and Crockett to stay in a motel in downtown L.A.

'Paul, I need a new love.'

Paul Watkins was describing for me how Manson would send him out to recruit young girls. Watkins admitted that he liked his special role in the Family. The only problem was, after he'd located a likely candidate, Charlie would insist on sleeping with her first.

Why didn't Manson pick up the girls himself? I asked.

'He was too old for most of the girls,' the 19-year-old Watkins replied. 'He frightened them. Also, I had a good line.' It was obvious that Watkins was better-looking than Charlie.

I asked Paul where he found the girls. He might go down to the Sunset Strip, where the teenyboppers hung out. Or drive the highways watching for girls who were hitchhiking. Once Charlie, through the connivance of an older woman who posed as Watkins' mother, even had him arrange a phony registration at a Los Angeles high school so he could be closer to the action.

Watkins also described the orgies that took place at the Gresham Street house and at Spahn. For a while there was one about every week. They would always start with drugs – grass, peyote,

LSD, whatever was available – Manson rationing them out, deciding how much each person needed. 'Everything was done at Charlie's direction,' Paul said. Charlie might dance around, everyone else following, like a train. As he'd take off his clothes, all the rest would take off their clothes. Then, when everyone was naked, they'd lie on the floor, 'and they'd play the game of taking twelve deep breaths and releasing them and close eyes and then rub against each other' until 'eventually all were touching'. Charlie would direct the orgy, arranging bodies, combinations, positions. 'He'd set it all up in a beautiful way like he was creating a masterpiece in sculpture,' Watkins said, 'but instead of clay he was using warm bodies.'

Manson often staged these events to impress outsiders. If there were guests who he felt could be of some use to him, he'd say to the Family, 'Let's get together and show these people how to make love.' Whatever the reaction, the impression was a lasting one. 'It was like the Devil buying your soul,' Watkins said.

Manson also used these occasions to 'eradicate hangups'. If a person indicated reluctance to engage in a certain act, Manson would force that person to commit it. Male-female, female-female, male-male, intercourse, cunnilingus, fellatio, sodomy – there could be no inhibitions of any kind. One 13-year-old girl's initiation into the Family consisted of her being sodomized by Manson while the others watched. Manson also 'went down on' a young boy to show the others he had rid himself of all inhibitions.

Charlie used sex, Paul said. For example when it became obvious that DeCarlo was making no effort to persuade his motorcycle gang to join the Family, Manson told the girls to withhold their favors from Danny.

The fact that Manson directed even the sex lives of his followers was powerful evidence of his domination. I asked Watkins for other examples specifically involving co-defendants. He recalled that once at Spahn Ranch, Charlie told Sadie: 'I'd like half a coconut, even if you have to go to Rio de Janeiro to get it.' Sadie got right up and was on her way out of the door when Charlie said, 'Never mind.'

It was a test. It was also, by inference, evidence that Susan Atkins would do anything Charles Manson asked her to do.

As with the others, I questioned Watkins about Manson's programming techniques. He told me something very interesting, which apparently the other Family members didn't know. He said that when Manson passed out the L S D, he always took a smaller dose than the others. Though Manson never told him why he did so, Paul presumed that during the 'trip' Manson wanted to retain control over his own mental faculties.

As Manson's second in command, Watkins had enjoyed Charlie's confidence more than most of the others. I asked him if Manson had ever mentioned Scientology or The Process. Watkins had never heard of The Process, but Manson had told him that while he was in prison he had studied Scientology, becoming a 'theta', which Manson defined as being 'clear'. Watkins said that in the summer of 1968 he and Charlie had dropped into a Church of Scientology in downtown Los Angeles, and Manson asked the receptionist, 'What do you do after "clear"?' When she was unable to tell him anything he hadn't already done, Manson walked out.

One aspect of Manson's philosophy especially puzzled me: his strange attitude toward fear. He not only preached that fear was beautiful, he often told the Family that they should live in a constant state of fear. What did he mean by that? I asked Paul.

To Charlie fear was the same thing as awareness, Watkins said. The more fear you have, the more awareness, hence the more love. When you're really afraid, you come to 'Now'. And when you are at Now, you are totally conscious.

Manson claimed that children were more aware than adults, because they were naturally afraid. But animals were even more aware than people, he said, because they always lived at Now. The coyote was the most aware creature there was, Manson maintained, because he was completely paranoid. Being frightened of everything, he missed nothing.

Charlie was always 'selling fear', Watkins continued. He *wanted* people to be afraid, and the more afraid the better. Using this same logic, 'Charlie said that death was beautiful, because people feared death.'

I would learn, from talking to other Family members, that Manson would seek out each individual's greatest fear – not so the person could confront and eliminate it, but so he could re-emphasize it. It was like a magic button, which he could push at will to control that person.

'Whatever you do,' Watkins advised me, as had both Crockett and Poston, 'don't ever let Charlie know you are afraid of him.' One day at Spahn, without warning or provocation, Manson had jumped on Watkins and started strangling him. At first Paul resisted, but then, gasping for breath, he suddenly gave up, stopped resisting. 'It was really weird,' Watkins said. 'The instant I stopped fearing him, his hands flew off my throat and he jumped back as if he'd been attacked by an unseen force.'

'Then it's like the barking dog,' I commented. 'If you show fear, it will attack; if you don't it won't?'

'Exactly. *Fear turns Charlie on.*'

Paul Watkins was inherently more independent than Brooks Poston, much less the follower type. Yet he too had remained with the Family for a long period. Other than the girls, was there some reason why he stayed?

'I thought Charlie was Christ,' he told me, not blinking an eye.

Both Watkins and Poston had severed the umbilical linking them to Manson. But both admitted to me that they still weren't completely free of him, that even now they would sometimes lapse back into a state where they could feel Manson's vibrations.

It was Paul Watkins who finally supplied the missing link in Manson's motive for the murders. Yet, if I hadn't talked to Jakobson and Poston, I might have missed its importance, for it was from all three, Gregg, Brooks, and Paul, that I obtained the keys to understanding (1) Charles Manson's unique interpretation of the Book of Revelation, and (2) his decidedly curious and complex attitude toward the English musical group the Beatles.

Several persons had told me Manson was fond of quoting from the Bible, particularly the ninth chapter of Revelation.

Once Charlie had handed Jakobson a Bible, already open to the chapter, and, while he read it, supplied his own interpretation of the verses. With only one exception, which will be noted, what Gregg told me tallied with what I later heard from Poston and Watkins.

The 'four angels' were the Beatles, whom Manson considered 'leaders, spokesmen, prophets', according to Gregg. The line 'And he opened the bottomless pit . . . And there came out of the smoke locusts upon the earth; and unto them was given power . . .' was still another reference to the English group, Gregg said. Locusts – Beatles – one and the same. 'Their faces were as the faces of men,' yet 'they had hair as the hair of women'. An obvious reference to the long-haired musicians. Out of the mouths of the four angels 'issued fire and brimstone'. Gregg: 'This referred to the spoken words, the lyrics of the Beatles' songs, the power that came out of their mouths.'

The 'breastplates of fire', Poston added, were their electric guitars. Their shapes 'like unto horses prepared unto battle' were the dune buggies. The 'horsemen who numbered two hundred thousand thousand', and who would roam the earth spreading destruction, were the motorcyclists.

'And it was commanded them that they should not hurt the grass of the earth, neither any green thing, neither any tree; but only those men which have not the seal of God on their foreheads.' I wondered about that seal on the forehead. How did Manson interpret that? I asked Jakobson.

'It was all subjective,' Gregg replied. 'He said there would be a mark on people.' Charlie had never told him exactly what the mark would be, only that he, Charlie, 'would be able to tell, he would know', and that 'the mark would designate whether they were with him or against him'. With Charlie, it was either one or the other, Gregg said; 'there was no middle road'.

One verse spoke of worshiping demons and idols of gold and silver and bronze. Manson said that referred to the material worship of the establishment: of automobiles, houses, money.

Q. 'Directing your attention to Verse 15, which reads: "And the four angels were loosed, which were prepared for an hour, and a day, and a month, and a year, for to slay the third part of men." Did he say what that meant?'

A. 'He said that those were the people who would die in Helter Skelter . . . one third of mankind . . . the white race.'

I now knew I was on the right track.

Only on one point did Jakobson's recollection of Manson's interpretation differ from that of the others. The first verse of Revelation 9 refers to a fifth angel; the chapter ends, however, referring to only four. Originally there were five Beatles, Gregg explained, one of whom, Stuart Sutcliffe, had died in Germany in 1962.

Poston and Watkins – who, unlike Jakobson, were members of the Family – interpreted this much differently. Verse 1 reads: 'And the fifth angel sounded, and I saw a star fall from heaven unto the earth: and to him was given the key of the bottomless pit.'

To members of the Family the identity of that fifth angel, the ruler of the bottomless pit, was never in doubt. It was Charlie.

Verse 11 reads: 'And they had a king over them, which is the angel of the bottomless pit, whose name in the Hebrew tongue is Abaddon, but in the Greek tongue hath his name Apollyon.'

The king also had a Latin name, which, though it appears in the Catholic Douai Version, was inadvertently omitted by the translators of the King James version. It was Exterminans.

Exterminans, t/n Charles Manson.

As far as Jakobson, Watkins, and Poston knew, Manson placed no special meaning on the last verse of Revelation 9. But I found myself thinking of it often in the months ahead:

'Neither repented they of their murders, nor of their sorceries, nor of their fornication, nor of their thefts.'

'The important thing to remember about Revelation 9,' Gregg told me, 'is that Charlie believed this was happening *now*, not in the future. It's going to begin now and it's time to choose sides . . . either that or flee with him to the desert.'

According to Jakobson, Manson believed 'the Beatles were spokesmen. They were speaking to Charlie, through their songs, letting him know from across the ocean that this is what was going to go down. He believed this firmly . . . He considered their songs prophecy, especially the songs in the so-called White Album . . . He told me that many, many times.'

Watkins and Poston also said that Manson and the Family were convinced that the Beatles were speaking to Charlie through their music. For example, in the song 'I Will' are the lines: 'And when at last I find you/Your song will fill the air/Sing it loud so I can hear you/Make it easy to be near you . . .' Charlie interpreted this to mean the Beatles wanted him to make an album, Poston and Watkins said. Charlie told them that the Beatles were looking for JC and he was the JC they were looking for. He also told them that the Beatles knew that Christ had returned to earth again and that he was living somewhere in Los Angeles.

'How in the world did he come up with that?' I asked them.

In the White Album is a song called 'Honey Pie', a lyric of which reads: 'Oh honey pie my position is tragic/Come and show me the magic/Of your Hollywood song.' A later lyric goes: 'Oh Honey pie you are driving me frantic/Sail across the Atlantic/To be where you belong.'

Charlie, of course, wanted *them* to sail across the Atlantic, to join him in Death Valley. While residing in the Gresham Street house (in January and February of 1969, just after the White Album was released), Manson and the girls sent several telegrams, wrote a number of letters, and made at least three telephone calls to England, attempting to reach the Beatles. No luck.

The line 'I'm in love but I'm lazy' from 'Honey Pie' meant to Charlie that the Beatles loved JC but were too lazy to go looking for him; too, they'd just gone all the way to India, following a man who they'd finally decided was a false prophet, the Maharishi. They were also calling for JC/Charlie in the first eight lines of the song 'Don't Pass Me By', in 'Yer Blues', and, in the earlier Magical Mystery Tour album, in 'Blue Jay Way'.

Much of this I would never use at the trial; it was simply too absurd.

The Beatles' White Album, Manson told Watkins, Poston, and others, 'set up things for the revolution'. *His* album, which was to follow, would in Charlie's words, 'blow the cork off the bottle. That would start it.'

Much of the time at the Gresham Street house, according to Poston, Watkins, and others, was spent composing songs for Charlie's album. Each was to be a message song, directed to a particular group of people, such as the bikers, outlining the part they'd play in Helter Skelter. Charlie worked hard on these songs; they had to be very subtle, he said, like the Beatles' own songs, their true meaning hidden beneath the awareness of all but the tuned-in people.

Manson was counting on Terry Melcher to produce this album. According to numerous Family members (both Melcher and Jakobson denied this), Terry had promised to come and listen to the songs one evening. The girls cleaned the house, baked cookies, rolled joints. Melcher didn't show. Manson, according to Poston and Watkins, never forgave Terry for this. Melcher's word was no good, he said angrily on a number of occasions.

Though the Beatles had made many records, it was the double-disk White Album, which Capitol issued in December 1968, that Manson considered most important. Even the fact that the cover was white – with no other design except the embossed name of the group – held significance for him.

It was, and remains, a startling album, containing some of the Beatles' finest music, and some of their strangest. Its thirty songs range from tender love ballads to pop parodies to cacophonies of noise made by taking loops of very diverse tapes and splicing them together. To Charles Manson, however, it was prophecy. At least this is what he convinced his followers.

That Charlie had renamed Susan Atkins 'Sadie Mae Glutz' long before the White Album appeared containing the song 'Sexy Sadie' was additional proof to the Family that Manson and the Beatles were mentally attuned.

Almost every song in the album had a hidden meaning, which Manson interpreted for his followers. To Charlie 'Rocky Raccoon' meant 'coon' or the black man. While to everyone except Manson and the Family it was obvious that the lyrics of 'Happiness Is a Warm Gun' had sexual connotations, Charlie interpreted the song to mean that the Beatles were telling blackie to get guns and fight whitey.

According to Poston and Watkins, the Family played five songs in the White Album more than all the others. They were: 'Blackbird', 'Piggies', 'Revolution 1', 'Revolution 9', and 'Helter Skelter'.

'Blackbird singing in the dead of night/Take these broken wings and learn to fly/All your life/You were only waiting for this moment to arise,' went the lyrics of 'Blackbird'. According to Jakobson, 'Charlie believed that the moment was now and that the black man was going to arise, overthrow the white man, and take his turn.' According to Watkins, in this song Charlie 'figured the Beatles were programming the black people to get it up, get it on, start doing it'.

On first hearing the song, I'd thought that the LaBianca killers had made a mistake, writing 'rise' instead of 'arise'. However, Jakobson told me that Charlie said the black man was going to 'rise' up against the white man. ' "Rise" was one of Charlie's big words,' Gregg said, providing me with the origin of still another of the key words.

Both the Tate and LaBianca murders had occurred in 'the dead of night'. However, if the parallel had special significance to Manson, he never admitted it to anyone I interviewed, nor, if he knew it, did he admit the probable meaning of the phrase 'helter skelter'. The song 'Helter Skelter' begins: 'When I get to the bottom I go back to the top of the slide/Where I stop and I turn and I go for a ride . . .' According to Poston, Manson said this was a reference to the Family emerging from the bottomless pit.

There was a simpler explanation. In England, home of the Beatles, 'helter skelter' is another name for a slide in an amusement park.

If you listen closely, you can hear grunts and oinks in the background of the song 'Piggies'.* By 'piggies', Gregg and the

---

* Unlike ex-Beatles John Lennon and Paul McCartney, George Harrison refused the authors permission to quote from the lyrics of any of his songs, including 'Piggies'.

others told me, Manson meant anyone who belonged to the establishment.

Like Manson himself, the song was openly critical of the piggies, noting that what they really needed was a damned good whacking.

'By that he meant the black man was going to give the piggies, the establishment, a damned good whacking,' Jakobson explained. Charlie really loved that line, both Watkins and Poston said; he was always quoting it.

I couldn't listen to the final stanza without visualizing what had happened at 3301 Waverly Drive. It describes piggy couples dining out, in all their starched finery, eating bacon with their forks and knives.

Rosemary LaBianca: forty-one knife wounds. Leno LaBianca: twelve knife wounds, punctured with a fork seven times, a *knife* in his throat, a *fork* in his stomach, and, on the wall, in his own blood, DEATH TO PIGS.

'There's a chord at the end of the song "Piggies",' Watkins said. 'It goes down and it's a really weird chord. After the sound of piggies snorting. And in the "Revolution 9" song, there's that same chord, and after it they have a little pause and snort, snort, snort. But in the pause, there is machine-gun fire.'

'And it's the same thing with the "Helter Skelter" song,' Paul continued. 'They had this really weird chord. And in the "Revolution 9" song there's the same chord again, with machine guns firing and people dying and screaming and stuff.'

The White Album contains two songs with the word 'revvolution' in their titles.

The printed lyrics of 'Revolution 1', as given on the jacket insert, read: 'You say you want a revolution/Well you know/We all want to change the world .../But when you talk about destruction/Don't you know that you can count me out.'

When you listen to the record itself, however, immediately after 'out' you hear the word 'in'.

Manson took this to mean the Beatles, once undecided, now favored the revolution.

Manson made much of these 'hidden lyrics', which can be found in a number of the Beatles' songs but are especially prevalent in the White Album. They were, he told his followers, direct communications to him, Charlie/JC.

Later on the lyrics go: 'You say you got a real solution/Well you know/We'd all love to see the plan.'

The meaning of this was obvious to Manson: Sing out, Charlie, and tell us how we can escape the holocaust.

Of all the Beatles' songs, 'Revolution 9' is easily the weirdest. Reviewers couldn't decide whether it was an exciting new direction for rock or an elaborate put-on. One critic said it reminded him of 'a bad acid trip'.

There are no lyrics as such, nor is it music in any conventional sense; rather it is a montage of noises – whispers, shouts, snatches of dialogue from the BBC, bits of classical music, mortars exploding, babies crying, church hymns, car horns, and football yells – which, together with the oft reinterated refrain 'Number 9, Number 9, Number 9', build to a climax of machine-gun fire and screams, to be followed by the soft and obviously symbolic lullaby 'Good Night'.

Of all the songs in the White Album, Jakobson said, Charlie 'spoke mostly of "Revolution 9".' He said 'it was the Beatles' way of telling people what was going to happen; it was their way of making prophecy; it directly paralleled the Bible's Revelation 9.' It was also the battle of Armageddon, the coming black-white revolution portrayed in sound, Manson claimed.

According to Poston: 'When Charlie was listening to it, he heard in the background noise, in and around the machine-gun fire and the oinking of pigs, a man's voice saying "Rise".' Listening to the recording again, I also heard it, twice repeated: the first time almost a whisper, the second a long-drawn-out scream.*

---

* It is first heard two minutes and thirty-four seconds into the song, just after the crowd sounds that follow 'lots of stab wounds as it were' and 'informed him on the third night' and just before 'Number 9, Number 9'.

This was potent evidence. Through both Jakobson and Poston, I'd now linked Manson, irrevocably, with the word 'rise' printed in blood at the LaBianca residence.

In 'Revolution 1' the Beatles had finally decided to commit themselves to the revolution. In 'Revolution 9' they were telling the black man that *now* was the time to rise and start it all. According to Charlie.

Manson found many other messages in this song (including the words 'Block that Nixon'), but as far as his philosophy of Helter Skelter was concerned, these were the most important.

Charles Manson was already talking about an imminent black-white war when Gregg Jakobson first met him, in the spring of 1968. There was an underground expression current at the time, 'the shit is coming down', variously interpreted as meaning the day of judgment was at hand or all hell was breaking loose, and Charlie often used it in reference to the coming racial conflict. But he wasn't rabid about it, Gregg said; it was just one of many subjects they discussed.

'When I first met Charlie [in June 1968], he really didn't have any of this Helter Skelter stuff going,' Paul Watkins told me. 'He talked a little bit about the "shit coming down", but just barely ... He said when the shit comes down the black man will be on one side and the white will be on the other, and that's all he said about it.'

Then, that December, Capitol issued the Beatles' White Album, one of the songs of which was 'Helter Skelter'. The final stanza went: 'Look out helter skelter helter skelter helter skelter/Look out [background scream] helter skelter/She's coming down fast/Yes she is/Yes she is.'

Manson apparently first heard the White Album in Los Angeles, while on a trip from Barker Ranch, where most of the Family remained. When Manson returned to Death Valley on December 31, 1968, he told the group, according to Poston, 'Are you hep to what the Beatles are saying? Helter Skelter is coming down. The Beatles are telling it like it is.'

It was the same expression, except that in place of the word for defecation Manson now substituted 'Helter Skelter'.

Another link had been made, this time to the bloody words on the refrigerator door at the LaBianca residence.

Though this was the first time Manson used the phrase, it was not to be the last.

Watkins: 'And he started rapping about this Beatle album and Helter Skelter and all these meanings that I didn't get out of it . . . and he builds this picture up and he called it Helter Skelter, and what it meant was the Negroes were going to come down and rip the cities all apart.'

After this, Watkins said, 'We started listening to the Beatles' album constantly . . .'

Death Valley is very cold in the winter, so Manson found a two-story house at 20910 Gresham Street in Canoga Park, in the San Fernando Valley, not too far from Spahn Ranch. In January 1969, Watkins said, 'we all moved into the Gresham Street house to get ready for Helter Skelter. So we could watch it coming down and see all of the things going on in the city. He [Charlie] called the Gresham Street house "The Yellow Submarine" from the Beatles' movie. It was like a submarine in that when you were in it you weren't allowed to go out. You could only peek out of the windows. We started designing dune buggies and motorcycles and we were going to buy twenty-five Harley sportsters . . . and we mapped escape routes to the desert . . . supply caches . . . we had all these different things going.

'I watched him building this big picture up,' Paul noted. 'He would do it very slowly, very carefully. I swallowed it hook, line, and sinker.

'Before Helter Skelter came along,' Watkins said with a sigh of wistful nostalgia, 'all Charlie cared about was orgies.'

Before Jakobson and I had ever discussed the Beatles, I asked him: 'Did Charlie ever talk to you about a black-white revolution?'

A. 'Yeah, that was Helter Skelter, and he believed it was going to happen in the near future, almost immediately . . . He used to explain how it would be so simple to start out. A couple of black people – some of the spades from Watts – would come up into the Bel Air and Beverly Hills district . . . up in the rich piggy district . . . and just really wipe some people out, just cutting bodies up and smearing blood and writing things on the wall in blood . . . all kinds of super-atrocious crimes that would really make the white man mad . . .'

Poston said very much the same thing before I ever talked to Watkins, but with the addition of one very important detail: 'He [Manson] said a group of real blacks would come out of the ghettos and do an atrocious crime in the richer sections of Los Angeles and other cities. They would do an atrocious murder with stabbing, killing, cutting bodies to pieces, smearing blood on the walls, writing "pigs" on the walls . . . in the victims' own blood.'

This was tremendously powerful evidence – linking Manson not only with the Tate murders, where PIG had been printed in Sharon Tate's blood on the front door of the residence, but also with the LaBianca murders, where DEATH TO PIGS had been printed in Leno LaBianca's blood on the living-room wall – and I questioned Poston in depth as to Manson's exact words, where the conversation had occurred, when, and who else was present. I then questioned everyone Poston mentioned who was willing to cooperate.

Ordinarily, I try to avoid repetitious testimony in a trial, knowing it can antagonize the jury. However, Manson's Helter Skelter motive was so bizarre that I knew if it was expounded by only one witness no juror would ever believe it.

The conversation had occurred in February 1969, at the Gresham Street house, Poston said.

We now had evidence that six months before the Tate-LaBianca murders Charles Manson was telling the Family exactly how the murders would occur, complete even to writing 'pigs' in the victims' own blood.

We now had also linked Manson with every one of the bloody words found at both the Tate and LaBianca residences.

But this would only be the beginning, Manson told Watkins. These murders would cause mass paranoia among the whites: 'Out of their fear they would go into the ghetto and just start shooting black people like crazy.' But all they would kill would be 'the ones that were with whitey in the first place.'

The 'true black race' – whom Manson identified at various times as the Black Muslims and the Black Panthers – 'wouldn't even be affected by it'. They would be in hiding, waiting, he said.

After the slaughter, the Black Muslims would 'come out and appeal to the whites, saying, "Look what you have done to my people." And this would split whitey down the middle,' Watkins said, 'between the hippie-liberals and all the uptight conservatives . . .' And it would be like the War between the States, brother against brother, white killing white. Then, after the whites had mostly killed off each other, 'the Black Muslims would come out of hiding and wipe them *all* out'.

All except Charlie and the Family, who would have taken refuge in the bottomless pit in Death Valley.

The karma would then have turned. 'Blackie would be on top.' And he would begin to 'clean up the mess, just like he always has done . . . He will clean up the mess that the white man made, and build the world back up a little bit, build the cities back up. But then he wouldn't know what to do with it. He couldn't handle it.'

According to Manson, Watkins said, the black man had a problem. He could only do what the white man had taught him to do. He wouldn't be able to run the world without whitey showing him how.

Watkins: 'Blackie then would come to Charlie and say, you know, "I did my thing. I killed them all and, you know, I am tired of killing now. It is all over."'

'And then Charlie would scratch blackie's fuzzy head and kick him in the butt and tell him to go pick cotton and go be a good nigger, and we would live happily ever after . . .' The Family, now grown to 144,000, as predicted in the Bible – a pure, white master race – would emerge from the bottomless pit. And 'It would be our world then. There would be no one else, except for us and the black servants.'

And, according to the gospel of Charlie – as he related it to his disciple Paul Watkins – he, Charles Willis Manson, the fifth angel, JC, would then rule that world.

Paul Watkins, Brooks Poston, and Gregg Jakobson had not only defined Manson's motive, Helter Skelter, Watkins had supplied that missing link. In his sick, twisted, disordered mind, Charles Manson believed that *he* would be the ultimate beneficiary of the black-white war and the murders which triggered it.

One day at the Gresham Street house, while they were on an acid trip, Manson had reiterated to Watkins and the others that blackie had no smart, 'that the only thing blackie knows is what whitey has told him or shown him' and 'so someone is going to have to show him how to do it'.

I asked Watkins: 'How to do what?'

A. 'How to bring down Helter Skelter. How to do all these things.'

Watkins: 'Charlie said the only reason it hadn't come down already was because whitey was feeding his young daughters to the black man in Haight-Ashbury, and he said that if his music came out, and all of the beautiful people – "love" he called it – left Haight-Ashbury, blackie would turn to Bel Air to get his rocks off.'

Blackie had been temporarily 'pacified' by the young white girls, Manson claimed. But when he took away the pacifier – when his album came out and all the young loves followed Pied Piper Charlie to the desert – blackie would need another means of getting his frustrations out and he would then turn to the establishment.

But Terry Melcher didn't come through. The album wasn't made. Sometime in late February of 1969 Manson sent Brooks and Juanita to Barker Ranch. The rest of the Family moved back to Spahn and began preparing for Helter Skelter. 'Now there was an actual physical effort to get things together, so they could move to the desert,' Gregg said. Jakobson, who visited the ranch during this period, was startled at the change in Manson. Previously he had preached oneness of the Family, complete in itself, self-sufficient; now he was cultivating outsiders, the motorcycle gangs. Before this he had been anti-materialistic; now he was accumulating vehicles, guns, money. 'It struck me that all this contradicted what Charlie had done and talked to me about before,' Gregg said, explaining that this was the beginning of his disenchantment and eventual break with Manson.

While at the Gresham Street house, Manson had told Watkins that the atrocious murders would occur that summer. It was almost summer now and the blacks were showing no signs of rising up to fulfill their karma. One day in late May or early June of 1969, Manson took Watkins aside, down near the old trailer at Spahn, and confided: 'The only thing black knows is what whitey has told him.' He then added, '*I'm* going to have to show him how to do it.'

According to Watkins: 'I got some weird pictures from that.' A few days later Watkins took off for Barker, fearful that if he stuck around he would see those weird pictures materialize into nihilistic reality.

It was September of 1969 before Manson himself returned to Barker Ranch, to find that Watkins and Poston had defected. Though Manson told Watkins about 'cutting Shorty into nine pieces', he made no mention whatsoever of the Tate-LaBianca murders. In discussing Helter Skelter with Watkins, however, Manson said, without explanation, 'I had to show blackie how to do it.'

On February 11, Kitty Lutesinger had given birth to Bobby Beausoleil's child. Even before this, she was an unwilling witness, and the little information I got from her came hard. Later she would return to the Family, leave it, go back. Unsure of what she might say on the stand, I eventually decided against calling her as a witness.

I made the same decision in relation to biker Al Springer, though for different reasons. Most of his testimony would be repetitive of DeCarlo's. Also, his most damning testimony – Manson's statement, 'We got five of them the other night' – was inadmissible because of *Aranda*. I did interview Springer, several times, and one remark Manson made to him, re the murders, gave me a glimpse into Manson's possible defense strategy. In discussing the many criminal activities of the Family, Manson had told Springer: 'No matter what happens, the girls will take the rap for it.'

I interviewed Danny numerous times, one session lasting nine hours, obtaining considerable information that hadn't come out in previous interviews. Each time I picked up a few more examples of Manson's domination: Manson would tell the Family when it was time to eat; he wouldn't permit anyone to be served until he was seated; during dinner he would lecture on his philosophy.

Although DeCarlo was extremely reluctant to testify, Sergeant Gutierrez and I eventually persuaded him that it was in his own best interests to do so.

I had less success with Dennis Wilson, singer and drummer for the Beach Boys. Though Wilson initially claimed to know nothing of importance, he finally agreed to 'level' with me, but he refused to testify.

It was obvious that Wilson was scared, and not without good reason. On December 4, 1969, three days after LAPD announced they had broken the case, Wilson had received an anonymous death threat. It was, I learned, not the only such threat, and the others were not anonymous.

Though denying any knowledge of the Family's criminal activities, Wilson did supply some interesting background information. In the late spring of 1968, Wilson had twice picked up the same pair of female hitchhikers while driving through Malibu. The second time he took the girls home with him. For Dennis, home was 14400 Sunset Boulevard, a palatial residence formerly owned by humorist Will Rogers. The girls – Ella Jo Bailey and Patricia Krenwinkel – stayed a couple of hours, Dennis said, mostly talking about this guy named Charlie.

Wilson had a recording session that night and didn't get home until 3 A.M. When he pulled into the driveway, a strange man stepped out of his back door. Wilson, frightened, asked, 'Are you going to hurt me?' The man said, 'Do I look like I'm going to hurt you, brother?' He then dropped to his knees and kissed Wilson's feet – obviously one of Charlie's favorite routines. When Manson ushered Wilson into his own home, he discovered he had about a dozen uninvited house guests, nearly all of them girls.

They stayed for several months, during which time the group more than doubled in number. (It was during Manson's 'Sunset Boulevard period' that Charles 'Tex' Watson, Brooks Poston, and Paul Watkins became associated with the Family.) The experience, Dennis later estimated, cost him about $100,000. Besides Manson's constantly hitting him for money, Clem demolished Wilson's uninsured $21,000 Mercedes-Benz by plowing it into a mountain on the approach to Spahn Ranch; the Family appropriated Wilson's wardrobe, and just about everything else in sight; and several times Wilson found it necessary to take the whole Family to his Beverly Hills doctor for penicillin shots. 'It was probably the largest gonorrhea bill in history,' Dennis admitted. Wilson even gave Manson nine or ten of the Beach Boys' gold records and paid to have Sadie's teeth fixed.

The newly divorced Wilson obviously found something attractive about Manson's life-style. 'Except for the expense,' Dennis told me, 'I got along very well with Charlie and the girls.' He and Charlie would sing and talk, Dennis said, while the girls cleaned house, cooked, and catered to their needs. Wilson said he liked the 'spontaneity' of Charlie's music, but added that 'Charlie never had a musical bone in his body'. Despite this, Dennis tried hard to 'sell' Manson to others. He rented a recording studio in Santa Monica and had Manson recorded. Wilson also introduced Manson to a number of people in or on the fringes of the entertainment industry, including Melcher, Jakobson, and Altobelli. At one party, Charlie gave Dean Martin's daughter, Deana, a ring and asked her to join the Family. Deana told me she kept the ring, which she later gave to her husband, but declined Manson's invitation. As did the other Beach Boys, none of whom shared Dennis' fondness for the 'scruffy little guru', as one described him.

Wilson denied having any conflicts with Manson during this period. However, in August 1968, three weeks before his lease was to expire, Dennis moved in with Gregg, leaving to his manager the task of evicting Charlie and the girls.

From Sunset Boulevard the Family moved to Spahn Ranch. Although Wilson apparently avoided the group for a time, he did see Manson occasionally. Dennis told me that he didn't have any trouble with Charlie until August 1969 – Dennis could not recall the exact date, but he did know it was after the Tate murders – when Manson visited him, demanding $1,500 so he could go to the desert. When Wilson refused, Charlie told him, 'Don't be surprised if you never see your kid again.' Dennis had a 7-year-old son, and obviously this was one reason for his reluctance to testify.

Manson also threatened Wilson himself, but Dennis did not learn of this until an interview I conducted with both Wilson and Jakobson. According to Jakobson, not long after Dennis refused Manson's request, Charlie handed Gregg a .44 caliber bullet and told him, 'Tell Dennis there are more where this came from.' Knowing how the other threat had upset Dennis, Gregg hadn't mentioned it to him.

This incident had occurred in late August or early September of 1969. Jakobson was startled by the change in Manson. 'The electricity was almost pouring out of him. His hair was on end. His eyes were wild. The only thing I can compare it to . . . is that he was just like an animal in a cage.'

Looking back on his involvement with the Family, Dennis told me: 'I'm the luckiest guy in the world, because I got off only losing my money.''

From rock star to motorcycle rider to ex-call girl, the witnesses in this case all had one thing in common: they were afraid for their lives. They needed only to pick up a newspaper or turn on

TV to see that many of the Family members were still roaming the streets; that Steve Grogan, aka Clem, was out on bail, while the Inyo County grand theft charges against Bruce Davis had been dismissed for lack of evidence. Neither Grogan, Davis, nor any of the others suspected of beheading Shorty Shea had been charged with that murder, there being as yet no physical proof that Shea was dead.

Perhaps in her cell at Sybil Brand, Susan Atkins recalled the lyrics of the Beatles' song 'Sexy Sadie':

> 'Sexy Sadie what have you done
> You made a fool of everyone . . .
> Sexy Sadie you broke the rules
> You laid it out for all to see . . .
> Sexy Sadie you'll get yours yet
> However big you think you are . . .'

Or perhaps it was simply that the numerous messages Manson was sending, by other Family members, were getting to her.

Susan called in Caballero and told him that under no circumstances would she testify at the trial. And she demanded to see Charlie.

Caballero told Aaron and me that it looked as if we'd lost our star witness.

We contacted Gary Fleischman, Linda Kasabian's attorney, and told him we were ready to talk.

From the start Fleischman, dedicated to the welfare of his client, had wanted nothing less than complete immunity for Linda Kasabian. Not until after I had talked to Linda myself did I learn that she had been willing to talk to us, immunity or not, and that only Fleischman had kept her from doing so. I also learned that she had decided to return to California voluntarily, against the advice of Fleischman, who had wanted her to fight extradition.

After a number of discussions, our office agreed to petition the Superior Court for immunity, *after* she had testified. In return it was agreed: (1) that Linda Kasabian would give us a full and complete statement of her involvement in the Tate-LaBianca murders; (2) that Linda Kasabian would testify truthfully at all trial proceedings against all defendants; and (3) that in the event Linda Kasabian did not testify truthfully, or that she refused to testify, for whatever reason, she would be prosecuted fully, but that any statement that she gave the prosecution would not be used against her.

When I interviewed Linda Kasabian, it was the first time she had discussed the Tate-LaBianca murders with anyone connected with law enforcement.

Small, with long light-brown hair, Linda bore a distinct resemblance to the actress Mia Farrow. As I got to know her, I found Linda a quiet girl, docile, easily led, yet she communicated an inner sureness, almost a fatalism, that made her seem much older than her 20 years. The product of a broken home, she herself had had two unsuccessful marriages, the last of which, to a young hippie, Robert Kasabian, had broken up just before she went to Spahn Ranch. She had one child, a girl named Tanya, age 2, and was now 8 months pregnant with another, conceived, she thought, the last time she and her husband were together. She had remained with the Family less than a month and a half – 'I was like a little blind girl in the forest, and I took the first path that came to me.' Only now, talking about what had happened, did she feel she was emerging from the darkness, she said.

On her own since 16, Linda had wandered from the east coast to the west, 'looking for God'. In her quest she had lived in communes and crash pads, taken drugs, had sex with almost anyone who showed an interest. She described all this with a candor that at times shocked me, yet which, I knew, would be a plus on the witness stand.

From the first interview I believed her story, and I felt that a jury would also. There were no pauses in her answers, no evasions, no attempts to make herself appear something she was not. She was brutally frank. When a witness takes the stand and tells the truth, even though it is injurious to his own image, you know he can't be impeached. I knew that if Linda testified truthfully about those two nights of murder, it would be immaterial whether she had been promiscuous, taken dope, stolen.

I talked to her from 1 to 4:30 P.M. on the twenty-eighth. It was the first of many long interviews, all of which took place at Sybil Brand, her attorney usually the only other person present. At the end of each interview I'd tell her that if, back in her cell, anything occurred to her which we hadn't discussed, to 'jot it down'. A number of these notes became letters to me, running to a dozen or more pages. All of which, together with my interview notes, became available to the defense under discovery.

Though she added many details, Linda Kasabian's story of those two nights was basically the same as Susan Atkins's. There were only a few surprises. But they were big ones.

Prior to my talking to Linda, we had assumed that she had probably witnessed only one murder, the shooting of Steve Parent. We now learned that she had also seen Katie chasing Abigail Folger across the lawn with an upraised knife and Tex stabbing Voytek Frykowski to death.

She also told me that on the night the LaBiancas were killed, Manson had attempted to commit three other murders.

10050 Cielo Drive.

Steven Earl Parent, 18, at his high-school prom.

Scale diagram of the Tate residence.

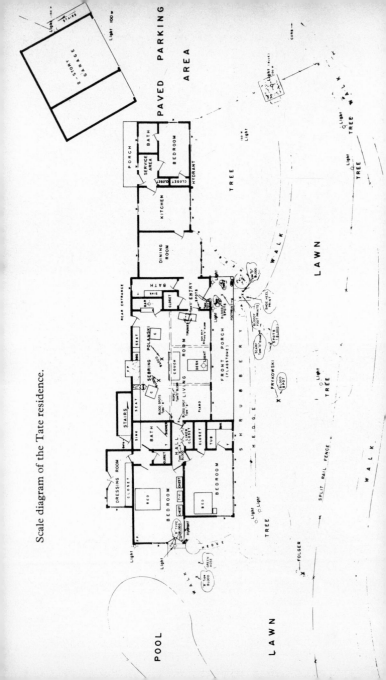

Jay Sebring, 35.

Sharon Tate, 26.

Abigail Folger, 25, and Voytek Frykowski, 32.

Leno LaBianca, 44.

Rosemary LaBianca, 38.

Spahn Ranch cowboy Donald 'Shorty' Shea.

Charles Manson, also known as
Jesus Christ, God.

Charles Manson at the time of the
Spahn Ranch raid,
August 16, 1969.

Manson after the October 10–12,
1969, raid on Barker Ranch in
Death Valley.

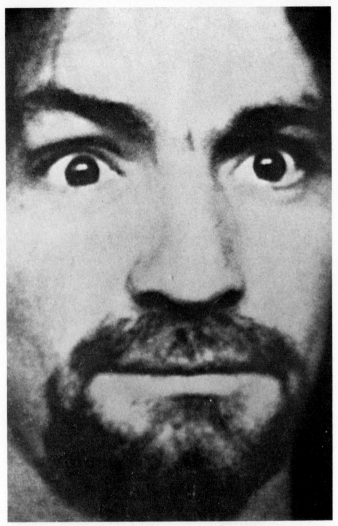

The most widely publicized photograph of Charles Manson.
Photo courtesy of Robert Hendrickson and Laurence Merrick.

Charles Watson, aka Tex, age 23.

Susan Denise Atkins, aka Sadie Mae Glutz, 21. *Photo courtesy of Robert Hendrickson and Laurence Merrick.*

Leslie Van Houten, aka LuLu, age 20. *Photo courtesy of Robert Hendrickson and Laurence Merrick.*

Patricia Krenwinkel, aka Katie, age 21. *Photo courtesy of Robert Hendrickson and Laurence Merrick.*

Robert 'Bobby' Beausoleil, aka
Cupid, age 22. *Photo courtesy of
Robert Hendrickson and Laurence
Merrick.*

Mary Theresa Brunner, age 25.
*Photo courtesy of Robert
Hendrickson and Laurence Merrick.*

Steve Grogan, aka Clem, age 17.
*Photo courtesy of Robert
Hendrickson and Laurence Merrick.*

Bruce McGregor Davis, age 26.

Lynette Fromme, aka Squeaky, age 20. *Photo courtesy of Robert. Hendrickson and Laurence Merrick.*

Catherine Share, aka Gypsy, age 27. *Photo courtesy of Robert Hendrickson and Laurence Merrick.*

During the August 16, 1969, raid on Spahn Ranch, sheriff's deputies arrested twenty-six persons. *From far left to right:* Straight Satan motorcycle gang member Danny DeCarlo, Charles Manson, Straight Satan Robert Reinhard, and ranch hand Juan Flynn.

Manson Family members and ranch hands alike were pulled in during the massive raid, which netted a huge cache of arms, including a submachine gun.

Among those arrested and taken to Independence to be booked were Gypsy (*far left*) and Katie, Brenda, Squeaky, and Sadie (*far right*). Standing along the jeep is Brenda.

The 'Helter Skelter' door found at Spahn Ranch.

Prosecutor Vincent Bugliosi. *Photo courtesy of Curt Gunther.*

Linda Kasabian, star witness for the prosecution.
Photo courtesy of Robert Hendrickson and Laurence Merrick.

The faces of Charles Manson. According to his disciple Squeaky: 'He was a changeling. He seemed to change every time I saw him.'

Manson's attorney Irving Kanarek.
Photo courtesy of Robert Hendrickson and Laurence Merrick.

During the trial Manson Family members conducted a vigil outside the Hall of Justice. *Left to right:* Sandy, Ouisch, Cathy, and Mary.
Photo courtesy of Robert Hendrickson and Laurence Merrick.

When Manson carved an X on his forehead, his followers did likewise. *Left to right :* Squeaky, Sandy, Ouisch, Cathy.
Photo courtesy of Robert Hendrickson and Laurence Merrick.

Following the guilty verdicts, Manson, Atkins, Krenwinkel, and Van Houten shaved their heads, as did the girls on the corner. *Left to right, facing camera :* Crystal, Mary, Kitty. *Backs to camera, left to right :* Sandy and Squeaky.
Photo courtesy of Robert Hendrickson and Laurence Merrick.

Charles Manson on his way to Death Row, San Quentin Prison.
Photo courtesy of Robert Hendrickson and Laurence Merrick.

Part Five

'Don't You Know
Who You're Crucifying?'

'For there shall arise false Christs,
and false prophets, and shall shew
great signs and wonders; insomuch that,
if it were possible, they shall deceive
the very elect . . . Wherefore, if they
shall say unto you. Behold, he is in
the desert; go not forth . . .'
Matthew 24:24, 26

'Just before we got busted in the desert,
there was twelve of us apostles and Charlie.'
Family member
Ruth Ann Moorehouse

'I may have implied on several occasions
to several different people that I may
have been Jesus Christ, but I haven't
decided yet what I am or who I am.'
Charles Manson

March 1970

On March 3, accompanied by attorney Gary Fleischman and some dozen LAPD and LASO officers, I took Linda Kasabian out of Sybil Brand. For Linda it was a trip back in time, to an almost unbelievable night nearly seven months ago.

Our first stop was 10050 Cielo Drive.

In late June of 1969, Bob Kasabian had called Linda at her mother's home in New Hampshire, suggesting a reconciliation. Kasabian was living in a trailer in Tapanga Canyon with a friend, Charles Melton. Melton, who had recently inherited $20,000, and had already given away more than half, planned to drive to the tip of South America, buy a boat, and sail around the world. He'd invited Linda and Bob, as well as another couple, to come along.

Linda, together with her daughter, Tanya, flew to Los Angeles, but the reconciliation was unsuccessful.

On July 4, 1969, Catherine Share, aka Gypsy, visited Melton, whom she had met through Paul Watkins. Gypsy told Linda about 'this beautiful man named Charlie', the Family, and how life at Spahn was all love, beauty, and peace. To Linda it was 'as if the answer to an unspoken prayer'.* That same day Linda and Tanya moved to Spahn. Though she didn't meet Manson that day, she did meet most of the other members of the Family, and they talked of little else. It was obvious to her that 'they worshiped him'.

That night Tex took her into a small room and told her 'far-

---

* My interviews with Linda Kasabian were not taped. Exact quotations are from either my interview notes, her trial testimony, or her narrative letters to me.

out things – nothing was wrong, all was right – things I couldn't comprehend'. Then 'He made love to me, and a strange experience took place – it was like being possessed.' When it was over, Linda's fingers were clenched so tightly they hurt. Gypsy later told her that what she had experienced was the death of the ego.

After making love, Linda and Tex talked, Linda mentioning Melton's inheritance. Tex told her that she should steal the money. According to Linda, she told him she couldn't do that – Melton was a friend, a brother. Tex told her that she could do no wrong and that everything should be shared. The next day Linda went back to the trailer and stole $5,000, which she gave to either Leslie or Tex. She had already turned over all her possessions to the Family, the girls having told her, 'What's yours is ours and what's ours is yours.'

Linda met Charles Manson for the first time that night. After all she had heard about him, she felt as if she were on trial. He asked why she had come to the ranch. She replied that her husband had rejected her. Manson reached out and felt her legs. 'He seemed pleased with them,' Linda recalled. Then he told her she could stay. Before making love to her, he told her that she had a father hangup. Linda was startled by his perception, because she disliked her stepfather. She felt that Manson could see inside her.

Linda Kasabian became a part of the Family – went on garbage runs, had sex with the men, creepy-crawled a house, and listened as Manson lectured about the Beatles, Helter Skelter, and the bottomless pit. Charlie told her that the black man was together but the white man was not. However, he knew a way to unite the white man, he said. It was the only way. But he didn't tell her what it was.

Nor did she ask. The first time they met, Manson had stressed, 'Never ask why.' When something he said or did puzzled her, she was reminded of this. Also of another of his favorite axioms, 'No sense makes sense.'

The whole Family, Linda said, was 'paranoid of blackie'. On weekends George Spahn did a brisk business renting horses. Occasionally among the riders there would be blacks. Manson maintained they were Panthers, spying on the Family. He always hid the young girls when they were around. At night everyone was required to wear dark clothing, so as to be less conspicuous, and eventually Manson posted armed guards, who roamed the ranch until dawn.

Gradually Linda became convinced that Charles Manson was Jesus Christ. He never told her this directly, but one day he asked her, 'Don't you know who I am?'

She replied, 'No, am I supposed to know something?'

He didn't answer, just smiled, and playfully twirled her around.

Yet she had doubts. The mothers were not allowed to care for their own children. They separated her and Tanya, Linda explained, because they wanted 'to kill the ego that I put in her' and 'at first I agreed to it, I thought that it was a good idea that she should become her own person'. Also, several times she saw Manson strike Dianne Lake. Linda had been in many communes – from the American Psychedelic Circus in Boston to Sons of the Earth Mother near Taos – but she'd never seen anything like this, and, forgetting Charlie's commandment, she did ask Gypsy why. Gypsy told her that Dianne really wanted to be beaten, and Charlie was only obliging her.

Overriding all doubts was one fact: she had fallen in love with Charles Manson.

Linda had been at Spahn Ranch a little over a month when, on the afternoon of Friday, August 8, 1969, Manson told the Family: *'Now is the time for Helter Skelter.'*

That Friday evening, about an hour after dinner, seven or eight members of the Family were standing on the boardwalk in front of the saloon when Manson came out and, calling Tex, Sadie, Katie, and Linda aside, told each to get a change of clothing and a knife. He also told Linda to get her driver's license. Linda, I later learned, was the only Family member with a valid license, excepting Mary Brunner, who had been arrested that afternoon. This was, I concluded, probably one of the reasons why Manson had picked Linda to accompany the others, each of whom, unlike her, had been with him a year or more.

Linda couldn't find her own knife (Sadie had it), but she obtained one from Larry Jones. The handle was broken and had been replaced with tape. Brenda found Linda's license and gave it to her just about the time Manson told Linda, 'Go with Tex and do whatever Tex tells you to do.'

Linda said that after Manson instructed her to go with Tex, the group piled into ranch hand Johnny Swartz's old Ford.

I asked Linda what each was wearing. She wasn't absolutely sure, but she thought Sadie had on a dark-blue T-shirt and dungarees, that Katie's attire was similar, and that Tex was wearing a black velour turtleneck and dark dungarees.

When shown the clothing the TV crew had found, Linda identified six of the seven items, failing to recall only the white T-shirt. The logical assumption was that she hadn't seen it because it had been worn under one of the other shirts.

What about footwear? I asked. The girls, she believed, were all barefoot. She thought, but couldn't be sure, that Tex had on cowboy boots.

A number of bloody footprints had been found at the Tate murder scene. After eliminating those belonging to LAPD personnel, two remained unidentified: a boot-heel print and the print of a bare foot – thus supporting Linda's recollections. Again, as with Susan Atkins, I badly needed independent corroboration of Linda's testimony.

I then asked Linda the same question I'd asked Susan – had any of them been on drugs that night? – and received the same reply: no.

As Tex started to drive off, Manson said, 'Hold it,' or 'Wait.' He then leaned in the window on the passenger side and said, 'Leave a sign. You girls know what to write. Something witchy.'

Tex handed Linda three knives and a gun, telling her to wrap them in a rag and put them on the floor. If stopped by the police, Tex said, she was to throw them out.

Linda positively identified the .22 caliber Longhorn revolver. Only at this time, she said, the grip had been intact and the barrel unbent.

According to Linda, Tex did not tell them their destination, or what they were going to do; however, she presumed they were going on another creepy-crawly mission. Tex did say that he had been to the house and knew the layout.

As we drove up Cielo Drive in the sheriff's van, Linda showed me where Tex had turned, in front of the gate at 10050, then parked, next to the telephone pole. He had then taken a pair of large, red-handled wire cutters from the back seat and shinnied up the pole. From where she was sitting, Linda couldn't see Tex cutting the wires, but she saw and heard the wires fall.

When shown the wire cutters found at Barker Ranch, Linda said they 'looked like' the pair used that night. Since the wire cutters had been found in Manson's personal dune buggy, her identification linked them not just to the Family but to Manson himself. I was especially pleased at this evidence, unaware that link would soon be severed, literally.

When Tex returned to the car, they drove to a spot near the bottom of the hill and parked. The four then took the weapons and extra clothing and stealthily walked back up to the gate. Tex also had some white rope, which was draped over his shoulder.

Linda pointed to the spot, to the right of the gate, where they had climbed the embankment and scaled the fence. As they were descending the other side, a pair of headlights suddenly appeared in the driveway. 'Lay down and be quiet,' Tex ordered. He then jumped up and ran to the automobile, which had stopped near the gate-control mechanism. Linda heard a man's voice saying, 'Please don't hurt me! I won't say anything!' She then saw Tex put the gun in the open window on the driver's side and heard four shots. She also saw the man slump over in the seat.

(Something here puzzled me, and still does. In addition to the gunshot wounds, Steven Parent had a defensive stab wound that ran from the palm across the wrist of his left hand. It severed the tendons as well as the band of his wristwatch. Obviously, Parent had raised his left hand, the hand closest to the open window, in an effort to protect himself, the force of the blow being sufficient to hurl his watch into the back seat. It therefore appeared that Tex must have approached the car with a knife in one hand, a gun in the other, and that he first slashed at Parent, then shot him. Yet neither Susan nor Linda saw Tex with a knife at this point, nor did either recall the stabbing.)

Linda saw Tex reach in the car and turn off the lights and ignition. He then pushed the car some distance up the driveway, telling the others to follow him.

The shooting put her in a state of shock, Linda said. 'My mind went blank. I was aware of my body, walking toward the house.'

As we went up the driveway, I asked Linda which lights had been on that night. She pointed to the bug light on the side of the garage, also the Christmas-tree lights along the fence. Little details, yet important if the defense contended Linda was fabricating her story from what she had read in the papers, since neither these, nor numerous other details I collected, had appeared in the press.

As we approached the residence, I noticed that Linda was shivering and her arms were covered with goose bumps. Though it wasn't cold that day, Linda was now nine months pregnant, and I slipped off my coat and put it over her shoulders. The shivering continued, however, all the time we were on the premises, and often, in pointing out something, she would begin crying. There was no question in my mind that the tears were real and that she was deeply affected by what had happened in this place. I couldn't help contrasting Linda with Susan.

When they reached the house, Linda said, Tex sent her around the back to look for an unlocked window or door. She reported that everything was locked, though she hadn't actually checked. (This explained why they ignored the open nursery window.) Tex then slit a screen on one of the front windows with a knife. Though the actual screen had since been replaced, Linda pointed to the correct window. She also said the slash was horizontal, as it had been. Tex then told her to go back and wait by the car in the driveway.

Linda did as she was told. Perhaps a minute or two later Katie came back and asked Linda for her knife (this was the knife with the taped handle) and told her, 'Listen for sounds.'

A few minutes later Linda heard 'horrifying sounds' coming from the house. A man moaned, 'No, no, no,' then screamed very loudly. The scream, which seemed continuous, was punctuated with other voices, male and female, begging and pleading for their lives.

Wanting 'to stop what was happening', Linda said, 'I started running toward the house.' As she reached the walk, 'there was a man, a tall man, just coming out of the door, staggering, and he had blood all over his face, and he was standing by a post, and we looked into each other's eyes for a minute, I don't know however long, and I said, "Oh, God, I'm so sorry." And then he just fell into the bushes.'

'And then Sadie came running out of the house, and I said, "Sadie, *please* make it stop! People are coming!" which wasn't true, but I wanted to make it stop. And she said, "It's too late." '

Complaining that she had lost her knife, Susan ran back into the house. Linda remained outside. (Susan had earlier told me, and the grand jury, that Linda had never entered the residence.) Turning, Linda saw a dark-haired woman in a white gown running across the lawn; Katie was pursuing her, an upraised knife in her hand. Somehow, the tall man managed to stagger from the bushes next to the porch onto the lawn, where he had again fallen. Linda saw Tex hit him over the head with something – it could have been a gun but she wasn't sure – then stab him repeatedly in the back as he lay on the ground.

(Shown a number of photographs, Linda identified the tall man as Voytek Frykowski, the dark-haired woman as Abigail Folger. Examining the autopsy report on Frykowski, I found that five of his fifty-one stab wounds were to the back.)

Linda turned and ran down the driveway. For what seemed like maybe five minutes, she hid in the bushes near the gate, then climbed the fence again and ran down Cielo to where they had parked the Ford.

Q. 'Why didn't you run to one of the houses and call the police?' I asked Linda.

A. 'My first thought was "Get help!" Then my little girl entered my mind – she was back [at the ranch] with Charlie. I didn't know where I was or how to get out of there.'

She got in the car and had started the engine when 'all of a sudden they were there. They were covered with blood. They looked like zombies. Tex yelled at me to turn off the car and get over. He had a terrible look in his eyes.' Linda slid over to the passenger side. 'Then he started in on Sadie and yelled at her for losing her knife.'

Tex had put the .22 revolver on the seat between them. Linda noticed that the grip was broken, and Tex told her it had smashed when he hit the man over the head. Sadie and Katie complained that their heads hurt because the people had pulled their hair while they were fighting with them. Sadie also said the big man had hit her over the head and that 'the girl' – it was unclear whether she meant Sharon or Abigail – had cried for her mother. Katie also complained that her hand hurt, explaining that when she stabbed, she kept hitting bones, and since the knife didn't have a regular handle, it bruised her hand.

Q. 'How did *you* feel, Linda?'

A. 'In a state of shock.'

Q. 'What about the others, how did they act?'

A. 'As if it was all a game.'

Tex, Sadie, and Katie changed their clothing while the car was in motion, Linda holding the wheel for Tex. Linda herself didn't change, since there was no blood on her. Tex told them he wanted to find a place to hose the blood off, and he turned off Benedict Canyon onto a short street not too far from the Tate residence.

Linda's account of the hosing incident paralleled Susan Atkins' and Rudolf Weber's. Weber's house was located 1.8 miles from the Tate premises.

From there Tex turned onto Benedict Canyon again and drove along through a dark, hilly country area. He stopped the car on a dirt shoulder off the road, and Tex, Sadie, and Katie gave Linda their bloody clothing, which, on Tex's instructions, she rolled up in one bundle and threw down the slope. Since it was dark, she couldn't see where it landed.

After driving off, Tex told Linda to wipe the knives clean of fingerprints, then throw them out the window. She did, the first knife hitting a bush at the side of the road, the second, which she tossed out a few seconds later, striking the curb and bouncing back into the road. Looking back, she saw it lying there. Linda believed she threw the gun out a few minutes later but she wasn't sure; it was possible that Tex did it.

After driving for a time, they stopped at a gas station – Linda was unable to recall the street – where Katie and Sadie took turns going into the rest room to wash the rest of the blood off their bodies. Then they drove back to Spahn Ranch.

Linda did not have a watch but guessed it must have been about 2 A.M. Charles Manson was standing on the boardwalk in the same spot where he had been when they drove off.

Sadie said she saw some blood on the outside of the car, and Manson had the girls get rags and sponges and wash the car inside and out.

He then told them to go to the bunkhouse. Brenda and Clem were already there. Manson asked Tex how it had gone. Tex told him that there was a lot of panic, that it was real messy, and that there were bodies lying all over the place, but that everyone was dead.

Manson asked the four, 'Do you have any remorse?' All shook their heads and said, 'No.'

Linda did feel remorse, she told me, but she didn't admit it to Charlie because 'I was afraid for my life. I could see in his eyes he knew how I felt. And it was against his way.'

Manson told them, 'Go to bed and say nothing to the others.'

Linda slept most of the day. It was almost sundown when Sadie told her to go into the trailer, that the TV news was coming on. Although Linda could not recall seeing Tex, she remembered Sadie, Katie, Barbara Hoyt, and Clem being there.

It was the big news. For the first time Linda heard the names of the victims. She also learned that one, Sharon Tate, had been pregnant. Only a few days earlier Linda had learned that she herself was pregnant.

'As we were watching the news,' Linda said, 'in my head I kept saying, "Why would they do such a thing?" '

After Linda and I left the Tate residence, I asked her to show us the route they had taken. She found the dirt shoulder where they had pulled off to dispose of the clothing, but was unable to find the street where Tex had turned off Benedict Canyon, so I had the sheriff's deputy who was driving take us directly to Portola. Once on the street, Linda immediately identified 9870, pointing to the hose in front. Number 9870 was Rudolf Weber's house. She also pointed to the spot where they had parked the car. It was the same spot Weber had indicated. Neither his address, nor even the fact that he had been located, had appeared in the press.

After Linda was back in jail, I asked Sergeant McGann to get some cadets from the Police Academy, or a troop of Boy Scouts, and conduct a search for the knives. From Linda's testimony, we knew that they had probably been thrown out of the car somewhere between the clothing site and the hill where young Steven Weiss had found the gun, an area of less than two miles. We also knew that since Linda had looked back and seen one of the knives lying in the road, there must have been some illumination nearby, which could be another clue.

The following day, March 4, Gypsy made another visit to Fleischman's office. She told him, in the presence of his law partner Ronald Goldman, 'If Linda testifies, thirty people are going to do something about it.'

I'd already checked out the security at Sybil Brand. Until her baby was born, Linda was being kept in an isolation cell off the infirmary. She had no contact with the other inmates; deputies brought her meals. After the baby was born, however, she would be reassigned to one of the open dormitories, where she might be threatened, even killed, by Sadie, Katie, or Leslie. I made a note to talk to Captain Carpenter to see if other arrangements could be made.

Attorney Richard Caballero had been able to postpone the inevitable, but he couldn't prevent it. The meeting between Susan Atkins and Charles Manson took place in the Los Angeles County Jail on March 5. It was like a 'joyous homecoming'. Sadie Mae Glutz had returned to the irresistible Charles Manson.

She fired Caballero the next day.

On March 6, Manson appeared in court and argued a number of novel motions. One asked that the 'Deputy District Attorneys in charge of the trial be incarcerated for a period of time under the same circumstances that I have been subject to . . .' Another requested that he 'be free to travel to any place I should deem fit in preparing my defense . . .'

There were more, and Judge Keene declared himself 'appalled' at Manson's 'outlandish' requests. Keene then said he had reviewed the entire file on the case, from his 'nonsensical' motions to his numerous violations of the gag order. He had also discussed Manson's conduct with Judges Lucas and Dell, before whom Manson had also appeared, concluding that it had become 'abundantly clear to me that you are incapable of acting as your own attorney'.

Infuriated, Manson shouted, 'It's not me that's on trial here as much as this court is on trial!' He also told the judge, 'Go wash your hands. They're dirty.'

THE COURT. 'Mr Manson, your status, at this time, of acting as your own attorney is now vacated.'

Against Manson's strong objections, Keene appointed Charles Hollopeter, a former president of the Los Angeles Criminal Courts Bar, as Manson's attorney of record.

'You can kill me,' Manson said, 'but you can't give me an attorney. I won't take one.'

Keene told Manson that if he found an attorney of his own choosing, he would consider a motion to substitute him for

Hollopeter. I knew Hollopeter by reputation. Since he'd never be Charlie's bootlicker, I guessed he'd last about a month; I was too generous.

Toward the end of the proceeedings, Manson shouted, *'There is no God in this courtroom!'* As if on cue, a number of Family members jumped up and yelled at Keene, 'You are a mockery of justice! You are a joke!' The judge found three of them – Gypsy, Sandy, and Mark Ross – in contempt, and sentenced each to five days in the County Jail.

When Sandy was searched prior to being booked, among the items found in her purse was a Buck knife.

After this, the sheriff's deputies, who are in charge of maintaining security in the Los Angeles criminal courts, began searching all spectators before they entered the courtroom.

On March 7, Linda Kasabian was taken to the hospital. Two days later she gave birth to a boy, whom she named Angel. On the thirteenth she was returned to the jail, without the child, Linda's mother having taken him back to New Hampshire.

In the interim I had talked to Captain Carpenter, and he had agreed to let Linda remain in her former cell just off the infirmary. I checked it out myself. It was a small room, its furnishings consisting of a bed, toilet bowl, washbasin, and a small desk and chair. It was clean but bleak. Far more important, it was safe.

Every few days I called McGann. No, he hadn't got around to looking for the knives yet.

On March 11, Susan Atkins, after formally requesting that Richard Caballero be relieved as her attorney, asked for Daye Shinn in Caballero's place.

Inasmuch as Shinn, one of the first attorneys to call on Manson after he was brought down from Independence, had represented Manson on several matters and had visited him more than forty times, Judge Keene felt there might be a possible conflict of interest involved.

Shinn denied this. Keene then warned Susan of the possible dangers of being represented by an attorney who had been so closely involved with one of her co-defendants. Susan said she didn't care; she wanted Shinn. Keene granted the substitution.

I hadn't come up against Shinn before. He was about forty, Korean born; according to the press, his main practice, before allying himself with the Manson defense, had been obtaining Mexican domestics for Southern California families.

On leaving the courtroom, Shinn told waiting reporters that Susan Atkins 'definitely will deny everything she told the grand jury'.

On March 15 we took Linda Kasabian out again. I wanted her to trace the route the killers had taken the night the LaBiancas were killed.

After dinner that night – Saturday, August 9, 1969 – Linda and several other Family members were standing outside the kitchen at Spahn. Manson called Linda, Katie, and Leslie aside and told them to get a change of clothing and meet him in the bunkhouse.

This time he mentioned nothing to Linda about knives, but he did tell her again to get her driver's license.

'I just looked at him and, you know, just sort of pleaded with my eyes, please don't make me go, because,' Linda said, 'I just knew we were going out again, and I knew it would be the same thing, but I was afraid to say anything.'

'Last night was too messy,' Manson told the group when they assembled in the bunkhouse. 'This time I'm going to show you how to do it.'

Tex complained that the weapons they had used the previous night weren't effective enough!

Linda saw two swords in the bunkhouse, one of which was the Straight Satans' sword. She did not see anyone pick them up, but later she noticed the Satans' sword and two smaller knives under the front seat of the car. In questioning DeCarlo, I'd learned that one night about this time he'd noticed that the sword had been taken out.

Again the group piled into Swartz's Ford. This time Manson himself slipped into the driver's seat, with Linda next to him, Clem on the passenger side, Tex, Sadie, Katie, and Leslie crowded in back. All wore dark clothing, Linda said, except for Clem, who had on an olive-drab field jacket. As he often did, Manson wore a leather thong around his neck, the two ends extending down to his breastbone, where they were looped together. I asked Linda if anyone else was wearing such a thong; she said no.

Before they left, Manson asked Bruce Davis for some money. Just as DeCarlo took care of the Family guns, Davis acted as comptroller for the group, taking care of the stolen credit cards, fake ID, and so forth.

As they drove off, Manson told them that tonight they would divide into two groups: each would take a separate house. He said he'd drop off one group, then take the second group with him.

When they stopped to buy gas (using cash, not a credit card), Manson told Linda to take over the driving. Questioning Linda, I established that Manson – and Manson alone – gave all the instructions as to where they were to go and what they were to do. At no time, she said, did Tex Watson instruct anyone to do anything. Charlie was in complete command.

Following Manson's directions, Linda took the freeway to Pasadena. Once off it, he gave her so many directions she was unsure where they were. Eventually he told her to stop in front of a house, which Linda described as a modern, one-story, middle-class-type home. This was the place where, as described by Susan Atkins, Manson got out, had them drive around the block, then got back in, telling them that, having looked in the window and seen photographs of children, he didn't want to 'do' that particular house, though, he added, in the future it might be necessary to kill children also. Linda's account was essentially the same as Susan's.

After riding around Pasadena for some time, Manson again

took over the driving. Linda: 'I remember we started driving up a hill with lots of houses, nice houses, rich houses, and trees. We got to the top of the hill and turned around and stopped in front of a certain house.' Linda couldn't remember if it was one story or two, only that it was big. Manson, however, said the houses were too close together here, so they drove off.

Shortly after this, Manson spotted a church. Pulling into the parking lot next to it, he again got out. Linda believed, but wasn't absolutely sure, that he told them he was going to 'get' the minister or priest.

However, he returned a few minutes later, saying the church door was locked.

Susan Atkins had neglected to mention the church in her account. I learned of it for the first time from Linda Kasabian.

Manson again told Linda to drive, but the route he gave her was so confusing that she soon became lost. Later, driving up Sunset from the ocean, there occurred another incident which Susan Atkins had neglected to mention.

Observing a white sports car ahead of them, Manson told Linda, 'At the next red light, pull up beside it. I'm going to kill the driver.'

Linda pulled up next to the car, but just as Manson jumped out, the light changed to green and the sports car zoomed away.

Another potential victim, unaware to this day how close to death he had come.

Thus far, their wanderings appeared totally at random, Manson seemingly having no particular victims in mind. As I'd later argue to the jury, up to this time no one in the vast, sprawling metropolis of seven million people, whether in a home, a church, or even a car, was safe from Manson's insatiable lust for death, blood, and murder.

But after the sports-car incident, Manson's directions became very specific. He directed Linda to the Los Feliz section of Los Angeles, not far from Griffith Park, having her stop on the street in front of a home in a residential area.

Linda recognized the house. In June of 1968 she and her husband had been driving from Seattle to Taos when they stopped off in Los Angeles. A friend had taken them to the house – 3267 Waverly Drive – for a peyote party.

Linda asked, 'Charlie, you're not going to do that house, are you?'

Manson replied, 'No, the one next door.'

Telling the others to stay in the car, Manson got out. Linda noticed him shove something into his belt, but she couldn't see what it was. She watched him walking up the driveway until it curved and he disappeared from sight.

I presumed, although I couldn't be sure of this, that Manson had a gun.

For Rosemary and Leno LaBianca, the horror that would end in their deaths had begun.

Linda guessed the time was about 2 A.M. Some ten minutes later, she said, Manson returned to the car.

I asked Linda if he was still wearing the leather thong around his neck. She said she hadn't noticed, though she did notice, later that night, that he no longer had it. I showed her the leather thong used to bind the wrists of Leno LaBianca, and she said it was 'the same kind' Manson had been wearing.

Manson told Tex, Katie, and Leslie to get out of the car and bring their clothing bundles with them. Obviously they were to be the first team. Linda heard some, though not all, of the conversation. Manson told the trio that there were two people inside the house, that he had tied them up and told them that everything was going to be all right, and that they shouldn't be afraid. He also instructed Tex, Katie, and Leslie that they were not to cause fear and panic in the people as had happened the night before.

The LaBiancas had been creepy-crawled, pacified with Charles Manson's unctuous assurances, then set up to be slaughtered.

Linda heard only bits and pieces of the rest of the conversation. She did not hear Manson specifically order the three to kill the two persons. Nor did she see them carrying any weapons. She believed she heard Manson say, 'Don't let them know you are going to kill them.' And she definitely heard him instruct them that when they were done they were to hitchhike back to the ranch.

As the trio started toward the house, Manson got back in the car and handed Linda a woman's wallet, telling her to wipe off the prints and remove the change. In opening it, she noticed the driver's license, which had a photo of a woman with dark hair. She recalled the woman's first name was 'Rosemary', while the last name 'was either Mexican or Italian'. She also remembered seeing a number of credit cards and a wrist watch.

When I asked Linda the color of the wallet, she said it was red. Actually it was brown. She also claimed to have removed all the change, but when the wallet was found there were still some coins in one of the inner compartments. Both were understandable errors, I felt, particularly overlooking the extra change compartment.

Manson again took over the driving. Linda was now on the passenger side, Susan and Clem in back. Manson told Linda that when they reached a predominantly colored area he wanted her to toss the wallet out onto a sidewalk, so a black person would find it, use the credit cards, and be arrested. This would make people think the Panthers had committed the murders, he explained.

Manson drove onto the freeway not far from where they had dropped off Tex, Katie, and Leslie. After driving for a long time, he pulled off the freeway and stopped at a nearby service station. Apparently having changed his plans, Manson now told Linda to put the wallet in the women's rest room. Linda did, only she hid it too well, lifting the top of the toilet tank and placing it over the bulb, where it would remain undiscovered for four months.

I asked Linda if she could remember anything distinctive about the station. She remembered there was a restaurant next door and that it seemed 'to radiate the color orange'.

There was a Denny's Restaurant next to the Standard station in Sylmar, with a large orange sign.

While Linda was in the rest room, Manson went to the restaurant, returning with four milk shakes.

Probably at the same time the LaBiancas were being murdered, the man who had ordered their deaths was sipping a milk shake.

Again Manson had Linda drive. After a long time, perhaps an hour, they reached the beach somewhere south of Venice. Linda recalled seeing some oil storage tanks. All four got out of the car, Sadie and Clem, at Charlie's instructions, dropping behind while he and Linda walked ahead in the sand.

Suddenly Manson was again all love. It was as if the events of the last forty-eight hours had never happened. Linda told Charlie that she was pregnant. Manson took Linda's hand and, as she described it, 'it was sort of nice, you know, we were just talking, I gave him some peanuts, and he just sort of made me forget about everything, made me feel good'.

Just as they reached a side street, a police car pulled up and two officers got out. They asked the pair what they were doing.

Charlie replied, 'We were just going for a walk.' Then, as if they should recognize him, he asked, 'Don't you know who I am?' or 'Don't you remember my name?' They said, 'No,' then returned to the patrol car and drove off, without asking either for identification. It was, Linda said, 'a friendly conversation', lasting only a minute.

Finding the two officers on duty in the area that night should be fairly easy, I thought, unaware how wrong I could be.

Clem and Sadie were already back in the car when they returned. Manson then told Linda to drive to Venice. En route he asked the three if they knew anyone there. None did. Manson then asked Linda, 'What about the man you and Sandy met in Venice? Wasn't he a piggy?' Linda replied, 'Yes, he's an actor.' Manson told her to drive to his apartment.

I asked Linda about the actor.

One afternoon in early August, Linda said, she and Sandy had been hitchhiking near the pier when this man picked them up. He told them he was Israeli or Arab – Linda couldn't recall which – and that he had appeared in a movie about Kahlil Gibran. The two girls were hungry, and he drove them to his apartment and fixed them lunch. Afterward, Sandy napped and Linda and the man made love. Before the girls left, he gave them some food and spare clothing. Linda couldn't remember the man's name, only that it was foreign. However, she felt sure she could find the apartment house, as she had located it when Manson asked her to drive there that night.

When they pulled up in front, Manson asked Linda if the man would let her in. 'I think so,' she replied. What about Sadie and Clem? Linda said she guessed so. Manson then handed her a pocketknife and demonstrated how he wanted her to slit the actor's throat.

Linda said she couldn't do it. 'I'm not you, Charlie,' Linda told Manson. 'I can't kill anybody.'

Manson asked her to take him to the man's apartment. Linda led Charlie up the stairs, but pointed to the wrong door.

On returning to the car, Manson gave the trio explicit instructions. They were to go to the actor's apartment. Linda was to knock. When the man let her in, Sadie and Clem were to go in also. Once they were inside, Linda was to slit the man's throat and Clem was to shoot him. When finished, they were to hitchhike back to the ranch.

Linda saw Manson hand Clem a gun, but was unable to describe it. Nor did she know if Sadie also had a knife.

'If anything goes wrong,' Manson told them, 'just hang it up, don't do it.' He then slid into the driver's seat and drove off.

Like the church and sports-car incidents, Susan Atkins had not mentioned the Venice incident to me, nor had she said anything about it when testifying before the grand jury. While I felt that she might have forgotten the two earlier incidents, I suspected the third was omitted intentionally, since it directly involved her as a willing partner in still another attempted murder. It was possible, however, that had I had more time to interview Susan, this too might have come out.

The actor's apartment was on the top, or fifth, floor, but Linda did not tell Clem or Sadie this. Instead, on reaching the fourth floor, she knocked on the first door she saw. Eventually a man sleepily asked, 'Who is it?' She replied, 'Linda.' When the man opened the door a crack, Linda said, 'Oh, excuse me, I have the wrong apartment.'

The door was open only a second or two and Linda caught just a glimpse of the man. She had the impression, though she was unsure of this, that he was middle-aged.

The three then left the building, but not before Sadie, ever the animal, defecated on the landing.

It was obvious that Linda Kasabian had prevented still another Manson-ordered murder. As independent evidence corroborating her story, it was important that we locate not only the actor but the man who answered the door. Perhaps he'd remember being awakened at 4 or 5 A.M. by a pretty young girl.

From the apartment house Clem, Sadie, and Linda walked to the beach, a short distance away. Clem wanted to ditch the gun. He disappeared from sight behind a sandpile, near a fence. Linda presumed that he had either buried the gun or tossed it over the fence.

Walking back to the Pacific Coast Highway, they hitched a ride to the entrance of Topanga Canyon. There was a hippie crash pad nearby, next door to the Malibu Feedbin, and Sadie said she knew a girl who was staying there. Linda recalled there was also an older man there, and a big dog. The three stayed about an hour, smoking some weed, then left.

They then hitched two rides, the last taking them all the way to the entrance of Santa Susana Pass Road, where Clem and Linda got out. Sadie, Linda learned the next day, remained in the car until it reached the waterfall area.

When Linda and Clem arrived at the ranch, Tex and Leslie were already there, asleep in one of the rooms. She didn't see Katie, though she learned the next day that, like Sadie, she had gone on to the camp by the waterfall. Linda went to bed in the saloon.

Two days later Linda Kasabian fled Spahn Ranch. The manner of her departure, however, would cause the prosecution a great deal of concern.

Rather than taking Linda directly to the LaBianca residence, I had the sheriff's deputy drive to the Los Feliz area, to see if

Linda could find the house itself. She did, pointing out both the LaBianca and True houses, the place where they had parked, the driveway up which Manson had walked, and so on.

I also wanted to find the two houses in Pasadena where Manson had stopped earlier that night, but, though we spent hours looking for them, we were, at this time, unsuccessful. Linda did find the apartment house where the actor had lived, 1101 Ocean Front Walk, and pointed out both his apartment, 501, and the door on which she had knocked, 403. I asked Patchett and Gutierrez to locate and interview both the actor and the man who had been living in 403.

Linda also showed us the sandpile near the fence where she believed Clem had disposed of the gun, but though we got out shovels and dug up the area, we were unable to locate the weapon.

That afternoon we returned to Pasadena and must have driven past forty churches before Linda found the one where Manson had stopped. I asked LAPD to photograph it and the adjoining parking lot as a trial exhibit.

Linda also identified the Standard station in Sylmar where she'd left the wallet, as well as Denny's Restaurant next door.

We took Linda out twice more, trying to find the two houses in Pasadena. On both occasions we were accompanied by South Pasadena PD officers who directed us to neighborhoods similar to those Linda had described. We finally found the large house atop the hill. Though I had it and the adjoining houses photographed – they were close together, as Manson had said – I decided against talking to the owners, sure they would sleep better not knowing how close to death they had come. We were never able to locate the first house – which both Susan and Linda had described – where Manson looked in the window and saw the photographs of the children.

We did grant Linda one special privilege, which might have been called a 'bonus'. On the three occasions we took her out of Sybil Brand, we let her call her mother in New Hampshire and talk to her two children. Her attorney paid for the calls. Though Angel was only a month old and much too young to understand, just speaking to them obviously meant a great deal to Linda.

Yet she never asked to do this. She never asked for anything. She told me not once but several times that although she was pleased to be getting immunity, because it meant that eventually she could be with her children, it didn't matter that much if she didn't get it. There was a sort of sad fatalism about her. She said she knew she had to tell the truth about what had happened, and that she had known she would be the one to tell the story ever since the murders occurred. Unlike the other defendants, she seemed burdened with guilt, though, again unlike them, she hadn't physically harmed anyone. She was a strange girl, marked by her time with Manson, yet not molded by him in the same way the others were. Because she was compliant, easily led, Manson apparently had had little trouble controlling her. Up to a point. But she had refused to cross that point. 'I'm not you, Charlie. I can't kill anybody.'

Once I asked her what she thought about Manson now. She was still in love with him, Linda said. 'Some things he said were the truth,' she observed thoughtfully. 'Only now I realize he could take a truth and make a lie of it.'

Two weeks had passed since I'd asked McGann to look for the knives; he still hadn't done it. I called Lieutenant Helder and a search crew went out the next day. No luck. However, at least during the trial we'd be prepared to prove that they had looked. Otherwise, the defense could contend that LAPD was so skeptical of Linda Kasabian's story that they hadn't even bothered to mount a search.

I had no idea how often the police had interviewed Winifred Chapman, the Polanskis' maid. I'd talked to her a number of times myself before I realized there was one question so obvious we'd all overlooked it.

Mrs Chapman had stated that she washed the front door of the Tate residence just after noon on Friday, August 8. This meant Charles Watson had to have left his print there sometime after this.

However, there was a *second* print found at the Tate residence, Patricia Krenwinkel's, located inside the door that led from Sharon Tate's bedroom to the pool.

I asked Mrs Chapman: 'Did you ever wash that door?' Yes. How often? A couple of times a week. She had to, she explained, because the guests usually used that door to get to the pool.

The big question: 'Did you wash it the week of the murders, and, if so, when?'

A. 'Tuesday was the last time. I washed it down, inside and out, with vinegar and water.'

Under discovery, I was only required to make a note of the conversation and put it in our tubs. However, in fairness to both Fitzgerald and his client, I called Paul and told him, 'If you're planning on having Krenwinkel testify that she went swimming at the Tate residence a couple of weeks before the murders and left her print at that time, better forget it. Mrs Chapman is going to testify she washed that door on Tuesday, August 5.'

Paul was grateful for the information. Had he based his defense on this premise, Mrs Chapman's testimony could have been devastating.

There was, in such conversations, something assumed though unstated. Whatever his public posture, I was sure that Fitzgerald knew that his client was guilty, and he knew that I knew it. Though only on rare occasions does a defense attorney slip up and admit this in court, when it comes to in-chambers discussions and private conversations, it's often something else.

There were two items of evidence in our files which I did not point out to the defense. I was sure they had already seen them – both were among the items photocopied for them – but I was hoping they wouldn't realize their importance.

One was a traffic ticket, the other an arrest report. Separately each seemed unimportant. Together they made a bomb that would demolish Manson's alibi defense.

On first learning from Fowles that Manson might claim that

he was not in the Los Angeles area at the time of the murders, I had asked LaBianca detectives Patchett and Gutierrez to see if they could obtain evidence proving his actual whereabouts on the subject dates. They did an excellent job. Together with information obtained from credit card transactions and interviews, they were able to piece together a timetable of Manson's activities during the week preceding the start of Helter Skelter.

On about August 1, 1969, Manson told several Family members that he was going to Big Sur to seek out new recruits.

He apparently left on the morning of Sunday, August 3, as sometime between seven and eight he purchased gas at a station in Canoga Park, using a stolen credit card. From Canoga Park, he headed north towards Big Sur. At about four the next morning, he picked up a young girl, Stephanie Schram, outside a service station some distance south of Big Sur, probably at Gorda. An attractive 17-year-old, Stephanie was hitchhiking from San Francisco to San Diego, where she was living with her married sister. Manson and Stephanie camped in a nearby canyon that night – probably Salmon or Limekiln Creek, both hippie hangouts – Manson telling her his views on life, love, and death. Manson talked a lot about death, Stephanie would recall, and it frightened her. They took LSD and had sex. Manson was apparently unusually smitten with Stephanie. Usually he'd have sex with a new girl a few times, then move on to a new 'young love'. Not so with Stephanie. He later told Paul Watkins that Stephanie, who was of German extraction, was the result of two thousand years of perfect breeding.

On August 4, Manson, still using the stolen credit card, purchased gas at Lucia. Ripping off the place, which bore a large sign reading 'Hippies Not Allowed', must have given him a special satisfaction, as he did it again the next day.

On the night of the fifth Manson and Stephanie drove north to a place whose name Stephanie couldn't recall but which Manson described as a 'sensitivity camp'. It was, he told her, a place where rich people went on weekends to play at being enlightened. He was obviously describing Esalen Institute.

Esalen was, at this time, just coming into vogue as a 'growth center', its seminars including such diverse figures as yogis and psychiatrists, salvationists and satanists. Obviously Manson felt Esalen a prime place to espouse his philosophies. It is unknown whether he had been there on prior occasions, those involved in the Institute refusing to even acknowledge his visits there.

Manson took his guitar and left Stephanie in the van. After a time she fell asleep. When she awakened the next morning, Manson had already returned. He was in less than a good mood, as, later that day, he unexpectedly struck her. Still later, at Barker Ranch, Manson would tell Paul Watkins – to quote Watkins – that while at Big Sur he had gone 'to Esalen and played his guitar for a bunch of people who were supposed to be the top people there, and they rejected his music. Some people pretended that they were asleep, and other people were saying, "This is too heavy for me," and "I'm not ready for that," and others were saying, "Well, I don't understand it," and some just got up and walked out.'

Still another rejection by what Manson considered the establishment – this occurring just three days before the Tate murders.

With his single recruit, Manson left Big Sur on August 6, making gas purchases that same day at San Luis Obispo and Chatsworth, a few miles from Spahn Ranch. According to Stephanie, they had dinner at the ranch that night and she met the Family for the first time. She felt uncomfortable with them, and, learning that Manson shared his favors with the other girls, told him she would stay only if he would promise to remain with her, and her alone, for two weeks. Surprisingly, Manson agreed. They spent that night in the van, parked not far from the ranch, then drove to San Diego the next day to pick up Stephanie's clothes.

En route, about ten miles south of Oceanside on Interstate 5, they were stopped by California Highway Patrol officer Richard C. Willis. Though pulled over for a mechanical violation, Manson was cited only for having no valid driver's license in his possession. Manson gave his correct name and the ranch address, and signed the ticket himself. Officer Willis noted on the ticket that Manson was driving a '1952 cream-colored Ford bakery van, license number K70683'. The date was Thursday, August 7, 1969; the time 6:15 P.M.

The ticket, which Patchett and Guiterrez found, proved Manson was in Southern California the day before the Tate murders.

While Stephanie was getting her clothes together, Manson talked to her sister, who was also a Beatles fan. She had the White Album, and Manson told her the Beatles had laid out 'the whole scene' in it. He warned her that the blacks were getting ready to overthrow the whites and that only those who fled to the desert and hid in the bottomless pit would be safe. As for those who remained in the cities, Manson said, 'People are going to be slaughtered, they'll be lying on their lawns dead.'

Just a little over twenty-four hours later, his prediction would be fulfilled, in all its gory detail, at 10050 Cielo Drive. With a little help from his friends.

That night, according to Stephanie, she and Charlie parked somewhere in San Diego and slept next to the van, returning to Spahn Ranch the following day, arriving there about two in the afternoon.

Stephanie was a bit vague when it came to dates. She 'thought' the day they returned to Spahn Ranch was Friday, August 8, but she wasn't sure. I anticipated that the defense would make the most of this, but I wasn't concerned, because that second piece of evidence conclusively placed Manson back at the ranch on Friday, August 8, 1969.

According to Linda Kasabian, on the afternoon of August 8 Manson gave Mary Brunner and Sandra Good a credit card and told them to purchase some items for him. At four that afternoon the two girls were apprehended while driving away from a Sears store in San Fernando, after store employees checked and found the credit card was stolen. The San Fernando PD arrest report stated that they were driving a 'van 1952 Ford license K70683'.

Because of the fine job of digging by the LaBianca detectives, we now had physical proof that Manson was back at Spahn Ranch on Friday, August 8, 1969.

Though both the traffic ticket and arrest report were in the discovery materials, so were hundreds of other documents. I was hoping that the defense would overlook their common denominator: that vehicle description with its telltale license number.

If Manson went with an alibi defense, and I proved that alibi was fabricated, this would be strong circumstantial evidence of his guilt.

There was, of course, other evidence placing Manson at Spahn Ranch that day. In addition to the testimony of Schram, DeCarlo, and others, Linda Kasabian said that when the Family got together that afternoon, Manson discussed his visit to Big Sur, saying that the people there were 'really not together, they were just off on their little trips' and that 'the people wouldn't go on his trip'.

It was just after this that Manson told them: 'Now is the time for Helter Skelter.'

Bits and pieces, often largely circumstantial. Yet patiently dug out and assembled, they became the People's case. And with almost every interview it became a little stronger.

I spent many hours interviewing Stephanie Schram, who, together with Kitty Lutesinger, had fled Barker Ranch just hours before the October 1969 raid, shotgun-wielding Clem in close pursuit. I often wondered what would have happened to the two girls had the raid been timed just a day later or Clem been a little faster.

Unlike Kitty, Stephanie had severed all contact with the Family. Though we had kept her current address from the defense, Squeaky and Gypsy found her working at a dog-grooming school. 'Charlie wants you to come back,' they told her. Stephanie replied, 'No thanks.' Considering what she knew, her forthright refusal was a brave act.

From Stephanie I learned that while at Barker Manson had

conducted a 'murder school'. He had given a Buck knife to each of the girls, and had demonstrated how they should 'slit the throats of pigs', by yanking the head back by the hair and drawing the knife from ear to ear (using Stephanie as a very frightened model). He also said they should 'stab them in either their ears or eyes and then wiggle the knife around to get as many vital organs as possible'. The details became even gorier: Manson said that if the police pigs came to the desert, they should kill them, cut them in little pieces, boil the heads, then put the skulls and uniforms on posts, to frighten off others.

Stephanie had told LAPD that Manson had spent the nights of Friday, August 8, and Saturday, August 9, with her. On questioning her, I learned that about an hour after dinner on August 8, Manson took her to the trailer at Spahn and told her to go to sleep, that he would join her soon. However, she didn't see him again until shortly before dawn the next morning, at which time he awakened her and took her with him to Devil's Canyon, the camp across the road from the ranch.

That night – August 9 – Stephanie said, 'when it got dark, he left and he came back either sometime during the night or early in the morning'.

If Manson was planning on using Stephanie Schram as an alternative abili, we were now more than ready for him.

On March 19, Hollopeter, Manson's court-appointed attorney, made two motions: that Charles Manson be given a psychiatric examination, and that his case be severed from that of the others.

Enraged, Manson tried to fire Hollopeter.

Asked whom he wished to represent him, Manson replied, 'Myself.' When Judge Keene denied the change, Manson picked up a copy of the Constitution and, saying it meant nothing to the Court, tossed it in a wastebasket.

Manson eventually requested that Ronald Hughes be substituted for Hollopeter. Like Reiner and Shinn, Hughes had been one of the first attorneys to call on Manson. He had remained on the periphery of the case ever since, his chief function being to run errands for Manson, as indicated by a document Manson had signed on February 17, designating him one of his legal runners.

Keene granted the substitution. Hollopeter, whom the press called 'one of L.A. county's most successful defense attorneys', was out, after thirteen days; Hughes, who had never before tried a case, was in.

Something of an intellectual, Hughes was a huge, balding man with a long, scraggly beard. His various items of apparel rarely matched and usually evidenced numerous food stains. As one reporter remarked, 'You could usually tell what Ron had for breakfast, for the past several weeks.' Hughes, whom I would get to know well in the months ahead, and for whom I developed a growing respect, once admitted to me that he had bought his suits for a dollar apiece at MGM; they were from Walter Slezak's old wardrobe. The press was quick to dub him 'Manson's hippie lawyer'.

Hughes' first two acts were to withdraw the motions for the psychiatric examination and the severance. Granted. His third and fourth were requests that Manson be allowed to revert to pro per status and to deliver a speech to the Court. Denied.

Although Manson was displeased with Keene's last two rulings, he couldn't have been too unhappy with the defense team, which now consisted of four attorneys – Reiner (Van Houten), Shinn (Atkins), Fitzgerald (Krenwinkel), and Hughes (Manson) – each of whom had been associated with him since early in the case.

Unknown to us, there were still changes ahead. Among the casualties would be both Ira Reiner and Ronald Hughes, each of whom dared go against Manson's wishes. Reiner would lose considerable time and money for having linked himself with the Manson defense. His loss would be small, however, compared to that of Hughes, who, just eight months later, would pay with his life.

On March 21, Aaron and I were walking down the corridor in the Hall of Justice when we spotted Irving Kanarek emerging from the elevator.

Although little known elsewhere, Kanarek was something of a legend in the Los Angeles courts. The attorney's obstructionist tactic had caused a number of judges to openly censure him from the bench. Kanarek stories were so common, and usually incredible, as to seem fictional when they were actually fact. Prosecutor Burton Katz, for example, recalled that Kanarek once objected to a prosecution witness's stating his own name because, having first heard his name from his mother, it was 'hearsay'. Such frivolous objections were minor irritations compared with Kanarek's dilatory tactics. As samples:

In the case of *People* vs *Goodman*, Kanarek had stretched a simple theft case, which should have taken a few hours or a day at most, to three months. The amount stolen: $100. The cost to the taxpayer: $130,212.

In the case of *People* vs *Smith and Powell*, Kanarek spent twelve and a half months on pre-trial motions. After an additional two months trying to pick a jury, Kanarek's own client fired him in disgust. *A year and a half* after Irving Kanarek came onto the case, the jury still hadn't been selected, nor a single witness called.

'All we need, Vince,' Aaron remarked jocularly to me, 'is to have Irving Kanarek on this case. We'd be in court ten years.'

The next day Ronald Hughes told a reporter that 'he may ask Van Nuys attorney I. A. Kanarek to enter the case as Manson's lawyer. He mentioned that he and Manson conferred with Kanarek at the County Jail Monday night.'

Though no miracle was involved, the Black Panther whom Charles Manson had shot and killed in July 1969 had resurrected. Only he wasn't a Panther, just a 'former dope dealer', and, contrary to what Manson and the Family had believed, after Manson shot him he hadn't died, though his friends had told Manson that he had. His name was Bernard Crowe, but he was best known by the descriptive nickname Lotsapoppa.

Crowe's story of the incident was essentially the same as that DeCarlo had told LAPD, although even Charlie didn't know the surprise ending.

After Manson and T.J. had left the Hollywood apartment where the shooting took place, Crowe, who had been playing dead, told his friends to call an ambulance. They did, then split. When questioned by the police at the hospital, Crowe said he didn't know who had shot him or why. He nearly didn't make it; he was on the critical list for eighteen days. The bullet was still lodged next to his spine.

I was interested in Crowe for two reasons. One, the incident proved that Charles Manson was quite capable of killing someone on his own. Though I knew I couldn't get this into evidence during the guilt phase of the trial, I was hopeful of introducing it during the penalty phase, when other crimes can be considered. Two, from the description it appeared that the gun Manson had shot Crowe with was the same .22 caliber Longhorn revolver which, just a little over a month later, Tex Watson would use in the Tate homicides. If we could remove the bullet from Crowe's body and match it up with the bullets test-fired from the .22 caliber revolver, we'd have placed the Tate murder weapon in Manson's own hand.

Sergeant Bill Lee of SID wasn't optimistic about the bullet. He told me that since it had been embedded in the body for over nine months, it was likely that acids had obliterated the stria to an extent where a positive identification would be difficult. Still, it might be possible. I then talked to several surgeons: they could take out the bullet, they told me, but the operation was risky.

I laid it out for Crowe. We'd like to have the bullet, and would arrange to have it removed at the Los Angeles County Hospital. But there were serious risks involved, and I didn't minimize them.

Crowe declined the operation. He was sort of proud of the bullet, he said. It made quite a conversation piece.

Eventually Manson would have learned, through discovery, of the resurrection of Bernard Crowe. Before this, however, Crowe was jailed on a marijuana charge. As he was being escorted down the hall, he passed Manson and his guard, who were on their way back from the attorney room. Charlie did a quick about-face, then told Crowe, according to the deputies who were present, 'Sorry I had to do it, but you know how it is.'

Crowe's response, if there was one, went unreported.

Toward the end of March the prosecution nearly lost one of its key witnesses.

Paul Watkins, once Manson's chief lieutenant, was pulled out of a flaming Volkswagen camper and rushed to Los Angeles County General Hospital with second-degree burns on 25 percent of his face, arms, and back. When sufficiently recovered to talk to the police, Watkins told them he had fallen asleep while reading by candlelight, and either that, or a marijuana cigarette he had been smoking, could have caused the fire.

These were only guesses, Watkins told them, as he was 'unsure of the origin of the blaze'.

Three days *before* the fire, Inyo County authorities had heard a rumor that Watkins was going to be killed by the Family.

April 1970

The words PIG, DEATH TO PIGS, RISE, and HEALTER SKEL-TER contain only thirteen different letters. Handwriting experts told me it would be extremely difficult – if not impossible – to match the bloody words found at the Tate and LaBianca residences with printing exemplars obtained from the defendants.

It wasn't only the small number of letters involved. The words were printed, not written; the letters were oversize; in both cases unusual writing implements had been used, a towel at the Tate residence, probably a rolled-up piece of paper at the LaBiancas; and all but the two words found on the refrigerator door at the latter residence had been printed high up on the walls, the person responsible having to stretch unnaturally high to make them.

As evidence, they appeared worthless.

However, thinking about the problem, I came up with an idea which, if successful, could convert them into very meaningful evidence. It was a gamble. But if it worked, it would be worth it.

We knew who had printed the words. Susan Atkins had testified before the grand jury that she had printed the word PIG on the front door of the Tate house, while Susan had told me, when I interviewed her, that Patricia Krenwinkel had admitted printing the words at the LaBiancas. Though Susan's grand jury testimony and her statements to me were inadmissable because of the deal we had made with her, she had confessed the printing at Tate to Ronnie Howard, so we had her on that. But we had nothing admissible on Krenwinkel.

The Fifth Amendment to the U.S Constitution provides that no person 'shall be compelled in any criminal case to be a witness against himself'. The U.S. Supreme Court has ruled that this is limited to verbal utterances, and that a defendant cannot refuse to give physical evidence of himself, like appearing in a lineup, submitting to a breath-analysis test for drunken driving, giving fingerprint and handwriting exemplars, hair samples, and so on. After researching the law, I drew up very explicit instructions for Captain Carpenter at Sybil Brand, stating exactly how to request the printing exemplars of Susan Atkins, Patricia Krenwinkel, and Leslie Van Houten.

Captain Carpenter assigned Senior Deputy H. L. Mauss to obtain the exemplars. According to my instructions, she informed Susan Atkins of the constitutional position, then told her: 'The word PIG was printed in blood at the Tate residence. We want you to print the word P I G.' Susan, without complaint, printed the exemplar as requested.

Leslie Van Houten and Patricia Krenwinkel were brought in individually and given similar instructions concerning their rights. However, each was told, *orally*: 'The words HELTER SKELTER, DEATH TO PIGS, and RISE were printed in blood at the LaBianca residence. We want you to print those words.'

In my memo to Captain Carpenter there was one additional instruction for the deputy: 'Do not write any of this for them.' I wanted to see if Krenwinkel misspelled 'helter' as 'healter' as she had on the refrigerator door.

Leslie Van Houten printed the exemplar.

Patricia Krenwinkel refused.

We'd won the gamble. We could now use her refusal in the trial as circumstantial evidence of her guilt.

As evidence, this was doubly important, since, before this, I'd had absolutely *no* independent evidence corroborating Linda Kasabian's testimony regarding Patricia Krenwinkel's involvement in the LaBianca murders. And without corroborating evidence, as a matter of law, Krenwinkel would have been entitled to an acquittal on those charges.

Though we'd won that gamble, we were less lucky when it came to putting the Tate–Sebring rope and the wire cutters in Manson's possession before the murders, evidence I was counting on to provide the necessary corroboration of Linda Kasabian's testimony as to Manson.

We knew from DeCarlo, who had been present, that Manson had purchased about 200 feet of the white, three-strand nylon rope at the Jack Frost surplus store in Santa Monica in June 1969. However, when Tate detectives finally interviewed Frost – three and a half months after my initial request – he was unable to find a purchase order for the rope. Nor could he definitely state that this was the same rope he had stocked. An attempt to identify the manufacturer, then trace it back to Frost, also failed. Frost usually picked up his stock in odd lots from jobbers or through auctions, rather than directly from the manufacturer.

Just as these were blind alleys, so was one other – literally. According to DeCarlo, Manson had given part of the rope to George Spahn, for use on the ranch. Spahn's near blindness, however, eliminated him as a witness.

It was then I thought of Ruby Pearl.

For some reason, though the police had visited Spahn Ranch numerous times, none of the officers had interviewed Ruby, George's ranch manager. I found her a fund of valuable information. Examining the Tate–Sebring rope, she not only said it looked like the rope Manson had, she also supplied numerous examples of Manson's domination; recalled seeing the .22 Longhorn at the ranch many times; identified the leather thong found at the LaBiancas' as similar to the ones Manson often wore; and told me that, prior to the arrival of the Family at Spahn, she had never seen any Buck knives there, but that in the summer of 1969 'suddenly it seemed everyone had one'.

While disappointed that we couldn't obtain documented proof of the rope sale, I was pleased with Ruby. Being an experienced horse wrangler – as well as a tough, gallant lady who showed not the slightest fear of the Family – her testimony would carry weight. There was a fine streak of stubborn authority about her.

Another find was Randy Starr, whom I interviewed the same day as Ruby. A sometime movie stunt man who specialized in fake hangings, Starr said the Tate–Sebring rope was 'identical' to a rope he'd once used to help Manson pull a vehicle out of the creek bed. Starr told me, 'Manson always kept the rope behind the seat in his dune buggy.'

Even more important was Randy Starr's positive identification of the .22 Longhorn revolver, for Starr had once owned the gun and had given it to Manson.

One question remained unanswered. Why, on the night of the Tate murders, did the killers bring along 43 feet 8 inches of rope? To tie up the victims? Manson accomplished this the next night with a single leather thong. I obtained a glimpse of a possible answer during one of my interviews with DeCarlo. According to Danny, in late July of 1969, Manson had told him that the establishment pigs 'ought to have their throats cut and be hung up by their feet'. This would really throw the fear into people, Manson said.

The logical inference, I felt, was that the killers brought along the rope intending to hang their victims.

The wire cutters presented their own problems. Linda Kasabian said the pair found in Manson's dune buggy looked like the pair that had been in the car that night. Fine. Joe Granado of of SID used them to test-cut a section of the Tate telephone wire and concluded that the two cuts were the same. Great. But then officer DeWayne Wolfer, considered LAPD's foremost expert on physical evidence, made some test cuts also, and he concluded that these wire cutters couldn't have been the ones used.

Not about to give up, I asked Wolfer if the tautness of the wire could have been a factor. Possibly, he said. I then asked Wolfer to accompany telephone company representatives to 10050 Cielo Drive and make another cut, only this time I wanted him to sever the wire while it was strung up and tight, the way it was the night of the murders. Wolfer eventually made the test, but his opinion remained unchanged: the actual cut made on the night of the murders and the test cut did not match.

When I'd accompanied LAPD to Spahn Ranch on November 19, 1969, we'd found a number of .22 caliber bullets and shell casings. Because of the terrific windstorm, and the necessity of following up other leads, our search had been cursory, however, and I'd asked Sergeant Lee to return and conduct a more thorough search. The much repeated request became even more important when, on December 16, 1969, LAPD obtained the .22 caliber Longhorn revolver. Yet it was not until April 15, 1970, that Lee returned to Spahn. Again concentrating on the gully area some two hundred feet behind George Spahn's residence, Lee found twenty-three more .22 caliber shell casings. Since twenty-two had been found during the first search, this brought the total to forty-five.*

It was not until after the latter search that Lee ran comparison tests on any of the Spahn shell casings. When he finally did, he concluded that fifteen of the forty-five had been fired from the Tate murder gun.

Belatedly, but fortunately in time for the trial, we now had scientific evidence linking the gun to Spahn Ranch.

For months one item of physical evidence had especially worried me: the pair of eyeglasses found near the trunks in the living room at the Tate murder scene. The natural conclusion was that if they didn't belong to any of the victims, they must belong to one of the killers. Yet neither Watson, Atkins, Krenwinkel, nor Kasabian wore glasses.

I anticipated that the defense would lean heavily on this, arguing that since they didn't belong to any of the defendants, at least one of the killers was still at large. From there it was only a short step to the conclusion that maybe the wrong people were on trial.

This posed an extremely serious problem for the prosecution. That problem, though not the mystery itself, vanished when I talked to Roseanne Walker.

Since Susan Atkins had confessed the murders to both Virginia Graham and Ronnie Howard, it occurred to me that she might have made incriminating statements to others, so I asked

---

* None of the .22 caliber bullets recovered during the two searches matched up with the bullets found at the murder scene or those test-fired from the weapon.

LAPD to locate any girls Atkins had been particularly close to at Sybil Brand.

One former inmate who agreed to talk to me, though she wasn't very happy about it, was Roseanne Walker. A pathetic, heavyset black girl who had been sent to Sybil Brand on five drug-related charges, Roseanne had been a sort of walking commissary, selling candy, cigarettes, and makeup to the other inmates. Not until the fifth or sixth time I interviewed her did Roseanne recall a conversation which, though it seemed unimportant to her, I found very significant.

Susan and Roseanne were listening to the radio one day, when the newscaster began talking about a pair of eyeglasses LAPD had found at the Tate murder scene. Amused, Susan remarked, 'Wouldn't it be too much if they arrested the person the glasses belonged to, when the only thing he was guilty of was losing his glasses?'

Roseanne replied that maybe the glasses did belong to the killer.

Susan said, 'That ain't the way it went down.'

Susan's remark clearly indicated that the glasses did *not* belong to the killers.

Other problems remained. One of the biggest concerned Linda Kasabian's escape from Spahn Ranch.

Linda told me that she decided to flee after the night of the LaBianca murders; however, Manson sent her to the waterfall area later that day (August 11) and she was afraid to leave that night because of the armed guards he had posted.

Early the next morning (August 12) Manson sought her out. She was to put on a 'straight' dress, then take a message to Mary Brunner and Sandra Good at Sybil Brand, as well as Bobby Beausoleil at the County Jail. The message: 'Say nothing; everything's all right.' After borrowing a car from Dave Hannum, a new ranch hand at Spahn, Linda went to Sybil Brand, but learned that Brunner and Good were in court; at the County Jail her identification was rejected and she wasn't allowed to see Beausoleil. When she returned to the ranch and told Manson she had been unsuccessful, he told her to try again the next day.

Linda saw her chance. That night she packed a shoulder bag with some clothing and Tanya's diapers and pins, and hid it in the parachute room. Early the next morning (August 13) she again borrowed Hannum's car. On going to get the bag, however, she found Manson and Stephanie Schram sleeping in the room. Deciding to forget the bag, she went to get Tanya, but discovered that the children had been moved to the waterfall area. There was no way she could go there to get Tanya, she said, without having to explain her actions. So she left the ranch without her.

Instead of going to Los Angeles as instructed, Linda began driving to Taos, New Mexico, where her husband was now living. Hannum's car broke down outside Albuquerque. When she tried to have it repaired, using a credit card Bruce Davis had earlier given her for gas, the gas station owner checked and learned the card was no longer valid. Linda then wrote a letter to Hannum, enclosing the keys, telling him where he could find the car, and apologizing. She then hitchhiked the rest of the way.

Linda found her husband living with another girl in a commune at Lorien, outside Taos. She told him about the Tate murders, the events of the second night, and leaving Tanya at Spahn. Bob Kasabian suggested they return to Spahn together and get Tanya, but Linda was afraid Manson would kill them all. Kasabian said he wanted to think about it for a few days. Unwilling to wait, Linda hitchhiked into Taos and went to see Joe Sage. Sage, who had a reputation for helping people, was a rather colorful character. When the 51-year-old Zen monk wasn't busy running his Macrobiotic Church, he was campaigning for president of the United States on an anti-pollution ticket. Linda asked Sage for enough money to return to Los Angeles to get her little girl. Sage, however, began questioning Linda, and eventually she told him and a youth named Jeffrey Jacobs about the murders.

Not believing Linda's tale, Sage placed a call to Spahn Ranch, talking first to an unidentified girl, then to Manson himself. Sage asked Manson – whose reaction can only be imagined – if

Linda's story was true. Manson told him Linda had flipped out; that her ego was not ready to die, and so she had run away.

Linda did not talk to Charlie, but she did talk to one of the other girls – she believed, but was not sure, it was Squeaky – who told her about the August 16 raid. The authorities had kept Tanya, she learned; she was now in a foster home. Linda also spoke to Patricia Krenwinkel, Katie saying something to the effect, 'You just couldn't wait to open your big mouth, could you?'

Linda subsequently called the Malibu police station and learned the name of the social worker who was handling Tanya's case.* Sage gave Linda enough money for round-trip air fare, as well as the name of a Los Angeles attorney, Gary Fleischman, who he felt might be able to help her reclaim Tanya. When Linda saw Fleischman, she did not tell him about the murders, only that she had left the ranch to look for her husband. Eventually, after a court hearing, the mother and daughter were reunited and flew back to Taos. Bob was still involved with the other girl, however, and Linda took Tanya and hitchhiked first to Miami, Florida, where her father was living, then to her mother's home in Concord, New Hampshire. It was here, on December 2, 1969, when the news broke that she was being sought in connection with the Tate murders, that Linda turned herself in to the local police. Waiving extradition, she was returned to Los Angeles the next day.

I asked Linda, 'Why, between the time you reclaimed Tanya and the date of your arrest in December, didn't you contact the police and tell them what you knew about the murders?'

She was afraid of Manson, Linda said, afraid that he might find and kill both her and Tanya. Also, she was pregnant, and didn't want to go through this ordeal until after the baby was born.

There were, of course, other reasons, the most important being

* On calling the social worker, Linda learned that another girl, posing as Tanya's mother, had attempted to reclaim Tanya a short time before. Though I couldn't prove it, I suspected that Manson had sent one of his girls to get Tanya, as insurance that Linda wouldn't talk.

her distrust of the police. In the drug-oriented world she inhabited, police were considered neither friends nor allies. I felt that this explanation, if properly argued, would satisfy the jury.

An even bigger question remained: 'How could you leave your daughter in that den of killers?'

Linda replied that she felt Tanya would be safe there, *just so long as she did not go to the police.* 'Something within me told me that Tanya would be all right,' Linda said, 'that nothing would happen to her, and that now was the time to leave. I knew I would come back and get her. I was just confident that she would be all right.'

Would the jury accept this? I didn't know. This was among my many concerns as the trial date drew ever closer.

When contacted by Lieutenant Helder and Sergeant Gutierrez, both Sage and Jacobs verified Linda's story. I was unable to use either as a witness, however, most of their testimony being inadmissible hearsay. Ranch hand David Hannum said he had begun work at Spahn on August 12, and that Linda had borrowed his car that same day, as well as the next. And a check of the hall records verified that Brunner and Good *had* been in court on August 12.

The various interviews yielded unexpected bonuses. Hannum said that once when he killed a rattlesnake, Manson had angrily castigated him, yelling, 'How would you like it if I chopped your head off?' He then added, 'I'd rather kill people than animals.' At the same time I interviewed Linda's husband, Robert Kasabian, I also talked to Charles Melton, the hippie philanthropist from whom Linda had stolen the $5,000. Melton said that in April 1969 (before Linda ever met the Family) he had gone to Spahn Ranch to see Paul Watkins. While there, Melton had met Tex, who, admiring Melton's beard, commented, 'Maybe Charlie will let me grow a beard someday.'

It would be difficult to find a better example of Manson's domination of Watson.

These were pluses. There were minuses. And they were big ones.

To prove to the jury that Linda's account of these two nights of murder wasn't fabricated out of whole cloth, I desperately needed some third person to corroborate any part of her story. Rudolf Weber provided that corroboration for the first night. But for the second night I had no one. I gave LAPD this all-important priority assignment: Find the two officers who spoke to Manson and Linda on the beach, the man whose door Linda knocked on that night, the man and woman at the house next to the Malibu Feedbin, or any of the drivers who gave them rides. I'd like to have had all these people, but if they could turn up even one, I'd be happy.

Linda had located the spot where the two police officers stopped and questioned them. It was near Manhattan Beach. But, Los Angeles being the megalopolis that it is, it turned out to be an area where there were overlapping jurisdictions, not one but three separate law-enforcement agencies patrolling it. And a check of all three failed to turn up anyone who could recall such an incident.

We had better luck when it came to locating the actor Linda had mentioned. LaBianca detectives Sartuchi and Nielsen found him still living in Apartment 501, 1101 Ocean Front Walk, Venice. Not Israeli but Lebanese, his name was Saladin Nader, age 39. He remembered picking up the two hitchhiking girls in early August 1969. He described both Sandy and Linda accurately, including the fact that Sandy was noticeably pregnant; picked out photos of each; and related essentially the same story Linda had told me, neglecting to mention only that he and Linda had gone to bed.

After questioning Nader, the investigating officers, according to their report, 'explained to subject the purpose of the interview, and he displayed amazement that such sweet and sociable young ladies would attempt to inflict any harm upon his body after he assisted them to the best of his ability'.

Though their stories jibed, Nader was only partial support for Linda's testimony, as (fortunately for him, and thanks to Linda) he did not encounter the group that night.

One floor down was the apartment of the man on whose door

Linda had knocked. Linda had pointed out the door, 403, for us, and I'd asked Gutierrez and Patchett to try to locate the man, hopeful he'd recall the incident. When I got their report, it was on the tenant of 404. Returning, they learned from the landlady that 403 had been vacant during August 1969. It was possible some transient may have been staying there, she said – it wouldn't have been the first time – but beyond that we drew a blank.

The LaBianca detectives handled all these investigations. Going over their reports, I was convinced they had done everything possible to run down the leads. But we were left with the fact that of the six to eight persons who could have corroborated Linda Kasabian's story of the events of that second night, we hadn't found even one. I anticipated that the defense would lean heavily on this.

Any defendant may file at least one affidavit of prejudice against a judge and have him removed from the case. It isn't even necessary to give a reason for such a challenge. On April 13, Manson filed such an affidavit against Judge William Keene. Judge Keene accepted Manson's challenge, and the case was reassigned to Judge Charles H. Older. Though more affidavits were expected – each defendant was allowed one – the defense attorneys, after a brief huddle, decided to accept Older.

I'd never tried a case before him. By reputation, the 52-year-old jurist was a 'no nonsense' judge. A World War II fighter pilot who had served with the Flying Tigers, he had been appointed to the bench by Governor Ronald Reagan in 1967. This would be his biggest case to date.

The trial date was set for June 15. Because of the delay, we were again hopeful that Watson might be tried with the others, but that hope was quickly dashed when Watson's attorney requested, and received, still another postponement in the extradition proceedings.

The retrial of Beausoleil for the Hinman murder had begun in late March. Chief witness for the prosecution was Mary

Brunner, first member of the Manson Family, who testified that she had witnessed Beausoleil stab Hinman to death. Brunner was given complete immunity in exchange for her testimony. Claiming that he had only been a reluctant witness, Beausoleil himself took the stand and fingered Manson as Hinman's murderer. The jury believed Brunner. In Beausoleil's first trial the case against him had been so weak that our office hadn't asked for the death penalty. This time prosecutor Burton Katz did, and got it.

Two things concerned me about the trial. One was that Mary Brunner did everything she could to absolve Manson – making me wonder just how far Sadie, Katie, and Leslie would be willing to go to save Charlie – and the other that Danny DeCarlo hedged on many of his previous statements to LAPD. I was worried that Danny might be getting ready to split, all too aware that he had little reason to stick around. Though the motorcycle engine theft charge had been dropped in return for his testimony in the Hinman case, we had made no deal with him on Tate–LaBianca. Moreover, although he had a good chance of sharing the $25,000 reward, it was not necessary that he testify to obtain it.

DeCarlo and Brunner did testify that same month before the grand jury, which brought additional indictments against Charles Manson, Susan Atkins, and Bruce Davis on the Hinman murder. But testifying before a grand jury in secret and having to face Manson himself in court were two different things.

Nor could I blame Danny for being apprehensive. As soon as the grand jury indictments were made public, Davis, who had been living with the Family at Spahn, vanished.

May 1970

In early May, Crockett, Poston, and Watkins encountered Clem, Gypsy, and a youth named Kevin, one of the newer Family members, in Shoshone. Clem told Watkins: 'Charlie says that when he gets out you all had better not be around the desert.'

From a source at Spahn Ranch we learned that Family members there appeared to be 'preparing for some activity'.

The Manson girls were interviewed so often that they were on a first-name basis with many of the reporters. Inadvertently, several times they implied that Charlie would be out soon. Perhaps significantly, the girls said nothing about his being 'acquitted' or 'released'.

It was obvious that something was being planned.

On May 11, Susan Atkins filed a declaration repudiating her grand jury testimony. Both Manson and Atkins used the declaration as basis for habeas corpus motions, which were subsequently denied.

Aaron and I conferred with District Attorney Younger. Sadie couldn't have it both ways. Either she had told the complete truth before the grand jury and, according to our agreement, we would not seek a first degree murder conviction against her, or, according to her recent declaration, she recanted her testimony, in which case the agreement was breached.

My personal opinion was that Susan Atkins had testified 'substantially truthfully' before the grand jury, with these exceptions: her omission of the three other murder attempts the second night; her hedging on whether she had stabbed Voytek Frykowski (which she had admitted to me when I interviewed her); and my instinctive, but strong, feeling (corroborated by her con-

359

fessions to Virginia Graham and Ronnie Howard) that she had lied when she testified that she had not stabbed Sharon Tate. Under Atkins' agreement with our office, 'substantially' wasn't good enough – she had to tell the complete truth.

With her declaration, however, the issue was closed. On the basis of her repudiation, Aaron and I asked Younger's permission to seek the death penalty against Susan Atkins as well as the other defendants. He granted it.

Sadie's about-face was not unexpected. Another change, however, caught almost everyone off guard. In court to petition for a new trial, Bobby Beausoleil produced an affidavit, signed by Mary Brunner, stating that her testimony in this trial 'was not true', and that she had lied when she said Beausoleil stabbed Hinman to death.

Although obviously stunned, prosecutor Burt Katz argued that the other evidence in the trial was sufficient to convict Beausoleil.

Investigating further, Burt learned that a few days before she was due to testify, Mary Brunner had been visited by Squeaky and Brenda at her parents' home in Wisconsin. She was again visited by Squeaky, this time accompanied by Sandy, two days before she signed the affidavit. Burt charged that the girls, representing Manson, had coerced Mary Brunner into repudiating her testimony.

Called to the stand, Mary Brunner first denied this, then, after conferring with counsel, did another about-face, and repudiated her repudiation. Her testimony in the trial was true, she said. Still later she *again* reversed herself.

Eventually, Beausoleil's motion for a new trial was denied, and he was sent to San Quentin's Death Row to wait out his appeal. The District Attorney's Office was left with a perplexing legal dilemma, however. After her testimony in the Beausoleil trial, the Court had granted Mary Brunner complete immunity for her part in the Hinman murder.

Except for the possibility that she might be tried for perjury, it looked as if Mary Brunner had managed to beat the rap.

Indicted on the Hinman murder, Manson appeared before Judge Dell to request that he be allowed to represent himself. When Dell denied the motion, Manson requested that Irving Kanarek and Daye Shinn be made his attorneys. Judge Dell ruled there would be 'a clear conflict of interest' if Shinn represented both Manson and Susan Atkins. This left Kanarek.

Commenting, 'I think we are well aware of Mr Kanarek and his record,' Manson told Judge Dell, 'I do not wish to hire this man as my attorney, but you leave me no alternative. I understand what I am doing. Believe me, I understand what I am doing. *This is the worst man in town I could pick*, and you are pushing him on me.' If Dell would permit him to represent himself, Manson said, then he would forget about having Kanarek.

'I am not going to be blackmailed,' Dell told Manson.

MANSON. 'Then I will take it up to the bigger father.'

Judge Dell said that Manson could, of course, appeal his decision. However, since Manson was already appealing the revocation of his pro per status in the Tate–LaBianca proceedings, Dell was willing to postpone a final decision until that writ was either accepted or rejected.

Aaron and I discussed the possible Kanarek substitution with District Attorney Younger. In view of his record, with Kanarek on the case the prospect that the trial might last two or more years was very real. Younger asked us if there was any legal basis for removing an attorney from a case. We told him we knew of none; however, I'd research the law. Younger asked me to prepare an argument for the Court, and suggested that it stress Kanarek's incompetency. From what I had learned of Kanarek, I did not feel that he was incompetent. His obstructionism, I felt, was the major issue.

I had no trouble obtaining evidence of this. From judges, deputy DAs, even jurors, I heard examples of his dilatory, obstructionist tactics. One deputy DA, on learning that he had to oppose Kanarek a second time, quit the office; life was too short for that, he said.

Anticipating that Manson would ask to substitute Kanarek on

Tate–LaBianca as well as Hinman, I began preparing my argument. At the same time I had another idea which just might make that argument unnecessary.

Maybe, with the right bait, I could persuade Manson to dump Kanarek himself.

On May 25, I was going through LAPD's tubs on the LaBianca case when I noticed, standing against the wall, a wooden door. On it was a multicolored mural; the lines from a nursery rhyme, '1, 2, 3, 4, 5, 6, 7 – All Good Children Go to Heaven'; and, in large letters, the words 'HELTER SKELTER IS COMING DOWN FAST.'

Stunned, I asked Gutierrez, 'Where in the hell did you get that?'

'Spahn Ranch.'

'When?'

He checked the yellow property envelope affixed to the door.

'November 25, 1969.'

'You mean for five months, while I've been desperately trying to link the killers with Helter Skelter, you've had this door, with those very words on it, the same bloody words that were found at the LaBianca residence?'

Gutierrez admitted they had. The door, it turned out, had been found on a cabinet in Juan Flynn's trailer. It had been considered so unimportant that to date no one had even bothered to book it into evidence.

Gutierrez did so the next day.

Again, as I had on numerous other occasions, I told the detectives that I wanted to interview Juan Flynn.

I had no idea how much Flynn actually knew. Along with Brooks, Poston, and Paul Watkins, the Panamanian cowboy had been interviewed by the authors of a quickie paperback that appeared even before the trial, but he obviously held back a great deal, since many of the incidents I'd learned about from Brooks and Paul were not included.

June 1–14, 1970

Two weeks before the start of the Tate–LaBianca trial, Manson requested, and obtained, the substitution of Irving Kanarek for Ronald Hughes.

I asked for a conference in chambers. Once there, I pointed out that the legal issues in this case were tremendously complex. Even with attorneys known to handle matters expeditiously, the trial could last four or more months. 'But,' I added, 'it is my frank opinion that if Mr Kanarek is permitted to represent Mr Manson, the case could last several years.' I noted, 'It is common knowledge among the legal profession that Mr Kanarek is a professional obstructionist. I believe the man is conscientious. I believe he is sincere.' However, I continued, 'there is no way for the Court to stop Mr Kanarek. Even holding him in contempt will not stop this man, because he will gladly spend the night in jail.'

Rather than have the trial become 'a burlesque on justice', I had an alternative suggestion, I told the Court. It was one I had considered for a long time and, though I had discussed it with Aaron, I knew it would come as a surprise to everyone else.

'As a possible solution, the prosecution has no objection to permitting Mr Manson to represent himself, as he has desired throughout, and let him have an attorney of his choice to assist him . . .'

Manson looked up at me with a startled expression. This was probably the last thing he had expected to hear from the prosecution.

Although I was hoping that, given this opportunity, Manson would dump Kanarek, I was sincere in making the suggestion. From the start Manson had maintained that only he could speak for himself. He'd strongly implied that, failing in this, he'd make trouble. And there was no question in my mind that this was his reason for choosing Kanarek.

Too, even though lacking formal education, Manson was bright. Having dominated them in the past, he could cross-examine such prosecution witnesses as Linda Kasabian, Brooks Poston, and other ex-Family members with probably more effectiveness than many 'straight' attorneys. And, to assist him in legal matters, he would have not only his own lawyer but three other experienced attorneys alongside him at the counsel table. Also, looking far ahead, I was concerned that the denial of Manson's request to defend himself might be an issue on appeal.

Aaron then quoted Manson's own statement, made in Judge Dell's court, that Kanarek was the worst man he could pick.

Kanarek objected so strongly to the proceedings that Judge Older remarked, 'Now the things that Mr Stovitz and Mr Bugliosi said about you, Mr Kanarek, while they might appear to be unfair, there certainly is, as a matter of common knowledge among the judges in this court, a good deal of truth in what they say. I am not impugning your personal motives, but you do have a reputation for taking an inordinately long time to do what someone else can do in a much shorter period . . .'

However, Older said, the only reason he was considering the matter was that he wanted to be absolutely sure Manson wanted Kanarek as his attorney. His remarks before Judge Dell had injected some doubt on that point.

In one respect, Manson replied, Kanarek would be the best attorney in town; 'in a lot of respects, he would be the worst attorney that I could take'. But, Manson continued, 'I don't think there is any attorney that can represent me as well as I can myself. I am smart enough to realize that I am not an attorney, and I will sit behind these men and I won't make a scene. I am not here to make trouble . . .

'There is a lot involved here that does not meet the eye. A person is born, he goes to school, he learns what he is told in a book, and he lives his life by what he knows. The only thing he knows is what someone has told him. He is educated; he does what an educated person does.

'But go out of this realm, you go into a generation gap, a free-love society, you get into insane drugs or smoking marijuana.' And in this other world the reality differs, Manson noted. Here experience alone is the teacher; here you discover 'there is no way that you can know the taste of water unless you drink it or unless it has rained on you or unless you jump in the river'.

THE COURT. 'All I want to do, Mr Manson, is find out if you are happy with Mr Kanarek or if you have second thoughts.'

MANSON. 'I thought I explained that. I would not be happy with anyone but myself. No man can represent me.'

I asked the Court's permission to question Manson. Though Kanarek objected, Charlie was agreeable. I asked him if he had consulted the other defense attorneys as to whether he should be represented by Kanarek. I had heard that two of them, Fitzgerald and Reiner, were very unhappy about Kanarek's entry into the case.

MANSON. 'I don't ask other men's opinions. I have my own.'

BUGLIOSI. 'Do you feel Mr Kanarek can give you a fair trial?'

MANSON. 'I do. I feel *you* can give me a fair trial. You showed me your fairness already.'

BUGLIOSI. 'I will give you a fair trial, Charlie, but I am out to convict you.'

MANSON. 'What's a fair trial?'

BUGLIOSI. 'That's when the truth comes out.'

Declaring, 'It would be a miscarriage of justice to permit you to represent yourself in a case having the complications this case has,' Older again asked Manson, 'Are you affirming Mr Kanarek as your attorney?'

'I am forced into a situation,' Manson replied. 'My second alternative is to cause you as much trouble as possible.'

A little over a week later we'd get our first sample of what he had in mind.

On being taken to Patton State Hospital in January, 16-year-old Dianne Lake had been labeled 'schizophrenic' by a staff psychologist. Though I knew the defense would probably try to use this to discredit her testimony, I wasn't too worried, since psychologists are not doctors and are not qualified to make medical diagnoses. The staff psychiatrists, who were doctors, said her problems were emotional, not mental: behavioral disorders of adolescence plus possible drug dependence. They also felt she had made excellent progress and were now sure she would be able to testify at the trial.

With Sergeant Patchett, I visited Patton in early June. The little ragamuffin I'd first seen in the jail in Independence now looked like any teen-ager. She was getting straight A's in school, Dianne told me proudly; not until getting away from the Family, she said, had she realized how good life was. Now, looking back, she felt she had been in a 'pit of death'.

In interviewing Dianne, I learned a number of things which hadn't come out in her earlier interviews. While they were in the desert together, at Willow Springs, Patricia Krenwinkel had told her that she had dragged Abigail Folger from the bedroom into the living room of the Tate residence. And Leslie Van Houten, after admitting to her that she had stabbed someone, had commented that at first she had been reluctant to do so, but then she'd discovered the more you stabbed, the more fun it was.

Dianne also said that on numerous occasions, in June, July, and August of 1969, Manson had told the Family, 'We have to be willing to kill pigs in order to help the black man start Helter Skelter.'

And several times – she believed it was in July, about a month before the Tate–LaBianca murders – Manson had also told them, '*I'm* going to have to start the revolution.'

The interview lasted several hours. One thing Dianne said struck me as very sad. Squeaky, Sandy, and the other girls in the family could never love anyone else, not even their parents, she told me. 'Why not?' I asked. 'Because,' she replied, 'they've given all their love to Charlie.'

In court on June 9, Manson suddenly turned in his chair so his back was to the judge. 'The Court has shown me no respect,'

Manson said, 'so I am going to show the Court the same thing.'
When Manson refused to face the Court, Judge Older, after
several warnings, had the bailiffs remove him from the courtroom. He was taken to the lockup adjoining the court, which was
equipped with a speaker system so he could hear, though not
participate in, the proceedings.

Although Older gave him several opportunities to return, on
the understanding that he would agree to conduct himself properly, Manson rejected them.

We had not given up in our attempt to have Irving Kanarek
taken off the case. On June 10, I filed a motion requesting an
evidentiary hearing on the Kanarek–Hughes substitution. The
thrust of my motion: Manson did not have the constitutional
right to have Kanarek as his lawyer.

The right of counsel of one's choice, I argued, was not an
unlimited, unqualified, absolute right. This right was given to
defendants seeking a favorable verdict for themselves. It was
obvious from Manson's statements that he wasn't picking Kanarek for this reason, but rather to subvert, thwart, and paralyze
the due and proper administration of justice. 'And we submit
that he cannot use the right to counsel of his choice in such an
ignoble fashion.'

Kanarek responded that he would be glad to let the Court read
the transcripts of his cases, to see if he used dilatory tactics. I
thought I saw Judge Older wince at this, but I wasn't sure. Older's
somber expression rarely changed. It was very difficult to guess
what he was thinking. Kanarek went on to point out that our
office hadn't tried to challenge Ronald Hughes, who had never
tried a case before, on the grounds that his representation might
hurt Manson. And, in conclusion, Kanarek, very much to the
point, asked that the prosecution's motion be struck 'on the basis
there is no basis for it in law'.

I'd frankly admitted this in my argument, but had noted that
this was 'a situation so aggravated that it literally cries out to the
Court to take a pioneer stand'.

367

Judge Older disagreed. My motion for an evidentiary hearing was denied.

Although District Attorney Younger had Older's ruling appealed to the California Supreme Court, it was let stand. Though we had tried to save the taxpayers perhaps several million dollars and everyone involved a great deal of time and unnecessary effort, Irving Kanarek would remain on the Tate–LaBianca cases just as long as Charles Manson wanted him.

'If Your Honor does not respect Mr Manson's rights, you need not respect mine,' Susan Atkins said, rising and turning her back to the Court. Leslie Van Houten and Patricia Krenwinkel followed suit. When Older suggested that the defense attorneys confer with their clients, Fitzgerald admitted that would do little good, 'because there is a minimum of client control in this case'. After several warnings, Older had the girls removed to one of the vacant jury rooms upstairs, and a speaker was placed there also.

I had mixed feelings about all this. If the girls parroted Mansons' actions during the trial, it would be additional evidence of his domination. However, their removal from the courtroom might also be considered reversible error on appeal, and the last thing we wanted was to have to try the whole case over again.

Under the current law, *Allen* vs *Illinois*, defendants can be removed from a courtroom if they engage in disruptive conduct. Another case, however, *People* vs *Zamora*, raised a subtler point. In that case, in which there were twenty-two defendants, the counsel tables were so situated that it was extremely difficult for the attorneys to communicate with their clients while court was in session. This led to a reversal by the Appellate Court, which ruled that the right of counsel implies the right of consultation between a defendant and his lawyer during the trial.

I mentioned this to Older, suggesting that some type of telephonic communication be set up. Older felt it unnecessary.

After the noon recess the girls professed a willingness to return. Speaking for all three, Patricia Krenwinkel told Older, 'We should be able to be present at this play here.'

To Krenwinkel it was just that – a play. Remaining standing, she turned her back to the bench. Atkins and Van Houten immediately mimicked her. Older again ordered all three removed.

Bringing all the defendants back into court the next day, Judge Older warned them that if they persisted in their conduct before a jury, they could badly jeopardize their cases. 'So I would ask you to seriously reconsider what you are doing, because I think you are hurting yourselves.' After again attempting to revert to pro per status, Manson said, 'O.K., then you leave me nothing. You can kill me now.'

Still standing, Manson bowed his head and stretched out his arms in a crucifixion pose. The girls quickly emulated him. When the deputies attempted to seat them, all resisted, Manson ending up scuffling with a deputy on the floor. Two deputies bodily carried him to the lockup, while the matrons took the girls out.

KANAREK. 'I would ask medical assistance for Mr Manson, Your Honor.'

THE COURT. 'I will ask the bailiff to check and see if he needs any. If he does, he will get it.'

He didn't. Once in the lockup, out of sight of the press and spectators, Manson became an entirely different person. He donned another mask, that of the complaisant prisoner. Having spent more than half his life in reformatories and prisons, he knew the role all too well. Thoroughly 'institutionalized', he played by the rules, rarely causing trouble in the jail itself.

After the noon recess we had several examples of Kanarek in action. Arguing a search-and-seizure motion, he said that Manson's arrest was illegal because 'Mr Caballero and Mr Bugliosi conspired to have Miss Atkins make certain statements' and that 'the District Attorney's Office suborned the perjury'.

As ridiculous as this was, subornation of perjury is an extremely serious charge, and since Kanarek was making it in open court, in front of the press, I reacted accordingly.

BUGLIOSI. 'Your Honor, if Mr Kanarek is going to have diarrhea of the mouth, I think he should make an offer of proof back in chambers. This man is totally irresponsible. I urgently request the Court we go back in chambers. God knows what this man is going to say next.'

THE COURT. 'Confine yourself to the argument, Mr Kanarek.'

The argument, when Kanarek did eventually get around to making it, left even the other defense attorneys looking stunned. Kanarek stated that since 'the warrant of arrest for the defendant Manson was based on illegally obtained and perjured testimony, therefore the seizure of the person of Mr Manson was illegal. The person of Mr Manson must, therefore, be suppressed from evidence.'

While I was wondering how you could suppress a person, Kanarek provided an answer: he asked that 'that piece of physical evidence which is Mr Manson's physical body' not 'be before the Court conceptually to be used in evidence'. Presumably, by Kanarek's convoluted logic, witnesses shouldn't even be allowed to identify Manson.

Older denied the motion. The preliminaries over, Older recessed court for the weekend. The trial would begin the following Monday – June 15, 1970.

Part Six

The Trial

'If the tale that is unfolding were not
so monstrous, aspects of it would break the heart.'
Jean Stafford

June 15–July 23, 1970

Judge Charles Older's court, Department 104, was located on the eighth floor of the Hall of Justice. As the first panel of sixty prospective jurors was escorted into the crowded courtroom, their expressions changed from boredom to curiosity. Then, as eyes alighted on the defendants, mouths dropped open in abrupt shock.

One man gasped, loud enough for those around him to hear, *'My God, it's the Manson trial!'*

In chambers the chief topic was sequestration. Judge Older had decided that once jury selection was completed, the jurors would be locked up until the end of the trial – 'to protect them from harassment and to prevent their being exposed to trial publicity'. Arrangements had already been made for them to occupy part of a floor at the Ambassador Hotel. Although spouses could visit on weekends, at their own expense, bailiffs would take all necessary precautions to see that the jury remained isolated from both outsiders and any news about the case. No one was sure how long this would be – estimates of the trial's length ranged from three to six months and up – but obviously it would be severe hardship for those chosen.

Although all the attorneys had some reservations about sequestration, only one strongly opposed it: Irving Kanarek. Since Kanarek had screamed the loudest about the taint of publicity adverse to his client, I concluded that Manson, not Kanarek, must have been behind the motion. And I had my own opinion as to why Charlie didn't want the jury locked up.

Rumor had it that Judge Older himself had already received several threats. A secret memo he'd sent the sheriff, outlining courtroom security measures, ended with the following paragraph:

'The sheriff shall provide the trial judge with a driver-bodyguard, and security shall be provided at the trial judge's residence on a 24-hour basis, until such time as all trial and post-trial proceedings have been concluded.'

Twelve names were drawn by lot. When the prospective jurors were seated in the jury box, Older explained that the sequestration could last 'as much as six months'. Asked if any felt this would constitute undue hardship, eight of the twelve raised their hands.*

Envisioning a mass exodus from the courtroom, Older was very strict when it came to excuses for cause. However, anyone who stated that he or she could not vote the death penalty under any circumstances was automatically excused, as was anyone who had read Susan Atkins' confession. This was usually approached obliquely, the prospective juror being asked something like 'Have you read where any defendant has made any type of incriminating statement or confession?' to which several answered on the order of 'Yes, that thing in the L.A. *Times*.' Questioning on this and other issues dealing with pre-trial publicity was done individually and in chambers, to avoid contaminating the whole panel.

After Older finished the initial questioning, the attorneys began their individual voir dire (examination). Lawyers are not supposed to 'educate' jurors during voir dire, but every lawyer worth his salt tries to predispose a jury to his side. For example, Reiner asked: 'Have you read anything in the press, or heard anything on TV, to the effect that Charles Manson has a kind of "hypnotic power" over the female defendants?' Obviously Reiner was less interested in the answer than in implanting this suggestion in the minds of the jurors. Similarly, walking the thin line between inquiry and instruction, I asked each juror: 'Do you understand that the People only have the burden of proving a

* Later, after obtaining revised estimates from the various attorneys, Judge Older changed this to 'three or more months', after which the hardship excuses abruptly declined.

defendant guilty beyond a *reasonable* doubt; we do not have the burden of proving his guilt beyond *all* doubt – only a *reasonable* doubt?'

Initially, Older would not permit the attorneys to instruct the prospective jurors in the law. I had a number of heated discussions with him about this before he let us couch such questions in general terms. This was, I felt, an important victory. For example, I didn't want to go through the whole trial only to have some juror decide, 'We can't convict Manson of the five Tate murders because he wasn't there. He was back at Spahn Ranch.'

The heart of our case against Manson was the 'vicarious liability' rule of conspiracy – each conspirator is criminally responsible for all the crimes committed by his co-conspirators if said crimes were committed to further the object of the conspiracy. This rule applies even if the conspirator was not present at the scene of the crime. For example: A, B and C decide to rob a bank. A plans the robbery, B and C carry it out. Under the law, A, though he never entered the bank, is as responsible as B and C.

From the prosecution's point of view, it was important that each juror understand such gut issues as reasonable doubt, conspiracy, motive, direct and circumstantial evidence, and the accomplice rule.

We hoped Judge Older would not declare Linda Kasabian an accomplice. But we were fairly sure he would,* in which case the defense would make much of the fact that no defendant can be convicted of any crime on the uncorroborated testimony of an accomplice. In researching the law, I found a California Supreme Court case, *People* vs *Wayne*, in which the Court said only 'slight' evidence was needed to constitute corroboration. After I brought this to Older's attention, he permitted me to use the word 'slight' in my questioning. This, too, I considered a significant victory.

Though Older had ascertained that each prospective juror could, if the evidence warranted it, vote a verdict of death, I went beyond this, asking each if he could conceive of circumstances

* He did later.

wherein he would be willing to vote such a verdict against (1) a young person; (2) a female defendant, or (3) a particular defendant even though the evidence showed that he himself did not do any actual killing. Obviously I wanted to eliminate anyone who answered any of these questions negatively.

Manson and the girls caused no disruptions during jury selection. In chambers during the individual voir dire, however, Manson would often stare at Judge Older for literally hours. I could only surmise that he had developed his incredible concentration while in prison. Older totally ignored him.

One day Manson tried it with me. I stared right back, holding his gaze until his hands started shaking. During the recess, I slid my chair over next to his and asked, 'What are you trembling about, Charlie? Are you afraid of me?'

'Bugliosi,' he said, 'you think I'm bad and I'm not.'

'I don't think you're all bad, Charlie. For instance, I understand you love animals.'

'Then you know I wouldn't hurt anyone,' he said.

'Hitler loved animals too, Charlie. He had a dog named Blondie, and from what I've read, Adolf was very kind to Blondie.'

Usually a prosecutor and a defendant won't exchange two words during an entire trial. But Manson was no ordinary defendant. And he loved to rap. In this, the first of many strange, often highly revealing, conversations we had, Manson asked me why I thought he was behind these murders. 'Because both Linda and Sadie told me you were,' I replied. 'Now, Sadie doesn't like me, Charlie, and she thinks you're Jesus Christ. So why would she tell me this if it wasn't true?'

'Sadie's just a stupid little bitch,' Manson said. 'You know, I only made love to her two or three times. After she had her baby and lost her shape, I couldn't have cared less about her. That's why she told that story, to get attention. I would never personally harm anyone.'

'Don't give me that crap, Charlie, because I won't buy it! What about Lotsapoppa? You put a bullet in his stomach.'

'Well, yeah, I shot that guy,' Manson admitted. 'He was going to come up to Spahn Ranch and get all of us. That was kinda in self-defense.'

Manson was enough of a jailhouse lawyer to know that I couldn't use anything he told me unless I'd first informed him of his constitutional rights. Yet this, and many subsequent admissions, surprised me. There was a strange sort of honesty about him. It was devious, it was never direct, but it was there. Whenever I pinned him down, he might evade, but not once in this, or the numerous other conversations we had, did he flatly deny that he had ordered the murders.

An innocent man protests his innocence. Instead, Manson played word games. If he took the stand and did this, I felt sure the jury would see through him.

Would Manson take the stand? The general consensus was that Manson's prodigious ego, plus the opportunity to use the witness stand as a forum to expound his philosophy before the world press, would impel him to testify. But – though I had already put in many hours preparing my cross-examination – no one but Manson really knew what he would do.

Toward the end of the recess, I told him, 'I've enjoyed talking to you, Charlie, but it would be much more interesting if we did it with you on the stand. I have lots and lots of things I'm curious about.'

'For instance?'

'For instance,' I replied, 'where in the world – Terminal Island, Haight-Ashbury, Spahn Ranch – did you get the crazy idea that other people don't like to live?'

He didn't answer. Then he began to smile. He'd been challenged. And knew it. Whether he'd decide to accept the challenge remained to be seen.

Though silent in court, Manson remained active behind the scenes.

On June 24, Patricia Krenwinkel interrupted Fitzgerald's voir dire to ask that he be relieved as her attorney. 'I have talked with him about the way I wish this to be handled right now, and he doesn't do as I ask,' she told the Court. 'He is to be my voice, which he is not . . .' Older denied her request.

Later the defense attorneys had a meeting with their clients. Fitzgerald, who had given up his Public Defender's job to represent Krenwinkel, emerged with tears in his eyes. I felt very badly about this and, putting my arm around his shoulder, told him, 'Paul, don't let it get you down. She'll probably keep you. And if she doesn't, so what? They're just a bunch of murderers.'

'They're savages, ingrates,' Fitzgerald said bitterly. 'Their only allegiance is to Manson.'

Fitzgerald didn't tell me what had occurred during the meeting, but it wasn't hard to guess. Directly, or through the girls, Manson had probably told the attorneys: Do it my way or you're off the case. Fitzgerald and Reiner told Los Angeles *Times* reporter John Kendall that all the attorneys had been instructed to 'remain silent' and not question prospective jurors.

When, the following day, Reiner disobeyed this order and continued his voir dire, Leslie Van Houten tried to fire him, repeating almost verbatim the words Krenwinkel had used. Older denied her request also.

What Reiner was going through could be gleaned from some instructed to 'remain silent' and not question prospective jurors. 'Even if it appears that Leslie Van Houten desired to stand or fall with the other defendants, could you nevertheless acquit her if the evidence against her was insufficient?'

On July 14 both the prosecution and the defense agreed to accept the jury. The twelve were then sworn. The jury consisted of seven men and five women, ranging in age from 25 to 73, in occupation from an electronics technician to a mortician.*

* The twelve jurors were: John Baer, an electrical tester; Alva Dawson, a retired deputy sheriff; Mrs Shirley Evans, a school secretary; Mrs Evelyn Hines, a dictaphone-teletype operator; William McBride II, a chemical company employee; Mrs Thelma McKenzie, a clerical supervisor; Miss Marie Mesmer, former drama critic for the now defunct Los Angeles *Daily News*; Mrs Jean Roseland, an executive secretary; Anlee Sisto, an electronics technician; Herman Tubick, a mortician; Walter Vitzelio, a retired plant guard; and William Zamora, a highway engineer.

It was very much a mixed jury, neither side getting exactly what it wanted.

Almost automatically, the defense will challenge anyone connected with law enforcement. Yet Alva Dawson, the oldest member of the jury, had worked sixteen years as a deputy sheriff with LASO while Walter Vitzelio had been a plant security guard for twenty years, and had a brother who was a deputy sheriff.

On the other hand, Herman Tubick, the mortician, and Mrs Jean Roseland, a secretary with TWA, each had two daughters in approximately the same age group as the three female defendants.

Studying the jurors' faces as they were sworn, I felt that most appeared pleased to have been selected. After all, they had been chosen to serve on one of the most famous trials of all time.

Older was quick to bring them back to earth. He instructed them that when they came to court the following morning they should bring their suitcases, clothing, and personal items, as from that point on they would be sequestered.

There remained the selection of the alternate jurors. Because of the anticipated length of the trial, Older decided to pick six, an unusually large number. Again we went through the whole voir dire.

Only this time it was without Ira Reiner. On July 17, Leslie Van Houten formally requested that Reiner be relieved as her attorney and Ronald Hughes appointed instead.

After questioning Hughes, Manson, and Van Houten on the possibility of a conflict of interest, Judge Older granted the substitution. Reiner was out, receiving not even so much as a thank-you for the eight months he had devoted to the case. Manson's former attorney, the 'hippie lawyer' Ronald Hughes, with his Santa Claus beard and Walter Slezak suits, became Leslie Van Houten's attorney of record.

Ira Reiner had been fired for one reason, and one reason only. He had tried to represent his client to the best of his ability. And he had properly decided that his client was not Charles Manson but Leslie Van Houten.

The Trial

There was a slight but perceptible smile on Manson's face. With good reason. He had succeeded in forming a united defense team. Although Fitzgerald remained its nominal head, it was obvious who was calling the shots.

On July 21 the six alternates were sworn, and they too were sequestered.* Jury selection had taken five weeks, during which 205 people had been examined and nearly 4,500 pages of transcript accumulated.

It had been a rough five weeks. Older and I had clashed on several occasions, Reiner and Older even oftener. And Older had threatened four of the attorneys with contempt, carrying through on one.

Three were for violations of the gag order: Aaron Stovitz was cited for an interview he had given the magazine *Rolling Stone*; Paul Fitzgerald and Ira Reiner for their quoted remarks in the Los Angeles *Times* story 'TATE SUSPECTS TRY TO SILENCE LAWYERS'. Though Older eventually dropped the contempt citations against all three, Irving Kanarek was less lucky. On July 8 he was seven minutes late to court. He had a valid reason – it was very difficult to find a parking space at the time court convened – but Older, who had previously threatened Kanarek with contempt when he was just three minutes late, was not sympathetic. He ruled Kanarek in contempt and fined him twenty-five dollars.

While we were busy selecting a jury, two of Manson's killers were set free.

Mary Brunner was reindicted and rearrested for the Hinman murder. Her attorneys filed a writ of habeas corpus. Ruling that she had fulfilled the conditions of the immunity agreement, Judge Kathleen Parker granted the writ and Brunner was released.

---

* The six alternate jurors were: Miss Frances Chasen, a retired civil service employee; Kenneth Daut, Jr, a state Division of Highways employee; Robert Douglass, an employee of the Army Corps of Engineers; John Ellis, a telephone installer; Mrs Victoria Kampman, a housewife; and Larry Sheely, a telephone maintenance man.

Meanwhile, Clem, t/n Steve Grogan, pleaded guilty to a grand theft auto charge stemming from the Barker raid. Van Nuys Judge Sterry Fagan heard the case. He was aware of Grogan's lengthy rap sheet. Moreover, the probation department, usually very permissive, in this case recommended that Grogan be sentenced to a year in the County Jail. Aaron also informed the judge that Clem was exceedingly dangerous; and that he had not only been along on the night the LaBiancas were killed, but we also had evidence that he had beheaded Shorty Shea. Yet unbelievably enough, Judge Fagan gave Clem straight probation!

On learning that Clem had returned to the Family at Spahn Ranch, I contacted his probation officer, asking him to revoke Clem's probation. There was more than ample cause. Among the terms of his probation were that he maintain residence at the home of his parents; seek and maintain employment; not use or possess any narcotics; not associate with known narcotics users. Moreover, he had been seen on several occasions, even photographed, with a knife and a gun.

His probation officer refused to act. He later admitted to LAPD that he was afraid of Clem.

Though Bruce Davis had gone underground, most of the other hard-core Family members were very much in evidence. Some dozen of them, including Clem and Mary, haunted the entrances and corridors of the Hall of Justice each day, where they would cast cold, accusing stares at the prosecution witnesses as they arrived to testify.

The problem of their presence in the courtroom – a concern since Sandy had been found carrying a knife – was solved by Aaron. Prospective witnesses are excluded when other witnesses are testifying. Aaron simply subpoenaed all the known Family members as prosecution witnesses, an act which raised a tremendous furor from the defense but made everyone else breathe a little easier.

July 24–26, 1970

Many of the spectators had been waiting since 6 A.M., hoping to get a seat and a glimpse of Manson. When he was escorted into the courtroom, several gasped. On his forehead was a bloody X. Sometime during the previous night he had taken a sharp object and carved the mark in his flesh.

An explanation was not long forthcoming. Outside court his followers passed out a typewritten statement bearing his name:

I have X'd myself from your world . . . You have created the monster. I am not of you, from you, nor do I condone your unjust attitude toward things, animals, and people that you do not try to understand . . . I stand opposed to what you do and have done in the past . . . You make fun of God and have murdered the world in the name of Jesus Christ . . . My faith in me is stronger than all of your armies, governments, gas chambers, or anything you may want to do to me. I know what I have done. Your courtroom is man's game. Love is my judge . . .

THE COURT. 'People vs Charles Manson, Susan Atkins, Patricia Krenwinkel, and Leslie Van Houten.

'All parties and counsel and jurors are present . . .

'Do the People care to make an opening statement?'

BUGLIOSI. 'Yes, Your Honor.'

I began the People's opening statement – which was a preview of the evidence the prosecution intended to introduce in the trial

– by summarizing the charges, naming the defendants, and, after relating what had occurred at 10050 Cielo Drive in the early-morning hours of August 9, 1969, and at 3301 Waverly Drive the following night, identifying the victims.

'A question you ladies and gentlemen will probably ask your-selves at some point during this trial, and we expect the evidence to answer that question for you, is this:

'What kind of a diabolical mind would contemplate or con-ceive of these seven murders? What kind of mind would want to have seven human beings brutally murdered?

'We expect the evidence at this trial to answer that question and show that defendant Charles Manson owned that diabolical mind. Charles Manson, who the evidence will show at times had the infinite humility, as it were, to refer to himself as Jesus Christ.

'Evidence at this trial will show defendant Manson to be a vagrant wanderer, a frustrated singer-guitarist, a pseudo-philo-sopher, but, most of all, the evidence will conclusively prove that Charles Manson is a killer who cleverly masqueraded behind the common image of a hippie, that of being peace loving . . .

'The evidence will show Charles Manson to be a megalo-maniac who coupled his insatiable thirst for power with an in-tense obsession for violent death.'

The evidence would show, I continued, that Manson was the unquestioned leader and overlord of a nomadic band of vaga-bonds who called themselves the 'Family'. After briefly tracing the history and composition of the group, I observed: 'We antici-pate that Mr Manson, in his defense, will claim that neither he nor anyone else was the leader of the Family and that he never ordered anyone in the Family to do anything, much less commit these murders for him.'

KANAREK. 'Your Honor, he is now making an opening state-ment for us!'

THE COURT. 'Overruled. You may continue, Mr Bugliosi.'

BUGLIOSI. 'We therefore intend to offer evidence at this trial showing that Charles Manson was in fact the dictatorial leader of the Family; that everyone in the Family was slavishly obedient to him; that he always had the other members of the Family do his bidding for him; and that eventually they committed the seven Tate–LaBianca murders at his command.

'This evidence of Mr Manson's total domination over the Family will be offered as circumstantial evidence that on the two nights in question it was he who ordered these seven murders.'

The principal witness for the prosecution, I told the jury, would be Linda Kasabian. I then briefly stated what Linda would testify to, interrelating her story with the physical evidence we intended to introduce: the gun, the rope, the clothing the killers wore the night of the Tate murders, and so forth.

We came now to the question that everyone had been asking since these murders occurred: *Why?*

The prosecution does not have the burden of proving motive, I told the jury. We needn't introduce one single, solitary speck of evidence as to motive. However, when we have evidence of motive we introduce it, because if one has a motive for committing a murder, this is circumstantial evidence that it was he who committed the murder. 'In this trial, we *will* offer evidence of Charles Manson's motives for ordering these seven murders.'

'We believe there to be more than one motive,' I told the jury. 'Besides the motives of Manson's passion for violent death and his extreme anti-establishment state of mind, the evidence in this trial will show that there was a further motive for these murders, which is perhaps as bizarre, or perhaps even more bizarre, than the murders themselves.

'Briefly, the evidence will show Manson's fanatical obsession with Helter Skelter, a term he got from the English musical group the Beatles.

'Manson was an avid follower of the Beatles and believed that they were speaking to him across the ocean through the lyrics of their songs. In fact, Manson told his followers that he found complete support for his philosophy in the words of those songs . . .

'To Charles Manson, Helter Skelter, the title of one of their songs, meant the black man rising up and destroying the entire white race; that is, with the exception of Charles Manson and his chosen followers, who intended to escape from Helter Skelter by going to the desert and living in a bottomless pit, a place that Manson derived from Revelation 9, a chapter in the last book of the New Testament . . .

'Evidence from several witnesses will show that Charles Manson hated black people, but that he also hated the white establishment, whom he called "pigs".

'The word "pig" was found printed in blood on the outside of the front door to the Tate residence.

'The words "death to pigs", "helter skelter", and "rise" were found printed in blood inside the LaBianca residence.

'The evidence will also show that one of Manson's principal motives for these seven savage murders was to ignite Helter Skelter; in other words, start the black-white revolution by making it look as though the black man had murdered these seven Caucasian victims. In his twisted mind, he thought this would cause the white community to turn against the black community, ultimately leading to a civil war between blacks and whites, a war which Manson told his followers would see bloodbaths in the streets of every American city, a war which Manson predicted and foresaw the black man as winning.

'Manson envisioned that black people, once they destroyed the entire white race, would be unable to handle the reins of power because of inexperience, and would therefore have to turn over the reins to those white people who had escaped from Helter Skelter, i.e., Charles Manson and his Family.

'In Manson's mind, his Family, and particularly he, would be the ultimate beneficiaries of a black-white civil war.

'We intend to offer the testimony of not just one witness but many witnesses on Manson's philosophy, because the evidence will show that it is so strange and so bizarre that if you heard it only from the lips of one person you probably would not believe it.'

Thus far all the emphasis had been on Manson. Convicting Manson was the first priority. If we convicted the others and not Manson, it would be like a war crimes trial in which the flunkies were found guilty and Hitler went free. Therefore I stressed that it was Manson who had ordered these murders, though his co-defendants, obedient to his every command, actually committed them.

There was a danger in this, however. I was giving the attorneys for the three girls a ready-made defense. In the penalty phase of the trial, they could argue that since Atkins, Krenwinkel, and Van Houten were totally under Manson's domination, they were not nearly as culpable as he, and therefore should receive life imprisonment rather than the death penalty.

Anticipating long in advance that I'd have to prove the very opposite, I laid the groundwork in my opening statement:

'What about Charles Manson's followers, the other defendants in this case, Susan Atkins, Patricia Krenwinkel, and Leslie Van Houten?

'The evidence will show that they, along with Tex Watson, were the actual killers of the seven Tate-LaBianca victims.

'The evidence will also show that they were *very willing* participants in these mass murders, that by their overkill tactics – for instance, Rosemary LaBianca was stabbed forty-one times, Voytek Frykowski was stabbed fifty-one times, shot twice, and struck violently over the head thirteen times with the butt of a revolver – these defendants displayed that *even apart* from Charles Manson, murder ran through their own blood.'

After mentioning Susan Atkins' confessions to Virginia Graham and Ronnie Howard; the fingerprint which placed Patricia Krenwinkel at the Tate murder scene; and the evidence which implicated Leslie Van Houten in the LaBianca murders, I observed: 'The evidence will show that Charles Manson started his Family in the Haight–Ashbury district of San Francisco in March of 1967. The Family's demise, as it were, took place in October of 1969 at Barker Ranch, a desolate, secluded, rock-strewn hideout from civilization on the shadowy perimeters of Death Valley. Between these two dates, seven human beings and an 8½-month baby boy fetus in the womb of Sharon Tate met their death at the hands of these members of the Family.

'The evidence at this trial will show that these seven incredible murders were perhaps the most bizarre, savage, nightmarish murders in the recorded annals of crime.

'Mr Stovitz and I intend to prove not just beyond a reasonable doubt, which is our only burden, but beyond *all* doubt that these defendants committed these murders, and are guilty of these murders; and in our final arguments to you at the conclusion of evidence, we intend to ask you to return verdicts of first degree murder against each of these defendants.'

Kanarek had interrupted my opening statement nine times with objections, all of which the Court had overruled. When I finished, he moved that the whole statement be stricken or, failing in that, a mistrial declared. Older denied both motions. Fitzgerald told the press my remarks were 'scurrilous and slanderous', and called the Helter Skelter motive 'a truly preposterous theory'.

I had a strong feeling that by the time of his closing argument to the jury, Paul wouldn't even bother to argue this.

The defense reserving its opening statements until after the prosecution had completed its case, the People called their first witness, Colonel Paul Tate.

With military erectness, Sharon's father took the stand and was sworn. Though 46, he looked younger, and sported a well-trimmed beard.

Our direct examination was brief. Colonel Tate described his last meeting with Sharon, and identified photos of his daughter, Miss Folger, Frykowski, Sebring, and the house at 10050 Cielo Drive.

Wilfred Parent, who followed Colonel Tate to the stand, broke down and cried when shown a photograph of his son, Steven.

Winifred Chapman, the Tate maid, was next. I questioned her in detail about the washing of the two doors; then, wanting to establish a chronology for the jurors, I took her up to her departure from the residence on the afternoon of August 8, 1969, intending to recall her to the stand later so she could testify to her discoveries the next morning.

On cross-examination Fitzgerald brought out that she hadn't

mentioned washing the door in Sharon's bedroom until months after the murders, and then she had told this not to LAPD but to me.

This was to be the start of a pattern. Having questioned each of the witnesses not once but a number of times, I had uncovered a great deal of information not previously related to the police. In many instances I had been the only one who had interviewed the witness. Though Fitzgerald initially planted the idea, Kanarek would nurture it until, in his mind at least, it budded into a full-bloomed conspiracy, with Bugliosi framing the whole case.

Kanarek had only one question for Mrs Chapman, but it was a good one. Had she ever seen the defendant Charles Manson before her appearance in court? She replied that she had not.

Although he had recently married and was not anxious to leave his bride, William Garretson had flown back from his home in Lancaster, Ohio, where he had returned after being released by LAPD. The former caretaker came across as sincere, though rather shy. Although I intended to call both officers Whisenhunt and Wolfer, the former to testify to finding the setting on Garretson's stereo at between 4 and 5, the latter to describe the sound tests he had conducted, I did question Garretson in detail as to the events of that night, and I felt the jury believed him when he claimed he hadn't heard any gunshots or screams.

I asked Garretson: 'How loud were you playing your stereo?'

A. 'It was about medium . . . It wasn't very loud.'

This, I felt, was the best evidence, Garretson was telling the truth. Had he been lying about hearing nothing, then surely he would have lied and said the stereo was loud.

Most of Fitzgerald's questions concerned Garretson's arrest and alleged rough handling by the police. At one point later in the trial Fizgerald would maintain that Garretson was involved in at least some of the Tate homicides. Since there wasn't even a hint of this in his cross-examination, I'd conclude that he was belatedly looking for a convenient scapegoat.

Kanarek again asked the same question. No, he'd never seen Manson before, Garretson replied.

By the end of the day we had finished with three more witnesses: Frank Guerrero, who had been painting the nursery that Friday; Tom Vargas, the gardener, who testified to the arrivals and departures of the various guests that day and to his signing for the two steamer trunks; and Dennis Hurst, who identified Sebring from a photograph as the man who came to the front door when he delivered the bicycle about eight that night.

The stage was now set for the prosecution's main witness, whom I intended to call to the stand first thing Monday morning.

On hearing my opening statement, Manson must have realized that I had his number.

At the conclusion of court that afternoon sheriff's deputy Sergeant William Maupin was escorting Manson from the lockup to the ninth floor of the jail when – to quote from Maupin's report –

inmate Manson stated to undersigned that it would be worth $100,000 to be set free. Inmate Manson also commented on how much he would like to return to the desert and the life he had before his arrest. Inmate Manson commented additionally that money meant nothing to him, that several people had contacted him regarding large sums of money. Inmate Manson also stated that an officer would only receive a six month sentence if caught releasing an inmate without authority.

Maupin reported the bribe offer to his superior, Captain Alley, who in turn informed Judge Older. Though the incident was never made public, Older gave the attorneys Maupin's report the next day. Reading it, I wondered what Manson would try next.

Over the weekend, Susan Atkins, Patricia Krenwinkel, and Leslie Van Houten lit matches, heated bobby pins red-hot, then burned X marks on their foreheads, after which they ripped open the burnt flesh with needles, to create more prominent scars.

When the jurors were brought into court Monday morning, the X's were the first thing they saw – graphic evidence that when Manson led, the girls followed.

A day or so later Sandy, Squeaky, Gypsy, and most of the other Family members did the same thing. As new disciples joined the group, this became one of the Family rituals, complete to tasting the blood as it ran down their faces.

July 27–August 3, 1970

Eight sheriff's deputies escorted Linda Kasabian from Sybil Brand to the Hall of Justice, through an entrance that circumvented those patrolled by the Family. When they reached the ninth floor, however, Sandra Good suddenly appeared in the corridor and screamed, *'You'll kill us all; you'll kill us all!'* Linda, according to those who witnessed the encounter, seemed less shaken than sad.

I saw Linda just after she arrived. Though her attorney, Gary Fleischman, had purchased a new dress for her, it had been misplaced, and she was wearing the same maternity dress she'd worn when pregnant. The baggy tent made her look more hippie-like than the defendants. After I'd explained the problem to Judge Older, he heard other matters in chambers until the dress was located and brought over. Later a similar courtesy would be extended to the defense when Susan Atkins lost her bra.

BUGLIOSI. 'The People call Linda Kasabian.'

The sad, resigned look she gave Manson and the girls contrasted sharply with their obviously hostile glares.

CLERK. 'Would you raise your right hand, please?'

KANAREK. 'Object, Your Honor, on the grounds this witness is not competent and she is insane!'

BUGLIOSI. 'Wait a minute! Your Honor, I move to strike that, and I ask the Court to find him in contempt for gross misconduct. This is unbelievable on his part!'

Unfortunately, it was all too believable – exactly the sort of thing we had feared since Kanarek came on the case. Ordering the jury to disregard Kanarek's remarks, Older called counsel to the bench. 'There is no question about it,' Older told Kanarek, 'your conduct is outrageous . . .'

BUGLIOSI. 'I know the Court cannot prevent him from speaking up, but God knows what he is going to say in the future. If I were to say something like this in open court, I would probably be thrown off the case by my office and disbarred . . .'

Defending Kanarek, Fitzgerald told the Court that the defense intended to call witnesses who would testify that Linda Kasabian had taken LSD at least three hundred times. The defense would contend, he said, that such drug use had rendered her mentally incapable of testifying.

Whatever their offer of proof, Older said, matters of law were to be discussed either at the bench or in chambers, *not* in front of the jury. As for Kanarek's outburst, Older warned him that if he did that once more, 'I am going to take some action against you.'

Linda was sworn. I asked her: 'Linda, you realize that you are presently charged with seven counts of murder and one count of conspiracy to commit murder?'

A. 'Yes.'

Kanarek objected, moving for a mistrial. Denied. It was some ten minutes later before I was able to get in the second question.

Q. 'Linda, are you aware of the agreement between the District Attorney's Office and your attorneys that if you testify to everything you know about the Tate-LaBianca murders, the District Attorney's Office will petition the Court to grant you immunity from prosecution and dismiss all charges against you?'

A. 'Yes, I am aware.'

Kanarek objected on four different grounds. Denied.

Q. 'Besides the benefits which will accrue to you under the agreement, is there any other reason why you have decided to tell everything you know about these seven murders?'

Another torrent of objections from Kanarek before Linda was able to answer: 'I strongly believe in the truth, and I feel the truth should be spoken.'

Thanks to Kanarek's objections, it took over an hour to get Linda up to her first meeting with Manson, her description of life at Spahn Ranch, and her definition of what she meant by the term 'Family'.

A. 'Well, we lived together as one family, as a family lives together, as a mother and father and children, but we were all just one, and Charlie was the head.'

I was questioning Linda about the various orders Manson had given the girls when, unexpectedly, Judge Older began sustaining Kanarek's hearsay objections. I asked to approach the bench.

Lay people believe hearsay is inadmissible. Actually there are so many exceptions to the hearsay rule that many lawyers feel the law should read, 'Hearsay is admissible except in these few instances.' I told Older: 'I had anticipated many legal problems in this case, and I have done research on them – because I kind of play the Devil's advocate – but I never anticipated I'd have any trouble showing Manson's directions to members of the Family.'

Older said he sustained the objections because he couldn't think of any exception to the hearsay rule that would permit the introduction of such statements.

This was crucial. If Older ruled such conversations inadmissible, there went the domination framework, and our case against Manson.

Shortly after this, court recessed for the day. Aaron, J. Miller Leavy, and I were up late that night, looking for citations of authority. Fortunately, we found two cases – *People* vs *Fratiano* and *People* vs. *Stevens* – in which the Court ruled you can show the existence of a conspiracy by showing the relationship between the parties, including statements made to each other. Shown the cases the next morning, Judge Older reversed himself and overruled Kanarek's objections.

Opposition now came from a totally unexpected direction: Aaron.

Linda had already testified that Manson ordered the girls to make love to male visitors to induce them to join the Family, when I asked her: 'Linda, do you know what a sexual orgy is?'

Kanarek immediately objected, as did Hughes, who remarked, in a somewhat revealing choice of words: 'We are not trying the sex lives of these people. We are trying the murder lives of these people.'

Not only were the defense attorneys shouting objections, many of which Older sustained; Aaron leaned over to me and said, 'Can't we skip this stuff? We're just wasting time. Let's get into the two nights of murder.'

'Look, Aaron,' I told him sotto voce, 'I'm fighting the judge, I'm fighting Kanarek, I'm not going to fight you. I've got enough problems. This is important and I'm going to get it in.'

As Linda finally testified, in between Kanarek's objections, *Manson* decided when an orgy would take place; *Manson* decided who would, and who would not, participate; and *Manson* then assigned the roles each would play. From start to finish he was the maestro, as it were, orchestrating the whole scene.

That Manson controlled even this most intimate and personal aspect of the lives of his followers was extremely powerful evidence of his domination.

Moreover, among the twenty-some persons involved in the particular orgy Linda testified to were Charles 'Tex' Watson, Susan Atkins, Leslie Van Houten, and Patricia Krenwinkel.

The sexual acts were not detailed, nor did I question Linda about other such 'group encounters'. Once the point was made, I moved on to other testimony – Helter Skelter, the black-white war, Manson's belief that the Beatles were communicating with him through the lyrics of their songs, his announcement, late on the afternoon of August 8, 1969, that 'Now is the time for Helter Skelter.'

Describing her appearance on the stand, the Los Angeles *Times* noted that even in discussing the group's sex life, Linda Kasabian was surprisingly 'serene, soft-spoken, even demure'.

Her testimony was also at times very moving. Telling how Manson separated the mothers and their children, and relating her own feelings on being parted from Tanya, Linda said, 'Sometimes, you know, when there wasn't anybody around, especially Charlie, I would give her my love and feed her.'

Linda was describing Manson's directions to the group just

before they left Spahn Ranch that first night when Charlie, seated at the counsel table, put his hand up to his neck and, with one finger extended, made a slitting motion across his throat. Although I was looking the other way and didn't see the gesture, others, including Linda, did.

Yet there was no pause in her reply. She went on to relate how Tex had stopped the car in front of the big gate; the cutting of the telephone wires; driving back down the hill and parking, then walking back up. As she described how they had climbed the fence to the right of the gate, you could feel the tension building in the courtroom. Then the sudden headlights.

A. 'And a car pulled up in front of us and Tex leaped forward with a gun in his hand ... And the man said, "Please don't hurt me, I won't say anything!" And Tex shot him four times.'

As she described the murder of Steven Parent, Linda began sobbing, as she had each time she had related the story to me. I could tell the jury was moved, both by the mounting horror and her reaction.

Sadie giggled. Leslie sketched. Katie looked bored.

By the end of the day I had brought Linda to the point where Katie was chasing the woman in the white gown (Folger) with a knife and Tex was stabbing the big man (Frykowski): 'He just kept doing it and doing it and doing it.'

Q. 'When the man was screaming, do you know what he was screaming?'

A. 'There were no words, it was beyond words, it was just screams.'

Reporters keeping track of Kanarek's objections gave up on the third day, when the count passed two hundred. Older warned Kanarek that if he interrupted either witness or the prosecution again, he would find him in contempt. Often a dozen transcript pages separated my question and Linda's answer.

BUGLIOSI. 'We are going to have to go back, Linda. There has been a blizzard of objections.'

KANAREK. 'I object to that statement.'

When Kanarek again interrupted Linda in mid-sentence, Older called us to the bench.

THE COURT. 'Mr Kanarek, you have directly violated my order not to repeatedly interrupt. I find you in contempt of Court and I sentence you to one night in the County Jail starting immediately after this court adjourns this afternoon until 7 A.M. tomorrow morning.'

Kanarek protested that 'rather than my interrupting the witness, the witness interrupted me'!

By day's end Kanarek would have company. Among the items I wished to submit for identification purposes was a photograph which showed the Straight Satans' sword in a scabbard next to the steering wheel of Manson's own dune buggy. Since the photograph had been introduced in evidence in the Beausoleil trial, I didn't get it until it was brought over from the other court. 'The District Attorney is withholding great quantities of evidence from us,' Hughes charged.

BUGLIOSI. 'For the record, I just saw it for the first time a few minutes ago myself.'

HUGHES. 'That is a lot of shit, Mr Bugliosi.'

THE COURT. 'I hold you in direct contempt of Court for that statement.'

Though in complete agreement with Older's earlier citing of Kanarek, I disagreed with his finding against Hughes, feeling if he was in contempt of anyone, it was me, not the Court. Too, it was based on a simple misunderstanding, one which, when explained to him, Hughes quickly accepted. Older was less understanding.

Given a choice between paying a seventy-five-dollar fine or spending the night in jail, Hughes told the Court: 'I am a pauper, Your Honor.' With no sympathy whatsoever, Older ordered him remanded into custody.

Kanarek learned nothing from his night in jail. The next morning he was right back interrupting both my questions and Linda's replies. Admonishments from the bench accomplished nothing; he'd apologize, then immediately do the same thing again. All this concerned me much less than the fact that he occasionally succeeded in keeping out testimony. Usually when Older sustained an objection, I could work my way around it, introducing the testimony in a different way. For example, when Older foreclosed me from questioning Linda about the defendants watching the news of the Tate murders on TV the day after those murders occurred, because he couldn't see the relevance of this, I asked Linda if, on the night of the murders, she was aware of the identities of the victims.

A. 'No.'

Q. 'When was the first time you learned the names of these five people?'

A. 'The following day on the news.'

Q. 'On television?'

A. 'Yes.'

Q. 'In Mr Spahn's trailer?'

A. 'Yes.'

Q. 'Did you see Tex, Sadie, and Katie during the day following these killings, other than when you were watching television with them?'

A. 'Well, I saw Sadie and Katie in the trailer. I cannot remember seeing Tex on that day.'

The relevance of this would become obvious when Barbara Hoyt took the stand and testified (1) that Sadie came in and told her to switch channels to the news; (2) that before this particular day Sadie and the others never watched the news; and (3) that immediately after the newscaster finished with Tate and moved on to the Vietnam war, the group got up and left.

In my questioning of Linda regarding the second night, there was one reiterated theme: Who told you to turn off the freeway? Charlie. Was anyone else in the car giving directions other than Mr Manson? No. Did anyone question any of Mr Manson's commands? No.

In her testimony regarding both nights, there were also literally a multitude of details which only someone who had been present on those nights of horrendous slaughter could have known.

Realizing very early how damaging this was, Manson had remarked, loud enough for both Linda and the jury to hear, 'You've already told three lies.'

Linda, looking directly at him, had replied, 'Oh, no, Charlie, I've spoken the truth, and you know it.'

By the time I had finished my direct examination of Linda Kasabian on the afternoon of July 30, I had the feeling the jury knew it too.

When I know the defense has something which might prove harmful to the prosecution's case, as a trial tactic I usually put on that evidence myself first. This not only converts a damaging left hook into a mere left jab, it also indicates to the jury that the prosecution isn't trying to hide anything. Therefore, I'd brought out, on direct, Linda's sexual permissiveness and her use of LSD and other drugs. Prepared to destroy her credibility with these revelations, the defense found itself going over familiar ground. In doing so, they sometimes even strengthened our case.

It was Fitzgerald, Krenwinkel's defense attorney, not the prosecution, who brought out that during the period Linda was at Spahn, 'I was not really together in myself ... I was extremely impressionistic ... I let others put ideas in me'; and – even more important – that she feared Manson.

Q. 'What were you afraid of?' Fitzgerald asked.

A. 'I was just afraid. He was a heavy dude.'

Asked to explain what she meant by this, Linda replied. 'He just had something, you know, that could hold you. He was a heavyweight. He was just heavy, period.'

Fitzgerald also elicited from Linda that she loved Manson; that 'I felt he was the Messiah come again'.

Linda then added one statement which went a long way toward explaining not only why she but also many of the others had so readily accepted Manson. When she first saw him, she said, 'I thought ... "This is what I have been looking for," and this is what I saw in him.'

Manson – a mirror which reflected the desires of others.

Q. 'Was it also your impression that other people at the ranch loved Charlie?'

A. 'Oh, yes. It seemed that the girls worshiped him, just would die to do anything for him.'

Helter Skelter, Manson's attitude toward blacks, his domination of his co-defendants: in each of these areas Fitzgerald's queries brought out additional information which bolstered Linda's previous testimony.

Often his questions backfired, as when he asked Linda: 'Do you remember who you slept with on August 8?'

A. 'No.'

Q. 'On the tenth?'

A. 'No, but eventually I slept with all the men.'

Time and again Linda volunteered information which could have been considered damaging, yet, coming from her, somehow seemed only honest and sincere. She was so open that it caught Fitzgerald off guard.

If possible, at the end of Fitzgerald's cross-examination Linda Kasabian looked even better than she had at the end of the direct.

It was Monday, August 3, 1970. I was on my way back to court from lunch, a few minutes before 2 P.M., when I was abruptly surrounded by newsmen. They were all talking at once, and it was a couple of seconds before I made out the words: 'Vince, have you heard the news, *President Nixon just said that Manson's guilty!*'

Fitzgerald had a copy of the AP wire. In Denver for a conference of law-enforcement officials, the President, himself an attorney, was quoted as complaining that the press tended 'to glorify and make heroes out of those engaged in criminal activities'.

He continued: 'I noted, for example, the coverage of the Charles Manson case . . . Front page every day in the papers. It usually got a couple of minutes in the evening news. Here is a man who was guilty, directly or indirectly, of eight murders. Yet here is a man who, as far as the coverage is concerned, appeared to be a glamorous figure.'

Following Nixon's remarks, presidential press secretary Ron Ziegler said that the President had 'failed to use the word "alleged" in referring to the charges'.*

We discussed the situation in chambers. Fortunately, the bailiffs had brought the jury back from lunch before the story broke. They remained sequestered in a room upstairs, and so, as yet, there was no chance of their having been exposed.

Kanarek moved for a mistrial. Denied. Ever suspicious that the sequestration was not effective, he asked that the jurors be

---

* On the way back to Washington on *Air Force One*, President Nixon issued a supplementary statement:

'I have been informed that my comment in Denver regarding the Tate murder trial in Los Angeles may continue to be misunderstood despite the unequivocal statement made at the time by my press secretary.

'The last thing I would do is prejudice the legal rights of any person, in any circumstances.

'To set the record straight, I do not now and did not intend to speculate as to whether the Tate defendants are guilty, in fact or not. All the facts in the case have not yet been presented. The defendants should be presumed to be innocent at this stage of the trial.'

voir dired to see if any had heard the news. As Aaron put it, 'It would be like waving a red flag. If they didn't know about it before, they certainly will after the voir dire.'

Older denied the motion 'without prejudice', so it could be renewed at a later time. He also said he would tell the bailiffs to inaugurate unusually stringent security measures. Later that afternoon the windows of the bus used to transport the jury to and from the hotel were coated with Bon Ami to prevent the jurors from seeing the inevitable headlines. There was a TV set in their joint recreation room at the Ambassador; ordinarily they could watch any program they wished, except the news, a bailiff changing the channels. Tonight it would remain dark. Newspapers would also be banned from the courtroom, Older specifically instructing the attorneys to make sure none were on the counsel table, where they might inadvertently be seen by the jury.

When we returned to court, there was a smug grin on Manson's face. It remained there all afternoon. It isn't every criminal who merits the attention of the President of the United States. Charlie had made the big time.

The jury was brought down, and Atkins' defense attorney, Daye Shinn, began his cross-examination of Linda.

Apparently intent on implying that I had coached Linda in her testimony, he asked: 'Do you recall what Mr Bugliosi said to you during your first meeting?'

A. 'Well he has always stressed for me to tell the truth.'

Q. 'Besides the truth, I'm talking about.'

As if anything else were important.

Q. 'Did Mr Bugliosi ever tell you that some of your statements were wrong, or some of your answers were not logical, or did not make sense?'

A. 'No, I told him; he never told me.'

Q. 'The fact that you were pregnant, wasn't that the reason that you stayed outside [the Tate residence] instead of going inside to participate?'

A. 'Whether I was pregnant or not, I would never have killed anybody.'

Shinn gave up after only an hour and a half. Linda's testimony remained unshaken.

With a heavy, ponderous shuffle, Irving Kanarek approached the witness stand. It was excruciatingly tiring listening to him. It was also very important that I do so, since, unlike the two attorneys who preceded him, Kanarek scored points. He brought out, for example, that when Linda returned to California to reclaim Tanya, she told the social worker that she'd left the state on August 6 or 7 – which, had this been true, would have been *before* the Tate-LaBianca murders occurred. If accurate, this meant that Linda had fabricated all of her testimony regarding those murders. And if she had lied to the social worker to get her daughter back, Kanarek implied, she could very well lie to this Court to get her own freedom.

But mostly he rambled and droned on and on, tiring the spectators as well as the witness. Many of the reporters 'wrote off' Kanarek early in the proceedings. Given a choice of defense attorneys, they quoted Fitzgerald, whose questions were better phrased. But it was Kanarek, in the midst of his verbosity, who was scoring.

He was also beginning to get to Linda. At the end of the day – her sixth on the stand – she looked a little fatigued and her answers were less sharp. No one knew how many days of this lay ahead, since Kanarek, unlike the other attorneys, consistently avoided answering Older's questions about the estimated length of his cross-examination.

On my way home that night I was again thankful the jury had been sequestered. You could see the headlines on every newsstand. The car radio had periodic updates. Hughes: 'I am guilty of contempt for uttering a dirty word, but Nixon has the contempt of the world to face.' Fitzgerald: 'It is very discouraging when the world's single most important person comes out against you.' The most reported quote was that of Manson, who had passed a statement to the press via one of the defense attorneys. Mimicking Nixon's remarks, it was unusually short and to the point: 'Here's a man who is accused of murdering hundreds of thousands in Vietnam who is accusing me of being guilty of eight murders.'

Just after the noon recess next day Manson suddenly stood and, turning toward the jury box, held up a copy of the front page of the Los Angeles *Times*.

A bailiff grabbed it but not before Manson had shown the jury the huge black headline:

MANSON GUILTY

NIXON DECLARES

Older had the jury taken out. He then demanded to know which attorney, against his express orders, had brought a newspaper into court. There were several denials but no one confessed.

There was no question now that the jury would have to be voir dired. Each member was brought in separately and questioned by the judge under oath. Of the twelve jurors and six alternates, eleven were aware of the full headline; two saw only the words MANSON GUILTY; four only saw the paper or the name MANSON and one, Mr Zamora, didn't see anything: 'I was looking at the clock at the time.'

After an extensive voir dire, all eighteen stated under oath that they had not been influenced by the headline and that they would consider only the evidence presented to them in court.

One aspect of this did concern me just a little. It was a subtler point. Although the headlines declared that Manson – not the girls – was guilty, it could be argued that as Manson's co-defendants the guilt 'slopped over' onto them. Although I assumed this would be an issue they would raise on appeal, I felt fairly certain it would not constitute 'reversible error'. There are errors in every trial, but most do not warrant a reversal by the appellate courts. This might have, had not Older voir dired the jury and obtained their sworn statements that they would not be influenced by the incident.

Nor did the three female defendants exactly help their case

when, the next day, they stood up and said in perfect unison: 'Your Honor, the President said we are guilty, so why go on with the trial?'

Older had not given up his search for the culprit. Daye Shinn now admitted that just before court resumed he'd walked over to the file cabinet where the bailiff had placed the confiscated papers and had picked up several and brought them back to the counsel table. He'd intended to read the sports pages, he said, unaware that the front pages were also attached.

Declaring Shinn in direct contempt of Court, Older ordered him to spend three nights in the County Jail, commencing as soon as court adjourned.

Irving Kanarek kept Linda Kasabian on the stand *seven days*. Unlike Fitzgerald and Shinn, he examined Linda's testimony regarding those two nights as if under a microscope. The problem with this, as far as the defense was concerned, was that some of her most damning statements were repeated two, three, even more times. Nor was Kanarek content to score a point and move on. Frequently he dwelt on a subject so long he negated his own argument. For example, Linda had testified that on the night of the Tate murders her mind was clear. She had also testified that after seeing the shooting of Parent she went into a state of shock. Kanarek did not stop at pointing out the seeming contradiction, but asked exactly when her state of shock ended.

A. 'I don't know when it ended. I don't know if it ever ended.'
Q. 'Your mind was completely clear, is that right?'
A. 'Yes.'
Q. 'You weren't under the influence of any drug, is that right?'
A. 'No.'
Q. 'You weren't under the influence of anything, right?'
A. 'I was under the influence of Charlie.'

Although Linda remained responsive to the questions, it was obvious that Kanarek was wearing her down.

On August 7 we lost a juror and a witness.

Juror Walter Vitzelio was excused because both he and his

wife were in ill health. The ex-security guard was replaced, by lot, by one of the alternates, Larry Sheely, a telephone maintenance man.

That same day I learned that Randy Starr had died at the Veterans Administration Hospital of an 'undetermined illness'.

The former Spahn ranch hand and part-time stunt man had been prepared to identify the Tate-Sebring rope as identical with one Manson had. Even more important, since Randy had given Manson the .22 caliber revolver, his testimony would have literally placed the gun in Manson's hand.

Though I had other witnesses who could testify to these key points, I was admittedly suspicious of Starr's sudden demise. Learning no autopsy had been performed, I ordered one. Starr, it was determined, had died of natural causes, from an ear infection.

KANAREK. 'Mrs Kasabian, I show you this picture.'

A. *'Oh, God!'* Linda turned her face away. It was the color photo of the very pregnant, and dead, Sharon Tate.

This was the first time Linda had seen the photograph, and she was so shaken Older called a ten-minute recess.

There was no evidence whatsoever that Linda Kasabian had been inside the Tate residence or that she had seen Sharon Tate's body. Aaron and I therefore questioned Kanarek's showing her the photograph. Fitzgerald argued that it was entirely possible that Mrs Kasabian had been inside both the Tate and LaBianca residences and had participated in all of the murders. Older ruled that Kanarek could show her the photo.

Kanarek then showed Linda the death photo of Voytek Frykowski.

A. 'He is the man that I saw at the door.'

KANAREK. 'Mrs Kasabian, why are you crying right now?'

A. 'Because I can't believe it. It is just – '

Q. 'You can't believe what, Mrs Kasabian?'

A. 'That they could do that.'

Q. 'I see. Not that *you* could do that, but that *they* could do that?'

A. 'I know I didn't do that.'

Q. 'You were in a state of shock, weren't you?'

A. 'That's right.'

Q. 'Then how do you know?'

A. 'Because I know. I do not have that kind of thing in me, to do such an animalistic thing.'

Kanarek showed Linda the death photos of all five of the Tate victims as well as those of Rosemary and Leno LaBianca. He even insisted that she handle the leather thong that had bound Leno's wrists.

Perhaps Kanarek hoped that he would so unnerve Linda that she would make some damaging admission. Instead, he only succeeded in emphasizing that, in contrast to the other defendants, Linda Kasabian was a sensitive human being capable of being deeply disturbed by the hideousness of these acts.

Showing Linda the photos was a mistake. And the other defense attorneys soon realized this. Each time Kanarek held up a picture, then asked her to look closely at some minute detail, the jurors winced or squirmed uncomfortably in their chairs. Even Manson protested that Kanarek was acting on his own. And still Kanarek persisted.

On Monday, August 10, 1970, the People petitioned the Court for immunity for Linda Kasabian. Though Judge Older signed the petition the same day, it was not until the thirteenth that he formally dropped all charges against her and she was released. She had been in custody since December 3, 1969. Unlike Manson, Atkins, Krenwinkel, and Van Houten, she had been in solitary confinement the whole time.

The next day Manson passed Linda a long handwritten letter. It seemed, at first, mostly nonsensical. Only on looking closer did one notice that key phrases had been marked with tiny check marks. Extracted, spelling errors intact, they read:

Love can never stop if it's love . . . The joke is over. Look at the end and begin again . . . Just give yourself to your love & give your love to be free . . . If you were not saying what your saying there would be no tryle . . . Don't lose your love its only there for you . . . Why do you

405

think they killed JC? Answer: Cause he was a Devil & bad. No one liked him ... Don't let anyone have this or they will find a way to use it against me ... This trile of Man's Son will only show the world that each man judges himself.

Coming just after she had been granted immunity, the message could only have one meaning: Manson was attempting to woo Linda back into the Family, in hopes that once freed she would repudiate her testimony.

Her answer was to give the letter to me.

Though a number of people had seen Manson pass Linda the letter, Kanarek maintained that she had grabbed it out of his hand!

The most effective cross-examination of Linda Kasabian was surprisingly that of Ronald Hughes. Though this was his first trial, and he frequently made procedural mistakes, Hughes was familiar with the hippie subculture, having been a part of it. He knew about drugs, mysticism, karma, auras, vibrations, and when he questioned Linda about these things, he made her look just a little odd, just a wee bit zingy. He had her admitting that she believed in ESP, that there were times at Spahn when she actually felt she was a witch.

Q. 'Do you feel that you are controlled by Mr Manson's vibrations?'

A. 'Possibly.'

Q. 'Did he put off a lot of vibes?'

A. 'Sure, he's doing it right now.'

HUGHES. 'May the record reflect, Your Honor, that Mr Manson is merely sitting here.'

KANAREK. 'He doesn't seem to be vibrating.'

Hughes asked Linda so many questions about drugs that, had an unknowing spectator walked into court, he would have assumed Linda was on trial for possession. Yet Linda's alert replies in themselves disproved the charge that LSD had destroyed her mind.

Q. 'Now, Mrs Kasabian, you testified that you thought Mr

Manson was Jesus Christ. Did you ever feel that anybody else was Jesus Christ?'

A. 'The biblical Jesus Christ.'

Q. 'When did you stop thinking that Mr Manson was Jesus Christ?'

A. 'The night at the Tate residence.'

Though I felt confident the jury was impressed with Linda, I was pleased to hear an independent evaluation. Hughes requested that the Court appoint psychiatrists to examine Linda. Older replied: 'I find no basis for a psychiatric examination in this case. She appears to be perfectly lucid and articulate. I find no evidence of aberration of any kind insofar as her ability to recall, to relate. In all respects she has been remarkably articulate and responsive. The motion will be denied.'

Hughes ended his cross-examination of Linda very effectively:

Q. 'You have testified that you have had trips on marijuana, hash, THC, morning-glory seeds, psilocybin, LSD, mescaline, peyote, methedrine, and Romilar, is that right?'

A. 'Yes.'

Q. 'And in the last year you have had the following major delusions: You have believed that Charles Manson is Jesus Christ, is that right?'

A. 'Yes.'

Q. 'And you believed yourself to be a witch?'

A. 'Yes.'

HUGHES. 'Your Honor, I have no further questions at this time.'

The basic purpose of redirect examination is to rehabilitate the witness. Linda needed little rehabilitating, other than being allowed to explain more fully replies which the defense had cut off. For example, I brought out that Linda meant 'state of shock' figuratively, not medically, and that she was very much aware of what was going on.

On redirect the prosecution can also explore areas first opened on cross-examination. Since the theft of the $5,000 had come out on cross, I was able to bring in the mitigating circumstances: that after stealing the money, Linda had turned it over to the Family and that she neither saw it again nor benefited from it.

Not until the re-redirect was I able to bring out why Linda had fled Spahn Ranch without Tanya.

The delay in getting this in was actually beneficial, I felt, for by this time the jury knew Linda Kasabian well enough to accept her explanation.

Direct. Cross. Redirect. Recross. Re-redirect. Re-recross. Just before noon on Wednesday, August 19, Linda Kasabian finally stepped down from the stand. She had been up there seventeen days – longer than most trials. Though the defense had been given a twenty-page summary of all my interviews with her, as well as copies of all her letters to me, *not once* had she been impeached with a prior inconsistent statement. I was very proud of her; it ever there was a star witness for the prosecution, Linda Kasabian was it.

Following the completion of her testimony, she flew back to New Hampshire for a reunion with her two children. For Linda, however, the ordeal was not yet over. Kanarek asked that she be subject to recall by the defense, and she would also have to testify when Watson was brought to trial.

Randy Starr was not the only witness the People lost during August.

Still afflicted with wanderlust, Robert Kasabian and Charles Melton had gone to Hawaii. I asked Linda's attorney, Gary Fleischman, if he could locate them, but he said they were off on some uncharted island, meditating in a cave, and there was no way to reach them. I'd wanted Melton especially, to testify to Tex's remark, 'Maybe Charlie will let me grow a beard someday.'

The loss of the other witness was a far greater blow to the prosecution. Saladin Nader, the actor whose life Linda had saved the night the LaBiancas were killed, had moved out of his apartment. He'd told friends he was going to Europe, but left no forwarding address. Although I requested the LaBianca detectives to try to locate him through the Lebanese Consulate and the Immigration Service, they were unsuccessful. I then asked them to interview his former landlady, Mrs Eleanor Lally, who could at least testify that during August 1969 the actor had occupied Apartment 501, 1101 Ocean Front Walk, Venice. But with Nader's disappearance, we lost the only witness who could even partially corroborate Linda Kasabian's story of that second night.

On August 18, however, we found a witness – one of the most important yet to appear.

Over seven months after I had first tried to get Watkins and Poston to persuade him to come in for an interview, Juan Flynn decided he was ready to talk.

Fearful that he would become a prosecution witness, the Family had launched a campaign of harassment that included threatening letters, hang-up phone calls, and cars racing past his trailer in the night, their occupants oinking or shouting 'Pig!' All this had made Juan mad – mad enough to contact LASO, who in turn called LAPD.

Since I was in court, Sartuchi interviewed Flynn that afternoon at Parker Center. It was a short interview; transcribed, it ran to only sixteen pages, but it contained one very startling disclosure.

SARTUCHI. 'When did you first become aware of the fact that Charles Manson was being charged with the crimes that he is presently on trial for?'

FLYNN. 'I became aware of the crimes that he is being charged with when he admitted to me of the killings that were taking place . . .'

In his broken English, Flynn was saying that Manson had admitted the murders to him!

Q. 'Was there any conversation about the LaBiancas, or was that all at the same time, or what?'

A. 'Well, I don't know if it was at the same time, but he led me to believe – he told me that he was the main cause for these murders to be committed.'

Q. 'Did he say anything more than that?'

A. 'He admitted – he boasted – of thirty-five lives taken in a period of two days.'

When LAPD brought him to my office, I hadn't yet talked to Sartuchi or heard the interview tape, so when in interviewing Flynn I learned of Manson's very incriminating admission, it came as a complete surprise.

In questioning Juan, I established that the conversation had taken place in the kitchen at Spahn Ranch, two to four days after news of the Tate murders broke on TV. Juan had just sat down to lunch when Manson came in and, with his right hand, brushed his left shoulder – apparently a signal that the others were to get out, since they immediately did. Aware that something was up, but not what, Juan started to eat.

(Ever since the arrival of the Family at Spahn Ranch, Manson had been trying to get the six-foot-five cowboy to join them. Manson had told Flynn: 'I will get you a big gold bracelet and put diamonds on it and you can be my head zombie.' There were other enticements. When first offered the same bait as the other males, Juan had sampled it eagerly, to his regret. 'That damn case of clap just wouldn't go away,' Juan told me, 'not for three, four months.' Though he had remained at Spahn, Juan had refused to be anybody's zombie, let alone little Charlie's. Of late, however, Manson had become more insistent.)

Suddenly Manson grabbed Juan by the hair, yanked his head back, and, putting a knife to his throat, said, '*You son of a bitch, don't you know I'm the one who's doing all of these killings?*'

Even though Manson had not mentioned the Tate-LaBianca murders by name, his admission was a tremendously powerful piece of evidence.*

The razor-sharp blade still on Juan's throat, Manson asked, 'Are you going to come with me or do I have to kill you?'

* Legally, Manson's statement was an admission rather than a confession. An admission is a statement by a defendant which, by itself, is not sufficient to warrant an inference of guilt, but which tends to prove guilt when considered with the rest of the evidence.

A confession is a statement by a defendant which discloses his intentional participation in the criminal act for which he is on trial and which discloses his guilt for that crime.

Juan replied, 'I am eating and I am right here, you know.'

Manson put the knife on the table. 'O.K.,' he said. 'You kill me.'

Resuming eating, Juan said, 'I don't want to do that, you know.'

Looking very agitated, Manson told him, 'Helter Skelter is coming down and we've got to go to the desert.' He then gave Juan a choice: he could oppose him or join him. If he wanted to join him, Charlie said, 'go down to the waterfall and make love to my girls'.

(Manson's 'my girls' was in itself a powerful piece of evidence.)

Juan told Charlie that the next time he wanted to contract a nine-month case of syphilis or gonorrhea, he'd let him know.

It was at this point that Manson boasted of killing thirty-five people in two days. Juan considered it just that, a boast, and I was inclined to agree. If there had been more than seven Manson-ordered murders during that two-day period, I was sure that at some point in the investigation we would have found evidence of them. Too, as far as the immediate trial was concerned, the latter statement was useless, as it was obviously inadmissible as evidence.

Eventually Manson picked up the knife and walked out. And Juan suddenly realized he didn't have much appetite left.

I talked to Juan over four hours that night. Manson's admission was not the only surprise. Manson had told Juan in June or July 1969, while Juan, Bruce Davis, and Clem were standing on the boardwalk at Spahn, 'Well, I have come down to it. The only way to get Helter Skelter going is for me to go down there and show the black man how to do it, by killing a whole bunch of those fuckin' pigs.'

Among Flynn's other revelations: Manson had threatened to kill him several times, once shooting at him with the .22 Longhorn revolver; on several occasions Manson had suggested that Juan kill various people; and Flynn had not only seen the group leave Spahn on probably the same night the LaBiancas were killed; Sadie had told him, just before they left, 'We're going to get some fucking pigs.'

Suddenly Juan Flynn became one of the prosecution's most important witnesses. The problem now was protecting him until he took the stand. Throughout our interview Juan had been extremely nervous; he'd tense at the slightest noise in the hall. He admitted that, because of his fear, he hadn't had a full night's sleep in months. He asked me if there was any way he could be locked up until it came time for him to testify.

I called LAPD and requested that Juan be put in either jail or a hospital. I didn't care which, just so long as he was off the streets.

Bemused by this unusual turnabout, Sartuchi, when he picked up Juan, asked him what he wanted to be arrested for. Well, Juan said, thinking a bit, he wanted to confess to drinking a beer in the desert a couple of months ago. Since he was in a National Park, that was against the law. Flynn was arrested and booked on that charge.

Juan remained in jail just long enough to decide he didn't like it one bit. After three or four days he tried to contact me. Unable to reach me right away, he called Spahn Ranch and left a message for one of the ranch hands to come down and bail him out. The Family intercepted the message, and sent Irving Kanarek instead.

Kanarek paid Juan's bail and bought him breakfast. He instructed Juan, 'Don't talk to anyone.'

When Juan had finished eating, Kanarek told him that he had already called Squeaky and the girls and that they were on their way over to pick him up. Hearing this, Juan split. Though he remained in hiding, he called in periodically, to assure me that he was still all right and that when the time came he would be there to testify.

Although it would never be mentioned in the trial, Juan had a special reason for testifying. Shorty Shea had been his best friend.

August 19–September 6, 1970

After Kasabian left the stand, I called a series of witnesses whose detailed testimony either supported or corroborated her account. These included: Tim Ireland, counselor at the girls' school down the hill from the Tate residence, who heard the cries and screams; Rudolf Weber, who described the hosing incident and dropped one bombshell: the license-plate number; John Swartz, who confirmed that was the number on his car and who told how, on two different nights in the first part of August 1969, Manson had borrowed the vehicle without asking permission; Winifred Chapman, who described her arrival at 10050 Cielo Drive on the morning of August 9, 1969; Jim Asin, who called the police after Mrs Chapman ran down Cielo screaming, 'Murder, death, bodies, blood!'; the first LAPD officers to arrive at the scene – DeRosa, Whisenhunt, and Burbridge – who described their grisly find. Bit by bit, piece by piece, from Chapman's arrival to the examination of the cut phone wires by the telephone company representative, the scene was re-created. The horror seemed to linger in the courtroom even after the witnesses had left the stand.

Since Leslie Van Houten was not charged with the five Tate murders, Hughes did not question any of these witnesses. He did, however, make an interesting motion. He asked that he and his client be permitted to absent themselves from the courtroom while those murders were discussed. Though the motion was denied, his attempt to separate his client from these events ran directly counter to Manson's collective defense, and I wondered how Charlie was reacting to it.

When McGann took the stand, I questioned him at some length as to what he had found at the Tate residence. The relevancy of many of the details – the pieces of gun grip, the dimensions and type of rope, the absence of shell casings, and so on – would become apparent to the jury later. I was especially interested in establishing that there was no evidence of ransacking or robbery. I also got in, ahead of the defense, that drugs had been found. And a pair of eyeglasses.

Anticipating the next witness, Los Angeles County Coroner Thomas Noguchi, Kanarek asked for a conference in chambers. He'd had a change of heart, Kanarek said. Though he'd earlier shown the death photos to Mrs Kasabian, 'I have thought about it, and I believe I was in error, Your Honor.' Kanarek asked that the photos, particularly those which were in color, be excluded. Motion denied. The photos could be used for identification purposes, Older ruled; as to their admissibility as evidence, that motion would be heard at a later time.

Each time Kanarek tried such a tactic, I thought, Surely he can't better this. And each time I found he not only could but did.

Although I had interviewed Dr Noguchi several times, I had a last conference with him in my office before we went to court. The coroner, who had conducted Sharon Tate's autopsy as well as supervised those of the other four Tate victims, had a habit of holding back little surprises. There are enough of these in a trial without getting them from your own witnesses, so I asked him outright if there was anything he hadn't told me.

Well, one thing, he admitted. He hadn't mentioned it in the autopsy reports, but, after studying the abrasions on her left cheek, he had concluded, 'Sharon Tate was hung.'

This was not the cause of death, he said, and she had probably been suspended less than a minute, but he was convinced the abrasions were rope burns.

I revised my interrogation sheets to get this in.

Although almost all of Dr Noguchi's testimony was important, several portions were especially so in terms of corroborating Linda Kasabian.

Noguchi testified that many of the stab wounds penetrated bones; Linda had testified that Patricia Krenwinkel had complained that her hand hurt from her knife striking bones.

Linda testified that the two knives she'd thrown out the car window had about the same blade length, estimating, with her hands, an approximate length of between 5½ and 6½ inches. Dr Noguchi testified that many of the wounds were a full 5 inches in depth. These was not only close to Linda's approximation, it also emphasized the extreme viciousness of the assaults.

Linda estimated the blade width at about 1 inch. Dr Noguchi said the wounds were caused by a blade with a width of between 1 and 1½ inches.

Linda estimated the thickness as maybe two or three times that of an ordinary kitchen knife. Dr Noguchi said the thickness varied from ⅛ to ½ inch, which corresponded to Linda's approximation.

Linda – who, on Manson's instructions, had several times honed knives similar to these while at Spahn Ranch – testified that the knives were sharpened on both sides, on one side all the way back to the hilt, on the other at least an inch back from the tip. Dr Noguchi testified that about two-thirds of the wounds had been made by a blade or blades that had been sharpened on both sides for a distance of about 1½ to 2 inches, one side then flattening out while the other remained keen.*

As I'd later argue to the jury, Linda's description of those two knives – their thickness, width, length, even the fine point of the double-edged blade – was strong evidence that the two knives she was talking about were the same knives Dr Noguchi had described.

In his cross-examination of Noguchi, Kanarek not only repeatedly referred to the victims' 'passing away', he spoke of Abigail Folger running to her 'place of repose'. It was beginning to sound like a guided tour of Forest Lawn.

The idiocy of all this was not lost on Manson. He complained: 'Your Honor, this lawyer is not doing what I am asking him to

---

* The other one-third of the wounds, Noguchi said, could have been made by a single-edged blade – but he didn't rule out the possibility that even these might have been made by a double-edged weapon, the unsharpened portion blunting the wound pattern so it appeared, on the surface, that a single-edged blade had been used.

do, not even by a small margin ... He is not my attorney, he is your attorney. I would like to dismiss this man and get another attorney.'

I was not sure whether Manson was serious or not. Even if he wasn't, it was still a good tactical move. Charlie was in effect telling the jury, 'Don't judge me by what this man says or does.'

Later, while the jury was out, Older asked Manson if he still desired to replace Kanarek. By this time Charlie had changed his mind. During the discussion Manson made an interesting observation as to his own feelings on the progress of the trial thus far: 'We did pretty good at the first of it. Then we kind of lost control when the testimony started.'

Denied access to the courtroom, the Family began a vigil outside the Hall of Justice, at the corner of Temple and Broadway. 'I'm waiting for my father to get out of jail,' Sandy told reporters as she knelt on the sidewalk next to one of the busiest intersections in the city of Los Angeles. 'We will remain here,' Squeaky told TV interviewers, as traffic slowed and people gawked, 'until all our brothers and sisters are set free.' In interviews the girls referred to the trial as 'the second crucifixion of Christ'.

At night they slept in the bushes next to the building. When the police stopped that, they moved their sleeping bags into a white van which they parked nearby. By day they knelt or sat on the sidewalk, granted interviews, tried to convert the curious young. It was easy to tell the hard-core Mansonites from the transient camp followers. Each of the former had an X carved on his or her forehead. Each also wore a sheathed hunting knife. Since the knives were in plain view, they couldn't be arrested for carrying concealed weapons. The police did bust them several times for loitering, but after a warning, or at most a few days in jail, they were back, and after a time the police left them alone.

Nearby city and county office buildings provided rest-room facilities. Also public phones, where, at certain prearranged times, one of the girls would await check-in calls from other Family members, including those wanted by the police. Several sob sisters who were covering the trial wrote largely sympathetic stories about their innocent, fresh, wholesome good looks and their devotion. They also often gave them money. Whether it was used for food or other purposes is not known. We did know the Family was adding to its hidden caches of arms and ammunition. And, since the Family was against hunting animals, it was a safe guess that they were stockpiling for something other than self-protection.

The deaths of her mother and stepfather had caused Susan Struthers to have a nervous breakdown. Though she was slowly recovering, we called Frank Struthers to the stand to identify photographs of Leno and Rosemary LaBianca and to describe what he'd found on returning home that Sunday night. Shown the wallet found in the Standard station, Frank positively identified it, and the watch in the change compartment, as his mother's. On questioning by Aaron, Frank also testified that he had been unable to find anything else missing from the residence.

Ruth Sivick testified to feeding the LaBianca dogs on Saturday afternoon. No, she saw no bloody words on the refrigerator door. Yes, she had opened and closed the door, to get the food for the dogs.

News vendor John Fokianos, who testified to talking to Rosemary and Leno between 1 and 2 A.M. that Sunday, was followed by Hollywood Division officers Rodriquez and Cline, who described their arrival and discoveries at the crime scene. Cline testified to the bloody writings. Galindo, the first of the homicide officers to arrive, gave a detailed description of the premises, also stating: 'I found no signs of ransacking. I found many items of value,' which he then enumerated. Detective Broda testified to seeing, just prior to the autopsy of Leno LaBianca, the knife protruding from his throat, which, because of the pillowcase over the victim's head, the other officers had missed.

This brought us to Deputy Medical Examiner David Katsuyama. And a host of problems.

According to the first LaBianca investigative report, 'The

bread knife recovered from [Leno LaBianca's] throat appeared to be the weapon used in both homicides.'

There was absolutely no scientific basis for this, since Katsuyama, who conducted both autopsies, had failed to measure the victims' wounds.

However, since the knife belonged to the LaBiancas, if this was let stand the defense could maintain that the killers had gone to the residence unarmed; ergo, they did not intend to commit murder. While a killing committed during the commission of a robbery is still first degree murder, this could affect whether the defendants escaped the death penalty. More important, it negated our whole theory of the case, which was that Manson, and Manson alone, had a motive for these murders, and that that motive was not robbery – a motive thousands of people could have – but to ignite Helter Skelter.

Shortly after I received the LaBianca reports, I ordered scale blowups of the autopsy photos, and asked Katsuyama to measure the length and thickness of the wounds. Initially I presumed there was no way to determine their depth, which would indicate the minimum length of the blade; however, in going over the coroner's original diagrams, I discovered that two of Rosemary LaBianca's wounds had been probed, one to the depth of 5 inches, the other 5½ inches, while two of Leno LaBianca's wounds were 5½ inches deep.

After many, many requests, Katsuyama finally measured the photos. I then compared his measurements with those of the bread knife. They came out as follows:

Length of blade of bread knife: 4⅞ inches.

Depth of deepest measurable wound: 5½ inches.

Thickness of blade of bread knife: just under 1/16 inch.

Thickness of thickest wound: 3/16 inch.

Width of blade of bread knife: from ⅜ to 1 3/16 inches.

Width of widest wound: 1¼ inches.

There was no way, I concluded, that the LaBiancas' bread knife could have caused all the wounds. Length, width, thickness – in each the dimensions of the bread knife were smaller than the wounds themselves. Therefore the killers must have brought their own knives.

Recalling, however, how Katsuyama had confused a leather thong for electrical cord before the grand jury, I showed him the two sets of figures and – questioning him in much the same manner as I would in court – asked him: Had he formed an opinion as to whether the bread knife found in Leno LaBianca's throat could have made all of the wounds? Yes, he had, Katsuyama replied. What was his opinion? Yes, it could have.

Suppressing a groan, I asked him to compare the figures again.

This time he concluded there was no way the LaBianca knife could have made all those wounds.

To be doubly safe, the day I was to call him to the stand I interviewed him again in my office. Again he decided the knife could have made the wounds, then again he changed his mind.

'Doctor,' I told him, 'I'm not trying to coach you. If it's your professional opinion that all the wounds were made by the bread knife, fine. But the figures that you yourself gave me indicate that the bread knife couldn't possibly have caused all the wounds. Now, which is it? Only don't tell me one thing now and something different on the stand. You've got to make up your mind.'

Even though he stuck to his last reply, I had more than a few apprehensive moments when it came time to question him in court. However, he testified: 'These dimensions [of the bread knife] are much smaller than many of the wounds which I previously described.'

Q. 'So it's your opinion that this bread knife, which was removed from Mr LaBianca's throat, could not have caused many of the other wounds, is that correct?'

A. 'Yes, it is.'

Rosemary LaBianca, Katsuyama also testified, had been stabbed forty-one times, sixteen of which wounds, mostly in her back and buttocks, having been made after she had died. Under questioning, Katsuyama explained that after death the heart stops pumping blood to the rest of the body, therefore postmortem wounds are distinguishable by their lighter color.

This was *very* important testimony, since Leslie Van Houten told Dianne Lake that she had stabbed someone who was already dead.

Susan Atkins had a stomach-ache. Though a fairly minor occurrence, in this instance it led to Aaron Stovitz's being yanked off the Tate-LaBianca case.

Four court days were lost when Susan Atkins complained of stomach pains which the doctors who examined and tested her said 'did not exist'. After sending the jury out, Judge Older called Susan to the stand, where she dramatically enumerated her ailments. Unimpressed, and convinced 'she is now putting on an act', Older brought the jury back in and resumed the trial. As he was leaving the courtroom, a reporter asked Aaron what he thought of Susan's testimony. He replied, 'It was a performance worthy of Sarah Bernhardt.'

The next morning Aaron was ordered to appear in District Attorney Younger's office.

After the *Rolling Stone* interview, Younger had told Aaron: 'No more interviews.' Being somewhat easygoing by nature, Aaron had trouble complying with the edict. Once, when Younger was in San Francisco, he'd turned on the radio to hear Aaron commenting on some aspect of the day's courtroom proceedings. Though Aaron's comments were not in violation of the gag order, on his return to L.A. Younger warned Aaron, 'One more interview and you're off the case.'

I accompanied Aaron to Younger's office. There was no way Aaron's comment could be called an interview, I argued. It was simply a passing remark. All of us had made many such during the trial. But Younger autocratically declared, 'No, I've made up my mind. Stovitz, you're off the case.'

I felt very badly about this. In my opinion, it was completely unfair. But in this case there was no appeal.

Sergeants Boen and Dolan of the Latent Prints Section of SID came across as the experts they were. Latents, exemplars, lift cards, smudges, fragmentary ridges, nonconductive surfaces, points of identity – by the time the two officers had finished, the jury had been given a mini-course in fingerprint identification.

Boen described how he had lifted the latent prints found at the Tate residence, particularly focusing on the latent found on the outside of the front door and the latent on the inside of the left French door in Sharon Tate's bedroom.

Using diagrams and greatly magnified photographs I'd ordered prepared, Dolan indicated eighteen points of identity between the print lifted from the front door of the Tate residence and the right ring finger on the Watson exemplar and seventeen points of identity between the print lifted from the door of the master bedroom and the left little finger on the Krenwinkel exemplar. LAPD, he testified, requires only ten points of identity to establish a positive identification.

After Dolan had testified that there has never been a reported case of two separate persons having an identical fingerprint, or of any single person having two matching prints, I brought out, through him, that in 70 percent of the crimes investigated by LAPD's fingerprint men not a single readable print is obtained. Therefore, I could later argue to the jury, the fact that none of Susan Atkins' prints were found inside the Tate residence did not mean she had not been there, since the absence of a clear, readable print is more common than uncommon.

No print belonging to Manson, Krenwinkel, or Van Houten had been found at the LaBianca residence. Anticipating that the defense would argue this proved that none of them had been there, I asked Dolan about the handle of the fork found protruding from Leno LaBianca's stomach. It was ivory, he said, a surface which readily lends itself to latent prints. I then asked him: 'Did you secure anything at all from that fork, a smudge, a trace, a fragmentary fingerprint, anything at all?'

A. 'No, sir, there was not so much as a slight smudge on it; in fact it gave the impression to me' – Kanarek objected, but Older let Dolan finish – 'it gave the impression to me that the handle of that particular fork had been wiped.' Later, Dolan testified, he'd run a test: he'd grasped the fork with his fingers, then dusted it, 'and found fragmentary ridges'.

Although Mrs Sivick had opened and closed the refrigerator door about 6 P.M. on the night of the murders, Dolan had found 'not a smudge' on the chrome handle or enamel surface of the door. However, in examining the door, he testified, he did find 'wipe-type marks'.

Also important were the locations of the Krenwinkel and Watson latents at the Tate residence. That Krenwinkel's print had been found on the inside of the door which led from Sharon Tate's bedroom outside to the pool not only proved that Patricia Krenwinkel had been inside the residence, together with other evidence it indicated that she had probably chased Abigail Folger out this door. Blood spots inside the house, on the door itself, and outside the door were determined to be B-MN, Abigail Folger's type and subtype. Therefore finding Krenwinkel's print here was completely consistent with Linda Kasabian's testimony that she saw Abigail running from this general direction chased by the knife-wielding Krenwinkel.

Even more conclusive was the position of the Watson print. Although Boen testified that it was on the outside of the front door, he'd also said that it was six to eight inches above the handle, near the edge, the tip of the finger pointing *downward*. As I illustrated to the jury, to leave the print where he did, Watson would have to be *inside* the Tate residence coming out. To make the print had he been outside, he would have had to twist his arm in a very uncomfortable and extremely unnatural direction. (Using the right ring finger and trying it both ways on a door, the reader will see what I mean.)

The logical assumption was that Watson left his print while chasing Frykowski, Krenwinkel while in pursuit of Folger.

These were the strong points of the fingerprint testimony. There was one weak spot. Anticipating that the defense would try to make the most of those unidentified latents – twenty-five of the fifty found at the Tate residence, six of the twenty-five found at the LaBianca residence – I brought this out myself. But with several possible explanations. Since, as Dolan testified, no person has two matching fingerprints, it was possible the twenty-five unmatched Tate latents could have been made by as few as three persons, while the six at the LaBiancas' could even have been made by one person. Moreover, I established through Dolan that latent fingerprints can have a long life; under ideal conditions those inside a residence may last for several months. I could afford to point this out, since I'd already established that the two prints I was most concerned about, Krenwinkel's and Watson's, were on surfaces Winifred Chapman had recently washed.

Kanarek, in his cross-examination of Dolan, tried to imply that in using benzidine to test for blood, Granado could have destroyed some of the prints at the LaBianca residence. Unfortunately for Kanarek, Dolan noted that he had arrived at the LaBianca residence *before* Granado did.

Though Kanarek did less well with Dolan than some of the the other prosecution witness, this didn't mean I could relax my guard. At any moment he was apt to do something like the following:

KANAREK. 'Your Honor, in view of the fact that the Los Angeles Police Department did not even choose to compare Linda Kasabian's fingerprints – '

BUGLIOSI. 'How do you know that, Mr Kanarek?'

KANAREK. ' – I have no further questions of this witness.'

THE COURT. 'Your comment is out of order.'

BUGLIOSI. 'Would Your Honor admonish the jury to disregard that gratuitous remark of Mr Kanarek's?'

Older did so.

Hughes' cross was brief and to the point. Had the witness compared a fingerprint exemplar of Leslie Van Houten with the latents found at the LaBianca residence? Yes. And none of those prints matched the prints of Leslie Van Houten, is that correct? Yes, sir. No further questions.

Hughes was learning, fast.

As much as possible, I tried to avoid embarrassing LAPD. It wasn't always possible. Earlier, for example, I'd had to bring in Sergeant DeRosa's pushing the gate-control button, so the jury wouldn't wonder why there was no testimony regarding that particular print. In my direct examination of 11-year-old Steven

Weiss, I stuck to his finding the .22 caliber revolver on September 1, 1969, and did not go into the subsequent events. However, Fitzgerald, on cross, brought out that although an officer had recovered the gun that same day, it was December 16, 1969, before LAPD Homicide claimed the weapon – after Steven's father called and told them they already had the gun they were looking for. Fitzgerald also brought out how, after Steven had taken care not to eradicate any prints, the officer who picked up the gun had done so literally, putting his hands all over it.

I felt sorry for the next witness. The spectators had barely stopped laughing when officer Watson of the Valley Services Division of LAPD took the stand to testify that he was the officer who recovered the gun.

Officer Watson's testimony was essential, however, for he not only identified the gun – bringing out that it was missing its right-hand grip and had a bent barrel and broken trigger guard – he also testified that it contained two live rounds and seven empty shell casings.

Sergeant Calkins then testified that on December 16, 1969, he had driven from Parker Center to the Valley Services Division to pick up the .22 caliber revolver.

On cross, Fitzgerald brought out that between September 3 and 5, 1969, LAPD had sent out some 300 gun flyers – containing a photograph and detailed description of the type of revolver they were looking for – to different police agencies in the United States and Canada.

Lest the jury begin wondering why LAPD hadn't recovered the gun from the Valley Services Division immediately after the flyers went out, I was forced to ask Calkins, on redirect: 'Did you ever send a flyer to the Valley Services Division of the Los Angeles Police Department in Van Nuys?'

A. 'Not to my knowledge, sir.'

To avoid further embarrassment to LAPD, I didn't ask how close the Valley Services Division was to the Tate residence.

September 7–10, 1970

Because of the State Bar Convention, court recessed for three days. I spent them working on my arguments, and worrying about a telephone call I'd received.

When court reconvened on the tenth, I made the following statement in chambers:

'One of our witnesses, Barbara Hoyt, has left her parents' home. I don't have all the details, but the mother said Barbara received a threat on her life, that if she testified at this trial she would be killed and so will her family.

'I know two things. I know the threat did not come from the prosecution and it did not come from an aunt I have that lives in Minnesota.

'I think the most reasonable inference is it came from the defense.

'I'm bringing this out because I want the defense attorneys and their clients to know that we are going to prosecute whoever is responsible for subornation of perjury. Not only will we prosecute, when our witnesses take the stand I will do my best to bring out, in front of the jury, that they received threats on their lives. It is relevant.

'I suggest the defendants tell their friends this.'

When we returned to the courtroom, I had to leave such concerns behind and focus completely on the evidence we were presenting. It was crucial. Piece by piece we were trying to link the gun to Spahn Ranch and Charles Manson.

On Friday, before our long adjournment, Sergeant Lee of the Firearms and Explosives Unit of SID positively identified the Sebring bullet as having been fired from the gun. Lee also stated

425

that while the other bullets recovered from the Tate scene lacked sufficient stria to make a positive identification, he found no markings or characteristics which would rule out the possibility that they too were fired from the same gun.

When I attempted to question Lee about still another link in this chain, the shell casings we had found at Spahn Ranch, Fitzgerald asked to approach the bench. It was the defense's contention, he said, that the shell casings were the product of an illegal search, and therefore inadmissible.

'Anticipating that just such an objection might be raised,' I told the Court, 'I obtained George Spahn's permission on tape. Sergeant Calkins should have it,' I said. 'He was there with me.'

Only Calkins didn't have the tape. And now, nearly a week later, he still hadn't found it. Finally, I called Calkins to the stand to testify that we had obtained Spahn's permission. Cross-examined by Kanarek, Calkins denied that the tape had 'disappeared' or was 'lost'; he just hadn't been able to locate it, he said.

Older finally ruled the search valid, and Lee testified that when examined under a comparison microscope the shell casing he'd test-fired from the gun and fifteen of the shell casings he'd found at Spahn Ranch had identical firing pin compression marks.

Stria, lands, grooves, firing pin marks: after hours of highly technical testimony, and more than a hundred objections, most of them by Irving Kanarek, we had placed the Tate murder gun at Spahn Ranch.

Although he had agreed to testify, Thomas Walleman, aka T.J., was a reluctant witness. He'd never completely broken with the Family. He'd drift away, drift back. He seemed attracted by the easy life style, repelled by the memory of the night he saw Manson shoot Bernard Crowe.

Though I knew I couldn't get the shooting itself in during our case in chief, I did question T.J. as to the events immediately prior to it. He recalled how, after receiving a telephone call, Manson borrowed Swartz's Ford, got a revolver, then, with T.J. accompanying him, drove to an apartment house on Franklin Avenue in Hollywood. After stopping the car, Manson handed T.J. the revolver and told him to put it in his belt.

Q. 'Then you both entered the apartment, is that correct?'

A. 'Yes.'

This was as far as I could go. I then showed T.J. the .22 caliber Hi Standard revolver and asked: 'Have you ever seen that particular revolver before?'

A. 'I don't think so. It looks like it, but I don't know for sure, you know.'

T.J. was hedging. I wasn't about to let him get away with it. Under further questioning, he admitted that this gun differed from the gun he had seen that night in only one particular: half the grip was missing.

Q. 'Now, your first statement, I believe, was to the effect that you didn't think this was the revolver, and then you said it looked like it.'

A. 'I mean, I don't know *for sure* whether it was the revolver, but *it looks like the revolver.* There are a lot of those made.'

I wasn't worried about that little qualification, for Lomax of Hi Standard had already testified that this model was relatively uncommon.

Though qualified, T.J.'s testimony was dramatic, as he was the first witness to connect Manson and the gun.

LAPD contacted me that night. Barbara Hoyt was in a hospital in Honolulu. Someone had given her what was believed to be a lethal dose of LSD. Fortunately, she had been rushed to the hospital in time.

I did not learn many of the details until I talked to Barbara.

After fleeing Barker Ranch, the pretty 17-year-old had returned home. Though she had cooperated with us, Barbara was extremely reluctant to testify, and when she was contacted by the Manson girls on the afternoon of September 5 and offered a free vacation in Hawaii in lieu of testifying, she'd accepted.

Among the Family members who'd helped persuade her were Squeaky, Gypsy, Ouisch, and Clem.

Barbara spent that night at Spahn Ranch. The next day Clem

drove Barbara and Ouisch to one of the Family hideouts, a house in North Hollywood which was being rented by one of the newer Family members, Dennis Rice.*

Rice took the pair to the airport, bought them tickets, and gave them fifty dollars in cash plus some credit cards, including, not inappropriately, a TWA 'Getaway' card. Using assumed names, the two girls flew to Honolulu, where they booked the penthouse suite of the Hilton Hawaiian Village Hotel. Barbara saw little of the islands, however, since Ouisch, sure the police would be look-ing for Barbara, insisted they remain in the suite.

While there, the pair, who had been close friends, had several long talks. Ouisch told Barbara. 'We all have to go through Helter Skelter. If we don't do it in our heads, we'll have to do it physi-cally. If you don't die in your head, you'll die when it comes down.' Ouisch also confided that Linda Kasabian was not long for this world; at the most, she had six months to live.

At approximately the same time each morning, Ouisch made a long-distance call. (The number was that of a pay phone in North Hollywood, three blocks from the Rice residence. At least one of these calls was to Squeaky, the unofficial leader of the Family in Manson's absence.)

Just after the call on the ninth, Ouisch's manner suddenly changed. 'She became very serious and looked at me kind of strangely,' Barbara said. Ouisch told Barbara that she had to go back to California, but that Barbara was to remain in Hawaii. She called and made a reservation on the 1:15 flight to Los Angeles that afternoon.

They caught a cab to the airport, arriving just before noon. Ouisch said she wasn't hungry, but suggested that Barbara eat something. They went into a restaurant and Barbara ordered a hamburger. When it arrived, Ouisch took it and went outside, telling Barbara to pay the check.

*Rice, thirty-one, had a rap sheet that went back to 1958 and, in common with Clem, had been convicted of offenses ranging from narcotics possession to indecent exposure. He was currently on probation for assaulting a police officer. Though new to the Family, he became one of its most hard-core members.

There was a line at the cash register, and for several minutes Barbara lost sight of Ouisch.

When she came out, Ouisch gave her the hamburger, and Barbara ate it while they were waiting for Ouisch's flight. Just before she was to board, Ouisch remarked, 'Imagine what it would be like if that hamburger had ten tabs of acid in it.' Barbara's response was, 'Wow!' She had never heard of anyone taking more than one tab of LSD, Barbara later said, and the thought was kind of frightening.

After Ouisch left, Barbara began feeling high. She tried to take a bus to the beach but became so sick and had to get off. Panicked, she then started running, and ran and ran and ran until she collapsed.

A social worker, Byron Galloway, saw the young girl sprawled on a curb near the Salvation Army headquarters. Fortuitously, Galloway was employed at the State Hospital, his specialty drug cases. Realizing that the girl was extremely ill, he rushed her to Queen's Medical Center, where her condition was diagnosed as acute psychosis, drug-induced. The doctor who examined her was able to get her name and her Los Angeles address, but the rest made little sense: according to the hospital records, 'Patient said, "Call Mr Bogliogi and tell him I won't be able to testify today in the Sharon Tate trial." '

After giving her emergency treatment, the hospital called the police and Barbara's parents. Her father flew to Hawaii and was able to bring her back to Los Angeles with him the next day.

On receiving the first fragmentary report, I told LAPD I wanted the persons involved charged with attempted murder.

Since Barbara was a witness in the Tate case, the investigation was given to Tate detectives Calkins and McGann.

September 11–17, 1970

Though I knew Danny DeCarlo was afraid of Manson, the motorcyclist did a good job of disguising it while on the stand. When Charlie and the girls smiled at 'donkey Dan', he grinned right back.

I was concerned that DeCarlo might qualify his answers, as he had in the Beausoleil trial. After only a few minutes of testimony, however, my concern suddenly shifted from DeCarlo to Older. When I tried to establish the Manson-Watson relationship through DeCarlo, Older repeatedly sustained the defense objections. He also sustained objections to Manson's dinnertime conversations when he discussed his philosophy about blacks and whites.

Back in chambers Older made two remarks which totally stunned me. He asked, 'What is the relevance of whether or not Manson was the leader?' And he wanted an offer of proof as to the relevance of Helter Skelter! It was as if Older hadn't even been present during the trial thus far.

That I was more than a little disturbed at his stance came across in my reply: 'The offer of proof is that he used to say that he wanted to turn blacks against whites. Of course, this is only the motive for these murders was *to ignite Helter Skelter*. I think it is not much else.'

I noted: 'The prosecution is alleging Mr Manson *ordered* these murders. It was his philosophy *that led up to* these murders. The motive for these murders was *to ignite Helter Skelter*. I think it is so obviously admissible that I am at a loss for words.'

THE COURT. 'I would suggest this to you, Mr Bugliosi. Over the noon hour give some careful thought as to what you contend your proof is going to show. Now, I realize that part of it may have to come in through one witness and part through another. This is not unusual. But so far I can't see any connection between what Mr Manson believed about blacks and whites in the abstract and any motive.'

I sweated through that noon hour. Unless I could establish Manson's domination of the other defendants, I wouldn't be able to convince the jury they had killed on his instructions. And if Older foreclosed me from bringing in Manson's beliefs about the black-white war from DeCarlo, when my heavyweight witnesses on this – Jakobson, Poston, and Watkins – were still to come, then we were in deep trouble.

I returned to chambers armed with citations of authority as to both the admissibility and the relevance of the testimony. Yet even after a long, impassioned plea, it appeared that I had not changed Older's mind. He still couldn't see, for instance, the relevance of Watson's subservience to Manson, or why I was trying to bring out, through DeCarlo, that Tex had an easygoing, rather weak personality. The relevance, of course, was that if I didn't establish both, the jury could very well infer that it was Watson, not Manson, who had ordered these murders.

BUGLIOSI. 'I think the Court can tell the relevancy by the fact the defense counsel are on their hind legs trying to keep it out.'

KANAREK. 'I think the heart of what we have here is this, that Mr Bugliosi has lost his cool, because he has a monomania about convicting Mr Manson.'

BUGLIOSI. 'He is charged with seven murders, and I am going to be tenacious on this ... I intend to go back with these witnesses and find out who Tex Watson was other than a name, Your Honor.'

THE COURT. 'I am not going to stop you from *trying*, Mr Bugliosi.'

On returning to court, I asked DeCarlo exactly the same question I had asked hours earlier: 'What was your impression of Tex Watson's general demeanor?'

KANAREK. 'Your Honor, I will object to that as calling for a conclusion.'

BUGLIOSI. '*People* vs *Zollner*, Your Honor.'

I so anticipated Older saying 'Sustained' that I almost thought I was imagining it when he said, 'Overruled. You may answer.'

DECARLO. 'He was happy-go-lucky. He was a nice guy. I liked Tex. He didn't have no temper or anything that I could see. He never said much.'

Glancing back, I saw both Don Musich and Steve Kay staring in openmouthed disbelief. Moments ago in chambers Older had objected to my whole line of inquiry. He'd now completely reversed himself. Going as fast as I could through the questioning, before he again changed his mind, I brought out that whenever Charlie told Tex to do anything, Tex did it.

That Older had gone along with us on the domination issue didn't mean that he saw the relevance of Helter Skelter. My fingers were crossed when I asked: 'Do you recall Mr Manson saying anything about blacks and whites? Black people and white people?'

Stunned and perturbed, Kanarek objected: 'It is the same question that he was asking previously!'

THE COURT. 'Overruled. You may answer.'

A. 'He didn't like black people.'

DeCarlo testified that Manson wanted to see the blacks go to war with the police and the white establishment, both of whom he referred to as 'pigs'; that Charlie had told him that the pigs 'ought to have their throats cut and be hung by their feet'; and that he had heard Manson use the term Helter Skelter many, many times. Through all this Kanarek objected repeatedly, often in the midst of DeCarlo's replies. Older told him: 'You are interrupting, Mr Kanarek. I have warned you several times today. I warn you now for the last time.' Within minutes, however, Kanarek was doing it again, and Older called him to the bench, found him in contempt of Court and, at the conclusion of the day's testimony, sentenced him to spend the weekend in the County Jail.

Danny DeCarlo had never really understood Helter Skelter, or cared to. As he admitted to me, his major interests while at Spahn were 'booze and broads'. He couldn't see how his testimony about this black-white stuff really hurt Charlie, and he testified to it freely and without qualification. But when it came to the physical evidence – the knives, the rope, the gun – he saw the link and pulled back, not much, but just enough to weaken his identifications.

In interviewing Danny, I'd learned a great many things which were not on the LAPD tapes. For example, he recalled that in early August 1969, Gypsy had purchased ten or twelve Buck knives, which had been passed out to various Family members at Spahn. The knives, according to DeCarlo, were about 6 inches in length, 1 inch in width, ⅛ inch in thickness – very close to the dimensions provided by Kasabian and Noguchi. In going through the sheriff's reports of the August 16 raid, I found that a large number of weapons had been seized (including a sub-machine gun in a violin case) but not a single Buck knife.

The logical presumption, I'd later argue to the jury, was that after the murders the rest of the Buck knives had been ditched.

I intended to call Sergeant Gleason from LASO to testify that no knives were found in the road. First, however, I wanted Danny to testify to the purchase. He did, but he qualified it somewhat. When I asked him who bought the Buck knives, he replied: 'I'm not sure. I think Gypsy did, I'm not sure.'

When it came to the Tate-Sebring rope, DeCarlo testified it was 'similar' to the rope Manson had purchased at the Jack Frost store. I persisted: 'Does it appear to be different in any fashion?'

A. 'No.'

DeCarlo had told me that Charlie preferred knives and swords to guns because 'in the desert guns could be heard for a long distance'. I asked DeCarlo if, among the guns at Spahn Ranch, Manson had a special favorite. Yeah, DeCarlo said, a Hi Standard .22 caliber Buntline revolver. I showed him the gun and asked him: 'Have you ever seen this revolver before?'

A. 'I saw one similar to it.'

Q. 'Does it appear to differ in any fashion?'

A. 'The trigger guard is broken.'

Other than that?

A. 'I can't be sure.'

S–HS–T

Q. 'Why can't you be sure?'

A. 'I don't know. I don't know the serial number of it. I am not sure that is it.'

DeCarlo had cleaned, cared for, and shot the gun. He had an extensive background in weapons. The model was unusual. And he had made a drawing of it for LAPD even before he was told that such a gun had been used in the Tate homicides. (I'd already introduced the drawing for identification purposes, over Kanarek's objection that it was 'hearsay'.) If anyone should have been able to make a positive identification of that revolver, it was Danny DeCarlo. He didn't do so, I suspected, because he was afraid to.

Though he was a shade weaker on the stand than in our interviews, I did succeed in getting a tremendous amount of evidence in through DeCarlo. Though court was interrupted for another three-day recess, DeCarlo's direct took less than a day and a half of actual court time. I completed it on September 17.

That morning Manson passed word through Fitzgerald and Shinn that he wanted to see me in the lockup during the noon recess. Kanarek was not present, though the other two attorneys were.

I asked Manson what he wanted to talk to me about.

'I just wanted you to know that I didn't have anything to do with the attempted murder of Barbara Hoyt,' Manson said.

'I don't know whether you ordered it or they did it on their own,' I replied, 'but you know, and I know, that in either case they did it because they thought it would please you.'

Manson wanted to rap, but I cut him off. 'I'm not really in the mood to talk to you, Charlie. Maybe, if you have enough guts to take the stand, we'll talk then.'

I asked McGann what was happening on the 'Honolulu hamburger case', as the papers had dubbed the Hoyt murder attempt. McGann said he and Calkins hadn't been able to come up with any evidence.

I asked Phil Sartuchi of the LaBianca team to take over. Phil efficiently turned in a detailed report, with information on the airline tickets, credit cards, long-distance calls, and so forth. It was December, however, before the case was taken to the grand jury. In the interim, Ouisch, Squeaky, Clem, Gypsy, and Rice remained at large. I'd often seen them with the other Family members at the corner of Temple and Broadway.

September 18, 1970

That afternoon we had a surprise visitor in court – Charles 'Tex' Watson.

After a nine-month delay that would necessitate trying him separately, Watson had finally been returned to California on September 11, after U.S. Supreme Court Justice Hugo Black refused to grant him a further stay of extradition. Sergeants Sartuchi and Gutierrez, who accompanied Watson on the flight, said he spoke little, mostly staring vacantly into space. He had lost about thirty pounds during his confinement, most of it during the last two months, when it became obvious his return to Los Angeles was imminent.

Fitzgerald had asked that Watson be brought into court, to see if DeCarlo could identify him.

Realizing that Fitzgerald was making a *very* serious mistake, Kanarek objected, strenuously, but Older granted the removal order.

The jury was still out when Watson entered the courtroom. Though he smiled slightly at the three female defendants, who grinned and blew him kisses, he seemed oblivious to Manson's presence. By the time the jury came in, Watson was already seated and appeared just another spectator.

FITZGERALD. 'Mr DeCarlo, you previously testified that a man by the name of Tex Watson was present at Spahn Ranch during the period of time that you were there in 1969, is that correct?'

A. 'Yeah.'

Q. 'Do you recognize Mr Watson in the courtroom?'

A. 'Yeah. Right over there.' Danny pointed to where Tex was

sitting. Obviously curious, the jury strained to see the man they had heard so much about.

FITZGERALD. 'Could I have this gentleman identify himself for the Court, Your Honor?'

THE COURT. 'Will you please stand and state your name.'

Watson stood, after being motioned to his feet by one of the bailiffs, but he remained mute.

DeCarlo made the identification.

Fitzgerald's mistake was obvious the moment Watson got up. One look and the jury knew that Charles 'Tex' Watson was not the type to order Charles Manson to do anything, much less instigate seven murders on his own. He looked closer to 20 than 25. Short hair, blue blazer, gray slacks, tie. Instead of the wild-eyed monster depicted in the April 1969 mug shot (when Watson had been on drugs) he appeared to be a typical clean-cut college kid.

Offstage, Watson could be made to seem the heavy. Having once seen him, the jury would never think this again.

Since our first meeting in Independence, I had remained on speaking terms with Sandy and Squeaky. Occasionally one or both would drop in at my office to chat. I usually made time for such visits, in part because I was still attempting to understand why they (and the three female defendants) had joined the Family, but also because I was remotely hopeful that if another murder was planned, one or the other might alert me. Neither, I was sure, would go to the police, and I wanted to leave at least one channel of communication open.

I'd had more hopes for Sandy than Squeaky. The latter was on a power trip – acting as Manson's unofficial spokesman, running the Family in his absence – and it seemed unlikely she would do anything to jeopardize her status. Sandy, however, had gone against Manson's wishes on several occasions, I knew; they were minor rebellions (when her baby was due, for example, she had gone to a hospital, rather than have it delivered by the Family), but they indicated that maybe, behind the pat phrases, I'd touch something responsively human.

437

On her first visit to my office, about two months earlier, we'd talked about the Family credo: Sandy had maintained it was peace; I'd maintained it was murder, and asked how she could stomach this.

'People are being murdered every day in Vietnam,' she'd countered.

'Assuming for the sake of argument that the deaths in Vietnam are murders,' I responded, 'how does this justify murdering seven more people?'

As she tried to come up with an answer, I told her, 'Sandy, if you really believe in peace and love, I want you to prove it. The next time murder is in the wind at Spahn Ranch, I want you to remember that other people like to live just as much as you do. And, as another human being, I want you to do everything possible to prevent it from happening. Do you understand what I mean?'

She quietly replied, 'Yes.'

I'd hoped she really meant that. That naïve hope vanished when, in talking to Barbara Hoyt, I learned that Sandy had been one of the Family members who had persuaded her to go to Hawaii.

As I left the court on the afternoon of the eighteenth, Sandy and two male followers approached me.

'Sandy, I'm very, very disappointed in you,' I told her. 'You were at Spahn when Barbara's murder was planned. There's no question in my mind that you knew what was going to happen. Yet, though Barbara was your friend, you said nothing, did nothing. Why?'

She didn't reply, but stared at me as if in a trance. For a moment I thought she hadn't heard me, that she was stoned on drugs, but then, very slowly and deliberately, she reached down and began playing with the sheath knife that she wore at her waist. That was her answer.

Disgusted, I turned and walked away. Looking back, however, I saw that Sandy and the two boys were following me. I stopped, they stopped. When I started walking again, they followed, Sandy still fingering the knife.

Gradually they were closing the distance between us. Deciding it was better to face trouble than have my back to it, I turned and walked back to them.

'Listen, you God damn bitch, and listen good,' I told her. 'I don't know for sure whether you were or weren't involved in the actual attempt to murder Barbara, but if you were, I'm going to do everything in my power to see that you end up in jail!' I then looked at the two males and told them if they followed me one more time, I was going to deck them on the spot.

I then turned and walked off. This time they didn't follow me.

My reaction was, I felt, exceptionally mild, considering the circumstances.

Kanarek felt otherwise. When court reconvened on Monday, the twenty-first, he filed a motion asking that I be held in contempt for interfering with a defense witness. He also asked that I be arrested for violating Section 415 of the Penal Code, charging that I had made obscene remarks in the presence of a female. Judge Older dismissed these motions.

September 21–26, 1970

Manson asked to see me in the lockup during the noon recess. He hoped I wasn't taking all this – the attempted murder, the knife incident, the trial – personally.

'No, Charlie,' I told him, 'I was assigned to this case; I didn't ask for it; this is my job.'

By now it should be obvious to me, Manson said, that the girls were acting on their own, that nobody was dominating them. When I raised a skeptical eyebrow, Manson said, 'Look, Bugliosi, if I had all the power and control that you say I have, I could simply say, "Brenda, go get Bugliosi," and that would be it.'

It was interesting, I thought, that Manson should single out Brenda McCann, t/n Nancy Pitman, as his chief assassin.

Later I'd have good reason to recall Manson's remarks.

Nothing personal. But immediately after this, the middle-of-the-night hang-up calls began. They'd continue even after we changed our unlisted number. And several times when I left the Hall of Justice at night, I was followed by various Family members, including Sandy. Only the first time disturbed me. Gail and the kids were circling the block in our car, and I was afraid they would be identified or the license number spotted. When I pretended not to see her, Gail quickly sized up the situation and drove around until I was able to shake my 'followers', though, as she later admitted to me, she was far less cool than she appeared.

Though concerned with the safety of my family, I didn't take any of this very seriously until one afternoon when, apparently enraged at the domination testimony that was coming in,

Manson told a bailiff, 'I'm going to have Bugliosi and the judge killed.'

By telling a bailiff this, Manson was making sure we got the message. Older was already under protection. The next day the District Attorney's Office assigned me a bodyguard for the duration of the trial. Additional precautions were taken, which, since they're probably used in protecting others, needn't be enumerated, though one might be noted. In order to prevent a repetition of the events at 10050 Cielo Drive, a walkie-talkie was installed in our home, which provided instant communication with the nearest police station, in case the telephone wires were cut.

Though Older and I were the only trial principals who had bodyguards, it was no secret that several, if not all, of the defense attorneys were frightened of the Family. Daye Shinn, I was told by one of his fellows, kept a loaded gun in each room of his house, in case of an unannounced visitation. What precautions, if any, Kanarek took I never learned, though Manson often assigned him top spot on his kill list. According to another defense attorney, Manson threatened numerous times to kill Kanarek; it was only fair, Manson supposedly said, since Kanarek was killing him in court.

The Family's attempt to silence Barbara Hoyt backfired. Once a reluctant witness, she was now very willing to testify.

Barbara not only confirmed Linda's story of the TV incident; she recalled that the previous night, the night of the Tate murders, Sadie called her on the field phone at the back house, asking her to bring three sets of dark clothing to the front of the ranch. When she arrived Manson told her, 'They already left.'

Barbara's story was both support for Linda Kasabian's testimony and powerful evidence of Manson's involvement, and, though unsuccessful, Kanarek fought hard to keep it out.

I was not able to bring out the Myers Ranch conversation until after a full half day of argument in chambers, and then, as I'd anticipated, I could only get in part of it.

One afternoon in early September 1969, Barbara had been

napping in the bedroom at Myers Ranch when she awoke to hear Sadie and Ouisch talking in the kitchen. Apparently thinking Barbara was still asleep, Sadie told Ouisch that Sharon Tate had been the last to die because, to quote Sadie, 'She had to watch the others die.'

During his cross-examination of Barbara, Kanarek asked: 'Have you been in any mental hospital for the last couple of years?'

Ordinarily I would have objected to such a question, but not this time, for Kanarek had just opened wide the door through which I could, on redirect, bring in the murder attempt.

Redirect is limited to the issues raised on cross-examination. For example, on redirect I had Barbara approximate the distance between the bedroom and the kitchen at Myers Ranch, then conducted a hearing experiment. She passed with no trouble.

Asking to approach the bench, I argued that since Kanarek had implied that Barbara Hoyt was in a mental hospital for an extended period of time, I had the right to bring out that she was in a mental ward only overnight and that it was not because of a mental problem. Older agreed, with one limitation: I couldn't ask who gave her the LSD.

Once I'd brought out the circumstances of her hospitalization, I asked: 'Did you take this overdose voluntarily?'

A. 'No.'

Q. 'Was it given to you by someone else?'

A. 'Yes.'

Q. 'Were you near death?'

KANAREK. 'Calls for conclusion, Your Honor.'

THE COURT. 'Sustained.'

It was good enough. I was sure the jury could put two and two together.

On Saturday, September 16, 1970, an era came to an end. A raging fire swept Southern California. Whipped by eighty-mile-an-hour winds, a wall of flame as high as sixty feet charred over

100,000 acres. Burned in the inferno was all of Spahn's Movie Ranch.

As the ranch hands tried to save the horses, the Manson girls, their faccs illuminated by the light of the conflagration, danced and clapped their hands, crying out happily, *'Helter Skelter is coming down! Helter Skelter is coming down!'*

September 27–October 5, 1970

Juan Flynn, who described his job at Spahn Ranch as 'manure shoveler', seemed to enjoy himself on the stand. Of all the witnesses, however, the lanky Panamanian cowboy was the only one who openly showed animosity to Manson. When Charlie tried to stare him down, Juan glared back.

After positively identifying the revolver, Juan remarked, 'And Mr Manson on one occasion fired this gun, you know, in my direction, you see, because I was walking with a girl on the other side of the creek.'

It was difficult to stop Juan once he got started. The girl had come to Spahn Ranch to ride horses; she'd ignored Manson but went off down the creek with amorous-minded Juan. Charlie was so miffed he'd fired several shots in their direction.

Kanarek succeeded in having all this, except Juan's seeing Manson fire the revolver, struck.

He also tried, but failed, to keep out the two most important pieces of evidence Juan Flynn had to offer.

One night in early August 1969, Juan had been watching TV in the trailer when Sadie came in, dressed in black. 'Where are you going?' Juan asked. 'We're going to get some fucking pigs,' Sadie replied. When she left, Juan looked out the window and saw her get into Johnny Swartz's old yellow Ford. Charlie, Clem, Tex, Linda, and Leslie got in also.

According to Juan, the incident had occurred after dark, about 8 or 9 P.M., and, though he wasn't able to pinpoint the date, he said it was about a week before the August 16 raid. The logical inference was that he was describing the night the LaBiancas were killed.

Juan's story was important both as evidence and as independent corroboration of Linda Kasabian's testimony. Not only did the time, participants, vehicle, and color of Susan Atkins' clothing coincide, Juan also noticed that Manson was driving.

Juan then testified to the kitchen conversation which occurred 'a day or so' later, when, putting a knife to his throat, Manson told him, 'You son of a bitch, don't you know I'm the one who's doing all of these killings?'

The newsmen rushed for the door.

MANSON ADMITTED MURDERS, SPAHN RANCH COWBOY CLAIMS

Kanarek's objections kept out another piece of extremely damaging evidence.

One night in June or July 1969, Manson, Juan, and three male Family members were driving through Chatsworth when Charlie stopped in front of a 'rich house' and instructed Juan to go in and tie up the people. When he'd finished, Manson said, he was to open the door and, to quote Manson, 'We'll come in and cut the motherfucking pigs up.' Juan had said, 'No thanks.'

This was in effect a dress rehearsal for the Tate-LaBianca murders. But ruling that 'the prejudicial effect far outweighs the probative value', Older wouldn't permit me to question Juan about this.

I was also unable, for the same reason, to get in a comment Manson made to Juan: 'Adolf Hitler had the best answer to everything.'

That answer, of course, was murder, but, owing to Kanarek's objections, neither of these two incidents were heard by the jury or ever made public.

On cross-examination Fitzgerald brought out an interesting anomaly. Even after Manson had allegedly threatened him, not once but several times, Juan still stuck around. After the raid he'd even accompanied the Family to Death Valley, remaining with them a couple of weeks before splitting to join Crockett, Poston, and Watkins.

That had puzzled me too. One possible explanation was that, as Juan testified, at first he had thought Manson was 'bullshitting' about the murders, that 'nobody in their right mind is going to kill somebody and then boast about it'. Also, Juan was easygoing and slow to anger. Probably more important, Juan was an independent cuss; like Paul Crockett, who didn't leave Death Valley until long after Manson threatened to kill him, he didn't like to be intimidated.

Kanarek picked up on Fitzgerald's discovery. 'Now, Mr Flynn, were you scared to be at the Myers Ranch with Mr Manson?'

A. 'Well, I was aware and precautious.'

Q. 'Just answer the question, Mr Flynn. I understand you are an actor, but would you just answer the question please.'

A. 'Well, I liked it there, you know, because I wanted to think nice things, you know. But every time I walked around the corner, well, that seemed to be the main subject, you know, about how many times they could do me in. Then, finally, I just left.'

Q. 'Now, Mr Flynn, will you tell me how you were aware and precautious? How did you protect yourself?'

A. 'Well, I just protected myself by leaving.'

Kanarek brought out that when Flynn was interviewed by Sartuchi he'd said nothing about Manson putting a knife to his throat. 'You were holding that back, is that it, Mr Flynn, to spring on us in this courtroom, is that right?'

A. 'No, I told the officers about this before, you see.'

Ignoring Flynn's response, Kanarek said: 'You mean, Mr Flynn, that you made it up for the purposes of this courtroom, is that correct, Mr Flynn?'

Kanarek was charging that Flynn had recently fabricated his testimony. I made a note of this, though as yet unaware how important this bit of dialogue would soon be.

After focusing on all the things I had brought out which were not in the Sartuchi interview, Kanarek asked Juan when he first mentioned the knife incident to anyone.

A. 'Well, there was some officers in Shoshone, you see, and I talked to them.' Flynn, however couldn't recall their names.

Kanarek strongly implied, several times, that Flynn was fictionalizing his story. Juan didn't take kindly to being called a liar. You could see his temper rising.

Intent on proving that Flynn was testifying so he could further his movie career (Juan had had bit parts in several Westerns), Kanarek asked: 'You recognize, do you not, that there is lots of publicity in this case against Mr Manson, right?'

A. 'Well, it is the type of publicity that I wouldn't want, you big catfish.'

THE COURT. 'On that note, Mr Kanarek, we will adjourn.'

After court I questioned Juan about the Shoshone interview. He thought one of the officers was from the California Highway Patrol, but he wasn't sure. That evening I called the DA's Office in Independence and learned that the man who had interviewed Juan was a CHP officer named Dave Steuber. Late that night I finally located him in Fresno, California. Yes, he'd interviewed Flynn, as well as Crockett, Poston, and Watkins, on December 19, 1969. He'd taped the whole conversation, which had lasted over nine hours. Yes, he still had the original tapes.

I checked my calendar. I guessed Flynn would be on the stand another day or two. Could Steuber be in L.A. in three days with the tapes and prepared to testify? Sure, Steuber said.

Steuber then told me something I found absolutely incredible. He had already made a copy of the tapes and given it to LAPD. On *December 29, 1969.* Later I learned the identity of the LAPD detective to whom the tapes had been given. The officer (since deceased) recalled receiving the tapes but admitted he hadn't played them. He thought he had given them to someone, but couldn't remember to whom. All he knew was that he no longer had them.

Perhaps it was because the interview was so long, nine hours. Or perhaps, it being the holiday season, in the confusion they were mislaid. Neither explanation, however, erases the unpleasant fact that as early as December 1969 the Los Angeles Police Department had a taped interview containing a statement in which Manson implied that he was responsible for the Tate-LaBianca murders, and as far as can be determined, no one even bothered to book it into evidence, much less play it.

Ordinarily there would have been no way I could introduce

447

the Steuber tape into evidence at the trial, for you cannot use a previously consistent statement to bolster a witness's testimony. However, there is an exception to that rule: such evidence is admissible if the opposing side contends the witness's testimony was recently fabricated and the prior consistent statement was made before the declarant had any reason to fabricate. When Kanarek asked, 'You mean, Mr Flynn, that you made it up for the purposes of this courtroom, is that correct, Mr Flynn?' he was charging recent fabrication, and opening the door for me to bring the prior consistent statement in.

A lot of doors were opened on cross-examination, but at first the biggest did not look like a door at all. The defense had made much of the fact that Juan did not tell his story to the authorities until long after the events occurred. With this opening, I argued, I should be allowed to bring out the reason why: he was in fear of his life.

Juan was permitted to testify that he didn't go to the police because 'I didn't think it was safe for me to do that, you see. I got a couple of threat notes . . .'

Actually, Juan had received three such notes, all handed him by Family members, the last as late as two weeks ago, when Squeaky and Larry Jones had discovered that Juan was living in John Swartz's trailer in Canoga Park. Arguing against their admission, Fitzgerald made an interesting statement: 'My life has been threatened three times, and I haven't come forward and talked about it.'

BUGLIOSI. 'Has the prosecution threatened you?'

FITZGERALD. 'No, I am not saying that.' He didn't elaborate.

Older ruled that Juan could testify to the notes, though not the identities of the persons who gave them to him. Juan also testified the hang-up calls, the cars that raced past in the night, their occupants oinking and screaming, 'Motherfucker!' and 'Pig!'

I asked him: 'And you considered these threats, is that correct?'

A. 'Well, they sounded, you know, pretty strong to me.'

Q. 'Are those among the reasons why you didn't want to come downtown and talk?'

A. 'Well, this was one of the reasons, yes.'

Q. 'Because of fear of your life?'

A. 'Yes.'

When I asked about the other reasons, Juan described how Manson, Clem, and Tex had creepy-crawled Crockett's cabin at Barker Ranch.

Because Kanarek had questioned Juan about Manson's 'programming' of Family members, I was able to bring in a conversation Manson had with Juan in which he explained that he had to 'unprogram' his followers to remove the programming placed upon them by their parents, schools, churches, and society. To get rid of the ego, Manson told him, you had to obliterate 'all the wants that you had . . . give up your mother and father . . . all the inhibitions . . . just blank yourself out'.

Since Manson's techniques differed depending on whether his subject was male or female, I asked what Manson had said about unprogramming the girls. I didn't anticipate that Juan would go into the detail he did.

A. 'Well, he says, you know, to get rid of the inhibitions, you know, you could just take a couple of girls and, you know, have them lay down, you know, and have them eat each other, or for me to take a girl up in the hills you know, and just lie back and let her suck my dick all day long . . .'

KANAREK. 'Your Honor, Your Honor! May we approach the bench, Your Honor?'

Earlier one of the alternate jurors had written Judge Older a letter complaining about the sexual explicitness of some of the testimony. I didn't look at him, but I suspected he must be having apoplexy. As I passed the counsel table on the way to the bench, I told Manson, 'Don't worry, Charlie, I'm keeping all the bad stuff out.'

Older struck the entire answer as nonresponsive.

I asked Juan: 'Did Mr Manson discuss with you – *without going into what he said, Juan* – plans that he had to "unprogram" the people in the Family?' When he replied 'Yes,' I let it go at that.

What Manson never explained to his Family was that in the process of unprogramming them, he was reprogramming them to be his abject slaves.

Throughout his cross-examination Kanarek had implied, as he had with many of the earlier witnesses, that Juan had been coached by me. I thought Kanarek was going to do this again, for the umpteenth time, when on recross he started: 'Mr Flynn, when a question is asked of you that you think may not help the prosecution in this case—'

BUGLIOSI. 'Oh, stop arguing.'

KANAREK. 'Your Honor, he's interrupting!'

BUGLIOSI. 'Be quiet.'

THE COURT. 'Mr Bugliosi, now, I'm not going to warn you again, sir.'

BUGLIOSI. 'What's he doing, Your Honor? He's accusing me of something and I don't like it.'

THE COURT. 'Approach the bench.'

BUGLIOSI. 'I am not going to take it. I've had it up to here.'

My indignation was as much a matter of trial tactics as anything else. If I let Kanarek get away with the same trick time after time, the jury might assume there was some truth in his charges. At the bench I told Older: 'I'm not going to be accused of a serious offense by this guy day in and day out.'

THE COURT. 'That's absurd. You interrupted Mr Kanarek. You made outrageous statements in front of the jury ... I find you in direct contempt of Court, and I fine you fifty dollars.'

To the amusement of the clerk, I had to call my wife to come down and pay the fine. Later the deputy D As in the office put up a buck each for a 'Bugliosi Defense Fund' and reimbursed her.

As with the earlier citation of Hughes, I felt if I was in contempt of anyone, it was Kanarek, not the Court. The following day, for the record, I responded to the contempt, noting among other things that 'in the future I would ask the Court to please consider two obvious points: this is a hotly contested trial and tempers become a little frayed; and also take into consideration what Mr Kanarek is doing which incites a response on my part'.

With my citation, we now had a perfect score: every attorney involved in the trial had been either cited for contempt or threatened with it.

The defense tried their best to ridicule Juan's fear of Manson.

Hughes brought out that since Manson was locked up, it was hardly likely he could hurt anyone; did Mr Flynn actually expect the jury to believe that he was afraid of Mr Manson?

Juan might have been speaking for all the prosecution witnesses when he answered: 'Well, not of Mr Manson himself, but the *reach* that he has, you know.'

By now I could see the pattern. The more damaging the testimony, the more chance Manson would create a disturbance, thereby assuring that he – and not the evidence itself – would get the day's headlines. Juan Flynn's testimony was hurting him badly. Several times while Flynn was on the stand, Older had to order Manson and the girls removed because of their outbursts. When it happened again, on October 2, Manson turned to the spectators and said: 'Look at yourselves. Where are you going? You're going to destruction, that's where you're going.' He then smiled a very odd little smile, and added, *'It's your Judgment Day, not mine.'*

Again the girls parroted Manson, and Older ordered all four removed.

Kanarek was livid. I'd just showed the judge the transcript pages where Kanarek accused Flynn of lying. Older ruled: 'There is no question: there was an implied, if not express, charge of recent fabrication.' Highway patrolman Dave Steuber would be permitted to play that portion of the taped interview dealing with Manson's incriminating admission.*

---

* Steuber had been investigating a stolen auto report, not murder, when he talked to Flynn, Poston, Crockett, and Watkins in Shoshone. However, realizing the importance of their story, he had spent over nine hours quizzing them on their knowledge of Manson and his Family. After the trial I wrote a letter to the California Highway Patrol, commending Steuber for the excellent job he had done.

After establishing the circumstances of the interview, Steuber set up the tape recorder and began playing the tape at the point where the statement had begun. There is something about such physical evidence that deeply impresses a jury. Again, in words very similar to those they had heard him use when he was on the stand, the jurors heard Juan say: 'Then he was looking at me real funny . . . And then he grabbed me by the hair like that, and he put a knife by my throat . . . And then he says, "Don't you know I'm the one who is doing all the killings?" '

Monday, October 5, 1970. Bailiff Bill Murray later said he had a very strong feeling that something was going to happen. You get a kind of sixth sense dealing with prisoners day after day, he said, noting that when he brought Manson into the lockup he was acting very tense and edgy.

Although they had made no assurances that they would conduct themselves properly, Older gave the defendants still another chance, permitting them to return to the courtroom.

The testimony was dull, undramatic. There was, at this point, no clue as to its importance, though I had a feeling Charlie just might suspect what I was up to. Through a series of witnesses, I was laying the groundwork for destroying Manson's anticipated alibi.

LASO detective Paul Whiteley had just finished testifying, and the defense attorneys had declined to cross-examine him, when Manson asked: 'May I examine him, Your Honor?'

THE COURT. 'No, you may not.'

MANSON. 'You are going to use this courtroom to kill me?'

Older told the witness he could step down. Manson asked the question a second time, adding, 'I am going to fight for my life one way or another. You should let me do it with words.'

THE COURT. 'If you don't stop, I will have to have you removed.'

MANSON. 'I will have *you* removed if you don't stop. *I have a little system of my own.*'

Not until Manson made that very startling admission did I realize that this time he wasn't playacting but deadly serious.

THE COURT. 'Call your next witness.'

BUGLIOSI. 'Sergeant Gutierrez.'

MANSON. *'Do you think I'm kidding?'*

It happened in less time that it takes to describe it. With a pencil clutched in his right hand, Manson suddenly leaped over the counsel table in the direction of Judge Older. He landed just a few feet from the bench, falling on one knee. As he was struggling to his feet, bailiff Bill Murray leaped too, landing on Manson's back. Two other deputies quickly joined in and, after a brief struggle, Manson's arms were pinned. As he was being propelled to the lockup, Manson screamed at Older: *'In the name of Christian justice, someone should cut your head off!'*

Adding to the bedlam, Atkins, Krenwinkel, and Van Houten stood and began chanting something in Latin. Older, much less disturbed than I would have expected, gave them not one but several chances to stop, then ordered them removed also.

According to the bailiffs, Manson continued to fight even after he had been taken into the lockup, and it took four men to put cuffs on him.

Fitzgerald asked if counsel might approach the bench. For the record, Judge Older described exactly how he had viewed the incident. Fitzgerald asked if he might inquire as to the judge's state of mind.

THE COURT. 'He looked like he was coming for me.'

FITZGERALD. 'I was afraid of that, and although – '

THE COURT. 'If he had taken one more step, I would have done something to defend myself.'

Because of the judge's state of mind, Fitzgerald said, he felt it incumbent upon him to move for a mistrial. Hughes, Shinn, and Kanarek joined. Older replied: 'It isn't going to be that easy, Mr Fitzgerald . . . They are not going to profit from their own wrong . . . Denied.'

Out of curiosity, after court Murray measured the distance of Manson's leap: ten feet.

Murray wasn't too surprised. Manson had very powerful leg and arm muscles. He was constantly exercising in the lockup.

Asked why, he'd once told a bailiff: 'I'm toughening myself up for the desert.'

Murray tried to re-create his own leap. Without that sudden shot of adrenaline, he couldn't even jump up on the counsel table.

Though Judge Older instructed the jury to 'disregard what you saw and what you have heard here this morning', I knew that as long as they lived they'd never forget it.

All the masks had been dropped. They'd seen the real face of Charles Manson.

From a reliable source, I learned that after the incident Judge Older began wearing a .38 caliber revolver under his robes, both in court and in chambers.

Judgment Day. Echoing Manson, the girls waiting outside on the corner spoke of it in conspiratorial whispers. 'Wait till Judgment Day. That's when Helter Skelter will really come down.'

Judgment Day. What was it? A plan to break out Manson? An orgy of retribution?

As important was the question of when. The day the jury returned their verdict of 'Not guilty' or 'Guilty'? Or, if the latter, the day the same jury decided 'Life' or 'Death'? Or perhaps the day of sentencing itself? Or might it even be tomorrow?

Judgment Day. We began to hear those words more and more often. Without explanation. As yet unaware that the first phase of Judgment Day had already begun, with the theft, from Camp Pendleton Marine Base, of a case of hand grenades.

October 6–31, 1970

Some weeks earlier, on returning to my office after court, I'd found a phone message from attorney Robert Steinberg, who was now representing Virginia Graham.

On the advice of her previous attorney, Virginia Graham had withheld some information. Steinberg had urged her to give this information to me. 'Specifically,' the phone message read, 'Susan Atkins laid out detailed plans to Miss Graham concerning other planned murders, including the murders of Frank Sinatra and Elizabeth Taylor.'

Since I was very busy, I arranged to have one of the co-prosecutors, Steve Kay, interview her.

According to Virginia, a few days after Susan Atkins told her about the Hinman, Tate, and LaBianca murders – probably on November 8 or 9, 1969 – Susan had walked over to Virginia's bed at Sybil Brand and begun leafing through a movie magazine. It reminded her, Susan said, about some other murders she had been planning.

She had decided to kill Elizabeth Taylor and Richard Burton, Susan matter-of-factly stated. She was going to heat a knife red-hot and put it against the side of Elizabeth Taylor's face. This was more or less to leave her mark. Then she'd carve the words 'helter skelter' on her forehead. After which, she was going to gouge her eyes out – Charlie had shown her how – and –

Virginia interrupted to ask what Richard Burton was supposed to be doing during all this.

Oh, both would be tied up, Susan said. Only this time the rope would be around their necks and their feet, so they couldn't get away 'like the others'.

Then, Susan continued, she would castrate Burton, placing his penis, as well as Elizabeth Taylor's eyes, in a bottle. 'And dig this, would you!' Susan laughed. 'And then I'd mail it to Eddie Fisher!'

As for Tom Jones, another of her intended victims, she planned to force him to have sex with her, at knife point, and then, just as he was climaxing, she would slit his throat.

Steve McQueen was also on the list. Before Susan could explain what she had in mind for McQueen, Virginia interrupted, saying, 'Sadie, you can't just walk up to these people and kill them!'

That would be no problem, Susan said. It was easy to find out where they lived. Then she'd simply creepy-crawl them, 'just like I did to Tate.'

She had something choice for Frank Sinatra, Susan continued. She knew that Frank liked girls. She'd just walk up to his door and knock. Her friends, she said, would be waiting outside. Once inside, they'd hang Sinatra upside down, then, while his own music was playing, skin him alive. After which they'd make purses out of the skin and sell them to hippie shops, 'so everyone would have a little piece of Frank'.

She had come to the conclusion, Susan said, that the victims had to be people of importance, so the whole world would know.

Shortly after this, Virginia terminated the conversation with Susan. When asked by Steve Kay why she hadn't come forward with the story before this, Virginia explained that it was just so insane that she didn't think anyone would believe her. Even her former attorney had advised her to say nothing about it.

Were these Sadie's own plans, or Charlie's? Knowing as much as I did about Susan Atkins, I doubted if all this came from her. Though I had no proof, it was a reasonable inference that she had probably picked up these ideas from Manson.

In any case, it didn't matter. Reading a transcript of the taped interview, I knew I'd never be able to introduce any of this in evidence: legally, its relevance to the Tate-LaBianca murders was negligible, and whatever limited relevance it did have would be outweighed by its extremely prejudicial effect.

Though Virginia Graham's statement was useless as evidence,

a copy of it was made available to each of the defense attorneys under discovery.

It would soon make its own kind of legal history.

Although it was Ronnie Howard who first went to the police, I called Virginia Graham to the stand first, since Susan had initially confessed to her.

Her testimony was unusually dramatic, since this was the first time the jury had heard what had happened inside the Tate residence.

The letters Susan Atkins had written to her former cellmates, Ronnie Howard, Jo Stevenson, and Kitt Fletcher, were also very incriminating. Although I was prepared to call a handwriting expert to testify to their authenticity, Shinn, in order to save time, stipulated that Susan had written them. However, before they could be introduced in evidence, we had to 'Arandize' them, excising any references to Atkins' co-defendants. This was done in chambers, outside the presence of the jury.

LIZ, SINATRA ON SLAY LIST

The Los Angeles *Herald Examiner* broke the story on October 9, in an exclusive article bearing the by-line of reporter William Farr. Learning the night before that the story was going to appear, Judge Older again ordered the windows of the jury bus covered so the jurors couldn't see the headlines on corner newsstands.

Farr's article contained direct quotes from the Virginia Graham statement, which we had turned over to the defense on discovery.

Questioned in chambers, Farr declined to identify his source or sources. After observing that under California law he could not order the reporter to do so, Older excused Farr.

It was obvious that one or more persons had violated the gag order. Older, however, did not press the issue, and there, it appeared, the matter rested. There was no indication at this time that the issue would eventually become a *cause célèbre* and result in the jailing of Farr.

Prior to his questioning by Older, Farr told Virginia Graham's attorney, Robert Steinberg, that he had received the statement from one of the defense attorneys. He did not say which one.

Gregg Jakobson was an impressive and very important witness. I had the tall, modishly dressed talent scout testify in detail to his many conversations with Manson, during which they discussed Helter Skelter, the Beatles, Revelation 9, and Manson's curious attitude toward death.

Shahrokh Hatami followed Jakobson to the stand, to testify to his confrontation with Manson at 10050 Cielo Drive on the afternoon of March 23, 1969. For the first time the jury, and the public, learned that Sharon Tate had seen the man who later ordered her murder.

In Rudi Altobelli, Kanarek finally met his match. On direct examination the owner of 10050 Cielo Drive testified to his first encounter with Manson at Dennis Wilson's home, and then, in considerable detail, he described Manson's appearance at the guest house the evening before he and Sharon left for Rome.

Extremely antagonistic because Altobelli had refused him permission to visit 10050 Cielo Drive, Kanarek asked: 'Now, presently, the premises on Cielo Drive where you live are quite secure, is that correct?'

A. 'I hope so.'

Q. 'Do you remember having a conversation with me when I tried to get into your fortress out there?'

A. 'I remember your insinuations or threats.'

Q. 'What were my insinuations or threats?'

A. 'That "We will take care of you, Mr Altobelli," "We will see about you, Mr Altobelli." "We will get the court up at your house and have the trial at your house, Mr Altobelli." '

Altobelli had told Kanarek that if the Court ordered it, he would be glad to comply. 'Otherwise, no. It is a home. It is not going to be a tourist attraction or a freak show.'

Q. 'Do you respect our courts of law, Mr Altobelli?'

A. 'I think more than you, Mr Kanarek.'

Despite defense objections, I had succeeded in getting in perhaps 95 percent of the testimony I'd hoped to elicit through Jakobson, Hatami, and Altobelli.

With the next witness, I suddenly found myself in deep trouble.

Charles Koenig took the stand to testify to finding Rosemary LaBianca's wallet in the women's rest room of the Standard station in Sylmar where he worked. He described how, on lifting the top of the toilet tank, he'd seen the wallet wedged above the mechanism, just above the waterline.

Kanarek cross-examined Koenig at great length about the toilet, causing more than a few snickers among spectators and press. Then I suddenly realized what he was getting at.

Kanarek asked Koenig if there was a standard procedure in connection with servicing the toilets in the rest room.

Koenig replied that the Standard station operating manual required that the rest room be cleaned every hour. The bluing agent, which is kept in the tank of the toilet, Koenig further testified, had to be replaced 'whenever it ran out'.

How often was that? Kanarek asked.

As 'lead man', or boss of the station, Koenig had not personally cleaned the rest rooms, but rather had delegated the task to others. Therefore I was able to object to this and similar questions as calling for a conclusion on Koenig's part.

Fortunately, court then recessed for the day.

Immediately afterward I called LAPD with an urgent request. I wanted the detectives to locate and interview every person who had worked in this particular station between August 10, 1969 (the date Linda Kasabian testified she left the wallet there) and December 10, 1969 (the date Koenig found it). And I wanted them interviewed before Kanarek could get to them, fearing that he might put words in their mouths. I told the officers: 'Tell them, "Forget what the Standard station operating manual says you should do; forget too what your employer might say if he found you didn't follow the instructions to the letter. Just answer truthfully: Did you personally, at any time during your employment, change the bluing agent in that toilet?" '

To replace the bluing agent, you had to lift the top off the tank. Had anyone done so, he would have immediately seen the wallet. If Kanarek could come up with just one employee who claimed to have replaced the bluing agent during that four-month period, the defense could forcefully contend that the wallet had been 'planted', not only destroying Linda Kasabian's credibility as to all of her testimony, but implying that the prosecution was trying to frame Manson.

LAPD located some, but not all, of the former employees. (None had ever changed the bluing agent.) Fortunately, Kanarek apparently had no better luck.

Hughes had only a few questions for Koenig, but they were devastating.

Q. 'Now, Sylmar is predominantly a white area, is it not?'

A. 'Yeah, I guess so.'

Q. 'Sylmar is not a black ghetto, is it?'

A. 'No.'

According to Linda, Manson had wanted a black to find the wallet and use the credit cards, so blacks would be blamed for the murders. My whole theory of the motive was based on this premise. Why, then, had Manson left the wallet in a white area?

In point of fact, the freeway exit Manson had taken was immediately north of Pacoima, the black ghetto of the San Fernando Valley. I tried to get this in through Koenig, but defense objections kept it out, and I later had to call Sergeant Patchett to so testify.

With a single witness, a service-station attendant, the defense – specifically Kanarek and Hughes – had almost knocked two huge holes in the prosecution's case.

By now I had narrowed down my opponents. Fitzgerald made a good appearance but rarely scored. Shinn was likable. For his first trial Hughes was doing damn well. But it was Irving Kanarek, whom most members of the press considered the trial's buffoon, who was scoring nearly all the points. Time and again Kanarek succeeded in keeping out important evidence.

For example, when Stephanie Schram took the stand, Kanarek objected to her testimony regarding the 'murder school' Manson had conducted at Barker Ranch, and Older sustained Kanarek's objection. Though I disagreed with Older's ruling, there was no way I could get around it.

On direct Stephanie had testified that she and Manson returned to Spahn Ranch from San Diego in a cream-colored van on the afternoon of Friday, August 8. On cross-examination Fitzgerald asked her: 'Could you be mistaken one day?' This indicated to me that Manson might still be planning to go alibi, so on redirect I brought in the traffic ticket they had been given the previous day. With the August 8 arrest report on Brunner and Good, which contained the license number of the same van, I was now ready to demolish Charlie if the defense claimed he wasn't even in Southern California at the time of the murders.

Yet I had no way of knowing whether Manson might have his own surprise bombshell, which he was waiting to explode.

As it happened, he had.

Sergeant Gutierrez, on the 'HELTER SKELTER' door. De-Wayne Wolfer, on the sound tests he'd conducted at the Tate residence, Jerrold Friedman, on the last telephone call Steven Parent made. Roseanne Walker, on Atkins' remarks about the eyeglasses. Harold True, on Manson's visits to the house next to the LaBianca residence. Sergeant McKellar, on Krenwinkel's attempts to avoid recognition just prior to her arrest in Mobile, Alabama. Bits and pieces, but cumulative. And eventually, I hoped, convincing.

Only a few prosecution witnesses remained. And I still didn't know what the defense would be. Although the prosecution had to give the defense a list of all our witnesses, the defense had no such obligation. Earlier Fitzgerald had told the press that he intended to call thirty witnesses, among them such celebrities as Mama Cass, John Phillips, and Beatle John Lennon, the latter to testify as to how he interpreted his own song lyrics. But that, and the rumors that Manson himself planned to testify, were the only clues to the defense. And even Manson's testifying was an iffy thing. In my talks with Charlie, he seemed to vacillate. I con-

tinued to goad him, but he was worried that perhaps I'd over-
played my hand.

The defendants hadn't been in court since Manson's attack on
the judge. The day Terry Melcher was to testify, however, Older
permitted their return. Not wanting to face Manson, Terry asked
me, 'Can't I go back in the lockup and testify through the
speaker?'

Of all the prosecution witnesses, Melcher was the most frightened of Manson. His fear was so great, he told me, that he had
been under psychiatric treatment and had employed a full-time
bodyguard since December 1969.

'Terry, they weren't after you that night,' I tried to reassure
him. 'Manson knew you were no longer living there.'

Melcher was so nervous, however, that he had to be given a
tranquilizer before taking the stand. Though he came over somewhat weaker than in our interviews, when he finished his testimony, he told me, with evident relief, that Manson had
smiled at him, therefore he couldn't be too unhappy with what
he'd said.

Kanarek, probably at Manson's request, did not question Melcher. Hughes brought out that when Wilson and Manson drove
Terry to the gate of 10050 Cielo Drive that night, they probably
saw him push the button. The defense could now argue that if
Manson was familiar with the gate-operating device, it would be
unlikely he'd have the killers climb over the fence, as Linda
claimed they had.

By this time I had proof that *both* Watson and Manson had
been to 10050 Cielo Drive on a *number* of occasions before the
murders. But the jury would never hear it.

Some months earlier I'd learned that after Terry Melcher had
moved out of the residence, but before the Polanskis had moved
in, Gregg Jakobson had arranged for a Dean Moorehouse to stay
there for a brief period. During this time Tex Watson had visited
Moorehouse at least three, and possibly as many as six, times. In
a private conversation with Fitzgerald, I told him this and he
replied that he already knew it.

Though I intended to introduce this evidence during the

Watson trial, I didn't want to bring it in during the current proceedings, and I was hoping that Fitzgerald wouldn't either, since it emphasized the Watson rather than the Manson link.

Though I suspected that Manson had visited there also during the same period, I had no proof of this until the trial was well under way, when I learned from the best possible source that Manson had been to 10050 Cielo Drive 'on five or six occasions'. My source was Manson himself, who admitted this to me during one of our rap sessions. Manson denied, however, having been in the house itself. He and Tex went up there, he said, to race dune buggies up and down the hills.

But I couldn't use this information against Manson, because, as he well knew, all of my conversations with him were at his instance and he was never advised of his constitutional rights.

It was a decidedly curious situation. Although Manson had vowed to kill me, he still asked to see me periodically – to rap.

Equally curious were our conversations. Manson told me, for example, that he personally believed in law and order. There should be 'rigid control' by the authorities, he said. It didn't matter what the law was – right and wrong being relative – but it should be strictly enforced by whoever had the power. And public opinion should be suppressed, because part of the people wanted one thing, part another.

'In other words, your solution would be a dictatorship,' I remarked.

'Yes.'

He had a simple solution to the crime problem, Manson told me. Empty the prisons and banish all the criminals to the desert. But first brand their foreheads with X's, so if they ever appeared in the cities they could be identified and shot on sight.

'Do I need two guesses as to who's going to be in charge of them in the desert, Charlie?'

'No.' He grinned.

On another occasion, Manson told me that he had just written to President Nixon, asking him to turn over the reins of power to him. If I was interested, I could be his vice-president. I was a brilliant prosecutor, he said, a master with words, and, 'You're right on about a lot of things.'

'What things, Charlie? Helter Skelter, the way the murders came down, your philosophy on life and death?'

Manson smiled and declined to answer.

'We both know you ordered these murders,' I told him.

'Bugliosi, it's the Beatles, the music they're putting out. They're talking about war. These kids listen to this music and pick up the message, it's subliminal.'

'You were along on the night of the LaBianca murders.'

'I went out a lot of nights.'

Never a direct denial. I couldn't wait to get him on the stand.

Manson told me that he liked prison, though he liked the desert, the sun, and women better. I told him he'd never been inside the green room at San Quentin before.

He wasn't afraid of death, Manson responded. Death was only a thought. He'd faced death before, many times, in both this and past lives.

I asked him if, when he shot Crowe, he'd intended to kill him.

'Sure,' he replied, adding, 'I could kill everyone without blinking an eye.' When I asked why, he said, 'Because you've been killing me for years.' Pressed as to whether all this killing bothered him, Manson replied that he had no conscience, that everything was only a thought. Only he, and he alone, was on top of his thought, in complete control, unprogrammed by anyone or anything.

'When it comes down around your ears, you'd better believe I'll be on top of my thought,' Manson said. 'I will know what I am doing. I will know *exactly* what I am doing.'

Manson frequently interrupted the testimony of Brooks Poston and Paul Watkins with asides. Kanarek's interruptions were so continuous that Older had to threaten to find him in contempt again.

It was all too obvious, to both Kanarek and Manson, that Poston and Watkins were impressively strong witnesses. Step by step they traced the evolution of Helter Skelter, not intellectually, as Jakobson understood it, but as onetime true believers, members of the Family who had watched a vague concept slowly material-ize into terrifying reality.

The cross-examination didn't shake their testimony in the slightest; rather, it elicited more details. When Kanarek ques-tioned Poston, for example, he accidentally brought out a good domination example: 'When Charlie would be around, things would be like when a schoolteacher comes back to class.'

Hughes asked Poston: 'Did you feel you were under Mr Manson's hypnotic spell?'

A. 'No, I did not think that Charlie had a hypnotic spell.'

Q. 'Did you feel he had some power?'

A. 'I felt he was Jesus Christ. That is power enough for me.'

Looking back on his time with Manson, Poston said: 'I learned a lot from Charlie, but it doesn't seem that he was making all those people free.' Watkins observed: 'Charlie was always preaching love. Charlie had no idea what love was. Charlie was so far from love it wasn't even funny. *Death is Charlie's trip*. It really is.'

Since his extradition to California, Charles 'Tex' Watson had been behaving peculiarly. At first he spoke little, then stopped speaking entirely. The prisoners in his cell block signed a petition complaining of the unsanitary condition of his cell. For hours he'd stare off into space, then inexplicably hurl himself against his cell wall. Placed in restraints, he stopped eating and, even though force-fed, his weight dropped to 110 pounds.

Though there was evidence that he was faking at least part of his symptoms, his attorney, Sam Bubrick, asked the Court to appoint three psychiatrists to examine him. Their conclusions differed but they agreed on one point: Watson was rapidly re-verting to a fetal state, which, unless immediately treated, could be fatal. Acting on the basis of their examination, on October 29 Judge Dell ruled Watson was at present incompetent to stand trial and ordered him committed to Atascadero State Hospital.

Manson asked to see me during the recess.

'Vince,' Manson pleaded through the lockup door, 'give me just half an hour with Tex. I'm positive I can cure him.'

'I'm sorry, Charlie,' I told him. 'I can't afford to take that chance. If you cured him, then everyone *would* believe you were Jesus Christ.'

November 1–19, 1970

The day before Watson was committed to Atascadero, two court-appointed psychiatrists found 17-year-old Dianne Lake competent to testify.

Following her release from Patton, Dianne had received some good news: Inyo County investigator Jack Gardiner and his wife, who had befriended Dianne after her arrest in the Barker raid, had been appointed her foster parents. She would live with them and their children until she finished high school.

Because of *Aranda*, there were some things the jury never heard – for example, that Tex had told Leslie to stab Rosemary LaBianca and, later, to wipe fingerprints off everything they had touched – since Katie had related these things to Dianne, and any reference by Katie to her co-defendants had to be excised.

Dianne could testify to what Leslie had told her she had done; however, the problem here was that Leslie never told Dianne *whom* she had stabbed. She said she had stabbed someone who was already dead; that this occurred near Griffith Park; and that there was a boat outside. From these facts I hoped the jury would conclude that she was talking about the LaBiancas. Dianne also testified that one morning in August Leslie had come into the back house at Spahn and proceeded to burn a purse, a credit card, and her own clothing, keeping only a sack of coins, which the girls divided and spent on food. Dianne, however, was unable to pinpoint the exact date, and though I hoped the jury would surmise this had occurred the morning after the LaBiancas were killed, there was no proof that this was so.

Since this was the only evidence, independent of Linda Kasabian's testimony, which I had linking Leslie Van Houten to the LaBianca homicides, it hurt, and badly, when Hughes on cross brought out that Dianne wasn't sure whether Leslie had told her about the boat or whether she had read about it in the newspapers.

Hughes also focused on a number of minor discrepancies in her previous statements (she'd told Sartuchi the coins were in the purse, while she'd told me they were in a plastic bag), and what could have been one very big bombshell. On direct Dianne had said that she, Little Patty, and Sandra Good, 'I believe,' had divided the money.

If Sandy was present, this couldn't have been August 10, the morning after the LaBianca murders, since Sandra Good, along with Mary Brunner, was still in custody. However, questioned further, Dianne said Sandy 'might not have been there'.

Fitzgerald also came up with a prior inconsistent statement: Dianne had told the grand jury that she was in Inyo County, rather than at Spahn Ranch, on August 8 and 9.

On redirect I asked Dianne: 'Why did you lie to the grand jury?'

A. 'Because I was afraid that I would be killed by members of the Family if I told the truth. And Charlie asked me not to – he told me not to say anything to anybody who had the power of authority.'

On November 4, Sergeant Gutierrez, in search of a cup of coffee, had wandered into the jury room where the female defendants stayed during recesses.

He found a yellow legal pad with the name Patricia Krenwinkel on it. Among the notes and doodlings, Katie had written the words 'healter skelter' three times – misspelling that first word exactly the same way it had been misspelled on the LaBianca refrigerator door.

Older would not permit me to introduce it in evidence, however. I felt he was 100 percent wrong about this: it was unquestionably circumstantial evidence; it had relevance; and it was admissible. But Older ruled otherwise.

Older also gave me a scare when I attempted to introduce Krenwinkel's refusal to make a printing exemplar. Older agreed it was admissible, but he felt Krenwinkel should be given another chance to comply, and ordered her to do so.

The problem here was that this time Krenwinkel just might, on the advice of counsel, make the exemplar, and if she did, I knew there would be real problems.

Katie refused – on the instructions of Paul Fitzgerald!

What Fitzgerald apparently did not realize was that it would be extremely difficult, if not impossible, for LAPD to match the two printing samples. And had LAPD failed to do so, by law Patricia Krenwinkel would have to be acquitted of the LaBianca murders. Her refusal to give an exemplar was the only speck of independent evidence I had supporting Kasabian's testimony regarding Krenwinkel's involvement in these crimes.

Krenwinkel had been given an excellent chance to 'beat the rap'. To this day I still don't understand why her attorney instructed her as he did and so lost her that chance.

The People's last two witnesses, Drs Blake Skrdla and Harold Deering, were the psychiatrists who had examined Dianne. On both direct and redirect examination, I elicited testimony from them to the effect that, although a powerful drug, LSD does not impair memory, nor is there any demonstrable medical evidence that it causes brain damage. This was important, since the defense attorneys had contended that the minds of various prosecution witnesses, in particular Linda and Dianne, had been so 'blown' by LSD that they could not distinguish fantasy from reality.

Skrdla testified that people on LSD *can* tell the difference between the real and the unreal; in fact, they often have a heightened awareness. Skrdla further stated that LSD causes illusions rather than hallucinations – in others words, that which is seen is actually there, only the perception of it is changed. This surprised a lot of people, since LSD is called a hallucinogenic drug.

When Watkins was on the stand, I personally brought out that although he was only 20, Paul had taken LSD between 150 and 200 times. Yet, as the jury undoubtedly observed, he was one of the brightest and most articulate of the prosecution witnesses.

Fitzgerald asked Skrdla: 'Would LSD in large doses over a period of time make someone sort of a zombie, or would it destroy rational thought processes?'

If, as I suspected, Fitzgerald was trying to lay the foundation for a defense based on these premise, that foundation collapsed when Skrdla replied: 'I have not seen this, counsel.'

Dr Deering was the People's last witness, He finished testifying on Friday November 13. Most of Monday, the sixteenth, was spent introducing the People's exhibits into evidence. There were 320 of these, and Kanarek objected to every one, from the gun to the scale map of the Tate premises. His strongest objections were to the color death photos. Responding, I argued: 'I grant the Court that these photographs are gruesome, there is no question about it, but if in fact the defendants are the ones who committed these murders, which the prosecution of course is alleging, they are the ones who are responsible for the gruesomeness and the ghastliness. It is their handiwork. The jury is entitled to look at that handiwork.'

Judge Older agreed, and they were admitted into evidence.

At 4:27 P.M. that Monday – exactly twenty-two weeks after the start of the trial, and two days short of a year after my assignment to the case – I told the Court: 'Your Honor, the People of the State of California rest.'

Court was recessed until Thursday, November 19, at which time each of the defense attorneys argued the standard motions to dismiss.

Back in December 1969 a great many attorneys predicted that when we reached this point Manson would have to be acquitted because of insufficiency of evidence.

I doubted if any lawyer in the country felt that way now, including the attorneys for the defense.

Older denied all the motions.

THE COURT. 'Are you ready to proceed with the defense?'

FITZGERALD. 'Yes, Your Honor.'

THE COURT. 'You may call your first witness, Mr Fitzgerald.'

FITZGERALD. 'Thank you, Your Honor. The defendants rest.'

Nearly everyone in the courtroom was caught completely off guard. For several minutes even Judge Older seemed too stunned to speak.

The biggest surprise, however, was still to come.

Part Seven

Murder In The Wind

'You could feel something in the air,
you know. You could feel something
in the air.'

Juan Flynn

'Snitches, and other enemies, will be
taken care of.'

Sandra Good

'Before his disappearance, Ronald Hughes,
the missing defense attorney in the Tate-
LaBianca murder trial, confided to close
friends that he was in fear of Manson.'

Los Angeles Times

November 19–December 20, 1970

Fitzgerald said the defense had rested. But the three female defendants now shouted that they wanted to testify.

Calling counsel into chambers, Judge Older demanded to know exactly what was going on.

There had been a split between the defense attorneys and their clients, Fitzgerald said. The girls wanted to testify; their attorneys opposed this, and wanted to rest their case.

Only after an hour of intense discussion did the real reason for the split come out, in an off-the-record admission by Fitzgerald:

Sadie, Katie, and Leslie wanted to take the stand and testify that they had planned and committed the murders – and that Manson was not involved!

Charlie had tried to explode his bombshell, but the attorneys for the girls had managed to defuse it, at least temporarily. Standing up against Manson for the first time, Ronald Hughes observed: 'I refuse to take part in any proceeding where I am forced to push a client out the window.'

The legal problems thus created were immense, but basically they came down to the question of which took precedence; the right to effective counsel or the right to testify. Worried that whichever course Older took might be reversible error on appeal, I suggested he take the matter to the State Supreme Court for a decision. Older, however, decided that even though the attorneys had rested, and had advised their clients not to take the stand, the right to testify 'supersedes any and all other rights'. The girls would be permitted to take the stand.

Older asked Manson if he also wished to testify. 'No,' he replied, then, after a moment's hesitation, added, 'That is, not at this time anyway.'

On returning to open court, Kanarek made a motion to sever Manson so he could be tried separately.

Charlie was now attempting to abandon ship, while letting the girls sink. After denying the motion, Older had the jury brought in and Susan Atkins took the stand and was sworn. Daye Shinn, however, refused to question her, stating that if he asked the questions she'd prepared, they would incriminate her.*

This created a whole new problem. Returning to chambers, Older remarked: 'It is becoming perfectly clear that this entire maneuver by the defense is simply one . . . to wreck the trial . . . I do not intend to permit this to happen.'

Still in chambers, and outside the presence of the jury, Susan Atkins told Judge Older that she wanted to testify to 'the way it happened. The way I *saw* it happen.'

Shinn said he would ask to be relieved as counsel if Older ordered him to question his client. Fitzgerald replied similarly, adding, 'As far as I am concerned, it would be sort of aiding and abetting a suicide.'

The matter was unresolved when court recessed for the day.

The following day Manson surprised everyone by saying that he too wanted to testify. In fact, he wanted to go on the stand before the others. Because of possible *Aranda* problems, however, it was decided that Manson should first testify outside the presence of the jury.

Manson was sworn. Rather than have Kanarek question him, he requested and received permission to make a statement.

He spoke for over an hour. He began almost apologetically, at first speaking so low that the spectators in the crowded courtroom had to lean forward to hear. But after a few minutes the voice changed, grew stronger, more animated, and, as I'd already discovered in my conversations with him, when this happened his face seemed to change too. Manson the nobody. Manson the martyr. Manson the teacher. Manson the prophet. He became all these, and more, the metamorphosis often occurring in mid-

---

* Shinn's remarks, in themselves incriminating, were later stricken from the record.

sentence, his face a light show of shifting emotions until it was not one face but a kaleidoscope of different faces, each real, but only for the moment.

He rambled, he digressed, he repeated himself, but there *was* something hypnotic about the whole performance. In his own strange way he was trying to weave a spell, not unlike the ones he had cast over his impressionable followers.

MANSON. 'There has been a lot of charges and a lot of things said about me and brought against the co-defendants in this case, of which a lot could be cleared up and clarified . . .

'I never went to school, so I never growed up to read and write too good, so I have stayed in jail and I have stayed stupid, and I have stayed a child while I have watched your world grow up, and then I look at the things that you do and I don't understand . . .

'You eat meat and kill things that are better than you are, and then you say how bad, and even killers, your children are. *You* made your children what they are . . .

'*These children that come at you with knives, they are your children. You taught them. I didn't teach them. I just tried to help them stand up.*

'Most of the people at the ranch that you call the Family were just people that you did not want, people that were alongside the road, that their parents had kicked out, that did not want to go to Juvenile Hall. So I did the best I could and I took them up on my garbage dump and I told them this: that in love there is no wrong . . .

'I told them that anything they do for their brothers and sisters is good if they do it with a good thought . . .

'I was working at cleaning up my house, something that Nixon should have been doing. He should have been on the side of the road, picking up his children, but he wasn't. He was in the White House, sending them off to war . . .

'I don't understand you, but I don't try. I don't try to judge nobody. I know that the only person I can judge is me . . . But I know this: that in your hearts and your own souls, you are as much responsible for the Vietnam war as I am for killing these people . . .

'I can't judge any of you. I have no malice against you and no ribbons for you. But I think that it is high time that you all start looking at yourselves, and judging the lie that you live in.

'I can't dislike you, but I will say this to you: you haven't got long before you are all going to kill yourselves, because you are all crazy. And you can project it back at me . . . but I am only what lives inside each and every one of you.

'My father is the jailhouse. My father is your system . . . I am only what you made me. I am only a reflection of you.

'I have ate out of your garbage cans to stay out of jail. I have wore your second-hand clothes . . . I have done my best to get along in your world and now you want to kill me, and I look at you, and then I say to myself, You want to kill *me*? Ha! I'm already dead, have been all my life. I've spent twenty-three years in tombs that you built.

'Sometimes I think about giving it back to you; sometimes I think about just jumping on you and letting you shoot me . . . If I could, I would jerk this microphone off and beat your brains out with it, because that is what you deserve, that is what you deserve . . .

'If I could get angry at you, I would try to kill every one of you. If that's guilt, I accept it . . .

'These children, everything they done, they done for the love of their brother . . .

'If I showed them that I would do anything for my brother – including giving my life for my brother on the battlefield – and then they pick up their banner, and they go off and do what they do, that is not my responsibility. I don't tell people what to do . . .

'These children [indicating the female defendants] were finding themselves. What they did, if they did whatever they did, is up to them. They will have to explain that to you . . .

'It's all your fear. You look for something to project it on, and you pick out a little old scroungy nobody that eats out of a garbage can, and that nobody wants, that was kicked out of the penitentiary, that has been dragged through every hellhole that you can think of, and you drag him and put him in a courtroom.

'*You expect to break me? Impossible! You broke me years ago. You killed me years ago* . . .'

Older asked Manson if he had anything further to say.

MANSON. 'I have killed no one and I have ordered no one to be killed.

'I may have implied on several different occasions to several different people that I may have been Jesus Christ, but I haven't decided yet what I am or who I am.'

Some called him Christ, Manson said. In prison his name was a number. Some now want a sadistic fiend, and so they see him as that. So be it. Guilty. Not guilty. They are only words. 'You can do anything you want with me, but you cannot touch me because I am only my love ... If you put me in the penitentiary, that means nothing because you kicked me out of the last one. I didn't ask to get released. I liked it in there because I like myself.'

Telling Manson, 'You seem to be getting far afield,' Older asked him to stick to the issues.

MANSON. 'The issues? ... Mr Bugliosi is a hard-driving prosecutor, polished education, a master of words, semantics. He is a genius. He has got everything that every lawyer would want to have except one thing: a case. He doesn't have a case. Were I allowed to defend myself, I could have proven this to you ...

'The evidence in this case is a gun. There was a gun that laid around the ranch. It belonged to everybody. Anybody could have picked that gun up and done anything they wanted to do with it. I don't deny having that gun. That gun has been in my possession many times.

'Like the rope was there.' Sure he'd bought the rope, Manson admitted, 150 feet of it, 'because you need rope on a ranch'.

The clothes? 'It is really convenient that Mr Baggot found those clothes. I imagine he got a little taste of money for that.'

The bloodstains? 'Well, they are not exactly bloodstains. They are benzidine reaction.'

The leather thong? 'How many people have ever worn moccasins with leather thongs?'

The photos of the seven bodies, 169 stab wounds? 'They put the hideous bodies on display and they imply: If he gets out, see what will happen to you.'

Helter Skelter? 'It means confusion, literally. It doesn't mean any war with anyone. It doesn't mean that some people are going to kill other people ... Helter Skelter is confusion. Confusion is coming down around you fast. If you can't see the confusion coming down around you fast, you can call it what you wish.'

Conspiracy? 'Is it a conspiracy that the music is telling the youth to rise up against the establishment because the establishment is rapidly destroying things? Is that a conspiracy?

'The music speaks to you every day, but you are too deaf, dumb, and blind to even listen to the music ...'

'It is not my conspiracy. It is not my music. I hear what it relates. It says "Rise," it says "Kill."

'Why blame it on me? I didn't write the music.'

About the witnesses. 'For example, Danny DeCarlo. He said that I hate black men, and he said that we thought alike ... But actually all I ever did with Danny DeCarlo or any other human being was reflect him back at himself. If he said he did not like the black man, I would say "O.K." So consequently he would drink another beer and walk off and say "Charlie thinks like I do."

'But actually he does not know how Charlie thinks because Charlie has never projected himself.

'I don't think like you people. You people put importance on your lives. Well, my life has never been important to anyone ...'

Linda Kasabian. She only testified against him because she saw him as her father and she never liked her father. 'So she gets on the stand and she says when she looked in that man's eyes that was dying, she knew that it was *my* fault. She knew it was my fault because she couldn't face death. And if she can't face death, that is not my fault. I can face death. I have all the time. In the penitentiary you live with it, with constant fear of death, because it is a violent world in there, and you have to be on your toes constantly.'

Dianne Lake. She wanted attention. She would make trouble, cause accidents to get it. She wanted a father to punish her. 'So as any father would do, I conditioned her mind with pain to keep her from burning the ranch down.'

Yes, he was a father to the young girls and boys in the Family.

But a father only in the sense that he taught them 'not to be weak and not to lean on me'. Paul Watkins wanted a father. 'I told him: "To be a man, boy, you have to stand up and be your own father." So he goes off to the desert and finds a father image in Paul Crockett.'

Yes, he put a knife to Juan Flynn's throat. Yes, he told him he felt responsible for all of these killings. 'I do feel some responsibility. I feel a responsibility for the pollution. I feel a responsibility for the whole thing.'

He didn't deny that he had told Brooks Poston to get a knife and go kill the sheriff of Shoshone. 'I don't know the sheriff of Shoshone. I am not saying that I didn't say it, but if I said it, at the time I may have thought it was a good idea.

'To be honest with you, I don't recall ever saying "Get a knife and a change of clothes and go do what Tex says." Or I don't recall saying "Get a knife and go kill the sheriff."

'In fact, it makes me mad when someone kills snakes or dogs or cats or horses. I don't even like to eat meat – that is how much I am against killing . . .

'I haven't got any guilt about anything because I have never been able to see any wrong . . . I have always said: Do what your love tells you, and I do what my love tells me . . . Is it *my* fault that your children do what *you* do?

'*What about your children?*' Manson asked angrily, rising slightly in the witness chair as if he were about to spring forward and attack everyone in the courtroom. '*You say there are just a few?*

'*There are many, many more, coming in the same direction.*

'*They are running in the streets – and they are coming right at you!*'

I had only a few questions for Manson, none of which came from the notebooks I'd kept.

Q. 'You say you are already dead, is that right, Charlie?'

A. 'Dead in your mind or dead in my mind?'

Q. 'Define it any way you want to.'

A. 'As any child will tell you, dead is when you are no more. It

481

is just when you are not there. If you weren't there, you would be dead.'

Q. 'How long have you been dead?'

Manson evaded a direct reply.

Q. 'To be precise about it, you think you have been dead for close to 2,000 years, don't you?'

A. 'Mr Bugliosi, 2,000 years is relative to the second we live in.'

Q. 'Suffice it to say, Department 104 is a long way from Calvary, isn't that true?'

Manson had testified that all he wanted was to take his children and return to the desert. After I reminded him that 'the only people who can set you free so that you can go back to the desert are the twelve jurors in this case', and noting that, though he had testified for over an hour, 'the jury in this case never heard a single, solitary word you said', I posed one final question: 'Mr Manson, are you willing to testify in front of the jury and tell them the same things that you have testified to here in open court today?'

Kanarek objected. Older sustained the objection, and I concluded my cross.

To my surprise, Older later asked me why I hadn't seriously cross-examined Manson. I'd thought the reason was obvious. I had nothing to gain. Even had I succeeded in goading Manson into confessing the murders, that confession would have been valueless, since the jury wasn't present. I had lots and lots of questions for Charlie, several notebooks full, *if* he took the stand in the presence of the jury, but in the meantime I had no intention of giving him a dry run.

However, when Older asked Manson if he now wished to testify before the jury, Charlies replied, 'I have already relieved all the pressure I had.'

As Manson left the stand and passed the counsel table, I overheard him tell the three girls: 'You don't have to testify now.'

The big question: what did he mean by 'now'? I strongly suspected that Manson hadn't given up but was only biding his time.

After the defense had introduced their exhibits, Judge Older recessed court for ten days to give the attorneys time to prepare their jury instructions and arguments.

This being his first trial, Ron Hughes had never argued before a jury before, or participated in drawing up the instructions which the judge would give the jury just before they began their deliberations. He was obviously looking forward to it, however. He confided to TV newscaster Stan Atkinson that he was convinced he could win an acquittal for Leslie Van Houten.

He wouldn't even get the chance to try.

When court resumed on Monday, November 30, Ronald Hughes was absent.

Quizzed by Older, none of the other defense attorneys knew where he was. Fitzgerald said that he had last talked to Ron on Thursday or Friday, and that he sounded O.K. at that time. Hughes often spent his weekends camping at Sespe Hot Springs, a rugged terrain some 130 miles northwest of Los Angeles. There had been floods in the area the past weekend. It was possible that Hughes had been stranded there.

The next day we learned that Hughes had gone to Sespe on Friday with two teen-agers, James Forsher and Lauren Elder, in Miss Elder's Volkswagen. The pair – who were questioned but not held – said that when it began raining, they had decided to return to L.A., but Hughes had decided to stay over until Sunday. When the two tried to leave, however, their auto became mired down, and they were forced to abandon it and hike out.

Three other youths had seen Hughes on the morning of the following day, Saturday the twenty-eighth. He was alone at the time and on high ground, well away from the flood area. Chatting with them briefly, he appeared neither ill nor in any danger.

Owing to the continued bad weather, it was two days before the Ventura Sheriff's Office could get up a helicopter to search the area. In the meantime, rumors abounded. One was to the effect that Hughes had deliberately skipped, either to avoid argument or to sabotage the trial. Knowing Ron, I seriously doubted if this was true. I became convinced it wasn't when reporters visited the place where Hughes lived.

He slept on a mattress in a garage behind the home of a friend. According to reporters, the place was a mess – one remarked that he wouldn't even let his dog sleep there. But on the wall of the garage, neatly framed and carefully hung, was Ronald Hughes' bar certificate.

Although there were numerous reports that a man fitting Hughes' description had been seen in various places – boarding a bus in Reno, driving on the San Bernardino freeway, drinking at a bar in Baja – none checked out. On December 2, Judge Older told Leslie Van Houten that he felt a co-counsel should be brought in to represent her during Hughes' absence. Leslie said she would refuse any other attorney.

On December 3, after consulting with Paul Fitzgerald, Older appointed Maxwell Keith co-counsel for Leslie.

A quiet, somewhat shy man in his mid-40s, whose conservative clothing and courtroom manner were in sharp contrast to those of Hughes, Keith had an excellent reputation in the legal community. Those who knew him well described him as conscientious, totally ethical, and completely professional, and it was clear from the start that he would be representing his client and not Manson.

Sensing this, Manson asked to have all the defence attorneys dismissed ('They aren't our lawyers; they won't listen to us') so he and the girls could represent themselves. He also demanded that the case be reopened so they could put on a defense. They had twenty-one witnesses waiting to testify, he said. Both requests were denied.

Keith had his work laid out for him. Before he could prepare his argument, he had to familiarize himself with 152 volumes of transcript, over 18,000 pages.

Though Older granted a delay until he could do so, he told all counsel: 'We will continue to meet every day at 9 A.M. until further notice.'

Older obviously wanted to count heads.

Several days earlier Steve Kay had overheard Manson tell the girls, 'Watch Paul; I think he's up to something. I made sure

Fitzgerald learned of the conversation. One missing attorney was one more than enough.

Neither the air search nor a subsequent ground search of the Sespe area yielded any trace of Hughes. The abandoned Volkswagen was found, with a batch of court transcripts inside, but other papers Hughes was known to have had, including a secret psychiatric report on Leslie Van Houten, were missing.

On December 6, Paul Fitzgerald told reporters, 'I think Ron is dead.' On December 7, an all-points bulletin was issued for Hughes, LASO admitting, 'This is something you do when you have no other leads.' On December 8, Judge Older went to the Ambassador Hotel to inform the jury of the reason for the delay. He also told them: 'It appears fairly certain that you will be sequestered over the Christmas holidays.' They took it much better than expected. On December 12, the search for Ronald Hughes was suspended.

The most persistent rumor was that Hughes had been murdered by the Family. There was, at this time, no evidence of this. But there was more than ample cause for speculation.

Though once little more than an errand boy for Manson, during the course of the trial Hughes had grown increasingly independent, until the two had finally split over whether there should be a defense – Hughes strongly opposing his client's taking the stand to absolve Charlie. I also heard from several sources, including Paul Fitzgerald, that Hughes was afraid of Manson. It was possible that he showed this fear, which, in Manson's case, was like waving a red flag before a bull. Fear turned Charlie on.

There could have been several reasons for his murder, if it was that. It may have been done to intimidate the other defense attorneys into letting Manson put on a defense during the penalty trial (one was so shaken by Hughes' disappearance that he went on a bender which ended in his arrest for drunken driving). Equally likely, it could have been a tactic to delay the trial – with the hope

485

that it would result in a mistrial, or set the stage for a reversal on appeal.

Speculation, nothing more. Except for one odd, perhaps unrelated, incident. On December 2, four days after Hughes was last seen alive, fugitives Bruce Davis and Nancy Pitman, aka Brenda McCann, voluntarily surrendered to the police. Two of the Family's most hard-core members, Pitman had been missing for several weeks after failing to appear for sentencing on a forgery charge, while Davis – who had been involved in both the Hinman and Shea murders, who had picked up the gun with which Zero had 'committed suicide' but had somehow left no prints, and who was the chief suspect in the slaying of two young Scientology students* – had evaded capture for over seven months.

Maybe it was just the proximity in time that linked the two events in my mind: Hughes' disappearance; Davis' and Pitman's surprise surrender. But I couldn't shake the feeling that in some way the two incidents might be related.

On December 18 – three days before the Tate-LaBianca trial reconvened – the Los Angeles County grand jury indicted Steve Grogan, aka Clem; Lynette Fromme, aka Squeaky; Ruth Ann Moorehouse, aka Ouisch; Catherine Share, aka Gypsy; and Dennis Rice on charges of conspiracy to prevent and dissuade a witness (Barbara Hoyt) from attending a trail. Three other charges, including conspiracy to commit murder, were dismissed by Judge Choate on a 995 motion by the defense.

Although we had presumed – as I suspected the involved Family members had also – that an overdose of LSD could be fatal, we learned from medical experts that there was no known case of anyone's dying from this cause. There were many cases, however, where LSD had resulted in death from misperception of surroundings: for example, a person, convinced he could fly, stepping out the window of a tall building. I thought of Barbara, running through the traffic in downtown Honolulu. That she hadn't been killed was no fault of the Family. The result, how-

---

* These murders will be discussed in a later chapter.

ever, was that, despite the best efforts of the LaBianca detectives, the D A's Office had a very weak case.

Pending trial, four of the five were released on bail. They immediately returned to the corner outside the Hall of Justice, where they would remain, on and off, during most of the remainder of the trial. Since Ouisch, who had given Barbara the LSD-laden hamburger, was nearly nine months pregnant, Judge Choate released her on her own recognizance. She promptly fled the state.

Nancy Pitman, who had been arrested with Davis, was freed on the forgery charge. She was rearrested a few weeks later while trying to pass Manson a tab of LSD in the visitors' room at the County Jail. After serving thirty days, she was again freed, to rejoin the group on the corner and, subsequently, to become involved in still another murder.

December 21, 1970–January 25, 1971

When court reconvened, the four defendants created a disturbance – Manson throwing a paper clip at the judge, the girls accusing him of 'doing away with Hughes' – all obviously planned actions to garner the day's headlines.

Older ordered the four removed. As Sadie was being escorted out, she passed behind me. Though I didn't see what happened, I felt it: she knocked over an exhibit board, hitting me on the back of the head. Those who witnessed the incident said it appeared she was lunging for the Buck knife, which was on a nearby table. Thereafter the knife was kept well out of the reach of the defendants.

Maxwell Keith then told the Court that though he now felt himself familiar with the evidence, from having read the transcripts and other documents, he was not at all sure he could effectively represent his client, since he had not been present when the witnesses testified and therefore could not judge their demeanor or credibility. On this basis, he requested a mistrial.

Though Keith argued persuasively, Judge Older denied the motion, observing that every day attorneys argue cases in appellate courts without having been present during the actual trials.

Once this and several other motions were out of the way, it was time for the People's opening argument.*

During the guilt phase of a trial in California, the prosecution delivers an opening argument, which is followed by the opening argument of the defense (or rebuttal), and, last, a closing argu-

---

* This is entirely separate from the opening statement, which is delivered at the start of the trial.

ment (or final summation) by the prosecution. Thus the People have the last word during the guilt trial.

During the penalty trial, if there is one, each side gives two arguments, with the defense being allowed to argue last.

I had spent several hundred hours preparing my opening argument for the guilt trial, starting even before the beginning of the trial itself. The result was contained in some 400 handwritten pages. But by this time I knew their contents so well I didn't even need to read them, but only glanced at them periodically.

I began by discussing in depth, with charts and other aids, the points of law the jury would have to consider: murder, conspiracy, and so on. The instructions which the judge would give the jury are printed, formal statements of law that use nebulous, abstract terms that often even lawyers don't understand. Moreover, the judge does not tell the jury how these rules of law apply to the facts of the case. Thus, in the jury's mind, the rules are floating lazily in the air with no thread connecting them to anything tangible. In each case I try, I make it a point to supply that link, by the liberal use of common-sense examples, by translating legalese into words and thoughts the jury will understand, and by literally tying those rules to the evidence.

After I had done this, I got into the principal part of my opening argument, summarizing the testimony of each witness, often quoting verbatim the words he had used on the stand, interrelating this testimony with the other evidence, and drawing inferences from it. Though the presentation took three days, it was a tight, cohesive package, and by the time I had finished I felt confident that I had established, beyond all doubt, Manson's control, his motives, his involvement, and the involvement of Watson, Atkins, Krenwinkel and Van Houten.

Apparently it got to Charlie. At the end of my opening statement, he had tried to bribe deputy Maupin to free him. The night after I completed the first day of my opening argument, he tried to break out of jail.

Though the incident was officially denied by LASO, one of the deputies told me the details. Despite daily searches of both his person and his cell, Manson had managed to obtain an incredibly long piece of string, at the end of which he had attached a small weight. By some unknown means or manner – for the area was supposedly under constant surveillance – he had got the string across the walkway in front of his cell and out a window, where it reached a full ten stories to the ground. One or more confederates then attached the contraband. However, something must have happened which prevented Manson from pulling it up, for when a deputy came around the corner of the Hall of Justice the next morning, he spotted the string and its cargo: a lid of marijuana and a hacksaw blade.

Accepting a promise that they would behave, Judge Older permitted the three female defendants to return to court the next afternoon. Manson, who said he had no desire to return, remained in the lockup, listening to the proceedings from there.

I had just resumed my argument when Leslie created a disturbance. Sadie and Katie followed suit, and each of the three was again ordered removed. This time Sadie was led in front of the lectern where I was standing. Suddenly, without warning, she kicked one of the female deputies in the leg, then grabbed some of my notes, tearing them in half. Grabbing them back, I involuntarily muttered, 'You little bitch!'

Though provoked, I regretted losing my cool.

The next day the Long Beach *Independent* bore the following front-page headline:

MANSON PROSECUTOR

TAKES SWING AT SUSAN

According to reporter Mary Neiswender: 'The chaos was capped by the chief prosecutor swearing at and attempting to slug one of the defendants . . . Bugliosi slapped the girl's hand, grabbed his notes and then swung at her shouting, "You little bitch!" '

In common with everyone else in the courtroom, Judge Older saw the incident somewhat differently. Describing it for the record, he branded the charge that I was struggling with Susan 'absolutely false. There was no struggle between Mr Bugliosi and anybody. What happened was [she] walked by the rostrum and grabbed the notes off the rostrum.'

After Krenwinkel had been removed, Judge Older called counsel to the bench and said that he had had it. 'It is perfectly obvious to the Court that after lo, these many months, the defendants are operating in concert with each other ... I don't think any American court is required to subject itself to this kind of nonsense day after day when it is perfectly obvious that the defendants are using it as a stage for some kind of performance ...' Older then stated that the defendants would not be permitted to return to court during the remainder of the guilt trial.

I had hoped to finish my argument before court recessed for the Christmas holiday, but Kanarek's multitudinous objections prevented my doing so.

The feelings of the jurors at being sequestered over Christmas were exemplified by one who hung up the hotel menu and wrote 'BAH HUMBUG' across it. Though they were permitted family visits, and special parties had been arranged at the Ambassador, it was for most a miserable time. None had anticipated being away from home this long. Many were worried whether they would still have their jobs when the trial ended. And no one, including the judge, would even venture a guess when that might be.

On weekends both jurors and alternates – always accompanied by two male and two female deputies – had taken trips to such places as Disneyland, the movie studios, the San Diego Zoo, many probably seeing more of Southern California than they had in the whole of their lives. They had dinner at restaurants all over Los Angeles. They went bowling, swimming, even nightclubbing. But this was only partial compensation for their long ordeal.

The strain was getting to them. Older people for the most part, they were set in their ways. Inevitably, arguments broke out, factions developed. One temperamental male juror slapped bailiff Ann Orr one night when, against his wishes, she changed channels on the communal TV. Often Murray and Orr sat up to 4 or

5 A.M., listening to a juror's complaints. As we neared the end of the guilt trial, I began worrying not about the evidence but about the personal disagreements the jurors might be carrying into the jury room with them when they began their deliberations.

It only takes one person to hang up a jury.

I concluded my opening argument on Monday, December 28, by telling the jury what I thought the defense's case would be, thereby lessening the psychological impact of the defense attorneys' arguments.

'The defense will probably argue that there is no conspiracy ... They will tell you that the Helter Skelter motive is absurd, ridiculous, unbelievable ... They will tell you that the interpretation of the Beatles' songs by Manson was normal ... They will tell you that Linda is insane with LSD; that she made up her story to be granted immunity; that Linda's testimony as an accomplice has not been corroborated ... Probably they will tell you the reason why they never put on a defense is because the prosecution never proved their case ... They will tell you that Charles Manson is not a killer; he wouldn't harm a flea.

'They will tell you that Charlie was not the leader of the Family; he never ordered these murders ... They will tell you that this has been a case of circumstantial evidence – as if there is something wrong with circumstantial evidence – completely disregarding the direct evidence by the way of Linda's testimony.

'Out of 18,000 pages of transcript, they will come up here and there with a slight discrepancy between the testimony of one witness and another witness, which of course has to be expected, but they will tell you this means that the People's witnesses are liars.'

I then asked the jury as intelligent men and women to conscientiously evaluate the evidence in this case, applying common sense and reason, and thereby reach a just and fair verdict.

'Under the law of this state and nation these defendants are entitled to have their day in court. They got that.

'They are also entitled to have a fair trail by an impartial jury. They also got that.

'That is all that they are entitled to!

'Since they committed these seven senseless murders, the People of the State of California are entitled to a guilty verdict.'

Toward the opening of his argument for Patricia Krenwinkel, Paul Fitzgerald said, 'If we set out to rebut every witness the prosecution put on that stand we would be here until 1974,' unthinkingly emphasizing the strength of the People's case, as well as the defense's inability to answer it.

Fitzgerald's argument was very disappointing. Not only were there many things he could have argued but didn't, he repeatedly misstated the evidence. He said that Sebring was hanged; that all the victims had been stabbed to death; that Tim Ireland heard Parent scream. He referred to Sharon as 'Mary Polanski'; he had the killers entering the Tate residence through a bedroom window; he confused how many times Frykowski had been stabbed and struck. He said Linda testified to five knives rather than three; he had Linda driving on the second night when Manson was, and vice versa; he had a deputy who wasn't even present arresting Manson during the Spahn raid; and so on.

Only a small portion of Fitzgerald's argument was devoted to the evidence against his client. And rebuttal it was not.

'If you were a mastermind criminal, if you had absolute power over the minds and bodies of bootlicking slaves, as they were referred to, would you send women out to do a man's job? ... Women, ladies and gentlemen, are life-givers. They make love, they get pregnant, they deliver babies. They are life-givers, not takers away. Women are adverse to violence ...'

He said that 'there is doubt as to whether or not that fingerprint [found at the Tate residence] belongs to Patricia Krenwinkel'. Even presuming it did, he said, 'It is entirely conceivable, possible, and reasonable that Patricia Krenwinkel was at that house as an invited guest or a friend.'

Some friend!

Fitzgerald did spend a great deal of time trying to destroy the credibility of Linda Kasabian. In my argument I had remarked: 'Linda Kasabian was on that witness stand, ladies and gentlemen, for eighteen days – an extraordinarily long period of time for any witness to testify in any case. I think you will agree with me that during those eighteen days Linda Kasabian and the truth were companions.' Fitzgerald challenged this. But he was unable to cite a single discrepancy in her account.

However, the greater portion of his argument dealt with the case against Charles Manson. All the testimony regarding Manson's philosophy proved, Fitzgerald said, was 'that he is some sort of right-wing hippie'. Manson, Manson, Manson.

Fitzgerald ended his argument with a long, impassioned plea – not for his client, Patricia Krenwinkel, but for Charles Manson. There was, he concluded, insufficient evidence against Manson.

Not once did he say that there was insufficient evidence against Patricia Krenwinkel.

Nor did he even ask the jury to come back with a not guilty verdict for his client!

Daye Shinn had prepared a chart listing all the witnesses who testified against his client, Susan Atkins. He said he would rebut each.

'The first one on the list is Linda Kasabian, and I believe Mr Fitzgerald has adequately covered Miss Kasabian's testimony.'

He then skimmed over the criminal records of DeCarlo, Howard, Graham, and Walker.

On Danny DeCarlo: 'How would you like to have him for your son-in-law? How would you like to have him meet your daughters?'

On Virginia Graham: 'How would you like to invite her to your house for Christmas? You would have to hide the silverware.

'Mr Bugliosi is laughing. As least I did not put him to sleep.'

Shinn's entire argument took only 38 pages of transcript.

Irving Kanarek, who followed Shinn, consumed 1,182.

For the most part, Kanarek ignored my argument against Manson. Remaining on the offense rather than taking the defense, he pounded home two names – Tex, Linda. Who was it Linda Kasabian first slept with at Spahn Ranch? Stole the $5,000 for? Accompanied to the Tate residence? Charles 'Tex' Watson. The most logical explanation for these murders was the simplest, Kanarek said. 'Love of a girl for a boy.'

As for his client, Kanarek portrayed him as a peaceful man whose only sin, if he had one, was that he preached and practiced love. 'Now the people who brought these charges, they want to get Charles Manson, for some ungodly reason, which I think is related to Manson's life style.'

Though many of his statements seemed to me to be too ridiculous for comment, I took many notes during Kanarek's argument. For he also planted little doubts, which, unless rebutted, could grow into bigger ones when the jury began its deliberations.

If the purpose was to start a black-white war, why did it stop the second night? Why wasn't there a third night, and a fourth? ... Why didn't the prosecution bring in Nader, and the policemen on the beach, and the man whose life Linda *claimed* to have saved? ... Are we to believe that by means of a wallet found in a toilet tank Mr Manson intended to start a race war? ... If Tex pushed Parent's car up the driveway, why weren't his prints found on it?

At the end of Kanarek's second day of argument, Judge Older told him that he was putting the jury to sleep. 'Now, I am not going to tell you how to make an argument,' Older said at the bench, 'but I would suggest to you that you may not be doing your client the utmost amount of good by prolonging it unduly ...'

He went on for a third day, and a fourth.

On the fifth day the jury sent a note to the bailiff, requesting NoDoz for themselves and sleeping pills for Mr Kanarek.

On the sixth day Older warned Kanarek, 'You are abusing your right to argue just as you have abused practically every other right you have in this case ... There is a point, Mr Kanarek, at which argument is no longer argument but a filibuster ... Yours is reaching that point.'

Kanarek went on another full day before bringing his argument to an end with the statement: 'Charles Manson is not guilty of *any* crime.'

Several times during Kanarek's argument Manson had interrupted with remarks from the lockup. Once he shouted, loud enough for the jury to hear, 'Why don't you sit down? You're just making things worse.'

During one of the noon recesses Manson asked to see me. I'd turned down several earlier requests, with the comment that I'd talk to him when he took the stand, but this time I decided to see what he wanted.

I was glad I did, as it was one of the most informative conversations we had – Manson telling me exactly how he felt about his three female co-defendants.

Manson wanted to clear up a couple of wrong impressions. One was Fitzgerald's reference to him as a 'right-wing hippie'. Though I personally thought the description had some validity, Manson felt otherwise. He'd never thought of himself as a hippie, he said. 'Hippies don't like the establishment so they back off and form their own establishment. They're no better than the others.'

He also didn't want me to think that Sadie, Katie, and Leslie were the best he could do. 'I've screwed girls that would make these three look like boys,' he said.

For some reason it was important to Manson that I believe this, and he re-emphasized it, adding, 'I'm a very selfish guy. I don't give a fuck for these girls. I'm only out for myself.'

'Have you ever told them that, Charlie?' I asked.

'Sure. Ask them.'

'Then why would they do what they're doing for you? Why would they be willing to follow you anywhere – even to the green room at San Quentin?'

'Because I tell them the truth,' Manson replied. 'Other guys bullshit them and say "I love you and only you" and all that baloney. I'm honest with them. I tell them I'm the most selfish guy in the world. And I am.'

Yet he was always saying that he would die for his brother, I reminded him. Wasn't that a contradiction?

'No, because that's selfish too,' he responded. 'He's not going to die for me unless I'm willing to die for him.'

I had the strong feeling that Manson was leveling with me. Sadie, Katie, and Leslie were willing to murder, even give their own lives, for Charlie. And Charlie personally couldn't have cared less about them.

Though he wasn't even present when the witnesses testified, Maxwell Keith, arguing for Leslie Van Houten, delivered the best of the four defense arguments. He also did what no other defense attorney had dared do during the entire trial. He put the hat on Charles Manson – albeit with a ten-foot pole.

'The record discloses over and over again that all of these girls at the ranch believed Manson was God, really believed it.

'The record discloses that the girls obeyed his commands without any conscious questioning at all.

'If you believe the prosecution theory that these female defendants and Mr Watson were extensions of Mr Manson – his additional arms and legs as it were – if you believe that they were mindless robots, they cannot be guilty of premeditated murder.' To commit first degree murder, Keith argued, you must have malice aforethought and you must think and plan. 'And these people did not have minds to make up . . . Each of the minds of these girls and Mr Watson were totally controlled by someone else.'

As for Leslie herself, Keith argued that even if she did all the things the prosecution contended, she still had committed no crime.

'At best, if you want to believe Dianne Lake, the evidence shows that she was there.

'At best, it shows that she did something after the commission of these homicides that wasn't very nice.

'And at best, it showed that she wiped some fingerprints off after the commission of these homicides, which does not make her an aider and abetter.

'As repugnant as you may feel this is, nobody in the world can be guilty of murder or conspiracy to commit murder who stabs somebody after they are already dead. I'm sure that desecrating somebody that is dead is a crime in this state, but she is not charged with that.'

This case, Keith concluded, must be decided on the basis of the evidence, and 'on the basis of the evidence, ladies and gentlemen, I say to you: You must acquit Leslie Van Houten.'

I began my final summation (closing argument) on January 13.

In my opinion, final summation is very often the most important part of the trial, since it's the last, final word to the jury. Again, several hundred hours had gone into the preparation. I began by meeting head on each of the defense contentions. In this way I hoped to dispose of any questions or lingering doubts that otherwise might distract the jury during the last phase of my argument, during which I summarized, as affirmatively as I could the highlights and strengths of my case.

Taking on each of the defense attorneys in turn, I cited twenty-four misstatements of either the law or the testimony in Fitzgerald's presentation. As for his suggestion that if Manson ordered these murders he would have sent men rather than women, I asked, 'Is Mr Fitzgerald suggesting that Katie, Sadie, and Leslie were inadequate to do the job? Isn't Mr Fitzgerald satisfied with their handiwork?'

Shinn had raised very few points that needed rebutting. Kanarek had raised a great many, and I took them on one by one. A few samples:

Kanarek had asked why the prosecution didn't have the defendants try on the seven articles of clothing to see if they fitted. I reversed this, asking why, if they didn't fit, the defense didn't illustrate this to the jury.

As for the absence of Watson's prints on Parent's vehicle, I reminded them of Dolan's testimony that 70 percent of the times LAPD goes to a crime scene no readable prints are found. I also noted that in moving his hand, it was very likely Watson had created an unreadable smudge.

When I lacked the answer to a question, I frankly admitted it.

But usually I offered at least one and often several possibilities. Why was there no blood on the Buck knife found in the chair? Kanarek had raised this point. It was a good one. We had no answer. We could speculate, however, that Sadie had lost the knife before she stabbed Voytek and Sharon, possibly while she was in the process of tying up Voytek, and that at some later point she borrowed another knife from Katie or Tex. 'Much more important than what knife she used was the fact that she confessed stabbing both of the victims to Virginia Graham and Ronnie Howard.'

The whole thrust of Irving Kanarek's seven-day argument, I told the jury, was that the prosecution had framed its case against his client, Charles Manson.

'In other words, ladies and gentlemen,' I observed, 'there are seven brutal murders, so the police and the District Attorney got together and said, 'Let's prosecute some hippie for these murders, someone whose life style we don't like. Just about any hippie will do,' and we just arbitrarily picked on poor Charles Manson.

'Charles Manson is not a defendant in this trial because he is some long-haired vagabond who made love to young girls and was a virulent dissenter.

'He is on trial because he is a vicious, diabolical murderer who gave the order that caused seven human beings to end up in the cold earth. That is why he is on trial.'

I also hit, and hard, Kanarek's claim that the prosecution was responsible for the excessive length of the trial. The jury had missed both Christmas and New Year's at home, and I didn't want them entering the jury chambers resenting the prosecution for this.

'Irving Kanarek, the Toscanini of tedium, is accusing the prosecution of tying up this court for over six months. You folks are the best witnesses. Every single, solitary witness that the prosecution called to the stand was asked brief questions, directly to the point. The witnesses were on that stand day after day on cross-examination, not on direct examination.'

As for Maxwell Keith, he did 'everything possible for his

client, Leslie Van Houten'. I observed. 'He gave his best. Unfortunately for Mr Keith, he had no facts and no law to support him. Mr Keith, if you look at his argument very closely, never really disputed that Linda Kasabian and Dianne Lake told the truth. Basically, his position was that even if Leslie did the things Linda and Dianne said she did, she is still not guilty of anything.

'I wonder if Max would concede that she is at least guilty of trespassing?'

KEITH. 'I will.'

Max's response surprised me. He was in effect admitting that Leslie had been in the LaBianca residence.

Even if Rosemary LaBianca was dead when Leslie stabbed her, I told the jury, she was guilty of first degree murder as both a co-conspirator and an aider and abetter. If a person is present at the scene of a crime, offering moral support, that constitutes aiding and abetting. But Leslie went far beyond this, stabbing, wiping prints, and so forth.

Also, we had only Leslie's word for it that Rosemary was dead when she stabbed her. 'Only thirteen of Rosemary's forty-one stab wounds were post-mortem. What about the other twenty-eight?'

Yes, Tex, Sadie, Katie, and Leslie were robots, zombies, automatons. No question about it. But only in the sense that they were totally subservient and obsequious and servile to Charles Manson. Only in that sense. 'This does not mean that they did not want to do what Charles Manson told them to do and weren't very willing participants in these murders. To the contrary, all the evidence goes the other way. There is no evidence that any of these defendants objected to Charles Manson about his two horrendous nights of murder.

'Only Linda Kasabian, down in Venice, said: "Charlie, I am not you. I can't kill." '

The others not only didn't complain, I noted, they laughed when the Tate murders were described on TV; Leslie told Dianne that stabbing was fun, that the more she stabbed the more she enjoyed it; while Sadie told Virginia and Ronnie that it was better than a sexual climax.

'The fact that these three female defendants obeyed Charles

Manson and did whatever he told them to do does not immunize them from a conviction of first degree murder. It offers no insulation, no protection whatsoever. If it did, then hired killers or trigger men for the Mafia would have a built-in defense for murder. All they would have to say is: 'Well, I did what my boss told me to do." '

Mr Keith also 'suggested that Watson and the three girls had some type of mental disability which prevented them from deliberating and premeditating, even prevented them from having malice aforethought'. The problem with this, I told the jury, was that the defense never introduced any evidence of insanity or diminished capacity; on the contrary, I reminded the jury, Fitzgerald described the girls as 'bright, intuitive, perceptive, well educated', while the evidence itself showed 'these defendants were thinking very, very clearly on these two nights of murder'.

Cutting telephone wires, instructing Linda to listen for sounds, hosing blood off their bodies, disposing of their clothing and weapons, wiping prints – 'their conduct clearly and unequivocally shows that on both nights they knew exactly what they were doing, that they intended to kill, they did kill, and they did everything possible to avoid detection.

'They were not suffering, ladies and gentlemen, from any diminished mental capacity. They were suffering from a diminished heart, a diminished soul.'

Still up to his old tricks, Kanarek had constantly interrupted my argument with frivolous objections. Even after another contempt citation and a $100 fine, Kanarek persisted. Calling counsel to the bench, Judge Older stated: 'I have come to the regretful conclusion during the course of the trial that Mr Kanarek appears to be totally without scruples, ethics, and professional responsibility so far as the trial of this lawsuit is concerned, and I want the record to clearly reflect that.'

KANEREK. 'May I be sworn?'

THE COURT. 'Mr Kanarek, I wouldn't believe you if you were.'

With the defense arguments out of the way, I spent an entire afternoon reviewing the eyewitness testimony of Linda Kasabian. Among the instructions Judge Older was going to give the jury was one regarding the testimony of an accomplice. Both Fitzgerald and Kanarek had read the start of it: 'The testimony of an accomplice ought to be viewed with distrust.' They stopped there, however. I read the jury the rest: 'This does not mean that you may arbitrarily disregard such testimony, but you should give it the weight to which you find it to be entitled after examining it with care and caution in the light of all the evidence in this case.'

I then took the evidence of other witnesses, totally independent of Linda Kasabian, and showed how it confirmed or supported her testimony. Linda testified that Watson shot Parent four times. Dr Noguchi testified that Parent was shot four times. Linda testified that Parent slumped over toward the passenger side. The police photographs show Parent slumped over toward the passenger side. Linda testified that Watson slit the screen horizontally. Officer Whisenhunt testified that the screen was slit horizontally. For the night of the Tate murders alone, I noted forty-five instances where other evidence confirmed Linda's account.

I concluded: 'Ladies and gentlemen, the fingerprint evidence, the firearms evidence, the confessions, and all of the other evidence would convince the world's leading skeptic that Linda Kasabian was telling the truth.'

I then cited every single piece of evidence against each of the defendants, starting with the girls and ending with Manson himself. I also noted that there were 238 references in the transcript to Manson's domination.

Helter Skelter. During the trail the evidence of this had come in piece by piece, from the mouths of many witnesses. I assembled those pieces now, in one devastating package. Very forcefully, and I felt convincingly, I proved that Helter Skelter was the motive for these murders, and that that motive belonged to Charles Manson and Charles Manson alone.

We were nearly finished now. Within a few hours the jury

would begin its deliberations. I ended my summation on a very powerful note.

'Charles Manson, ladies and gentlemen, said that he had the power to give life. On the nights of the Tate-LaBianca murders, he thought he had the concomitant right to take human life.

'He never had the right, but he did it anyway.

'On the hot summer night of August the eighth, 1969, Charles Manson, the Mephistophelean guru who raped and bastardized the minds of all those who gave themselves so totally to him, sent out from the fires of hell at Spahn Ranch three heartless, bloodthirsty robots and – unfortunately for him – one human being, the little hippie girl Linda Kasabian.

'The photographs of the victims show how very well Watson, Atkins, and Krenwinkel carried out their master Charles Manson's mission of murder ...

'What resulted was perhaps the most inhuman, nightmarish, horror-filled hour of savage murder and human slaughter in the recorded annals of crime. As the helpless, defenseless victims begged and screamed out into the night for their lives, their lifeblood gushed out of their bodies, forming rivers of gore.

'If they could have, I am sure that Watson, Atkins, and Krenwinkel would gladly have swum in that river of blood, and with orgasmic ecstasy on their faces. Susan Atkins, the vampira, actually tasted Sharon Tate's blood ...

'The very next night, Leslie Van Houten joined the group of murderers, and it was poor Leno and Rosemary LaBianca who were brutally butchered to death to satisfy Charles Manson's homicidal madness ...

'The prosecution put on a monumental amount of evidence against these defendants, much of it scientific, all of it conclusively proving that these defendants committed these murders.

'Based on the evidence that came from that witness stand, not only isn't there any reasonable doubt of their guilt, which is our only burden, there is absolutely no doubt whatsoever of their guilt ...

'Ladies and gentlemen, the prosecution did its job in gathering and presenting the evidence. The witnesses did their job by taking that witness stand and testifying under oath. Now you are the last link in the chain of justice.

'I respectfully ask that after your deliberations you come back into this courtroom with the following verdict.' I then read in full the verdict the People wished.

I came now to the end of my argument, what the newspapers would call the 'roll call of the dead'. After each name I paused, so the jurors could recall the person.

'Ladies and gentlemen of the jury,' I quietly began, 'Sharon Tate ... Abigail Folger ... Voytek Frykowski ... Jay Sebring ... Steven Parent ... Leno LaBianca ... Rosemary LaBianca ... are not here with us now in this courtroom, *but from their graves they cry out for justice.* Justice can only be served by coming back to this courtroom with a verdict of guilty.'

Gathering up my notes, I thanked the jury for the patience and attention they had shown throughout the proceedings. It had been a very, very long trial, I noted, and an immense imposition on their personal and private lives. 'You have been an exemplary jury. The plaintiff at this trial is the People of the State of California. I have all the confidence in the world that you will not let them down.'

After the noon recess, Judge Older instructed the jury. At 3:20 P.M., on Friday, January 15, 1971 – exactly seven months after the start of the trial – the jury filed out to begin their deliberations.

The jury deliberated all day Saturday, then took Sunday off. On Monday they sent out two requests: that they be given a phonograph so they could play the Beatles' White Album, which, though introduced in evidence and much discussed, had never been played in court; and that they be permitted to visit the Tate and La Bianca residences.

After lengthy conferences with counsel, Older granted the first request but denied the second. Though admitting that, not having been to either of the death scenes, he too was naturally curious, the judge decided such visits would be tantamount to reopening the case, complete to the recalling of witnesses, cross cross-examination, and so on.

On Tuesday the jury asked to have Susan Atkins' letters to her former cellmates reread to them. This was done. Probably unprecedented in a case of this magnitude and complexity, at no time did the jury request that any of the actual testimony be reread. I could only surmise they were relying on the extensive notes each had taken throughout the trial.

Wednesday, Thursday, Friday – no further messages were received from the jury. Long before the end of the week the New York *Times* was reporting that the jury had been out too long, that it appeared they were deadlocked.

I wasn't bothered by this. I'd already told the press that I didn't expect them to come back for four or five days at the very minimum, and I wouldn't have been surprised had they stayed out a week and a half.

Nor did I worry about our having proven our case.

What did worry me was human nature.

Twelve individuals, from completely different backgrounds, had been locked up together longer than any jury in history. I thought a great deal about those twelve persons. One juror had let it be known that he intended to write a book about his experiences, and some of the other jurors were apprehensive about how they might be portrayed. The same juror also wanted to be elected foreman, and when he wasn't even in the running, was so piqued that for a day or two he wouldn't eat with the others.* Would he – or any of the other eleven – hang up the jury because of some personal animosity or slight? I didn't know.

Both Tubick and Roseland had daughters about the same age as Sadie, Katie, and Leslie. Would this affect their decision, and if so, how? Again I didn't know.

It was rumored, largely on the basis of glances they had exchanged in court, that the youngest member of the jury, William

---

* Alva Dawson, the ex-deputy sheriff, and Herman Tubick, the mortician, had tied. A coin was tossed, and Tubick was made foreman. A deeply religious man, who began and ended each day of deliberations with silent prayer, Tubick had been a stabilizing influence during the long sequestration.

McBride II, had become slightly enamored of defendant Leslie Van Houten. It was unsubstantiated gossip, yet in the long hours the press waited for some word from the jury room, reporters made bets on whether McBride would vote second degree for Leslie, or perhaps even acquittal.

Immediately after my assignment to the case, I'd requested as much information as was available on the background of Charles Manson. Like must of the evidence, it came in piecemeal. Not until after the People had rested their case did I finally receive the records covering the seven months Manson spent at the National Training School for Boys in Washington, D.C. I found most of the information already familiar, with one startling exception.

If true, it could very well be the seed which – nurtured with hate, fear, and love – flowered into Manson's monstrous, grotesque obsession with the black-white revolution.

Manson had been sent to the institution in March 1951, when he was 16 years old. In his admission summary, which was drawn up after he had been interviewed, there was a section on family background. The first two sentences read: 'Father: unknown. He is alleged to have been a colored cook by the name of Scott, with whom the boy's mother had been promiscuous at the time of pregnancy.'

Was Manson's father *black*? Reading through the rest of the records, I found two similar statements, though no additional details.

There were several possible explanations for the inclusion of this statement in Manson's records. The first was that it was totally erroneous: some bureaucratic snafu of which Manson himself may even have been unaware. Another possibility was that Manson had lied about this in his interviews, though I couldn't imagine any conceivable benefit he would derive, particularly in a reform school located in the South. It was also possible that it was true.

There was one further possibility, and in a sense it was even more important than whether the information was true or false.

Did young Charles Manson *believe* it to be true? If so, this would go a long way toward explaining the genesis of his bizarre philosophy, in which the blacks finally triumph over the whites but eventually have to hand over the reins of power to Manson himself.

I knew only one thing for sure. Even had I received this information earlier, I wouldn't have used it. It was much too inflammatory. I did decide, however, to ask Manson himself about it, if I got the chance.

I was in bed with the flu when, at 10:15 A.M. on Monday, January 25, court clerk Gene Darrow telephoned and said, 'Just got the word. The jury has reached a verdict. Judge Older wants to see all the attorneys in his chambers as soon as they can get here.'

The Hall of Justice resembled a fortress, as it had since the jury went out. A secret court order had been issued that same day, which began: 'Due to intelligence reports indicating a possible attempt to disrupt proceedings on what has been described as "Judgment Day" additional security measures will be implemented . . .' There followed twenty-seven pages of detailed instructions. The entire Hall of Justice had been sealed, anyone entering the building for whatever reason being given a personal effects and body search. I now had three bodyguards, the judge a like number.

The reason for this intensive security was never made public. From a source close to the Family, L A S O had heard what they initially believed to be an incredible tale. While working at Camp Pendleton Marine Base, one of Manson's followers had stolen a case of hand grenades. These were to be smuggled into court on 'Judgment Day' and used to free Manson.

Again, we didn't know precisely what the Family meant by Judgment Day. But by this time we did know that at least a part of the story was true. A Family member *had* been working in the arms depot at Pendleton, and after he quit, a case of hand grenades *was* missing.

By 11:15 all counsel were in chambers. Before bringing the jury in, Judge Older said he wanted to discuss the penalty trial.

California has a bifurcated trial system. The first phase, which we had just completed, was the guilt trial. If any of the defendants were convicted, a penalty trial would follow, in which the same jury would determine the penalty for the offense. In this case we had requested first degree murder verdicts against all the defendants. If the jury returned such verdicts, there were only two possible penalties: life imprisonment or death.

The penalty trial is, in most cases, very short.

After conferring with counsel, Judge Older decided that if there was a penalty phase, it would commence in three days. Older also said he had decided to seal the courtroom until after the verdicts were read and all the jurors polled. Once the jurors and the defendants had been removed, the press would be allowed out, and then the spectators.

The three girls were brought in first. Though they had usually worn fairly colorful clothing during the trial, apparently there hadn't been time for them to change, as all were wearing drab jail dresses. They seemed in good spirits, however, and were giggling and whispering. On being brought in, Manson winked at them and they winked back. Charlie was wearing a white shirt and blue scarf, and sporting a new, neatly trimmed goatee. Another face, for judgment day.

Single file, the jurors entered the jury box, taking their assigned seats, just as they had hundreds of times before. Only this time was different, and the spectators searched the twelve faces for clues. Perhaps the most common of all courtroom myths is that a jury won't look at the accused if they have reached a guilty verdict. This is rarely true. None held Manson's gaze when he stared at them, but then neither did they quickly look away. All you could really read in their faces was a tired tenseness.

THE COURT. 'All jurors and alternates are present. All counsel but Mr Hughes are present. The defendants are present. Mr Tubick, has the jury reached a verdict?'

TUBICK. 'Yes, Your Honor, we have.'

THE COURT. 'Will you hand the verdict forms to the bailiff.'

Foreman Tubick handed them to Bill Murray, who in turn

gave them to Judge Older. As he scanned them, saying nothing, Sadie, Leslie, and Katie fell silent and Manson nervously fingered his goatee.

THE COURT. 'The clerk will read the verdicts.'

CLERK. 'In the Superior Court of the State of California, in and for the County of Los Angeles, the People of the State of California vs Charles Manson, Patricia Krenwinkel, Susan Atkins, and Leslie Van Houten, Case No. A–253,156. Department 104.'

Darrow paused before reading the first of the twenty-seven separate verdicts. It seemed minutes but was probably only seconds. Everyone sat as if frozen, waiting.

'We, the jury in the above-entitled action, find the defendant, Charles Manson, *guilty* of the crime of murder of Abigail Folger in violation of Section 187, Penal Code of California, a felony, as charged in Count 1 of the Indictment, and we further find it to be murder of the first degree.'

Glancing at Manson, I noticed that, though his face was impassive, his hands were shaking. The girls displayed no emotion whatsoever.

The jury had deliberated for forty-two hours and forty minutes, over a nine-day period, a remarkably short time for such a long and complicated trial. The reading of the verdicts took thirty-eight minutes.

The People had obtained the verdicts they had requested against Charles Manson, Patricia Krenwinkel, and Susan Atkins: each had been found guilty of one count of conspiracy to commit murder and seven counts of murder in the first degree.

The People had also obtained the verdicts requested against Leslie Van Houten: she had been found guilty of one count of conspiracy to commit murder and two counts of murder in the first degree.

I later learned that although McBride had suggested the possibility of a lesser finding against Leslie Van Houten, when it came time to vote there was only one ballot and it was unanimous.

While the individual jurors were being polled, Leslie turned to Katie and said, 'Look at the jury; don't they look sad?' She was right, they did. Obviously it had been a very rough ordeal.

As the jury was being taken out, Manson suddenly yelled at Older: 'We are still not allowed to put on a defense? You won't outlive that, old man!'

The Manson girls on the corner outside the Hall of Justice first heard the news over the radio. They were strangely calm. Though Brenda told newsmen, 'There's a revolution coming, very soon,' and Sandy said, 'You are next, all of you,' these were Manson's words, delivered in court months before, which they had been mouthing ever since. There were no tears, no outward display of emotion. It was as if they really didn't care. Yet I knew this wasn't true.

Watching the interview later on TV, I surmised that perhaps they had conditioned themselves to expect the worst.

In retrospect, another possibility emerges. Once the lowest of the low in the Manson hierarchy, good only for sex, procreation, and serving men, the girls had now become his chief apostles, the keepers of the faith. Now Charlie was dependent on them. It appears quite likely that they were undisturbed by the verdict because they were already formulating a plan which, if all went well, could set not only Manson but all the other Family members free.

Part Eight

Fires In Your Cities

'Mr and Mrs America – you are wrong.
I am not the King of the Jews nor am
I a hippie cult leader. I am what you
have made of me and the mad dog devil
killer fiend leper is a reflection of
your society . . . Whatever the outcome of
this madness that you call a fair trial
or Christian justice, you can know
this: In my mind's eye my thoughts
light fires in your cities.'

> Statement issued by
> Charles Manson after
> his conviction for the
> Tate-LaBianca murders

January 26–March 17, 1971

During the penalty trial the sole issue for the jury to decide was whether the defendants should receive life imprisonment or the death penalty. Considerations like mitigating circumstances, background, remorse, and the possibility of rehabilitation were therefore now relevant.

To avoid prolonging the trial and risk alienating the jury, I called only two witnesses: officer Thomas Drynan and Bernard 'Lotsapoppa' Crowe.

Drynan testified that when he arrested Susan Atkins outside Stayton, Oregon, in 1966, she was carrying a .25 caliber pistol. 'I asked Miss Atkins what she intended to do with the gun,' Drynan recalled, 'and she told me that if she had the opportunity she would have shot and killed me.'

Drynan's testimony proved that even before Susan Atkins met Charles Manson she had murder in her heart.

Crowe described how, on the night of July 1, 1969, Manson had shot him in the stomach and left him for dead. The importance of Crowe's testimony was that it proved that Manson was quite capable of committing murder on his own.

On February 1, I rested the People's case. That afternoon the defense called their first witnesses: Katie's parents, Joseph and Dorothy Krenwinkel.

Joseph Krenwinkel described his daughter as an 'exceedingly normal child, very obedient'. She was a Bluebird, Camp Fire Girl, and Job's daughter, and belonged to the Audubon Society.

FITZGERALD. 'Was she gentle with animals?'

MR KRENWINKEL. 'Very much so.'

Patricia had sung in the church choir, Mr Krenwinkel testified. Though she was not an exceptional student, she re-

513

ceived good grades in the classes she liked. She had attended one semester of college, at Spring Hill College, a Jesuit school in Mobile, Alabama, before returning to Los Angeles, where she shared an apartment with her half sister.

The Krenwinkels had divorced when Patricia was seventeen. According to Joseph Krenwinkel, there was no bitterness; he and his wife had parted, and remained, friends.

Yet just a year later, when Patricia was eighteen, she had abandoned her family and job to join Manson.

Dorothy Krenwinkel said of her daughter, 'She would rather hurt herself than harm any living thing.'

FITZGERALD. 'Did you love your daughter?'

A. 'I did love my daughter; I will always love my daughter; and no one will ever convince me she did anything terrible or horrible.'

FITZGERALD. 'Thank you.'

BUGLIOSI. 'No questions, Your Honor.'

Fitzgerald wanted to introduce into evidence a number of letters Patricia Krenwinkel had written to various persons, including her father and a favorite priest at Spring Hill.

All were hearsay and clearly inadmissible. All I would have needed to do was object. But I didn't. Though aware that they would appeal to the sympathies of the jury, I felt that justice should prevail over technicalities. The issue now was whether this girl should be sentenced to death. And this was an issue for the jury to decide, not me. I felt that in reaching that extremely serious decision, they should have any information even remotely relevant.

Keith handled the direct examination of Jane Van Houten, Leslie's mother. Keith later told me that although Leslie's father didn't want to testify, he was behind Leslie 100 percent. Although, like the Krenwinkels, the Van Houtens were divorced, they too had stuck by their daughter.

According to Mrs Van Houten, 'Leslie was what you would call a feisty little child, fun to be with. She had a wonderful sense of humor.' Born in the Los Angeles suburb of Altadena, she had an older brother and a younger brother and sister, the latter Korean orphans whom the Van Houtens had adopted.

When Leslie was fourteen, her parents separated and divorced. 'I think it hurt her very much,' Mrs Van Houten testified. That same year Leslie fell in love with an older youth, Bobby Mackey; became pregnant; had an abortion; and took LSD for the first time. After that she dropped acid at least once and often two or three times a week.*

During her freshman and sophomore years at Monrovia High School, Leslie was one of the homecoming princesses. She tried out again her junior year, but this time she didn't make it. Bitter over the rejection, she ran away with Mackey to Haight-Ashbury. The scene there frightened her, however, and she returned home to finish high school and to complete a year of secretarial training. Mackey, in the meantime, had become a novitiate priest in the Self Realization Fellowship. In an attempt to continue their relationship, Leslie became a novitiate nun, giving up both drugs and sex. She lasted about eight months before breaking with both Mackey and the yoga group. Mrs Van Houten did not testify to the period which followed; possibly she knew little if anything about it. From interviews I'd learned that Leslie went full spectrum. The former nun was now anxious to 'try anything' be it drugs or answering sex-partner ads in the Los Angeles *Free Press*. A long-time friend stopped dating her because she had become 'too kinky'.

For a few months Leslie lived in a commune in Northern California. During this period she met Bobby Beausoleil, who had his own wandering 'family', consisting of Gypsy and a girl named Gail. Leslie became a part of the *ménage à quatre*. Gail, however, was jealous, and the arguments became near constant. First Gypsy split, moving to Spahn Ranch. Then, shortly after, Leslie followed, also joining Manson. She was nineteen.

---

*Patricia Krenwinkel had also taken LSD before meeting Manson. Very obese in her early teens, she began using diet pills at fourteen or fifteen, then tried reds, mescaline, and LSD, provided by her half sister Charlene, now deceased, who was a heroin addict.

About this time Leslie called her mother and told her that she had decided to drop out and that she wouldn't be hearing from her again. She didn't, until Leslie's arrest.

Keith asked Mrs Van Houten: 'How do you feel about your daughter now?'

A. 'I love Leslie very much.'

Q. 'As much as you always have?'

A. 'More.'

As the parents testified, one realized that they too were victims, just as were the relatives of the deceased.

Calling the defendants' parents first was a bad tactical error on the part of the defense. The testimony and plight evoked sympathy from everyone in the courtroom. They should have been called at the very end of the defense's case, just before the jury went out to deliberate. As it was, by the time the other witnesses had testified, they were almost forgotten.

Shinn called no witnesses on behalf of Susan Atkins. Her father, Shinn told me, had refused to have anything more to do with her. All he wanted, he said, was to get his hands on Manson.

A reporter from the Los Angeles *Times* had located Charles Manson's mother in a city in the Pacific Northwest. Remarried and living under another name, she claimed Charles' tales of childhood deprivation were fictions, adding, 'He was a spoiled, pampered child.'

Kanarek did not use her as a witness. Instead, he called Samuel Barrett, Manson's parole officer.

Barrett was a most unimpressive witness. He thought he first met Manson 'about 1956, around that'; he couldn't remember whether Manson was on probation or parole; he stated that since he was responsible for 150 persons, he couldn't be expected to recall everything about each one.

Repeatedly, Barrett minimized the seriousness of the various charges against Manson prior to the murders. The reason he did this was obvious: otherwise, one might wonder why he hadn't revoked Manson's parole. One still did wonder. Manson associated with ex-cons, known narcotics users, and minor girls. He failed to report his whereabouts, made few attempts to obtain employment, repeatedly lied regarding his activities. During the first six months of 1969 alone, he had been charged, among other things, with grand theft auto, narcotics possession, rape, contributing to the delinquency of a minor. There was more than ample reason for parole revocation.

During a recess one of the reporters approached me in the hall. 'God, Vince,' he exclaimed, 'did it ever occur to you that if Barrett had revoked Manson's parole in, say, April of 1969, Sharon and the others would probably still be alive today?'

I declined comment, citing the gag order as an excuse. But it had occurred to me. I had thought about it a great deal.

The parade of perjurers began with little Squeaky.

Lynette Alice Fromme, 22, testified that she was from an upper-middle-class background, her father an aeronautical engineer. When she was 17, she said, her father kicked her out of the house. 'And I was in Venice, sitting down on a curb crying, when a man walked up and said, "Your father kicked you out of the house, did he?" '

'And that was Charlie.'

Squeaky placed great importance on the fact that she had met Manson before any of the other girls, excepting only Mary Brunner.

In questioning her about the family, Fitzgerald asked: 'Did you have a leader?'

A. 'No, we were riding on the wind.'

No leader, but –

'Charlie is our father in that he would – he would point out things to us.'

Charlie was just like everyone else, but –

'I would crawl off in a corner and be reading a book, and he would pass me and tell me what it said in the book ... And also he knew our thoughts ... He was always happy, always ... He would go into the bathroom sometimes to comb his hair, and there would be a whole crowd of people in their watching him because he had so much fun.'

Squeaky had trouble denying the teachings of her lord and master. When Fitzgerald tried to minimize the importance of the Beatles' White Album, she replied, 'There is a lot in that album, there is a lot.' Although she claimed, 'I never heard Charlie utter the words "helter skelter," ' she went on to say that 'it is a matter of evolution and balance' and 'the black people are coming to the top, as it should be'.

Altogether, Squeaky was so helpful to the prosecution that there was little need for cross-examination. Among the questions I had intended to ask her, for example, was one Kanarek now asked: 'Did you think that Charles Manson was Jesus Christ?'

Squeaky hesitated a moment before answering. Would she be the apostle who denied Jesus? Apparently she decided she would not, for she replied: 'I think that the Christians in the caves and in the woods were a lot of kids just living and being without guilt, without shame, being able to take off their clothes and lay in the sun . . . And I see Jesus Christ as a man who came from a woman who did not know who the father of her'baby was.'

Squeaky was the least untruthful of the Family members who testified. Yet she was so damaging to the defense that thereafter Fitzgerald let the other defense attorneys call the witnesses.

Keith called Brenda McCann, t/n Nancy Laura Pitman, 19. Though not unattractive, Brenda came across as a tough, vicious little girl, filled with hostility that was just waiting to erupt.

Her father 'designed the guidance controls of missiles over in the Pentagon', she said. He also kicked her out of the house when she was 16, she claimed. The dropout from Hollywood High School asserted there was no such thing as a Family, and Charlie was not a leader at all. It was more like Charlie followed us around and took care of us.'

But, as with Squeaky and the girls who would follow her, it was obvious that Brenda's world revolved around a single axis. He was nobody special but 'Charlie would sit down and all the animals would gather round him, donkeys and coyotes and things . . . And one time he reached down and petted a rattle-snake.'

Questioned by Kanarek, Brenda testified that Linda 'would take LSD every day . . . took speed . . . Linda loved Tex very much . . . Linda followed Tex everywhere . . .'

On cross-examination I aked Brenda: 'Would you give up your life for Charles Manson if he asked you to?'

A. 'Many times he has given you his life.'

Q. 'Just answer the question, Brenda.'

A. 'Yes, I would.'

Q. 'Would you lie on the stand for Charles Manson?'

A. 'No, I would tell the truth on the stand.'

Q. 'So you would die for him, but not lie for him?'

A. 'That's right.'

Q. 'Do you feel that lying under oath is a more serious matter than dying, Brenda?'

A. 'I don't take dying all that seriously myself.'

All these witnesses were extremely antagonistic toward their real families. Sandra Good for example, claimed that her father, a San Diego stockbroker, had disowned her, neglecting to mention that this was only after he had sent her thousands of dollars and was threatened by Manson if he didn't give her more.

Manson had severed their umbilical cords while fastening one of his own. And throughout their testimony it showed. Even more than Squeaky and Brenda, Sandy rhapsodized on Manson's 'magical powers'. She told the story of how Charlie had breathed on a dead bird and brought it back to life. 'I believe his voice could shatter this building if he so desired . . . Once he yelled and a window broke.'

It was not until the penalty trial that the jury learned of the vigil of the Family members on the corner of Temple and Broadway. Rather movingly, Sandy testified to life there. 'You can hardly see the sky most of the time for the smog. They are always digging; every day there is a new project going; something is always under construction. They are always ripping out something and putting something in, usually of a concrete nature. It is insane out there. It's madness, and the more I am out there the more I feel this X. I am X'd out of it.'

After I'd declined to cross-examine Sandy, she very angrily asked, 'Why didn't you ask me any questions?'

'Because you said nothing which hurt the People's case, Sandy,' I replied. 'In fact, you helped it.'

I had anticipated that Sandy would testify that Manson wasn't even at Spahn Ranch at the time the murders had occurred. When she didn't, I knew the defense had decided to abandon the idea of using an alibi defense. Which meant they had something else in mind. But what?

Manson and the three female defendants had been allowed to return to court during the penalty phase. They were much quieter now, far more subdued, as if it had finally got through to them that this 'play', as Krenwinkel had characterized it, might cost them their lives. While Squeaky and the other Manson girls testified, their mentor looked thoughtful and pulled on his goatee, as if to say: They're telling it like it is.

The female witnesses wore their best clothes for the occasion. It was obvious that they were both proud and happy to be up there helping Charlie.

The jurors shared a common expression – incredulity. Few even bothered to take notes. I suspected that all of them were mulling over the astonishing contrast. On the stand the girls talked of love, music, and babies. Yet while the love and the music and the babies were going on, this same group was going out and butchering human beings. And to them, amazingly enough, there was no inconsistency, no conflict between love and murder!

By February 4, I was fairly sure, from the questions Kanarek had been asking the witnesses, that Manson was not going to take the stand. This was my biggest disappointment during the entire trial, that I wouldn't have the chance to break Charlie on cross-examination.

That same day our office learned that Charles 'Tex' Watson had been returned to Los Angeles and ruled competent to stand trial.

Only three days after his transfer to Atascadero, Watson had begun eating regular meals. Within a month, one of the psychiatrists who examined him wrote: 'There is no evidence of abnormal behavior at the present time except his silence, which is purposeful and with reason.' Another later noted: 'Psychological testing gave a scatter pattern of responses inconsistent with any recognized form of mental illness . . .' In short, Tex was faking it. All this information would be useful, I knew, if Tex tried to plead insanity during his trial, which was now scheduled to follow the current proceedings.

Catherine Share, aka Gypsy, was the defense's most effective liar. She was also, at twenty-eight, the oldest female member of the Family. And, of all its members, she had the most unusual background.

She was born in Paris in 1942, her father a Hungarian violinist, her mother a German-Jewish refugee. Both parents, members of the French underground, committed suicide during the war. At eight, she was adopted and brought to the United States by an American family. Her adoptive mother, who was suffering from cancer, committed suicide when Catherine was sixteen. Her adoptive father, a psychologist, was blind. She cared for him until he remarried, at which time she left home.

A graduate of Hollywood High School, she had attended college for three years; married; divorced a year later. A violin virtuoso since childhood, with an unusually beautiful singing voice, she had obtained work in a number of movies. It was on the set of one, in Topanga Canyon, that she became involved with Bobby Beausoleil, who had a minor role. About two months later Beausoleil introduced her to Charles Manson. Though it was, on her part, love at first sight, she continued traveling with the Beausoleil menage for another six months, before splitting for Spahn Ranch. Although she was an avowed Communist when she joined the Family, Manson soon convinced her that his dogma was ordained. 'Of all the girls,' Paul Watkins had told me, 'Gypsy was most in love with Charlie.'

She was also the most eloquent in his defense. But, though

brighter and more articulate than most of the others, she too occasionally slipped up.

'We are all facing the same sentence,' she told the jury. 'We are all in a gas chamber right here in L.A., a slow-acting one. The air is going away from us in every city. There is going to be no more air, and no more water, and the food is dying. They are poisoning you. The food you are eating is poisoning you. There is going to be no more earth, no more trees. Man, especially white man, is killing this earth.

'But those aren't Charles Manson's thoughts, those are my thoughts,' she quickly added.

During her first day on the stand Gypsy dropped no bombshells. It was not until her second day on the stand, on *redirect* by Kanarek, and immediately after Kanarek had asked to approach the witness and speak to her privately, that Gypsy suddenly came up with an alternative motive – one that was designed to clear Manson of any involvement in the murders.

Gypsy claimed that it was Linda Kasabian, not Charles Manson, who had masterminded the Tate-LaBianca murders! Linda was in love with Bobby Beausoleil, Gypsy said. When Bobby was arrested for the Hinman murder, Linda proposed that the girls commit other murders which were similar to the Hinman slaying, in the belief that the police would connect the crimes and, realizing that Beausoleil was in custody when these other murders occurred, set him free.

The 'copycat' motive was in itself not a surprise. In fact, Aaron Stovitz had suggested it as one of several possible motives in his interview with the reporters from *Rolling Stone*. There was only one thing wrong with it. It wasn't true. But in an attempt to clear Manson and to cast doubt on the Helter Skelter motive, the defense witnesses, starting with Gypsy, now began manufacturing their own bogus evidence.

Gypsy claimed that on the afternoon of August 8, 1969, Linda explained the plan to her and asked her if she wanted to go along. Horrified, Gypsy instead fled to the mountains. When she returned, the murders had already occurred and Linda was gone.

Gypsy further testified that Bobby Beausoleil was innocent of the Hinman murder; all he had done was drive a car belonging to Hinman. And Manson wasn't involved either. The Hinman murder had been committed by Linda, Sadie, and *Leslie*!

Maxwell Keith quickly objected. At the bench he told Judge Older: 'It sounds to me like this girl is leading up to testimony of an admission by my client to her participation in the Hinman, Tate, and LaBianca murders. This is outrageous!'

THE COURT. 'I don't know if Mr Kanarek has the faintest idea of what he wants to do.'

FITZGERALD. 'I am afraid so.'

KANAREK. 'I know exactly.'

Keith observed: 'I talked to this witness yesterday at the County Jail about her testimony. It was sort of innocuous testimony regarding Leslie. And all of a sudden, boom, we are being bombed out of the courtroom.'

On cross-examination I asked: 'Isn't it true, Gypsy, that what you are trying to do is clear Charles Manson at the expense of Leslie and Sadie?'

A. 'I wouldn't say that. No, it isn't true.'

To destroy her credibility, I then impeached Gypsy with a number of inconsistent statements she had previously made. Only then did I return to the bogus motive.

Gypsy had testified that immediately after hearing of the Tate-LaBianca murders, she was sure that Linda, Leslie, and Sadie were involved.

I asked her: 'If in your mind Linda, Sadie, and Leslie were somehow involved in the Tate-LaBianca murders, and Mr Manson was innocent and had nothing to do with it, why haven't you come forward before today to tell the authorities about this conversation you had with Linda?'

A. 'I didn't want anything to do with it. I don't believe in coming to you at all.'

Earlier on cross-examination Gypsy had admitted that she loved Manson, that she would willingly die for him. After reminding her of these statements, I said: 'All right, and you believe he had nothing to do with these murders, right?'

A. 'Right.'

523

Q. 'And yet you let him stay in jail all these months without coming forward with this valuable information?'

Gypsy evaded a straight reply.

Q. 'When was the first time you told anyone about this infamous conversation that you had with Linda when she asked you to go out and murder someone?'

A. 'Right here.'

Q. 'Today?'

A. 'Uh-huh.'

Q. 'So today on the witness stand was the first time that you decided to release all this valuable information, is that right?'

A. 'That's right.'

I had her. I could now argue to the jury that here's Manson, being tried for seven counts of murder, and there's Gypsy, out on the corner of Temple and Broadway twenty-four hours a day since the start of the trial, a girl who loves Manson and would give her life for him, but who waits until well into the penalty trial, and on redirect at that, before she decides to tell anyone what she knows.

At 6:01 A.M. on February 9, 1971, a monster earthquake shook most of Southern California. Measuring 6.5 on the Richter scale, it claimed sixty-five lives and caused millions of dollars' worth of damage.

I awoke thinking the Family was trying to break into our house.

The jurors awoke to find water cascading on them from broken pipes above their rooms.

The girls on the corner told reporters Charlie had caused the quake.

Despite the disaster, court resumed at the usual time that morning, with Susan Atkins taking the stand to trigger an earthquake of her own.

Daye Shinn's first question of his client was: 'Susan, were you personally involved in the Tate and LaBianca homicides?'

Susan, who was wearing a dark jumper and a white blouse, and looking very little-girlish, calmly replied, 'Yes.'

524

Although by this time all counsel knew that the three girls intended to take the stand and 'confess', Fitzgerald having mentioned in it chambers nearly a week before, the jury and spectators were stunned. They looked at each other as if disbelieving what they had heard.

Shinn then took Susan through her background: her early religious years ('I sang in the church choir'); the death of her mother from cancer ('I couldn't understand why she died, and it hurt me'); her loss of faith; her problems with her father ('My father kept telling me, "You're going downhill," so I just went downhill'); her experiences as a topless dancer in San Francisco; her explanation for why she was carrying a gun when arrested in Oregon ('I was afraid of snakes'); and her introduction to drugs, Haight-Ashbury, and her first fateful meeting with Charles Manson.

Returning to the crimes, she testified: 'This whole thing started when I killed Gary Hinman, because he was going to hurt my love . . .'

Judge Older called the noon recess. Before leaving the stand, Susan turned toward me and said, 'Look at it, Mr Bugliosi. Your whole thing, man, is just gone, your whole motive. It is so silly. So dumb.'

That afternoon, Sadie recited the newly revised version of how the Hinman murder went down. According to Susan, when Manson arrived at the Hinman residence, to persuade Gary to sign over the pink slip on a car they had already purchased, Gary drew a gun on him. As Manson fled, Gary tried to shoot him in the back. 'I had no choice. He was going to hurt my love. I had my knife on me and I ran at him and I killed him . . . Bobby was taken to jail for something that I did.'

The holes in her story were a mile wide. I noted them for my cross-examination.

After the arrest of Beausoleil, Susan testified, Linda proposed committing copycat murders. '. . . and she told me to get a knife and a change of clothes . . . she said these people in Beverly Hills had burned her for $1,000 for some new drug, MDA . . .'

Before leaving Spahn Ranch, Susan said, 'Linda gave me

some LSD, and she gave Tex some STP . . . Linda issued all the directions that night . . . No one told Charlie where we were going or what we were going to do . . . Linda had been there before, so she knew where to go . . . Tex went crazy, shot Parent . . . Linda went inside the house . . . Linda gave me her knife.' At this point in her narrative, Daye Shinn opened the blade of the Buck knife and started to hand the knife to Susan.

THE COURT. 'Put that knife back the way it was!'

SHINN. 'I only wanted to get the dimensions, Your Honor.'

Susan skipped ahead in her narrative. She was holding Sharon Tate and 'Tex came back and he looked at her and he said, "Kill her." And I killed her . . . And I just stabbed her and she fell, and I stabbed her again. I don't know how many times I stabbed her . . .' Sharon begged for the life of her baby, and 'I told her, "Shut up. I don't want to hear it." '

Though Susan's words were horrifyingly chilling, her expression for the most part remained simple, even childlike.

There was only one way to describe the contrast: it was incredibly obscene.

In discussing the Hinman murder, Susan had placed Leslie Van Houten at the murder scene. There had never been any evidence whatsoever that Leslie was involved in the Hinman murder.

In discussing the night the LaBiancas were killed, Susan made some additional changes in the cast of characters. Manson didn't go along, she said. Linda drove; Tex creepy crawled the LaBianca residence; Linda instructed Tex, Katie, and Leslie what to do; Linda suggested killing the actor in Venice. And when they returned to Spahn Ranch, 'Charlie was there sleeping.'

Just as improbable was another of her fictional embellishments. She had implicated Manson in her conversation with me and in her testimony before the grand jury, she claimed, because I had promised her that if she did so I would personally see that none of the defendants, including Manson, would receive the death penalty.

The best refutation of this was that she had implicated Manson on the tape she made with Caballero, days before our first meeting.

Shinn then began questioning Susan about Shorty! I asked to approach the bench.

BUGLIOSI. 'Your Honor, I can't believe what is going on here. He is talking about Shorty Shea now!' Turning to Daye, I said, 'You are hurting yourself if you bring in other murders, and you are hurting the co-defendants.' Older agreed and cautioned Shinn to be extremely careful.

I was worried that, if Shinn continued, the case might be reversed on appeal. What conceivable rationale could there be for having your client take the stand and confess to a murder with which she isn't even charged?

Fitzgerald took over the direct. He asked Susan why the Tate victims were killed.

A. 'Because I believed it was right to get my brother out of jail. And I still believe it was right.'

Q. 'Miss Atkins, were any of these people killed as a result of any personal hate or animosity that you had toward them?'

A. 'No.'

Q. 'Did you have any feeling toward them at all, any emotional feeling toward any of these people – Sharon Tate, Voytek Frykowski, Abigail Folger, Jay Sebring, Steven Parent?'

A. 'I didn't know any of them. How could I have felt any emotion without knowing them?'

Fitzgerald asked Susan if she considered these mercy killings.

A. 'No. As a matter of fact, I believe I told Sharon Tate I didn't have any mercy for her.'

Susan went on to explain that she knew what she was doing 'was right when I was doing it'. She knew this because, when you do the right thing, 'it feels good'.

Q. 'How could it be right to kill somebody?'

A. 'How could it not be right when it is done with love?'

Q. 'Did you ever feel any remorse?'

A. 'Remorse? For doing what was right to me?'

Q. 'Did you ever feel sorry?'

A. 'Sorry for doing what was right to me? I have no guilt in me.'

Fitzgerald looked beaten. By bringing out her total lack of remorse, he had made it impossible for the defense to persuasively argue that she was capable of rehabilitation.

We had reached a strange situation. Suddenly, in the penalty phase, long after the jury had found the four defendants guilty, I was in a sense having to prove Manson's guilt all over again.

If I cross-examined too strenuously, it would appear that I did not feel that we had proven our case. If I eschewed cross-examination, there was the possibility of leaving a lingering doubt as to guilt, which, when it came time for their deliberations, could influence the jury's vote on penalty. Therefore I had to proceed very carefully, as if trying to walk between raindrops.

The defense, and specifically Irving Kanarek, had tried to plant such a doubt by providing an alternative to Helter Skelter – the copycat motive. Though I felt the testimony on this was thoroughly unconvincing, this didn't mean I could sit back and presume the jury would feel as I did.

As an explanation for why she was lying to save him, it was important that I conclusively prove to the jury Susan Atkins' total commitment to Manson. At the start of my cross-examination I asked her: 'Sadie, do you believe Charles Manson is the second coming of Christ?'

A. 'Vince, I have seen Christ in so many people in the last four or five years, it is hard for me to say which one exactly is the second coming of Christ.'

I repeated the question.

A. 'I have thought about it. I have thought about it quite a bit . . . I have entertained the thought that he was Christ, yes . . . I don't know. Could be. If he is, wow, my goodness!'

After confronting her with her letter to Ronnie Howard, in which she stated, 'If you can believe in the second coming of Christ, M is he who has come to save,' I asked her: 'Even now on the witness stand, Sadie, you think that maybe Charles Manson, the man over there who is playing with his hair, might be Jesus Christ?'

A. 'Maybe. I will leave it at that. Maybe yes. Maybe no.'

I persisted until Susan admitted: 'He represented a God to me that was so beautiful that I'd do anything for him.'

Q. 'Even commit murder?' I asked instantly.

A. 'I'd do anything for God.'

Q. 'Including murder?' I pressed.

A. 'That's right. If I believed it was right.'

Q. 'And you murdered the five people at the Tate residence for your God, Manson, didn't you?'

Susan paused, then said: 'I murdered them for my God Bobby Beausoleil.'

Q. 'Oh, so you have two Gods?'

Evasively she replied: 'There is only one God and God is in all.'

Since Susan had already testified to these matters, the prosecution was able to use her prior inconsistent statements – including her grand jury testimony – for impeachment purposes.

On cross-examination I had Susan repeat the alleged reasons why they went to the Tate residence: Once she'd restated the copycat nonsense, I hit her with her statements regarding Helter Skelter's being the motive – made to me, to the grand jury, and in the Howard letter.

I also brought out that she had told me, and the grand jury, that Manson had ordered the seven Tate-LaBianca murders; that Charlie had directed all their activities the second night; and that none of them had been on drugs either night.

I then led her back through her scenario of the Hinman, Tate, and LaBianca murders, step by step, knowing she would slip up, which she did, repeatedly.

For example, I asked: 'Where was Charles Manson when you stabbed Gary Hinman to death?'

A. 'He left. He left right after he cut Gary's ear.' Having inadvertently admitted this, she quickly added that she had tried to sew up Hinman's ear.

529

I then took her back again: Hinman drew a gun on Manson; Manson ran; Hinman started to shoot Manson; to protect her love, she stabbed Hinman to death. Just when, I asked, did she have time to play Florence Nightingale?

Susan further claimed that she didn't tell Manson that she had killed Hinman until after their arrest in the Barker raid. In other words, though she had lived with Manson from July to October 1969, she hadn't got around to mentioning this? 'That's right.' Why? 'Because he never asked.'

She hadn't even told him she committed the Tate and La-Bianca murders, she claimed. Nor, until two days ago, had she told anyone that Linda Kasabian masterminded the murders.

Q. 'Between August 9, 1969, and February 9, 1971, how come you never told anyone that Linda was behind these murders?'

A. 'Because I didn't. It's that simple.'

Q. 'Did you tell *anyone* in the Family that you committed all these murders?'

A. 'No.'

Q. 'If you told outsiders like Ronnie Howard and Virginia Graham, how come you didn't tell members of your own Family, Sadie?'

A. 'Nothing needed to be said. What I did was what I did with those people, and that is what I did.'

Q. 'Just one of those things, seven dead bodies?'

A. 'No big thing.'

I paused to let this incredible statement sink in before asking: 'So killing seven people is just business as usual, no big deal, is that right, Sadie?'

A. 'It wasn't at the time. It was just there to do.'

I asked her how she felt about the victims. She responded, 'They didn't even look like people ... I didn't relate to Sharon Tate as being anything but a store mannequin.'

Q. 'You have never heard a store mannequin talk, have you, Sadie?'

A. 'No, sir. But she just sounded like an I BM machine ... She kept begging and pleading and pleading and begging, and I got sick of listening to her, so I stabbed her.'

A. 'And the more she screamed, the more you stabbed, Sadie?'

A. 'Yes. So?'

Q. 'And you looked at her and you said, "Look, bitch, I have no mercy for you." Is that right, Sadie?'

A. 'That's right. That's what I said then.'

BUGLIOSI. 'No further questions.'

On Tuesday, February 16, after lengthy discussions in chambers, Judge Older told the jury that he had decided to end the sequestration.

Their surprise and elation were obvious. They had been locked up for over eight months, the longest sequestration of any jury in American history.

Though I remained worried about possible harassment from the Family, most of the other reasons for the sequestration – such as mention of the Hinman murder, Susan Atkins' confession in the Los Angeles *Times*, her grand jury testimony, and so on – no longer existed, since the jury heard this evidence when Sadie and the others took the stand.

It was almost as if we had a new jury. When the twelve entered the box the next day, there were smiles on all their faces. I couldn't remember when I'd last seen them smiling.

The smiles would not remain there long. Patricia Krenwinkel now took the stand, to confess her part in the Tate and LaBianca homicides.

An even more improbable witness than Susan Atkins, her testimony regarding the copycat motive was vague, nebulous, and almost devoid of supporting detail. The point in her taking the stand was to take the focus off Manson. Instead, like the other Family members who had preceded her, she repeatedly highlighted his importance. For example, describing life at Spahn Ranch, she said: 'We were just like wood nymphs and wood creatures. We would run through the woods with flowers in our hair, and Charlie would have a small flute . . .'

On the murder of Abigail Folger: 'And I had a knife in my hands, and she took off running, and she ran – she ran out through the back door, one I never even touched, I mean, nobody got fingerprints because I never touched that door ... and I stabbed her and I kept stabbing her.'

Q. 'What did you feel after you stabbed her?'

A. 'Nothing – I mean, like what is there to describe? It was just there, and it's like it was right.'

On the murder of Rosemary LaBianca: According to Katie, she and Leslie took Rosemary LaBianca into the bedroom and were looking through the dresses in her closet when, hearing Leno scream, Rosemary grabbed a lamp and swung at them.

On the mutilation of Leno LaBianca: After murdering Rosemary, Katie remembered seeing Leno lying on the floor in the living room. She flashed, 'You won't be sending your son off to war,' and 'I guess I put WAR on the man's chest. And then I guess I had a fork in my hands, and I put it in his stomach ... and I went and wrote on the walls ...'

On cross-examination I asked her: 'When you were on top of Abigail Folger, plunging your knife into her body, was she screaming?'

A. 'Yes.'

Q. 'And the more she screamed, the more you stabbed?'

A. 'I guess.'

Q. 'Did it bother you when she screamed for her life?'

A. 'No.'

Katie testified that when she stabbed Abigail she was really stabbing herself. My next question was rhetorical. 'But you didn't bleed at all, did you, Katie; just Abigail did, isn't that right?'

The defense was contending, through these witnesses, that the words POLITICAL PIGGY (Hinman), PIG (Tate), and DEATH TO PIGS (LaBianca) were the clue which the killers felt would cause the police to link the three crimes. But when I'd asked Sadie why she'd written POLITICAL PIGGY on the wall of the Hinman residence in the first place, she had no satisfactory answer. Nor could she tell me why, if these were to be copycat murders, she'd only written PIG and not POLITICAL PIGGY at Tate. Nor was Katie now able to give a convincing explanation as to why she'd written HEALTER SKELTER on the LaBiancas' refrigerator door.

It was obvious that Maxwell Keith wasn't buying the copycat motive either. On redirect he asked Katie: 'The homicides at the Tate residence and the LaBianca residence had nothing to do, did they, with trying to get Bobby Beausoleil out of jail?'

A. 'Well, it's hard to explain. It was just a thought, and the thought came to be.'

Maxwell Keith very reluctantly called his client, Leslie Van Houten, to the stand. After taking her through her background, Keith asked to approach the bench. He told Older that his client was going to involve herself in the Hinman murder. He had discussed this with her for 'hours and hours' but to no avail.

Once she began reciting her tale, the transparency of her fictions became obvious. According to Leslie, Mary Brunner was never at the Hinman residence, while both Charles Manson and Bobby Beausoleil left before the actual killing took place. It was Sadie, she said, who killed Gary.

Though implicating herself in the Hinman murder, at least by her presence, Leslie did try to provide some mitigating circumstances for her involvement in the LaBianca murders. She claimed she knew nothing about the Tate murders and that when she went along the next night she had no idea where they were going or what they were going to do. The murder of Rosemary LaBianca was made to seem almost like self-defense. Only after Rosemary swung at her with the lamp did she 'take one of the knives and Patricia had a knife, and we started stabbing and cutting up the lady'.

Q. 'Up to that time, did you have any intention of hurting anybody?'

A. 'No.'

Q. 'Did you stab her after she appeared to be dead, Les?'

A. 'I don't know if it was before or after she was dead, but I stabbed her . . . I don't know if she was dead. She was lying there on the floor.'

Q. 'Had you stabbed her at all before you saw her lying on the floor?'

A. 'I don't remember.'

Leslie's forgetting such things was almost as improbable as her claim that she hadn't mentioned the murders to Manson until they were in the desert.

Very carefully, Keith tried to establish that Leslie had remorse for her acts.

Q. 'Leslie, do you feel sorrow or shame or a sense of guilt for having participated in the death of Mrs LaBianca?'

A. [Pause]

Q. 'Let me go one by one. Do you feel sorrowful about it; sorry; unhappy?'

You could almost feel the chill in the courtroom when Leslie answered: 'Sorry is only a five-letter word. It can't bring back anything.'

Q. 'I am trying, Leslie, to discover how you feel about it.'

A. 'What can I feel? It has happened. She is gone.'

Q. 'Do you wish that it hadn't happened?'

A. 'I never wish anything to be done another way. That is a foolish thought. It never will happen that way. You can't undo something that is done.'

Q. 'Do you feel as if you wanted to cry for what happened?'

A. 'Cry? For her dead? If I cry for death, it is for death itself. She is not the only person who has died.'

Q. 'Do you think about it from time to time?'

A. 'Only when I am in the courtroom.'

Through most of the trial Leslie Van Houten had maintained her innocent-little-girl act. She'd dropped it now, the jury seeing for the first time how cold and unfeeling she really was.

Another aspect of her real nature surfaced when Kanarek examined her. Angry and impatient at some of his questions, she snapped back hostile, sarcastic replies. With each spurt of venom, you could see the jurors drawing back, looking at her as if anew. Whatever sympathy she may have generated earlier was gone now.

Leslie Van Houten had been found guilty of two homicides. I felt she deserved the death penalty for her very willing participation in those acts. But I didn't want the jury to vote death on the basis of a crime she didn't even commit. I told her attorney, Maxwell Keith, that I was willing to stipulate that Leslie was not at the Hinman residence. 'I mean, the jury is apt to think she was, and hold it against your client, and I don't think that is right.'

Also, during cross-examination I asked: 'Did you tell anyone – prior to your testimony on the witness stand – that it was you who was along with Sadie and Bobby Beausoleil at Gary Hinman's house?'

A. 'I told Patricia about it.'

Q. 'Actually it was Mary Brunner who was inside the residence, not you, isn't that correct?'

A. 'That is what you say.'

Although I was attemping to exonerate Leslie of any complicity in the Gary Hinman murder, I did the opposite when it came to the murder of Rosemary LaBianca. By the time I'd finished my cross-examination on this, Leslie had admitted that Rosemary might still have been alive when she stabbed her; and that she not only stabbed her in the buttocks and possibly the neck, but 'I could have done a couple on the back'. (As I'd later remind the jury, many of the back wounds were not postmortem, while one, which severed Rosemary LaBianca's spine, would have been in and of itself fatal.)

As with Sadie and Katie, I emphasized the improbabilities in her copycat tale. For example, though she had testified that she was 'hopelessly in love' with Bobby Beausoleil, and became aware that these murders had been committed in an attempt to free him, I brought out that she hadn't even offered to testify in either of his trials, when her story, had it been true, could have resulted in his release.

At this point I decided to go on a fishing expedition. Though I had no definite knowledge that this was so, I strongly suspected that Leslie had told her first attorney, Marvin Part, the true story of these murders. I did know that Part had recorded her story and, though I never heard the tape, I recalled Part almost begging the judge to listen to it.

BUGLIOSI. 'Isn't it true, Leslie, that before the trial started you told someone that Charles Manson ordered these murders?'

A. 'I had a court-appointed attorney, Marvin Part, who was insistent on the fact that I was – '

Keith interrupted her, objecting that we were getting into the area of privileged communications. I noted to Judge Older that Leslie herself had mentioned Part by name and that she had the right to waive the privilege. Kanarek also objected, well aware of what I was hoping to bring out.

VAN HOUTEN. 'Mr Kanarek, will you shut up so I can answer his question? . . . I had a court-appointed attorney by the name of Marvin Part. He had a lot of different thoughts, which were all his own, on how to get me off. He said he was going to make some tape recordings, and he told me the gist of what he wanted me to say. And I said it.'

Q. 'What did you tell Mr Part?'

A. 'I don't remember. It was a long time ago.'

I asked her if she told Part that Manson had ordered these murders.

A. 'Sure I told him that.'

Did she tell Part that Manson was along the second night, and that when they stopped on Waverly Drive, Manson got out and entered the LaBianca house?

After a number of evasive replies, Leslie angrily answered: 'Sure I told him that!'

THE COURT. 'We will take our recess at this time – '

VAN HOUTEN. 'Mr Bugliosi, you are an evil man!'

Each of the Family witnesses denied that Manson hated blacks. But in the light of what I'd recently learned, several put it in a very curious way. When Fitzgerald asked Squeaky: 'Did he love the black man or did he hate him?' she had replied: 'He loved them. He is his father – the black man is Charlie's father.' Gypsy had testified: 'First of all, Charlie spent nearly all of his life in jail. So he got to know the black people very, very well. In fact, I mean, they were like his father, you know.' Leslie had said something very similar, adding: 'If Charlie hated black people he would hate himself.'

During a recess I asked Manson, 'Charlie, was your father black?'

'*What?*' He seemed startled by the question, yet whether because it was such a crazy idea or because I'd found out something he didn't want known I couldn't tell. There was nothing evasive about his eventual response, however; he emphatically denied it.

He seemed to be telling the truth. Yet I wondered. I still do.

The next witness was no stranger to the stand. Brought back from New Hampshire at the request of Irving Kanarek, Linda Kasabian was again sworn. Fitzgerald, Keith, and Shinn had opposed calling her; Kanarek should have listened to their advice, as Linda again came over so well that I didn't even cross-examine her. None of her previous testimony was shaken in the slightest.

Linda, her husband, and their two children were living together on a small farm in New Hampshire. The footloose Bob Kasabian had turned out to be a pillar of strength, and I was pleased to hear that their marriage now seemed to be working.

Ruth Ann Moorehouse, aka Ouisch, age 20, who'd once told Danny DeCarlo she couldn't wait to get her first pig, repeated the now familiar refrain: 'Charlie was no leader.' But 'the rattlesnakes liked him, he could play with them' and 'he could change old men into young men'.

Adding a few more fictional touches to the copycat motive, Ouisch claimed that Bobby Beausoleil was the father of Linda Kasabian's second child.

I asked her: 'You would do anything to help Charles Manson and these three female defendants, wouldn't you, Ouisch?'

When she evaded a direct reply, I asked: 'You would even murder for them, wouldn't you?'

A. 'I could not take a life.'

Q. 'All right, let's talk about that, Ouisch. Do you know a girl by the name of Barbara Hoyt?'

On the advice of her attorney, Ouisch refused to answer any questions about the Hoyt murder attempt. By law, when a witness refuses to be cross-examined, that witness's entire testimony can be stricken. This was done in Ouisch's case.

Easily the weirdest of all the witnesses was Steve Grogan, aka Clem, age 19. He spoke of the 'engrams' on his brain; answered questions about his father by talking about his mother; and claimed that the real leader of the Family was not Manson but Pooh Bear, Mary Brunner's child.

The youth who beheaded Shorty Shea appeared to be a complete idiot. He grinned incessantly, made funny faces, and played with his beard even more than Manson. Yet it was more than partly role playing, as several of his very careful replies indicated.

Clem recalled accompanying Linda, Leslie, Sadie, Tex, and Katie one night in a car; he claimed that Linda had given them all LSD first; and he insisted that Manson was not along. But he was very careful not to say that this was the night of the LaBianca murders, to avoid implicating himself.

Many of his responses were almost exact quotations from Manson. For example, when I asked him, 'When did you join the Family, Clem?' he replied, 'When I was born of white skin.'

The defense called their next witness: Vincent T. Bugliosi. At the bench Fitzgerald admitted that this was an unusual situation: 'On the other hand, in this case Mr Bugliosi has been an investigator as well as a prosecutor.'

Daye Shinn questioned me about my interview with Susan Atkins and her testimony before the grand jury. Why did I feel Susan hadn't told the grand jury the whole truth? he asked. I enumerated the reasons, noting, among other things, my belief that she had stabbed Sharon Tate.

Q. 'How did you come to that conclusion?'

A. 'She admitted it on the witness stand, Mr Shinn, for one thing. Also, she told Ronnie Howard and Virginia Graham that she stabbed Sharon Tate.'

Shinn was trying to reinstate the 'deal' in which the DA's Office agreed not to seek the death penalty against Susan if she testified truthfully. As Older told him at the bench: 'Susan

Atkins took the stand in this case under oath and testified that she was lying at the grand jury. If there'd been any agreement, that in itself would have been enough to negate it.'

Keith asked me if I had either heard the tape Leslie made with Part or discussed its contents with him. I replied that I had not. Kanarek's cross-examination went so far afield that Judge Older finally terminated it.

Others who took the stand in succeeding days included Aaron Stovitz; Evelle Younger, former Los Angeles District Attorney and now California State Attorney General; attorneys Paul Caruso and Richard Caballero; and promoter Lawrence Schiller. During the examination of these witnesses, Kanarek scored one of the biggest points – for the prosecution. In questioning Caballero, Atkins' former attorney, he asked: 'What did [Susan Atkins] tell you about the language written in blood at these three homes?'

CABALLERO. 'I told you not to ask me that question, Irving'

Apparently convinced that Caballero was hiding something favorable to his client, Kanarek repeated the question.

Caballero sighed and said: 'She told me that Charles Manson had wanted to bring on Helter Skelter and it wasn't happening fast enough, and the use of the word "pig" was for the purpose of making them think that Negroes were committing these crimes, because the Panthers and people like that are the ones that used the name "pig" to mean the establishment, and that was the whole purpose of it, that Helter Skelter wasn't happening fast enough, and Charlie was going to bring on the ruination of the world, and this is why all the murders were committed.

'I asked you not to ask me these questions, Mr Kanarek.'

Having failed abysmally in their attempt to sell the copycat motive, the defense now switched to a new tactic. They called a number of psychiatrists to the stand, hoping to establish that LSD had affected the minds of the three female defendants to the extent that they were not responsible for their acts.

It was not a real defense, but it could be made to seem a mitigating circumstance which, unless thoroughly rebutted, might tip the scales in favor of life imprisonment.

Their first witness, Dr Andre Tweed, professed to be an expert on LSD, but almost all of his testimony was contrary to that of acknowledged experts in the field.

On December 24, 1969, Patricia Krenwinkel had been examined by a Mobile, Alabama psychiatrist, a Dr Claude Brown. Since Tweed had based his conclusions in part on Brown's report, I was given a copy of it just prior to my cross-examination.

It was a bombshell, as my question to Dr Tweed indicated:

Q. 'In forming your opinions with respect to Patricia Krenwinkel, did you take into consideration that she told Dr Brown that on the night of the Tate murders Charles Manson told her to go along with Tex Watson?'

After numerous objections and lengthy conferences at the bench, Dr Tweed admitted that he had considered this. Still later, Patricia Krenwinkel was recalled to the stand, where, though she denied the truth of the statement, she admitted that she had told Dr Brown that this was so.

We now had a perfect score. Manson had called Sadie, Katie, and Leslie to the stand in an attempt to exonerate him. Instead, I had now proven that each of the three had previously told others that Manson was behind these murders.

There were other surprises in the Brown report. Krenwinkel also told the doctor that she had fled to Mobile 'because she was afraid of Manson finding her and killing her';* that on the day of the Tate murders she was coming *off* an acid trip and wasn't on any drugs that night; and that following the murders 'she was always fearful that they would be arrested for what they had done, but "Charlie said nobody could touch us" '.

This latter statement proved that Katie was well aware of the consequences of her acts.

* Although harmful to Manson, this could only be helpful to Fitzgerald's client, Patricia Krenwinkel. However, it was not Fitzgerald who brought this out but Keith, after Fitzgerald had concluded his examination.

This was important, since it was obvious from their questions that the defense attorneys were trying to imply that the three female defendants were insane at the time they committed these murders.

Under California law an insanity plea must be entered *before* the start of the trial. A separate sanity phase is then held, after the guilt trial. The defense, however, had not entered such a plea at the proper time. Therefore, in one sense, the question of whether the defendants were sane or insane was irrelevant, since this was not an issue which the jury would have to decide. In another sense, however, it was crucial. If the defense could cause the jury to doubt the sanity of the defendants, this could strongly influence their vote on the penalty they were to pay.

Suddenly I was not only having to prove Manson's guilt all over again, I was also having to prove that the girls were legally sane.

In most states, including California, the legal test of insanity is the M'Naghten Rule. Among other things, M'Naghten provides that if a defendant, as a result of mental disease or defect, does not realize that what he did was wrong, then he is legally insane. It is not enough, however, that he personally believe his acts were not wrong. Were this so, every man would be a law unto himself. For instance, a man could rape a dozen women, say, 'I don't think it's wrong to rape,' and therefore evade criminal punishment. The clincher is whether he knows that society thinks his actions are wrong. If he does, then he cannot be legally insane. And deliberate acts to avoid detection – such as cutting telephone wires, eradicating prints, changing identities, disposing of incriminating evidence – constitute circumstantial evidence that the defendant knows society views his acts as wrong.

Earlier Dr Tweed had testified that Patricia Krenwinkel didn't believe these murders were wrong. I now asked him on cross: 'In your opinion, when Patricia Krenwinkel was committing these murders, did she believe that society thought it was wrong to do what she was doing?'

A. 'I believe so.'

BUGLIOSI. 'No further questions.'

On March 4, Manson trimmed his beard to a neat fork and completely shaved his head, because, he told newsmen, 'I am the Devil and the Devil always has a bald head.'

Interestingly enough, this time the three female defendants did not follow Manson's example. Nor, when he occasionally acted up in court, did they parrot him, as they had in the guilt trial. Obviously it had got across to them, albeit belatedly, that such antics only proved Manson's domination.

While denying that LSD can cause brain damage, the next witness, psychiatrist Keith Ditman, testified that the drug can have a detrimental effect on a person's personality. He also stated that a person using LSD is more susceptible to the influence of a second party, and that Leslie's use of the drug, *plus* Manson's influence over her, could have been significant factors in causing her to participate in a homicide.

VAN HOUTEN. 'This is all such a big lie. I was influenced by the war in Vietnam and TV.'

On cross-examination I got Ditman to concede that not all people react the same to LSD, that it depends upon the personality structure of the person ingesting the drug. I then brought out that Ditman had never examined Leslie; therefore, not knowing what her personality structure was, he couldn't say what effect, if any, LSD had on her mental state.

Nor, turning this around, not having examined her, could he say for certain whether she did or did not have inherent homicidal tendencies.

Keith, on redirect, asked Ditman: 'What is meant by inherent homicidal tendencies?'

A. 'That a person has, let's say, more than the average human being, a killer instinct . . .'

Q. 'Psychiatrically speaking, do some people have greater killer instincts than others, in your opinion?'

A. 'Well, some people have a more covert and overt hostility and aggression. In that sense, they are *more capable* of committing crimes of violence, such as murder.'

Dr Ditman had just articulated one of the chief points of the final argument I was preparing to give at the close of the penalty phase.

Dr Joel Fort, the almost legendary 'hippie doctor of the Haight', didn't look the part. The founder of the National Center for Solving Social and Health Problems was fortyish, dressed conservatively, talked quietly, didn't have long hair (in fact he was bald). Angered by his testimony, Manson shouted, 'If he ever seen a hippie, it was in the street while he was driving by in his car.'

Manson's anger had good cause. Even on direct, Dr Fort was more helpful to the prosecution than the defense. The author of one book on drugs and co-author of eleven others, Dr Fort stated that 'a drug by itself does not perform a magical transformation – there are many other factors'.

On cross-examination I brought out one. Fort said, 'It was my feeling [after examining Leslie Van Houten] that Mr Manson's influence played a very significant role in the commission of the murders.'

Another very crucial point came out on cross. I asked Fort: 'Isn't it true, Doctor, that people under the influence of LSD do not tend to be violent?'

A. 'That is true.'

Still attacking the prosecution's theory of Manson's domination, Kanarek asked Fort: 'Now, do you know of any cases where someone has – I mean, other than in the Frankenstein type of picture – do you know where someone has sat down and programmed people to go out, let's say, and commit armed robberies, burglaries, assaults? Do you know of any such instances?'

A. 'Yes. In one sense, that is what we do when we program soldiers in a war ... The Army uses a peer group technique and the patriotic ideals that are instilled in citizens of a particular country to bring about this pattern of behavior.'

Dr Fort was typical of many persons who, though opposed to capital punishment in principle, felt that these murders were so savage and senseless, so totally lacking in mitigating circumstances, that justice demanded that these persons be sentenced to death. I learned this in a conversation with him in the hall outside court, in which he stated that he was extremely unhappy that he had been called to testify for the defense in this case. Greatly concerned about the stain the Manson Family had cast on all young people, Dr Fort offered to testify for the prosecution when I brought Charles 'Tex' Watson to trial, an offer which I later accepted.

It was just such a hallway interview that I discovered how potentially damaging to the defense their next witness could be. Learning that Keith intended to call Dr Joel Simon Hochman during the afternoon session, I cut my lunch hour short so I could spend a half hour interviewing the psychiatrist.

To my amazement, I learned that Maxwell Keith hadn't even interviewed his own witness. He was calling him to the stand 'cold'. Had he talked to him for just five minutes, Keith would never have called Hochman. For the doctor, who *had* interviewed Leslie, felt that the use of LSD wasn't an important influence on her; rather, he felt there was something very seriously wrong with Leslie Van Houten.

In his testimony and the psychiatric report he wrote following the examination, Dr Hochman called Leslie Van Houten 'a spoiled little princess' who was unable 'to suffer frustration and delay of gratification'. From childhood on, she'd had extreme difficulties with impulse control. When she didn't get her way, she went into rages, for example beating her adopted sister with a shoe.

'From a position of over-all perspective,' Hochman noted, 'it is quite clear that Leslie Van Houten was a psychologically loaded gun which went off as a consequence of the complex intermeshing of highly unlikely and bizarre circumstances.'

Hochman confirmed something I had long suspected. Of the three female defendants, Leslie Van Houten was the least committed to Charles Manson. 'She listened to [Manson's] talk of philosophy, but it wasn't her trip.' Nor could she 'get that in to Charlie sexually, and that bothered her a lot. "I couldn't get it on with Charlie like I could with Bobby," she said . . .' According to Hochman, Leslie was obsessed with beauty. 'Bobby was beautiful, Charles was not, physically. Charles was short. That is something that always turned me off.'

Yet she killed at his command.

Keith asked Hochman: 'Doctor, did you ask her whether or not Mr Manson, during her association with him, had any influence over her in her thought process and in her conduct and activity?'

A. 'She denies it. But I don't buy that.'

Q. 'Why don't you buy that?'

A. 'Well, I don't understand why she would stay on the scene that long if there was nothing there for her, on some unconscious basis.'

According to Hochman, in talking to him Leslie professed 'a kind of primitive Christianity, love for the world, acceptance of all things. And I asked her, "Well, professing that, how can it be you would murder someone?" She said, "Well that was something inside of me too." '

Maxwell Keith should have stopped right there. Instead, he asked Hochman: 'How do you interpret that?'

A. 'I think it's rather realistic. I think that in reality it *was* something inside of her, despite her chronic denial of the emotional aspects of herself, that a rage was there.'

Nor did Keith leave it at that. He now asked: 'When you say a rage was there, what do you mean by that?'

A. 'In my opinion it would take a rage, an emotional reaction to kill someone. I think it is unquestionable that that feeling was inside of her.'

Q. 'Bearing in mind that she had never seen or heard of Mrs LaBianca, in your opinion there was some hate in her when this occurred?'

A. 'Well, I think it would make it easier for her not to know Mrs LaBianca . . . It is hard to kill someone that you have good feelings towards. I don't think there was anything specific about Mrs LaBianca.

'Let me make myself clear: Mrs LaBianca was an object, a

blank screen upon which Leslie projected her feelings, much as a patient projects his feeling on an analyst whom he doesn't know ... feelings towards her mother, her father, toward the establishment ...

'I think she was a very angry girl for a long time, a very alienated girl for a long time, and the anger and rage was associated with that.'

Hochman was articulating one of the main points of my final summation: namely, that Leslie, Sadie, Katie, and Tex had a hostility and rage within them that pre-existed Charles Manson. They were different from Linda Kasabian, Paul Watkins, Brooks Poston, Juan Flynn, and T.J. When Manson asked them to kill for him, each said no.

Tex Watson, Susan Atkins, Patricia Krenwinkel, and Leslie Van Houten said yes.

So there had to be something special about these people that caused them to kill. Some kind of inner flaw. Apart from Charlie.

Though he had badly damaged his own case, Keith had tried to put the hat on Manson. Fitzgerald, in his examination of Hochman, did just the opposite. He sought to minimize the importance of Manson's influence over Leslie. Asking Hochman what Manson's influence actually was, he received this reply: 'His ideas, his presence, the role he played in his relationship to her, served to reinforce a lot of her feelings and attitudes. It served to reinforce and give her a way of continuing her general social alienation, her alienation from the establishment.'

Q. 'So, really, all you are saying is that (A) Manson could possibly have had some influence, and (B), if he did have some influence, it would only contribute to the lowering of her restraints on her impulsiveness, is that correct?'

A. 'Yes.'

Q. 'So any influence Manson had on Leslie Van Houten, in terms of your professional opinion, is tenuous at best, is that correct?'

A. 'Let me give you another example that may make it clearer ... Suppose someone comes in and says, "Let's eat the whole apple pie." Obviously your temptation is stimulated by the suggestion, but your final decision on whether or not to eat the whole pie or just one piece comes out of you. So the other person is influential, but is not a final arbiter or decider of that situation . . .

'Someone can tell you to shoot someone, but your decision to do that comes from inside you.'

Kanarek, when his turn came, picked up the scent. 'And so you are telling us then, in layman's language, that when someone takes a knife and stabs, the decision to do that is a personal decision?'

A. 'In the ultimate analysis it is.'

Q. 'It is a personal decision of the person who does the stabbing?'

A. 'Yes.'

Ironically, Kanarek and I were now on the same side. Both of us were seeking to prove that, even independent of Manson, these girls had murder within them.

Hochman found in all three girls 'much evidence in their history of early alienation, of early antisocial or deviant behavior'. Of the three, Hochman felt Sadie had a little more remorse than the other two – she often talked of wishing her life were over. Yet he also noted, 'One is struck by the absence of a conventional sense of morality or conscience in this girl.' And he testified, 'She does not seem to manifest any evidence of discomfort or anxiety about her present circumstances, or her conviction and possible death sentence. On the contrary, she seemed to manifest a remarkable peacefulness and self-acceptance in her present state.'

According to Hochman, all three girls denied 'any sense of guilt whatever about anything'. And he felt that intellectually they actually believed there is no right or wrong, that morality is a relative thing. 'However, I, as a psychiatrist, know that you cannot rationally do away with the feelings that exist on the irrational, unconscious level. You cannot tell yourself that killing is O.K. intellectually when you have grown up all your life feeling that killing is wrong.'

In short, Hochman believed that as human beings the girls felt some guilt deep down inside, even though they consciously suppressed it.

Keith asked Hochman: 'In your opinion, Doctor, would Leslie be susceptible or respond to intensive therapy?'

A. 'Possibly.'

Q. 'In other words, you don't feel that she is such a lost soul that she could never be rehabilitated?'

A. 'No, I don't think she is *that* lost a soul, no.'

To a psychiatrist, no one is beyond redemption. This is essential, standard testimony. Yet only one of the defense attorneys, Maxwell Keith, asked the question, and then only on redirect.

Earlier I'd brought out that Hochman had only the word of the girls that they were on LSD either night. I now asked him: 'Have you ever read a reported case in the literature of LSD of any individual who committed murder while under the influence of LSD?'

A. 'No. Suicide, but not murder.'

On recross-examination I had Hochman define the word 'psychotic'. He replied that it meant 'a loss of contact with reality'.

I then asked him: 'At the present time, Doctor, do you feel any of these three female defendants are psychotic?'

A. 'No.'

Q. 'In your opinion, do you feel that any of these three female defendants have ever been psychotic?'

A. 'No.'

BUGLIOSI. 'May I approach the witness, Your Honor? I want to ask the witness a question privately.'

THE COURT. 'Yes, you may.'

I had already questioned Dr Hochman once about this. But I wanted to be absolutely certain of his reply. Once I had received it, I returned to the counsel table and asked him a number of unrelated questions, so the jury wouldn't know what we had been talking about. I then gradually worked up to the big one.

Q. 'The term "insanity", Doctor, you are familiar with that term, of course?'

A. 'Yes.'

Q. 'Basically, you define the word "insanity" to be the layman's synonym for "psychotic"?'

A. 'I would say that the word "insanity" is used generally to mean "psychotic".'

Q. 'Then, from a psychiatric standpoint, I take it that in your opinion none of these three female defendants are presently insane nor have they ever been insane, is that correct?'

A. 'That is correct.'

As far as the psychiatric testimony was concerned, with Hochman's reply the ball game was over.

The defense called only three more witnesses during the penalty trial, all hard-core Family members. Each was on the stand only a short time, but their testimony, particularly that of the first witness, was as shocking as anything that had gone before.

Catherine Gillies, whose grandmother owned Myers Ranch, parroted the Family line: Charlie never led anyone; there was never any talk of a race war; these murders were committed to free Bobby Beausoleil.

Coldly, matter-of-factly, the 21-year-old girl testified that on the night of the LaBianca murders, 'I followed Katie to the car, and I asked if I could go with her. Linda, Leslie, and Sadie were all in the car. And they said that they had plenty of people to do what they were going to do, and that I didn't need to go.'

On direct examination by Kanarek, Cathy stated: 'You know, I am willing to kill for a brother, we all are.'

Q. 'What do you mean by that?'

A. 'In other words, to get a brother out of jail, I would kill. I would have killed that night except I did not go . . .'

Q. 'What prevented you from going with them, if anything?'

A. 'Just the fact that they didn't need me.'

Apparently Fitzgerald hoped to soften the harshness of her reply when he asked her: 'Have you killed anybody to get someone out of jail?'

With a strange little smile, Cathy turned her head and, looking directly at the jury, replied: 'Not yet.'

Cathy had testified on direct examination that Katie had told her about the Tate–LaBianca murders. On cross-examination I asked her: 'When Katie told you that they had murdered these people, did this disturb you at all?'

A. 'Actually it had very little effect on me because I knew why they had done it.'

Q. 'So it didn't upset you?'

A. 'No, it definitely didn't upset me.'

Mary Brunner, first member of the Manson Family, claimed that the police had told her that she would be charged with murder if she did not implicate Manson in the Hinman slaying. She now repudiated this testimony and further denied even being at the Hinman residence.

Keith brought out that Mary Brunner had testified both in the second trial of Bobby Beausoleil and before the Hinman grand jury, and neither time did she say anything about Leslie Van Houten being present when Hinman was killed.

I had no questions for her. The point was made.

Brenda McCann was recalled to the stand, to testify that on the nights of the Tate and LaBianca murders she had seen Manson sleeping with Stephanie Schram in Devil's Canyon.

The groundwork for my cross-examination of Brenda had been laid fifteen months before. I impeached her with her testimony before the grand jury, when she stated that she couldn't remember where she, or Manson, was on either night.

Brenda was the last witness. She completed her testimony on Tuesday, March 16, 1971. That afternoon, after a number of delays – Kanarek, for example, refused to stipulate that Gary Hinman was dead – the defense rested. Wednesday we worked on the jury instructions, and on Thursday the trial entered its final stage. All that now remained were the arguments, the deliberations, and the verdict.

March 18–29, 1971

My opening argument in the penalty trial was brief, lasting less than ten minutes. As with all my arguments during the trial, Manson decided to sit this one out, in the lockup. The psychology behind this was obvious: he didn't want the jury focusing on him when I discussed him.

I began by saying: 'I am not going to address myself to the frantic effort by the three female defendants and the defense witnesses to make it look like Charles Manson wasn't involved in these murders. I am sure all of you clearly saw that they were lying on that witness stand to do what they could for their God, Charles Manson.

'Well, Charles Manson has already been convicted. He has already been convicted of seven counts of first degree murder and one count of conspiracy to commit murder.

'The difficulty in your decision, as I see it, is not whether these defendants deserve the death penalty, ladies and gentlemen. In view of the incredibly savage, barbaric, and inhuman murders they committed, the death penalty is the only proper verdict.' I then stated the very heart of my argument: '*If this case were not a proper case for the imposition of the death penalty, no case ever would be.* In view of what they did, life imprisonment would be the greatest gift, the greatest charity, the greatest handout, as it were, ever given.

'The difficulty in your decision, as I see it, is whether you will have the fortitude to return verdicts of death against all four defendants.'

The defense attorneys, I anticipated, would beg for their clients' lives. This was not only commendable, I told the jury, it was also understandable, just as it was understandable that they 'argued during the guilt phase that their clients were not involved in these murders, even though during the penalty phase the three female defendants took the stand and said: "Yes, we were involved" '.

There was absolutely no reason for these defendants to viciously and inhumanly snuff out the lives of these seven human beings, I noted. There were *no* mitigating circumstances.

'These defendants are not human beings, ladies and gentlemen. Human beings have a heart and a soul. No one with a heart and a soul could have done what these defendants did to these seven victims.

'These defendants are human monsters, human mutations.

'There is only one proper ending to the Tate-LaBianca murder trial,' I concluded, 'verdicts of death for all four defendants.'

Kanarek stipulated, at the start of his argument, that 'Mr Manson is not all good'. However, he continued, 'Mr Manson is innocent of these matters that are before us.'

Why was he on trial then? Kanarek returned to his two favorite themes: 'Mr Manson has had quite a share of troubles because of the fact that he likes girls.' And he was only brought to trial 'so someone in the District Attorney's Office can have a gold star and say, "I got Charles Manson" '.

Kanarek's argument stretched over three days. It was occasionally ridiculous, as when he said, 'We can perform a public service for the United States of America by giving these people life, because if there is a revolution, this is the kind of thing that could spark it.' It was sometimes unintentionally funny, as when he stated that, unlike Patricia Krenwinkel and Leslie Van Houten, 'Charles Manson has no family to come here to testify.' But mostly he tried to plant little seeds of doubt.

Why, if Susan Atkins lied on the stand to absolve Manson, would she have implicated him in the Hinman murder? Wasn't the fact that Manson himself shot Crowe, to protect the people at Spahn Ranch, evidence that he didn't need to order others to act for him? If these girls were lying about Manson's non-involvement in the murders, wouldn't they have also lied and said they had sorrow and remorse?

Kanarek only briefly mentioned the copycat motive; he didn't even try to argue it. Instead, he suggested still another alternative motive. 'But for the fact that at least some of these people [supposedly referring to the Tate victims] were engaged in a narcotic episode of some type, these events would not have taken place.'

Daye Shinn, who argued next, fastened on Dr Hochman's statement that he believed these girls had subconscious if not conscious remorse.

As for Susan, 'She is still young,' Shinn argued. 'She is only 22 years old. I believe there is still a hope of rehabilitating her . . . Maybe someday she may be rehabilitated to the extent that she may finally realize what she has done was not right. I believe that she deserves the chance, an opportunity, so that maybe someday she may be released and live the rest of her life out of prison.'

This was very bad strategy on Shinn's part, implying that if Susan Atkins was given life imprisonment she might someday be released on parole. By law, the prosecution can't argue this, it is so prejudicial to the defendant.

Of the four defense attorneys, Maxwell Keith gave the best opening argument. He was also the only one who really attempted to rebut my contentions.

'Mr Bugliosi tells you that if the death penalty is not appropriate in this case, it would never be appropriate. Well, I wonder if it ever is appropriate?

'Mr Bugliosi read to you at the close of his argument on the guilt phase the roll call of the dead. Let me read to you now, ladies and gentlemen, the roll call of the living dead: Leslie, Sadie, Katie, Squeaky, Brenda, Ouisch, Sandy, Cathy, Gypsy, Tex, Clem, Mary, Snake, and no doubt many more. These lives, and the lives of these three young girls in particular, have been so damaged that it is possible, in some cases, their destruction is beyond repair. I hope not, but it is possible.'

Leslie Van Houten, he strongly argued, was capable of rehabilitation. She should be studied, not killed. 'I am not asking you to forgive her, although to forgive is divine. I am asking you to give her the chance to redeem herself. She deserves to live. What she did was not done by the real Leslie. Let the Leslie of today die – she will, slowly and maybe painfully. And let the Leslie as she once was live again.'

Nowhere in Paul Fitzgerald's argument, which followed, did he state, or even imply, that Manson was responsible for what had happened to Patricia Krenwinkel.

'Patricia Krenwinkel is 23 years old,' Fitzgerald observed. 'With 365 days in the year, there are approximately 8,400 days in 23 years, and approximately 200,000 hours in her lifetime.

'The perpetration of these offences took at best approximately three hours.

'Is she to be judged solely on what occurred during three of 200,000 hours?'

Just before court commenced on March 23, I walked over to the water cooler. Manson, in the nearby lockup, called out to me, rather loudly, 'If I get the death penalty, there is going to be a lot of bloodletting. Because I am not going to take it.'

Both the court clerk and Steve Kay overheard the remark. Kay intemperately rushed out of the courtroom and repeated it to the press. Learning of this, I asked the reporters not to print it. The *Herald Examiner* wouldn't agree, and it broke the story with a banner headline:

MANSON DEATH THREAT
Warns of Terror
If Doomed to Die

Before this, however, Judge Older, made aware of what had happened, decided that, rather than wait to the close of arguments, he would sequester the jury immediately.

In my final argument I rebutted point by point the earlier defense contentions. For example, the defense had claimed that Linda got her story from listening to the Susan Atkins tapes. Why would Linda need to listen to the tapes, I asked, when she was present both nights?

Kanarek had told the jury that if they returned death penalty verdicts, they would be murderers. This was a very heavy argument. As support, he cited the Fifth Commandment: 'Thou shalt not kill.'

In answer, I told the jury that most biblical scholars and historians interpret the original language to mean: 'Thou shalt not commit murder,' which is exactly how it appears in the New English Bible, dated 1970.

Kanarek argued that there was no domination. In addition to all the evidence during the guilt trial I observed, during the penalty trial, 'When Atkins, Krenwinkel, and Van Houten played the part of the sacrificial lamb and admitted their participation in these murders, and then lied on that witness stand and said that Manson wasn't involved, the fact that they were willing to lie on that witness stand just proves, all the more, Manson's domination over them . . .' As for the other Family witnesses, Squeaky, Sandy, and the others, 'All of them sounded like a broken record on that witness stand. They all have the same thought; they use the same language; each one was a carbon copy of the other. They are all still totally subservient and subject to Charles Manson. They are his X'd-out slaves.'

I came now to the copycat motive. My objective was to completely demolish it, yet not dwell on it so long that it would seem that I was giving it credence.

'It is really laughable, ladies and gentlemen,' I began, 'the way the three female defendants and the defense witnesses sought to take the hat off Charles Manson.

'They had to come up with a motive for these murders other than Helter Skelter. Why? Because no less than ten witnesses during the guilt trial had irrevocably connected Manson with Helter Skelter, so they certainly could not say from that witness stand that the motive for these murders was Helter Skelter. If they said that, they would be saying, "Yes, Charles Manson masterminded these murders." So they came up with the copycat motive.

'I could give you between twenty and thirty reasons why it's obvious that this nonsensical story of the defense was fabricated out of whole cloth, but I won't take up your time with it, and I am not going to insult your intelligence.' I did point out a few:

Linda Kasabian testified during the penalty trial that she had never heard anyone discuss committing these murders to free Bobby Beausoleil.

Gary Hinman was stabbed not more than four times. Voytek Frykowski was stabbed fifty-one times, Rosemary LaBianca forty-one times, Leno LaBianca twenty-six times. Rather a great difference, if these were copycat slayings.

And, if these murders were to be carbon copies, why weren't the words 'political piggy' used at the Tate and LaBianca residences? And why no bloody paw print at the latter two houses?

The most powerful evidence demolishing this ridiculous motive, I noted, was that as early as February 1969, 'long before there was any Hinman murder to copy, long before there were any words "political piggy" to copy, Manson told Brooks Poston and other Family members – including all of his co-defendants – that, quoting Poston: "He said a group of real blacks would come out of the ghettos and do an atrocious crime in the richer sections of Los Angeles and other cities. They would do an atrocious murder with stabbing, killing, cutting bodies to pieces, smearing blood on the walls, writing 'pigs' on the walls."

'Writing "pigs" on the walls,' I repeated.

'So writing "pig" at the Tate and LaBianca residences was simply a part of Manson's blueprint for starting Helter Skelter, not an effort to copy the Hinman murder.

'Yes,' I admitted, 'there is a connection between the Hinman murder and the Tate-LaBianca murders. But it was not this silly Bobby Beausoleil nonsense. Here is the connection. Mr Manson not only ordered the Tate-LaBianca murders, he also ordered the Hinman murder. That is the connection.'

As for Susan Atkins' claim that Linda Kasabian masterminded these murders, I noted that not until the penalty phase did she say anything about this, and then 'all of a sudden Linda Kasabian is Charles Manson'.

The most preposterous thing about all this was that supposedly for one and a half years both Sadie and Gypsy kept this secret in their perjurous bosoms. They not only didn't tell the other members of the Family, they didn't even tell Manson's attorney, though both testified they loved and would willingly die for Charlie.

'And why didn't they tell him about this motive? Because it didn't exist. It was recently fabricated.'

As for Manson's alibi, that he was with Stephanie Schram in Devil's Canyon on both of these nights, 'Isn't it strange that all of Mr Manson's X'd-out slaves have testified to this during the penalty trial, and the very person, Stephanie Schram, whom they claim Manson was with, testified that Manson was not with her?'

I then addressed myself to the issue of whether the four defendants should receive the death penalty.

The strongest argument that can be made in support of capital punishment is, I feel, deterrence – that it may save additional lives. Unfortunately, under California law the prosecution could not argue deterrence, only retribution.

'These weren't typical murders, ladies and gentlemen. This was a one-sided war where unspeakable atrocities were committed. If all of these defendants don't receive the death penalty, the typical first-degree murderer only deserves ten days in the County Jail.'

In regard to the defense contention that the three female defendants were insane, I reminded the jury that Dr Hochman, the only psychiatrist to examine all three, said they are not and have never been insane.

Dr Hochman testified that we are all capable of killing, I noted. 'He did not say that we are all capable of murder. There is a vast difference between killing – as in justifiable homicide, self-defense, or defense of others – and murder. And no one can convince me, ladies and gentlemen, that all of us are capable of murdering strangers for no reason whatsoever like these three female defendants did.

'It takes a special type of person to do what they did. It takes a person who places no value on the life of a fellow human being.

'True, Watson, Atkins, Krenwinkel, and Van Houten committed these murders because Charles Manson told them to, but they would never have committed these murders in a million years if they did not already have murder in their guts, in their system. Manson merely told them to do what they were already capable of doing.'

Moreover, there was no evidence that Manson *forced* Watson and the girls to murder for him. 'In fact, the inference is that they wanted to go along. That seemed to be the general feeling in the Family. Witness the statement of Cathy Gillies. Witness Susan Atkins' telling Juan Flynn, "We're going to get some fucking pigs." Does that sound like someone who is being forced to go out?'

Manson ordered the murders, but Watson and the three girls personally committed them 'because they wanted to. Make no mistake about that. If they did not want to murder these victims, *all they had to do was not do it.*'

I examined now the backgrounds of the three girls. Like the other female members of the Family, they had 'one common denominator among them. It was obvious that each of them had a revulsion, an antipathy, a seething feeling of disgust for society, for their own parents.'

'Manson was simply the catalyst, the moving force that translated their pre-existing disgust and hatred for society and human beings into violence.'

I anticipated an argument that I felt Maxwell Keith might give. 'The thought certainly may enter your mind that, as wicked and as vicious as these three female defendants are, by comparison to Charles Manson they are nowhere as wicked and vicious as he is; therefore, let's give Manson the death penalty and these three female defendants life imprisonment.

'The only problem with that type of approach is that these female defendants are given credit, as it were, because of Manson's extreme wickedness and viciousness. Under that type of reasoning, if Adolf Hitler were Charles Manson's co-defendant, Manson should receive life imprisonment because of the indescribably evil Adolf Hitler.' Rather than compare the three female defendants with Manson, I told the jury, they should evaluate the conduct of *each* of the defendants and determine whether it warranted the imposition of the death penalty. I then went into the acts of each, starting with Manson, enumerating one by one the reasons they deserved death rather than life.

One question the jury would surely ask, I noted, was: Why no remorse? The answer was simple: 'Manson and his co-defendants like to kill human beings. That is why they have no remorse. As Paul Watkins testified, "Death is Charlie's trip." '

I came to the end of my argument.

'Now the defense attorneys want you to give these defendants a break. Did these defendants give the seven victims in this case a break?

'Now the defense attorneys want you to give their clients another chance. Did these defendants give the seven victims in this case any chance at all?

'Now the defense attorneys want you to have mercy on their clients. Did these defendants have any mercy at all on the seven victims in this case when they begged and pleaded for their lives?'

I then reminded the jurors that nine months earlier, during voir dire, each had told me he would be willing to vote death if he felt this was a proper case. I reiterated: '*If the death penalty is to mean anything in the State of California, other than two empty words, this is a proper case.*'

I concluded: 'On behalf of the People of the State of California, I can't thank you enough for the enormous public service you have rendered as jurors in this very long, historic trial.'

That night after dinner I said to Gail, 'There must be *something* I have to do tonight.' But there wasn't. For a year and a half, seven days a week, I had been totally immersed in the case. Now all I could do was listen to the closing arguments of the defense attorneys and wait until the jury reached its verdict.

Kanarek began by implying that perhaps I had poisoned the glass of water on the lectern and ended, more than a day later, by reading chapter after chapter from the New Testament.

'Now, this being the Easter season, there is an analogy here between Mr Manson – this may sound at first blush to be ridiculous, and we are not suggesting that Mr Manson is the deity or Christlike or anything like that – *but how can we know?*'

Judge Older, who had several times warned Kanarek that he had exhausted all relevant rebuttal, finally brought his sermon to an end at the point of resurrection.

Shinn spent his time attacking the D A's Office and in particular me: 'Miss Atkins was drowning without friends ... and she saw Mr Bugliosi with an oar. She said: Oh, here comes help now. Miss Atkins reached out for that oar. And what do you think Mr Bugliosi did? He hit her over the head with the oar.'

Keith delivered a strong argument against the death penalty itself. Before this, however, he said: 'Now strangely, or perhaps not so strangely, I accepted wholeheartedly certain areas of Mr Bugliosi's argument.

'I accept his exposition to you that Mr Manson dominated these girls and ordered the homicides.

'I accept that the "free Bobby Beausoleil" motive is nonsense.

'I accept his telling you that you shouldn't hold the Hinman murder against Leslie.

'I accept his argument that Leslie's testimony and the testimony of the other girls in this case shows Mr Manson's domination and influence still persists and is all-pervasive.'

To deny these things, Keith said, would be to deny the evidence. Thus Keith became the first, and only, defense attorney to accuse Manson of these murders.

Keith, however, said that he did not agree that any of the defendants should receive the death penalty, not even Charles Manson. For in his opinion, Keith said, 'Mr Manson is insane,' and in instilling his thoughts into the minds of the three female defendants he had also infected them with his madness.

Keith concluded: 'Give Leslie the chance for redemption, to which she is entitled. Remember, Linda Kasabian cut the umbilical cord, in Mr Bugliosi's words, that tied her to Manson and his Family. Give Leslie the chance to do the same. Give her life. I thank you.'

Fitzgerald read a short argument, at the end of which he began describing in detail how the three female defendants would be executed in the gas chamber at San Quentin Prison if the jury returned verdicts of death. This was improper argument, and I objected. When we approached the bench, Paul literally begged Judge Older to let him proceed. 'This is extremely important! I can't impress on the Court how important it is!' Because he was so desperate, I decided to back off, agreeing not to object if he would describe this as a hypothetical situation – 'Imagine that this is happening' – and not as fact. He did so, after which Judge Older instructed the jury. They left the courtroom at 5:25 P.M. on Friday, March 26, 1971.

While I felt confident that the jury would return a death penalty verdict against Charles Manson, I was less sure when it came to the girls. Only four females had been executed in California history, none of them as young as the defendants.

I had anticipated that the jury would be out at least four days. When I received the call Monday afternoon, after only two days, I knew there could be only one verdict. It was too fast for anything else. Their actual deliberations, I later learned, had taken only ten hours.

Again under extraordinary security precautions, the jury was brought back into the courtroom, at 4:24 P.M. on Monday, March 29, with their verdicts.

Manson and the girls had been brought into the courtroom earlier – the three female defendants now, when it was too late to influence the jury, having shaved their heads also – but before the clerk read the first verdict, Manson yelled, 'I don't see how you can get by with this without letting me put on some kind of defense . . . You people have no authority over me . . . Half of you in here ain't as good as I am . . .' and Older ordered him removed.

Manson's no-defense claim was nonsense. It was obvious that the defense he intended to put on during the guilt phase had been delivered in toto during the penalty phase. The jury's reaction to it was now being delivered, in a courtroom jammed with spectators and press.

The clerk read the first verdict: 'We, the jury in the above-entitled action, having found the defendant Charles Manson guilty of murder in the first degree as charged in Count I of the Indictment, do now fix the penalty as death.'

KRENWINKEL. 'You have just judged yourselves.'

ATKINS. 'Better lock your doors and watch your own kids.'

VAN HOUTEN. 'Your whole system is a game. You blind, stupid people. Your children will turn against you.'

Judge Older had the three girls removed. They too listened over the loudspeaker as the clerk fixed the penalty for all four defendants as death on all counts.

Judge Older left the bench to shake hands with each juror. 'If it were within the power of a trial judge to award a medal of honor to jurors,' he told them, 'believe me, I would bestow an award on each of you.'

For the first time the jurors could speak to the press about their ordeal.

Jury foreman Herman Tubick told reporters that the jury was convinced 'the motive was Helter Skelter'. Mrs Thelma McKenzie said the jury had 'certainly tried' to find points upon which they could sentence the female defendants to a verdict less severe, 'but we couldn't'. William McBride remarked: 'I felt sympathy for the women but sympathy can't interfere with justice. What they did deserves the death penalty.' Marie Mesmer said she felt more pity for Susan Atkins than for the other two girls, because of her background, but that she was shocked when all three showed no signs of remorse. As for Manson, she said: 'I wanted to protect society. I think Manson is a very dangerous influence.' Jean Roseland, mother of three teeen-agers, two of them girls, said the most terrible part of the whole trial was Leslie Van Houten 'looking at me with those big brown eyes'. Mrs Roseland was convinced Manson's power to manipulate others came not from within himself but 'from the voids within the minds and souls of his followers'.

Colonel Paul Tate was reported to have said, regarding the death sentence verdicts: 'That's what we wanted. That's what we expected. But there's no jubilation in something like this, no sense of satisfaction. It's more a feeling that justice has been done. Naturally I wanted the death penalty. They took my daughter and my grandchild.'

Mrs Tate told reporters that she didn't believe any human being should have the power to take a life, that that was up to God.

Roman Polanski declined comment, as did the other relatives of the victims whom the media contacted.

Sandy, Cathy, and the other girls on the corner had threatened to burn themselves to death with gasoline if any of the four were given death sentences. They didn't carry out their threat, though all did later shave their heads.

On learning of the decision, Sandy looked into the TV cameras and screamed: *'Death? That's what you're all going to get!'*

With the exception of the sentencing, the trial was over. It had been the longest murder trial in American history, lasting nine and a half months; the most expensive, costing approximately $1 million; and the most highly publicized; while the jury had been sequestered 225 days, longer than any jury before it. The trial transcript alone ran to 209 volumes, 31,716 pages, approximately eight million words, a mini-library.

For almost everyone, the ordeal was not only long but expensive. A number of the jurors, anticipating that they would be paid by their employers, now found themselves either unpaid or without jobs. Mrs Roseland, for example, claimed that TWA did not honor a verbal agreement to keep her on salary until the end of the trial, and estimated she lost about $2,700 in back pay. TWA denied there was any such agreement. There were several such denials.

The financial sacrifice on the part of the defense attorneys was enormous. Fitzgerald said: 'It's just really wiped me out.' He told a reporter that he had lost about $30,000 in income and incurred $10,000 in trial expenses. He had been forced to sell his stereo and other possessions, and had spent $5,000 which he didn't have. Six-times-married Daye Shinn said: 'I'm behind in my house payments and child support and my alimonies.' Shinn had received $19,000 in royalties from the Atkins book, he said, but he claimed that about $16,000 of it went back to the Manson Family. Kanarek refused to discuss his financial situation. Another of the defense attorneys did tell me, however, that at one point during the trial Manson had ordered Shinn to give Kanarek $5,000 from the Atkins account, to help defray his expenses, but how much more he received, if any, is unknown. Keith, who received a fee from the county, since he was court-appointed, admitted his private practice had gone downhill and that he didn't expect to gain any new clients as a result of the publicity.

The trial cost another attorney his life.

In the avalanche of stories on the Manson verdict, one small item which appeared that same day went almost unnoticed.

The Ventura County Sheriff's Office reported that they had found a body believed to be that of the missing defense attorney, Ronald Hughes. The badly decomposed corpse had been found face down, wedged between two boulders, in Sespe Creek, miles from where Hughes had last been seen alive.

Two fishermen had discovered the body early Saturday but didn't report it until Sunday night, because 'we didn't want to spoil our fishing trip'.

The cause of death was at this time unknown. Through our office, I ordered an immediate autopsy.

April 19, 1971

Judge Older had set Monday, April 19, 1971, as the date of sentencing.

There was speculation that Older might decide on his own to reduce at least some of the verdicts from death to life. In a previous case Older had done this for a defendant who had poured gasoline on two beds where four children were sleeping, killing one of them. However, I personally felt that since Older had complimented the jurors, he wouldn't turn right around and set aside their verdict.

On the nineteenth the Court heard, and rejected, a number of defense motions, including those for a new trial. Judge Older then asked the defendants if they had anything to say. Only Manson did.

Charlie's left hand was trembling and he seemed near tears. Very meekly, with a quivering voice, he said: 'I accept this court as my father. I have always done my best in my life to uphold the laws of my father, and I accept my father's judgment.'

THE COURT. 'After nine and a half months of trial, all of the superlatives had been used, all of the hyperbole had been indulged in, and all that remains are the bare, stark facts of seven senseless murders, seven people whose lives were snuffed out by total strangers . . .

'I have carefully looked, in considering this action, for mitigating circumstances, and I have been unable to find any . . .

'It is my considered judgment that not only is the death penalty appropriate, but it is almost compelled by the circumstances. I must agree with the prosecutor that if this is not a proper case for the death penalty, what would be?'

Speaking to Manson, Judge Older said: 'The Department of

Corrections is ordered to deliver you to the custody of the Warden of the State Prison of the State of California at San Quentin to be by him put to death in the manner prescribed by law of the State of California.'

There was at this time no Death Row for women. A special isolation wing was being constructed at the California Institute for Women at Frontera, and Atkins, Krenwinkel, and Van Houten were sent there to await execution.

It was anticipated that the appeals would take at least two and possibly as long as five years.

In actuality, their fate would be decided in less than one.

After the sentencing, I didn't anticipate ever seeing Charles Manson again. But I'd see him twice more, the last time under very peculiar circumstances.

Epilogue

A Shared Madness

'A more comprehensive description of her
condition will necessitate further study.
But at this time we might suggest the
possibility that she may be suffering from
a condition of *folie à famille*, a kind of
shared madness within a group situation.'

Dr Joel Hochman,
in his psychiatric
report on Susan Atkins

'I lived with Charlie for one year straight
and on and off for two years. I know Charlie.
I know him inside and out. I became Charlie.
Everything I once was, was Charlie. There was
nothing left of me anymore. And all of the
people in the Family, there's nothing left of
them anymore, they're all Charlie too.'

Paul Watkins

'We are what you have made us. We were brought
up on your TV. We were brought up watching
"Gunsmoke", "Have Gun Will Travel", "FBI", "Combat".
"Combat" was my favorite show. I never missed
"Combat".'

Brenda

'Whatever is necessary, you do it. When somebody
needs to be killed, there's no wrong. You do it,
and then you move on. And you pick up a child and
you move him to the desert. You pick up as many
children as you can and you kill whoever gets in
your way. That is us.'
                              Sandy

'If you find an apple that has a little spot on it,
you cut out that spot.'
                              Squeaky

'You just better hope I never get out.'
                              Bobby Beausoleil

A Shared Madness

Although Manson and the girls had been convicted, the trials, and the murders, were not yet over.

For their part in the attempted murder of prosecution witness Barbara Hoyt, four of the five defendants served ninety days in the County Jail, while the fifth escaped punishment entirely.

Although I was not assigned to the case, I questioned the way it was handled. Because it was felt that the evidence against the defendants was weak, and because of the expense of flying in witnesses from Hawaii, the DA's Office, LAPD, and the defense attorneys agreed to a 'deal'. In return for the defendants pleading 'no contest' to one count of conspiracy to dissuade a witness from testifying, the prosecutor made a motion to reduce the charge from a felony to a misdeameanor. Judge Stephen Stothers granted the motion, and on April 16, 1971, he sentenced four of the five defendants – Lynette Fromme, aka Squeaky; Steve Grogan, aka Clem; Catherine Share, aka Gypsy; and Dennis Rice – to ninety days in the County Jail. Since they had already served fifteen days, they were back on the streets in seventy-five days.

The fifth defendant, Ruth Ann Moorehouse, aka Ouisch, the girl who actually gave Barbara Hoyt the LSD-laden hamburger, got off scot-free. When it came time for sentencing, she failed to appear. Although a bench warrant was issued for her arrest and she was known to be living in Carson City, Nevada, the DA's Office decided it wasn't worth the trouble to extradite her.

Of the five, three would later be involved in other murders, some attempted, some successful.

Epilogue

Charles 'Tex' Watson went on trial in August 1971. A good portion of my preparation took place not in a law library but in a medical library, since I was relatively sure that Watson was going to plead not guilty by reason of insanity and put on a psychiatric defense.

The trial had three possible phases – guilt, sanity, and penalty – each of which presented its own special problems.

Even though defense attorney Sam Bubrick told me that Watson intended to take the stand and confess, I knew I still had to present a strong case during the guilt phase, since it was a safe bet that Watson's testimony would be self-serving. Too, I had to prove (by evidence such as Watson's instructing Linda to steal the $5,000) that although Watson was dominated by Manson, he still had enough independence to make him legally responsible for his acts. One of the key issues during the guilt trial, then, was whether Watson was suffering from diminished mental capacity at the time of the murders. If he was, and it was of such a nature that it prevented him from deliberating and premeditating, the jury would have to find the chief Tate-LaBianca killer guilty of second rather than first degree murder.

If convicted of any degree of criminal homicide, then there would be a sanity trial, in which the sole issue would be whether Watson was sane or insane at the time of the murders. I anticipated, and quite rightly, that the defense would call a number of prominent psychiatrists (eight were called), many of whom would testify that in their opinion Watson was insane. Therefore I'd not only have to subject their testimony to withering cross-examination, I'd also have to present an abundance of evidence showing that Watson was in full command of his mental faculties at the time of the murders and that he was well aware that in the eyes of society what he was doing was wrong. In short, I had to prove that he wasn't legally insane. Such evidence as his cutting of the telephone wires, his telling Linda to wipe the knives of fingerprints, his manner when talking to Rudolf Weber, and his using an alias when questioned by the authorities in Death Valley a few weeks after the murders thus became extremely important to proving my case, in that all were circumstantial evidence of a consciousness of wrongdoing and guilt on Watson's part.

If Watson was convicted of first degree murder and also found sane, then the jury would have to decide the ultimate question: whether he was to be given life or death. And this meant I would again face many of the same problems I had with the girls in the penalty phase of the earlier trial.

Still another problem was Watson's demeanor. In an obvious attempt to project a college-boy image, Watson dressed very conservatively in court — short hair, shirt and tie, blue blazer, slacks. But he still looked strange. His eyes were glassy, and never seemed to focus. He reacted not at all to the damning testimony of such witnesses as Linda Kasabian, Paul Watkins, Brooks Poston, and Dianne Lake. And his mouth was always slightly gaping, giving him the appearance of being mentally retarded.

Taking the stand on direct examination by the defense, Tex played the part of Manson's abject slave. He admitted shooting or stabbing six of the Tate-LaBianca victims, but denied stabbing Sharon Tate. And everything which showed either premeditation or deliberation he put on Manson or the girls.

My cross-examination so shook Tex that he often forgot he was supposed to be playing the idiot. By the time I'd finished, it was obvious to the jury that he was in complete command of his mental faculties and probably always had been. I also got him to admit that he had stabbed Sharon Tate too; that he didn't think of the victims as people but as 'just blobs'; that he had told Dr Joel Fort that the people at the Tate residence 'were running around like chickens with their heads cut off', and that when he said this he had smiled; and I tore to shreds his story that he was simply an unthinking zombie programmed by Charles Manson, as well as cast considerable doubt on his claim that he now felt remorse for what he had done.

Watson's testimony cleared up some mysteries:

Contrary to the findings of LAPD evidence-expert DeWayne Wolfer, Watson identified the pair of red wire cutters found in Manson's dune buggy as the pair he had used to cut the Tate telephone wires that night.

Also revealed for the first time were Manson's exact instructions to Watson on the night of the murders at 10050 Cielo Drive. Watson testified: 'Charlie called me over behind a car . . . and handed me a gun and a knife. He said for me to take the gun and knife and go up to where Terry Melcher used to live. He said to kill everybody in the house as gruesome as I could. I believe he said something about movie stars living there.'

And Watson admitted that when he entered the LaBianca residence, he was already armed with a knife.

My greatest difficulty during the entire Watson trial came not from the evidence, the defense attorneys, or the defense witnesses, but from the judge, Adolph Alexander, who was a personal friend of defense attorney Sam Bubrick.

Alexander not only repeatedly favored the defense in his rulings, he went far beyond that. During voir dire he remarked: 'Many of us are opposed to the death penalty.' When prosecution witnesses were testifying, he gave them incredulous, unbelieving looks; when defense witnesses took the stand, he industriously took note. All this was done right in front of the jury. He also frequently cross-examined the prosecution witnesses. Finally, I'd had it. Asking to approach the bench, I reminded Alexander that this was a jury trial, not a court trial, and that I was immensely concerned that by cross-examining the prosecution witnesses he was giving the jury the impression that he didn't believe the witnesses, and since a judge has substantial stature in the eyes of a jury, this could be extremely harmful to the People. I suggested that if he wanted to have certain questions asked, he write them out and give them to the defense attorneys to ask.

Thereafter Alexander cut down on his cross-examination of the prosecution witnesses. However, he still continued to amaze me. When the jury went out to deliberate, he didn't even have the exhibits sent back to the jury room – a virtually automatic act – until after I had demanded that he do so. And once, in chambers and off the record, he referred to the defendant as 'poor Tex'.

Also off the record was a remark I made to him toward the end of the trial: 'You're the biggest single obstacle to my obtaining a conviction of first degree murder in this case.'

Despite the problems presented by Judge Alexander, on October 12, 1971, the jury found Watson guilty of seven counts of first degree murder and one count of conspiracy to commit murder. That I had effectively destroyed the testimony of the defense psychiatrists on cross-examination was borne out by the fact that on October 19 it took the jury only two and a half hours to decide that Watson was sane. And on October 21, after remaining out only six hours, they returned with a verdict of death.

The trial had lasted two and a half months and cost a quarter of a million dollars. It also added another forty volumes, 5,916 pages, to the mini-library on the Tate-LaBianca murders.

Although Judge Alexander thanked the jury for the conscientious job they had done, he remarked, on the day he sentenced Watson, 'If I had tried this case without a jury, I possibly would have arrived at a different verdict.'

In still other proceedings, Susan Atkins pleaded guilty to the murder of Gary Hinman and was given life imprisonment. In sentencing her, Judge Raymond Choate called her 'a danger to any community', who should spend 'her entire life in custody'.

The defense obtained separate trials for Charles Manson, Bruce Davis, and Steve Grogan on the combined Hinman-Shea murder charges. Despite the fact that the body of Donald 'Shorty' Shea hadn't been found (and hasn't to this day), prosecutors Burt Katz, Anthony Manzella, and Steven Kay succeeded in the difficult task of obtaining guilt verdicts against each of the defendants on all of the counts. Verdicts of life imprisonment were returned for Manson and Davis. The Grogan jury voted death, but when it came time for sentencing – two days before Christmas 1971 – Judge James Kolts, commenting that 'Grogan was too stupid and too hopped up on drugs to decide anything on his own', and declaring that it was really Manson 'who decided who lived or died', reduced the sentence to life imprisonment.

During voir dire in his trial, Manson, angered by the judge's refusal to let him represent himself, told the Court: 'I enter a plea of guilty. I chopped off Shorty's head.' The judge refused to accept the plea, and the next day Manson withdrew it. During another angry outburst, Manson turned to the press and said, 'I've told my people to start killing you.'

Again Manson was represented by Irving Kanarek. With Irving, he knew it would be a long trial, postponing his trip to San Quentin's Death Row.

Through all the trials, the Manson girls continued their vigil on the corner of Temple and Broadway. Literally in the shadow of the Hall of Justice, in view of the thousands of people who passed that corner every day, they fashioned a bizarre plot to free all the imprisoned Manson Family members.

In late July of 1971 my co-author learned from a Family member in the San Francisco Bay Area that the Family was planning to break out Manson sometime within the next month. Though he was not told how they intended to accomplish this, he was given some additional details: the Family was stockpiling arms and ammunition; they had secretly rented a house in South Los Angeles and were hiding an escaped convict there; and with Manson's escape 'Helter Skelter will really start; the revolution will be on'.

Wishful thinking? I wasn't sure, and passed the information along to LAPD. When I did, I learned that among the witnesses Manson had called in the Hinman-Shea trial was a Folsom convict named Kenneth Como, also known by the colourful aka Jesse James. Though it hadn't been publicized, when brought to Los Angeles less than a week before, Como had managed to escape from the Hall of Record. LAPD doubted, however, that he was still in the area. As for the Manson escape, they had heard rumors also, but nothing definite. They were inclined to doubt the tale.

On schedule, less than a month later, the Manson Family made their attempt.

Shortly after closing time on the night of Saturday, August 21,

1971, six armed robbers entered the Western Surplus Store in the Los Angeles suburb of Hawthorne. While one kept a shotgun on the female clerk and two customers, the others began carrying rifles, shotguns, and pistols to a van parked in the alley outside. They had collected about 140 guns when they spotted the first police car. LAPD, alerted by a silent alarm, had already sealed off the alley.

The robbers came out shooting. In the ten-minute gun battle that followed, the van was riddled with over fifty bullets, and some twenty bullets crashed into the police cars. Surprisingly, no one was killed, though three of the suspects received slight wounds.

All six robbers were Manson Family members. Apprehended were Mary Brunner, 27, first member of the Family; Catherine Share, aka Gypsy, 29, and Dennis Rice, 32, both recently freed after serving ninety-day sentences for their part in the attempted silencing of Barbara Hoyt; Lawrence Bailey, aka Larry Jones, 23, who was present the night the Tate killers left Spahn; and escaped convict Kenneth Como, 33. Another Family member, Charles Lovett, 19, got away during the gun fight but was subsequently apprehended.

After their arrest it was learned that the same group was also responsible for the robbery of a Covina beer distributorship on August 13, which netted them $2,600.

The police surmised that through the robberies the group intended to get enough guns and ammunition to stage a San Rafael-type commando raid on the courthouse. Steve Grogan had called Manson as a witness in his trial. It was believed that the day Manson appeared in court the Family intended to storm the Hall of Justice, breaking out both.

Actually, the real plan was far more spectacular. And, given the right circumstances and enough public pressure, it just *might* have worked.

Although never made public before this, according to a Family member who was privy to the planning of the Hawthorne robbery, the real plan was as follows:

Using the stolen weapons, the Family was going to hijack a 747

575

and kill one passenger every hour until Manson and all the other imprisoned Family members were released.

Extraordinary security measures were taken during the trial of the Hawthorne robbery defendants, in part because the defense had called as witnesses what Judge Arthur Alarcon labeled 'the biggest collection of murderers in Los Angeles County at one time'. Twelve convicted killers, including Manson, Beausoleil, Atkins, Krenwinkel, Van Houten, Grogan, and Davis, took the stand. Their presence in one place made everyone a little nervous. Especially since by this time the Family had discovered that the Hall of Justice was not escapeproof.

In the early-morning hours of October 20, 1971, Kenneth Como hacksawed his way through the bars of his thirteenth-floor cell, climbed down to the eighth floor on a rope made of bed sheets, kicked in a window in the courtroom of Department 104 (where just a few months earlier I'd prosecuted Manson and his three female co-defendants), then left the building by way of the stairs. Sandra Good picked up Como in the Family van. Though Sandy later smashed up the van and was arrested, Como managed to elude capture for seven hours. Also arrested – but subsequently released, there being no positive proof that they had aided and abetted the escape – were Squeaky, Brenda, Kitty, and two other Family members.

No attempt was made to break out Manson during the Hawthorne trial. However, two of the jurors had to be replaced by alternates after receiving telephone threats that they would be killed if they voted for conviction. The calls were linked to an unidentified female Family member.

Although Gypsy and Rice had previously been given only ninety days for their part in the attempted murder of a prosecution witness, they and their co-defendants found that the courts take shooting at police officers a little more seriously. All were charged with two counts of armed robbery. Rice pleaded guilty and was sent to state prison. The others were convicted on both counts and given the following sentences: Lovett, two consecutive five-year-to-life terms; Share, ten years to life;

Como, fifteen years to life; Brunner and Bailey, twenty years to life.

Sandra Good was subsequently tried for aiding and abetting an escape. Her attorney, the one and only Irving Kanarek, claimed she had been kidnaped by Como. The jury didn't buy it, and Sandy was given six months in jail.

The day Como escaped, Kanarek, appearing in Judge Raymond Choate's court, claimed in his patented way: 'I allege with no proof at this particular time that this escape was deliberately allowed to take place.'

Judge Choate asked Kanarek if he could explain why Como was forced to climb down a rope from the thirteenth to the eighth floor.

'That makes it look good, Your Honor,' Kanarek explained.

While Manson was still on trial for the Hinman-Shea murders, I dropped into the courtroom one day. It was a welcome relief to be a spectator for a change.

Manson, who had recently taken to wearing a black storm trooper's uniform in court, spotted me and sent a message by the bailiff that he wanted to speak to me. There were a few things I wanted to ask him about also, so I stayed over after court recessed. Sitting in the prisoner's dock in the courtroom, we talked from 4:30 P.M. to nearly 6 P.M. None of the talk concerned the current charges against him. Mostly we discussed his philosophy. I was especially interested in learning the evolution of some of his ideas, and questioned him at length about his relationship with Scientology and with the satanic cult known as The Process, or the Church of the Final Judgement.

Manson had wanted to speak to me, he said, because he wanted me to know 'I don't have no hard feelings'. He told me that I had done 'a fantastic, remarkable job' in convicting him, and he said, 'You gave me a fair trial, like you promised.' He was not bitter about the result, however, because to him 'prison has always been my home; I didn't want to leave it the last time and you're only sending me back there'. There were regular meals, not great, but better than the garbage at Spahn Ranch. And since you don't have to work if you don't want to, he'd have plenty of time to play his guitar.

'That may be, Charlie, but you don't have any women there,' I said.

'I don't need broads,' he replied. 'Every women I ever had, *she* asked *me* to make love to her. I never asked them. I can do without them.' There was plenty of sex in prison, he said.

Although Manson again claimed that the Beatles' music and LSD were responsible for the Tate-LaBianca murders, he admitted that he had known they were going to happen, 'because I even knew what the mice were doing at Spahn Ranch'. He then added, 'So I said to them: "Here, do you want this rope? Do you want this gun?" And later I told them not to tell anyone about what happened.'

Though careful never to do so in open court, in our private conversations Manson often referred to blacks as 'niggers'. He claimed he didn't dislike them. 'I don't hate anyone,' he said, 'but I know they hate me.'

Returning to the familiar theme of Helter Skelter, I asked him when he thought the black man was going to take over.

'I may have put a clog in them,' he replied.

'You mean the trial alerted whitey?'

His reply was a simple, and sad, 'Yeah.'

Our conversation took place on June 14, 1971. The following day one of the attorneys complained, and Judge Choate conducted an evidentiary hearing in open court. I testified to the gist of our conversation, noting that Manson had asked to speak to me, and not vice versa, and that the current charges were not discussed. There was nothing unethical about this, I observed. Moreover, I'd told Kanarek that Manson wanted to talk to me, but Kanarek had merely walked away.

The bailiff, Rusty Burrell, who had sat in on the conversation, staying overtime because he found it interesting, supported my account. As did Manson himself.

MANSON. 'The version the man [indicating me] gave was right on. I am almost sure Mr Kanarek knew that I had asked to see him. I had wanted to speak to this man for the last year, and it was my request that motivated it.'

As for the hearing itself, Manson said: 'Your Honor, I don't think this is fair at all. You know, this was my mistake.'

Agreeing, and ruling that there had been no impropriety involved, Judge Choate brought the hearing to an end.

The irony of all this was not lost on the press, which reported, with some incredulity, that Manson had taken the stand to defend the man who had convicted him of seven murders!

My interest in the sources of Manson's beliefs stretched back to my assignment to the case. Some of those sources have been mentioned earlier. Others, though inadmissible as evidence in the trial, have more than a passing interest, if only as clues to the genesis of such a sick obsession.

I knew, from Gregg Jakobson and others, that Manson was an eclectic, a borrower of ideas. I knew too, both from his prison records and from my conversations with him, that Manson's involvement with Scientology had been more than a passing fad. Manson told me, as he had Paul Watkins, that he had reached the highest stage, 'beta clear', and no longer had any connection with or need for Scientology. I was inclined to accept at least the latter portion of his claim. In my rather extensive investigation, I found no evidence of any kind that Manson was involved with Scientology after his release from prison in 1967.* By this time, he had gone on to do his own thing.

What effect, if any, Scientology had on Manson's mental state cannot be measured. Undoubtedly he picked up from his 'auditing' sessions in prison some knowledge of mind control, as well as some techniques which he later put to use in programming his followers.

---

* One of Manson's chief disciples, Bruce Davis, was very closely involved with Scientology for a time, working in its London headquarters from about November or December of 1968 to April of 1969. According to a Scientology spokesman, Davis was kicked out of the organization for his drug use. He returned to the Manson Family and Spahn Ranch in time to participate in the Hinman and Shea slayings.

Manson's link with The Process, or the Church of the Final Judgement, is more tenuous, yet considerably more fascinating. The leader of the satanic cult is one Robert Moore, whose cult name is Robert DeGrimston. Himself a former disciple of Scientology founder L. Ron Hubbard, Moore broke with Scientology about 1963 to form his own group, after apparently attaining a high position in the London headquarters. He and his followers later traveled to various parts of the world, including Mexico and the United States, and for at least several months, and possibly longer, he lived in San Francisco. He also reportedly participated in a seminar at the Esalen Institute in Big Sur, though whether this coincided with any of Manson's visits there is unknown.

One of DeGrimston's most fervent disciples is one Victor Wild, a young leather goods manufacturer whose Process name is Brother Ely.

Up until December of 1967, Victor Wild's residence, and the San Francisco headquarters for The Process, was 407 Cole Street, in Haight-Ashbury.

From about April through July 1967, Charles Manson and his still fledgling Family lived just two blocks away, at 636 Cole. In view of Manson's curiosity, it appears very likely that he at least investigated the satanists, and there is fairly persuasive evidence that he 'borrowed' some of their teachings.

In one of our conversations during the Tate-LaBianca trial, I asked Manson if he knew Robert Moore, or Robert DeGrimston. He denied knowing DeGrimston, but said he had met Moore. 'You're looking at him,' Manson told me. 'Moore and I are one and the same.' I took this to mean that he felt they thought alike.

Not long after this I was visited by two representatives of The Process, a Father John and a Brother Matthew. Having heard that I was asking questions about the group, they had been sent from their Cambridge, Massachusetts, headquarters to assure me that Manson and Moore had never met and that Moore was opposed to violence. They also left me a stack of Process literature. The following day the names 'Father John' and 'Brother Matthew' appeared on Manson's visitor's list. What they discussed is unknown. All I know is that in my last conversation with Manson, Charlie became evasive when I questioned him about The Process.

In 1968 and 1969, The Process launched a major recruiting drive in the United States. They were in Los Angeles in May and June of 1968 and for at least several months in the fall of 1969, returning to England in about October, after claiming to have converted some 200 American hippies to their sect. Manson was in Los Angeles during both periods. It is possible that there may have been some contact with Manson and/or his group, but I found no evidence of this. I'm inclined to think that Manson's contact with the group probably occurred in San Francisco in 1967, as indicated, at a time when his philosophy was still being formulated. I believe there was at least some contact, in view of the many parallels between Manson's teachings and those of The Process, as revealed in their literature.

Both preached an imminent, violent Armageddon, in which all but the chosen few would be destroyed. Both found the basis for this in the Book of Revelation. Both conceived that the motorcycle gangs, such as Hell's Angels, would be the troops of the last days. And both actively sought to solicit them to their side.

The three great gods of the universe, according to The Process, were Jehovah, Lucifer, and Satan, with Christ the ultimate unifier who reconciles all three. Manson had a simpler duality; he was known to his followers as both Satan and Christ.

Both preached the Second Coming of Christ, a not unusual belief, except in their interpretation of it. According to a Process pamphlet: 'Through Love, Christ and Satan have destroyed their enmity and come together for the End: Christ to Judge, Satan to execute the Judgement.' When Christ returned this time, Manson said, it would be the Romans, i.e. the establishment, who went up on the cross.

Manson's attitude toward fear was so curious I felt it to be almost unique. At least I felt that until reading in a special issue of *The Process* magazine devoted to fear: 'Fear is beneficial ... Fear is the catalyst of action. It is the energizer, the weapon built into the game in the beginning, enabling a being to create an effect upon himself, to spur himself on to new heights and to brush aside the bitterness of failure.' Though the wording differs, this is almost exactly what Manson preached.

Manson spoke frequently of the bottomless pit, The Process of the bottomless void.

Within the organization, The Process was called (at least until 1969) 'the family', while its members were known as brothers, sisters, mothers, fathers.

The symbol of The Process is similar, though not identical, to the Swastika Manson carved on his forehead.

Among the precepts of The Process which parallel Manson's own: 'The Time of the End is now . . . The Ultimate Sin is to kill an animal . . . Christ said love your enemy. Christ's enemy was Satan. Love Christ and Satan . . . The Lamb and the Goat must come together. Pure Love descended from the Pinnacle of Heaven, united with Pure Hatred raised from the depths of Hell.'

One former Process member, being interrogated by LAPD in connection with two motorcycle gang slayings (neither of which was connected with The Process), said of the cult, 'They don't like anybody that they can't indoctrinate or anybody that is not with them. They are just totally against what they call the "gray forces", the rich establishment or the Negroes – '

Q. 'Why don't they like Negroes?'

A. 'I don't know. They just don't.'

Q. 'They have a natural hate for the Negro?'

A. 'They have a natural hate but they would also like to use the Negro as a whole to begin some kind of militant thing . . . They are really good at picking out angry people.'

This was merely the opinion of one disaffiliated member, and may well not be the official position of The Process itself, but the similarities to Manson's own philosophy are still chilling.

These are only some of the parallels I found. They are enough to convince me, at least, that even if Manson himself may never have been a member of The Process, he borrowed heavily from the satanic cult.*

*There is at least one precept Manson did not borrow from the group: unmarried adherents are expected to remain chaste.

Nor are these the only connections between the Manson Family and satanists.

Bobby Beausoleil was for a time closely associated with filmmaker Kenneth Anger, who was himself deeply involved in both the motorcycle gang mystique and the occult. Beausoleil starred in Anger's film *Lucifer Rising*, playing the part of Lucifer. This was before he ever met Manson.

In his psychiatric report on Susan Atkins, Dr Joel Hochman wrote of a portion of her San Francisco period, apparently sometime in 1967 or 1968, before she too met Manson:

At this time she entered into what she now calls her Satanic period. She became involved with Anton LaVey, the Satanist.* She took a part in a commercial production of a witch's sabbath, and recalls the opening night when she took LSD. She was supposed to lie down in a coffin during the act, and lay down in it while hallucinating. She stated that she didn't want to come out, and consequently the curtain was 15 minutes late. She stated that she felt alive and everything else in the ugly world was dead. Subsequently, she stayed on her 'Satanic trip' [for] approximately eight months . . .

During the Tate-LaBianca trial, Patricia Krenwinkel doodled. Her two favorite subjects, according to bailiff Bill Murray, were Devil's heads and the Mendes Goat, both satanist symbols.

Before he killed him, Charles 'Tex' Watson told Voytek Frykowski: 'I am the Devil and I'm here to do the Devil's business.'

An apparently important influence on Manson, in both precept and example, was a dead man: Adolf Hitler. Manson looked up to Hitler and spoke of him often. He told his followers that 'Hitler had the best answer to everything' and that he was 'a tuned-in guy who leveled the karma of the Jews'. Manson saw himself as no less a historical figure, a leader who would not only reverse the karma of the blacks but level all but his own Aryan race – his all-white, all-American Family.

* LaVey, founder of the San Francisco-based First Church of Satan, is known, by those knowledgeable in such matters, more as a spectacular showman than as a demonic satanist. He has stated numerous times that he condemns violence and ritual sacrifice.

There were both surface and substantive parallels between Hitler and Manson.

The births of both men are shrouded in mystery; both were little men; both suffered deep wounds in their youth, the psychological scars at least contributing to, if not causing, their deep hatred for society; both suffered the stigma of illegitimacy, in Manson's case because he himself was a bastard, in Hitler's because his father was.

Both were vagrant wanderers; both were frustrated, and rejected, artists; both liked animals more than people; both were deeply engrossed in the occult; both had others commit their murders for them.

Both were racists; yet there is some evidence that both also believed they carried the blood of the very people they despised. Many historians believe that Hitler was secretly obsessed with the fear that he had a Jewish ancestor. If Manson's prison records are correct, he may have believed his father was black.

Both surrounded themselves with bootlicking slaves; both sought out the weaknesses of others, and used them; both programmed their followers through repetition, repeating the same phrases over and over; both realized and exploited the psychological impact of fear.

Both had a favorite epithet for those they hated: Hitler's was '*Schweinhund*', Manson's was 'pigs'.

Both had eyes which their followers described as 'hypnotic'; beyond that, however, both had a presence, a charisma, and a tremendous amount of personal persuasive power. Generals went to Hitler intent on convincing him that his military plans were insane; they left true believers. Dean Moorehouse went to Spahn Ranch to kill Manson for stealing his daughter, Ruth Ann; he ended up on his knees worshiping him.

Both Manson's and Hitler's followers were able to explain away the monstrous acts their leaders committed by retreating into philosophical abstractions.

Probably the single most important influence on Hitler was Nietzsche. Manson told Jakobson that he had read Nietzsche. Whether true or not – Manson read with difficulty and Nietzsche is not easy reading – both Manson and Hitler believed in what are popularly thought to be the three basic tenets of Nietzsche's philosophy: women are inferior to men; the white race is superior to all other races; it is not wrong to kill if the end is right.

And kill they both did. Both believed that mass murder was all right, even desirable, if it furthered the atttainment of some grand plan. Each had such a plan; each had his own grandiose obsession: Hitler's was the Third Reich, Manson's was Helter Skelter.

At some point parallels become more than coincidence. How much of this was conscious borrowing on Manson's part, how much unconscious emulation, is unknown. I do believe that if Manson had had the opportunity, he would have become another Hitler. I can't conceive of his stopping short of murdering huge masses of people.

Some mysteries remain. One is the exact number of murders committed by members of the Manson Family.

Manson bragged to Juan Flynn that he had committed thirty-five murders. When Juan first told me this, I was inclined to doubt that it was anything more than sick boasting on Charlie's part. There is now evidence, however, that even if this wasn't true *then,* the total to date may be very close to, and may even exceed, Manson's estimate.

In November 1969, Susan Atkins told Ronnie Howard, 'There are eleven murders that they will never solve.' Leslie Van Houten used the same number in her interrogation by Mike McGann, while Ouisch told Barbara Hoyt that she knew of ten people the Family had killed 'besides Sharon'.

Susan told Virginia Graham that, in addition to the eight Hinman-Tate-LaBianca slayings, 'there's more – and more before'. One was undoubtedly Shea. Another was probably the 'Black Panther' (Bernard Crowe), whom Susan, like Manson himself, erroneously believed dead.

Susan may have been referring to Crowe when, in the tape she made with Caballero, she said that the .22 caliber Longhorn revolver used in the Tate homicides had been used in 'other killings', though on the tape this was clearly plural, not singular.

Susan also told Virginia, 'There's also three people out in the desert that they done in.' According to Virginia, Susan 'just said it very nonchalant like, mentioning no names'. When Steve Zabriske tried unsuccessfully to convince Portland police that a Charlie and a Clem were involved in both the Tate and the LaBianca murders, he also said that Ed Bailey had told him that he had seen this Charlie shoot a man in the head. The murder had occurred in Death Valley, according to Bailey, and the gun was a .45 caliber automatic. When interrogated by LAPD in May 1970, Bailey, t/n Edward Arthur Bailey, denied this. However, another source, who was for a time close to the Family, claims he heard 'there are supposed to be two boys and a girl buried about eight feet deep behind Barker Ranch'.

No bodies have ever been found. But then the body of Donald 'Shorty' Shea has never been found either.

On October 13, 1968, two women, Clida Delaney and Nancy Warren, were beaten, then strangled to death with leather thongs a few miles south of Ukiah, California. Several members of the Manson Family were in the area at the time. Two days later Manson suddenly moved the whole Family from Spahn to Barker Ranch. The Mendocino County Sheriff's Office believed there might be a link. But a belief is not evidence.

At about 3:30 A.M. on December 30, 1968, 17-year-old Marina Habe, daughter of writer Hans Habe, was abducted outside the West Hollywood home of her mother as she was returning home from a date. Her body was found on New Year's Day, off Mulholland near Bowmont Drive. Cause of death: multiple stab wounds in the neck and chest.

It has been rumored, but never confirmed, that the victim was acquainted with one or more members of the Family. Though most of his followers were at Barker Ranch, Manson was apparently in Los Angeles on December 30, returning to Barker the following day. Though several persons, including KNXT newscaster Carl George, believed there was a connection, nothing definite has been established, and the murder remains unsolved.

On the night of May 27, 1969, Darwin Orell Scott was hacked

to death in his Ashland, Kentucky, apartment. The killing was so savage that the victim, who was stabbed nineteen times, was pinned to the floor with a butcher knife.

Sixty-four-year-old Darwin Scott was the brother of Colonel Scott, the man alleged to be Charles Manson's father.

In the spring of 1969 a motorcycle-riding guru from California who called himself 'Preacher' appeared in the Ashland area with several female followers. Dispensing free LSD to local teen-agers, he attempted to set up a commune in an abandoned farmhouse near Huntington. He remained in the area until April, at which time vigilantes burned down the house and drove off the group, because, quoting the Ashland paper, 'they didn't like hippies and didn't want any more around'. At least four local residents later told reporters that Manson and Preacher were one and the same person. Despite their positive IDs, Manson's presence in California during at least part of this period is fairly well documented, and it would appear that he was in California on the day of Scott's murder.

On May 22, 1969, Manson telephoned his parole officer, Samuel Barrett, requesting permission to travel to Texas with the Beach Boys. Permission was withheld pending verification of Manson's employment with the group. In a letter dated May 27, the same day as Scott's murder, Manson said that the group had left without him and that he had moved from Death Valley back to Spahn Ranch. To categorize Barrett's control over Manson as minimal would be an exaggeration. Barrett did not again talk to Manson until June 18.

Barrett did not note the postmark on the letter. He did note that he didn't receive it until June 3, seven days after it was supposedly written. It is possible that Manson was using the letter as an alilbi; it is also possible that he sent one of his killers to murder Scott. But both possibilities are strictly conjecture. The murder of Darwin Scott also remains unsolved.

Early on the morning of July 17, 1969, 16-year-old Mark Walts left his parents' home in Chatsworth and hitchhiked to the Santa Monica Pier to go fishing. His pole was later found on the pier. His body was found about 4 A.M. on July 18, off Topanga

Canyon Boulevard a short distance from Mulholland. Young Walts' face and head were badly bruised and he had been shot three times in the chest by a .22 caliber weapon.

Though neither a ranch hand nor a Family member, Walts occasionally hung around Spahn Ranch. Although LASO sent investigators to Spahn, they were unable to uncover any evidence linking the killing to anyone there.

Walts' brother, however, called the ranch and told Manson, 'I know you done my brother in, and I'm going to kill you.' Though he didn't carry through, he obviously felt Manson was responsible.

When Danny DeCarlo had his marathon session with LAPD, he was asked: 'What do you know about a 16-year-old boy that was shot?'

DeCarlo replied: 'That had nothing to do with anybody up there. I'll tell you why, because they were just as shocked about it [as I was]. If they had done it they would have told me.'

DeCarlo informed the officers about the brother's call. One asked: 'Why do you think he suspected Charlie?' DeCarlo replied: 'Because there aren't too many maniacs on the street that would just pull a gun on someone and blow their head off for no reason at all.'

LAPD didn't pursue it further, since this was LASO's case. The murder remains unsolved.

In a period of one month – between July 27 and August 26, 1969 – Charles Manson and his murderous Family slaughtered nine people: Gary Hinman, Steven Parent, Jay Sebring, Abigail Folger, Voytek Frykowski, Sharon Tate, Leno LaBianca, Rosemary LaBianca, and Donald Shea.

Though it is known that a number of female Family members were involved in the 'cleanup' operation that followed Shea's murder, none has ever been tried as an accessory after the fact. Some are still on the streets today.

Manson's arrest on October 12, 1969, did not stop the murders.

As already mentioned, on November 5, 1969, John Philip Haught, aka Christopher Jesus, aka Zero, was shot to death in a beach house in Venice. The four Family members still present when the police arrived claimed he had killed himself while playing Russian roulette.

Three big questions remain: why was Zero playing Russian roulette with a fully loaded gun; why, if he took the gun out of the leather case, was the case clean of prints; and why, though Bruce Davis admitted picking up the gun, were neither his prints nor those of Zero on it?

About a week after the story of Manson's involvement in the Tate-LaBianca murders broke in the press, Los Angeles *Times* reporter Jerry Cohen was contacted by a man who claimed he had been present when Zero was shot. Only Zero hadn't been playing Russian roulette; he had been murdered.

The man was about 25, five feet eight, blond, of slight build. He refused to give Cohen his name. He was, he admitted, 'scared to death'.

Six or eight persons had been in the Venice pad that night, smoking hash. 'It was one of the chicks that killed Zero,' he told Cohen. But he wouldn't say which one, only that recently, at another Manson Family gathering, she had sat staring at him for three hours, all the while fingering her knife.

In questioning him, Cohen established that he had become involved with the Family after the Tate-LaBianca murders. He had never met Manson, he said, but he had heard from other Family members that there had been 'many more murders than the police know of' and that 'the Family is a whole lot larger than you think'.

The youth wanted money to get to Marin County, in Northern California. Cohen gave him twenty-five dollars, implying there would be more if he returned to identify Zero's murderer. He never saw him again.

On November 16, 1969, the body of a young girl was found dumped over an embankment at Mulholland and Bowmont Drive near Laurel Canyon, in almost the same spot where

Marina Habe's body was found. A brunette in her late teens, five feet nine, 115 pounds, she had been stabbed 157 times in the chest and throat. Ruby Pearl remembered seeing the girl with the Family at Spahn, and thought her name was 'Sherry'. Though the Manson girls traded aliases often, LASO was able to identify only one Sherry, Sherry Ann Cooper, aka Simi Valley Sherri. She had fled Barker Ranch at the same time as Barbara Hoyt and was, fortunately, still alive. The victim, who had been dead less than a day, became Jane Doe 59 in police files. Her identity is still unknown.

The proximity in time of her death to that of Zero suggests the possibility that she may have been present at the murder, then killed so she wouldn't talk. But this is strictly conjecture, and there is no evidence to support it. Her murder remains unsolved.

On November 21, 1969, the bodies of James Sharp, 15, and Doreen Gaul, 19, were found in an alley in downtown Los Angeles. The two teen-agers had been killed elsewhere, with a long-bladed knife or bayonet, then dumped there. Each had been stabbed over fifty times.

Ramparts Division Lieutenant Earl Deemer investigated the Sharp-Gaul murders, as did Los Angeles *Times* reporter Cohen. Although the two men felt there was a good possibility that a Family member was involved in the slayings, the murders remain unsolved.

Both James Sharp and Doreen Gaul were Scientologists, the latter a Scientology 'clear' who had been residing in a Church of Scientology commune less than two miles from the LaBianca residence. According to several sources, Doreen Gaul was a former girl friend of Manson Family member Bruce Davis, who, like Manson himself, was an ex-Scientologist.

Davis' whereabouts at the times of the murders of Sharp, Gaul, and Jane Doe 59 are not known. He disappeared shortly after being questioned in connection with the death of Zero.

On December 1, 1969, Joel Dean Pugh, husband of Family member Sandy Good, was found with his throat slit in a London hotel room. As noted, local police ruled the death a suicide. On learning of Pugh's demise, Inyo County DA Frank Fowles made official inquiries, specifically asking Interpol to check visas to determine if one Bruce Davis was in England at the time.

Scotland Yard replied as follows:

It has been established that Davis is recorded as embarking at London airport for the United States of America on 25th April 1969 while holding United States passport 612 2568. At this time he gave his address as Dormer Cottage, Felbridge, Surrey. This address is owned by the Scientology Movement and houses followers of this organization.

The local police are unable to give any information concerning Davis but they understand that he has visited our country more recently than April 1969. However, this is not borne out by our official records.

Davis did not reappear until February 1970, when he was picked up at Spahn Ranch, questioned briefly on the Inyo County grand theft auto charges, then released. After the grand jury indicted him for the Hinman murder, he vanished again, this time not surfacing until December 2, 1970, four days after the mysterious disappearance of Ronald Hughes. When he gave himself up he was accompanied by Family member Brenda McCann.

With three exceptions, these are all the known murders which have been proven, or are suspected to be, linked to the Manson Family. Are there more? I've discussed this with officers from LAPD and LASO, and we tend to think that there probably are, because these people liked to kill. But there is no hard evidence.

As for those three other murders, two of them occurred as late as 1972.

On November 8, 1972, a hiker near the Russian River resort community of Guerneville, in Northern California, saw a hand protruding from the ground. When police exhumed the body, it was found to be that of a young man wearing the dark-blue tunic of a Marine dress uniform. He had been shotgunned and decapitated.

The victim was subsequently identified as James T. Willett, 26, a former Marine from Los Angeles County. This information appeared on radio and TV newscasts on Friday, November 10.

On Saturday, November 11, Stockton, California, police spotted Willett's station wagon parked in front of a house at 720 West Flora Street. When refused entry to the house, they broke in, arresting two men and two women and confiscating a number of pistols and shotguns.

Both women had Manson Family X's on their foreheads. They were Priscilla Cooper, 21, and Nancy Pitman, aka Brenda McCann, 20. A few minutes after police entered the residence, a third female called, asking to be picked up and given a ride to the house. The police obliged, and also arrested Lynette Fromme, aka Squeaky, 24, ex-officio leader of the Family in Manson's absence.

The two men were Michael Monfort, 24, and James Craig, 33, both state prison escapees wanted for a number of armed robberies in various parts of California. Both had the letters 'AB' tattooed on their left breasts. According to a spokesman for the state Department of Corrections, the initials stood for the Aryan Brotherhood, described as 'a cult of white prison inmates, dedicated largely to racism but also involved in hoodlum activities, including murder contracts . . .'

While in the house, the police noticed freshly turned earth in the basement. After obtaining a search warrant, they began digging, and early the following morning exhumed the body of Lauren Willett, 19. She had been shot once in the head, her death occurring either late Friday night or early Saturday morning, not long after the identity of her slain husband was revealed on news broadcasts.

Questioned by the police, Priscilla Cooper claimed that Lauren Willett had killed herself 'playing Russian roulette'.

Although, like Zero, Mrs Willett was not able to contradict

this story, the Stockton police were far more skeptical than had been LASO. The three women and two men were charged with her murder.

They were scheduled to go on trial in May 1973. On April 2, however, four of the five surprised the Court by entering guilty pleas. Michael Monfort, who pleaded guilty to the murder of Lauren Willett, was sentenced to seven years to life in state prison. Superior Court Judge James Darrah also ordered consecutive terms of up to five years and two years for James Craig, who had pleaded guilty to being an accessory after the fact to murder and to possessing an illegal weapon, i.e. a sawed-off shotgun. Both girls also pleaded guilty to being an accessory after the fact, and both Priscilla Cooper and Nancy Pitman, aka Brenda, who Manson once indicated to me was his chief candidate for Family assassin, were sent to state prison for up to five years.

Still another Family member, Maria Alonzo, aka Crystal, 21, arrested while trying to smuggle a switchblade knife into the Stockton jail, was subsequently released.

As was Squeaky. There being insufficient evidence to link Lynette Fromme to Lauren Willett's murder, the charges against her were dropped and she was freed, to again assume leadership of the Manson Family.

Monfort, and an accomplice, William Goucher, 23, subsequently pleaded guilty to second degree murder in the death of James Willett, and were sent to state prison for five years to life. Craig, who pleaded guilty to being an accessory after the fact to the murder, was given another prison term of up to five years.

The motive for the two murders is not known. It is known that the Willetts had been associated with the Manson Family for at least a year, and possibly longer. Police surmised that Lauren Willett was killed after learning of the murder of her husband, to keep her from going to the police. As for the murder of James Willett, the official police theory is that Willett himself may have been about to inform about the robberies the group had committed.

There is another possibility. It may be that both James and

Lauren Willett were killed because they knew too much about still another murder.

James and Lauren. Something about those first names seemed familiar. Then it connected. On November 27, 1970, a James Forsher and a Lauren Elder drove defense attorney Ronald Hughes to Sespe Hot Springs. After Hughes disappeared, the couple were questioned but not polygraphed, the police being satisfied that when they left the flooded area Hughes was still alive.

At first I thought 'Elder' might be Lauren Willett's maiden name, but it wasn't. Nor, in checking the police reports and newspaper articles, was I able to find any description of Forsher and Elder. All I did find were their ages, both given as 17, and an address, from which I subsequently learned they had long since moved. All other efforts to track them down were unsuccessful.

It appears unlikely that James Forsher and James Willett were the same person: Willett would have been 24 in 1970, not 17. But Lauren is a decidedly uncommon name. And, 19 in 1972, she would have been 17 in 1970.

Coincidence? There had been far stranger ones in this case.

One thing is now known, however. If an admission by one of Manson's most hard-core followers is correct, Ronald Hughes *was* murdered by the Manson Family.

It was some weeks after the conclusion of the Tate-LaBianca trial before I received the autopsy report I'd requested from Ventura County. The identification, made through dental X-rays, was positive. The body was that of Ronald Hughes. Yet the rest of the autopsy report added little to the newspaper accounts. It noted: 'The decedent was observed face down in a pool of water with the head and shoulder wedged under a large rock.' One arm was almost completely severed at the shoulder, and there were large open areas in the chest and back. Other than this, 'no outward evidence of violence was noted' while 'no evidence of foul play [was] indicated by the X-rays'. All this was qualified more than a little by the fact that the body was badly decomposed. As for the report's primary findings, there were none: 'Nature of death: Undetermined. Cause of death: Undetermined.'

The report did note that the stomach contained some evidence of 'medication residue'. But its exact composition – drugs, poison, whatever – was, like the nature and cause of death, left undetermined.

Completely dissatisfied with the report, I requested that our office conduct an investigation into the death of Hughes. The request was denied, it being decided that since there was no evidence of foul play, such an investigation was unnecessary.

There the matter remained, until very recently. While the Tate-LaBianca trial was still in progress, motion-picture director Laurence Merrick began work on a documentary on the Manson Family. The film, simply titled *Manson,* dealt only briefly with the murders and focused primarily on life at Spahn and Barker ranches. I narrated a few segments, and there were interviews with a number of Manson's followers. The movie was shown at the Venice Film Festival in 1972 and nominated for an Academy Award the following year. During its filming Merrick gained the confidence of the Manson girls. Sandra Good admitted, for example, on film, that when she and Mary Brunner learned of the Tate murders, while still in the Los Angeles County Jail, 'Mary said, "Right on" and I said "Wow, looks like we did it!" '

Off camera, and unrecorded, Sandy made a number of other admissions to Merrick. She told him, in the presence of one other witness, that to date the Family had killed 'thirty-five to forty people'. And that 'Hughes was the first of the retaliation murders'.

The trials did not write finis to the Manson saga. As Los Angeles *Times* reporter Dave Smith observed in *West* magazine: 'To pull the curtain over the Manson case is to deny ourselves any possible hint of where the beast may come from next, and so remain afraid of things that go bump in the night, the way we were in August in 1969.'

Mass murders have occurred throughout history. Since the Tate-LaBianca slayings, in California alone: labor contractor

595

Juan Corona has been convicted of killing twenty-five migrant farm workers; John Linley Frazier slaughtered Dr Victor Ohta, his wife, two of his sons, and his secretary, then dumped their bodies in the Ohta swimming pool; in a rampage that lasted several months, Herbert Mullin killed thirteen persons, ranging in age from 3 to 73; Edmund Kemper III, ruled insane after slaying his grandmother and grandfather, was ruled sane and released, to later kill his mother, one of her friends, and six college coeds; and a possible total of seventeen murders has been attributed to two young ex-convict drifters.

With the exception of the latter pair, however, these were the work of loners, obviously deranged, if not legally insane, individuals.

The Manson case was, and remains, unique. If, as Sandra Good claimed, the Family has to date committed thirty-five to forty murders, this may be near the U.S. record. Yet it is not the number of victims which makes the case intriguing and gives it its continuing fascination, but a number of other elements for which there is probably no collective parallel in the annals of American crime: the prominence of the victims; the months of speculation, conjecture, and pure fright before the killers were identified; the incredibly strange motive for the murders, to ignite a black-white Armageddon; the motivating nexus between the lyrics of the most famous rock group ever, the Beatles, and the crimes; and, behind it all, pulling the strings, a Mephistophelean guru who had the power to persuade others, most of them young girls, to go out and savagely murder total strangers at his command, with relish and gusto, and no evident signs of guilt or remorse – all these things combine to make these murders perhaps the most bizarre in American history.

How Manson gained control remains the most puzzling question of all.

During the Tate-LaBianca trials, the issue was not so much how he did this but proving that he did it. Yet in understanding the whole Manson phenomenon, the *how* is extremely important.

We have some of the answers.

During the course of his wanderings Manson probably encountered thousands of persons. Most chose not to follow him, either because they sensed that he was a very dangerous man or because they did not respond to the sick philosophy he preached.

Those who did join him were not, as noted, the typical girl or boy next door. Charles Manson was not a Pied Piper who suddenly appeared on the basketball court at Texas State, handed Charles Watson a tab of LSD, then led him into a life of crime. Watson had quit college with only a year to go, gone to California, immersed himself in the selling as well as the using of drugs, before he ever met Charles Manson. Not just Watson but nearly ever other member of the Family had dropped out before meeting Manson. Nearly all had within them a deep-seated hostility toward society and everything it stood for which pre-existed their meeting Manson.

Those who chose to go with him did so, Dr Joel Hochman testified, for reasons 'which lie within the individuals themselves'. In short, there was a need, and Manson seemed to fulfill it. But it was a double process of selection. For Manson decided who stayed. Obviously he did not want anyone who he felt would challenge his authority, cause dissension in the group, or question his dogma. They chose, and Manson chose, and the result was the Family. Those who gravitated to Spahn Ranch and stayed did so because basically they thought and felt alike. This was his raw material.

In shaping that material into a band of cold-blooded assassins, Manson employed a variety of techniques.

He sensed, and capitalized on, their needs. As Gregg Jakobson observed, 'Charlie was a man of a thousand faces' who 'related to all human beings on their level of need'. His ability to 'psych out' people was so great that many of his disciples felt he could read their minds.

I doubt seriously if there was any 'magic' in this. Having had many, many years to study human nature in prison, and being the sophisticated con man that he is, Manson probably realized that there are certain problems that nearly every human being is beset with. I strongly suspect that his 'magical powers' were nothing more, and nothing less, than the ability to utter basic truisms to the right person at the right time. For example, any girl, if she is a runaway, has probably had problems with her father, while anyone who came to Spahn Ranch was searching for something. Manson made it a point to find out what that something was, and supply at least a semblance of it, whether it was a father surrogate, a Christ figure, a need for acceptance and longing, or a leader in leaderless times.

Drugs were another of his tools. As brought out in the psychiatric testimony during the trials, LSD was not a causal agent but a catalyst. Manson used it very effectively, to make his followers more suggestible, to implant ideas, to extract 'agreements'. As Paul Watkins told me, Charlie always took a smaller dose of LSD than the others, so he would remain in command.

He used repetition. By constantly preaching and lecturing to his subjects on an almost daily basis, he gradually and systematically erased many of their inhibitions. As Manson himself once remarked in court: 'You can convince anybody of anything if you just push it at them all of the time. They may not believe it 100 percent, but they will still draw opinions from it, especially if they have no other information to draw their opinions from.'

Therein lies still another of the keys he used: in addition to repetition, he used isolation. There were no newspapers at Spahn Ranch, no clocks. Cut off from the rest of society, he created in this timeless land a tight little society of his own, with its own value system. It was holistic, complete, and totally at odds with the world outside.

He used sex. Realizing that most people have sexual hangups, he taught, by both precept and example, that in sex there is no wrong, thereby eradicating both their inhibitions and their guilt.

But there was more than sex. There was also love, a great deal of love. To overlook this would be to miss one of the strongest bonds that existed among them. The love grew out of their sharing, their communal problems and pleasures, their relationship with Charlie. They were a real family in almost every sense of that word, a sociological unit complete to brothers, sisters, substitute mothers, linked by the domination of an all-knowing, all-powerful patriarch. Cooking, washing dishes, cleaning, sewing –

all the chores they had hated at home they now did willingly, because they pleased Charlie.

He used fear, very, very effectively. Whether he picked up this technique in prison or later is not known, but it was one of his most effective tools for controlling others. It may also have been something more. As Stanford University professor Philip Zimbardo, a long-time student of crime and its effects, noted in a *Newsweek* article: 'By raising the level of fear around you, your own fear seems more normal and socially acceptable.' Manson's own fear bordered on paranoia.

He taught them that life was a game, a 'magical mystery tour'. One day they would be pirates with cutlasses, slashing at anyone who dared board their imaginary ship; the next they'd change costumes and identities and become Indians stalking cowboys; or devils and witches casting spells. A game. But there was always a pattern behind it: them versus us. Dr Hochman testified: 'I think that historically the easiest way to program someone into murdering is to convince them that they are alien, that they are them and we are us, and that they are different from us.'

Krauts. Japs. Gooks. Pigs.

With the frequent name changing and role playing, Manson created his own band of schizophrenics. Little Susan Atkins, who sang in the church choir and nursed her mother while she was dying of cancer, couldn't be held responsible for what Sadie Mae Glutz had done.

He brought to the surface their latent hatred, their inherent penchant for sadistic violence, focusing it on a common enemy, the establishment. He depersonalized the victims by making them symbols. It is easier to stab a symbol than a person.

He taught his followers a completely amoral philosophy, which provided complete justification for their acts. If everything is right, then nothing can be wrong. If nothing is real, and all of life is a game, then there need be no regret.

If they needed something that couldn't be found in the garbage bins or communal clothing pile, they stole it. Step by step. Panhandling, petty theft, prostitution, burglaries, armed robberies, and, last of all, for no motive of gain but because it was Charlie's will, and Charlie's will is Man's Son, the final step, the ultimate act of defiance of the establishment, the most positive proof of their total commitment – murder.

Comedians punned that 'the family that slays together stays together'. But behind the grim jest there was truth. Knowing they had violated the strictest of all commandments created a bond not less but more binding in that it was *their* secret.

He used religion. Not only did he find support for much of his philosophy in the Bible, he often implied that he was the Second Coming of Christ. He had his twelve apostles, several times over; not one but two Judases, Sadie and Linda; his retreat to the desert, Barker Ranch; and his trial, in the Hall of Justice.

He also used music, in part because he was a frustrated musician but also because he must have known it was the one thing that could get through to more young people than any other.

He used his own superior intelligence. He was not only older than his followers, he was brighter, more articulate and savvy, far more clever and insidious. With his prison background, his ever adaptable line of con, plus a pimp's knowledge of how to manipulate others, he had little trouble convincing his naïve, impressionable followers that it was not they but society which was sick. This too was exactly what they wanted to hear.

All of these factors contributed to Manson's control over others. But when you add them all up, do they equal murder without remorse? I think not. I tend to think that there is something more, some missing link that enabled him to so rape and bastardize the minds of his followers that they would go against the most ingrained of all commandments, Thou shalt not kill, and willingly, even eagerly, murder at his command.

It may be something in his charismatic, enigmatic personality, some intangible quality or power that no one has yet been able to isolate and identify. It may be something he learned from others. Whatever it is, I believe Manson has full knowledge of the formula he used. And it worries me that we do not. For the frightening legacy of the Manson case is that it could happen again.

I believe Charles Manson is unique. He is certainly one of the most fascinating criminals in American history, and it appears unlikely that there will ever be another mass murderer even remotely similar to him. But it does not take a prophet to see at least some of the potentials of his madness in the world today. Whenever people unquestioningly turn over their minds to authoritarian figures to do with as they please – whether it be in a satanic cult or some of the more fanatic offshoots of the Jesus Movement, in the right wing or the far left, or in the mind-bending cults of the new sensitivity – those potentials exist. One hopes that none of these groups will spawn other Charles Mansons. But it would be naïve to suggest that that chilling possibility does not exist.

There are some happy endings to the Manson story. And some not so happy.

Both Barbara Hoyt and Dianne Lake returned to and graduated from high school, with apparently few if any permanent scars from their time with Manson. Barbara is now studying to be a nurse.

Stephanie Schram has her own dog-grooming shop. Paul Watkins and Brooks Poston formed their own combo and appear at various clubs in the Inyo County area. Their songs were good enough to be used as background music in the Merrick documentary on Manson.

After the fire George Spahn sold his ranch to an investment firm, which planned to turn it into a dude ranch for German visitors to the United States. He's since purchased another ranch, near Klamath Falls, Oregon, and Ruby Pearl is running it for him.

I haven't heard from Juan Flynn recently, but I'm not worried about him. Juan was always able to take care of himself. Though I last saw him in my office, for some reason I visualize him on a big white horse, his pretty girl friend behind him holding on for dear life as they gallop off into the sunset. Which, I suspect, is Juan's own image of himself.

Since the murder of his wife, Roman Polanski has produced several motion pictures, including a new version of *Macbeth*. Critics noticed in his interpretation disturbing parallels to the Tate murders. Polanski himself posed for an *Esquire* interview, holding aloft a shiny knife, and, according to the press, he has recently moved back to Los Angeles, into a home not far from 10050 Cielo Drive.

Polanski's attorney, working in conjunction with LAPD, divided the $25,000 reward as follows: Ronnie Howard and Virginia Graham each received $12,000, while Steven Weiss, the young boy who found the .22 caliber murder weapon, received $1,000.

Neither Danny DeCarlo nor Alan Springer was around to share in the reward. Shortly before the Watson trial, Danny skipped bail on the federal gun charge and fled to Canada; his exact whereabouts are unknown. According to LAPD, biker Al Springer simply 'vanished'. It is not known whether he is alive or dead.

Ronnie Howard tried working as a cocktail waitress but found it difficult to hold a job. Everywhere she went, she said, she was identified as the 'Manson case snitch'. Several times she was beaten up on her way home from work, and one night someone fired a bullet through the living-room window of her apartment, missing her head by inches. The would-be assailant was never identified. The next day she told reporters: 'I should have kept my mouth shut in the first place.'

Virginia Graham had a job as a receptionist in a legal office and seemed well on the way to rehabilitation, when she jumped parole. As this is written, she is still a fugitive.

Many, though not all, of the hard-core Manson Family members are now serving time in various penal institutions. Other Family members split to follow new leaders. Cathy Gillies, according to the last information I received, was a 'mom' with one of the motorcycle gangs. Still others continue to make headlines. Maria Alonzo, aka Crystal, who was released shortly after the Stockton murder, was arrested in March 1974 and charged with allegedly plotting to kidnap a foreign consul general in an attempt to secure the release of two prisoners in the Los Angeles County Jail. As this is written, she has yet to be brought to trial.

For a time there was a spate of books, plays and motion pictures which, if not glorifying Manson, depicted him in a not wholly unfavorable light. And, for a time, it looked as if a Manson cult was emerging. Not only were there buttons reading 'FREE THE MANSON FOUR', that cancerous growth known as the Family again began growing. When interviewed, the new converts – who had never had any personal contact with Manson – looked and talked exactly like Squeaky, Sandy, and the others, giving rise to the very disturbing possibility that Manson's madness might be communicable. But the strange phase quickly passed, and there is little left of the Manson Family now, though little Squeaky, chief cheerleader of the Manson cause, is still keeping the faith.

Although undisputed leader of the Family while Charlie is in absentia, and presumably involved in the planning of their activities, and though arrested more than a dozen times on charges ranging from robbery to murder, she has only been convicted a few times, and always on minor charges. Moreover, not long ago she found a champion in, of all places, the District Attorney's Office in Los Angeles.

One of the young deputy DAs, William Melcher, first became acquainted with Squeaky while the group was holding its vigil on the corner of Temple and Broadway. For Christmas 1970, Melcher's wife baked cookies for the Manson girls, and a friendship developed. Not long after Squeaky was released on the Stockton murder charge, she was rearrested as a suspect in a Granada Hills armed robbery. Convinced they had the wrong person, Melcher successfully proved this to the police and she was freed. Clearing her was, Melcher told the Los Angeles *Times*, 'my greatest satisfaction in three years as a prosecutor'. Noting that the group had 'a lot of ill-feeling about the police and courts, I wanted them to know that justice also works on their side of the street'. Someday he would like to write a book on the girls, Melcher added. 'I'd like to write not an exposé of the tragedy and violence, which I do not condone, but a book about the beauty I've seen in that group – their opposition to war, their truthfulness and their generosity.'

The fate of Charles Manson, Charles Watson, Susan Atkins, Patricia Krenwinkel, Leslie Van Houten, and Robert Beausoleil was decided on February 18, 1972. That day the California State Supreme Court announced that it had voted 6–1 to abolish the death penalty in the state of California. The opinion was based on Article 1, Section 6, of the State Constitution, which forbids 'cruel or unusual punishment'.*

The sentences of the 107 persons awaiting execution in California were automatically reduced to life imprisonment.

Manson, in Los Angeles as a defense witness in the Bruce Davis trial, grinned broadly on hearing the news.

In California a person sentenced to life imprisonment is eligible to apply for parole in seven years.

By August 1972 the last prisoners had left California's Death Rows, most to be transferred to the 'yards', or general inmate population, of various state penal institutions. Although at this writing Atkins, Krenwinkel, and Van Houten remain in the special security unit constructed for them at the California Institute for Women at Frontera, it is likely that in time they will join the general population also.

In his psychiatric report on Patricia Krenwinkel, Dr. Joel Hochman said that of the three girls Katie had the most tenuous hold on reality. It was his opinion that if she were ever separated from the others and the Manson mystique, it was quite possible she would lose even that, and lapse into complete psychosis.

With regard to Leslie Van Houten, who of the three girls was

---

* In June 1972 the United States Supreme Court ruled, in a 5–4 decision, that the death penalty, if imposed in an arbitrary fashion with the jury being given absolute discretion and no guidelines, constituted 'cruel and unusual punishment' in violation of the Eighth Amendment to the U.S. Constitution.

Although a number of states, including California, have since passed laws restoring the death penalty and making it mandatory for certain crimes, including mass murders, at the time this is written the United States Supreme Court has yet to rule on their constitutionality.

Even if the California law is let stand, it would not affect the Manson Family killers, since the new statute is not retroactive.

least committed to Manson, yet still murdered for him, I fear that she may grow harder and tougher; I have very little hope for her eventual rehabilitation.

Writing of Susan Atkins, Los Angeles *Times* reporter Dave Smith expressed something which I had long felt. 'Watching her behavior – bold and actressy in court, cute and mincing when making eye-play with someone, a little haunted when no one pays attention – I get the feeling that one day she might start screaming, and simply never stop.'

As for the other convicted Manson Family killers – Charles Watson; Robert Beausoleil; Steve Grogan, aka Clem; and Bruce Davis – all are now in the general inmate population. Tex is no longer playing insane and has a girl friend who visits him regularly. Bobby received a certain amount of national attention when he was interviewed by Truman Capote during a TV documentary on American prisons. Not long afterward his jaw was broken and his hand dislocated in a brawl in the yard of San Quentin. The fight was the result of a power struggle over the leadership of the Aryan Brotherhood, with which Beausoleil had become affiliated. The AB, which is believed responsible for more than a dozen fatal stabbings in various California prisons in the last few years, is the successor to several earlier groups, including a neo-Nazi organization. Its total membership is not known, but it is believed to have about two hundred hard-core inmate followers, and it espouses many of the same racial principles that Charles Manson did. The legacy lives on.

Of all the Manson Family killers, only their leader merits special handling. In October 1972, Charles Manson was transferred to the maximum security adjustment center at Folsom Prison in Northern California. Described as 'a prison within a prison', it provides special housing for 'problem inmates' who cannot be safely controlled in the general prison population. With the transfer Manson lost not only all of the special privileges afforded those awaiting execution, he also lost his regular inmate privileges, because of his 'hostile and belligerent attitude'.

'Prison is my home, the only home I ever had,' Manson often said. In 1967 he begged the authorities not to release him. Had anyone heeded his warning, this book need never have been written, and perhaps thirty-five to forty people now dead might still be alive.

In convicting him, Manson said, I was only sending him home. Only this time it won't be the same. Observed San Quentin warden Louis Nelson, before Manson was transferred to Folsom: 'It would be dangerous to put a guy like Manson into the main population, because in the eyes of other inmates he didn't commit first-class crimes. He was convicted of killing a pregnant woman, and that sort of thing doesn't allow him to rank very high in the prison social structure. It's like being a child molester. Guys like that are going to do hard time wherever they are.'

Too, like Sirhan Sirhan, convicted slayer of Senator Robert Kennedy, his notoriety is his own worst enemy. For as long as he remains in prison, Manson will be looking over his shoulder, aware that any con hoping to make a reputation need only put a shiv in his back.

That Manson, Watson, Beausoleil, Davis, Grogan, Atkins, Van Houten, and Krenwinkel will be eligible for parole in 1978 does not mean that they will get it, only that this is the earliest date they will be eligible to apply. The average incarceration in California for first degree murder is ten and a half to eleven years. Because of the hideous nature of their crimes and the total absence of mitigating circumstances, my guess is that all will serve longer periods; the girls fifteen to twenty years, the men – with the exception of Manson himself – a like number.

As for the leader of the Family, my guess is that he will remain in prison for at least twenty-five years, and quite possibly the rest of his life.

In mid-October of 1973 some thirty prisoners in California's toughest lockup, Folsom Prison's 4–A adjustment center, staged what was described by the San Francisco *Chronicle* as a 'peaceful protest' against prison conditions.

The man who used and championed fear did not participate. According to the *Chronicle* story: 'Mass murderer Charles Manson is among the inmates in 4–A, although prison spokesmen say he is not involved in this demonstration. Manson has been threatened by other inmates in the past, and authorities say he seldom ventures out of his cell for fear of being attacked.'

Index

Index

Index

Index

Index

Manson Charles Milles (*cont.*)

180; Bugliosi's analysis of criminal record, 180–81; rumor will go alibi, Bugliosi asks LaBianca detectives for detailed report on activities week of the murders, 183; Manson Family girls interviewed concerning, 184–91; Jacobson fascination with 'Manson package', 192; Melcher interview, recalls time Manson outside gate 10050 Cielo, 193–4; not mentioned by name in LAPD press conference, 198; Hoyt disclosures, 201; birth of Family recounted, speculation regarding how developed incredible control over others, birth of son, 201–4; revelations on Atkins tape, 206–7; Atkins-Bugliosi interview, 210–11; Atkins' grand jury testimony re how she met Manson, his direction of Family, his ordering of Tate and LaBianca murders, 212–29; DeCarlo's grand jury testimony concerning, 232; charged with Tate-LaBianca murders, brought to L.A., 233; arraignment, Court appoints Fitzgerald to represent, watch-stopping incident, 235; Atkins 'kite' to Howard re Manson second coming of Christ, 239; Bugliosi discovers Springer statement with Manson confession, 241; need to link murder gun to, 245; request to dismiss attorney and defend self, Judge Keene reluctantly grants, 247–8; Swartz interview re borrowing car, Shea disappearance, 250–51; efforts to have Krenwinkel return, plans for umbrella defense, 252; prosecution's apprehension that might demand immediate trial, 255–6; rope purchase, 260; importance of establishing domination, 261; granted discovery, 261; manipulation of the defense, 263–4; unique motion by 'Charles Manson, also known as Jesus Christ, Prisoner,' denied, 264; claim of DA pressure on Atkins, 265; problems establishing motive, 265–7; pressures on other defendants and their attorneys, 267–8; arson charges refiled, 268–9; unlikely emergence as counterculture hero,

270–71; request for early trial, 272; Jakobson's talks with Manson, revelations concerning his philosophy, domination, race ideas, Helter Skelter, 272–6; Melcher reluctantly reveals Manson visited Altobelli at guest house, Altobelli and Hatami confirm, Sharon Tate saw man who would order her murder, 276–82; Crockett and Poston taped recollections, 282–6; importance of name change, 287–8; Poston on programming techniques, 288; Watkins provides missing link in Helter Skelter motive, 292–4; unique interpretation of Bible and Beatles lyrics, 292–305; hint of possible defense strategy, 306; additional examples of domination, 306; messages to Atkins, 309; quotation from, 313; Kasabian interviews, revelations concerning, 311, 315–24; meeting with Atkins, persuades her to change attorneys, 325; Judge Keene revokes pro per status, Hollopeter appointed attorney, 325–6; Kasabian re Manson's activities the night of the LaBianca murders, 327–35; LaBianca detectives report on activities week of murders, proof of presence at Spahn Ranch on August 8, 1969, 337–41; link with Esalen Institute, 338–9; Schram testimony re conducting murder school at Barker, 341–2; substitution of Hughes for Hollopeter, 342–3; resurrection of Crowe and reaction, 344–6; linked to rope, gun, and wire cutters, 349–51; conversation with Sage re Kasabian murder claims, 353–4; Kasabian's fear of, 354; files affidavit of prejudice against Judge Keene, trial assigned to Judge Older, 357; indictment on Hinman murder, Kanarek substituted for Hughes, conversation with Bugliosi re fair trial, 361–2, 363–5; turns back on judge, removed to lockup, refusals to return, 366–7; Kanarek asserts arrest illegal, Bugliosi retort, 369–70; first reaction of prospective jurors, 373; conversation with Bugliosi, challenged to take stand, 376–7; carving

Index

Index